FOR
MICHAEL TURNER
WHO SHARED HIS ADVENTURE WITH US.

WE ALSO DEDICATE THIS BOOK TO
GRACE, JAKE, KELLY C,
KELLY M, SAM C, STEVE, PILI,
SANDI, SAM L, AUDREY, GEOFF J,
MIKE E, DANIEL, JOHN, PETE W,
JOE W, GEOFF R, PETER J,
AURORE, CARRIE, GABE

AND ALL THE COUNTLESS OTHER FRIENDS, FAMILY,

AND OUR FANS,

WHO SUPPORTED US AND SHARED THIS ADVENTURE WITH US TOO.

THANK YOU.
FOR EVERYTHING.

*A*LL
YOU
NEED
ARE
WINGS...
to fly

MICHAEL TURNER'S SOULFIRE
THE DEFINITIVE EDITION
THE COMPLETE FIRST VOLUME

SOULFIRE CREATED BY:

MICHAEL TURNER

MICHAEL TURNER'S: SOULFIRE™ VOLUME I - THE DEFINITIVE EDITION
ISBN: 978-0-9823628-6-0
FIRST PRINTING, 2012.
Collects material originally published as Michael Turner's Soulfire: Beginnings, Soulfire: Preview, Soulfire Issues 0, 1-10, and Aspen Seasons: Winter 2009

PUBLISHED BY ASPEN MLT, INC.
Office of Publication: 5855 Green Valley Circle. Suite. 111, Culver City, CA 90230.
The Aspen MLT, Inc. logo® is a registered trademark of Aspen MLT, Inc. Michael Turner's Soulfire® and the Soulfire logo
are the trademarks of Aspen MLT, Inc. The entire contents of this book, all artwork, characters and their likenesses are ©
2012 Aspen MLT, Inc. All Rights Reserved. Any similarities between names, characters, persons, and/or institutions in this
publication with persons living or dead or institutions is unintended and is purely coincidental. With the exception of artwork
used for review purposes, none of the contents of this book may be reprinted, reproduced or transmitted by any means or in
any form without the express written consent of Aspen MLT, Inc. For information regarding the CPSIA on this printed material
call: 203-595-3636 and provide reference # EAST – 999999

Address correspondence to:
SOULFIRE c/o
Aspen MLT Inc.
5855 Green Valley Circle. Suite. 111
Culver City, CA. 90230-6946

or email us: fanmail@aspencomics.com

Visit us on the web at:
www.aspencomics.com
www.aspenstore.com
www.facebook.com/aspencomics
www.twitter.com/aspencomics

COLLECTED EDITION EDITORS: MARK ROSLAN AND FRANK MASTROMAURO
ORIGINAL SERIES EDITORS: FRANK MASTROMAURO AND VINCE HERNANDEZ
COVER AND BOOK DESIGN: PETER STEIGERWALD AND MARK ROSLAN
COVER ILLUSTRATIONS: MICHAEL TURNER AND PETER STEIGERWALD

For Aspen:

FOUNDER: MICHAEL TURNER
CO-OWNER, PRESIDENT: FRANK MASTROMAURO
CO-OWNER, V. PRESIDENT: PETER STEIGERWALD
EDITOR IN CHIEF: VINCE HERNANDEZ
EDITORIAL ASSISTANT: JOSH REED
DIRECTOR OF DESIGN AND PRODUCTION: MARK ROSLAN
MARKETING ASSISTANT: CJ WILSON
OFFICE COORDINATOR: ERICK RAYMUNDO
ASPENSTORE.COM: CHRIS RUPP

To follow the continuing saga of *Michael Turner's Soulfire*, be sure to
also check out the regular issues available at a comic shop near you!

To find the Comic Shop
nearest you...

Table of Contents

· *Colors:* PETER STEIGERWALD ·
· *Additional Colors:* BETH SOTELO, CHRISTINA STRAIN & DAVID MORÁN ·

· *Letters:* RICHARD STARKINGS & COMICRAFT *(Chapter 1-4)*
· DREAMER DESIGN *(Chapter 5-9)* · JOSH REED *(Chapter 10-13)* ·

· *Special Thanks:* Koi Turnbull, Marcus To, Joel Gomez & Martin Montiel Luna ·

Table of Contents

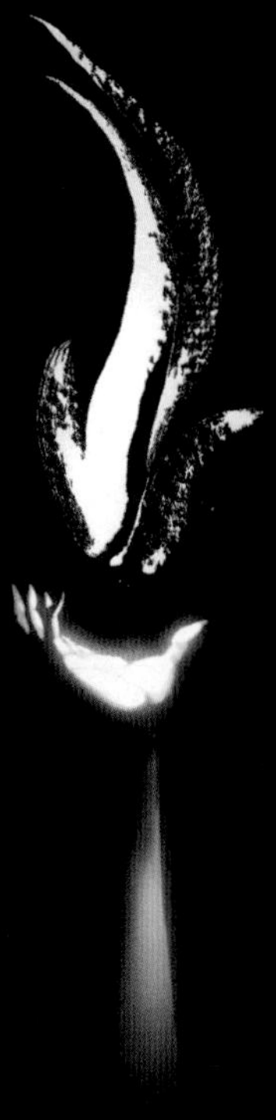

INTRODUCTION

by J.T. Krul

TO SAY THAT THIS BEAUTIFUL BOOK YOU HOLD IN YOUR HANDS IS A LABOR OF LOVE WOULD BE A GROSS UNDERSTATEMENT. THE BRAINCHILD OF MICHAEL TURNER, SOULFIRE WAS THE FLAGSHIP NEW PROPERTY PREMIERING UNDER THE ASPEN STUDIOS BANNER WHEN THE COMPANY BEGAN IN 2003. AND IN MANY WAYS, THE STORY WITHIN THESE PAGES EMBODIES EVERYTHING MIKE AND HIS COMPANY STOOD FOR - CELEBRATING THE WONDROUS AND SPECIAL MAGIC IN LIFE. I'LL NEVER FORGET HAVING DINNER WITH MIKE, FRANK, AND PETER - SITTING ACROSS THE TABLE AS THEY UNVEILED THE INCREDIBLE WORLD THEY HAD STARTED CREATING WITH JEPH LOEB. AN INFECTIOUS ENERGY BUZZED AMONGST US IN THE FORM OF FAST WORDS, BRIGHT EYES, AND WILD HAND GESTURES - NOT TO BE CONTAINED, EVEN WITH MOUTHS FULL OF FOOD. I JUMPED IN WITH BOTH FEET AND HAVEN'T LOOKED BACK.

SOULFIRE IS THE FUTURISTIC TALE OF A VERY SPECIAL BOY NAMED MALIKAI AND HIS INTIMATE CONNECTION TO A LOST MAGIC THAT A WORLD, OVERWHELMED BY TECHNOLOGY, DESPERATELY NEEDS TO SEE RETURN. IT'S A WORLD THAT'S LOST ITS SPIRIT, ITS HUMANITY, AND ITS SOUL. AS HE EMBARKS ON HIS QUEST, MALIKAI IS CHALLENGED BY SEEMINGLY INSURMOUNTABLE OBSTACLES, AND MUST RELY ON HIS FEW FRIENDS AND ALLIES TO HELP SEE HIM THROUGH HIS PERIL - ULTIMATELY KNOWING THAT THE BATTLE IS HIS TO FACE ALONE. AT THE TIME, NOBODY REALIZED JUST HOW PROPHETIC THIS JOURNEY WOULD BE IN TERMS OF PARALLELING MIKE'S OWN BATTLE WITH CANCER.

OVER THE NEXT FEW YEARS, WE ALL STOOD BY MIKE DURING HIS STRUGGLE, OFFERING WHAT LITTLE HELP AND COMFORT WE COULD. SOME DAYS WERE GOOD; SOME WERE NOT. WHEN HE COULD PUT PENCIL TO PAPER, THE WORLD OF SOULFIRE CAME ALIVE - JUST AS VIBRANT AS EVER. HIS SICKNESS NEVER CREPT INTO THE ART BECAUSE HE NEVER LET IT INTO HIS SOUL. THROUGHOUT IT ALL, MIKE WAS A TOWER OF WILLPOWER AND POSITIVE ENERGY. HE REFUSED TO LET THE PAIN TAKE CONTROL OF HIS LIFE. HE

FOUGHT WITH EVERY FIBER OF HIS BEING - STANDING STRONG AGAINST THE OBSTACLES BEFORE HIM.

IN THE END, MIKE WOULD BE UNABLE TO FINISH THIS FIRST VOLUME BEFORE HIS PASSING, BUT I REMEMBER TALKING ABOUT THE BOOK WITH HIM EVEN IN THE FINAL FEW WEEKS OF HIS LIFE. AND THERE WAS NO WAY WE WERE GOING TO LET THE BOOK GO UNFINISHED. MIKE'S JOURNEY WAS CONTINUING ON ELSEWHERE, AND FOR US MALIKAI'S JOURNEY MUST CONTINUE AS WELL. LONG TIME FRIEND AND EQUALLY TALENTED ARTIST JOE BENITEZ STEPPED IN TO COMPLETE MIKE'S VISION WITH HEART, FLAIR, AND LOVE.

I COULD TALK AT GREAT LENGTH ABOUT MIKE'S STRUGGLE - ABOUT HIS DAYS OF PAIN, DAYS WHERE DRAWING WAS SIMPLY AN IMPOSSIBLE FEAT - BUT THAT'S NOT THE REAL STORY. THE REAL STORY IS THE CORE OF SOULFIRE. IT IS A STORY OF LIGHT. AND THAT'S EXACTLY WHAT MIKE WAS - A SOURCE OF LIGHT FOR ANY AND ALL THAT EVER MET HIM. WHETHER FAMILY MEMBERS OR INTIMATE FRIENDS OR EVEN THE RANDOM FAN HE TALKED WITH FOR A FEW MOMENTS AT A SIGNING - MIKE'S SPIRIT WAS A BEACON FOR ALL TO SEE. HE TOUCHED COUNTLESS LIVES THROUGH HIS ART, AND EVEN MORE WITH HIS HEART. IT'S HARD TO WRITE ABOUT SOULFIRE WITHOUT TALKING ABOUT MIKE AND WHAT HE MEANT TO ALL OF US - AND THAT'S BECAUSE (AS I STATED EARLIER) HIS SPIRIT AND IMPACT IN THIS WORLD MIRRORS THE MAGICAL ONE MALIKAI PRESENTS IN THE STORY YOU ARE ABOUT TO READ.

BUT MIKE WOULDN'T WANT ME TO LEAVE IT AT THAT. HE'D TELL ME TO GET TO THE GOOD STUFF - THE ACTION, THE ADVENTURE, AND ESPECIALLY THE DRAGONS - MIKE LOVED DESIGNING THIS WORLD WHICH CAME TO LIFE BEGINNING WITH A HULKING, MONSTROUS MECHANICAL DRAGON LOOMING OVER THE SKIES OF SAN FRANCISCO. SO, STRAP YOURSELF IN AND GET READY FOR THE RIDE OF A LIFETIME BECAUSE MAGIC IS BACK...AND THE WORLD WILL NEVER BE THE SAME AGAIN.

J.T. KRUL
Writer *Teen Titans, Green Arrow, Fathom*
Los Angeles, January 2012

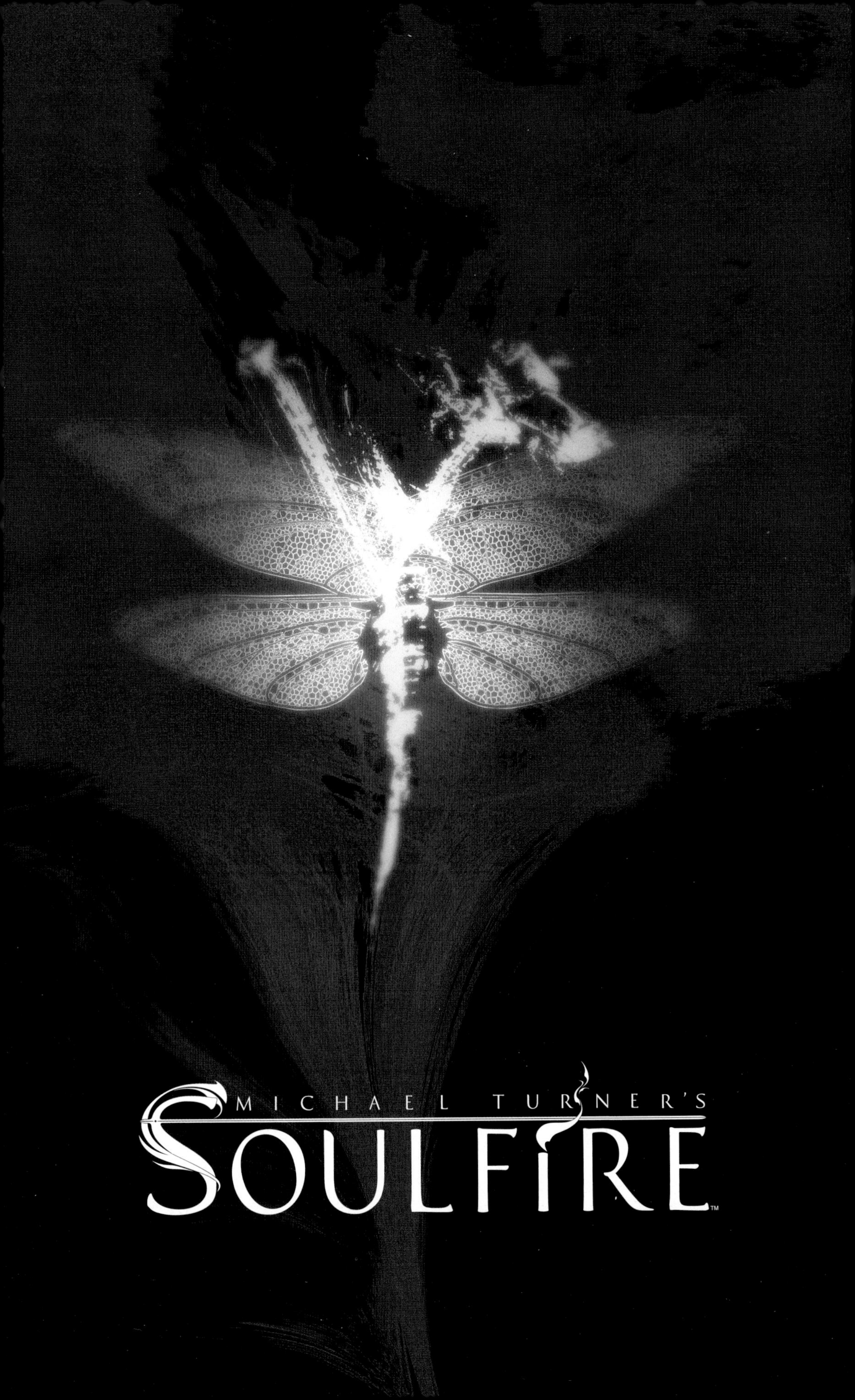
MICHAEL TURNER'S
SOULFIRE™

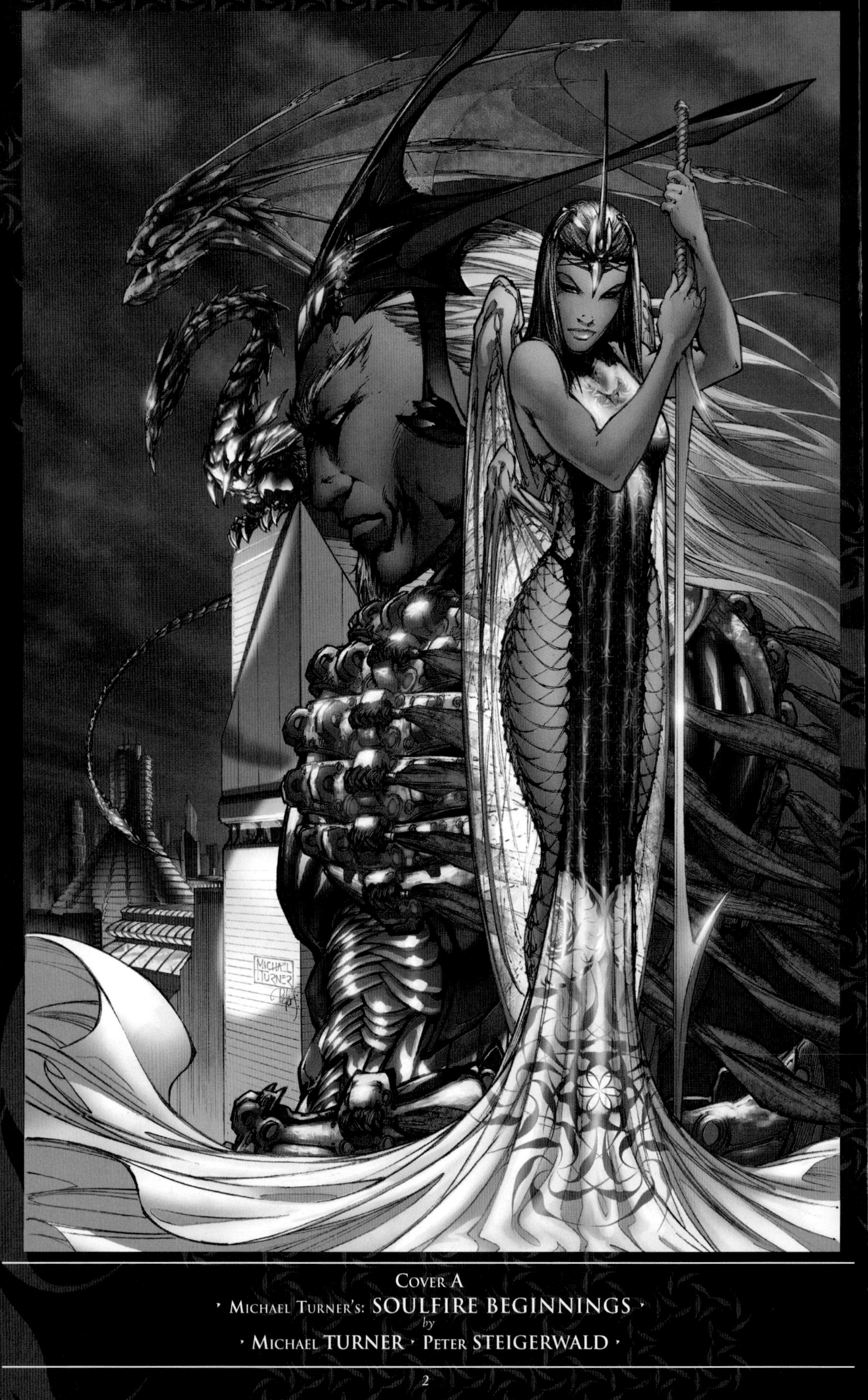
MICHAEL TURNER

Cover A

‣ Michael Turner's: SOULFIRE BEGINNINGS ‣

by

‣ Michael TURNER ‣ Peter STEIGERWALD ‣

In the summer of 2003, Aspen released the Soulfire: Beginnings nine-page prelude story exclusively at the Wizard World Philadelphia comic book convention. The story, featuring Soulfire's main antagonist Rainier and his quest for power beyond his means, quickly went on to sell out all first print copies its debut weekend. It has never been reprinted until now.

---

story Jeph Loeb - *story and pencils:* Michael Turner
colors: Peter Steigerwald - *letters:* Richard Starkings

SOULFIRE BEGINNINGS

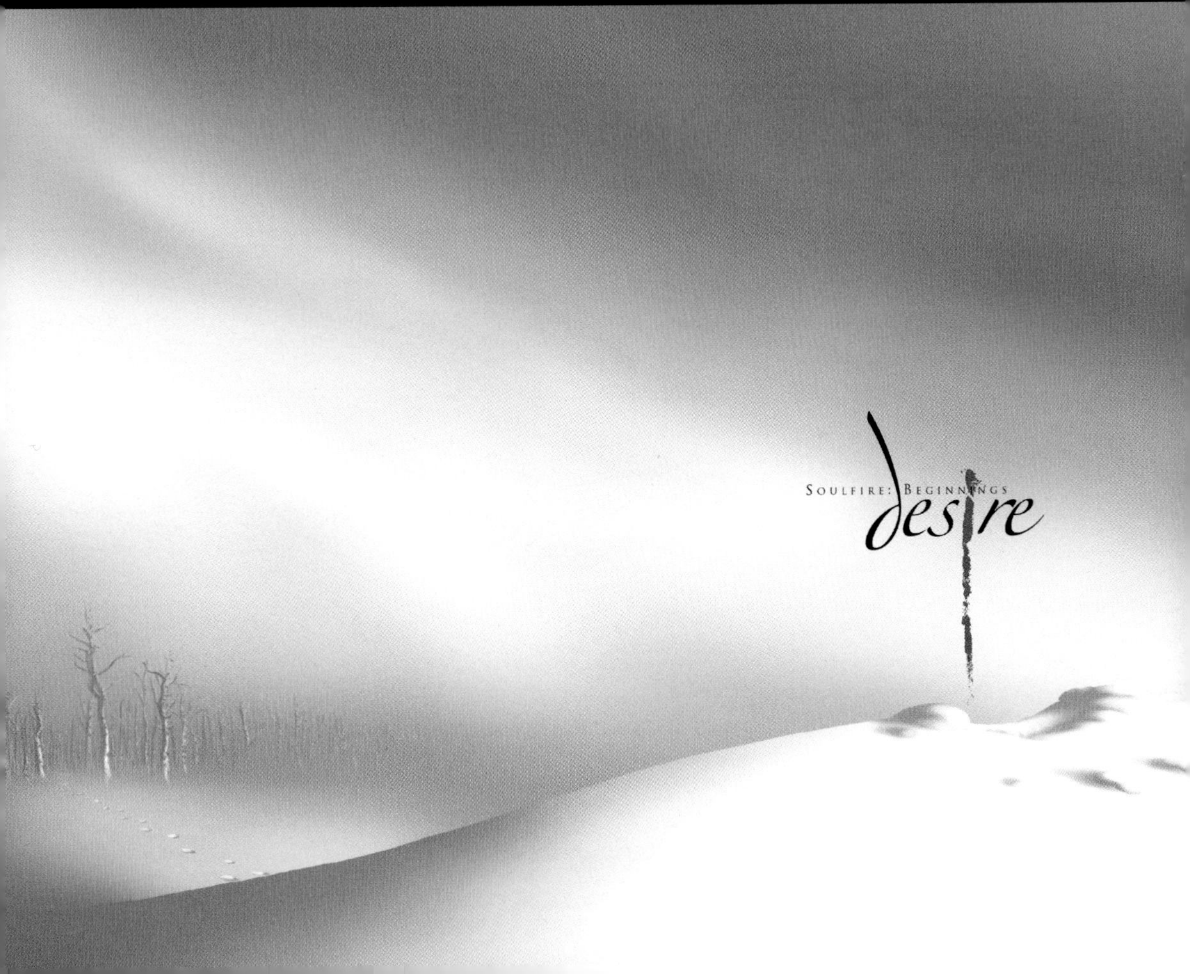
Soulfire: Beginnings
desire

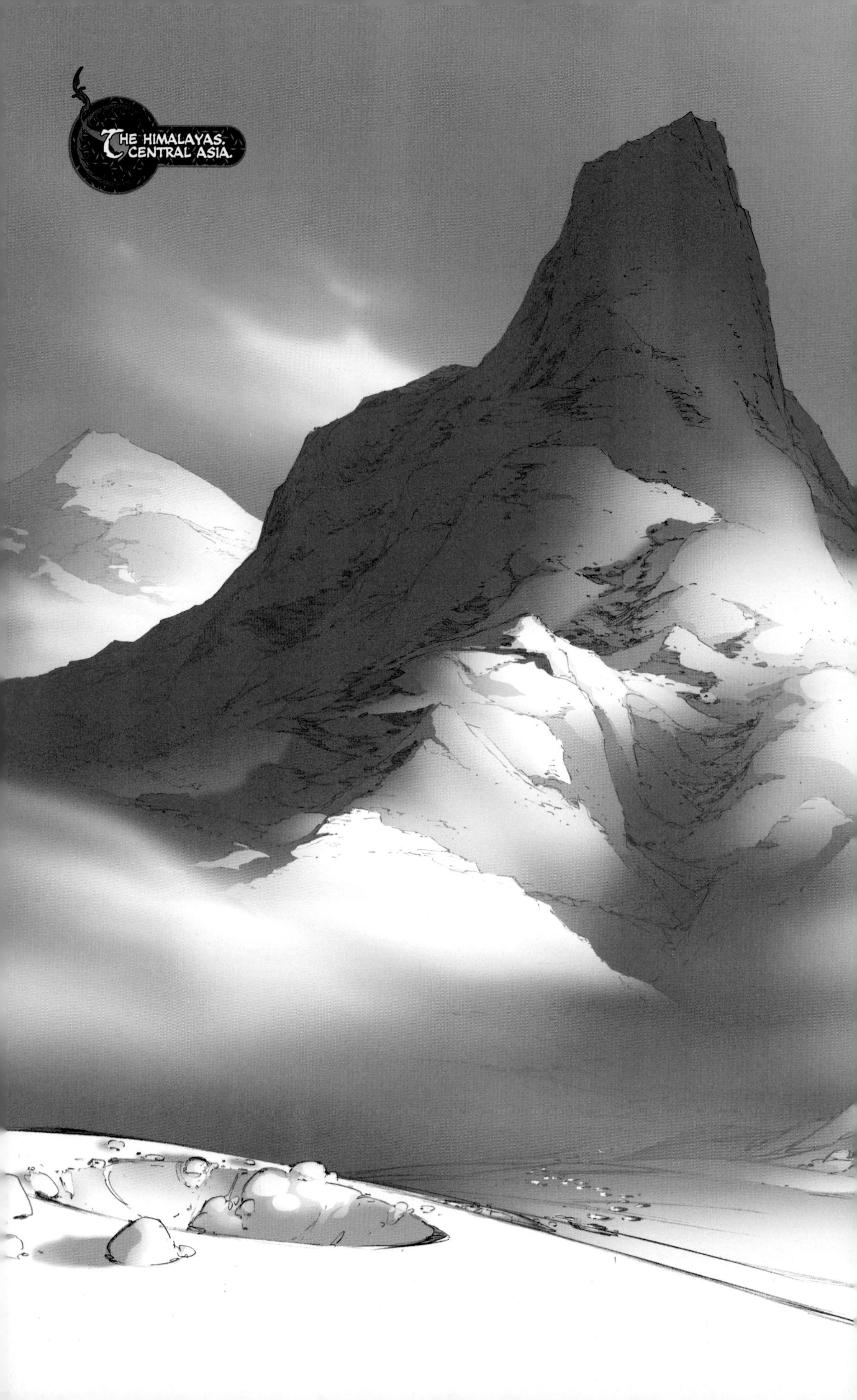
THE HIMALAYAS.
CENTRAL ASIA.

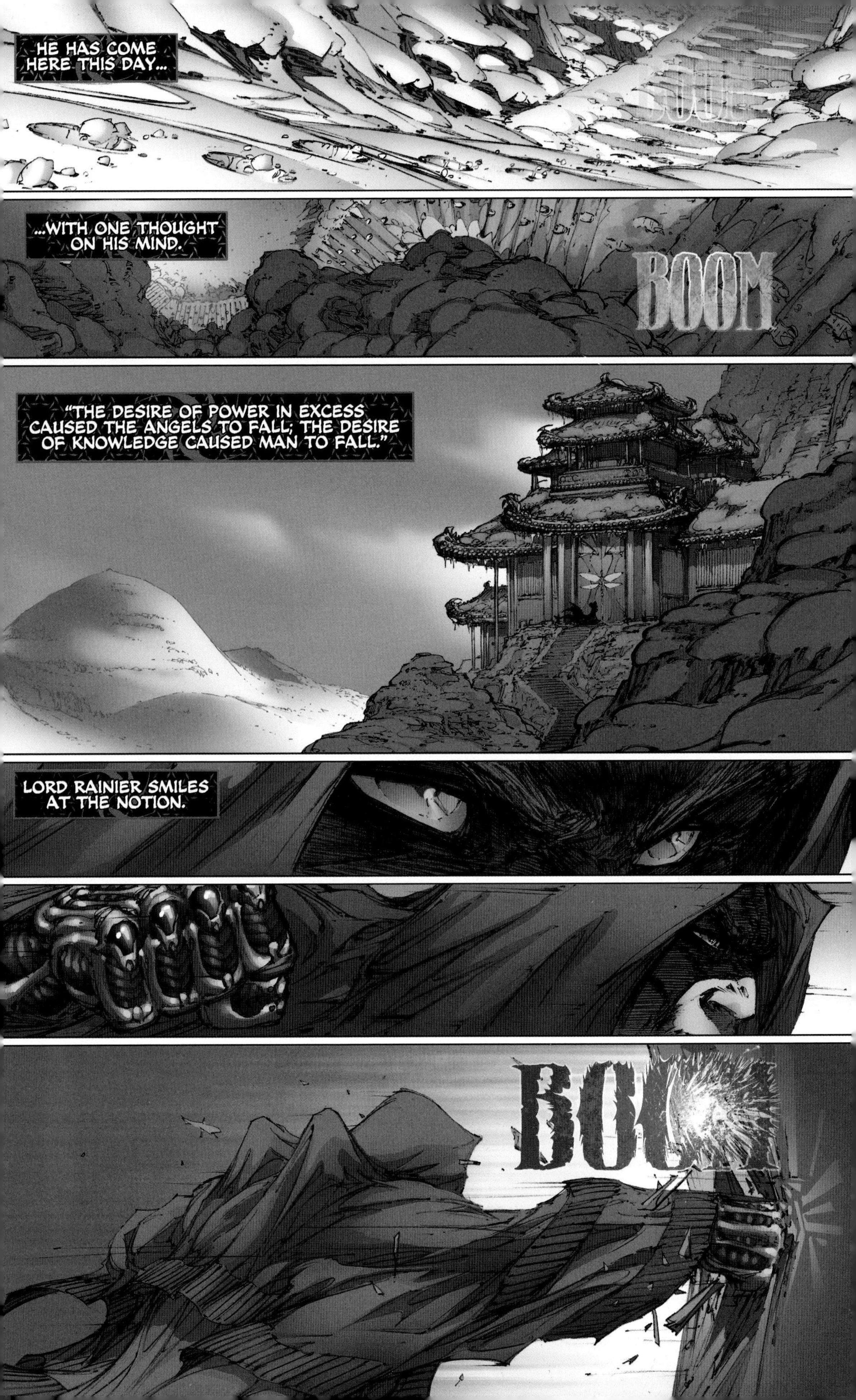
HE HAS COME HERE THIS DAY...
...WITH ONE THOUGHT ON HIS MIND.
BOOM
"THE DESIRE OF POWER IN EXCESS CAUSED THE ANGELS TO FALL; THE DESIRE OF KNOWLEDGE CAUSED MAN TO FALL."
LORD RAINIER SMILES AT THE NOTION.

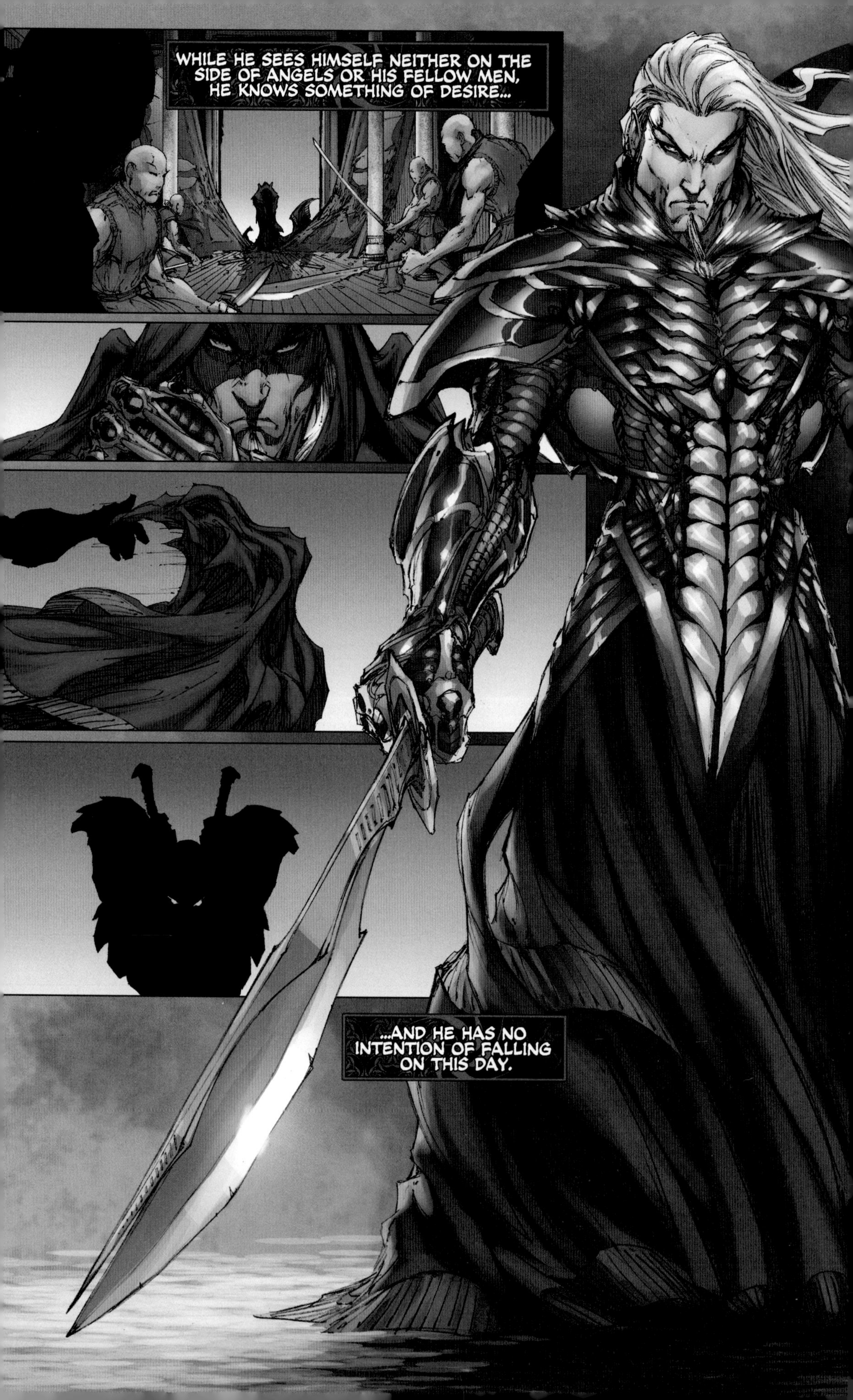
WHILE HE SEES HIMSELF NEITHER ON THE SIDE OF ANGELS OR HIS FELLOW MEN, HE KNOWS SOMETHING OF DESIRE...
...AND HE HAS NO INTENTION OF FALLING ON THIS DAY.

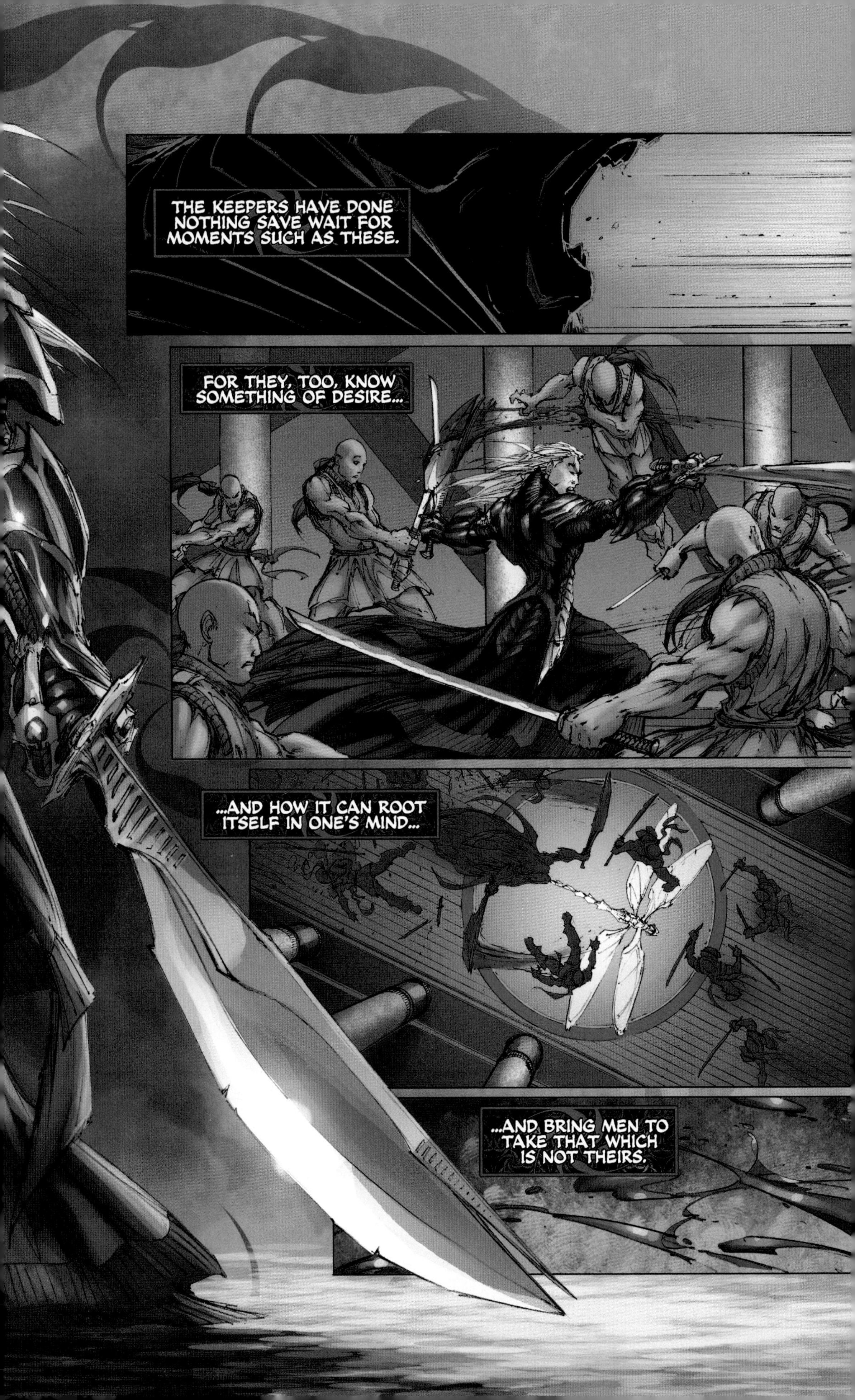
THE KEEPERS HAVE DONE NOTHING SAVE WAIT FOR MOMENTS SUCH AS THESE.
FOR THEY, TOO, KNOW SOMETHING OF DESIRE...
...AND HOW IT CAN ROOT ITSELF IN ONE'S MIND...
...AND BRING MEN TO TAKE THAT WHICH IS NOT THEIRS.

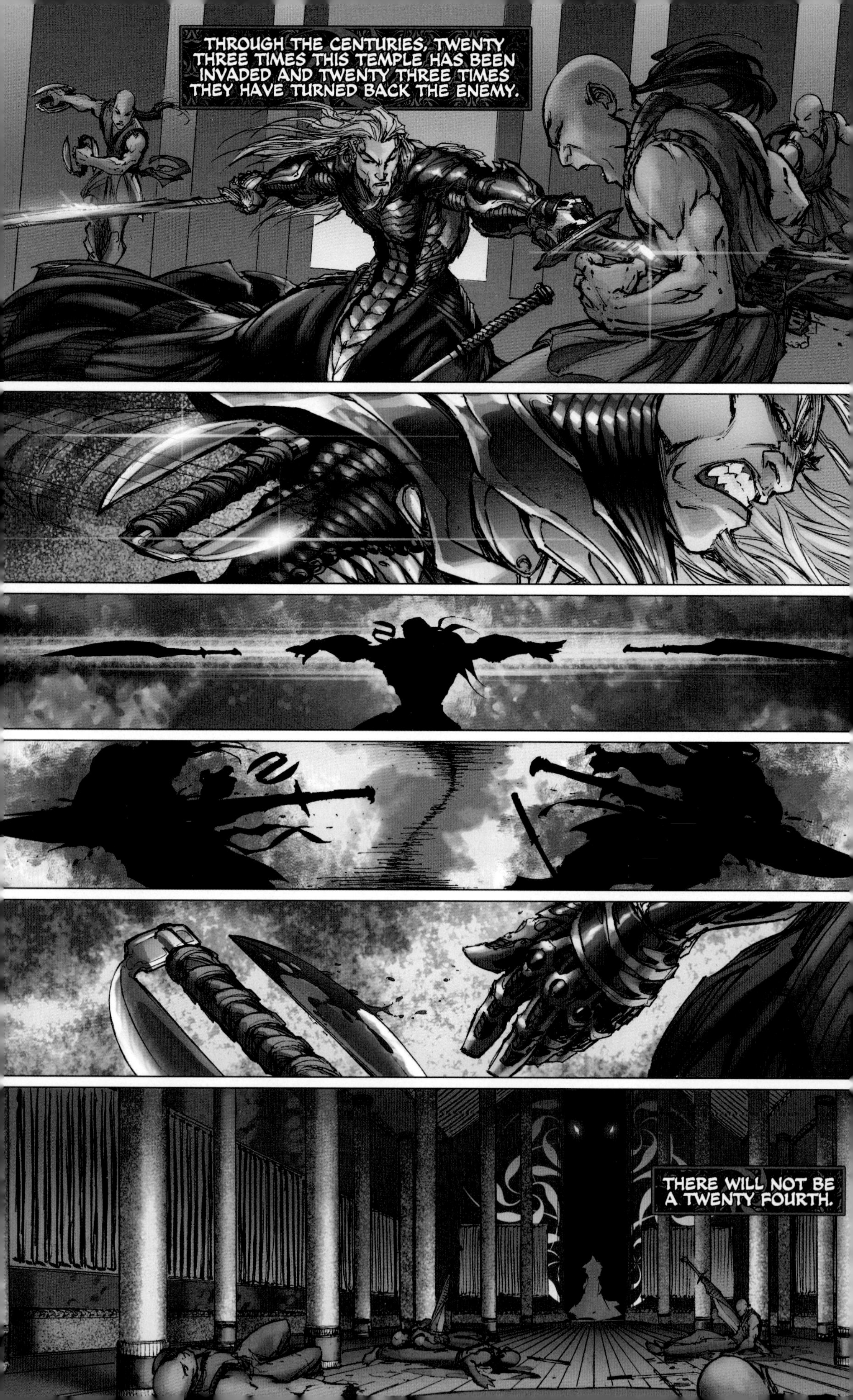
THROUGH THE CENTURIES, TWENTY THREE TIMES THIS TEMPLE HAS BEEN INVADED AND TWENTY THREE TIMES THEY HAVE TURNED BACK THE ENEMY.
THERE WILL NOT BE A TWENTY FOURTH.

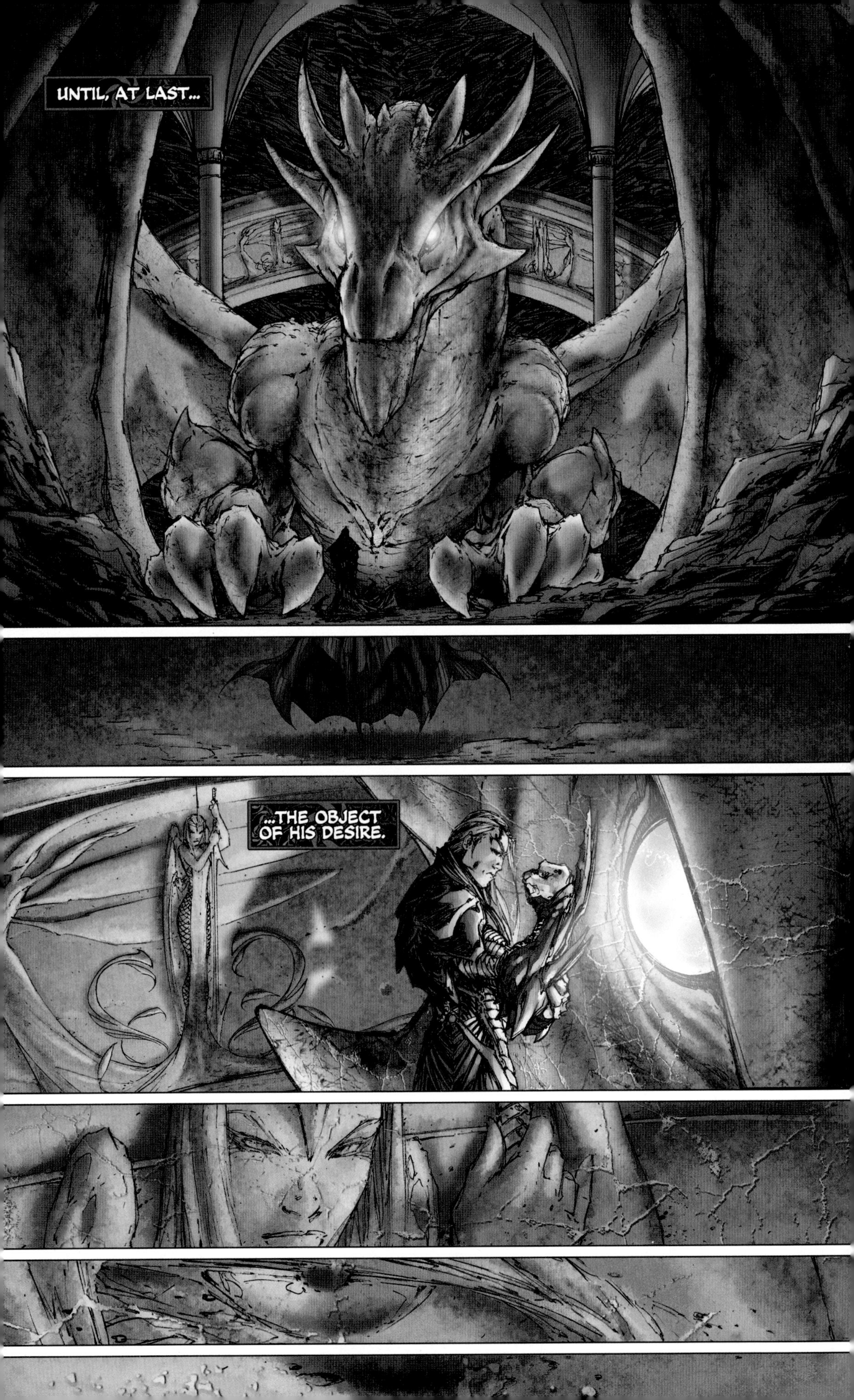
UNTIL, AT LAST...
...THE OBJECT OF HIS DESIRE.

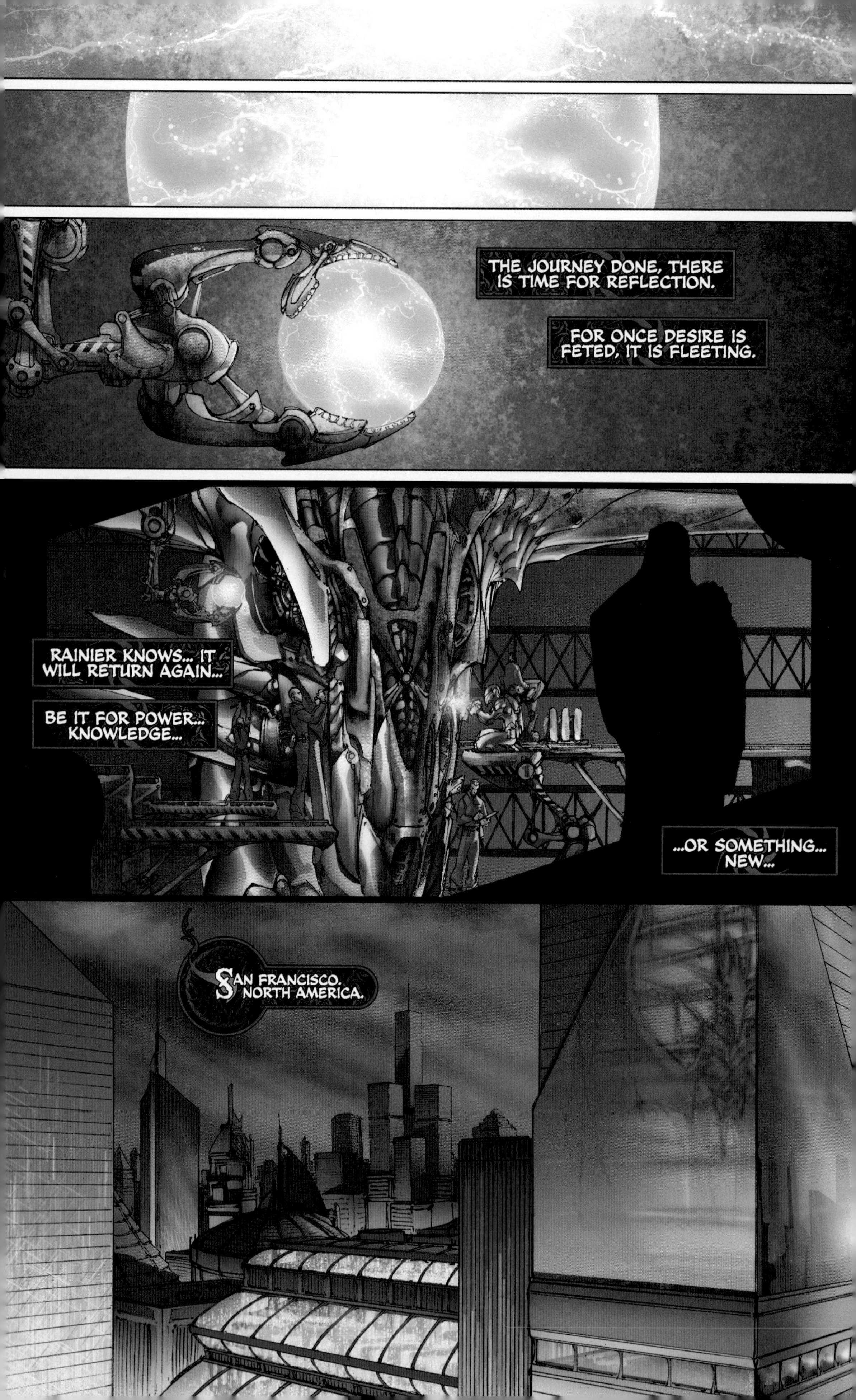
THE JOURNEY DONE, THERE IS TIME FOR REFLECTION.
FOR ONCE DESIRE IS FETED, IT IS FLEETING.
RAINIER KNOWS... IT WILL RETURN AGAIN...
BE IT FOR POWER... KNOWLEDGE...
...OR SOMETHING... NEW...
SAN FRANCISCO. NORTH AMERICA.

The Soulfire Preview issue was originally released within the pages of Wizard Magazine in March of 2003 as part of a voting contest for the fans to decide upon Michael Turner's next published property. It then became Aspen Comics' first ever-printed title, debuting to popular acclaim at that year's Pittsburgh Comic Con. This six-page preview book went on to become the most rare Aspen Comics issue to date, and features the introduction of principal Soulfire characters Malikai and Grace.

story Jeph Loeb - *story and pencils:* Michael Turner - *colors:* Peter Steigerwald
letters: Richard Starkings, Josh Reed

SOULFIRE PREVIEW

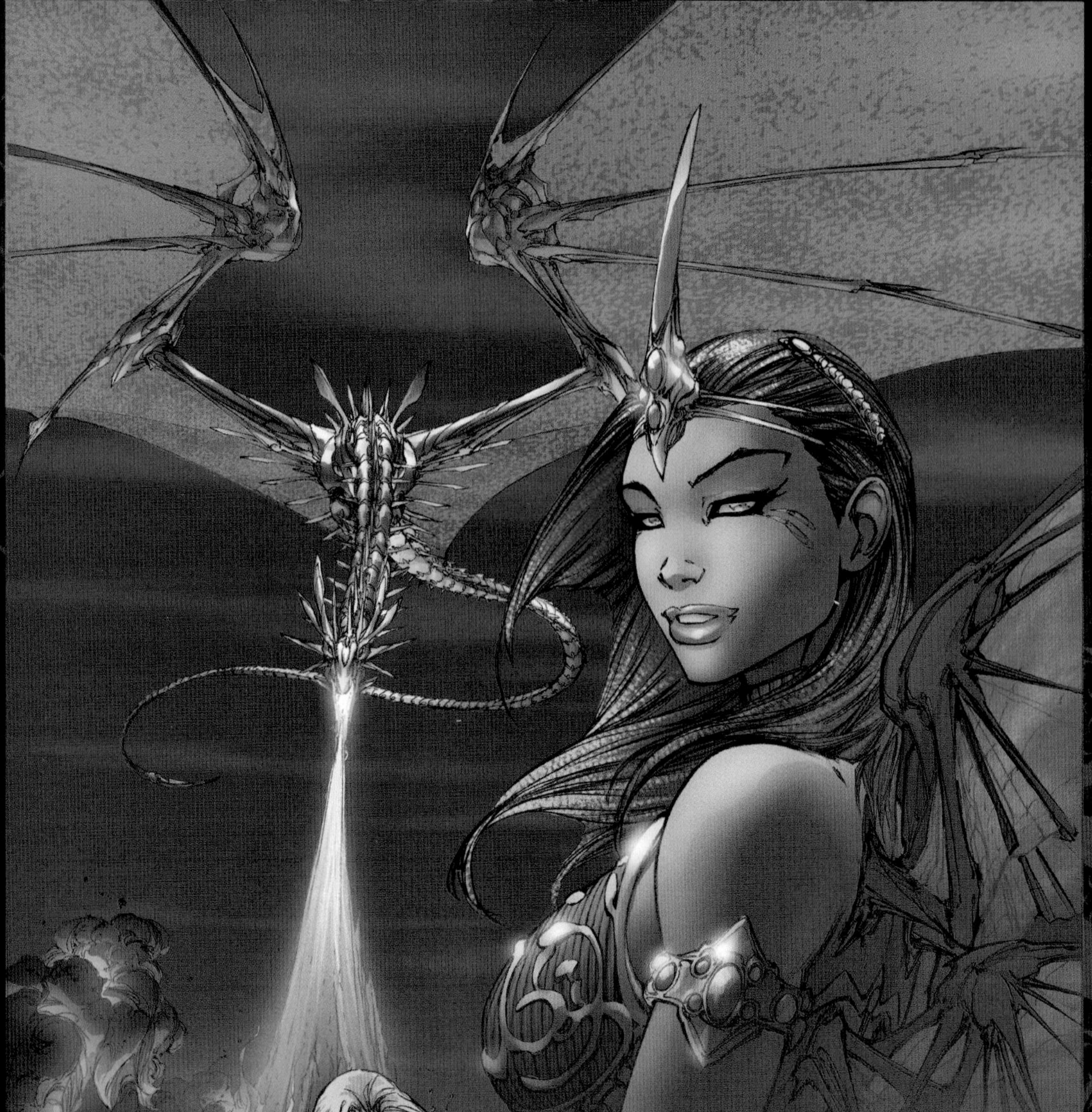
MICHAEL TURNER

Cover A

Michael Turner's: SOULFIRE PREVIEW

by

Michael TURNER · Peter STEIGERWALD

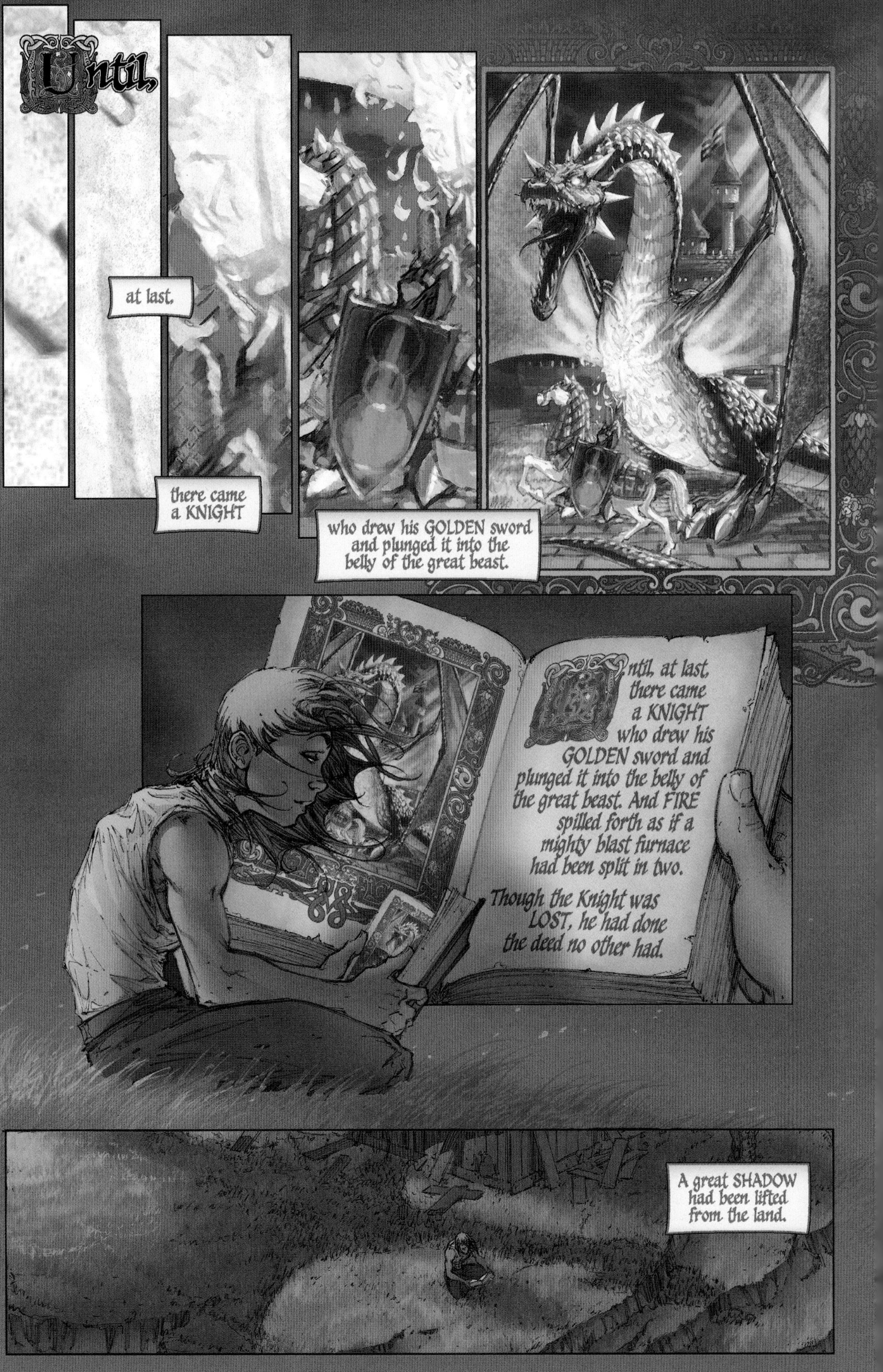
Until,
at last,
there came a KNIGHT
who drew his GOLDEN sword and plunged it into the belly of the great beast.
Until, at last, there came a KNIGHT who drew his GOLDEN sword and plunged it into the belly of the great beast. And FIRE spilled forth as if a mighty blast furnace had been split in two.
Though the Knight was LOST, he had done the deed no other had.
A great SHADOW had been lifted from the land.

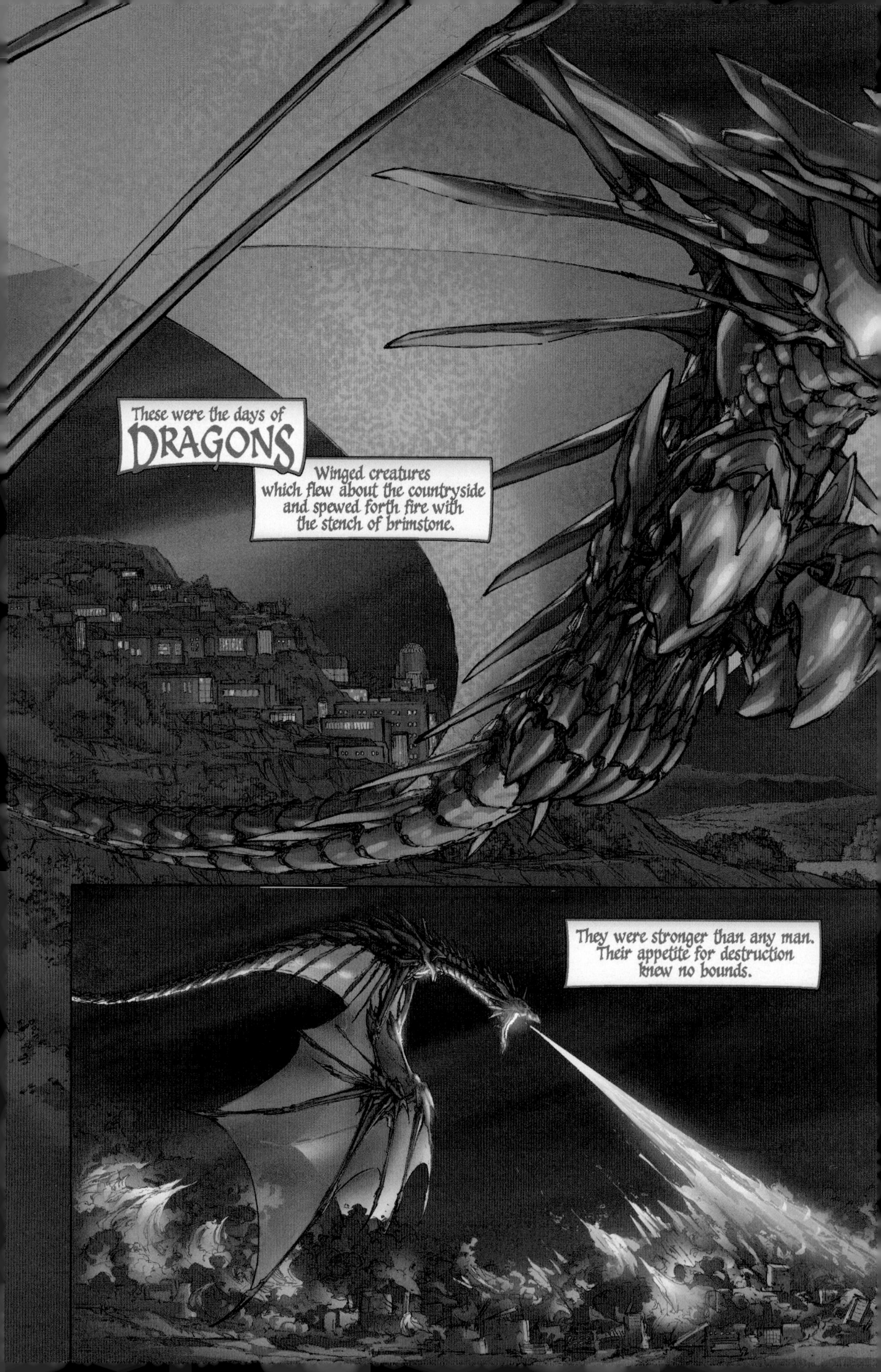
These were the days of DRAGONS
Winged creatures which flew about the countryside and spewed forth fire with the stench of brimstone.
They were stronger than any man. Their appetite for destruction knew no bounds.

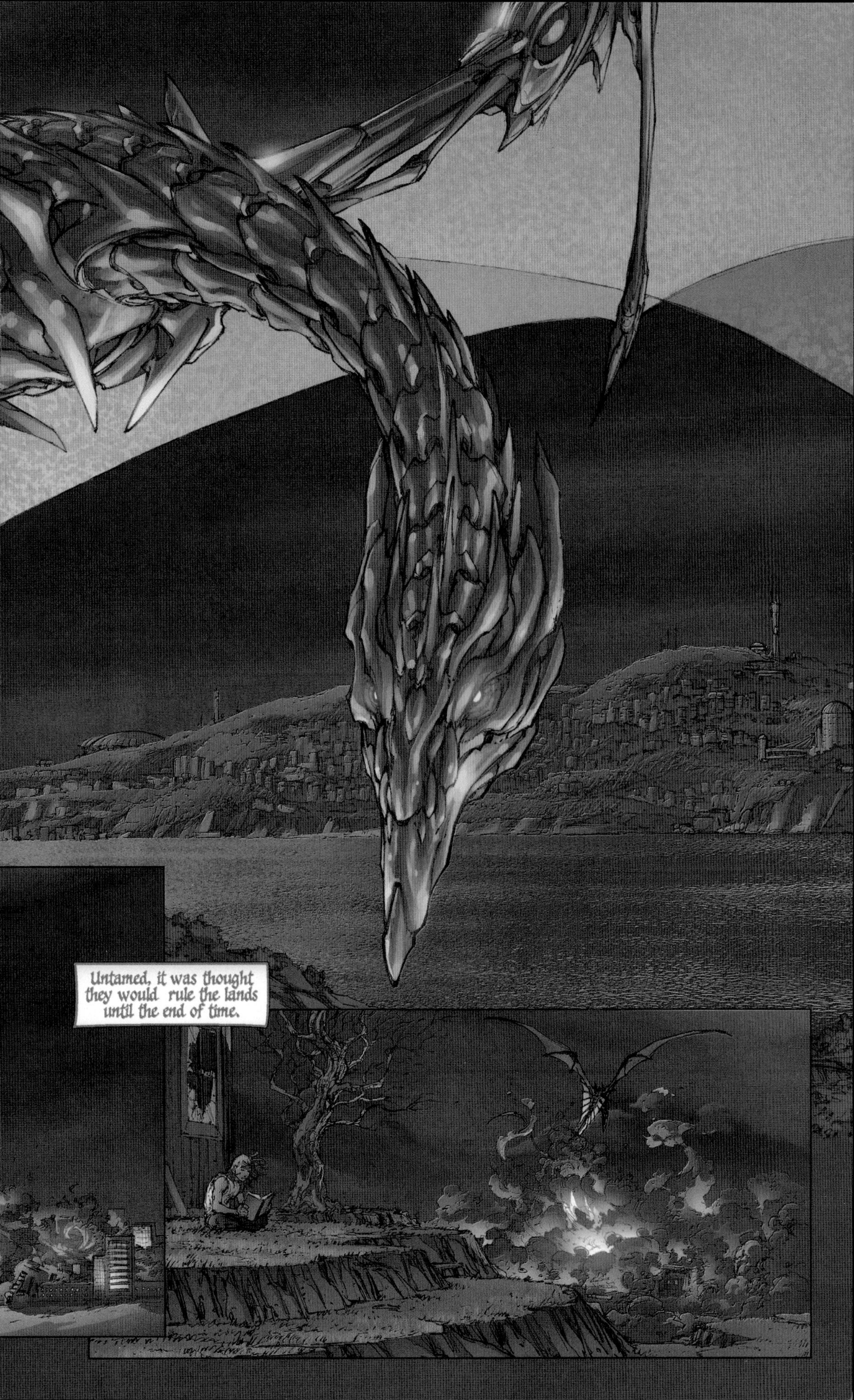
Untamed, it was thought they would rule the lands until the end of time.

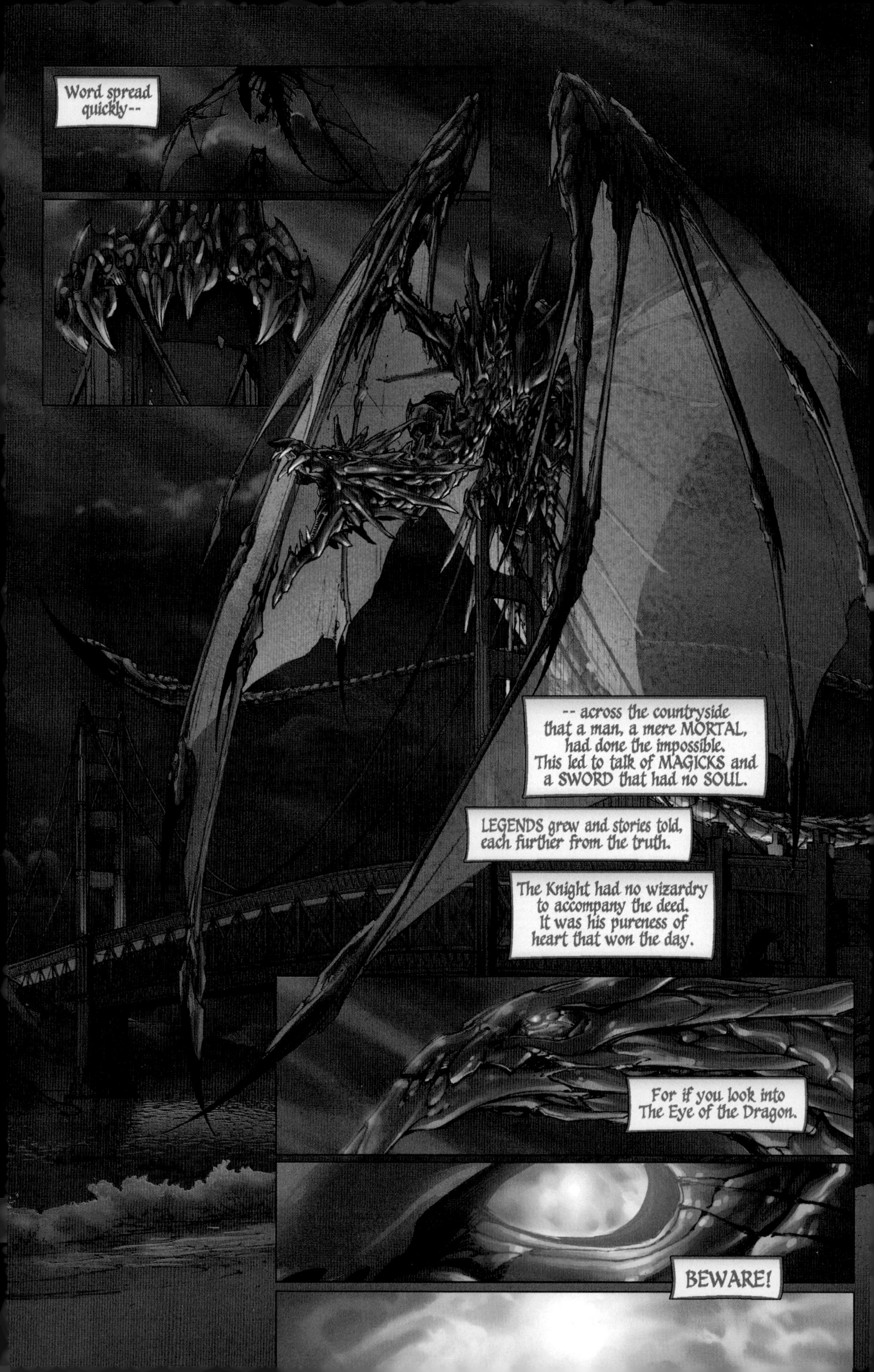
Word spread quickly--
-- across the countryside that a man, a mere MORTAL, had done the impossible. This led to talk of MAGICKS and a SWORD that had no SOUL.
LEGENDS grew and stories told, each further from the truth.
The Knight had no wizardry to accompany the deed. It was his pureness of heart that won the day.
For if you look into The Eye of the Dragon.
BEWARE!

Lest the Dragon look back into thee.
MALIKAI..?
DOES IT STILL HURT?
IT DOES.
THAT'S TO BE EXPECTED.
THEN, WHY DID YOU ASK?
GRACE...?
THEY SAID YOU WERE... GONE.
PEOPLE WILL SAY WHAT THEY THEMSELVES WANT TO HEAR.
IT'S UP TO YOU WHETHER OR NOT TO LISTEN.

COME WITH ME, MAL.
WE HAVE MUCH TO DISCUSS...
...AND PRECIOUS LITTLE TIME TO DO IT IN...
THE BEGINNING...

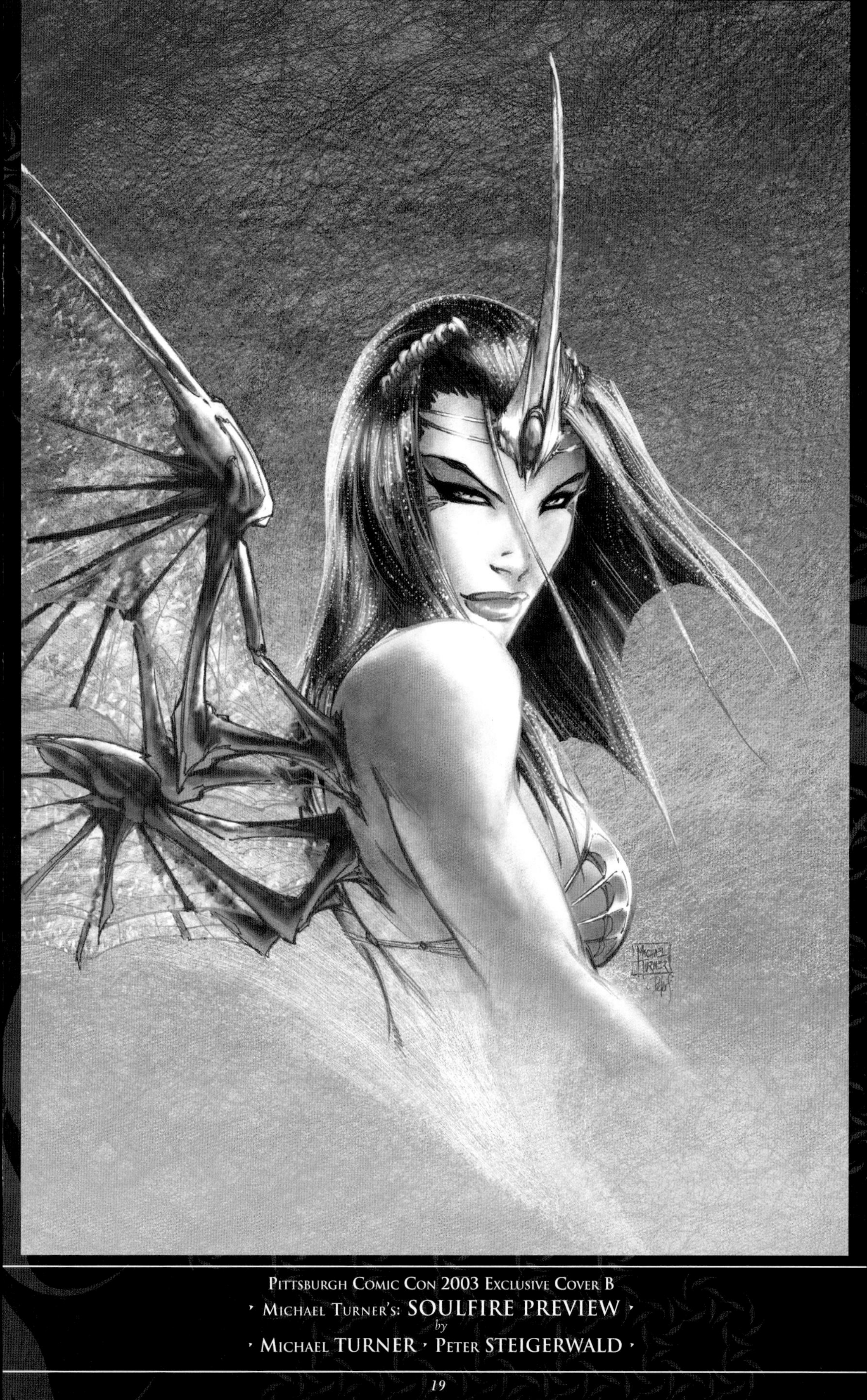
MICHAEL TURNER

Pittsburgh Comic Con 2003 Exclusive Cover B

· Michael Turner's: SOULFIRE PREVIEW ·

by

· Michael TURNER · Peter STEIGERWALD ·

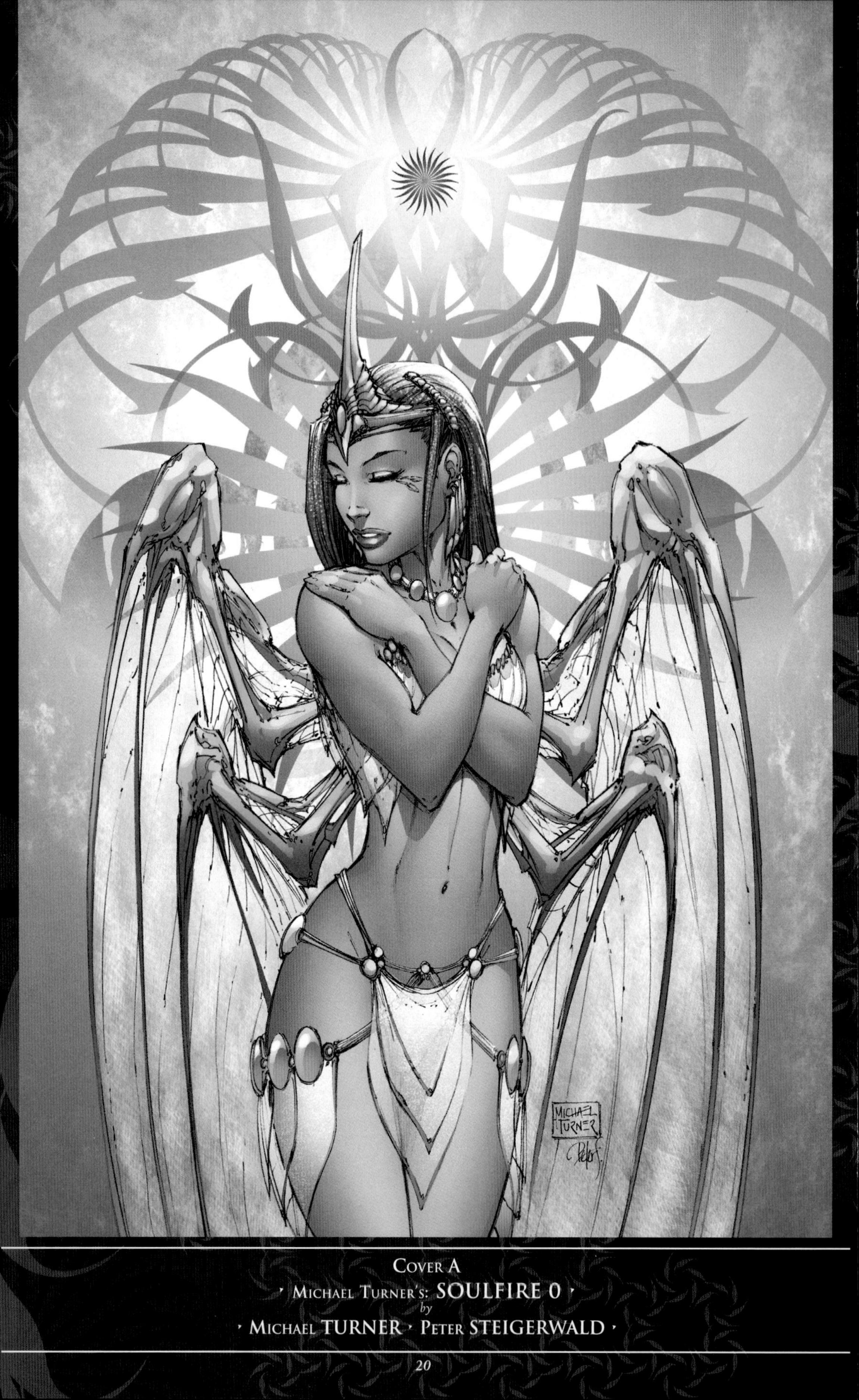
MICHAEL TURNER

Cover A

· Michael Turner's: SOULFIRE 0 ·

by

· Michael TURNER · Peter STEIGERWALD ·

The debut of Michael Turner's classic first volume launched with this lavish prologue story detailing the history of magic throughout the timeline of the Soulfire universe, as well as the malevolent rise of technology that would soon eclipse it. This introductory 12-page issue was one of the top selling independent comic books of the year.

story Jeph Loeb - *story and pencils:* Michael Turner
colors: Peter Steigerwald - *letters:* Richard Starkings, Josh Reed

SOULFIRE ZERO

SOULFIRE ZERO

The Day the Magic Died

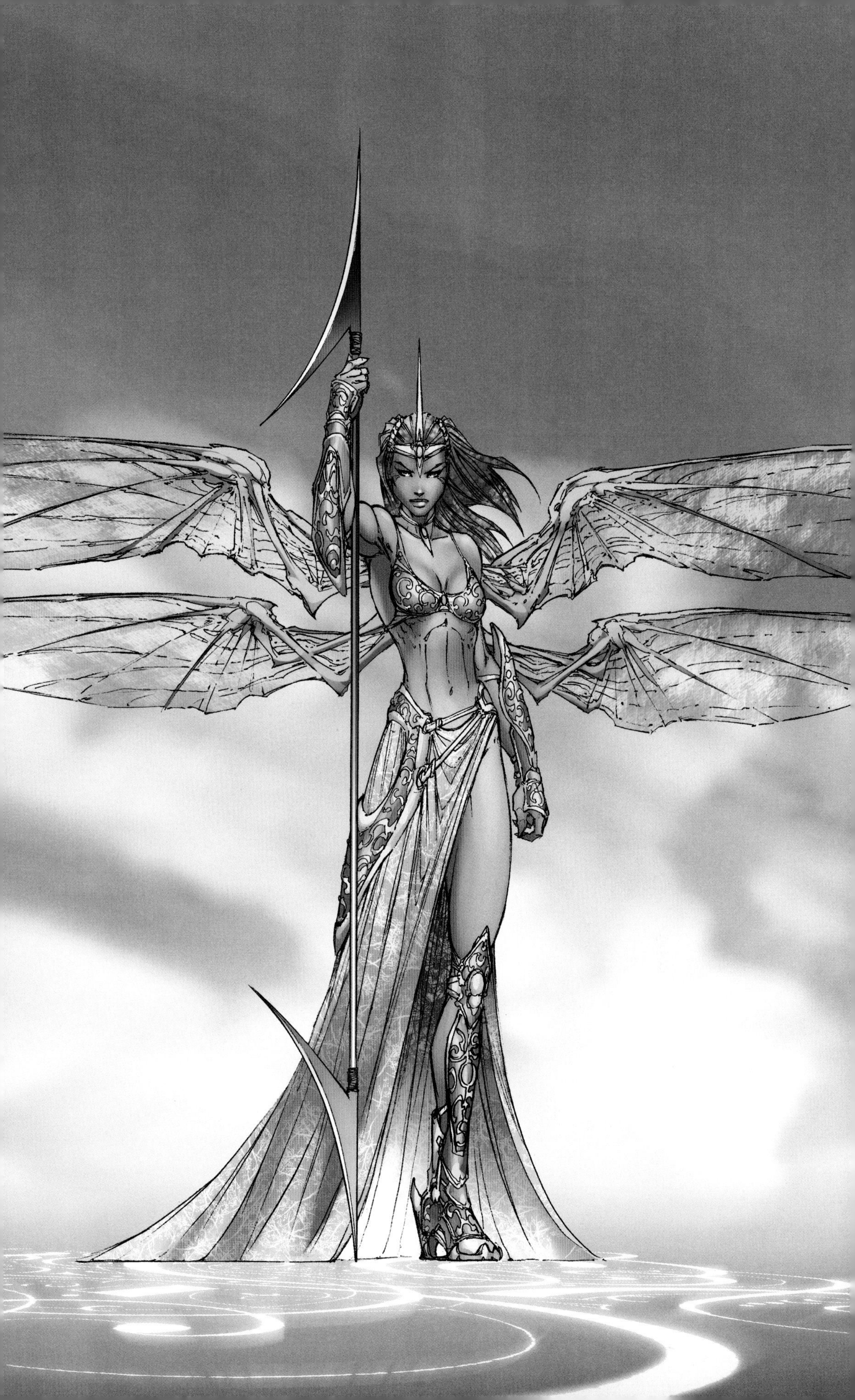

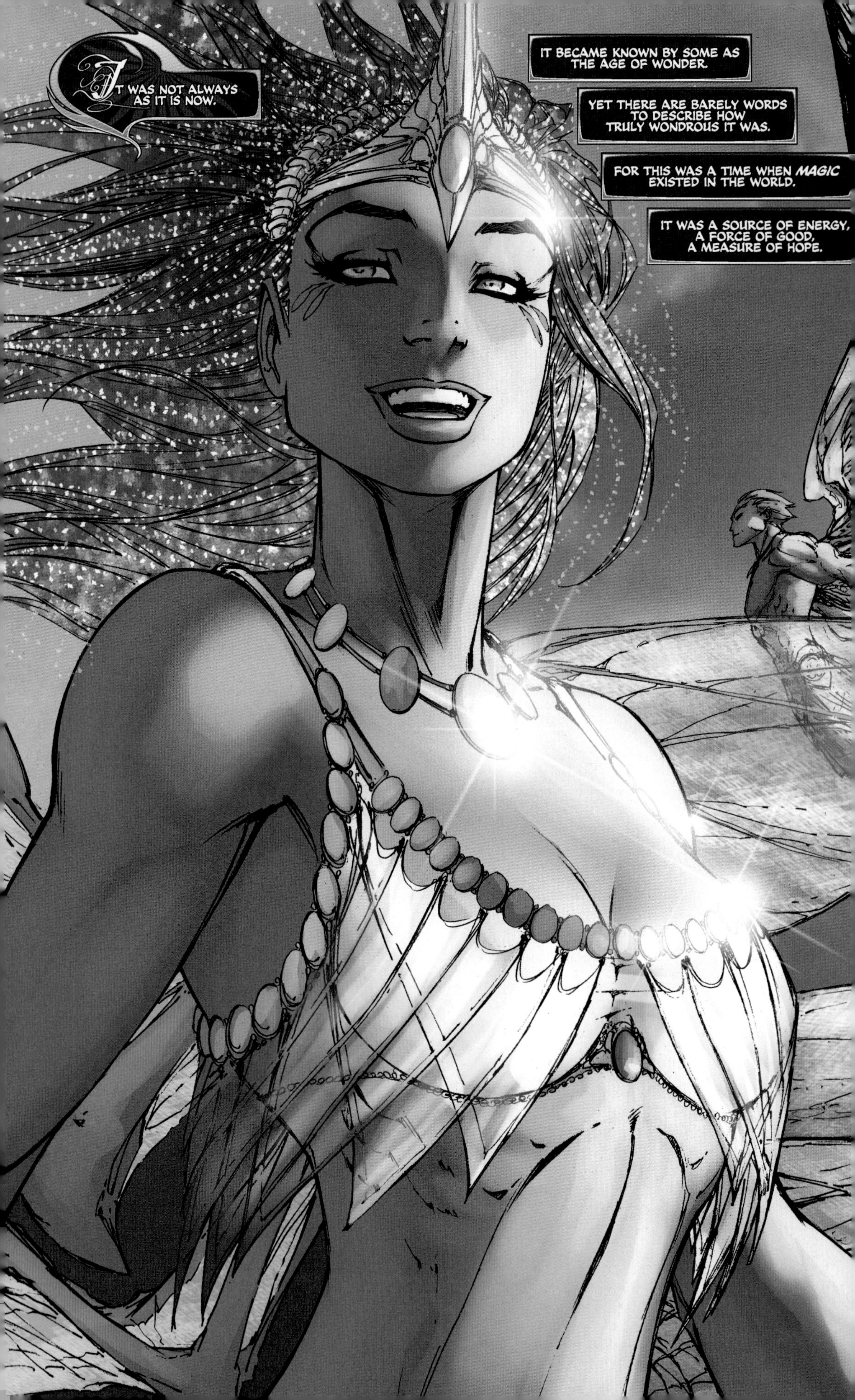
IT WAS NOT ALWAYS AS IT IS NOW.
IT BECAME KNOWN BY SOME AS THE AGE OF WONDER.
YET THERE ARE BARELY WORDS TO DESCRIBE HOW TRULY WONDROUS IT WAS.
FOR THIS WAS A TIME WHEN MAGIC EXISTED IN THE WORLD.
IT WAS A SOURCE OF ENERGY, A FORCE OF GOOD, A MEASURE OF HOPE.

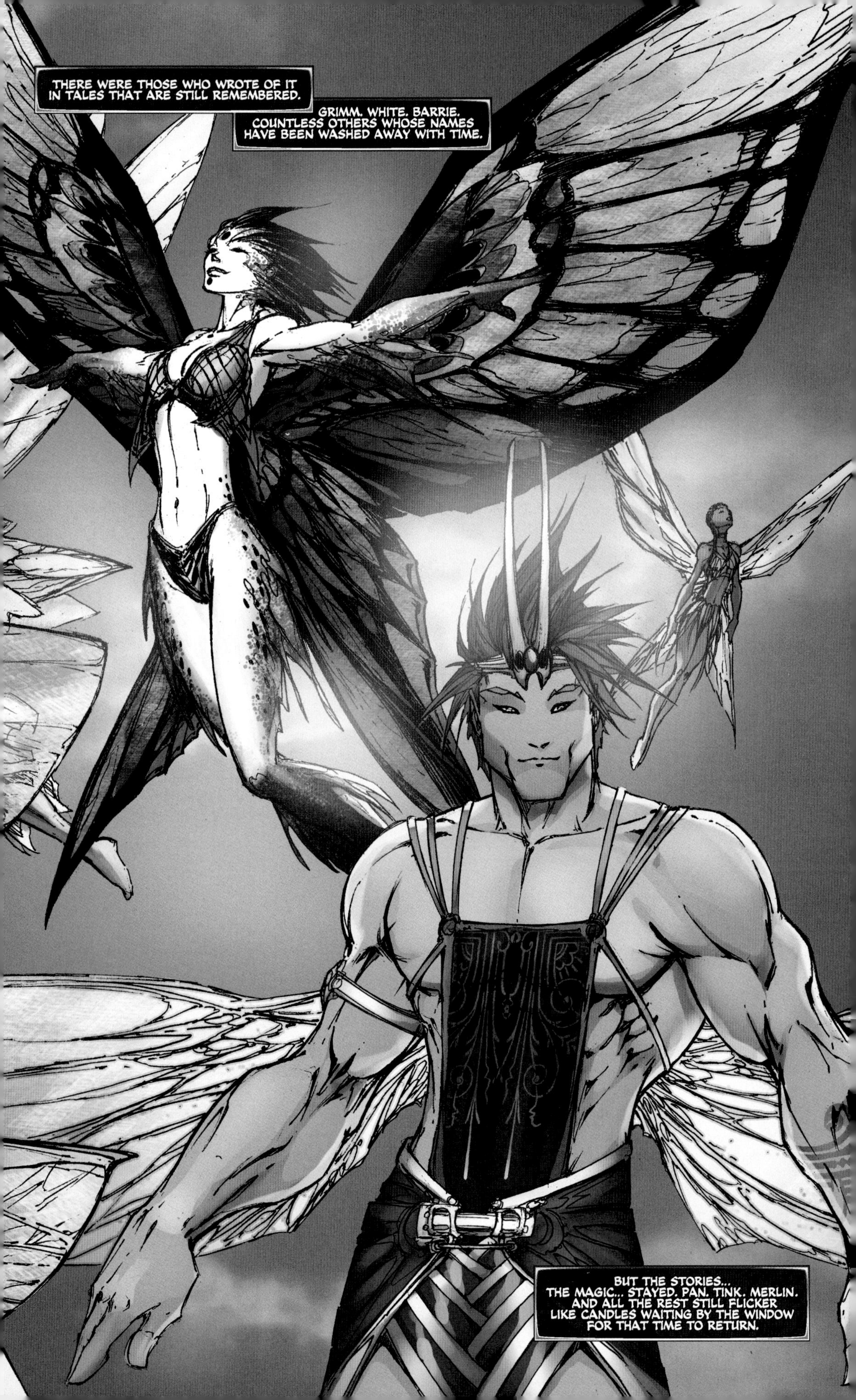
THERE WERE THOSE WHO WROTE OF IT IN TALES THAT ARE STILL REMEMBERED.
GRIMM. WHITE. BARRIE. COUNTLESS OTHERS WHOSE NAMES HAVE BEEN WASHED AWAY WITH TIME.
BUT THE STORIES... THE MAGIC... STAYED. PAN. TINK. MERLIN. AND ALL THE REST STILL FLICKER LIKE CANDLES WAITING BY THE WINDOW FOR THAT TIME TO RETURN.

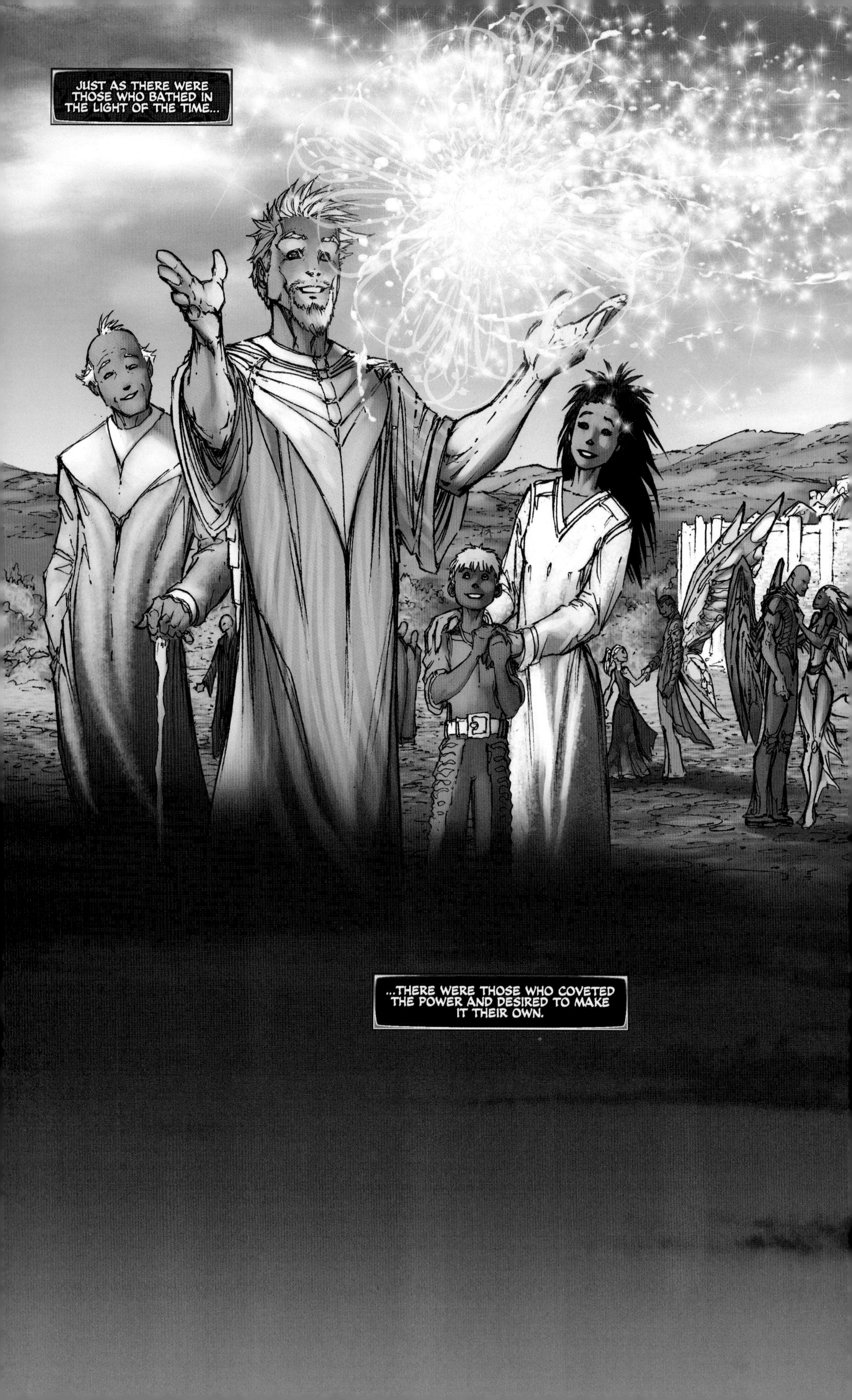
JUST AS THERE WERE THOSE WHO BATHED IN THE LIGHT OF THE TIME...
...THERE WERE THOSE WHO COVETED THE POWER AND DESIRED TO MAKE IT THEIR OWN.

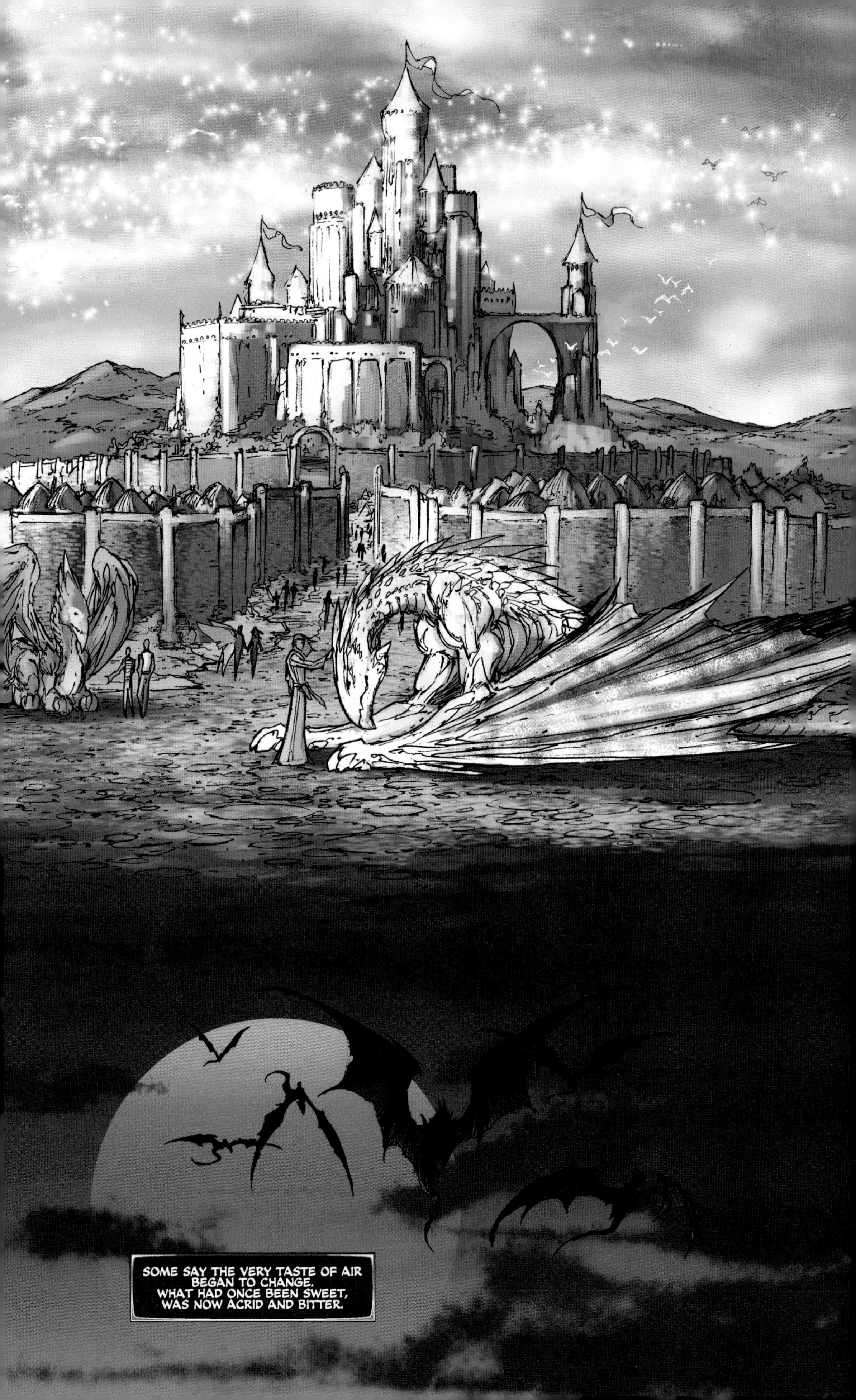
SOME SAY THE VERY TASTE OF AIR
BEGAN TO CHANGE.
WHAT HAD ONCE BEEN SWEET,
WAS NOW ACRID AND BITTER.

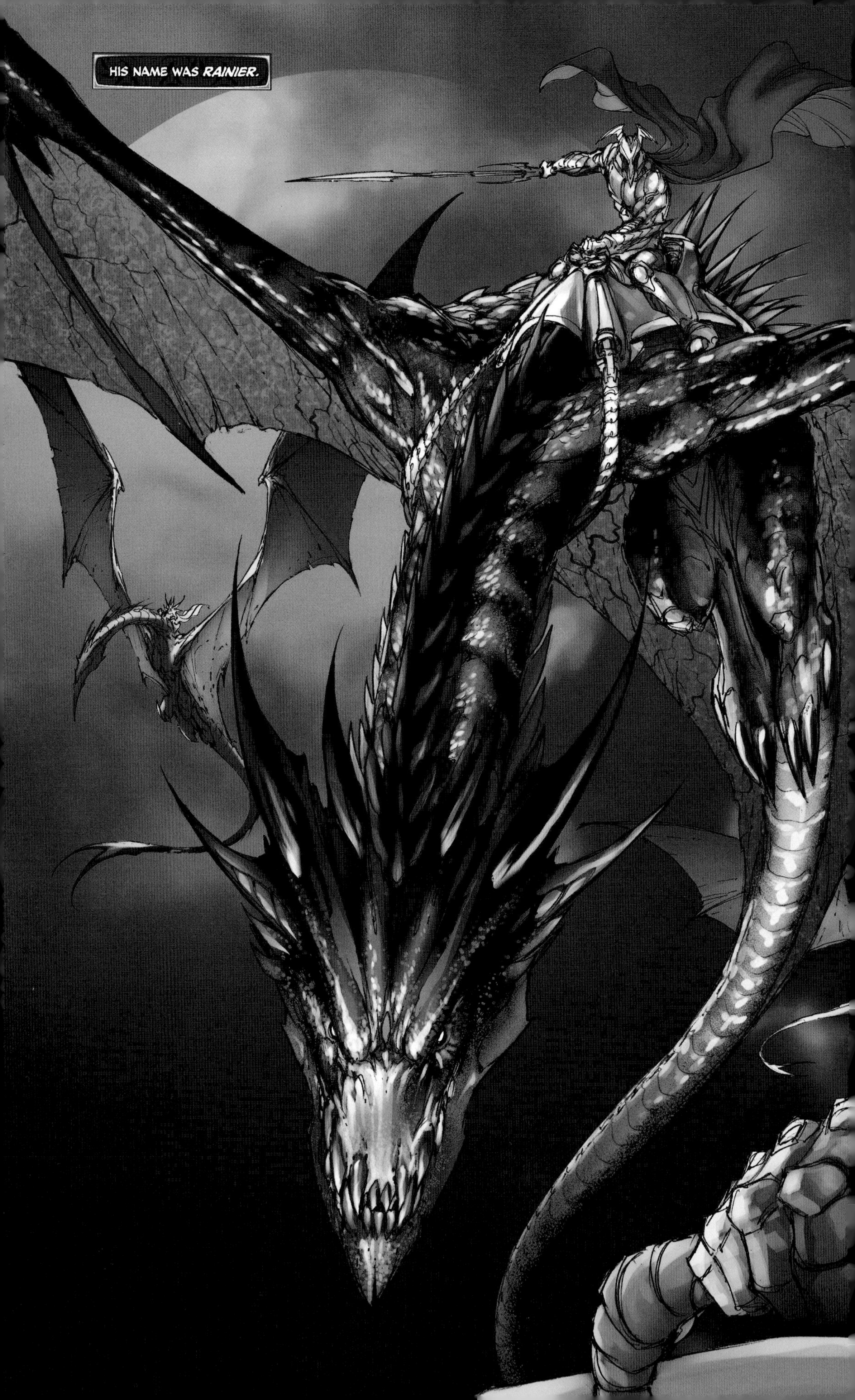
HIS NAME WAS RAINIER.

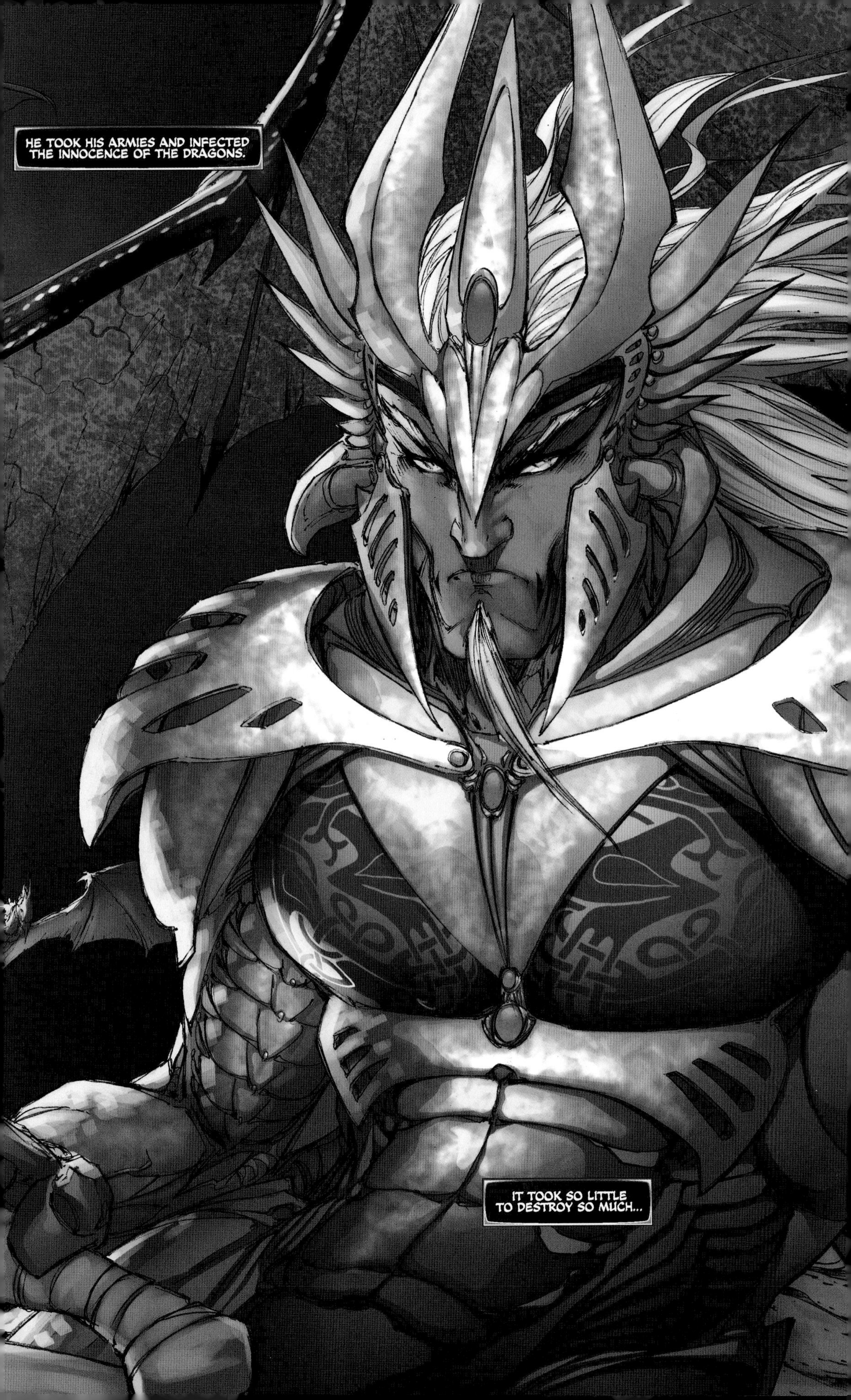
HE TOOK HIS ARMIES AND INFECTED THE INNOCENCE OF THE DRAGONS.
IT TOOK SO LITTLE TO DESTROY SO MUCH...

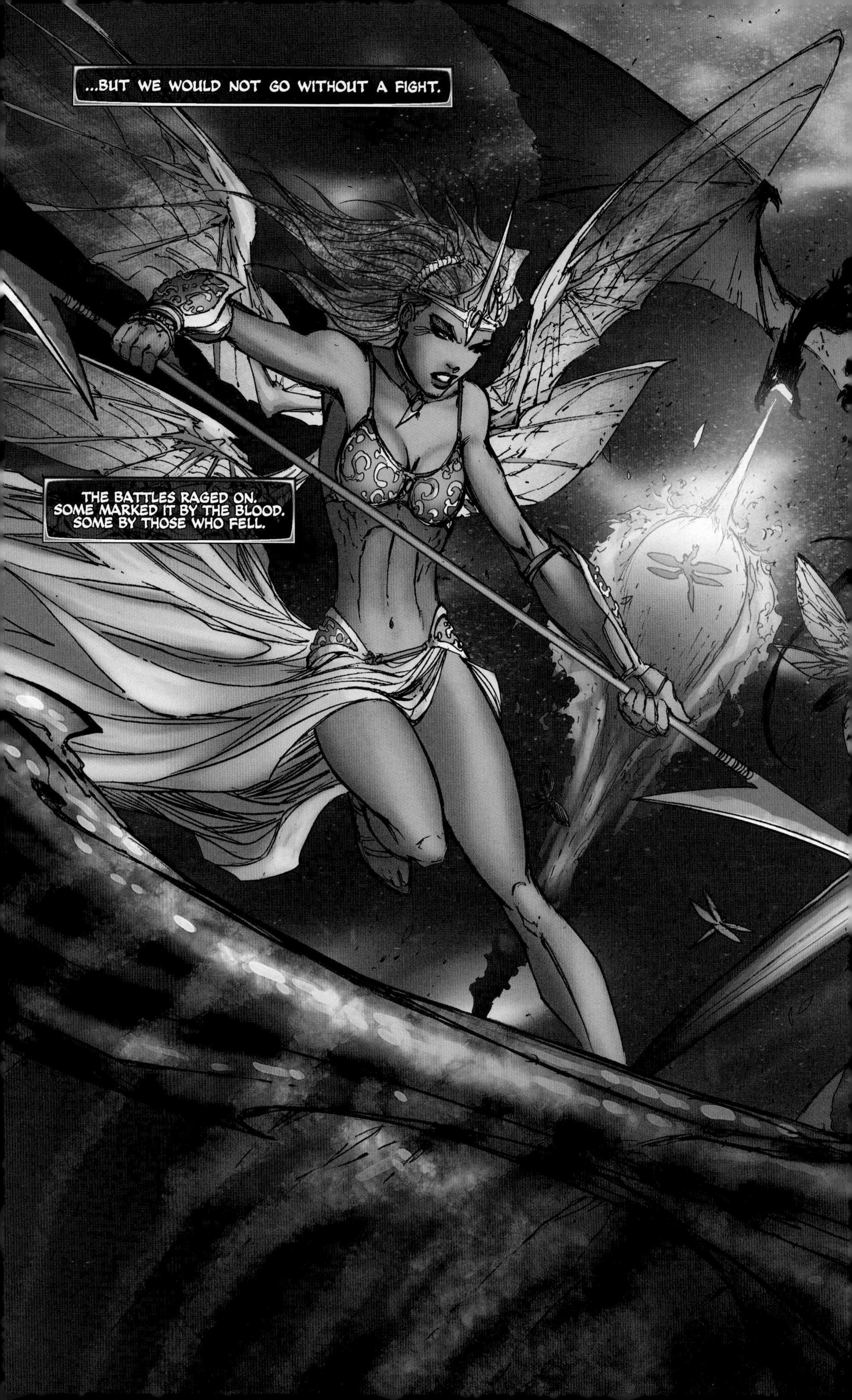
...BUT WE WOULD NOT GO WITHOUT A FIGHT.
THE BATTLES RAGED ON. SOME MARKED IT BY THE BLOOD. SOME BY THOSE WHO FELL.

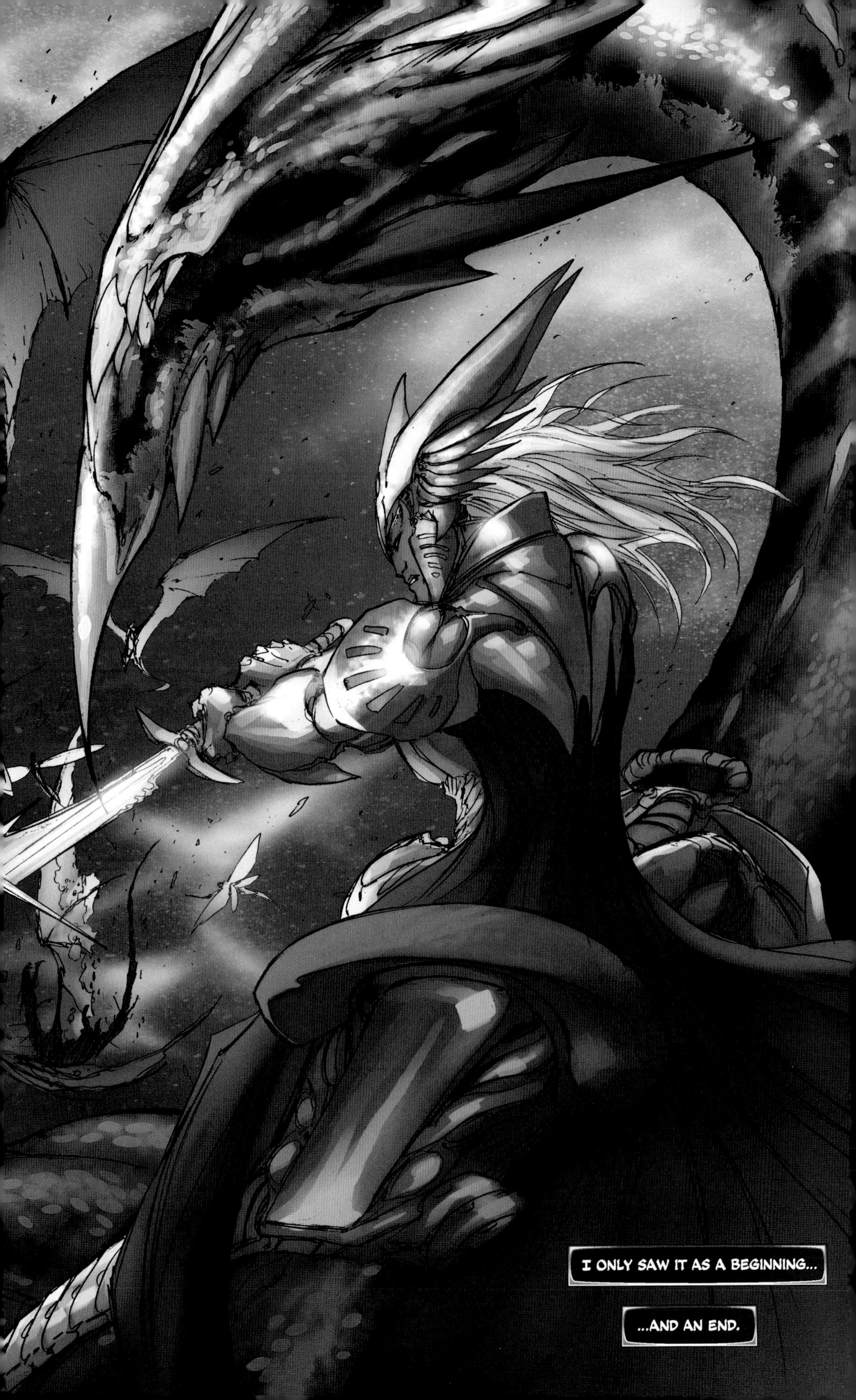
I ONLY SAW IT AS A BEGINNING...
...AND AN END.

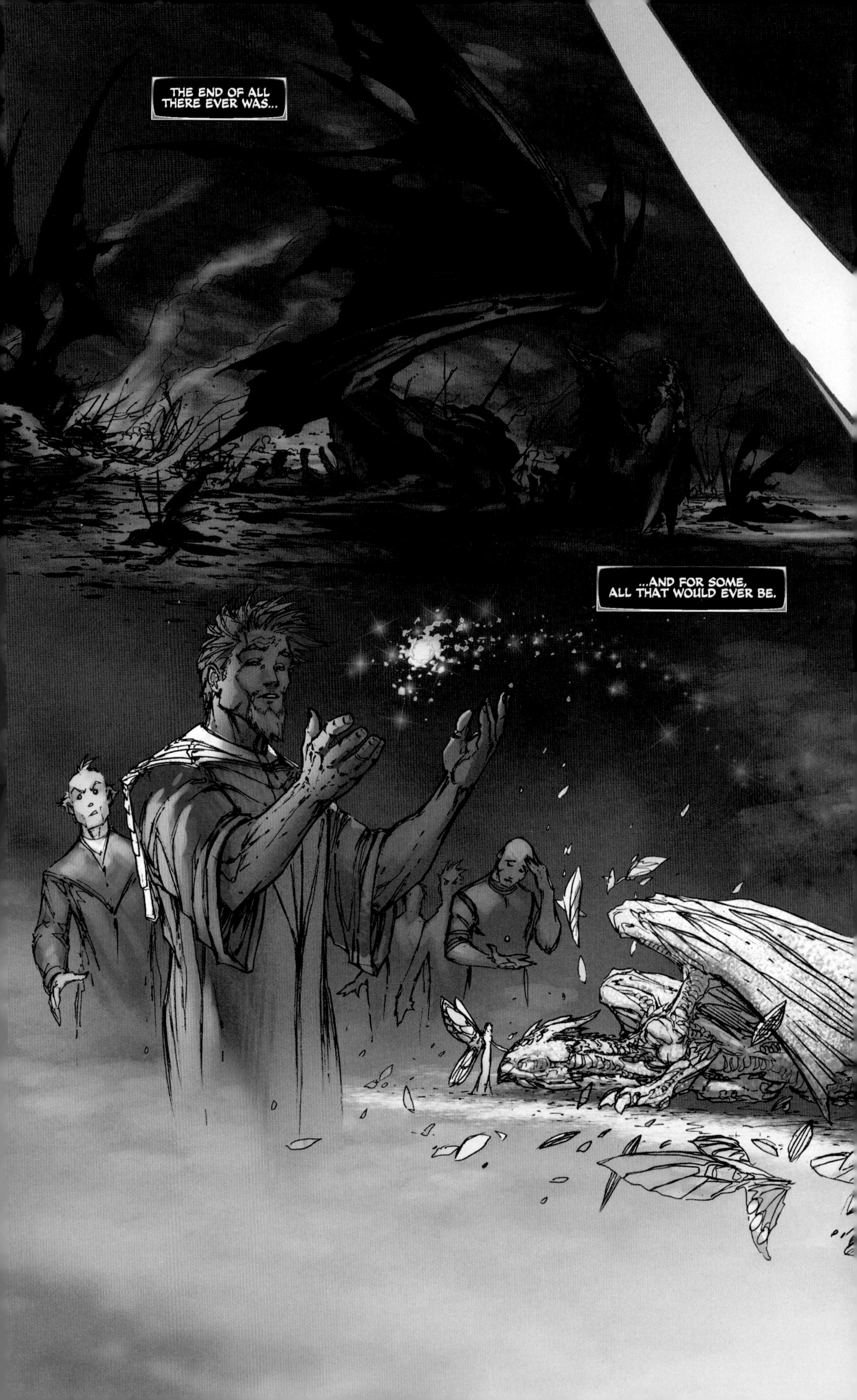
THE END OF ALL THERE EVER WAS...
...AND FOR SOME, ALL THAT WOULD EVER BE.

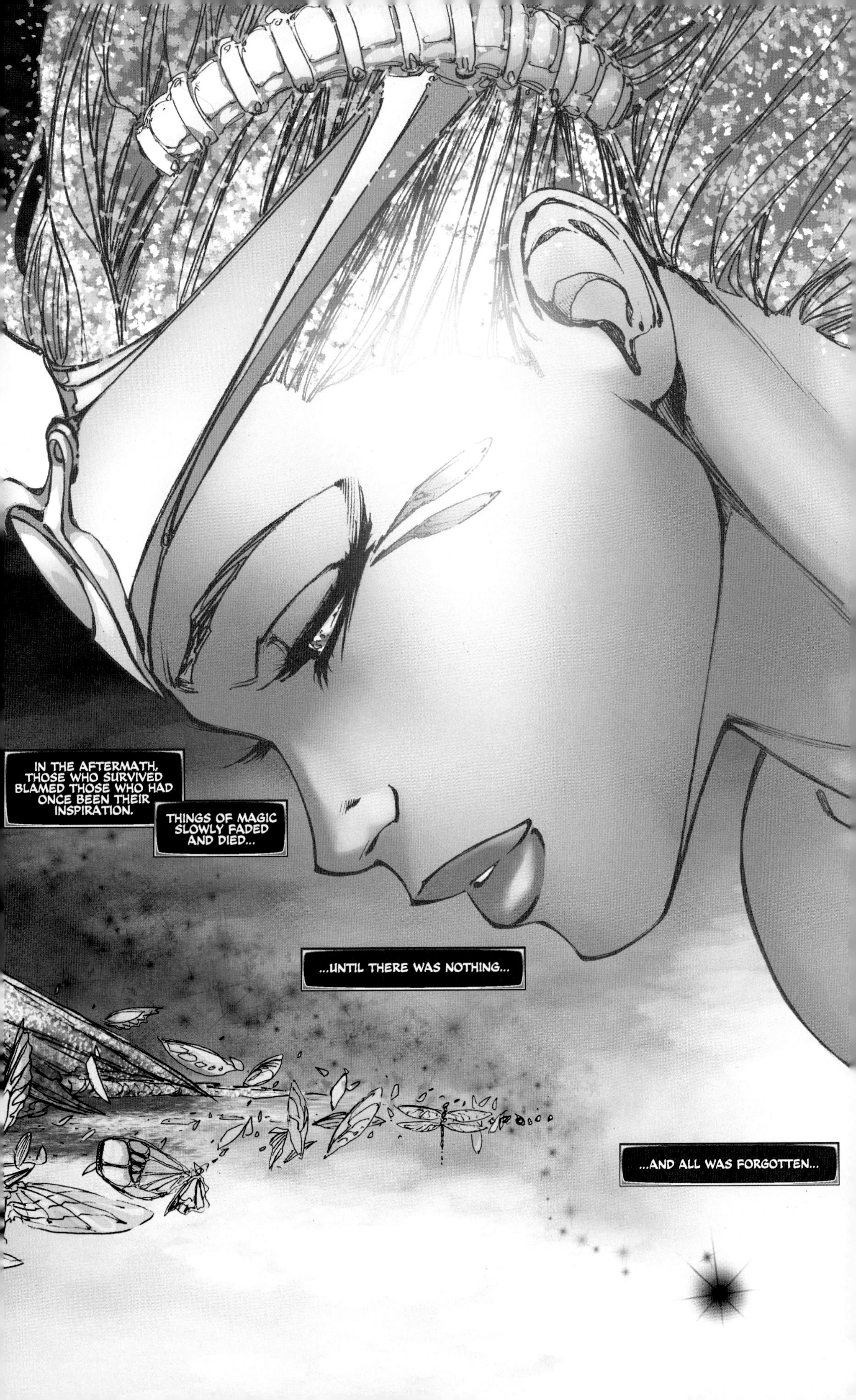
IN THE AFTERMATH, THOSE WHO SURVIVED BLAMED THOSE WHO HAD ONCE BEEN THEIR INSPIRATION.
THINGS OF MAGIC SLOWLY FADED AND DIED...
...UNTIL THERE WAS NOTHING...
...AND ALL WAS FORGOTTEN...

THERE ARE THOSE WHO SAY WE CAN REKINDLE THE AGE OF WONDER.
THAT MAGIC CANNOT EVER TRULY DIE BUT LAYS DORMANT...
...WAITING...
WAITING FOR A TIME WHEN THERE ARE THOSE WHO BELIEVE IN IT AGAIN AND SEE THE GOOD IT CAN BRING TO THE EARTH AND TO THE UNIVERSE.
QUESTION IS...
...DO YOU BELIEVE?

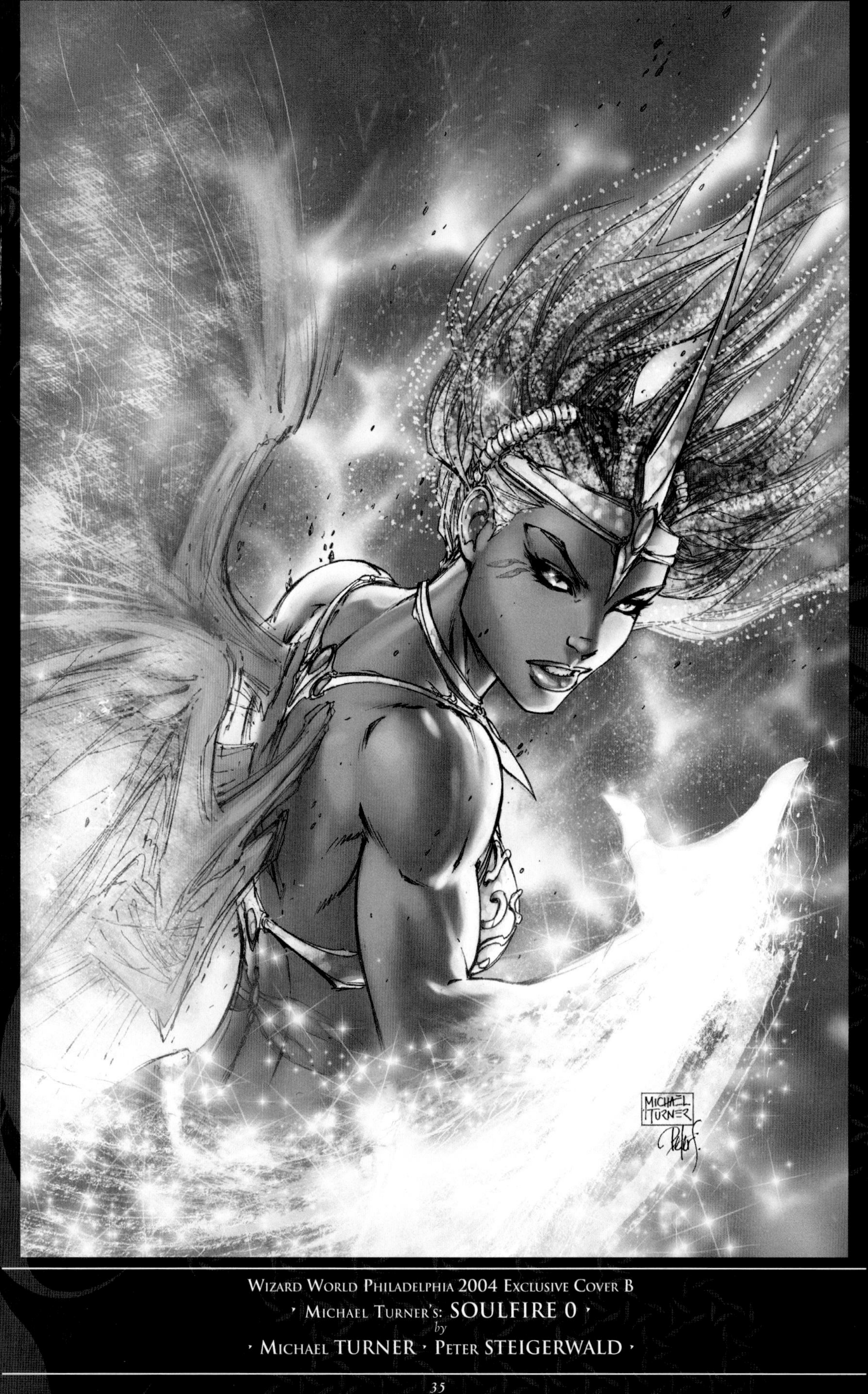
MICHAEL TURNER

Wizard World Philadelphia 2004 Exclusive Cover B

· Michael Turner's: SOULFIRE 0 ·

by

· Michael TURNER · Peter STEIGERWALD ·

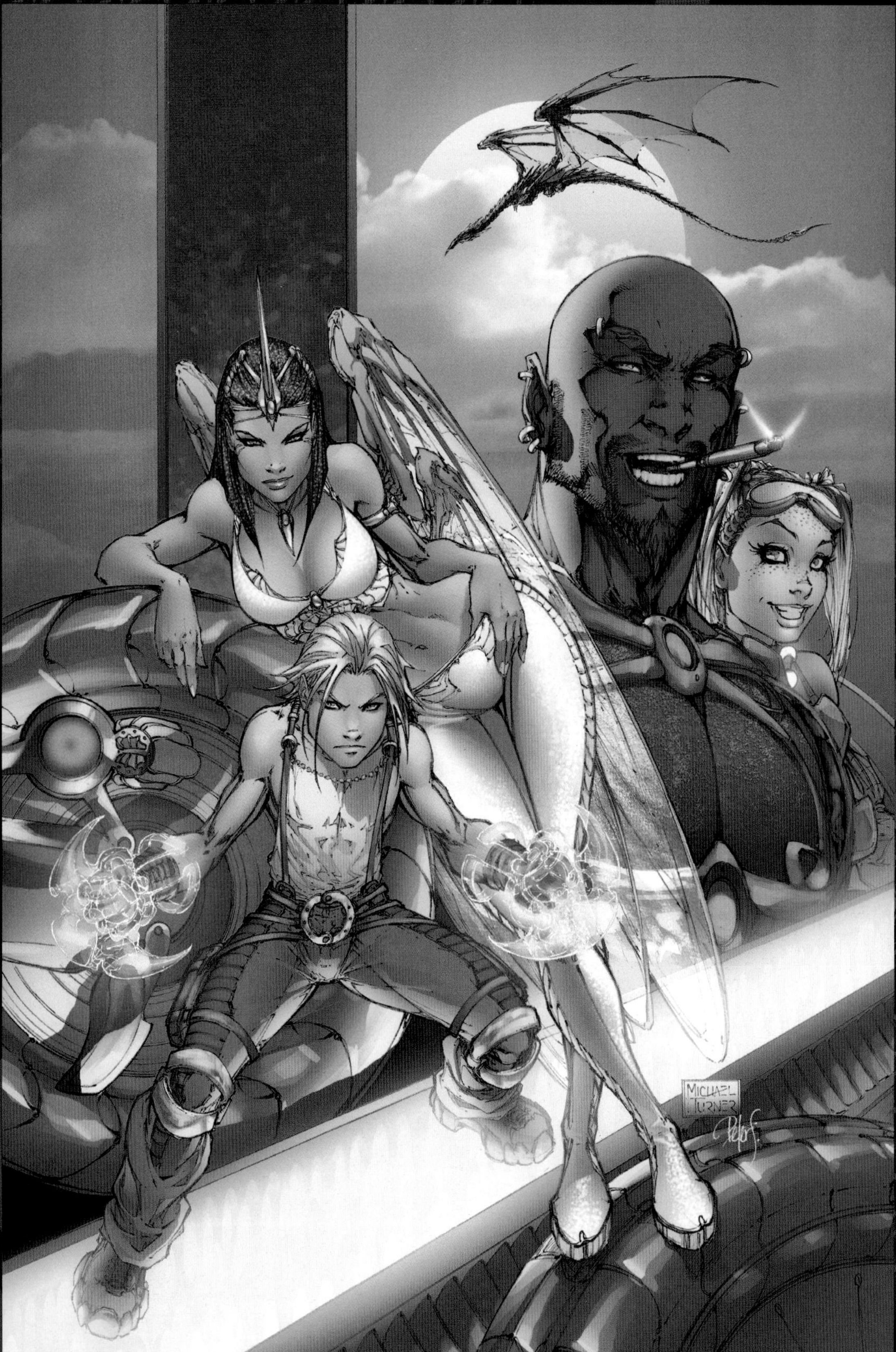
MICHAEL TURNER
Peter S.

Cover A
· Michael Turner's: SOULFIRE 1 ·
by
· Michael TURNER · Peter STEIGERWALD ·

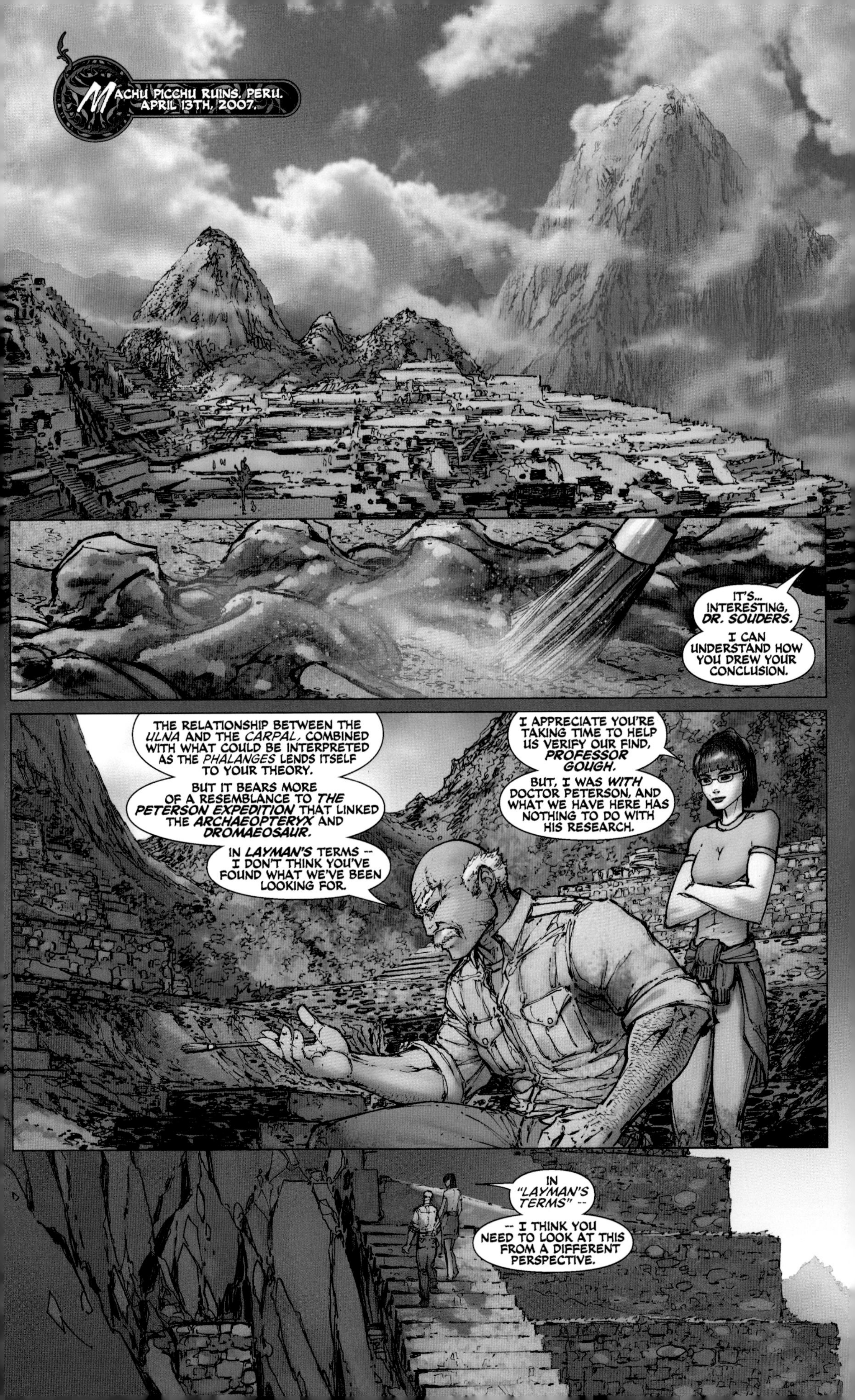

MACHU PICCHU RUINS, PERU.
APRIL 13TH, 2007.
IT'S... INTERESTING, DR. SOUDERS.
I CAN UNDERSTAND HOW YOU DREW YOUR CONCLUSION.
THE RELATIONSHIP BETWEEN THE ULNA AND THE CARPAL, COMBINED WITH WHAT COULD BE INTERPRETED AS THE PHALANGES LENDS ITSELF TO YOUR THEORY.
BUT IT BEARS MORE OF A RESEMBLANCE TO THE PETERSON EXPEDITION THAT LINKED THE ARCHAEOPTERYX AND DROMAEOSAUR.
IN LAYMAN'S TERMS -- I DON'T THINK YOU'VE FOUND WHAT WE'VE BEEN LOOKING FOR.
I APPRECIATE YOU'RE TAKING TIME TO HELP US VERIFY OUR FIND, PROFESSOR GOUGH.
BUT, I WAS WITH DOCTOR PETERSON, AND WHAT WE HAVE HERE HAS NOTHING TO DO WITH HIS RESEARCH.
IN "LAYMAN'S TERMS" --
-- I THINK YOU NEED TO LOOK AT THIS FROM A DIFFERENT PERSPECTIVE.

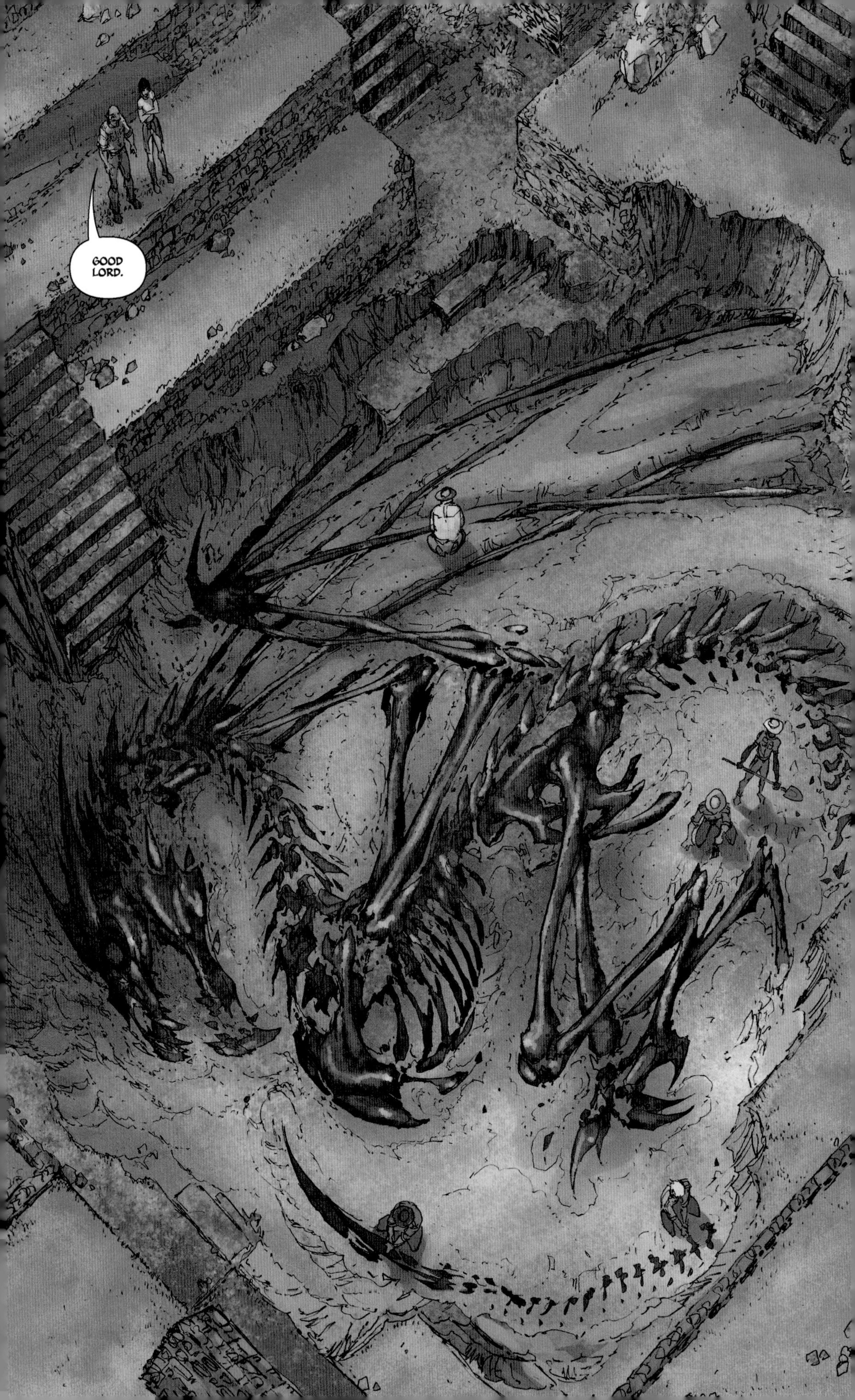
GOOD LORD.

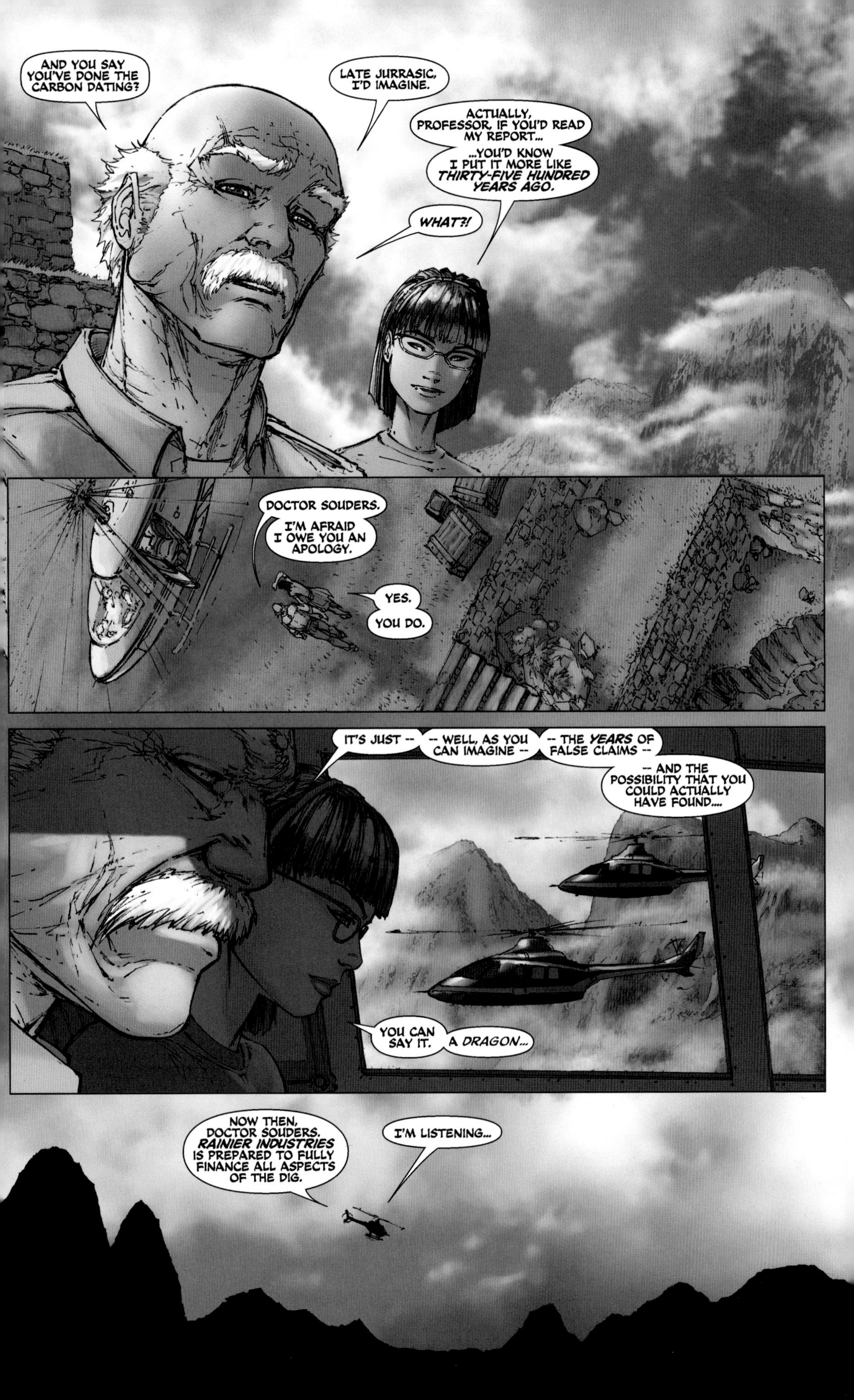
AND YOU SAY YOU'VE DONE THE CARBON DATING?
LATE JURRASIC, I'D IMAGINE.
ACTUALLY, PROFESSOR, IF YOU'D READ MY REPORT...
...YOU'D KNOW I PUT IT MORE LIKE *THIRTY-FIVE HUNDRED YEARS AGO.*
WHAT?!
DOCTOR SOUDERS. I'M AFRAID I OWE YOU AN APOLOGY.
YES.
YOU DO.
IT'S JUST --
-- WELL, AS YOU CAN IMAGINE --
-- THE *YEARS* OF FALSE CLAIMS --
-- AND THE POSSIBILITY THAT YOU COULD ACTUALLY HAVE FOUND....
YOU CAN SAY IT.
A *DRAGON*...
NOW THEN, DOCTOR SOUDERS. *RAINIER INDUSTRIES* IS PREPARED TO FULLY FINANCE ALL ASPECTS OF THE DIG.
I'M LISTENING...

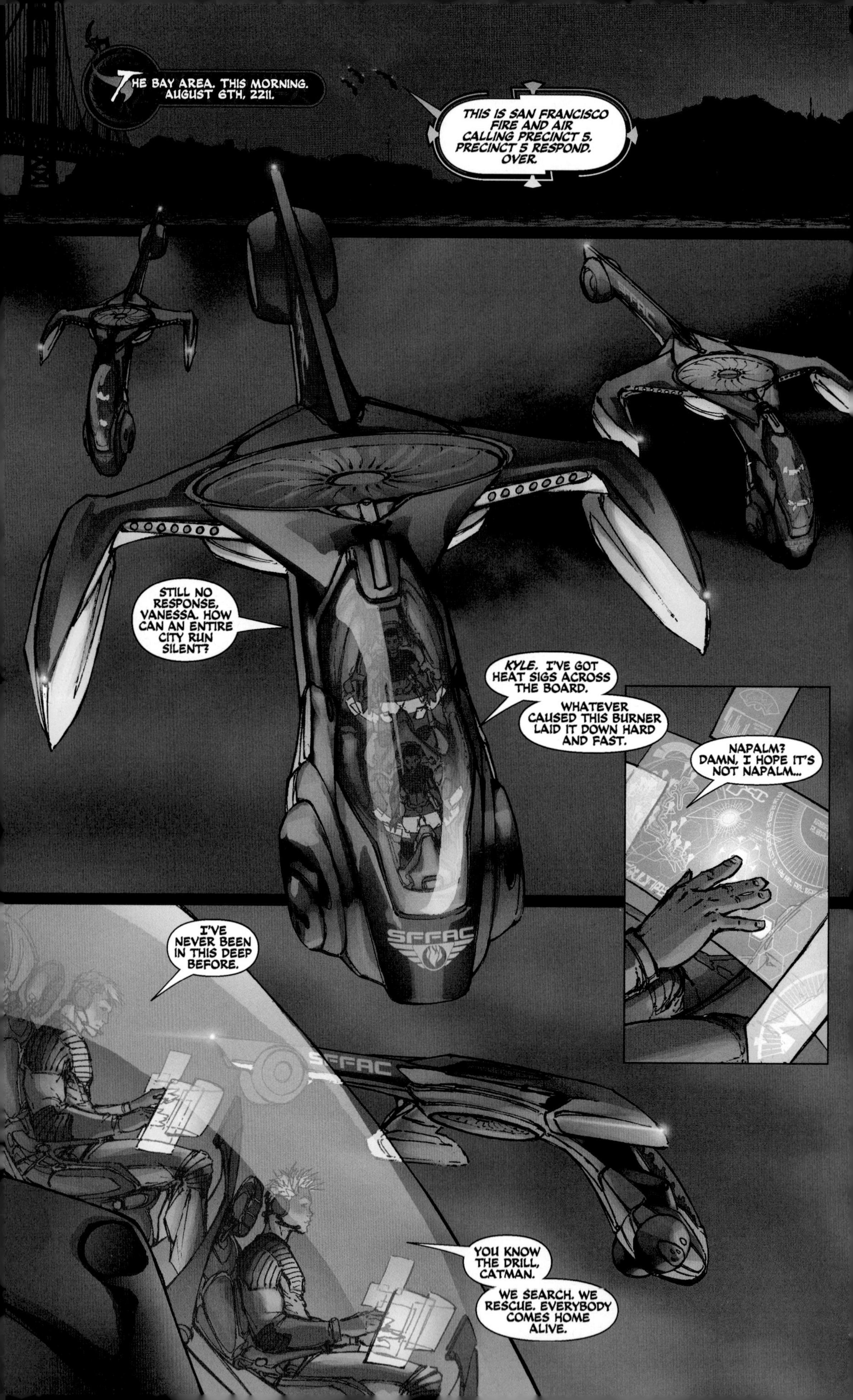
THE BAY AREA. THIS MORNING. AUGUST 6TH, 2211.
THIS IS SAN FRANCISCO FIRE AND AIR CALLING PRECINCT 5. PRECINCT 5 RESPOND. OVER.
STILL NO RESPONSE, VANESSA. HOW CAN AN ENTIRE CITY RUN SILENT?
KYLE. I'VE GOT HEAT SIGS ACROSS THE BOARD.
WHATEVER CAUSED THIS BURNER LAID IT DOWN HARD AND FAST.
NAPALM? DAMN, I HOPE IT'S NOT NAPALM...
I'VE NEVER BEEN IN THIS DEEP BEFORE.
YOU KNOW THE DRILL, CATMAN.
WE SEARCH. WE RESCUE. EVERYBODY COMES HOME ALIVE.

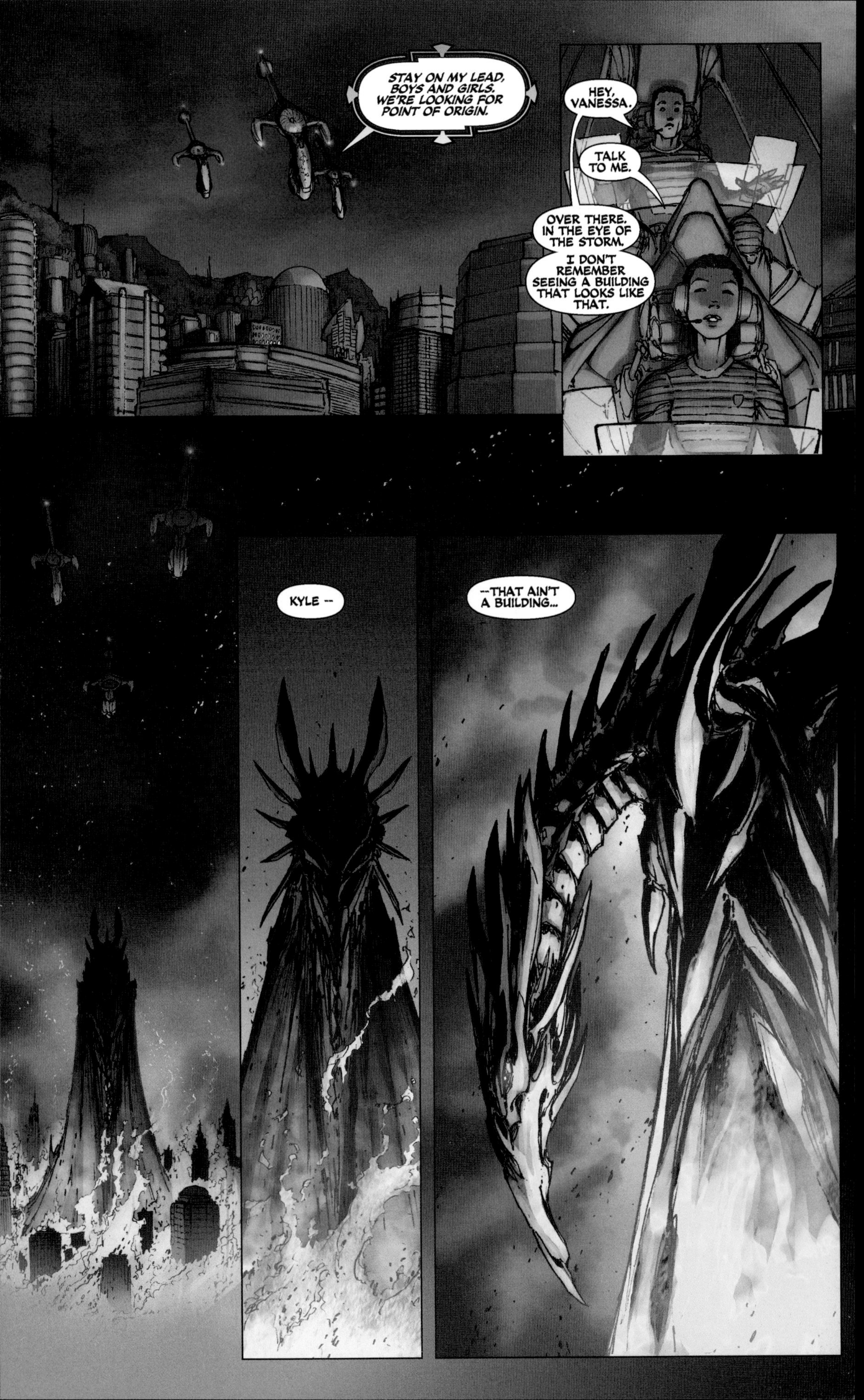
STAY ON MY LEAD, BOYS AND GIRLS. WE'RE LOOKING FOR POINT OF ORIGIN.
HEY, VANESSA.
TALK TO ME.
OVER THERE. IN THE EYE OF THE STORM.
I DON'T REMEMBER SEEING A BUILDING THAT LOOKS LIKE THAT.
KYLE --
--THAT AIN'T A BUILDING...

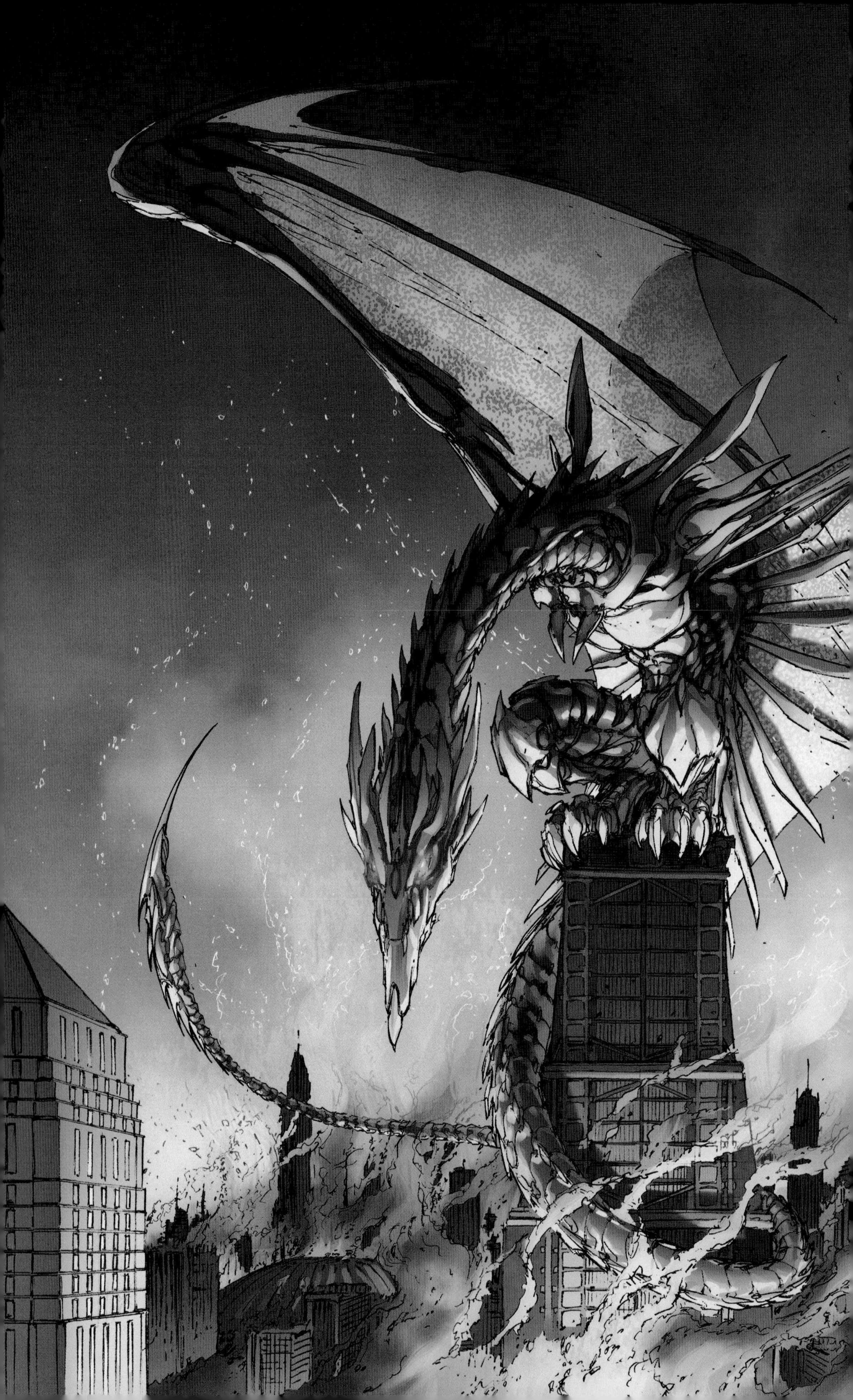

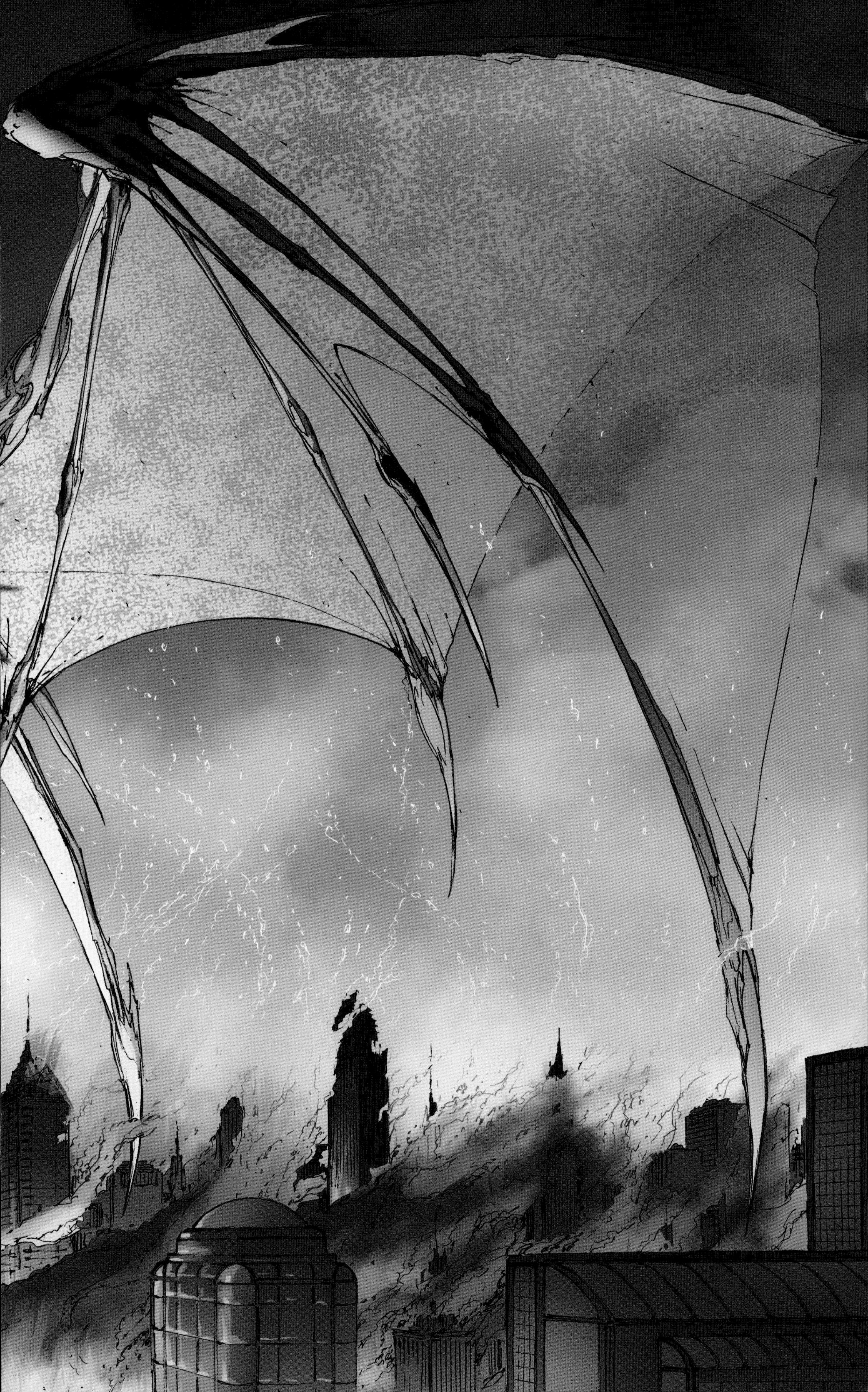

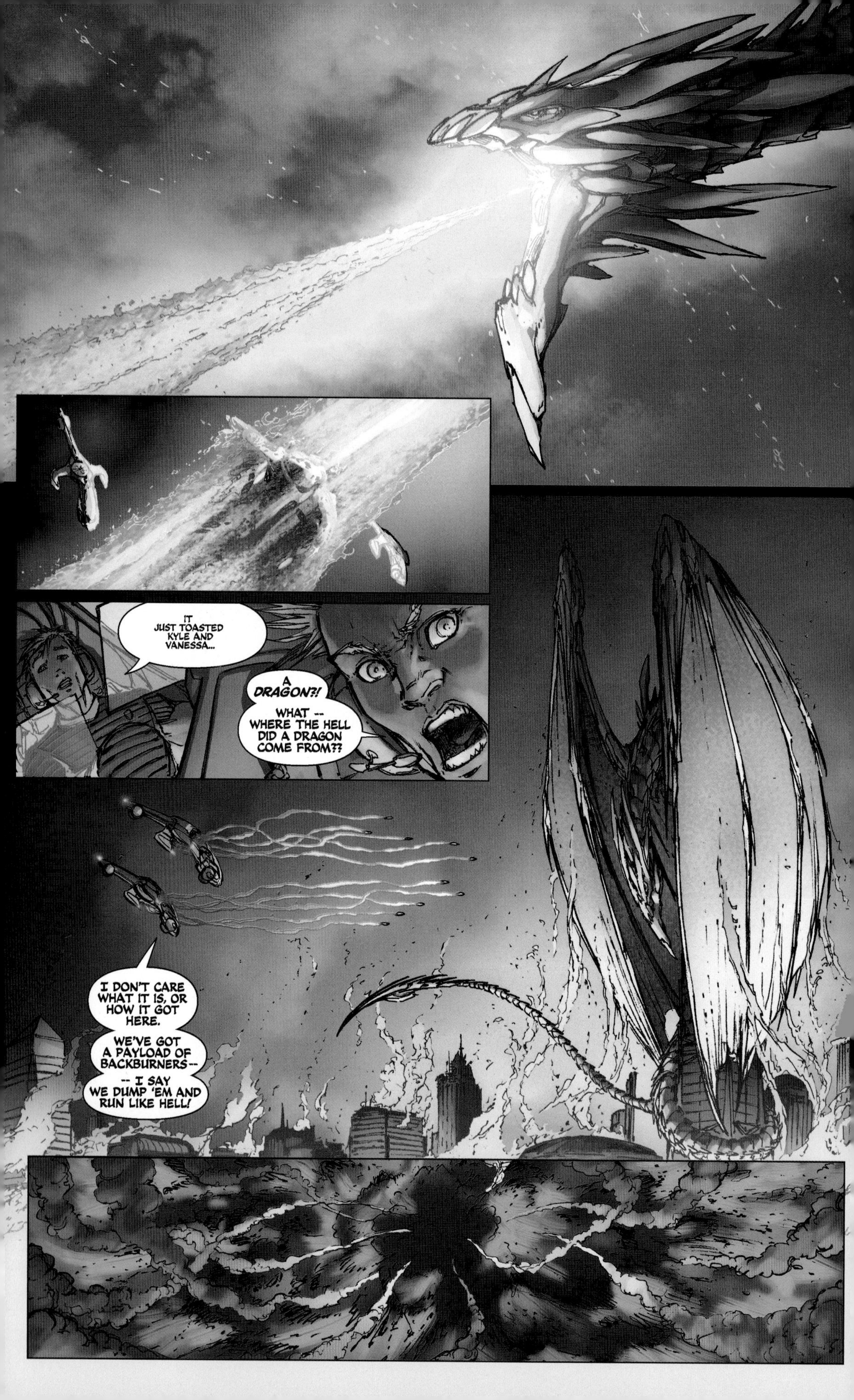
IT JUST TOASTED KYLE AND VANESSA...
A DRAGON?!
WHAT -- WHERE THE HELL DID A DRAGON COME FROM??
I DON'T CARE WHAT IT IS, OR HOW IT GOT HERE.
WE'VE GOT A PAYLOAD OF BACKBURNERS--
-- I SAY WE DUMP 'EM AND RUN LIKE HELL!

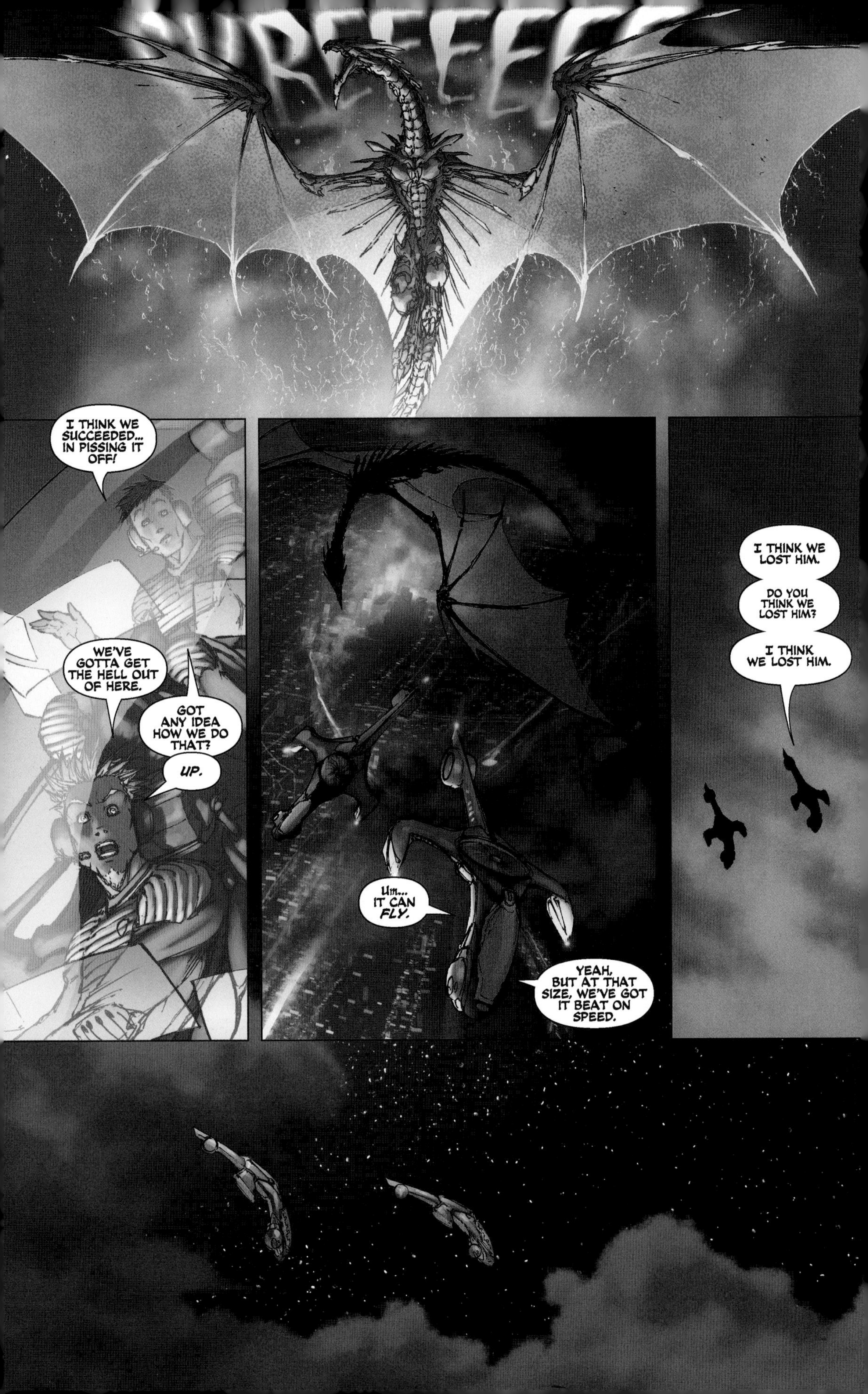
I THINK WE SUCCEEDED... IN PISSING IT OFF!
WE'VE GOTTA GET THE HELL OUT OF HERE.
GOT ANY IDEA HOW WE DO THAT?
UP.
Um... IT CAN *FLY.*
YEAH, BUT AT THAT SIZE, WE'VE GOT IT BEAT ON SPEED.
I THINK WE LOST HIM.
DO YOU THINK WE LOST HIM?
I THINK WE LOST HIM.

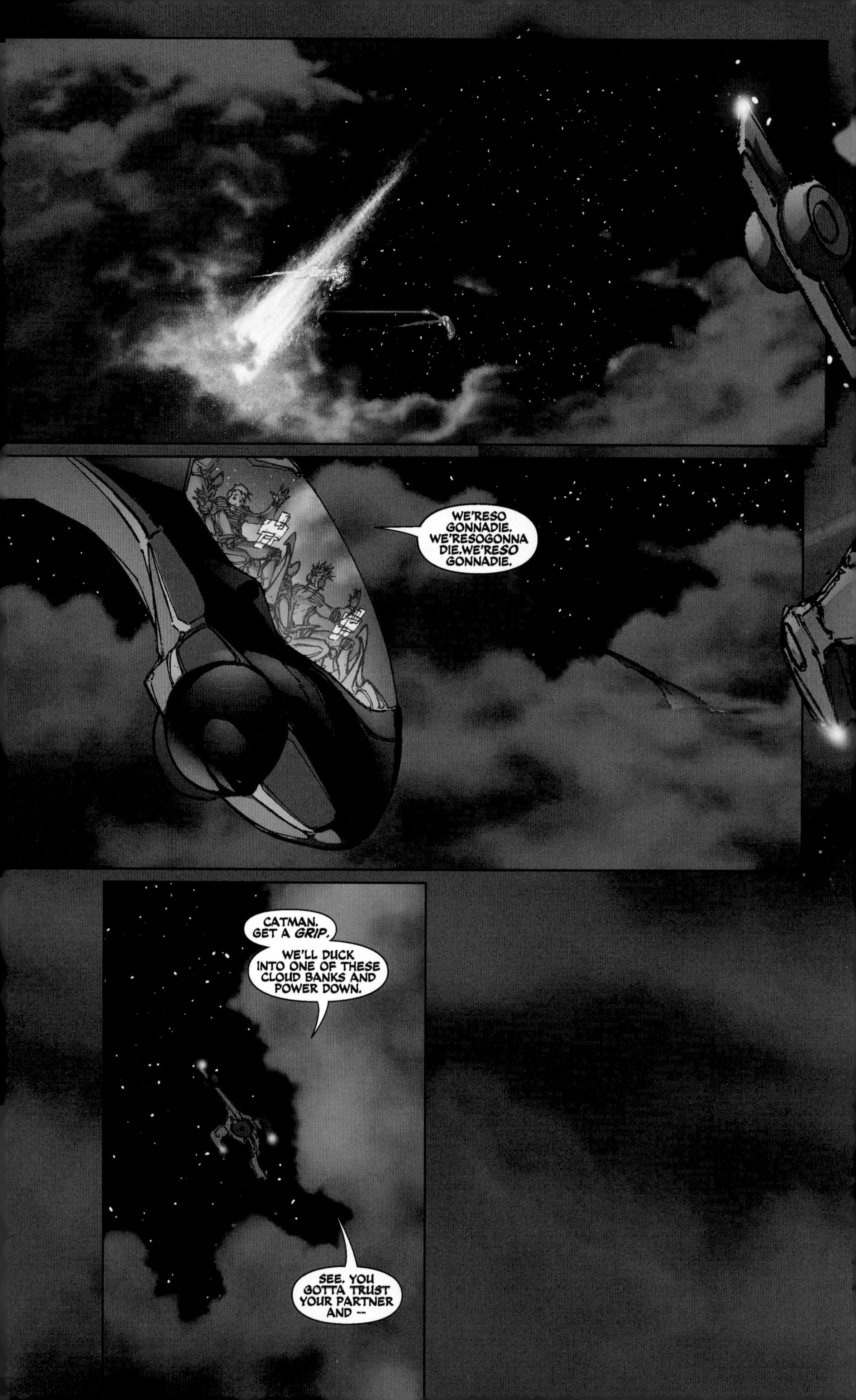
WE'RESO GONNADIE. WE'RESOGONNA DIE.WE'RESO GONNADIE.
CATMAN. GET A GRIP.
WE'LL DUCK INTO ONE OF THESE CLOUD BANKS AND POWER DOWN.
SEE. YOU GOTTA TRUST YOUR PARTNER AND --

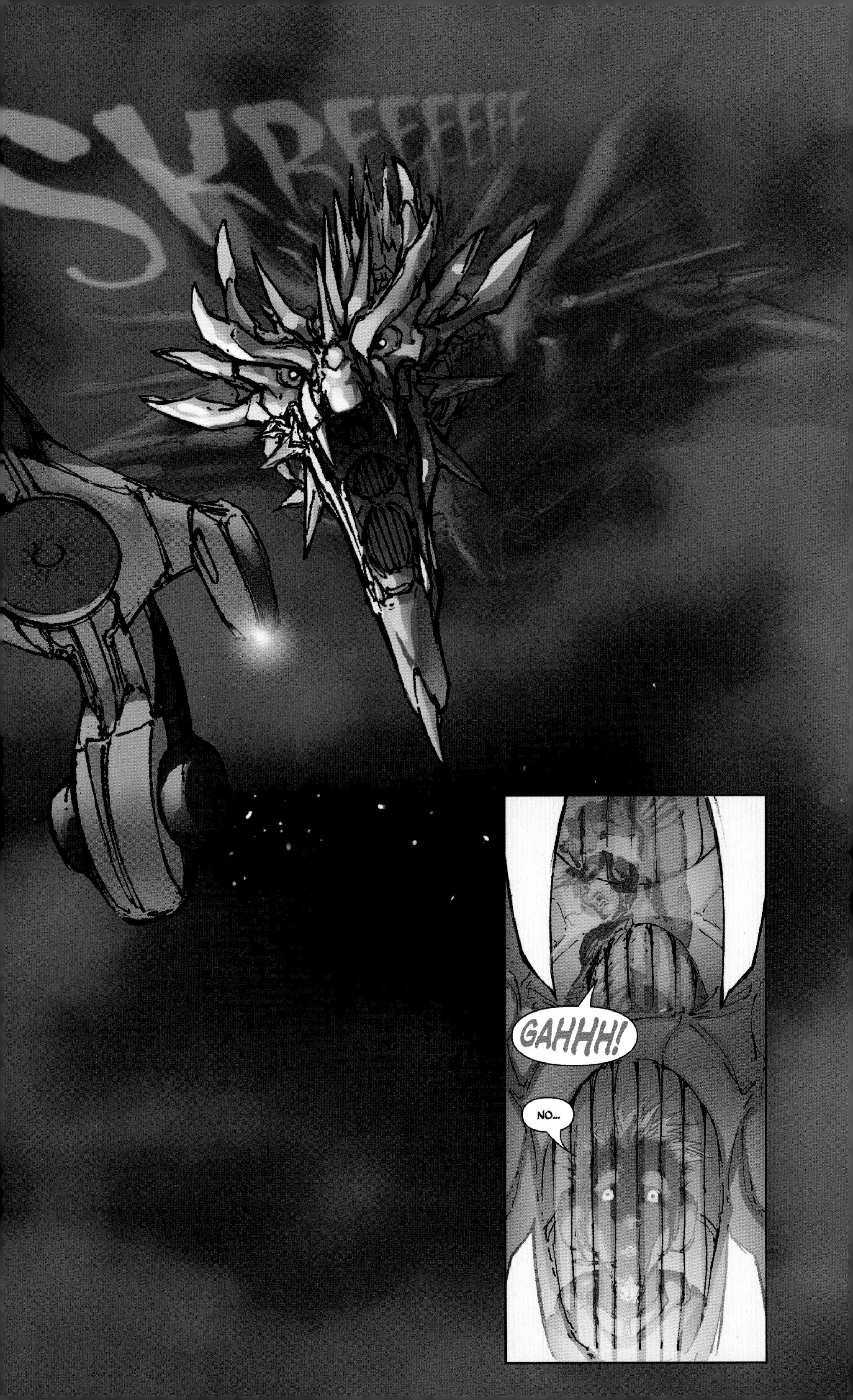
SHREEEEE
GAHHH!
NO...

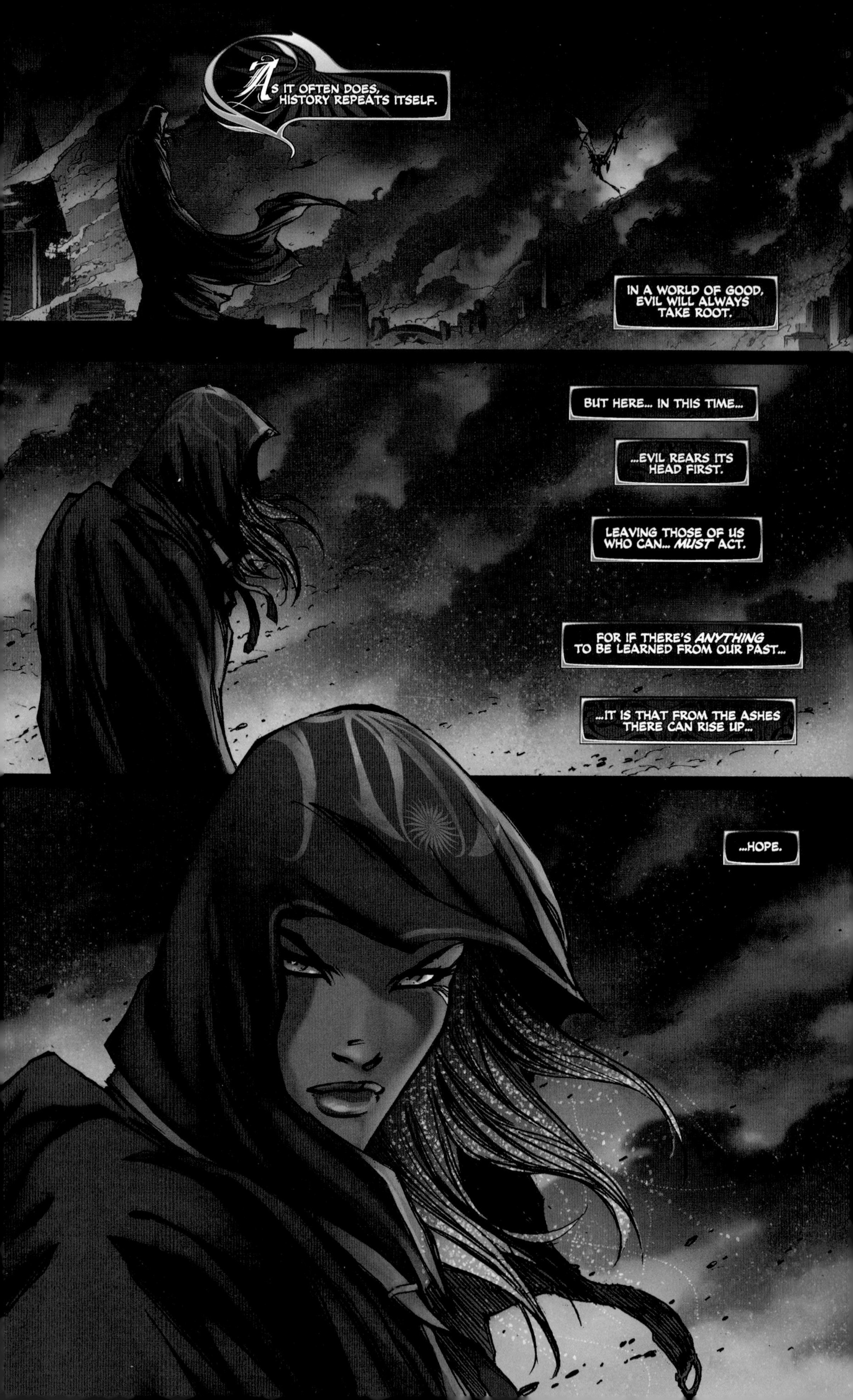
As it often does, history repeats itself.
In a world of good, evil will always take root.
But here... in this time...
...evil rears its head first.
Leaving those of us who can... *must* act.
For if there's *anything* to be learned from our past...
...it is that from the ashes there can rise up...
...hope.

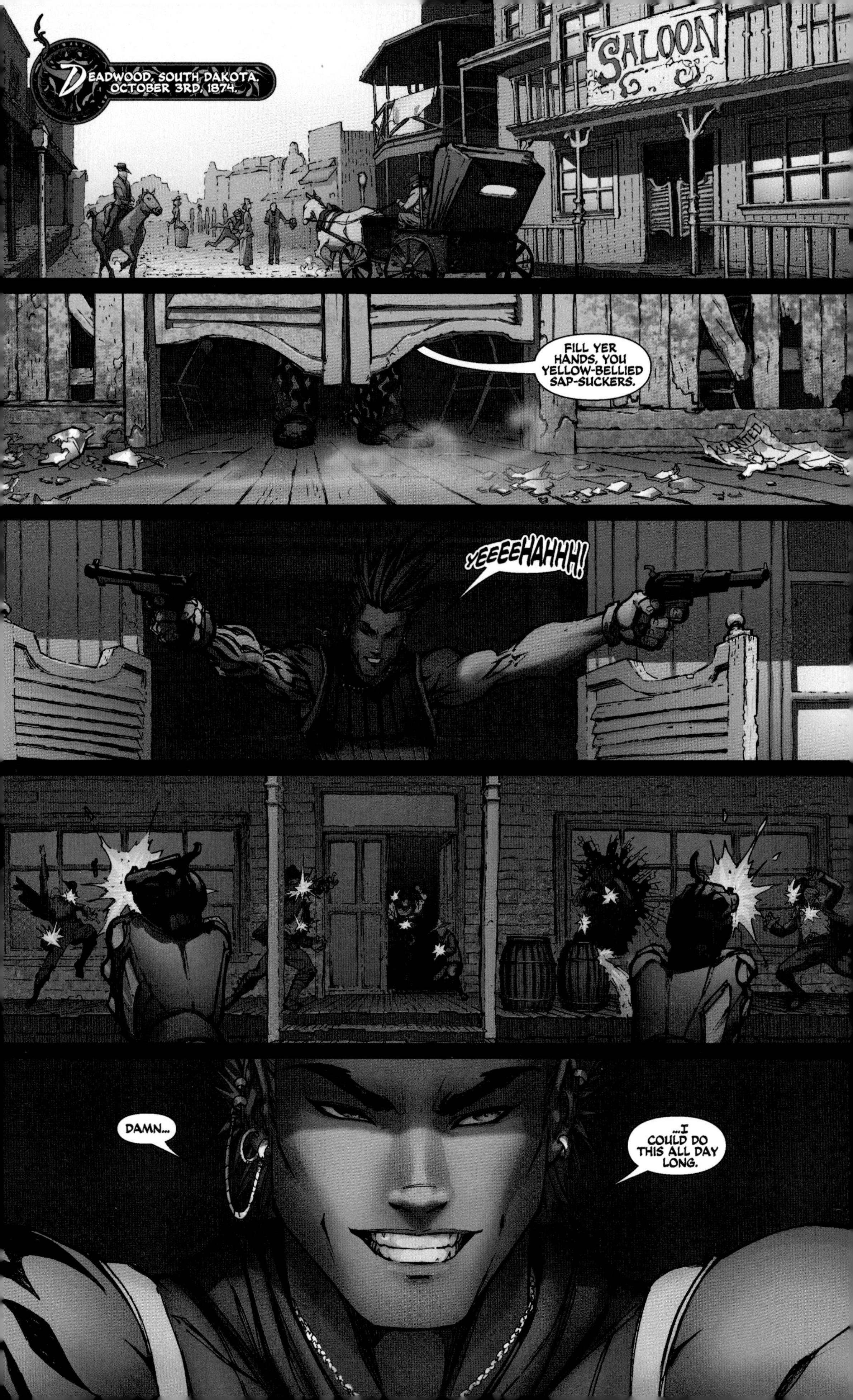

DEADWOOD, SOUTH DAKOTA. OCTOBER 3RD, 1874.
SALOON
FILL YER HANDS, YOU YELLOW-BELLIED SAP-SUCKERS.
WANTED
YEEEEHAHHH!
DAMN...
...I COULD DO THIS ALL DAY LONG.

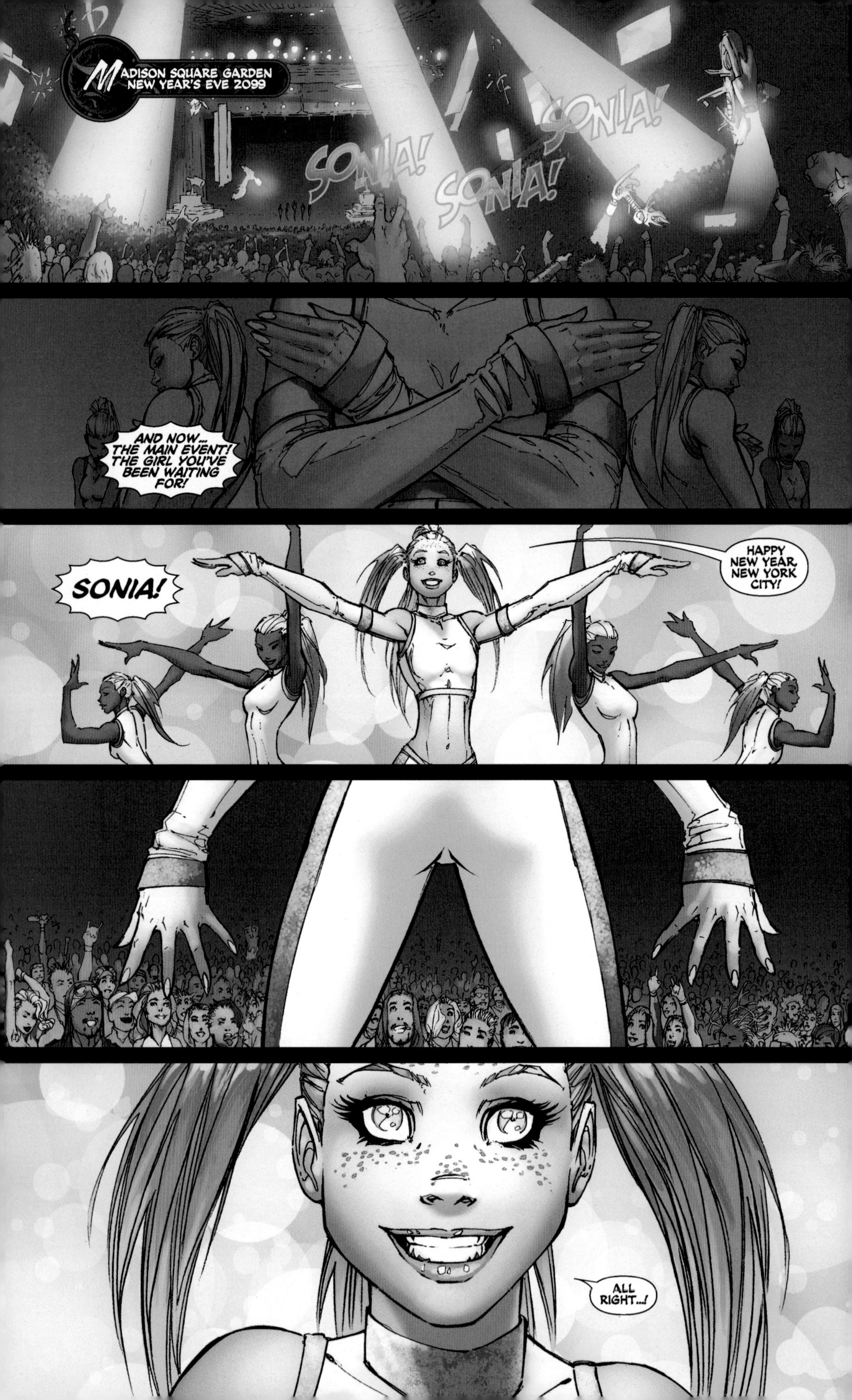
MADISON SQUARE GARDEN
NEW YEAR'S EVE 2099
SONIA!
SONIA!
SONIA!
AND NOW... THE MAIN EVENT! THE GIRL YOU'VE BEEN WAITING FOR!
SONIA!
HAPPY NEW YEAR, NEW YORK CITY!
ALL RIGHT...!

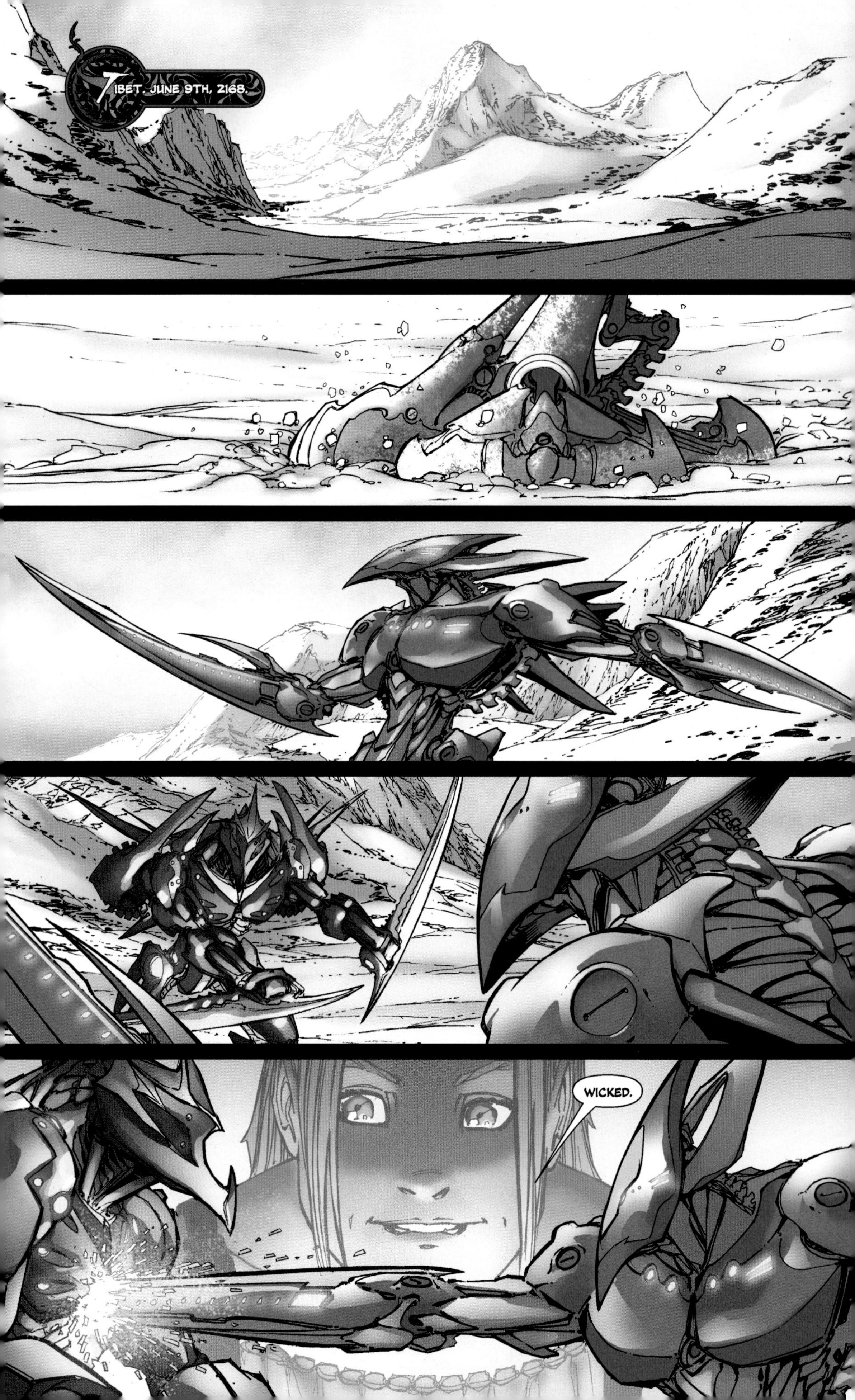

TIBET. JUNE 9TH, 2168.
WICKED.

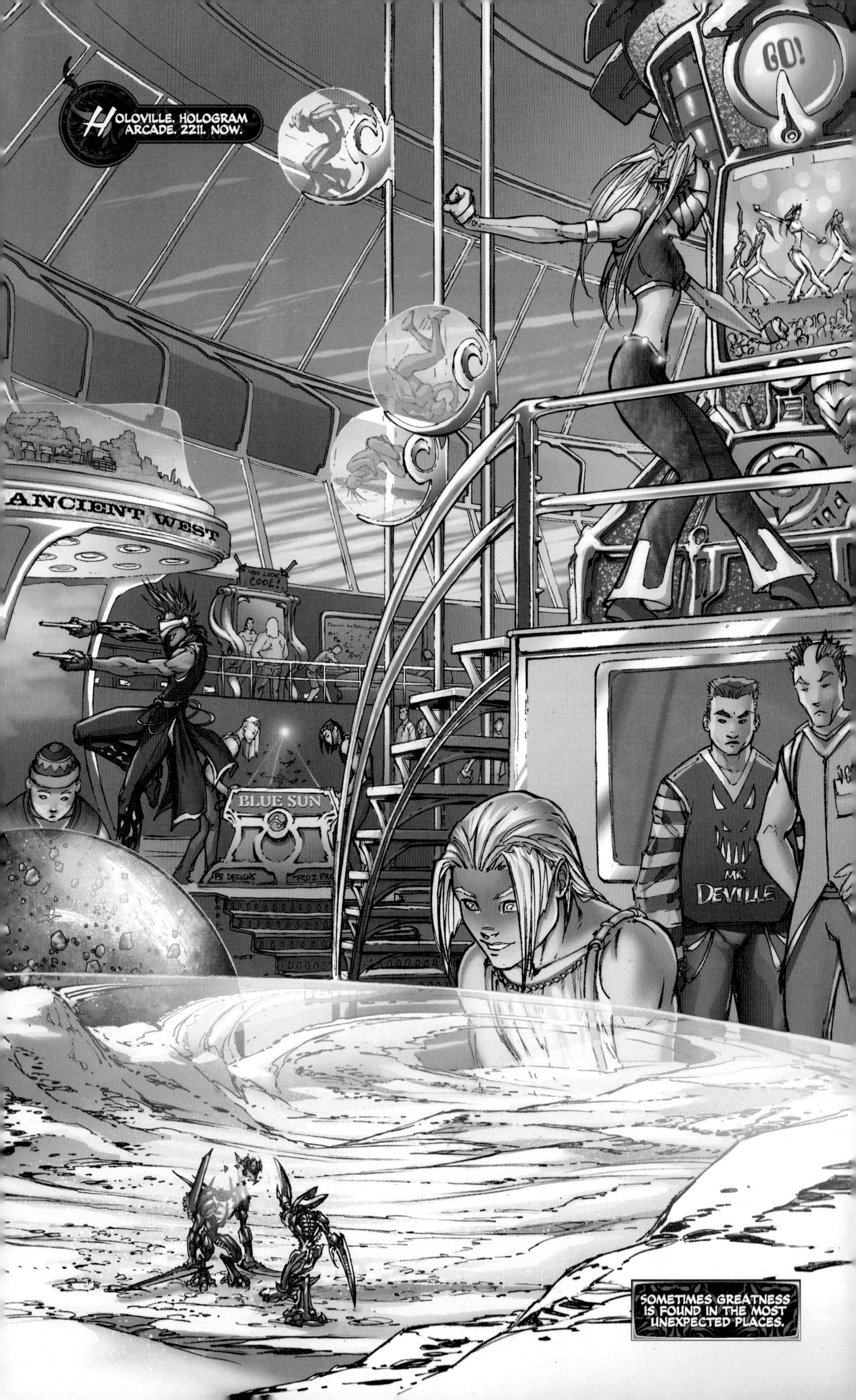
HOLOVILLE. HOLOGRAM ARCADE. 2211. NOW.
GO!
ANCIENT WEST
YOU LOOK COOL!
BLUE SUN
PS DESIGNS
MR. DEVILLE
SOMETIMES GREATNESS IS FOUND IN THE MOST UNEXPECTED PLACES.

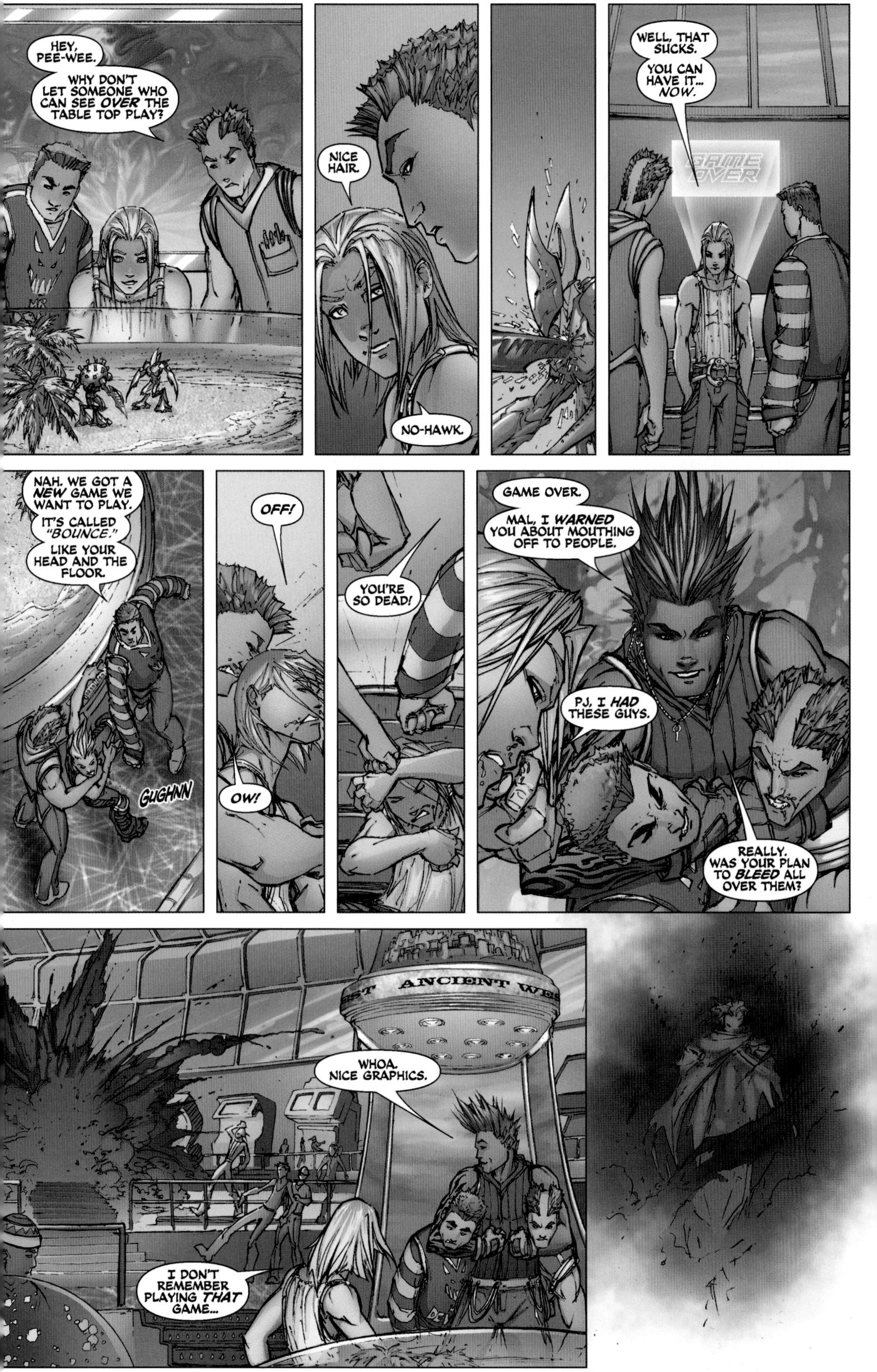
HEY, PEE-WEE.
WHY DON'T LET SOMEONE WHO CAN SEE *OVER* THE TABLE TOP PLAY?
NICE HAIR.
NO-HAWK.
WELL, THAT SUCKS.
YOU CAN HAVE IT... *NOW.*
GAME OVER
NAH. WE GOT A *NEW* GAME WE WANT TO PLAY.
IT'S CALLED *"BOUNCE."*
LIKE YOUR HEAD AND THE FLOOR.
GUGHNN
OFF!
OW!
YOU'RE SO DEAD!
GAME OVER.
MAL, I *WARNED* YOU ABOUT MOUTHING OFF TO PEOPLE.
PJ, I *HAD* THESE GUYS.
REALLY. WAS YOUR PLAN TO *BLEED* ALL OVER THEM?
ANCIENT WE
WHOA. NICE GRAPHICS.
I DON'T REMEMBER PLAYING *THAT* GAME...

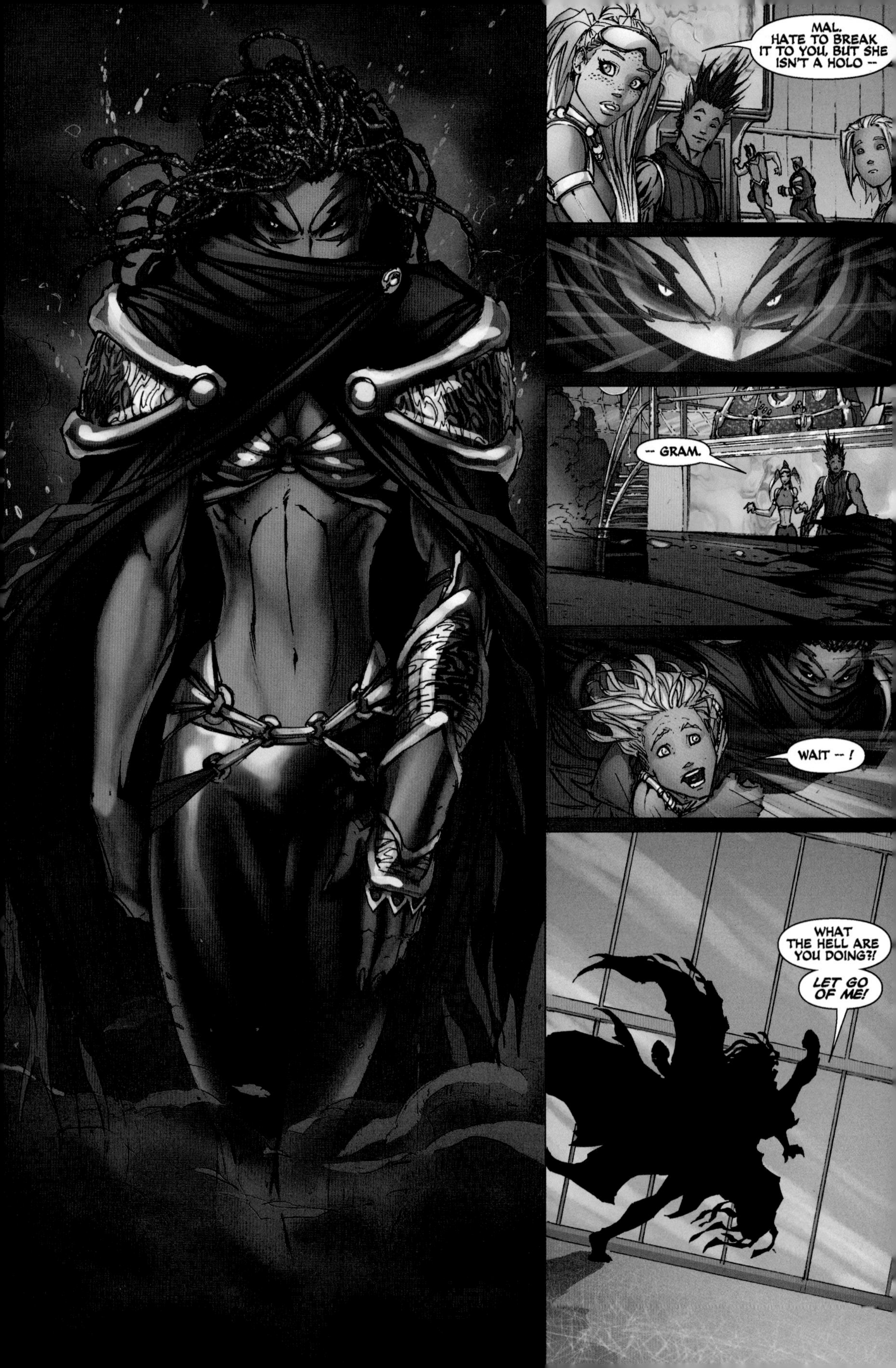
MAL. HATE TO BREAK IT TO YOU, BUT SHE ISN'T A HOLO --
-- GRAM.
WAIT -- !
WHAT THE HELL ARE YOU DOING?!
LET GO OF ME!

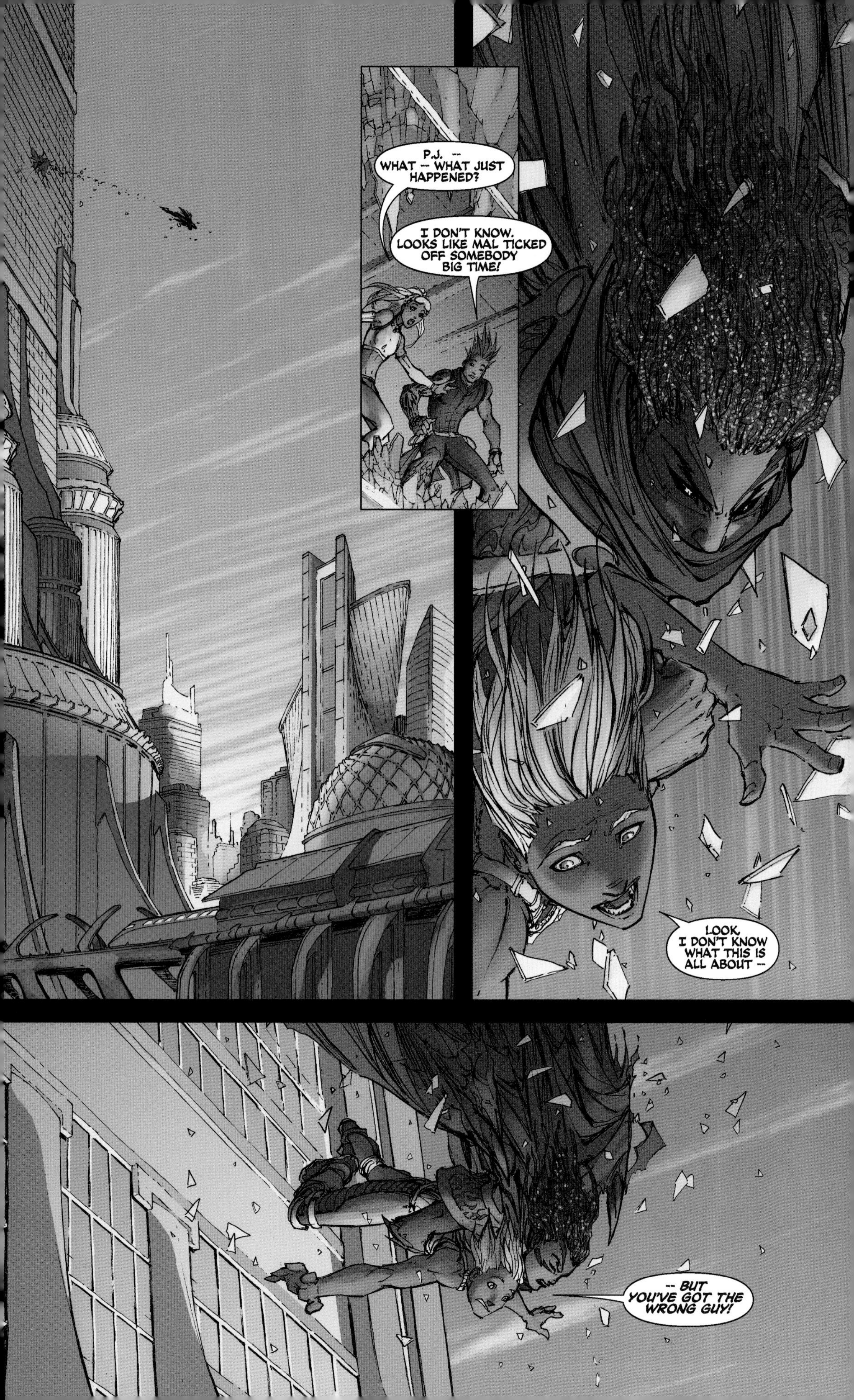
P.J. -- WHAT -- WHAT JUST HAPPENED?
I DON'T KNOW. LOOKS LIKE MAL TICKED OFF SOMEBODY BIG TIME!
LOOK, I DON'T KNOW WHAT THIS IS ALL ABOUT --
-- BUT YOU'VE GOT THE WRONG GUY!

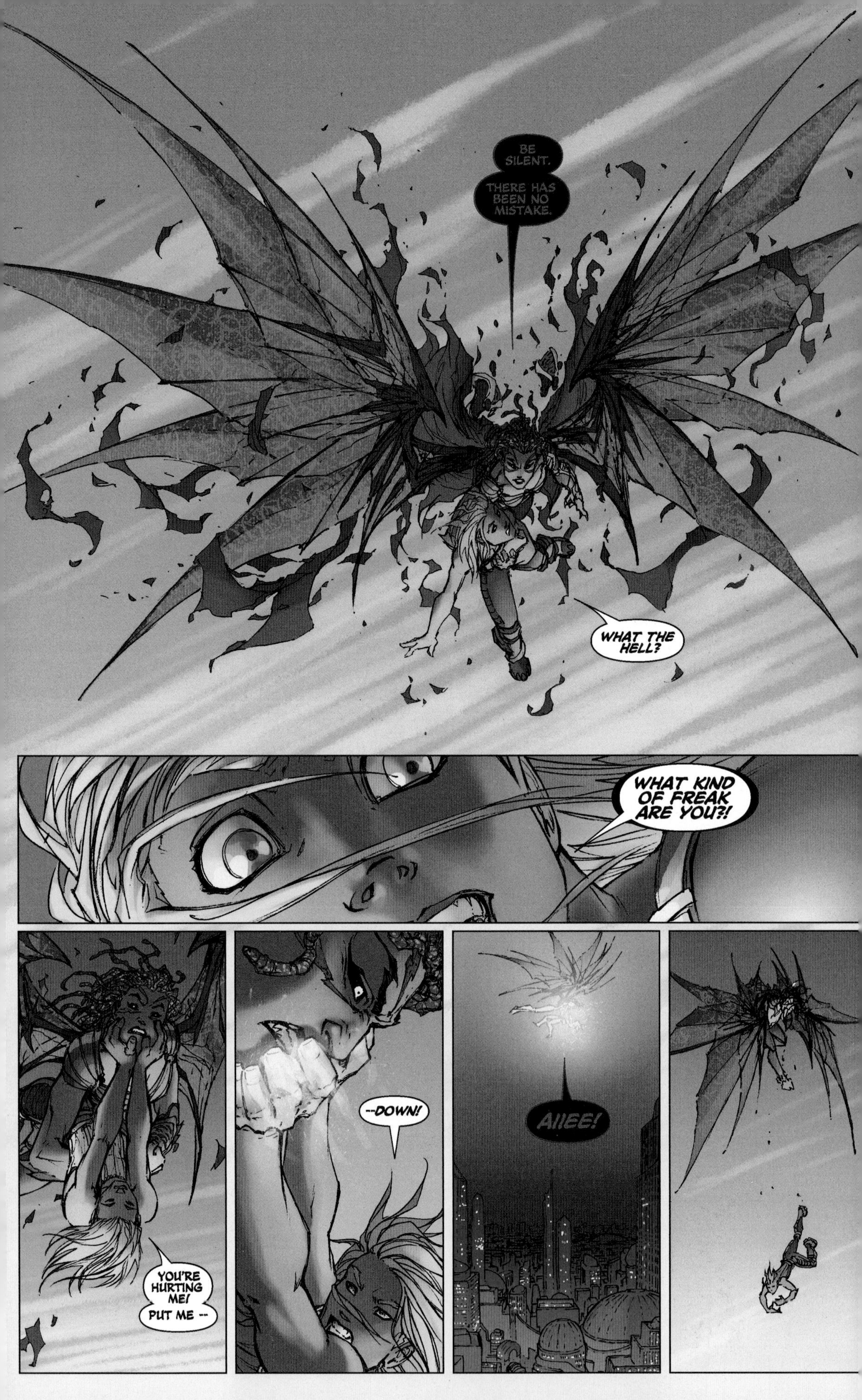
BE SILENT.
THERE HAS BEEN NO MISTAKE.
WHAT THE HELL?
WHAT KIND OF FREAK ARE YOU?!
YOU'RE HURTING ME! PUT ME --
--DOWN!
AIIEE!

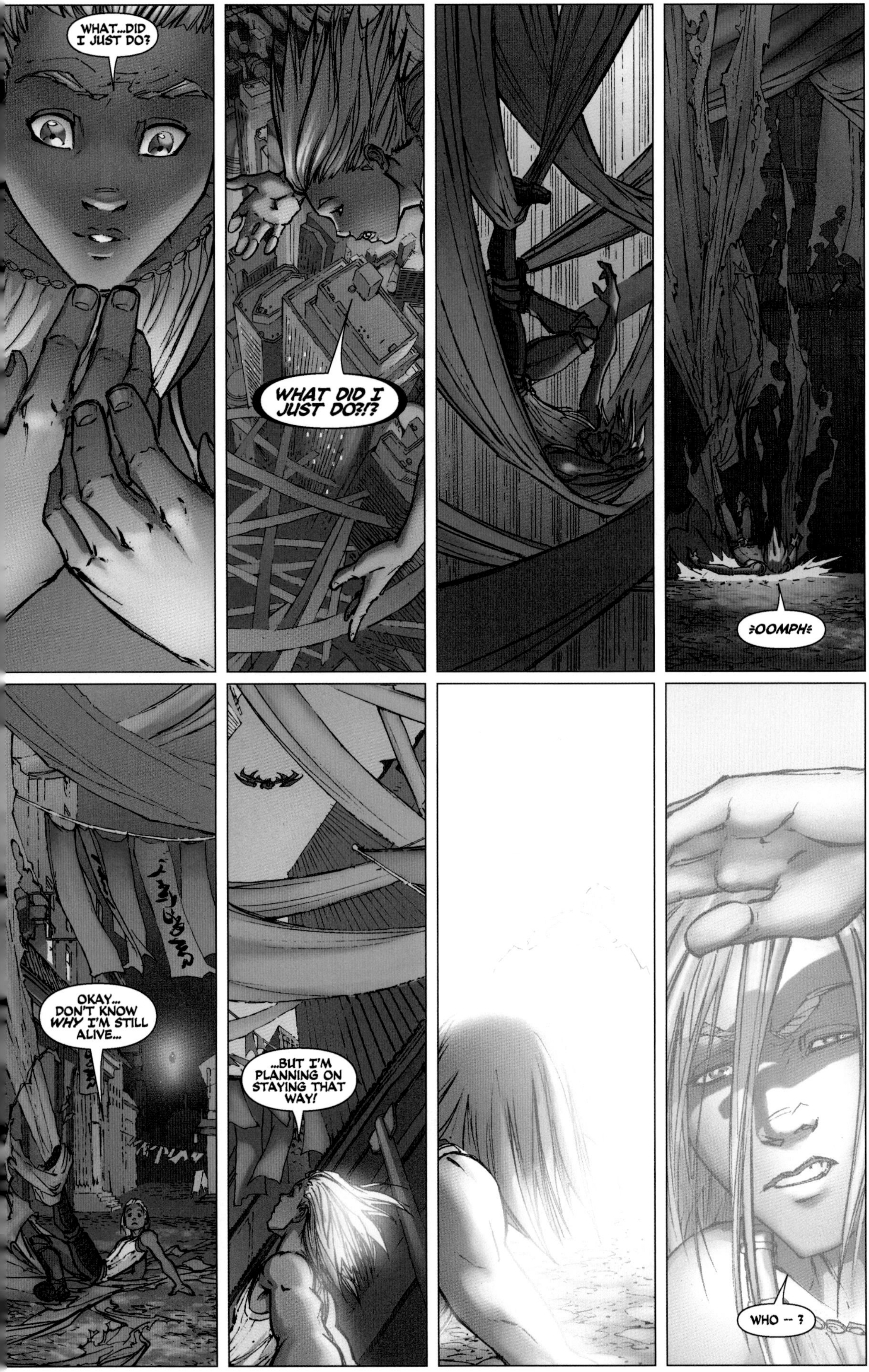
WHAT...DID I JUST DO?
WHAT DID I JUST DO?!?
OOMPH
OKAY... DON'T KNOW WHY I'M STILL ALIVE...
...BUT I'M PLANNING ON STAYING THAT WAY!
WHO -- ?

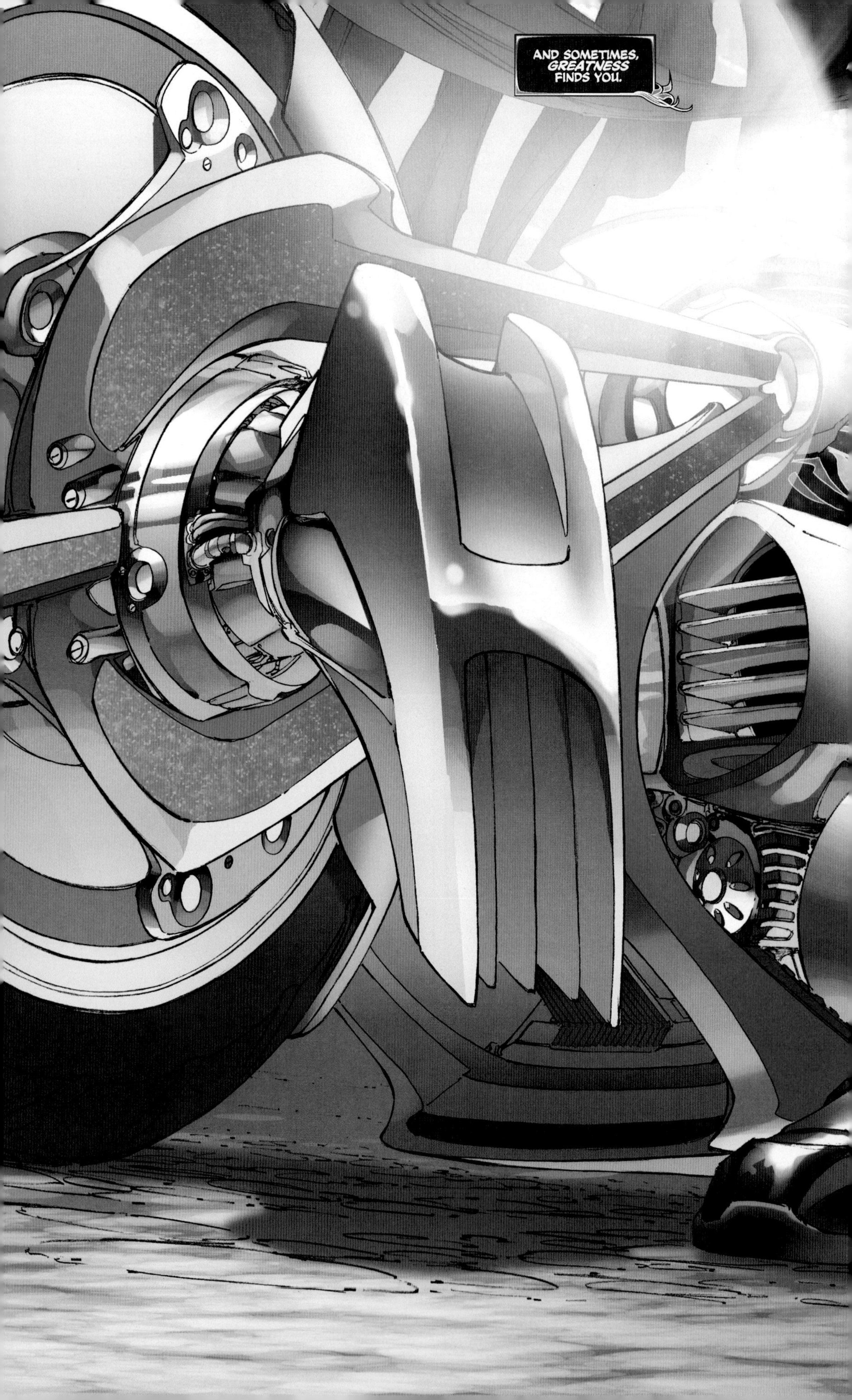
AND SOMETIMES,
GREATNESS
FINDS YOU.

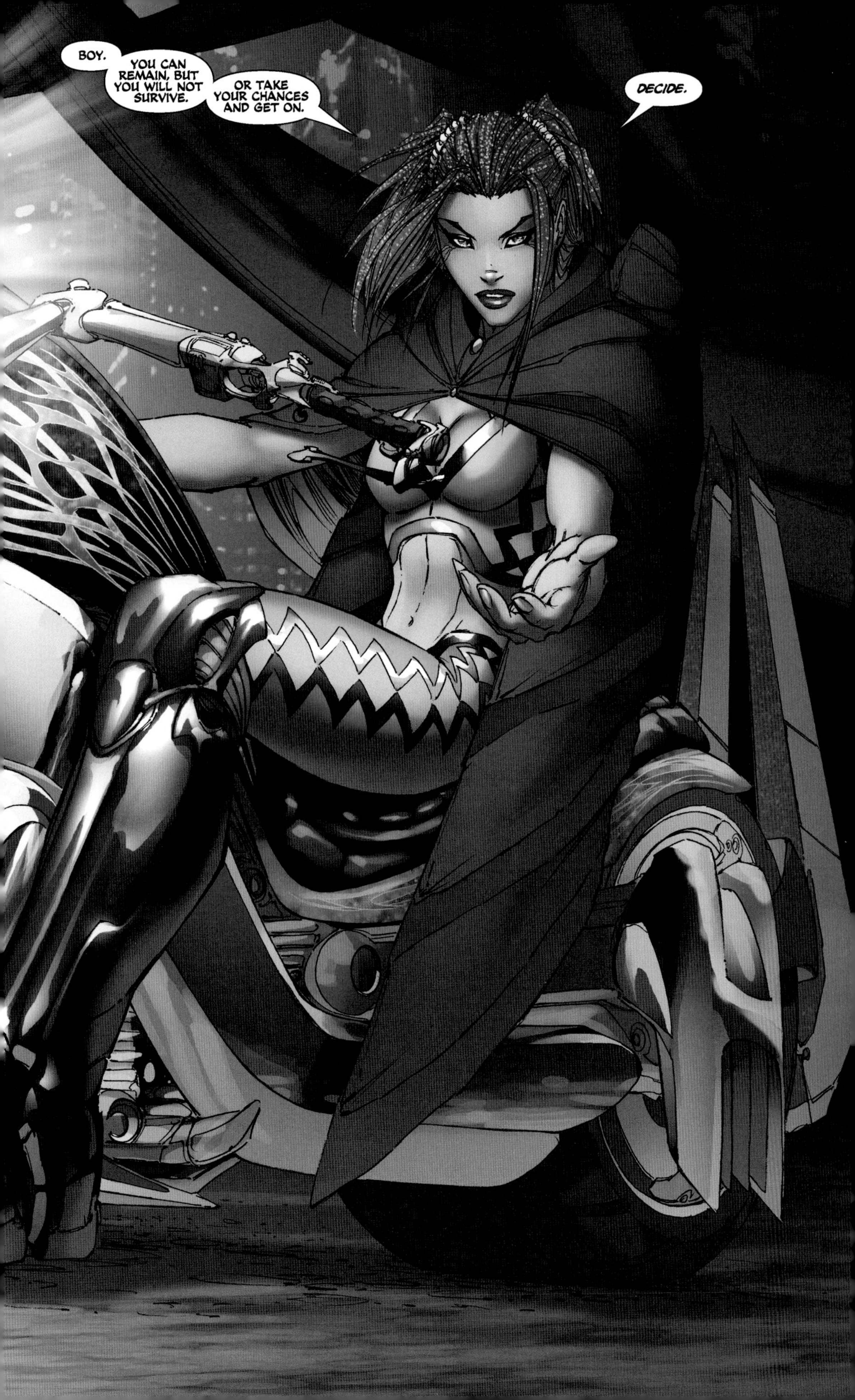
BOY.
YOU CAN REMAIN, BUT YOU WILL NOT SURVIVE.
OR TAKE YOUR CHANCES AND GET ON.
DECIDE.

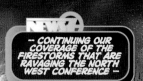

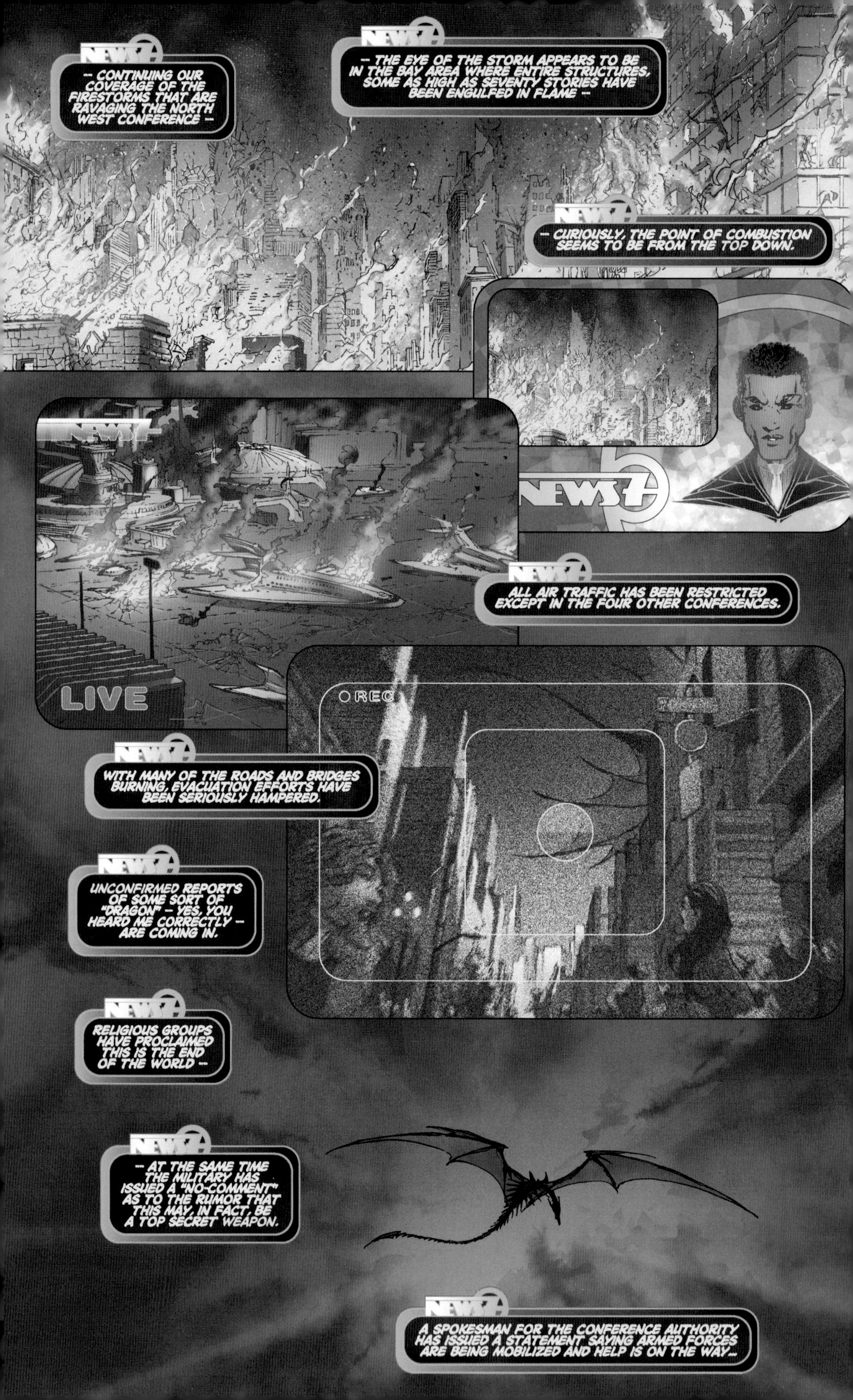

NEWS7
-- CONTINUING OUR COVERAGE OF THE FIRESTORMS THAT ARE RAVAGING THE NORTH WEST CONFERENCE --
NEWS7
-- THE EYE OF THE STORM APPEARS TO BE IN THE BAY AREA WHERE ENTIRE STRUCTURES, SOME AS HIGH AS SEVENTY STORIES HAVE BEEN ENGULFED IN FLAME --
NEWS7
-- CURIOUSLY, THE POINT OF COMBUSTION SEEMS TO BE FROM THE TOP DOWN.
NEWS7
NEWS7
LIVE
NEWS7
ALL AIR TRAFFIC HAS BEEN RESTRICTED EXCEPT IN THE FOUR OTHER CONFERENCES.
REC
NEWS7
WITH MANY OF THE ROADS AND BRIDGES BURNING, EVACUATION EFFORTS HAVE BEEN SERIOUSLY HAMPERED.
NEWS7
UNCONFIRMED REPORTS OF SOME SORT OF "DRAGON" -- YES, YOU HEARD ME CORRECTLY -- ARE COMING IN.
NEWS7
RELIGIOUS GROUPS HAVE PROCLAIMED THIS IS THE END OF THE WORLD --
NEWS7
-- AT THE SAME TIME THE MILITARY HAS ISSUED A "NO-COMMENT" AS TO THE RUMOR THAT THIS MAY, IN FACT, BE A TOP SECRET WEAPON.
NEWS7
A SPOKESMAN FOR THE CONFERENCE AUTHORITY HAS ISSUED A STATEMENT SAYING ARMED FORCES ARE BEING MOBILIZED AND HELP IS ON THE WAY--

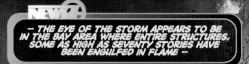

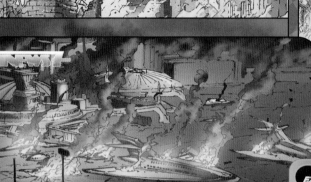

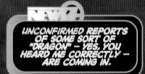

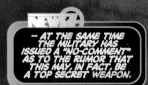

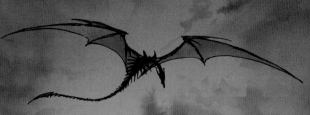

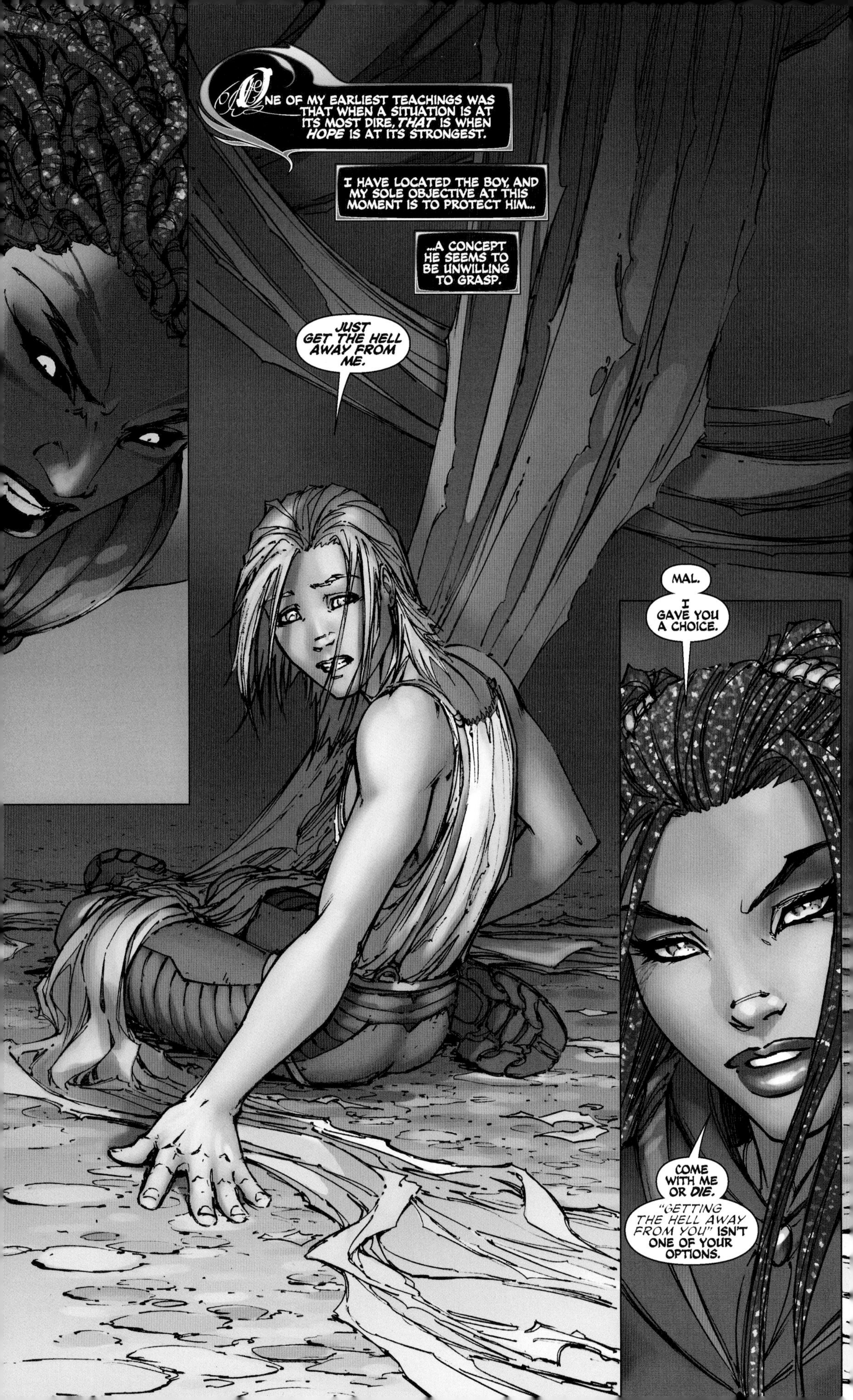

ONE OF MY EARLIEST TEACHINGS WAS THAT WHEN A SITUATION IS AT ITS MOST DIRE, *THAT* IS WHEN *HOPE* IS AT ITS STRONGEST.
I HAVE LOCATED THE BOY, AND MY SOLE OBJECTIVE AT THIS MOMENT IS TO PROTECT HIM...
...A CONCEPT HE SEEMS TO BE UNWILLING TO GRASP.
JUST GET THE HELL AWAY FROM ME.
MAL.
I GAVE YOU A CHOICE.
COME WITH ME OR *DIE.*
"GETTING THE HELL AWAY FROM YOU" ISN'T ONE OF YOUR OPTIONS.

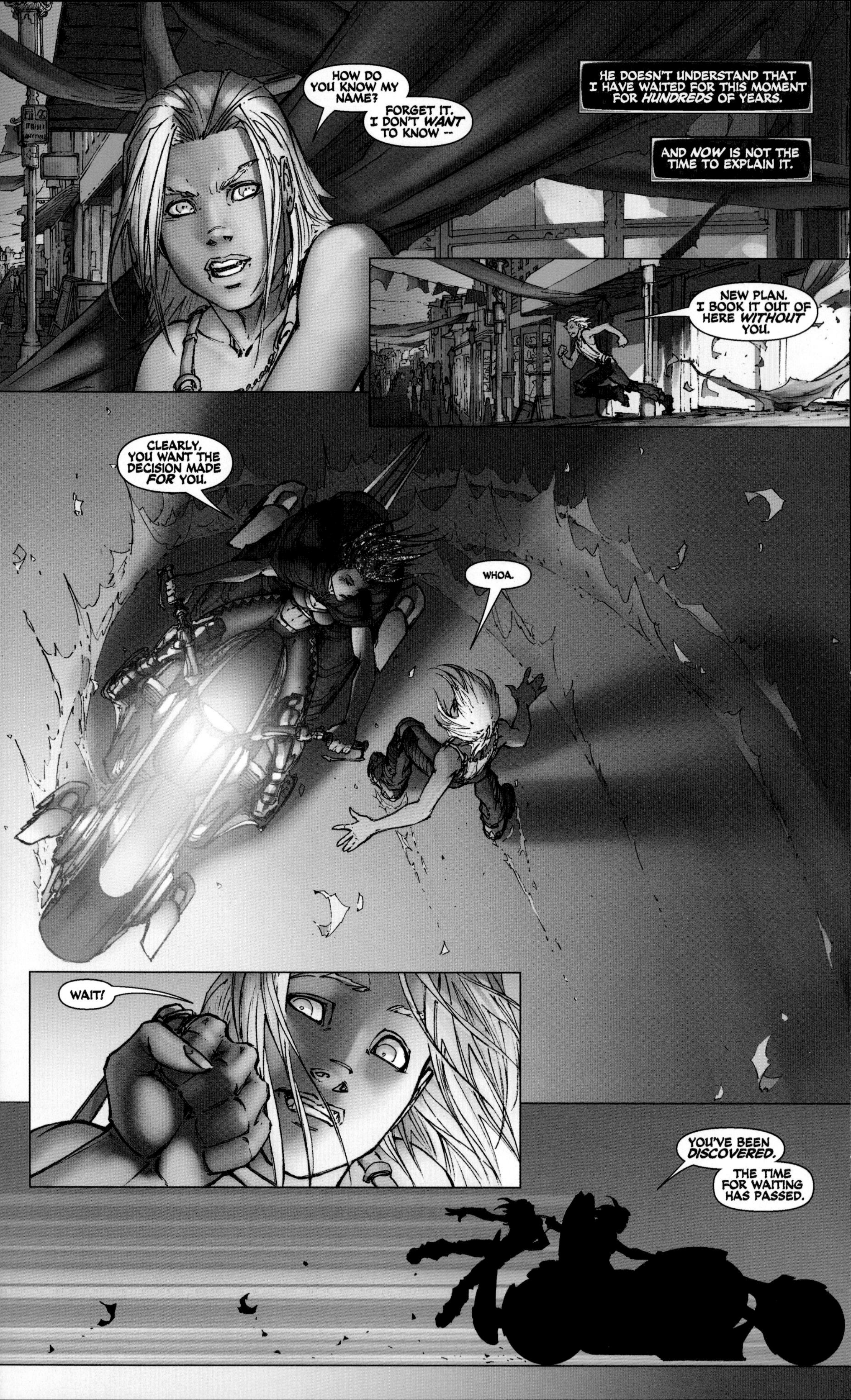
HOW DO YOU KNOW MY NAME?
FORGET IT. I DON'T WANT TO KNOW --
HE DOESN'T UNDERSTAND THAT I HAVE WAITED FOR THIS MOMENT FOR HUNDREDS OF YEARS.
AND NOW IS NOT THE TIME TO EXPLAIN IT.
NEW PLAN. I BOOK IT OUT OF HERE WITHOUT YOU.
CLEARLY, YOU WANT THE DECISION MADE FOR YOU.
WHOA.
WAIT!
YOU'VE BEEN DISCOVERED.
THE TIME FOR WAITING HAS PASSED.

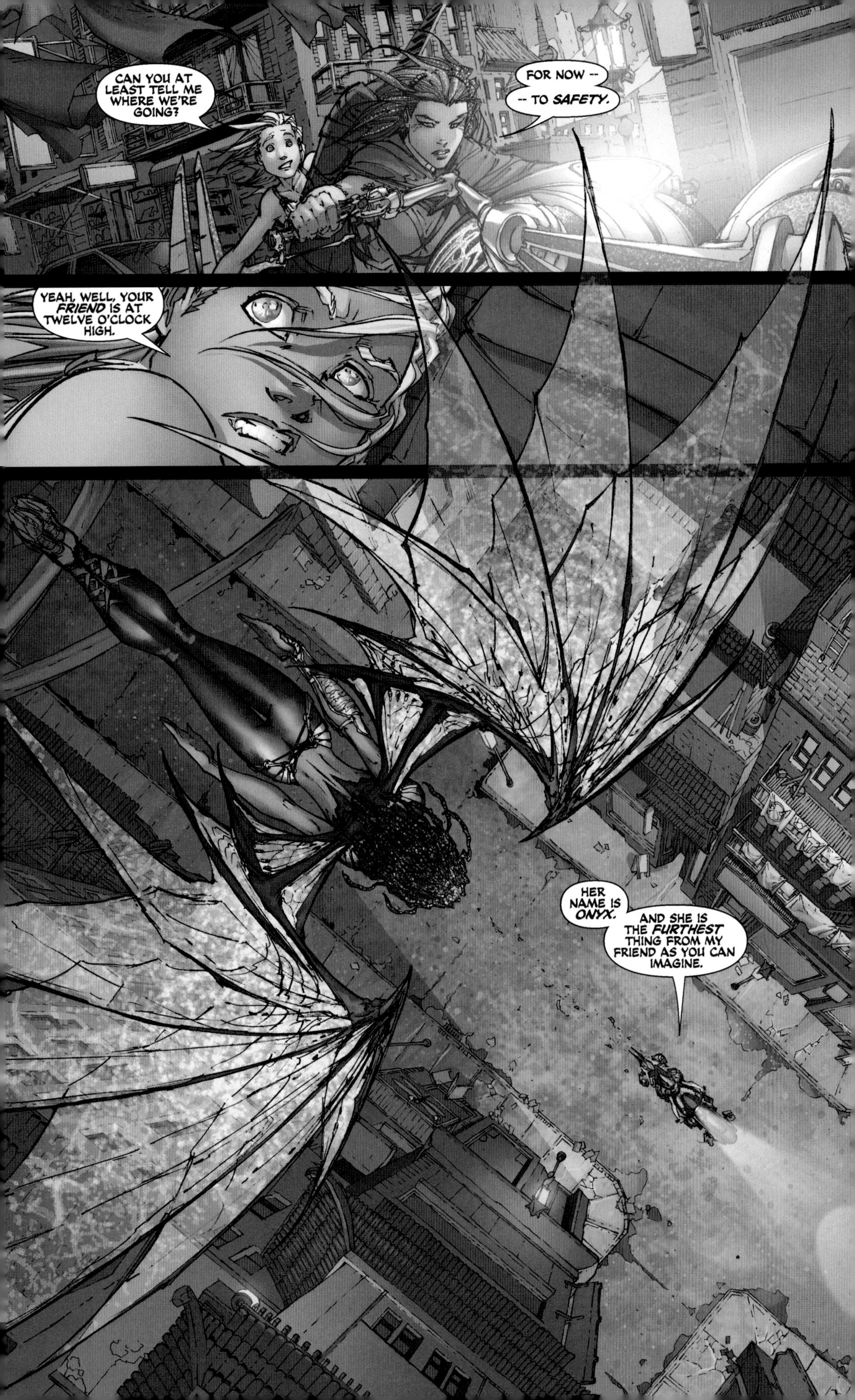
CAN YOU AT LEAST TELL ME WHERE WE'RE GOING?
FOR NOW --
-- TO *SAFETY.*
YEAH, WELL, YOUR *FRIEND* IS AT TWELVE O'CLOCK HIGH.
HER NAME IS *ONYX.*
AND SHE IS THE *FURTHEST* THING FROM MY FRIEND AS YOU CAN IMAGINE.

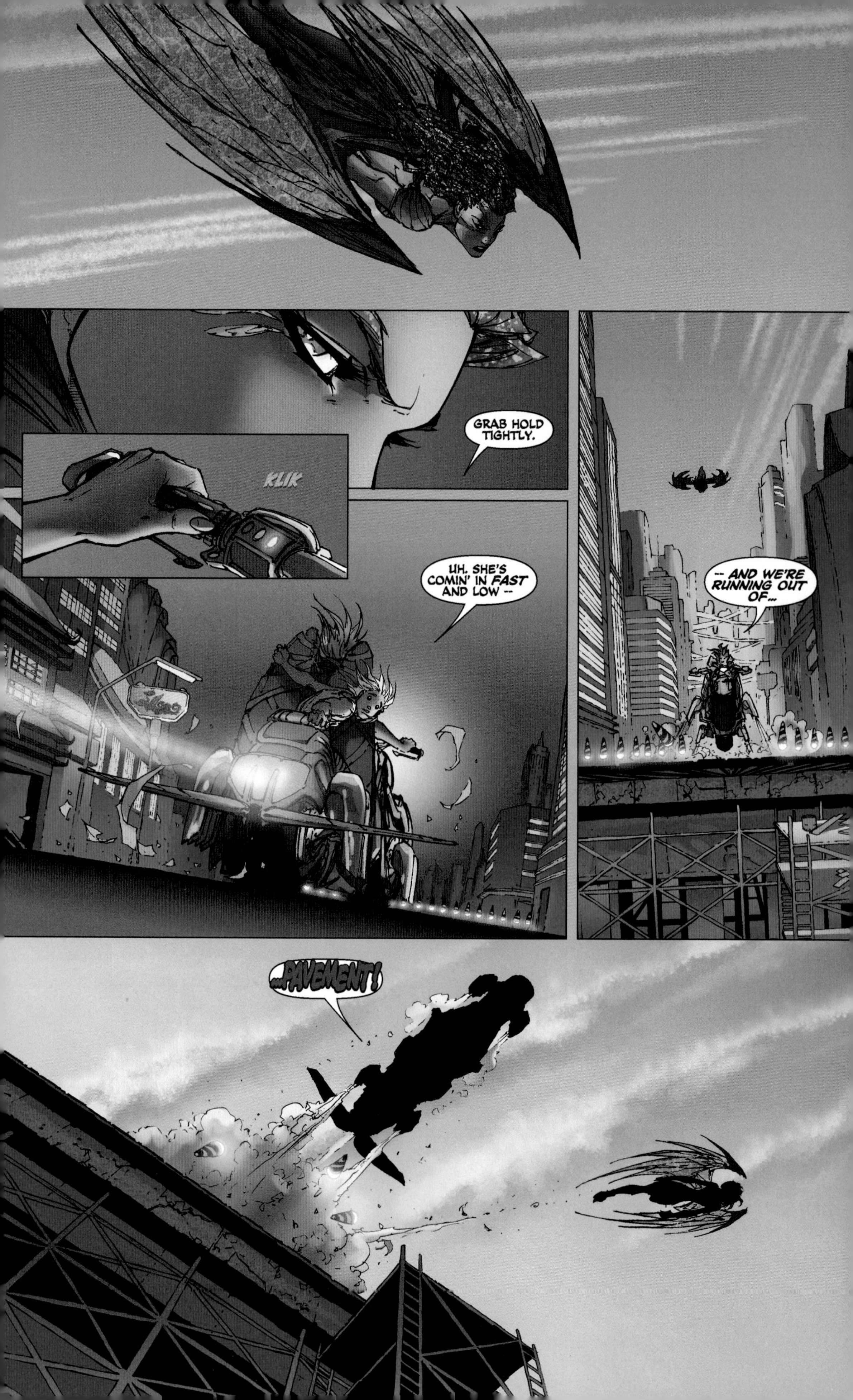
GRAB HOLD TIGHTLY.
KLIK
UH, SHE'S COMIN' IN FAST AND LOW --
-- AND WE'RE RUNNING OUT OF...
...PAVEMENT!

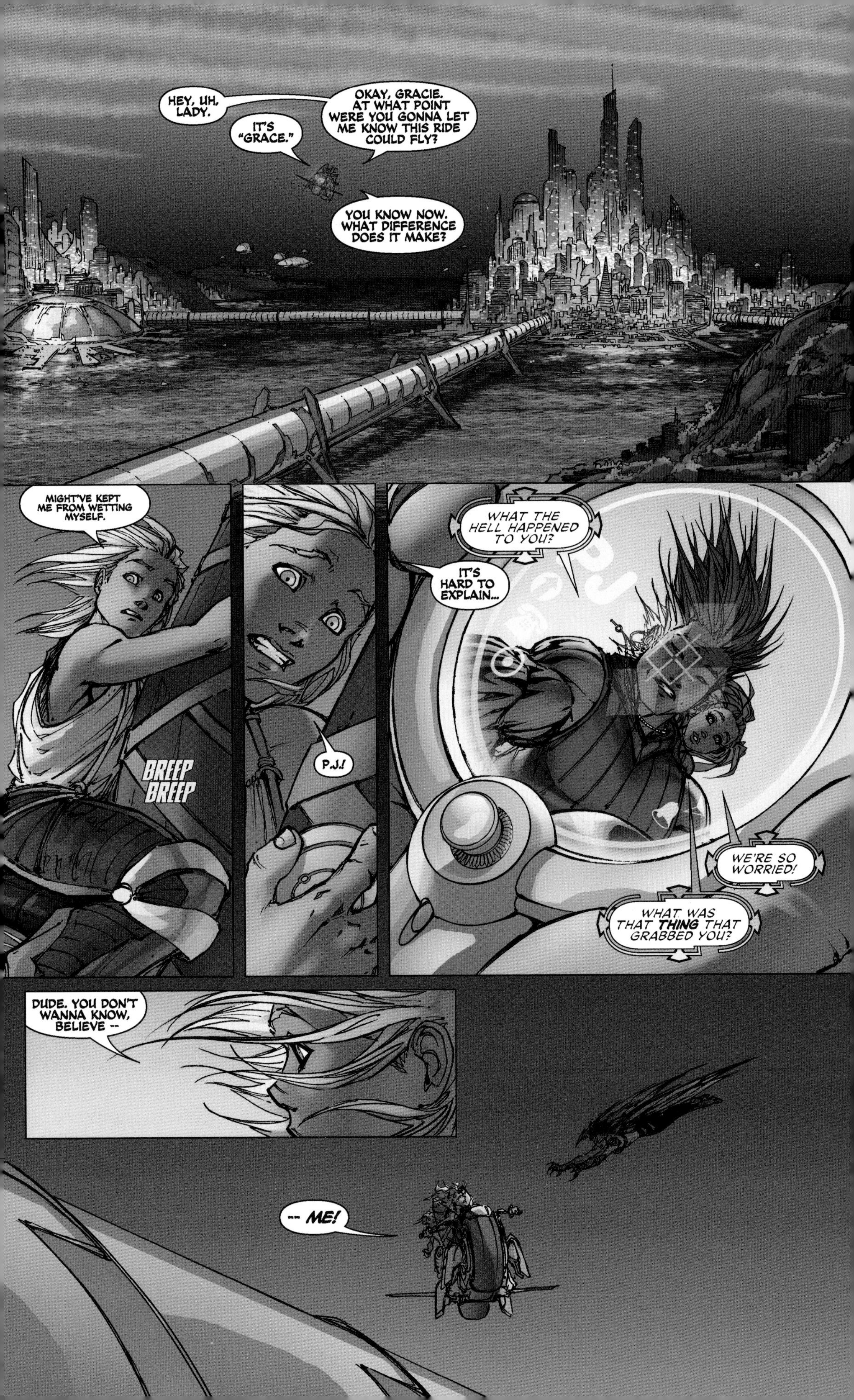

HEY, UH, LADY.
OKAY, GRACIE. AT WHAT POINT WERE YOU GONNA LET ME KNOW THIS RIDE COULD FLY?
IT'S "GRACE."
YOU KNOW NOW. WHAT DIFFERENCE DOES IT MAKE?
MIGHT'VE KEPT ME FROM WETTING MYSELF.
BREEP BREEP
P.J.!
WHAT THE HELL HAPPENED TO YOU?
IT'S HARD TO EXPLAIN...
WE'RE SO WORRIED!
WHAT WAS THAT THING THAT GRABBED YOU?
DUDE. YOU DON'T WANNA KNOW, BELIEVE --
-- ME!

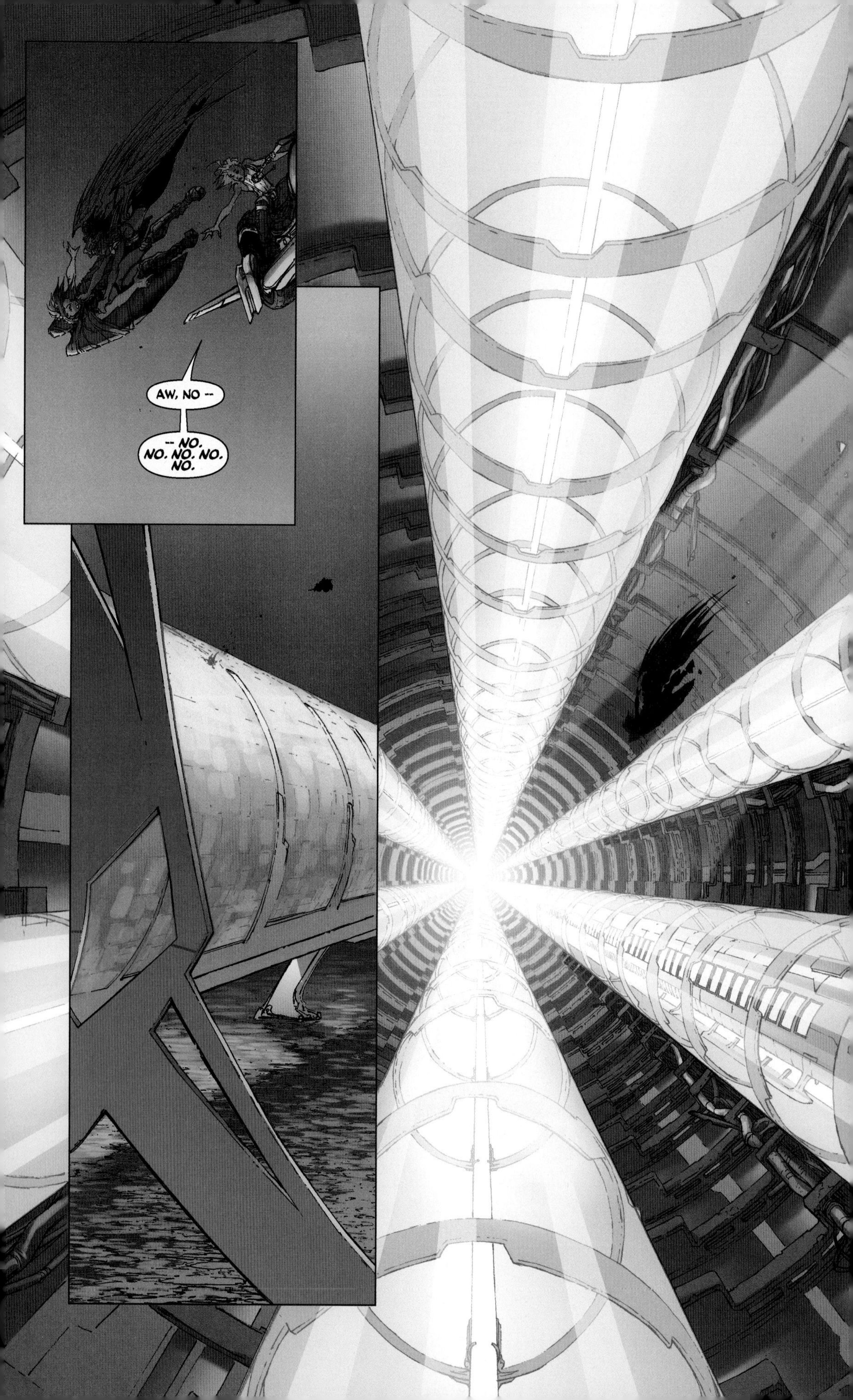
AW, NO --
-- NO. NO. NO. NO. NO.

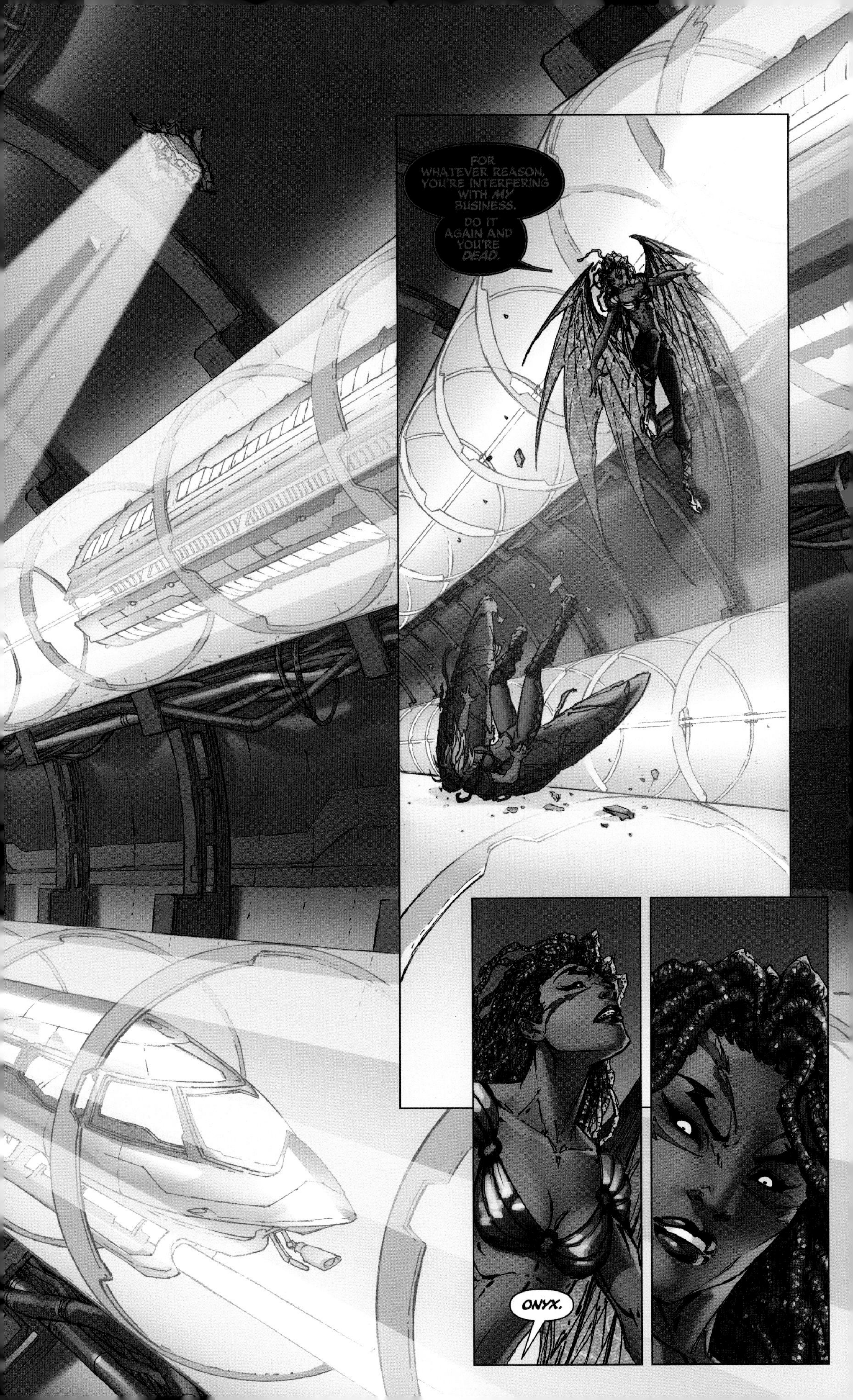
FOR WHATEVER REASON, YOU'RE INTERFERING WITH *MY* BUSINESS.
DO IT AGAIN AND YOU'RE *DEAD*.
ONYX.

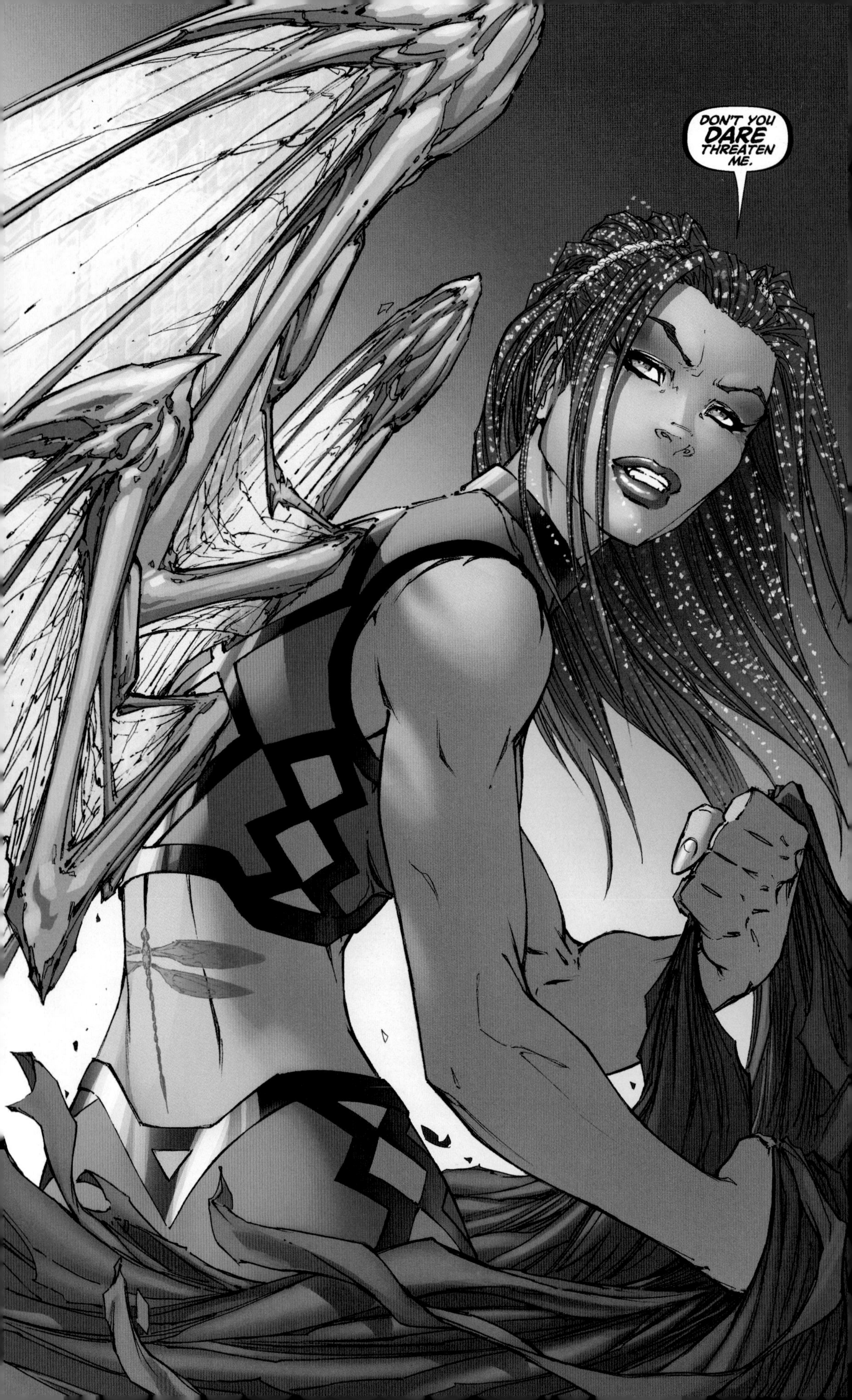
DON'T YOU DARE THREATEN ME.

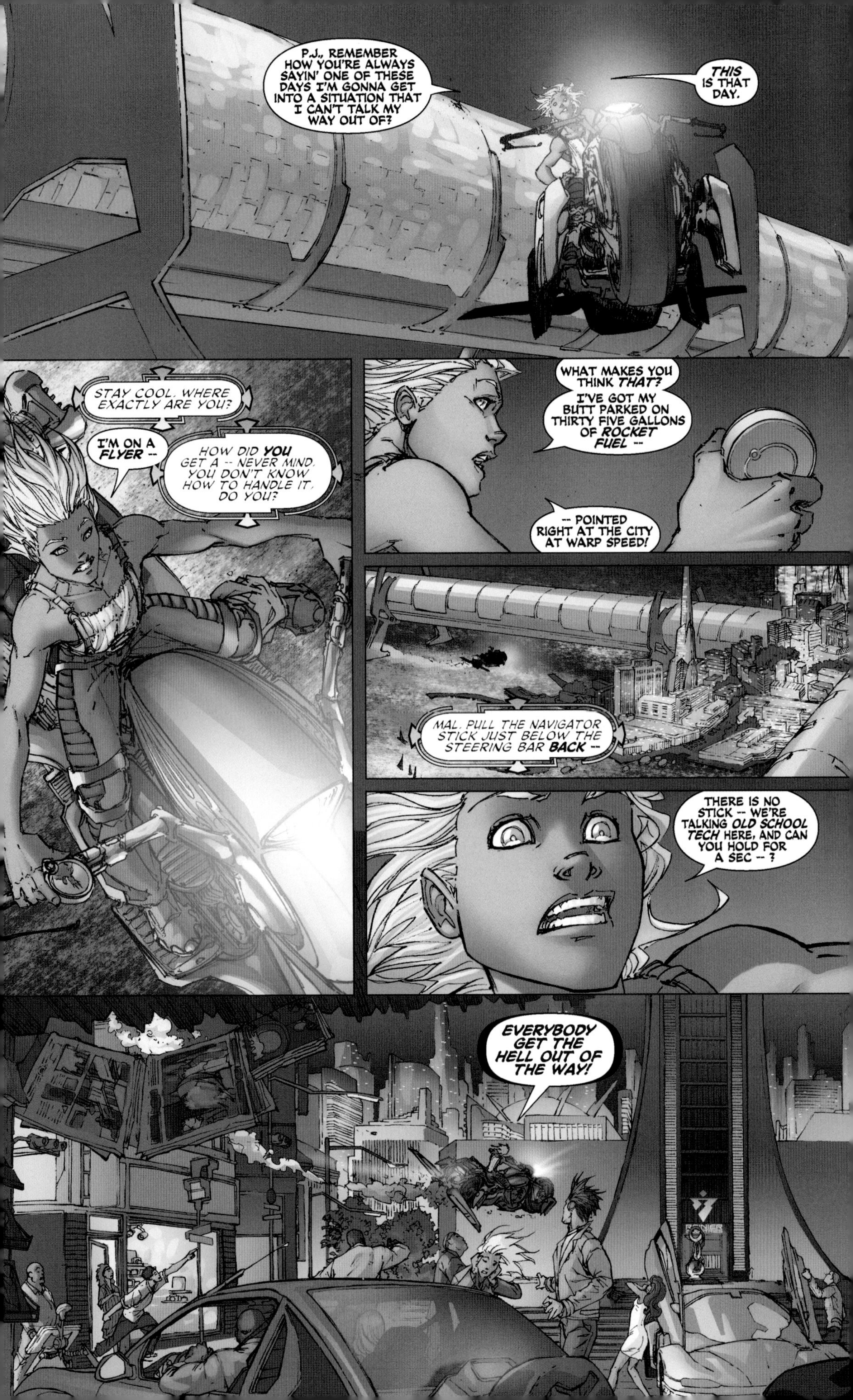
P.J., REMEMBER HOW YOU'RE ALWAYS SAYIN' ONE OF THESE DAYS I'M GONNA GET INTO A SITUATION THAT I CAN'T TALK MY WAY OUT OF?
THIS IS THAT DAY.
STAY COOL. WHERE EXACTLY ARE YOU?
I'M ON A FLYER --
HOW DID YOU GET A -- NEVER MIND. YOU DON'T KNOW HOW TO HANDLE IT, DO YOU?
WHAT MAKES YOU THINK THAT? I'VE GOT MY BUTT PARKED ON THIRTY FIVE GALLONS OF ROCKET FUEL --
-- POINTED RIGHT AT THE CITY AT WARP SPEED!
MAL. PULL THE NAVIGATOR STICK JUST BELOW THE STEERING BAR BACK --
THERE IS NO STICK -- WE'RE TALKING OLD SCHOOL TECH HERE, AND CAN YOU HOLD FOR A SEC -- ?
EVERYBODY GET THE HELL OUT OF THE WAY!

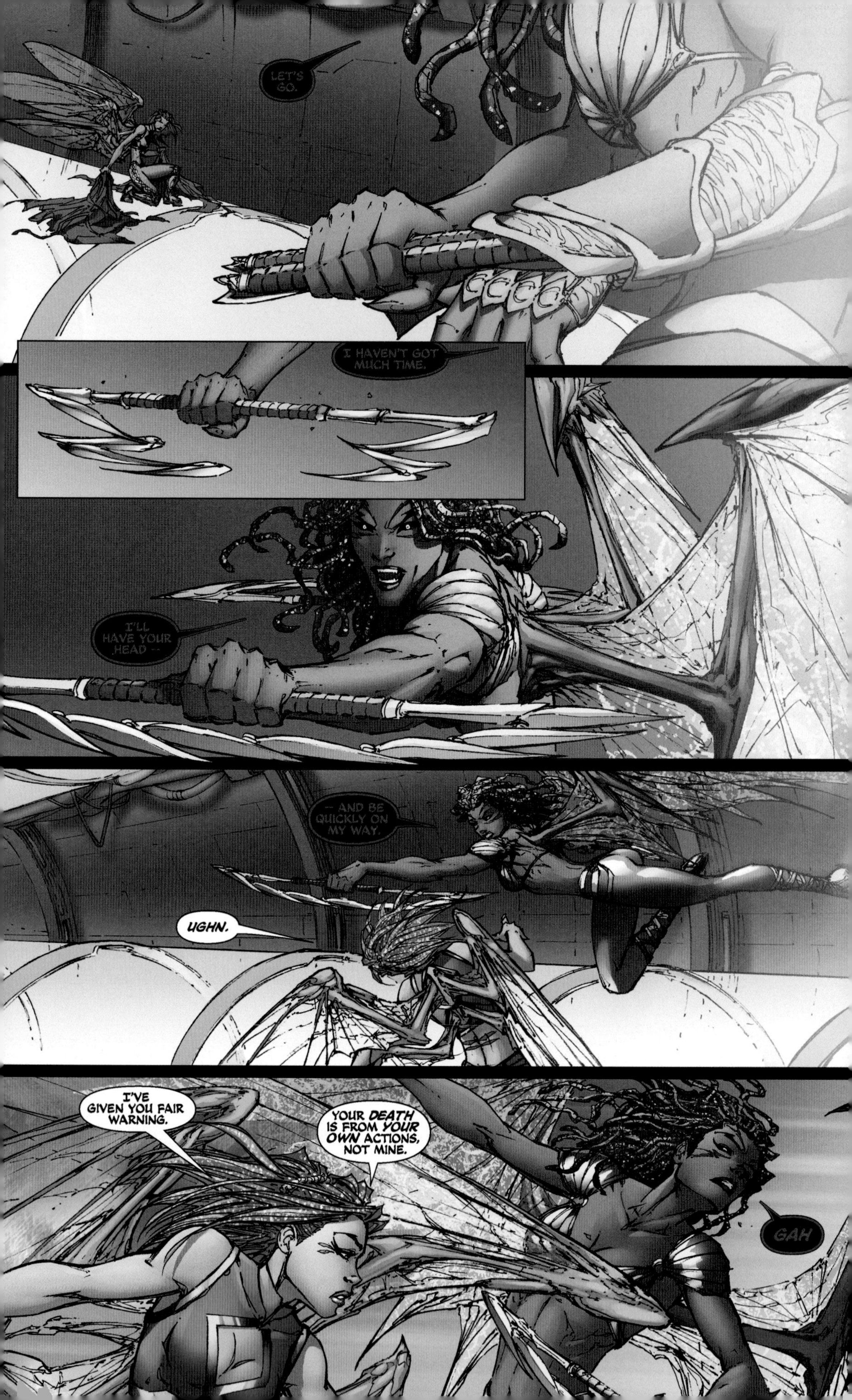
LET'S GO.
I HAVEN'T GOT MUCH TIME.
I'LL HAVE YOUR HEAD --
-- AND BE QUICKLY ON MY WAY.
UGHN.
I'VE GIVEN YOU FAIR WARNING.
YOUR *DEATH* IS FROM *YOUR OWN* ACTIONS, NOT MINE.
GAH

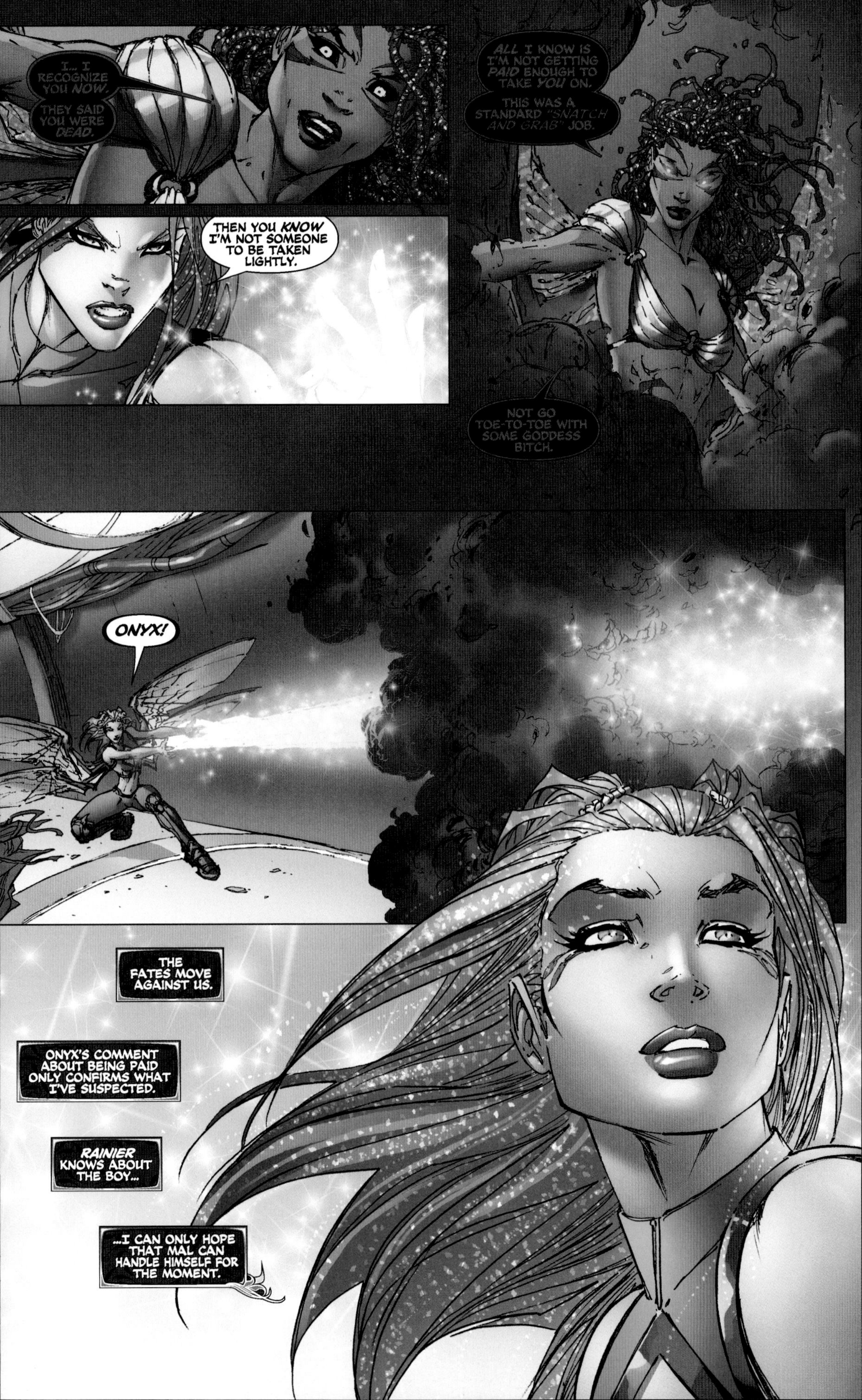
I... I RECOGNIZE YOU NOW.
THEY SAID YOU WERE DEAD.
THEN YOU KNOW I'M NOT SOMEONE TO BE TAKEN LIGHTLY.
ALL I KNOW IS I'M NOT GETTING PAID ENOUGH TO TAKE YOU ON.
THIS WAS A STANDARD "SNATCH AND GRAB" JOB.
NOT GO TOE-TO-TOE WITH SOME GODDESS BITCH.
ONYX!
THE FATES MOVE AGAINST US.
ONYX'S COMMENT ABOUT BEING PAID ONLY CONFIRMS WHAT I'VE SUSPECTED.
RAINIER KNOWS ABOUT THE BOY...
...I CAN ONLY HOPE THAT MAL CAN HANDLE HIMSELF FOR THE MOMENT.

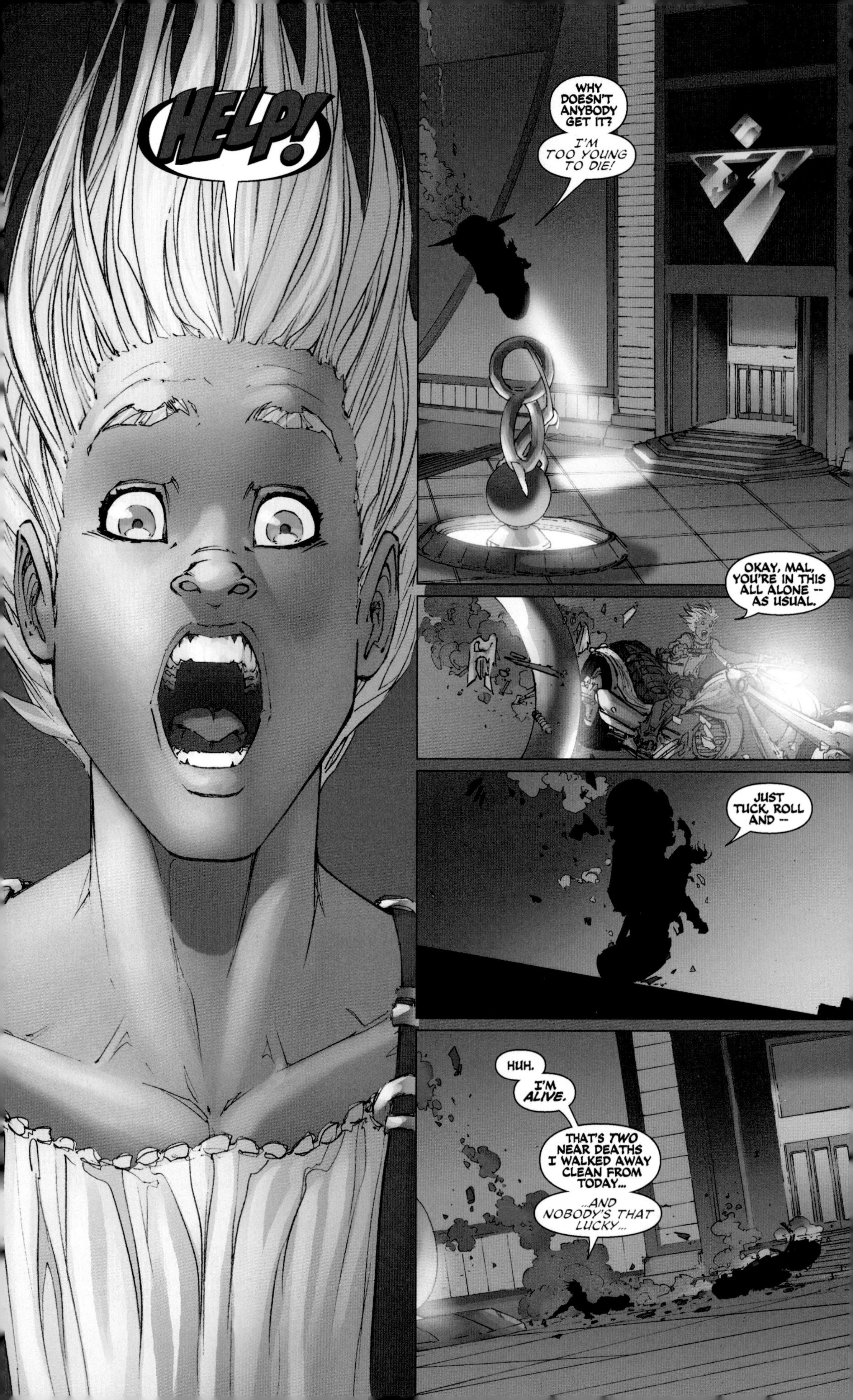
HELP!
WHY DOESN'T ANYBODY GET IT?
I'M TOO YOUNG TO DIE!
OKAY, MAL, YOU'RE IN THIS ALL ALONE -- AS USUAL.
JUST TUCK, ROLL AND --
HUH. I'M ALIVE.
THAT'S TWO NEAR DEATHS I WALKED AWAY CLEAN FROM TODAY...
...AND NOBODY'S THAT LUCKY...

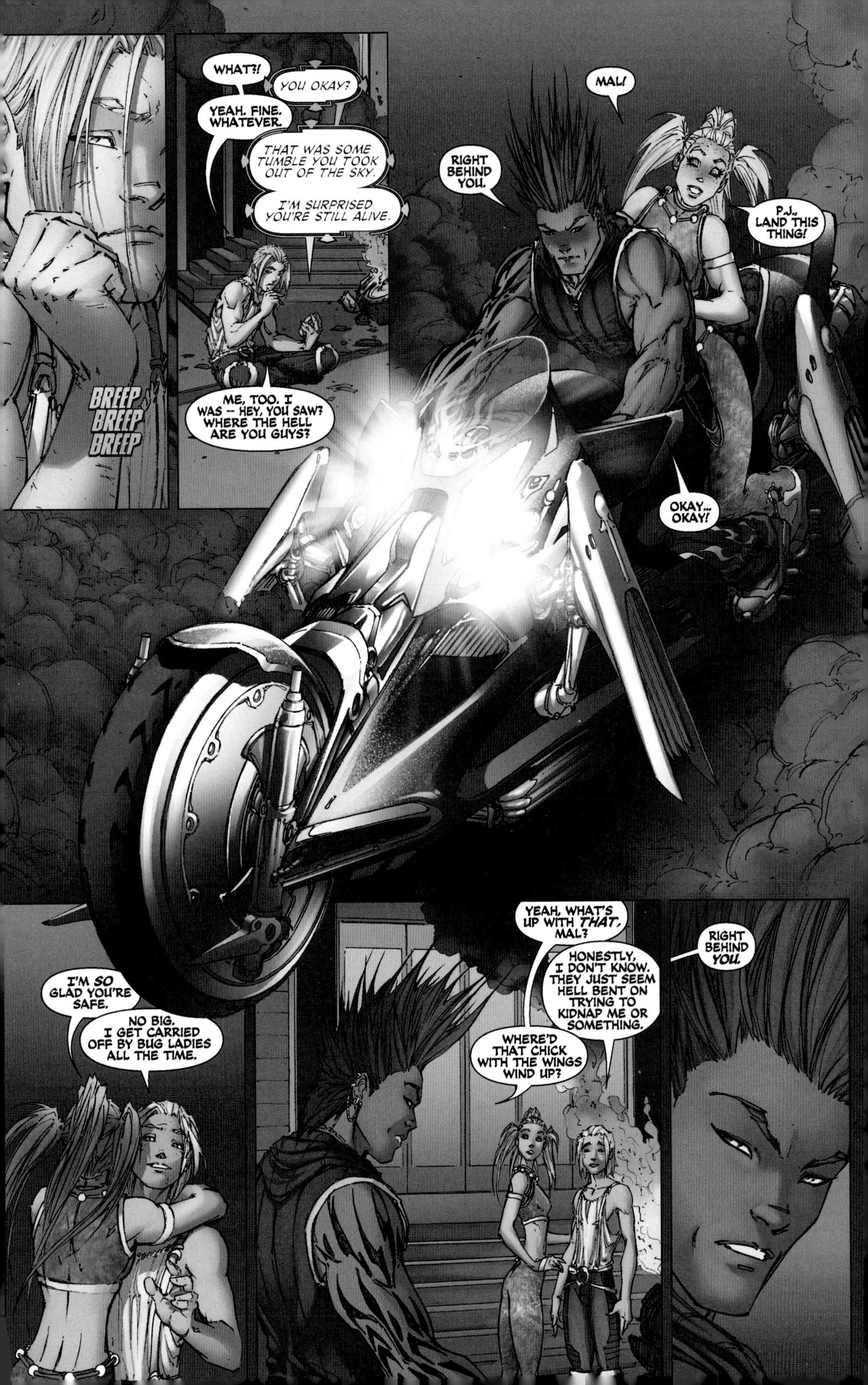
BREEP
BREEP
BREEP
WHAT?!
YOU OKAY?
YEAH. FINE. WHATEVER.
THAT WAS SOME TUMBLE YOU TOOK OUT OF THE SKY.
I'M SURPRISED YOU'RE STILL ALIVE.
ME, TOO. I WAS -- HEY, YOU SAW? WHERE THE HELL ARE YOU GUYS?
MAL!
RIGHT BEHIND YOU.
P.J., LAND THIS THING!
OKAY... OKAY!
I'M SO GLAD YOU'RE SAFE.
NO BIG. I GET CARRIED OFF BY BUG LADIES ALL THE TIME.
YEAH, WHAT'S UP WITH THAT, MAL?
HONESTLY, I DON'T KNOW. THEY JUST SEEM HELL BENT ON TRYING TO KIDNAP ME OR SOMETHING.
WHERE'D THAT CHICK WITH THE WINGS WIND UP?
RIGHT BEHIND YOU.

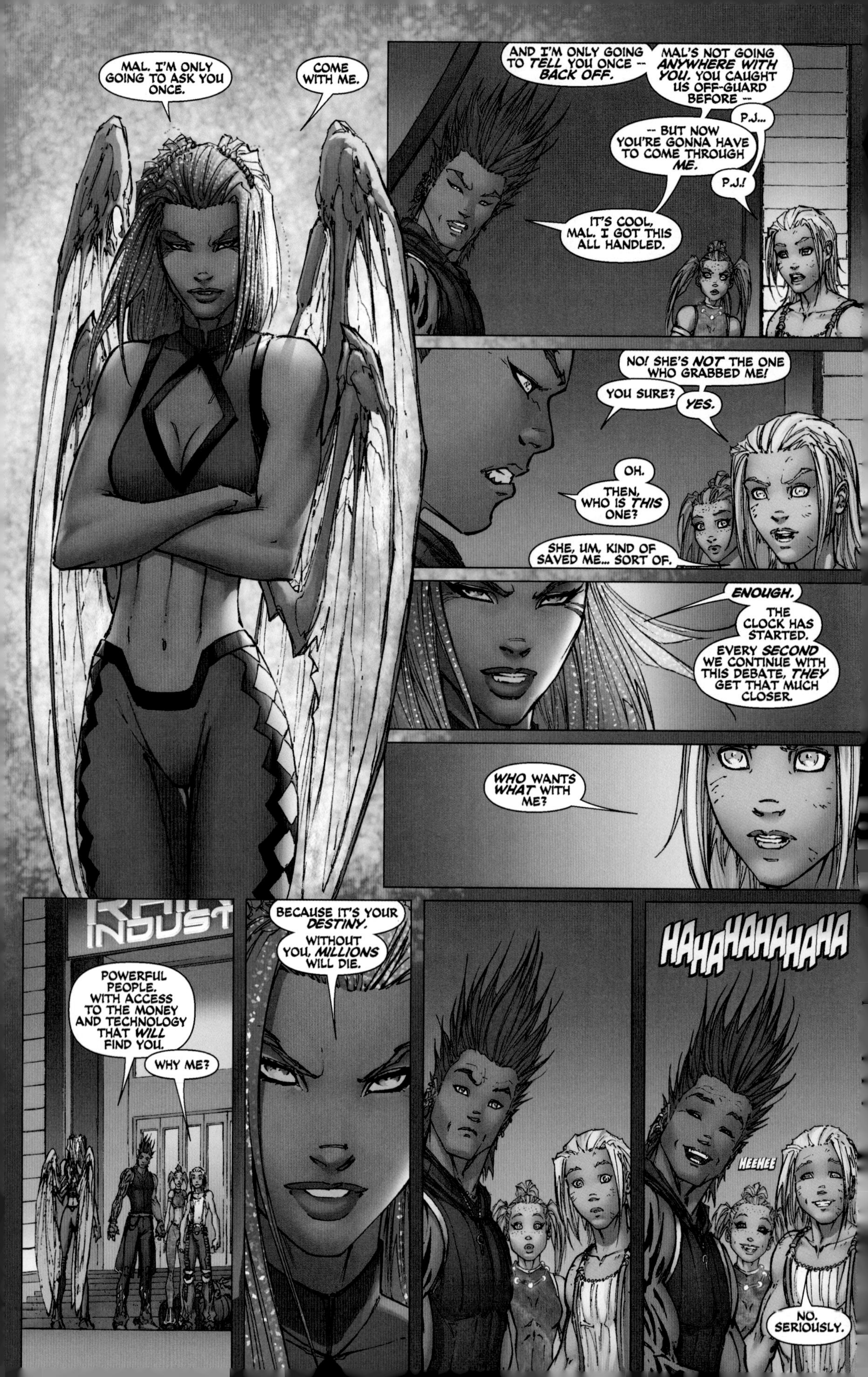
MAL. I'M ONLY GOING TO ASK YOU ONCE.
COME WITH ME.
AND I'M ONLY GOING TO TELL YOU ONCE -- BACK OFF.
MAL'S NOT GOING ANYWHERE WITH YOU. YOU CAUGHT US OFF-GUARD BEFORE --
P.J...
-- BUT NOW YOU'RE GONNA HAVE TO COME THROUGH ME.
P.J.!
IT'S COOL, MAL. I GOT THIS ALL HANDLED.
NO! SHE'S NOT THE ONE WHO GRABBED ME!
YOU SURE?
YES.
OH. THEN, WHO IS THIS ONE?
SHE, UM, KIND OF SAVED ME... SORT OF.
ENOUGH.
THE CLOCK HAS STARTED.
EVERY SECOND WE CONTINUE WITH THIS DEBATE, THEY GET THAT MUCH CLOSER.
WHO WANTS WHAT WITH ME?
INDUST
POWERFUL PEOPLE. WITH ACCESS TO THE MONEY AND TECHNOLOGY THAT WILL FIND YOU.
WHY ME?
BECAUSE IT'S YOUR DESTINY.
WITHOUT YOU, MILLIONS WILL DIE.
HAHAHAHAHAHAHA
HEEHEE
NO, SERIOUSLY.

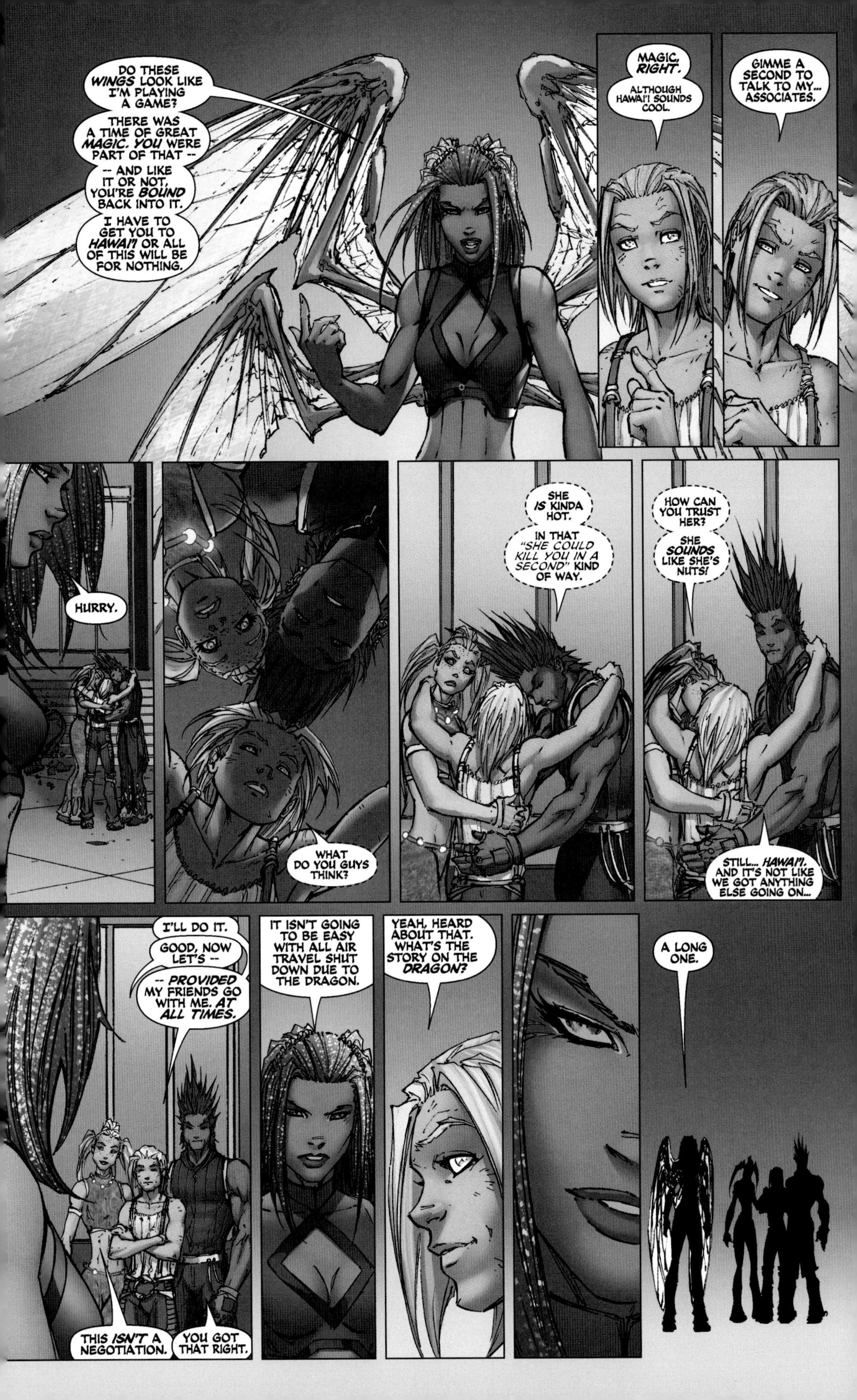
DO THESE WINGS LOOK LIKE I'M PLAYING A GAME?
THERE WAS A TIME OF GREAT MAGIC. YOU WERE PART OF THAT --
-- AND LIKE IT OR NOT, YOU'RE BOUND BACK INTO IT.
I HAVE TO GET YOU TO HAWAI'I OR ALL OF THIS WILL BE FOR NOTHING.
MAGIC, RIGHT.
ALTHOUGH HAWAI'I SOUNDS COOL.
GIMME A SECOND TO TALK TO MY... ASSOCIATES.
HURRY.
WHAT DO YOU GUYS THINK?
SHE IS KINDA HOT.
IN THAT "SHE COULD KILL YOU IN A SECOND" KIND OF WAY.
HOW CAN YOU TRUST HER?
SHE SOUNDS LIKE SHE'S NUTS!
STILL... HAWAI'I. AND IT'S NOT LIKE WE GOT ANYTHING ELSE GOING ON...
I'LL DO IT.
GOOD, NOW LET'S --
-- PROVIDED MY FRIENDS GO WITH ME. AT ALL TIMES.
THIS ISN'T A NEGOTIATION.
YOU GOT THAT RIGHT.
IT ISN'T GOING TO BE EASY WITH ALL AIR TRAVEL SHUT DOWN DUE TO THE DRAGON.
YEAH, HEARD ABOUT THAT. WHAT'S THE STORY ON THE DRAGON?
A LONG ONE.

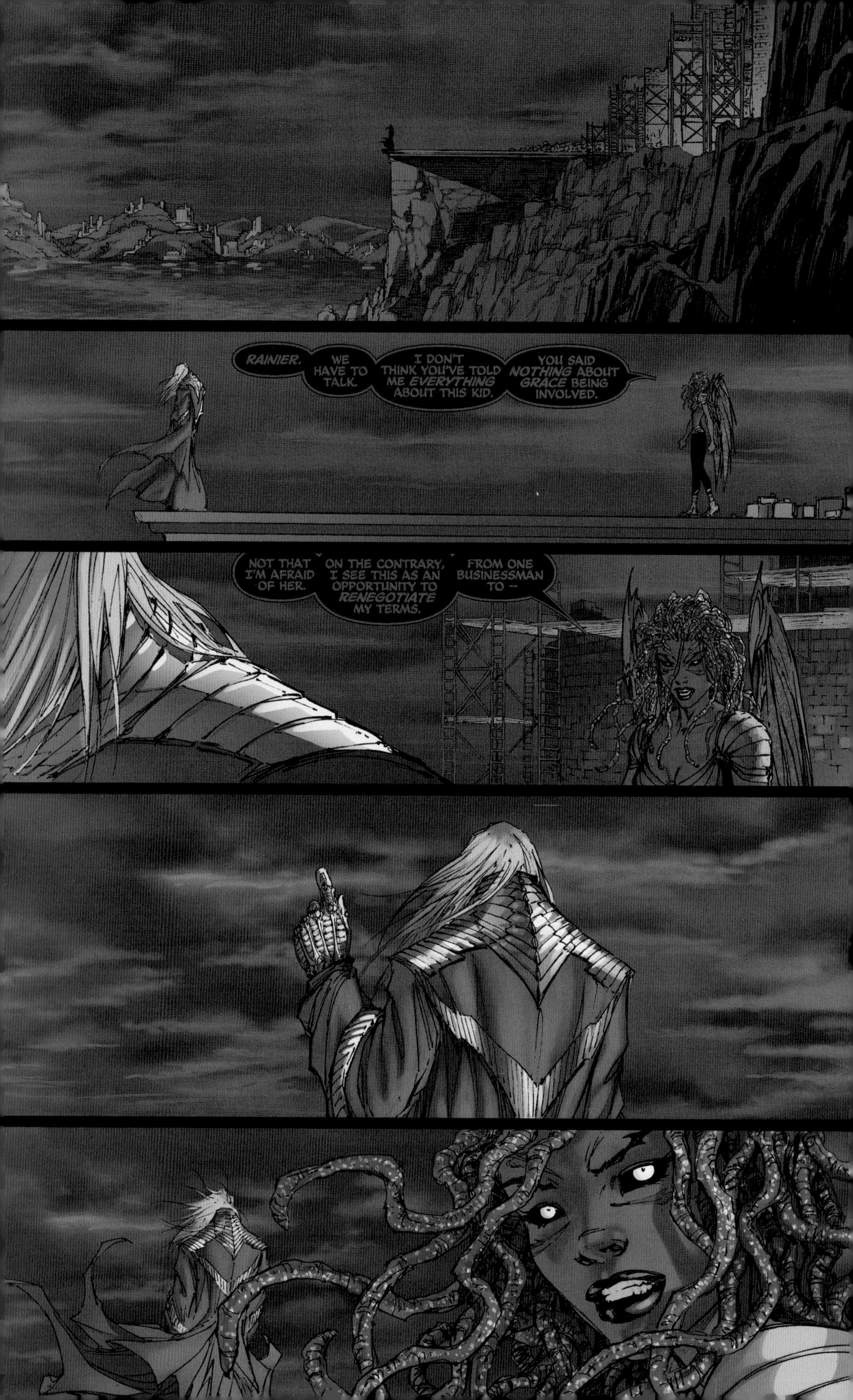
RAINIER.
WE HAVE TO TALK.
I DON'T THINK YOU'VE TOLD ME EVERYTHING ABOUT THIS KID.
YOU SAID NOTHING ABOUT GRACE BEING INVOLVED.
NOT THAT I'M AFRAID OF HER.
ON THE CONTRARY, I SEE THIS AS AN OPPORTUNITY TO RENEGOTIATE MY TERMS.
FROM ONE BUSINESSMAN TO --

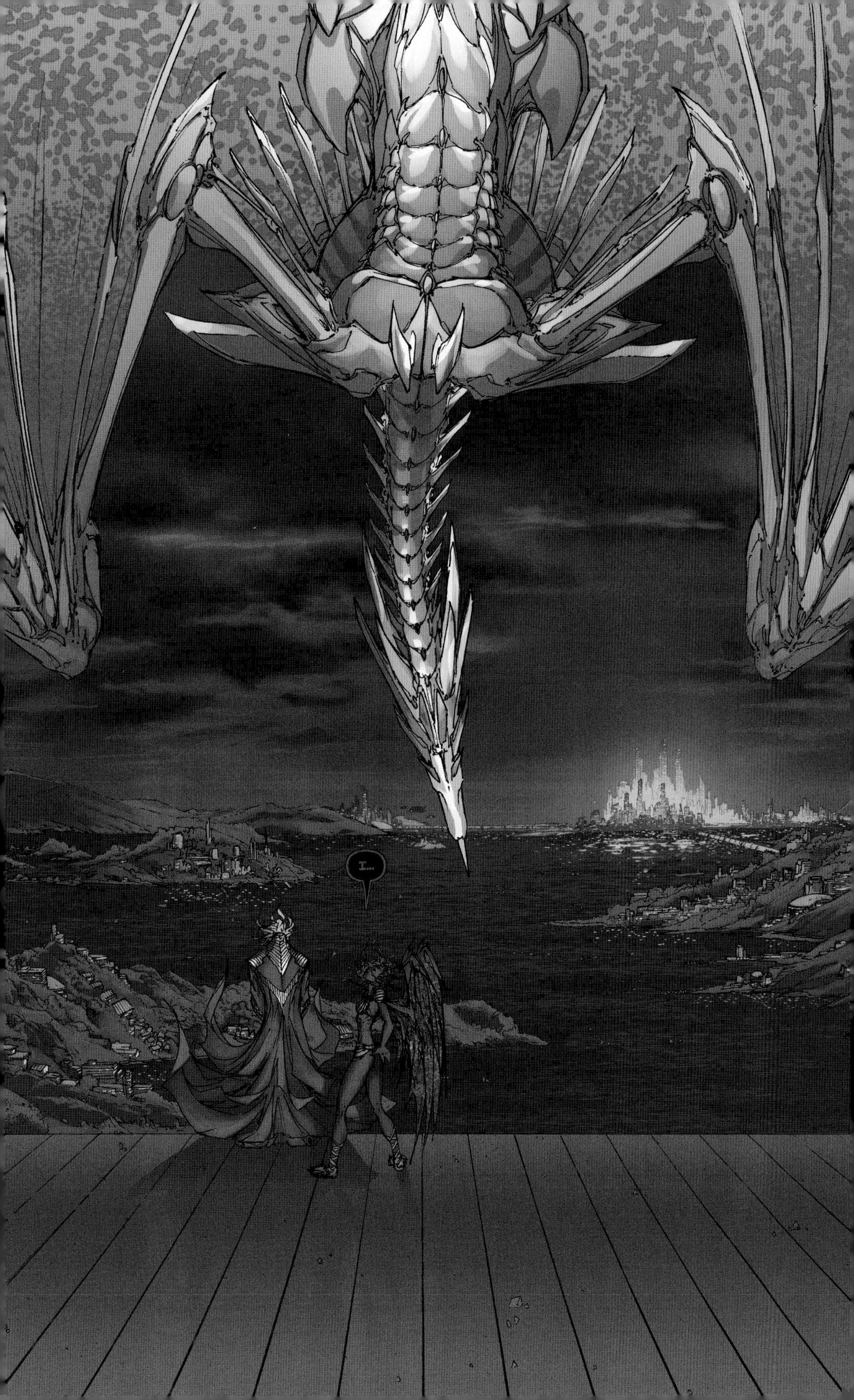
I...

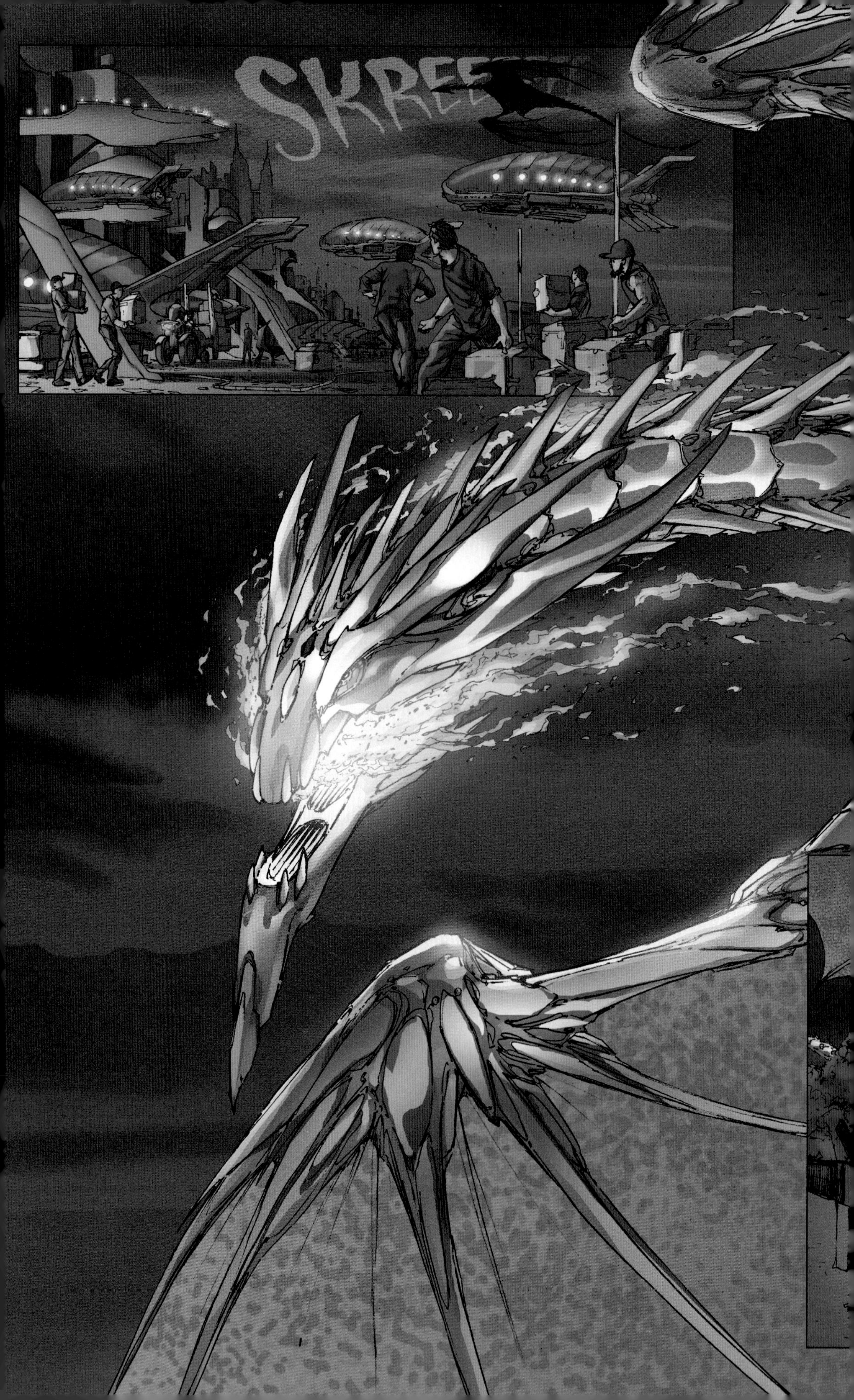
SKREE

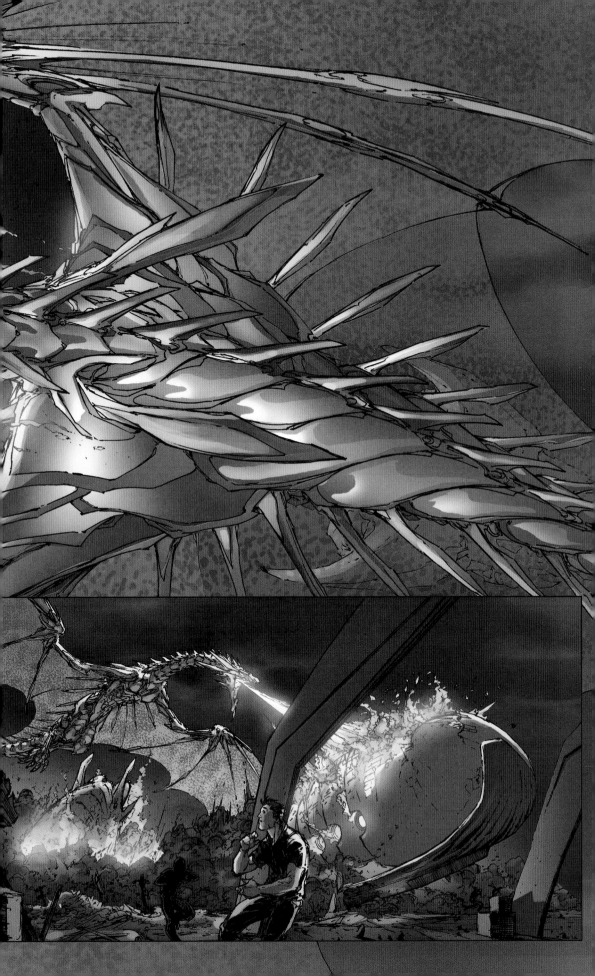

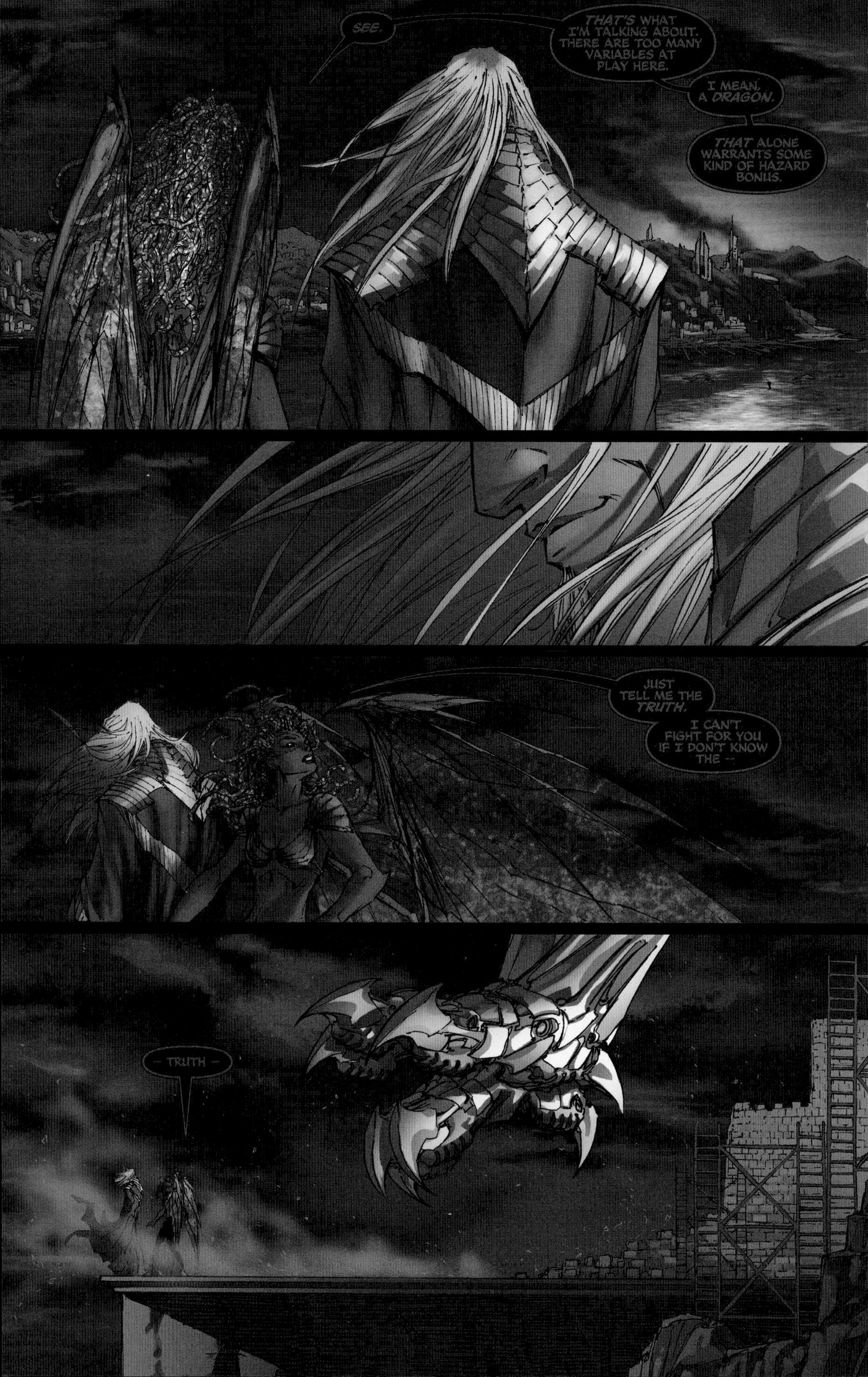
SEE.
THAT'S WHAT I'M TALKING ABOUT. THERE ARE TOO MANY VARIABLES AT PLAY HERE.
I MEAN, A DRAGON.
THAT ALONE WARRANTS SOME KIND OF HAZARD BONUS.
JUST TELL ME THE TRUTH.
I CAN'T FIGHT FOR YOU IF I DON'T KNOW THE --
-- TRUTH --

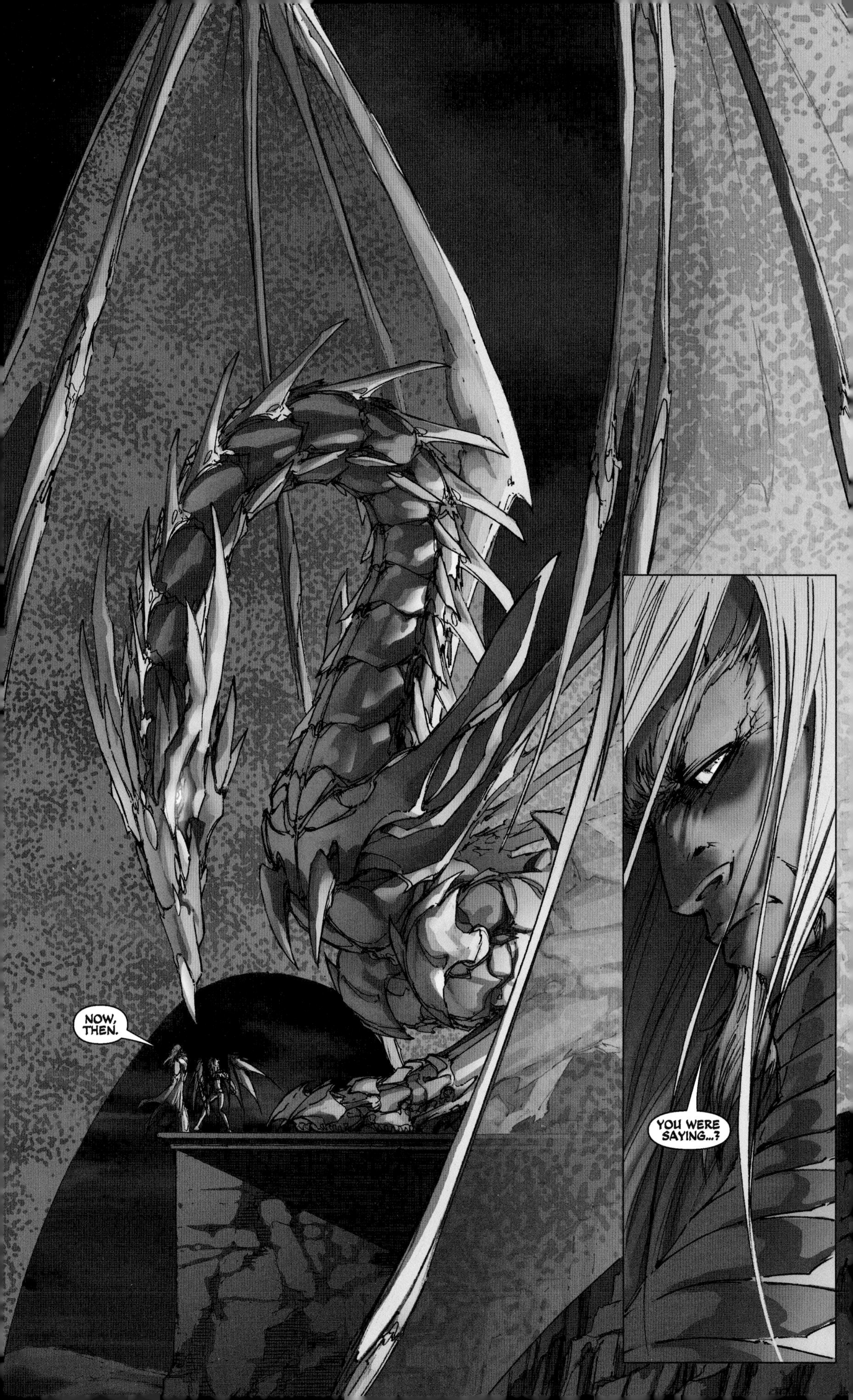
NOW, THEN.
YOU WERE SAYING...?

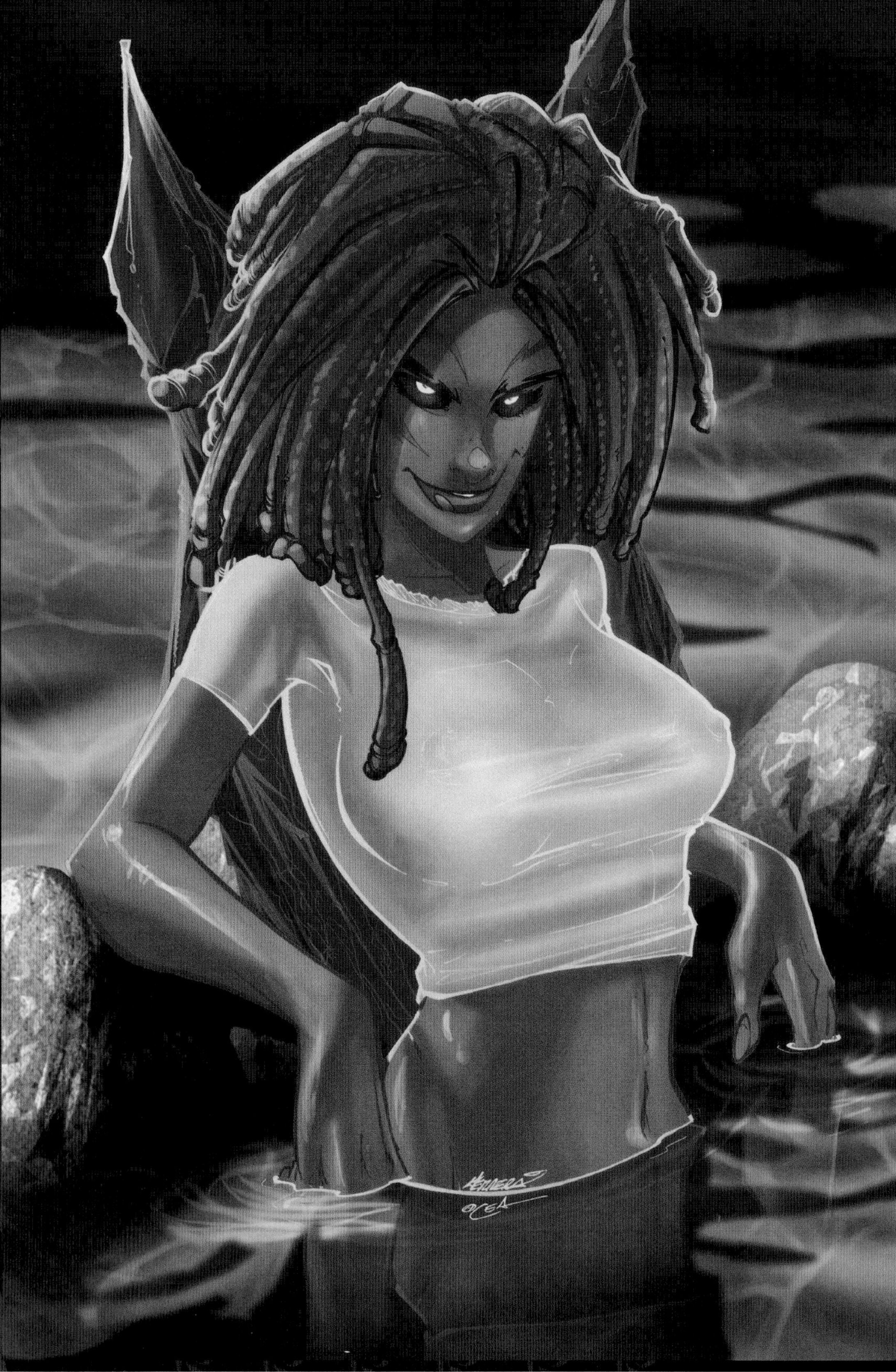

ONYX

· PIN-UP FROM ASPEN SPLASH: 2007 SWIMSUIT SPECTACULAR ·

by

· FRANCISCO HERRERA · LEONARDO OLEA ·

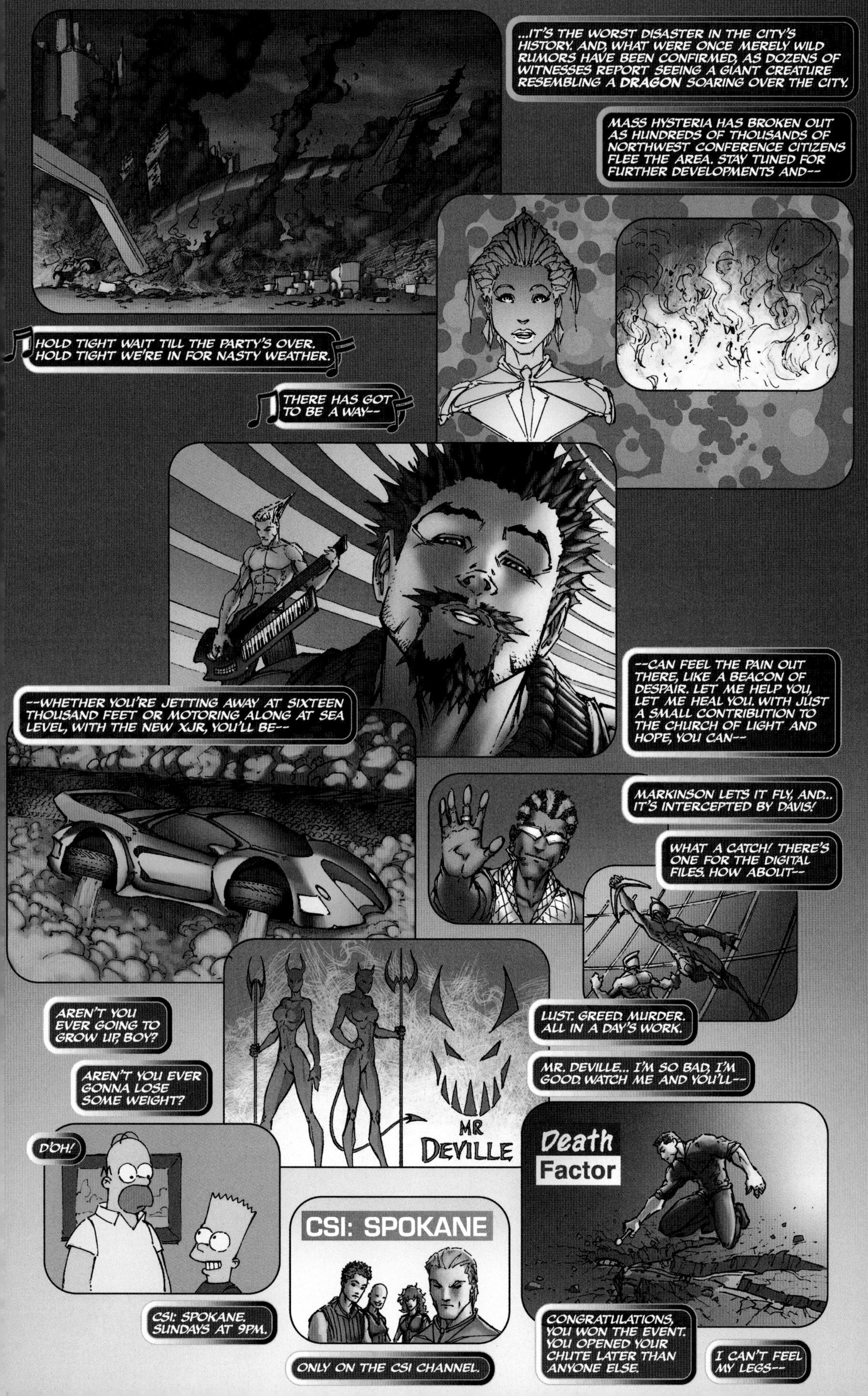
...IT'S THE WORST DISASTER IN THE CITY'S HISTORY. AND, WHAT WERE ONCE MERELY WILD RUMORS HAVE BEEN CONFIRMED, AS DOZENS OF WITNESSES REPORT SEEING A GIANT CREATURE RESEMBLING A DRAGON SOARING OVER THE CITY.
MASS HYSTERIA HAS BROKEN OUT AS HUNDREDS OF THOUSANDS OF NORTHWEST CONFERENCE CITIZENS FLEE THE AREA. STAY TUNED FOR FURTHER DEVELOPMENTS AND--
HOLD TIGHT WAIT TILL THE PARTY'S OVER. HOLD TIGHT WE'RE IN FOR NASTY WEATHER.
THERE HAS GOT TO BE A WAY--
--CAN FEEL THE PAIN OUT THERE, LIKE A BEACON OF DESPAIR. LET ME HELP YOU, LET ME HEAL YOU. WITH JUST A SMALL CONTRIBUTION TO THE CHURCH OF LIGHT AND HOPE, YOU CAN--
--WHETHER YOU'RE JETTING AWAY AT SIXTEEN THOUSAND FEET OR MOTORING ALONG AT SEA LEVEL, WITH THE NEW XJR, YOU'LL BE--
MARKINSON LETS IT FLY, AND... IT'S INTERCEPTED BY DAVIS!
WHAT A CATCH! THERE'S ONE FOR THE DIGITAL FILES. HOW ABOUT--
AREN'T YOU EVER GOING TO GROW UP, BOY?
AREN'T YOU EVER GONNA LOSE SOME WEIGHT?
D'OH!
LUST. GREED. MURDER. ALL IN A DAY'S WORK.
MR. DEVILLE... I'M SO BAD, I'M GOOD. WATCH ME AND YOU'LL--
MR DEVILLE
CSI: SPOKANE
CSI: SPOKANE. SUNDAYS AT 9PM.
ONLY ON THE CSI CHANNEL.
Death Factor
CONGRATULATIONS, YOU WON THE EVENT. YOU OPENED YOUR CHUTE LATER THAN ANYONE ELSE.
I CAN'T FEEL MY LEGS--

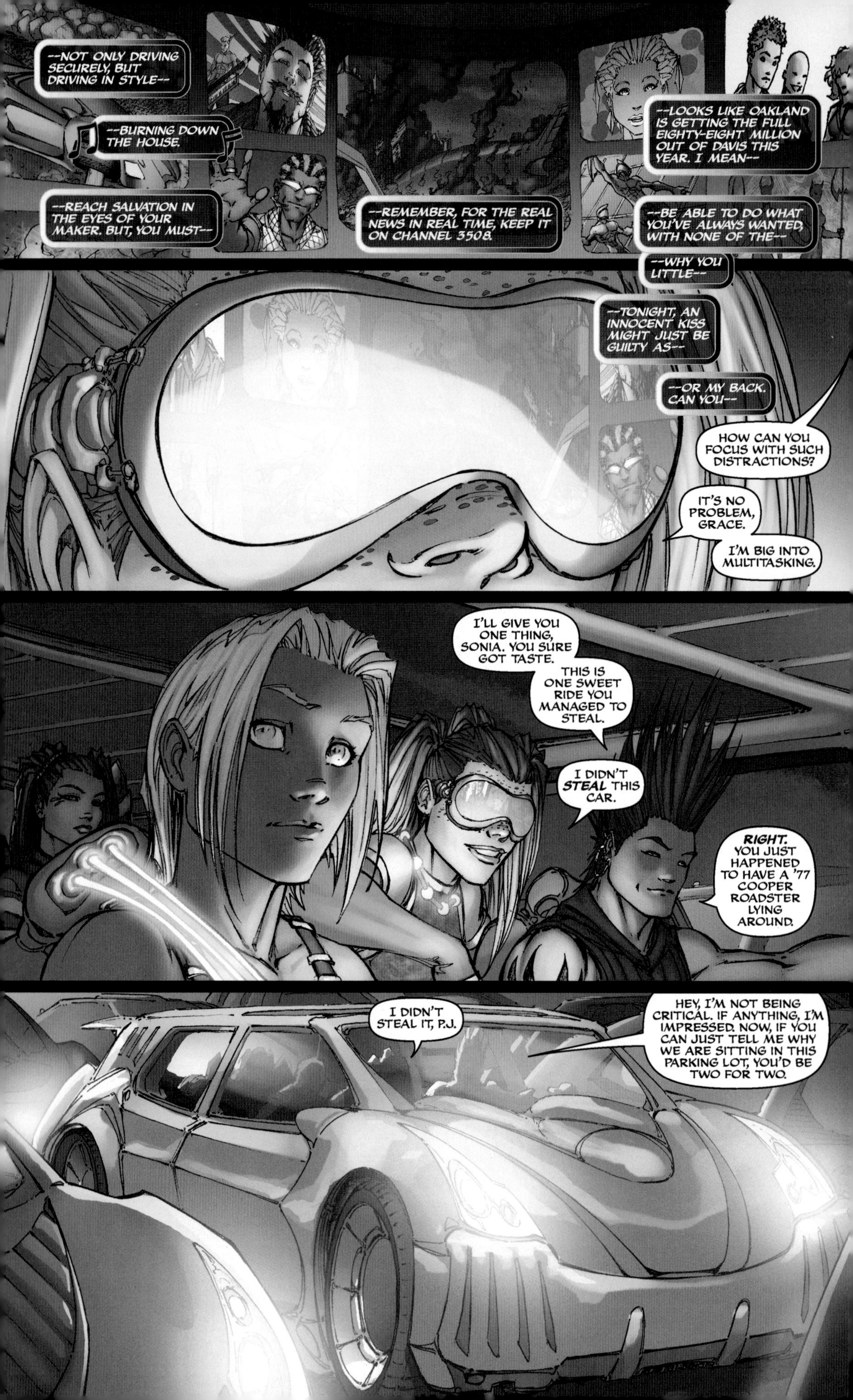

--NOT ONLY DRIVING SECURELY, BUT DRIVING IN STYLE--
--BURNING DOWN THE HOUSE.
--REACH SALVATION IN THE EYES OF YOUR MAKER. BUT, YOU MUST--
--REMEMBER, FOR THE REAL NEWS IN REAL TIME, KEEP IT ON CHANNEL 3508.
--LOOKS LIKE OAKLAND IS GETTING THE FULL EIGHTY-EIGHT MILLION OUT OF DAVIS THIS YEAR. I MEAN--
--BE ABLE TO DO WHAT YOU'VE ALWAYS WANTED, WITH NONE OF THE--
--WHY YOU LITTLE--
--TONIGHT, AN INNOCENT KISS MIGHT JUST BE GUILTY AS--
--OR MY BACK. CAN YOU--
HOW CAN YOU FOCUS WITH SUCH DISTRACTIONS?
IT'S NO PROBLEM, GRACE.
I'M BIG INTO MULTITASKING.
I'LL GIVE YOU ONE THING, SONIA. YOU SURE GOT TASTE.
THIS IS ONE SWEET RIDE YOU MANAGED TO STEAL.
I DIDN'T STEAL THIS CAR.
RIGHT. YOU JUST HAPPENED TO HAVE A '77 COOPER ROADSTER LYING AROUND.
I DIDN'T STEAL IT, P.J.
HEY, I'M NOT BEING CRITICAL. IF ANYTHING, I'M IMPRESSED. NOW, IF YOU CAN JUST TELL ME WHY WE ARE SITTING IN THIS PARKING LOT, YOU'D BE TWO FOR TWO.

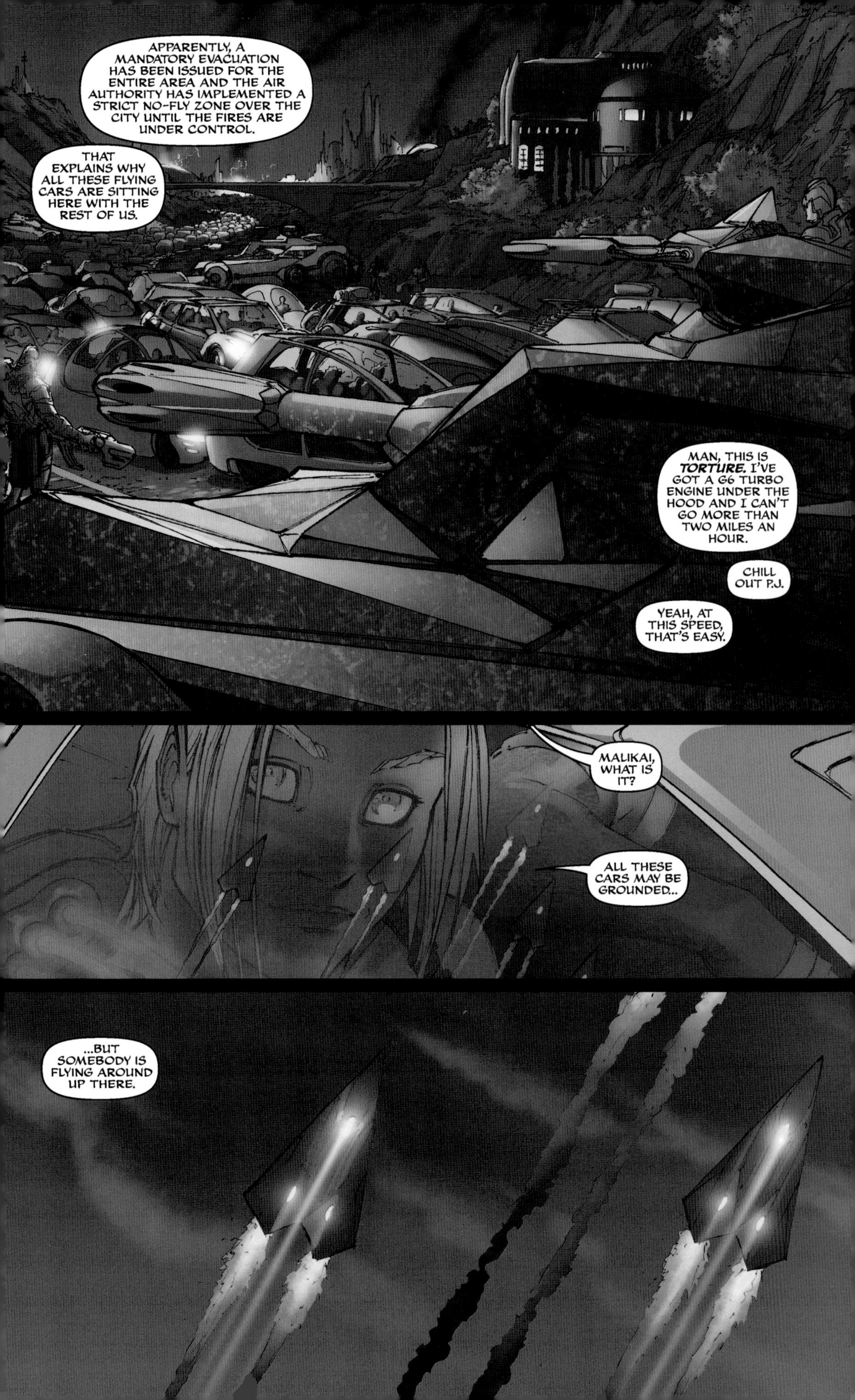
APPARENTLY, A MANDATORY EVACUATION HAS BEEN ISSUED FOR THE ENTIRE AREA AND THE AIR AUTHORITY HAS IMPLEMENTED A STRICT NO-FLY ZONE OVER THE CITY UNTIL THE FIRES ARE UNDER CONTROL.
THAT EXPLAINS WHY ALL THESE FLYING CARS ARE SITTING HERE WITH THE REST OF US.
MAN, THIS IS ***TORTURE.*** I'VE GOT A G6 TURBO ENGINE UNDER THE HOOD AND I CAN'T GO MORE THAN TWO MILES AN HOUR.
CHILL OUT P.J.
YEAH, AT THIS SPEED, THAT'S EASY.
MALIKAI, WHAT IS IT?
ALL THESE CARS MAY BE GROUNDED...
...BUT SOMEBODY IS FLYING AROUND UP THERE.

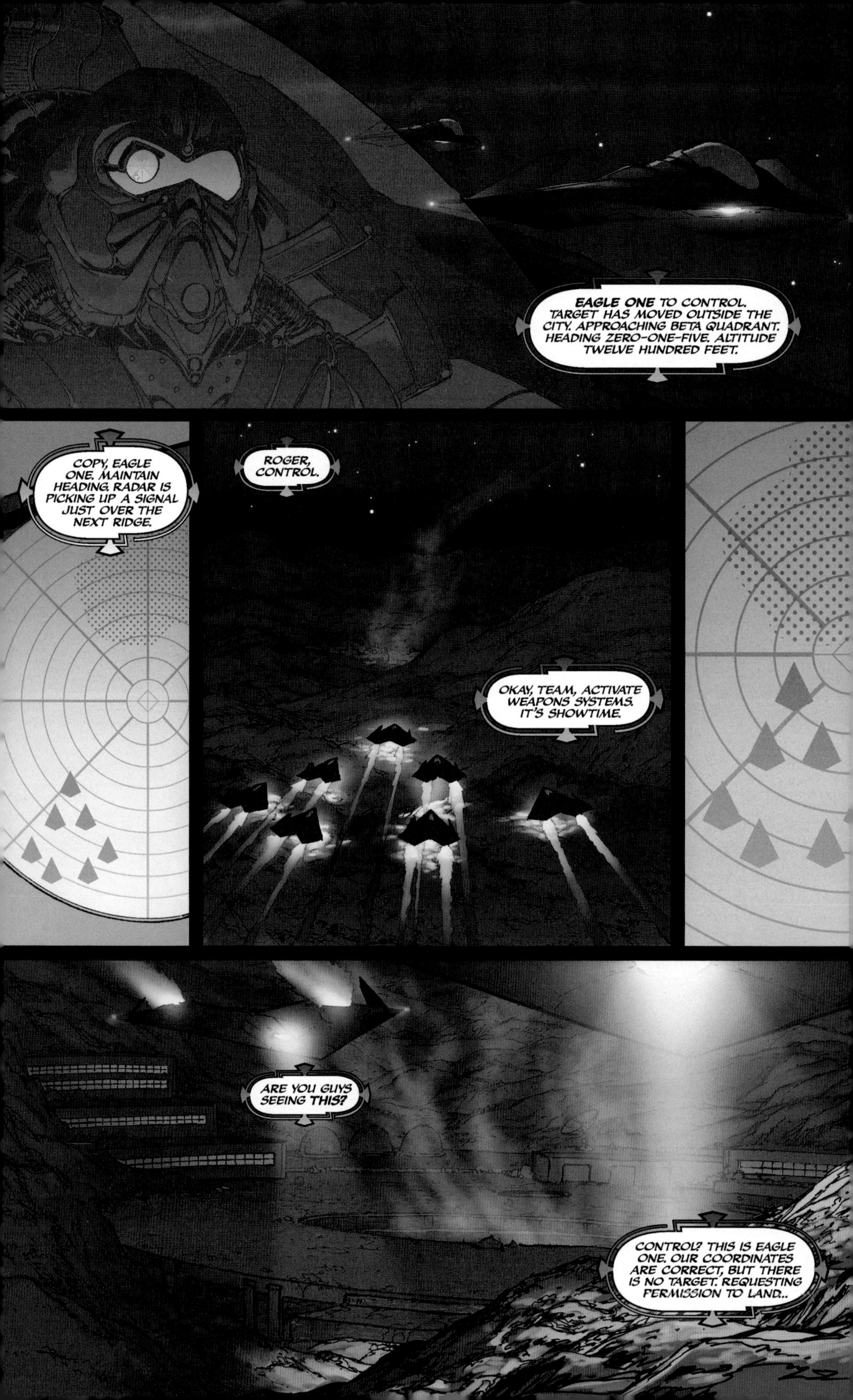
EAGLE ONE TO CONTROL. TARGET HAS MOVED OUTSIDE THE CITY. APPROACHING BETA QUADRANT. HEADING ZERO-ONE-FIVE. ALTITUDE TWELVE HUNDRED FEET.
COPY, EAGLE ONE. MAINTAIN HEADING. RADAR IS PICKING UP A SIGNAL JUST OVER THE NEXT RIDGE.
ROGER, CONTROL.
OKAY, TEAM, ACTIVATE WEAPONS SYSTEMS. IT'S SHOWTIME.
ARE YOU GUYS SEEING THIS?
CONTROL? THIS IS EAGLE ONE. OUR COORDINATES ARE CORRECT, BUT THERE IS NO TARGET. REQUESTING PERMISSION TO LAND...

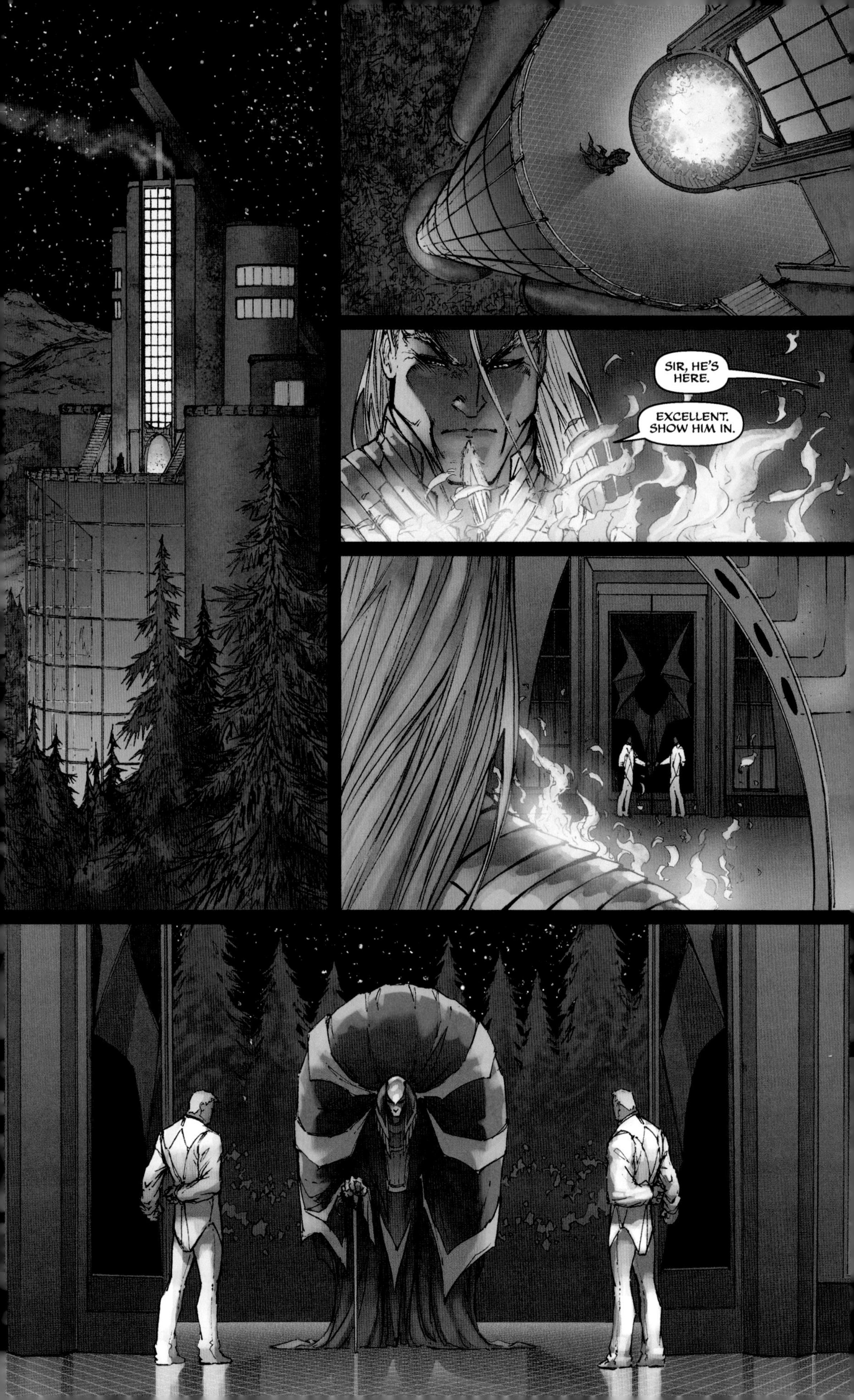
SIR, HE'S HERE.
EXCELLENT. SHOW HIM IN.

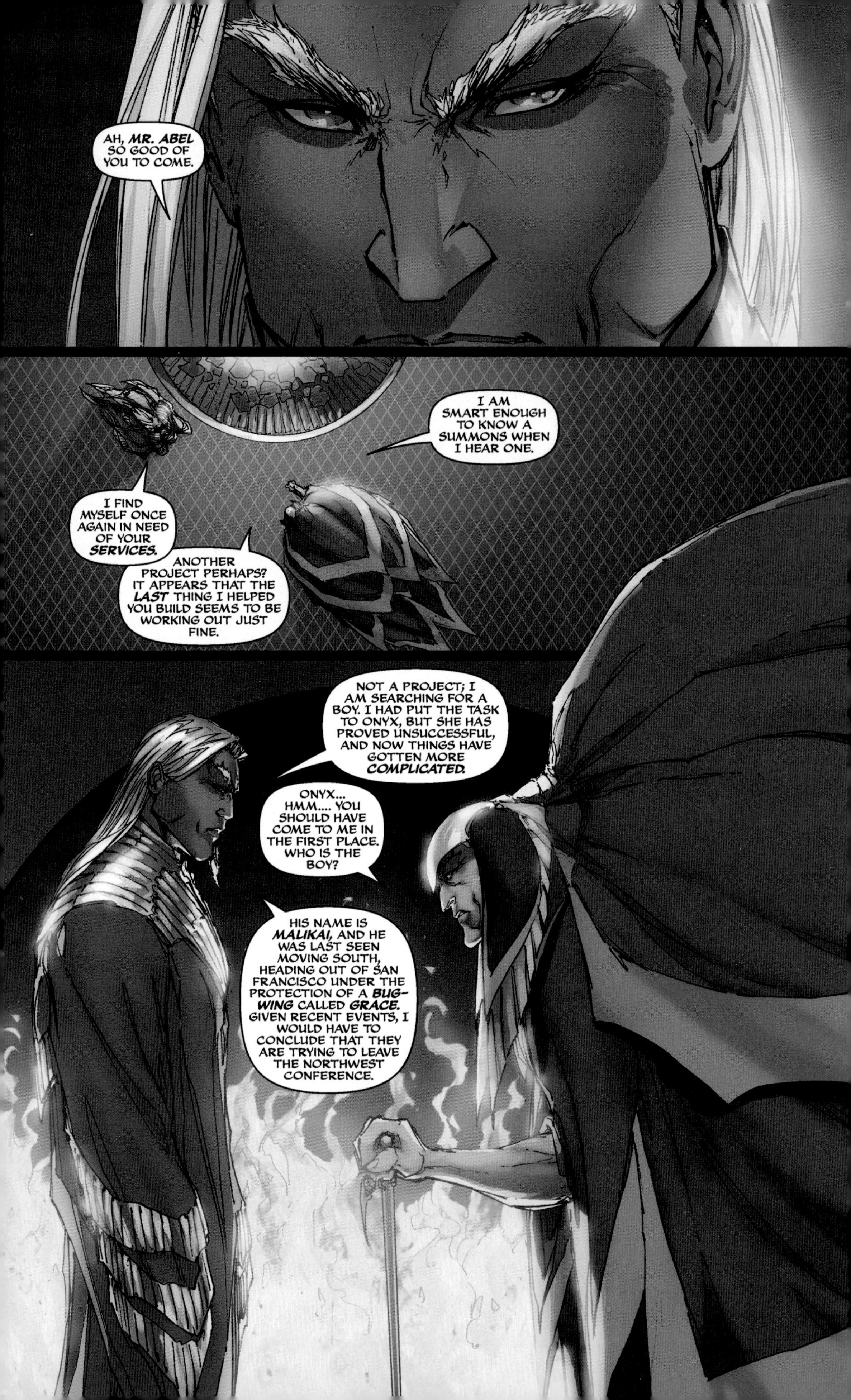
AH, **MR. ABEL** SO GOOD OF YOU TO COME.
I AM SMART ENOUGH TO KNOW A SUMMONS WHEN I HEAR ONE.
I FIND MYSELF ONCE AGAIN IN NEED OF YOUR **SERVICES.**
ANOTHER PROJECT PERHAPS? IT APPEARS THAT THE **LAST** THING I HELPED YOU BUILD SEEMS TO BE WORKING OUT JUST FINE.
NOT A PROJECT; I AM SEARCHING FOR A BOY. I HAD PUT THE TASK TO ONYX, BUT SHE HAS PROVED UNSUCCESSFUL, AND NOW THINGS HAVE GOTTEN MORE **COMPLICATED.**
ONYX... HMM.... YOU SHOULD HAVE COME TO ME IN THE FIRST PLACE. WHO IS THE BOY?
HIS NAME IS **MALIKAI,** AND HE WAS LAST SEEN MOVING SOUTH, HEADING OUT OF SAN FRANCISCO UNDER THE PROTECTION OF A **BUG-WING** CALLED **GRACE.** GIVEN RECENT EVENTS, I WOULD HAVE TO CONCLUDE THAT THEY ARE TRYING TO LEAVE THE NORTHWEST CONFERENCE.

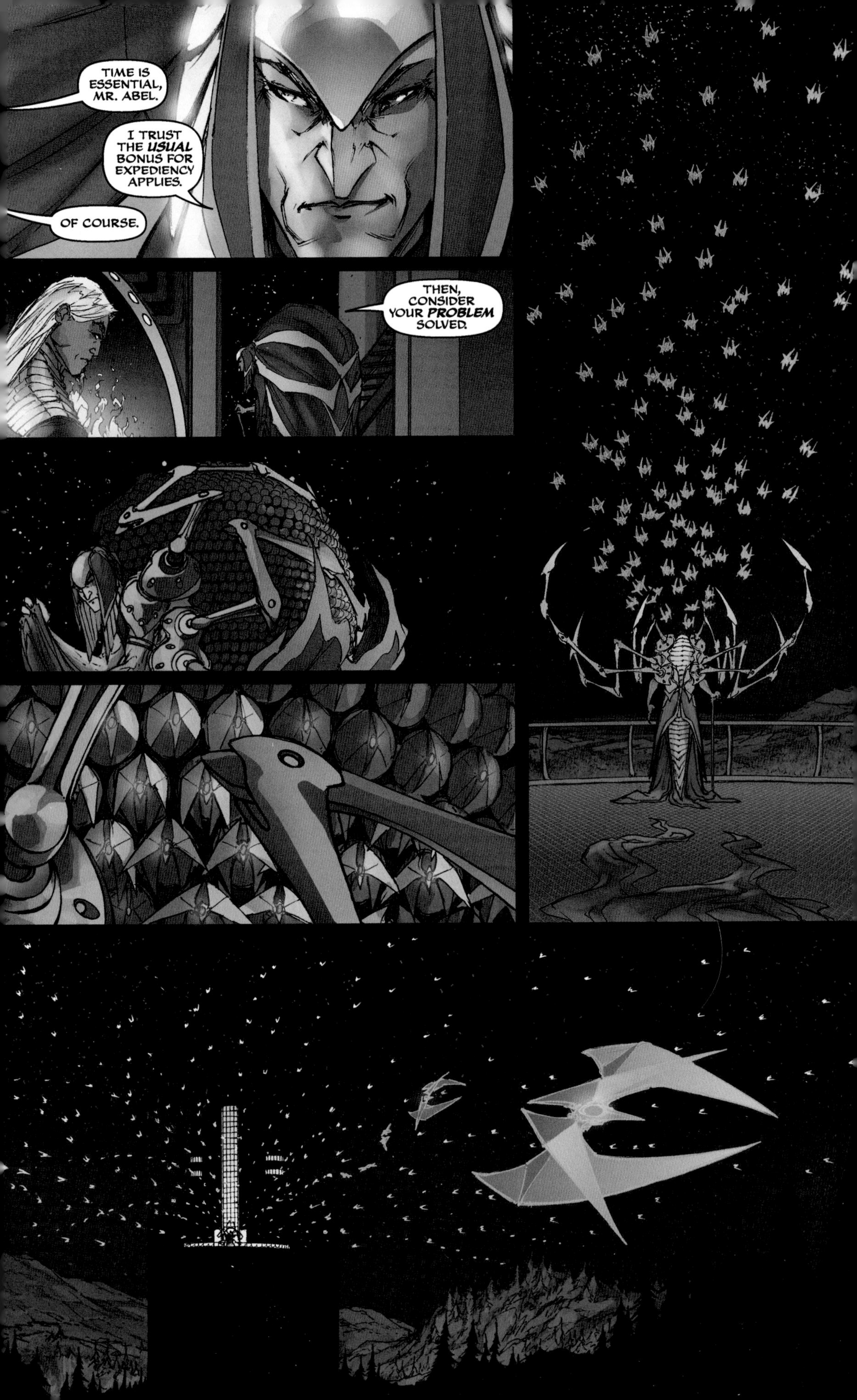
TIME IS ESSENTIAL, MR. ABEL.
I TRUST THE USUAL BONUS FOR EXPEDIENCY APPLIES.
OF COURSE.
THEN, CONSIDER YOUR PROBLEM SOLVED.

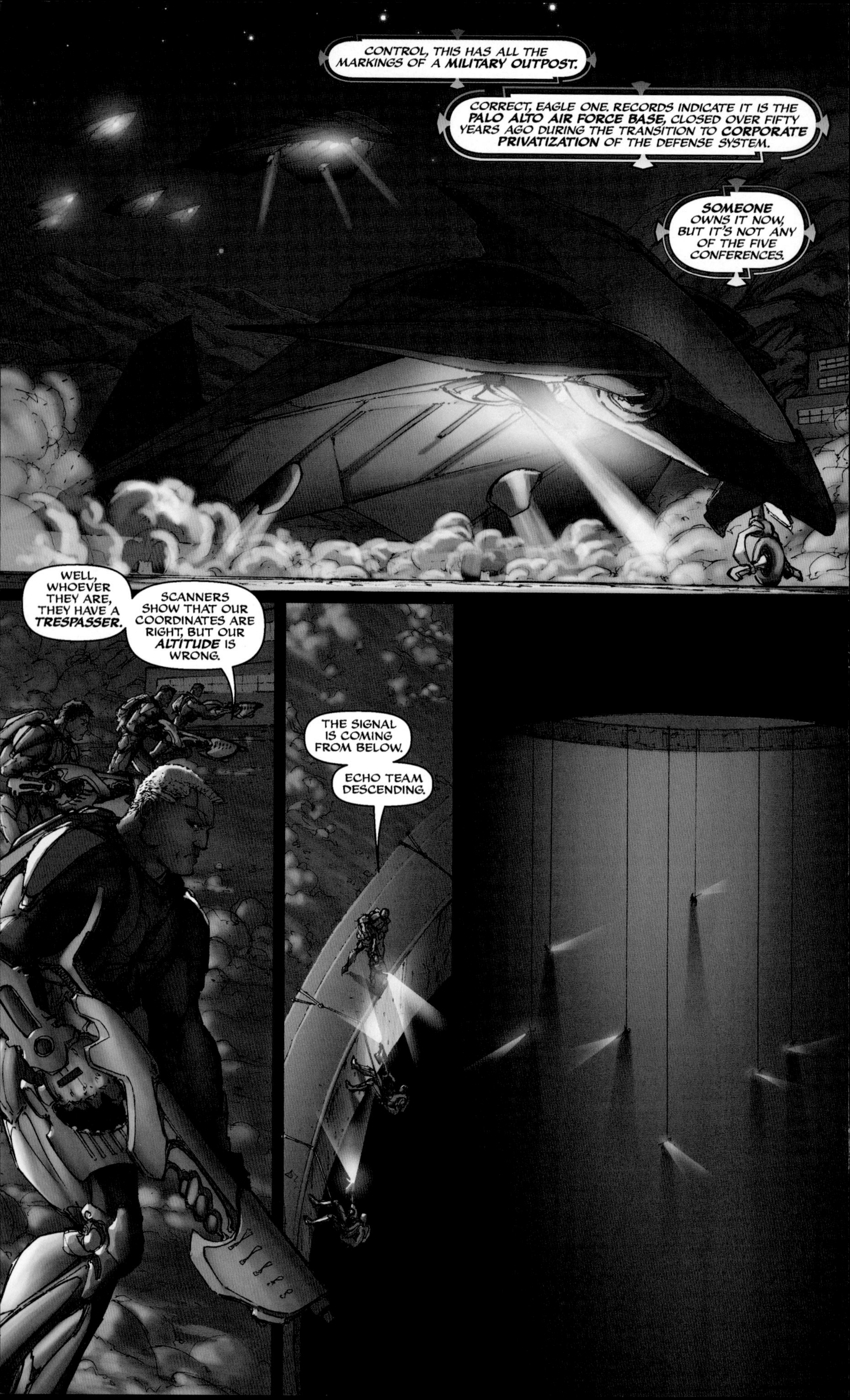
CONTROL, THIS HAS ALL THE MARKINGS OF A **MILITARY OUTPOST.**
CORRECT, EAGLE ONE. RECORDS INDICATE IT IS THE **PALO ALTO AIR FORCE BASE,** CLOSED OVER FIFTY YEARS AGO DURING THE TRANSITION TO **CORPORATE PRIVATIZATION** OF THE DEFENSE SYSTEM.
SOMEONE OWNS IT NOW, BUT IT'S NOT ANY OF THE FIVE CONFERENCES.
WELL, WHOEVER THEY ARE, THEY HAVE A ***TRESPASSER.***
SCANNERS SHOW THAT OUR COORDINATES ARE RIGHT, BUT OUR ***ALTITUDE*** IS WRONG.
THE SIGNAL IS COMING FROM BELOW.
ECHO TEAM DESCENDING.

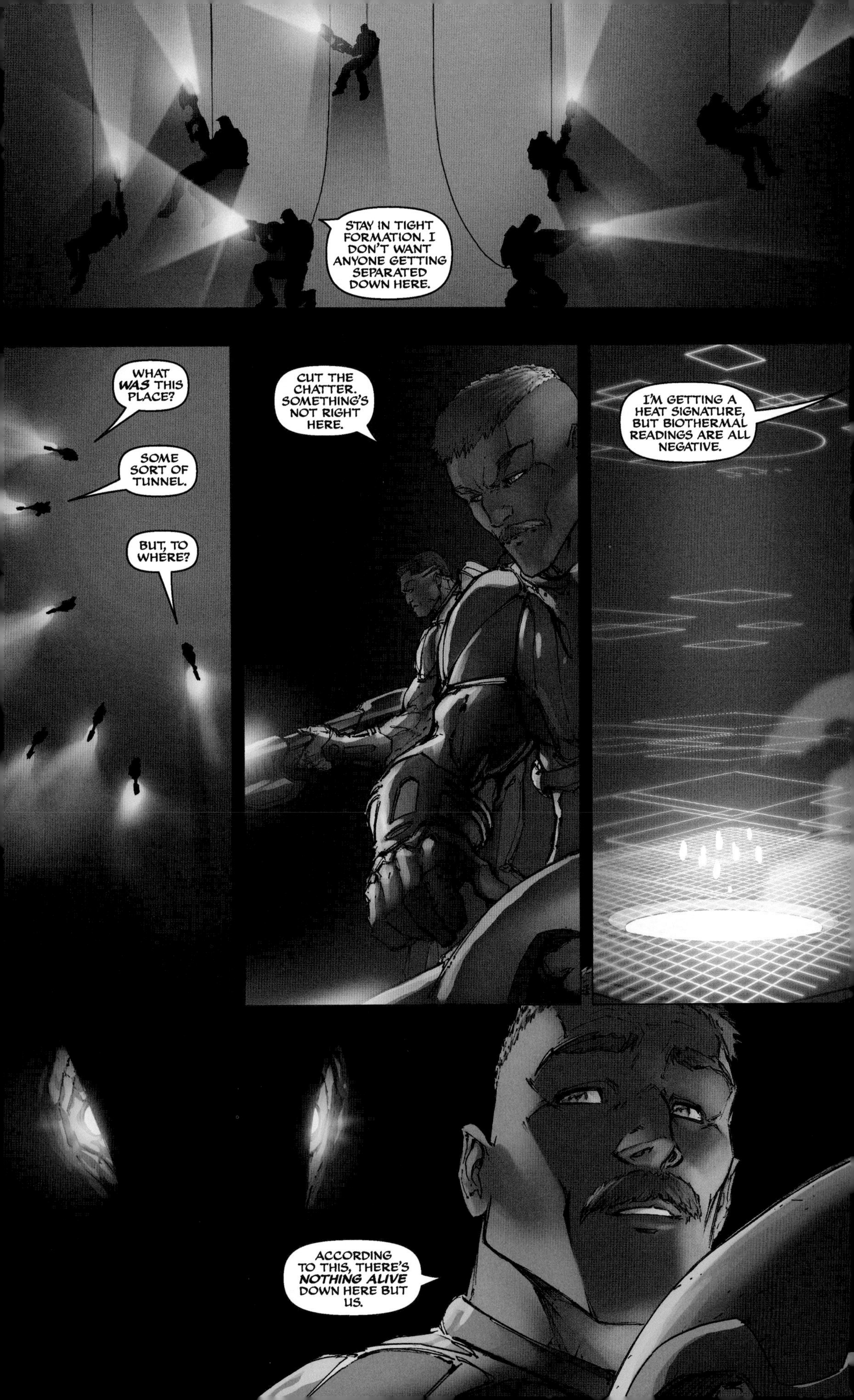
STAY IN TIGHT FORMATION. I DON'T WANT ANYONE GETTING SEPARATED DOWN HERE.
WHAT *WAS* THIS PLACE?
SOME SORT OF TUNNEL.
BUT, TO WHERE?
CUT THE CHATTER. SOMETHING'S NOT RIGHT HERE.
I'M GETTING A HEAT SIGNATURE, BUT BIOTHERMAL READINGS ARE ALL NEGATIVE.
ACCORDING TO THIS, THERE'S *NOTHING ALIVE* DOWN HERE BUT US.

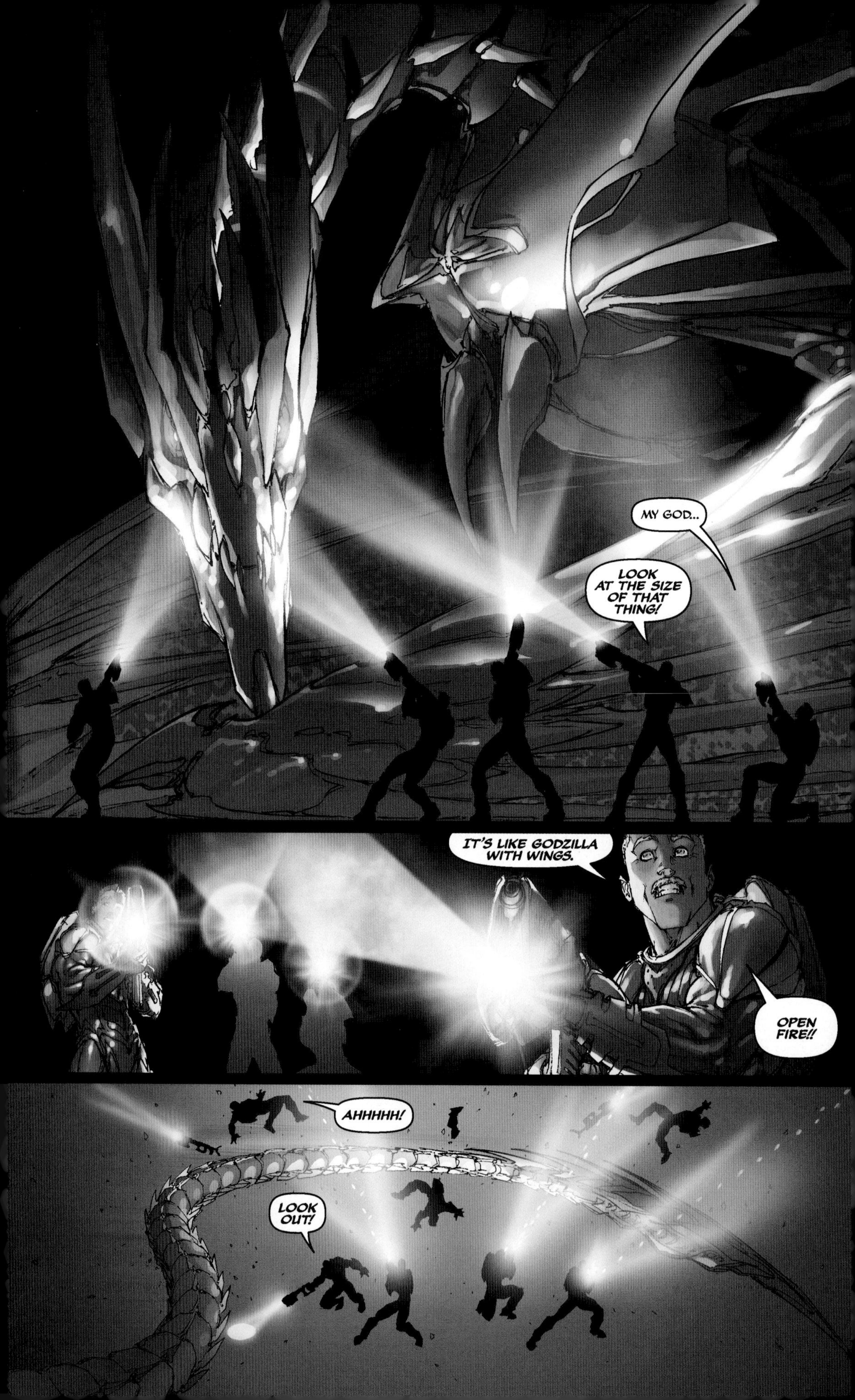
MY GOD...
LOOK AT THE SIZE OF THAT THING!
IT'S LIKE GODZILLA WITH WINGS.
OPEN FIRE!!
AHHHHH!
LOOK OUT!

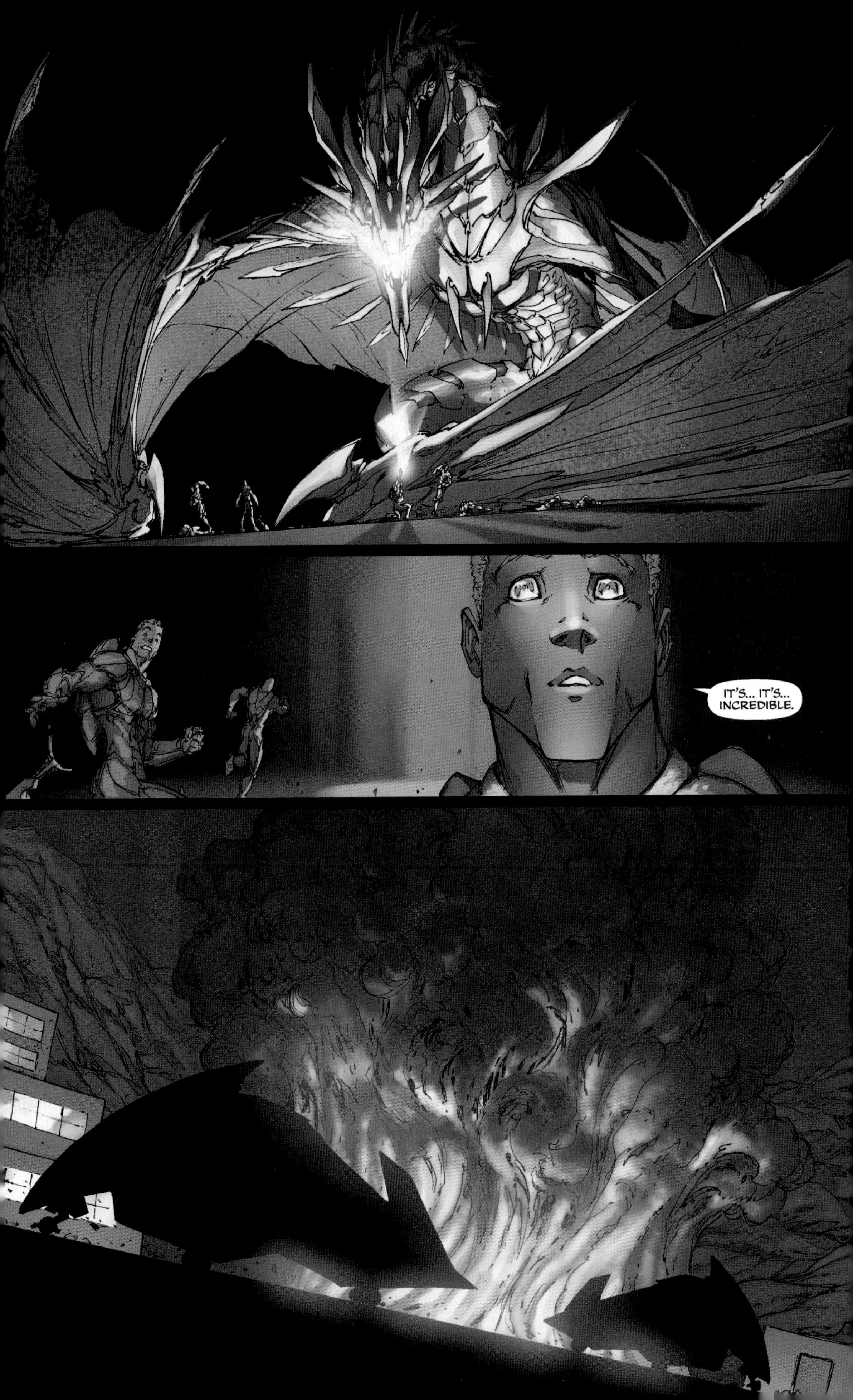
IT'S... IT'S... INCREDIBLE.

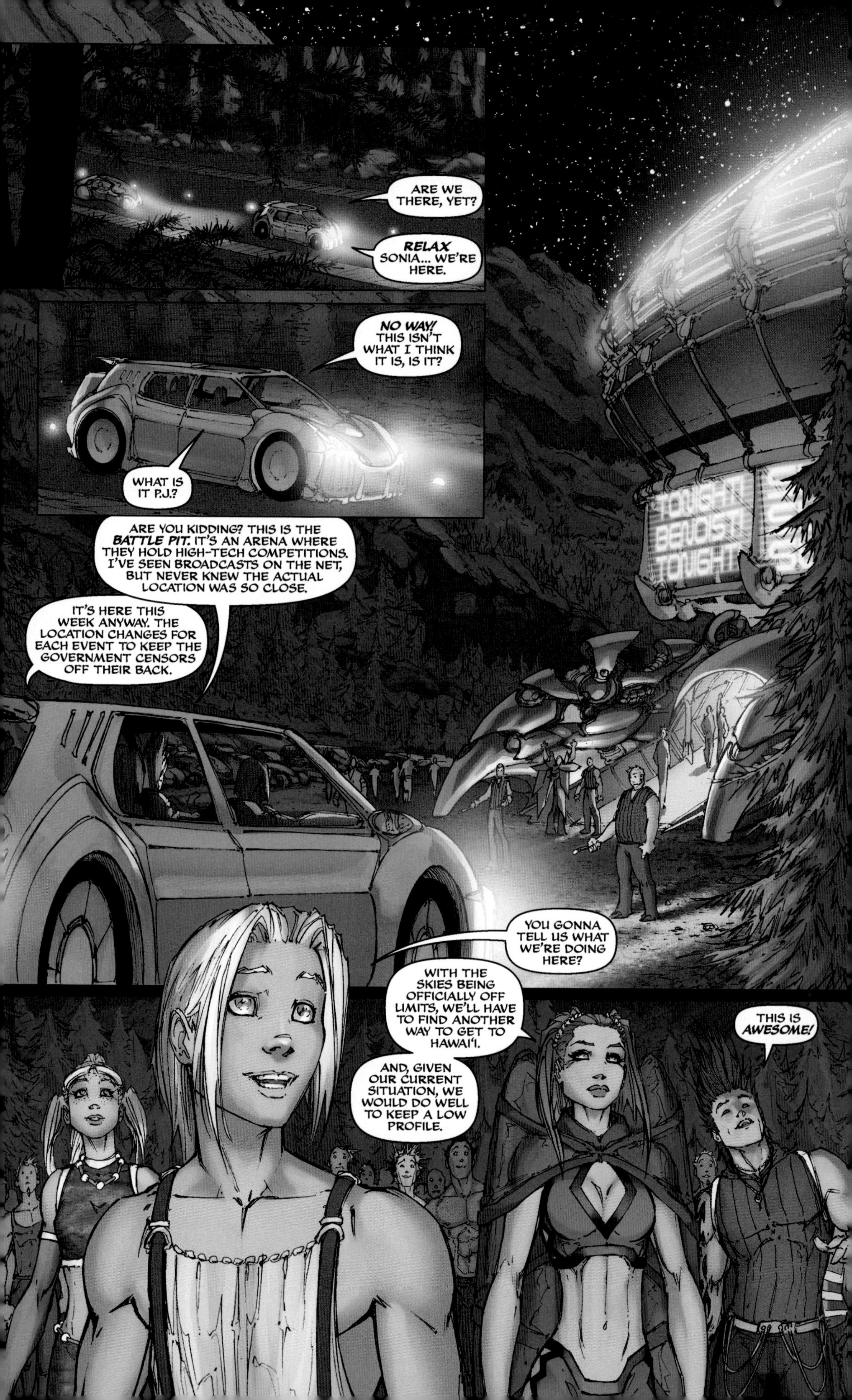

ARE WE THERE, YET?
RELAX SONIA... WE'RE HERE.
NO WAY! THIS ISN'T WHAT I THINK IT IS, IS IT?
WHAT IS IT P.J.?
TONIGHT! BENOIST! TONIGHT!
ARE YOU KIDDING? THIS IS THE *BATTLE PIT.* IT'S AN ARENA WHERE THEY HOLD HIGH-TECH COMPETITIONS. I'VE SEEN BROADCASTS ON THE NET, BUT NEVER KNEW THE ACTUAL LOCATION WAS SO CLOSE.
IT'S HERE THIS WEEK ANYWAY. THE LOCATION CHANGES FOR EACH EVENT TO KEEP THE GOVERNMENT CENSORS OFF THEIR BACK.
YOU GONNA TELL US WHAT WE'RE DOING HERE?
WITH THE SKIES BEING OFFICIALLY OFF LIMITS, WE'LL HAVE TO FIND ANOTHER WAY TO GET TO HAWAI'I.
AND, GIVEN OUR CURRENT SITUATION, WE WOULD DO WELL TO KEEP A LOW PROFILE.
THIS IS *AWESOME!*

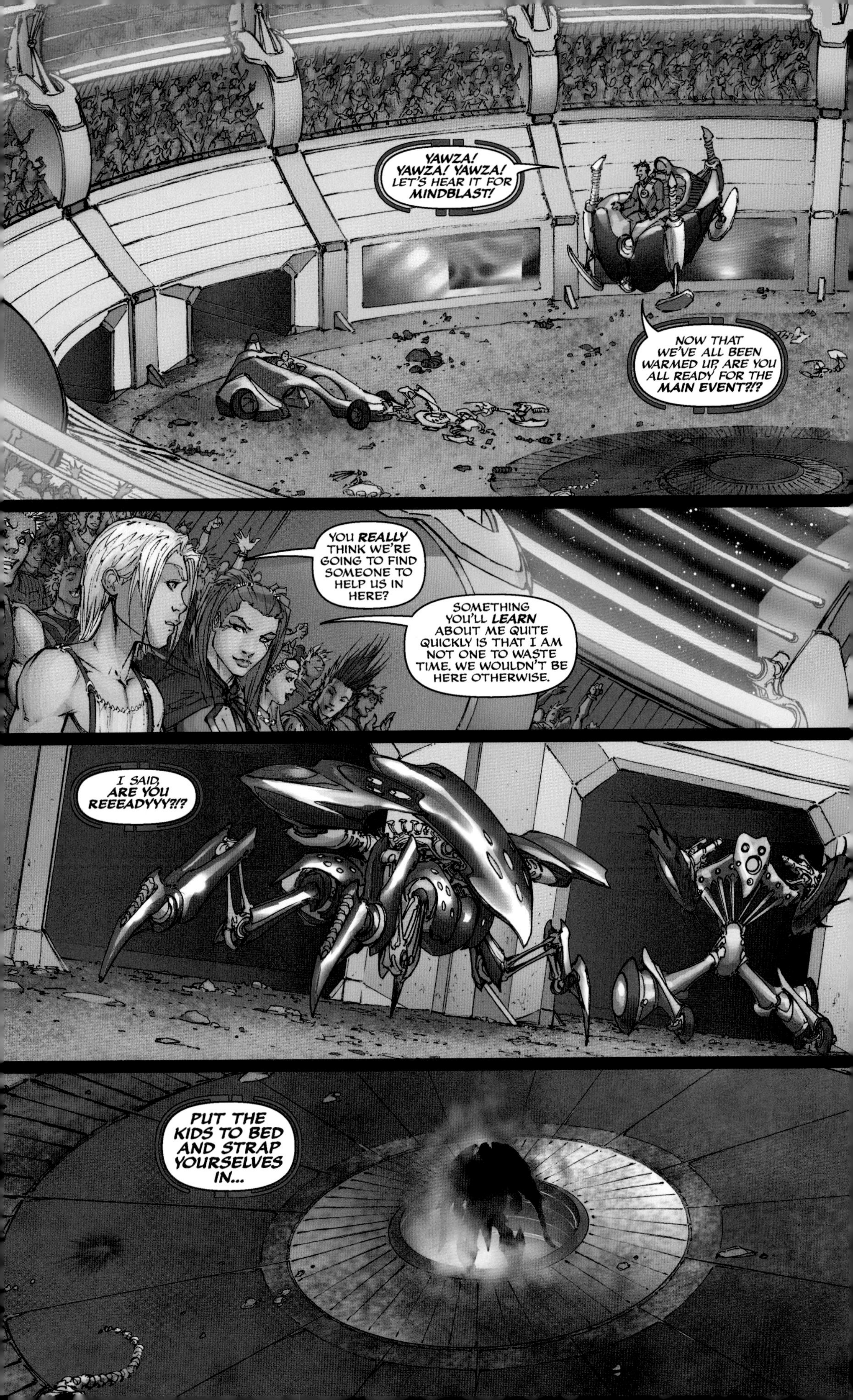
YAWZA! YAWZA! YAWZA! LET'S HEAR IT FOR MINDBLAST!
NOW THAT WE'VE ALL BEEN WARMED UP, ARE YOU ALL READY FOR THE MAIN EVENT?!?
YOU REALLY THINK WE'RE GOING TO FIND SOMEONE TO HELP US IN HERE?
SOMETHING YOU'LL LEARN ABOUT ME QUITE QUICKLY IS THAT I AM NOT ONE TO WASTE TIME. WE WOULDN'T BE HERE OTHERWISE.
I SAID, ARE YOU REEEADYYY?!?
PUT THE KIDS TO BED AND STRAP YOURSELVES IN...

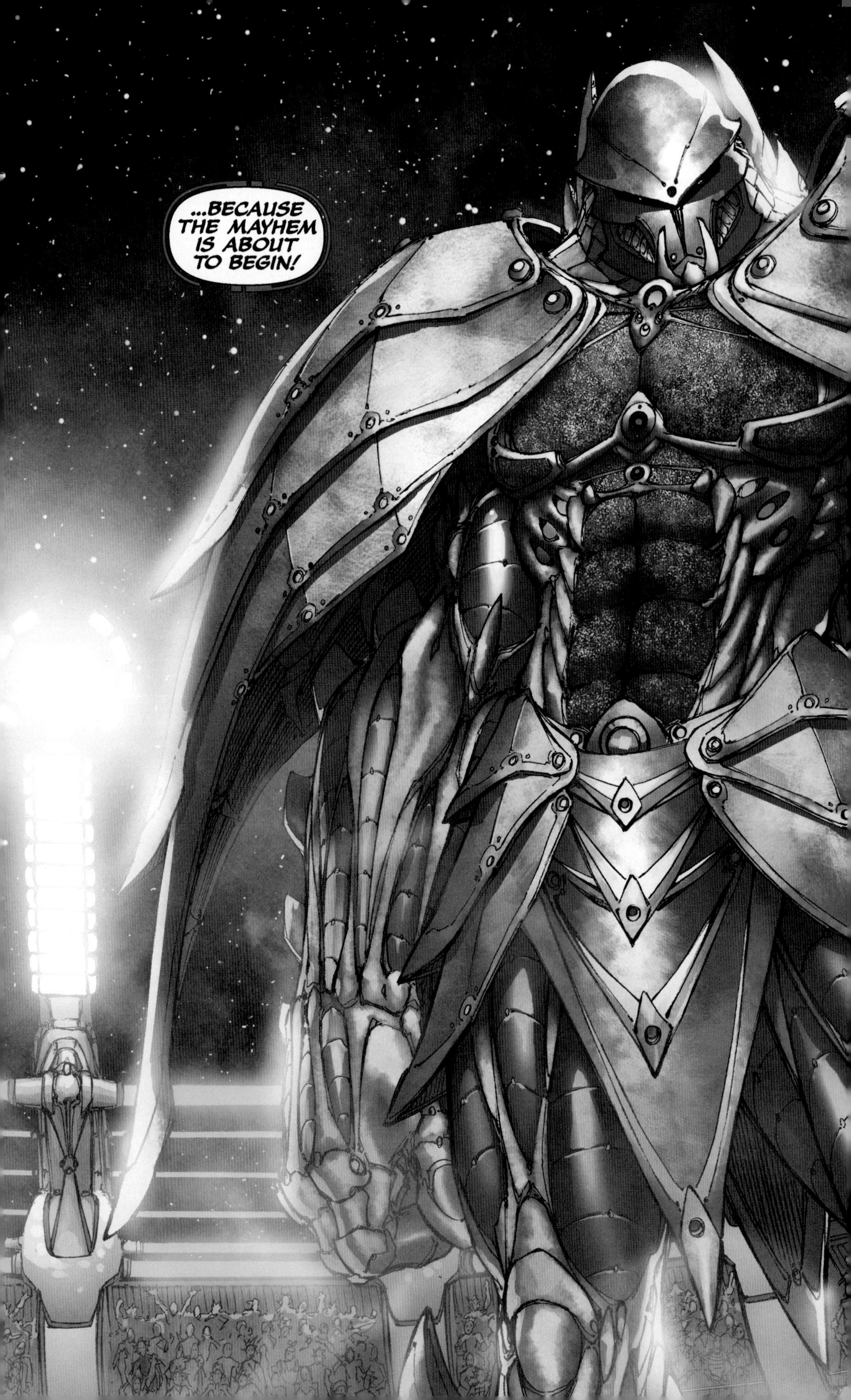
...BECAUSE THE MAYHEM IS ABOUT TO BEGIN!

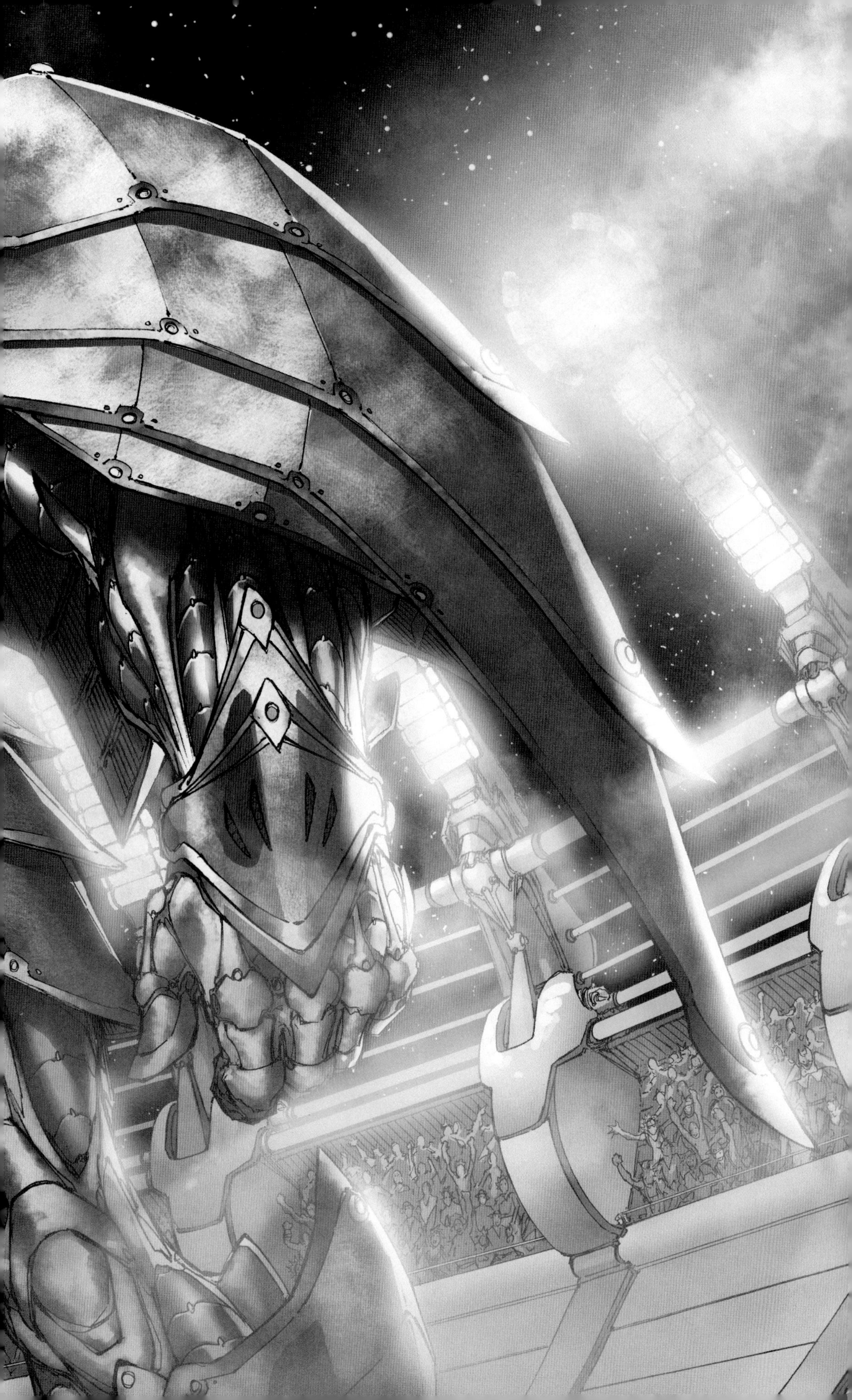

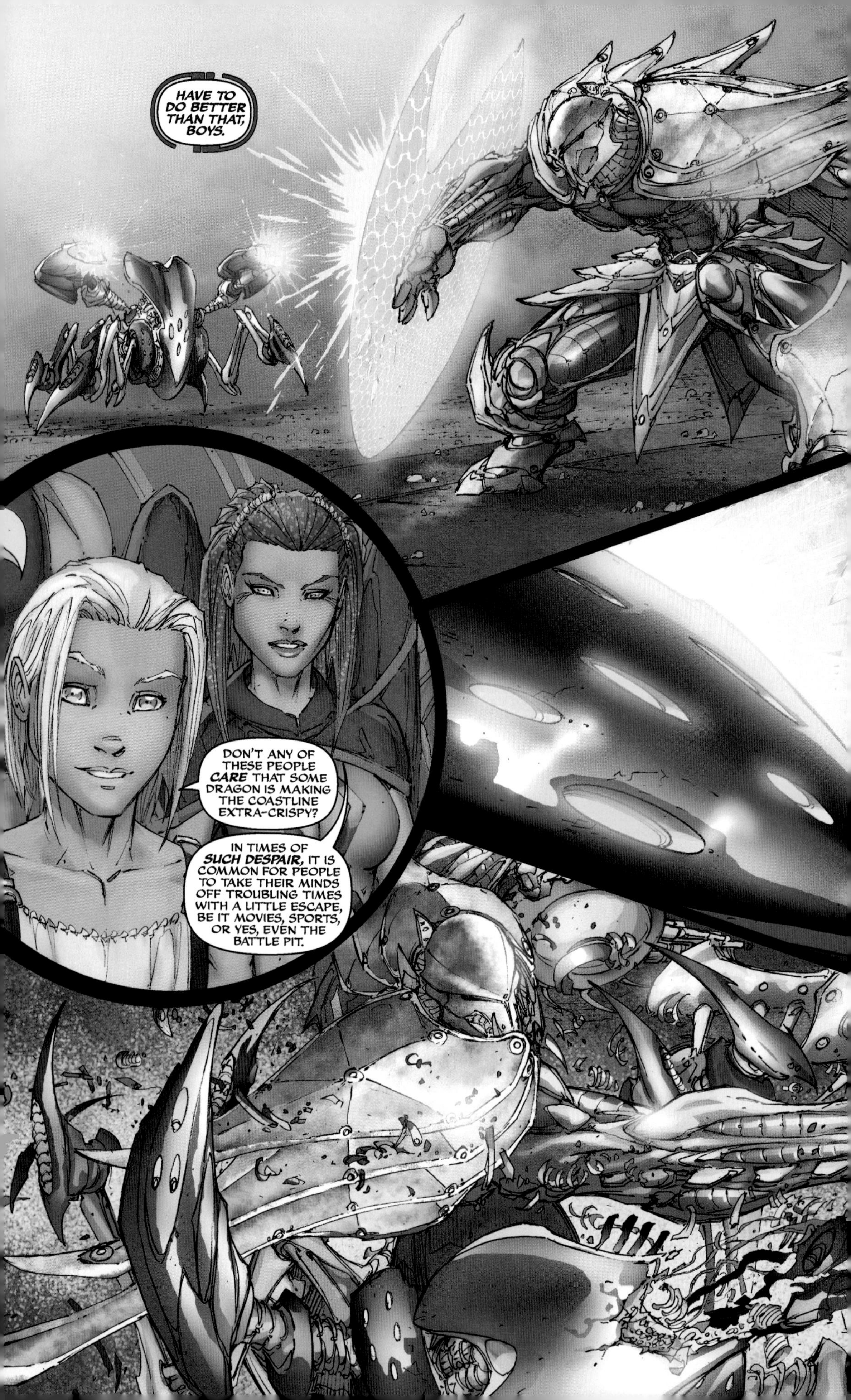
HAVE TO DO BETTER THAN THAT, BOYS.
DON'T ANY OF THESE PEOPLE CARE THAT SOME DRAGON IS MAKING THE COASTLINE EXTRA-CRISPY?
IN TIMES OF SUCH DESPAIR, IT IS COMMON FOR PEOPLE TO TAKE THEIR MINDS OFF TROUBLING TIMES WITH A LITTLE ESCAPE, BE IT MOVIES, SPORTS, OR YES, EVEN THE BATTLE PIT.

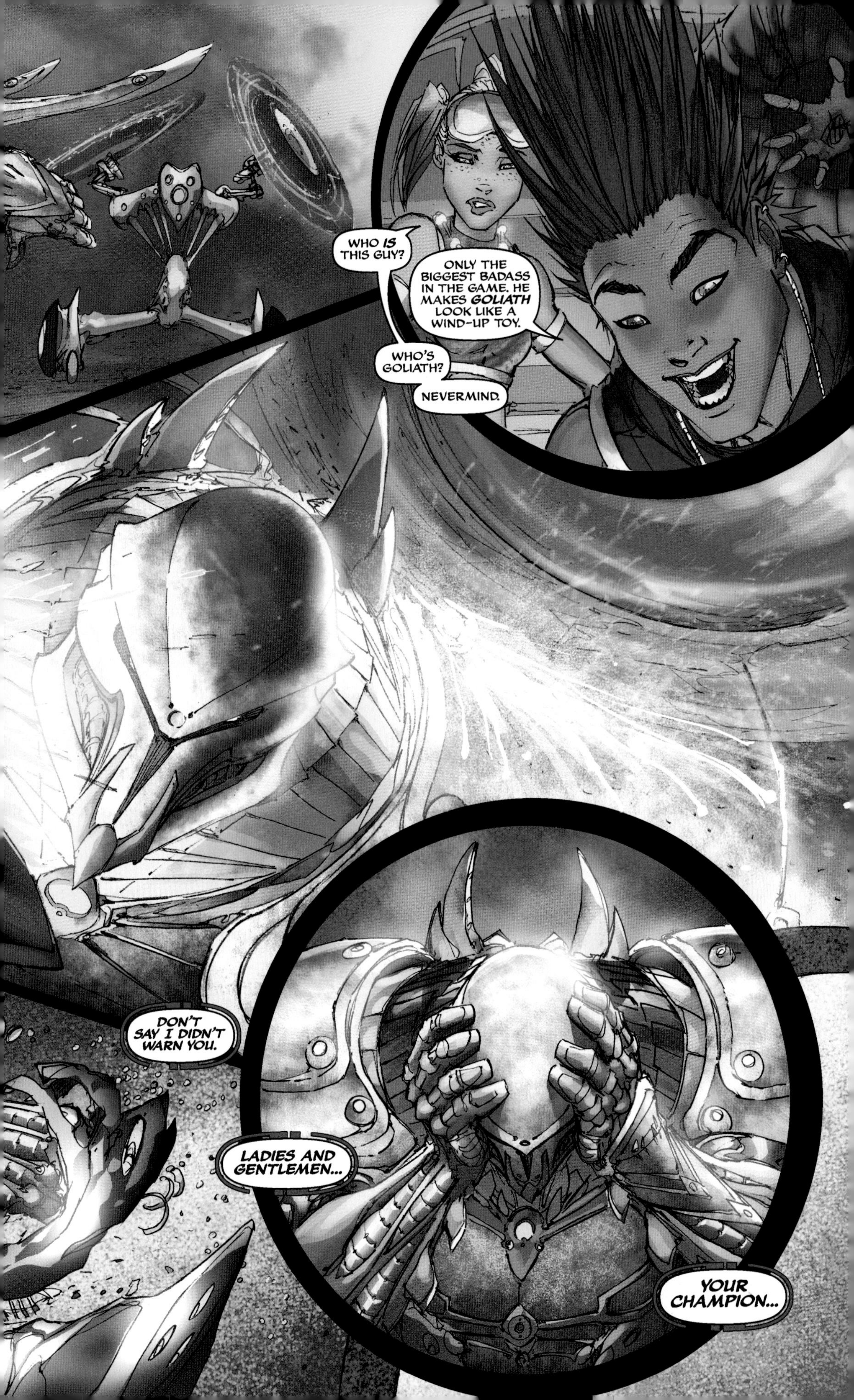
WHO IS THIS GUY?
ONLY THE BIGGEST BADASS IN THE GAME. HE MAKES GOLIATH LOOK LIKE A WIND-UP TOY.
WHO'S GOLIATH?
NEVERMIND.
DON'T SAY I DIDN'T WARN YOU.
LADIES AND GENTLEMEN...
YOUR CHAMPION...

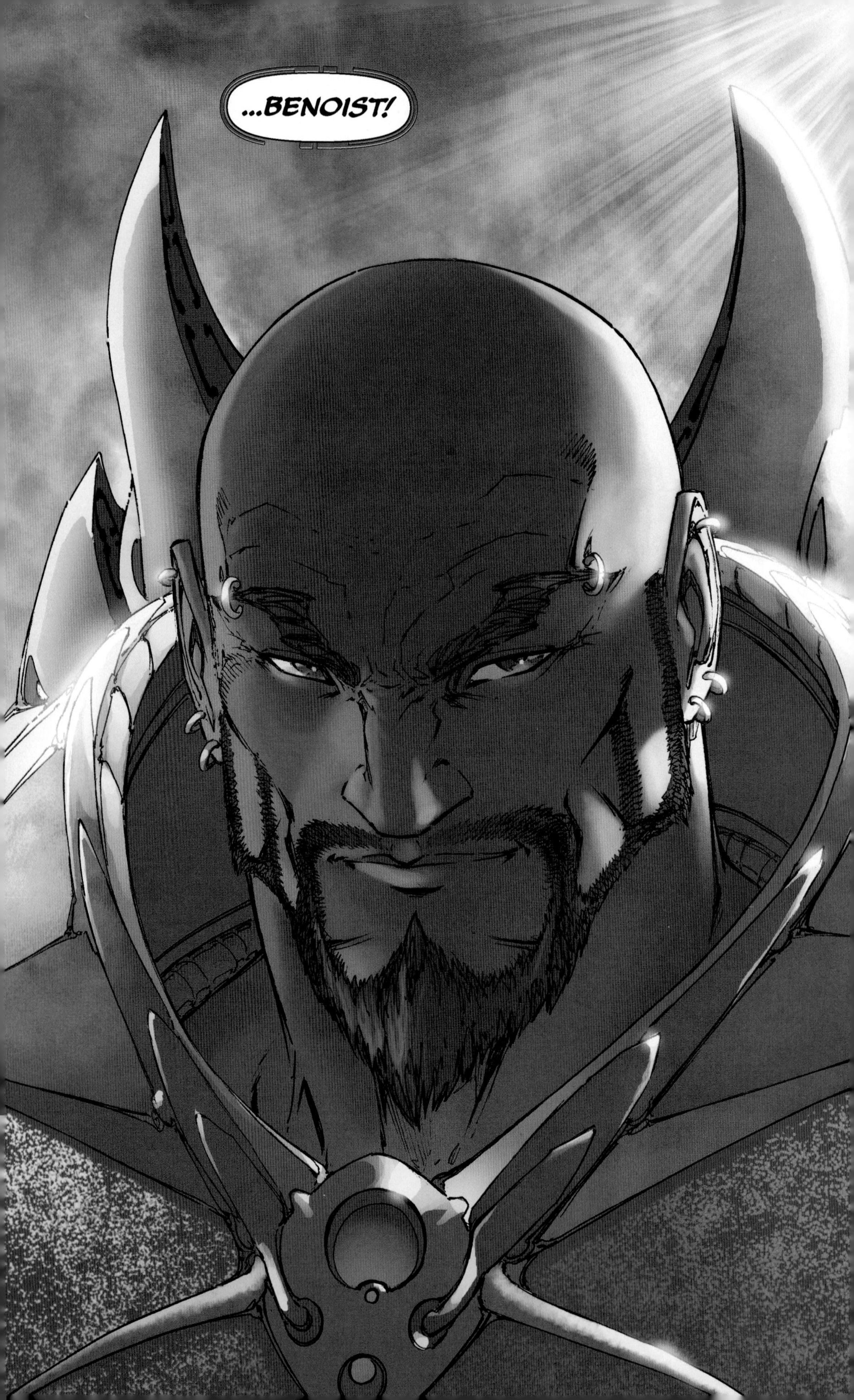
...BENOIST!

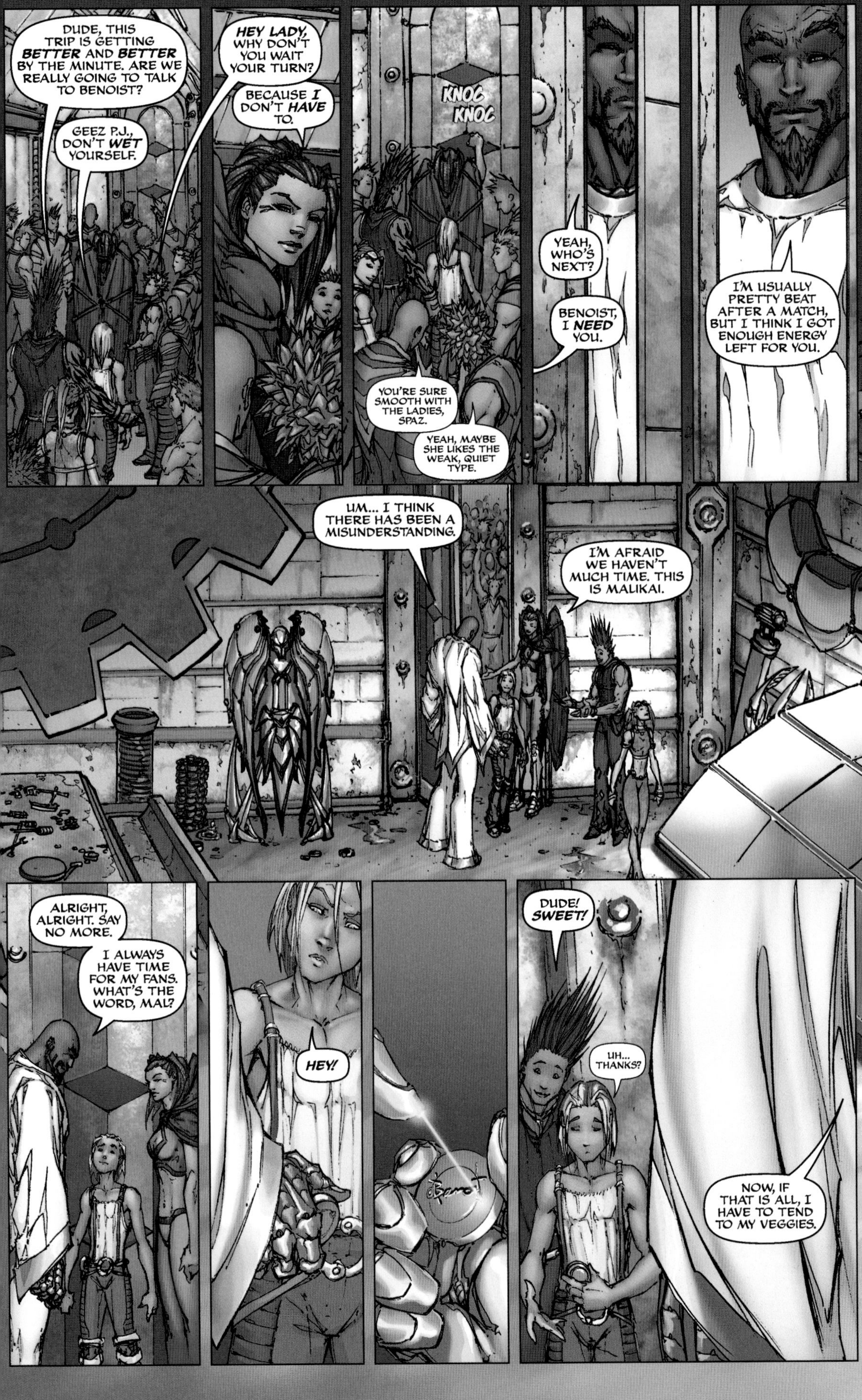

DUDE, THIS TRIP IS GETTING BETTER AND BETTER BY THE MINUTE. ARE WE REALLY GOING TO TALK TO BENOIST?
GEEZ P.J., DON'T WET YOURSELF.
HEY LADY, WHY DON'T YOU WAIT YOUR TURN?
BECAUSE I DON'T HAVE TO.
KNOC KNOC
YOU'RE SURE SMOOTH WITH THE LADIES, SPAZ.
YEAH, MAYBE SHE LIKES THE WEAK, QUIET TYPE.
YEAH, WHO'S NEXT?
BENOIST, I NEED YOU.
I'M USUALLY PRETTY BEAT AFTER A MATCH, BUT I THINK I GOT ENOUGH ENERGY LEFT FOR YOU.
UM... I THINK THERE HAS BEEN A MISUNDERSTANDING.
I'M AFRAID WE HAVEN'T MUCH TIME. THIS IS MALIKAI.
ALRIGHT, ALRIGHT. SAY NO MORE.
I ALWAYS HAVE TIME FOR MY FANS. WHAT'S THE WORD, MAL?
HEY!
DUDE! SWEET!
UH... THANKS?
NOW, IF THAT IS ALL, I HAVE TO TEND TO MY VEGGIES.

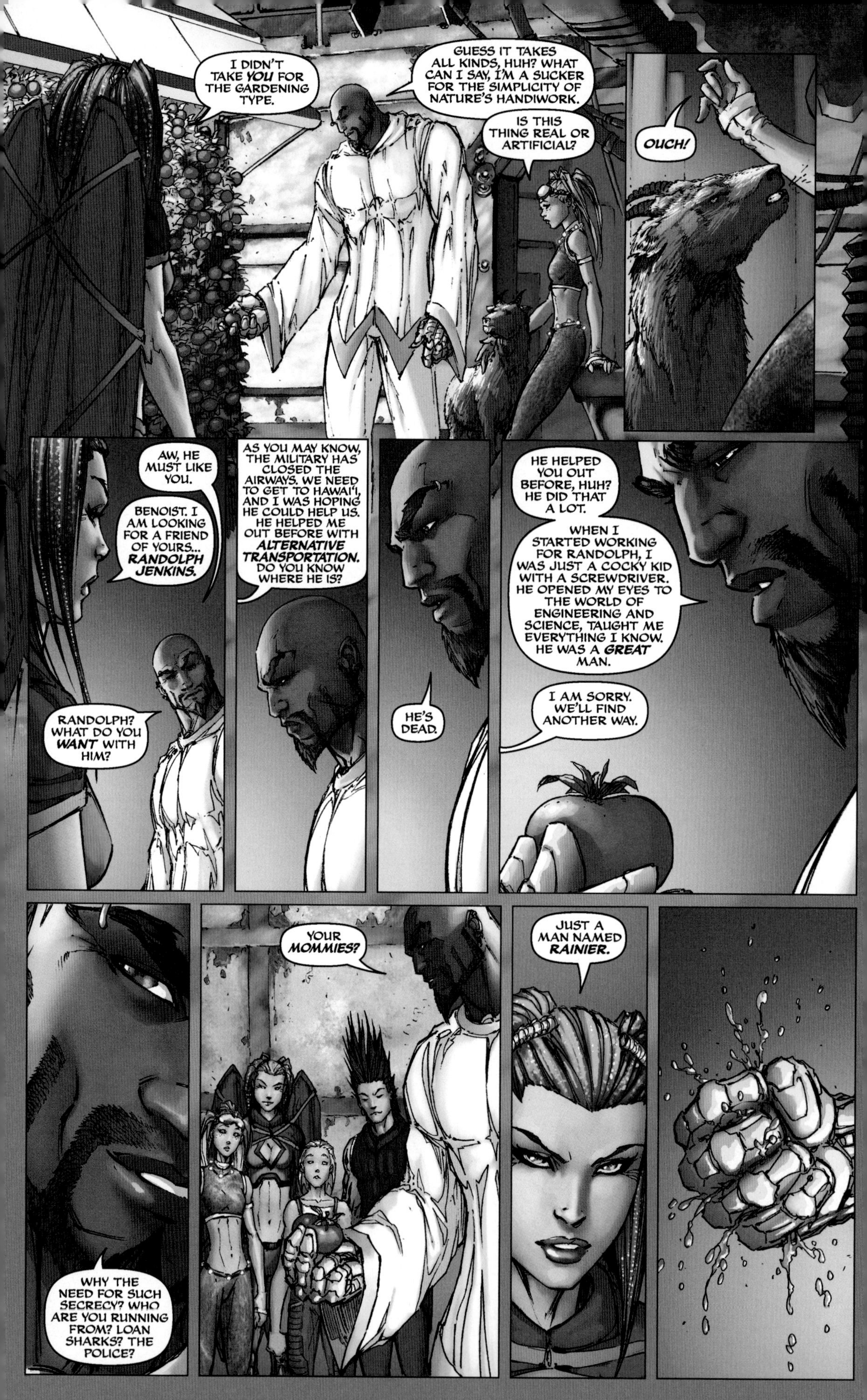
I DIDN'T TAKE YOU FOR THE GARDENING TYPE.
GUESS IT TAKES ALL KINDS, HUH? WHAT CAN I SAY, I'M A SUCKER FOR THE SIMPLICITY OF NATURE'S HANDIWORK.
IS THIS THING REAL OR ARTIFICIAL?
OUCH!
AW, HE MUST LIKE YOU.
BENOIST. I AM LOOKING FOR A FRIEND OF YOURS... RANDOLPH JENKINS.
RANDOLPH? WHAT DO YOU WANT WITH HIM?
AS YOU MAY KNOW, THE MILITARY HAS CLOSED THE AIRWAYS. WE NEED TO GET TO HAWAI'I, AND I WAS HOPING HE COULD HELP US. HE HELPED ME OUT BEFORE WITH ALTERNATIVE TRANSPORTATION. DO YOU KNOW WHERE HE IS?
HE'S DEAD.
HE HELPED YOU OUT BEFORE, HUH? HE DID THAT A LOT.
WHEN I STARTED WORKING FOR RANDOLPH, I WAS JUST A COCKY KID WITH A SCREWDRIVER. HE OPENED MY EYES TO THE WORLD OF ENGINEERING AND SCIENCE, TAUGHT ME EVERYTHING I KNOW. HE WAS A GREAT MAN.
I AM SORRY. WE'LL FIND ANOTHER WAY.
WHY THE NEED FOR SUCH SECRECY? WHO ARE YOU RUNNING FROM? LOAN SHARKS? THE POLICE?
YOUR MOMMIES?
JUST A MAN NAMED RAINIER.

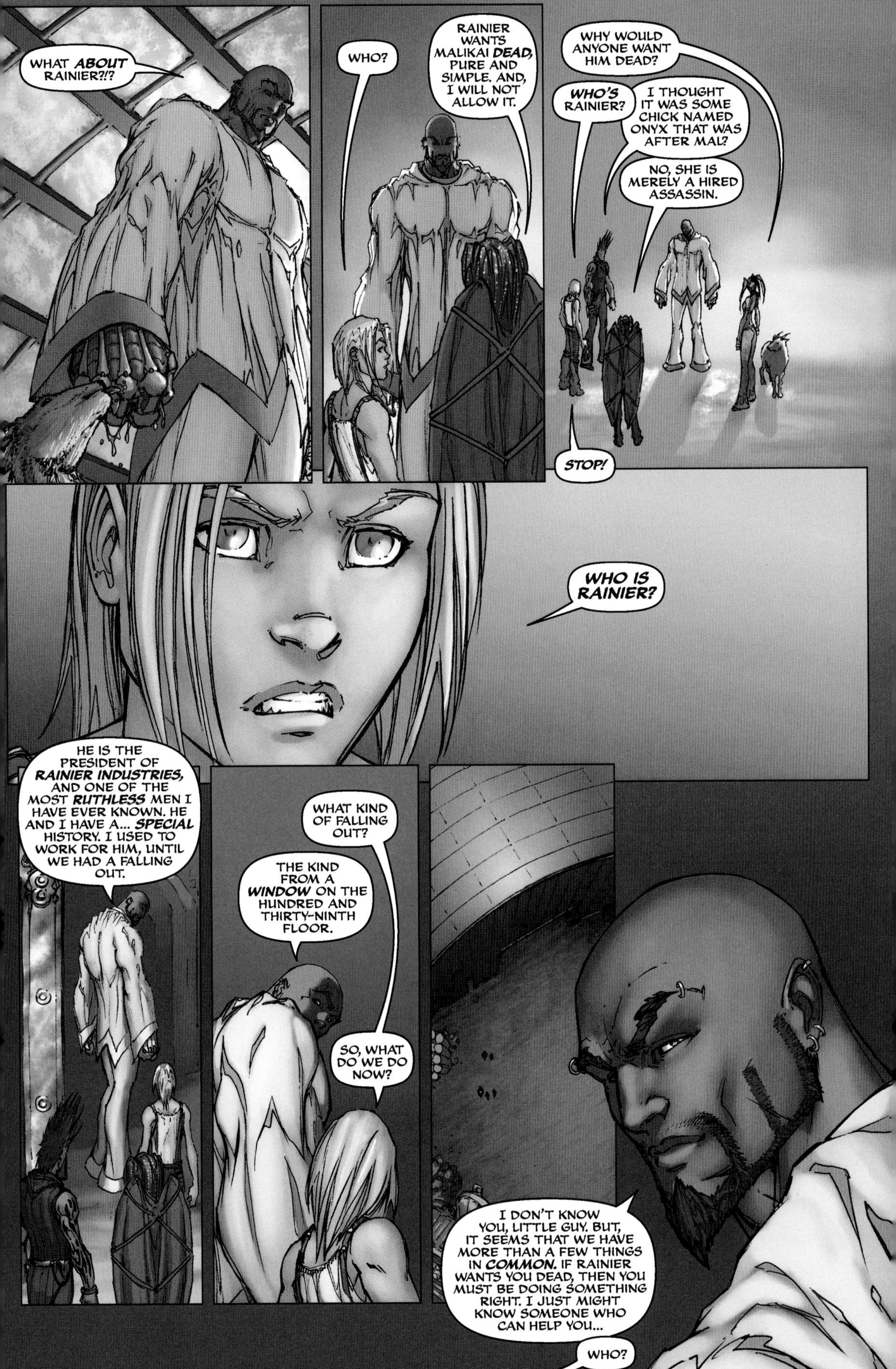
WHAT ABOUT RAINIER?!?
WHO?
RAINIER WANTS MALIKAI DEAD, PURE AND SIMPLE. AND, I WILL NOT ALLOW IT.
WHY WOULD ANYONE WANT HIM DEAD?
WHO'S RAINIER?
I THOUGHT IT WAS SOME CHICK NAMED ONYX THAT WAS AFTER MAL?
NO, SHE IS MERELY A HIRED ASSASSIN.
STOP!
WHO IS RAINIER?
HE IS THE PRESIDENT OF RAINIER INDUSTRIES, AND ONE OF THE MOST RUTHLESS MEN I HAVE EVER KNOWN. HE AND I HAVE A... SPECIAL HISTORY. I USED TO WORK FOR HIM, UNTIL WE HAD A FALLING OUT.
WHAT KIND OF FALLING OUT?
THE KIND FROM A WINDOW ON THE HUNDRED AND THIRTY-NINTH FLOOR.
SO, WHAT DO WE DO NOW?
I DON'T KNOW YOU, LITTLE GUY. BUT, IT SEEMS THAT WE HAVE MORE THAN A FEW THINGS IN COMMON. IF RAINIER WANTS YOU DEAD, THEN YOU MUST BE DOING SOMETHING RIGHT. I JUST MIGHT KNOW SOMEONE WHO CAN HELP YOU...
WHO?

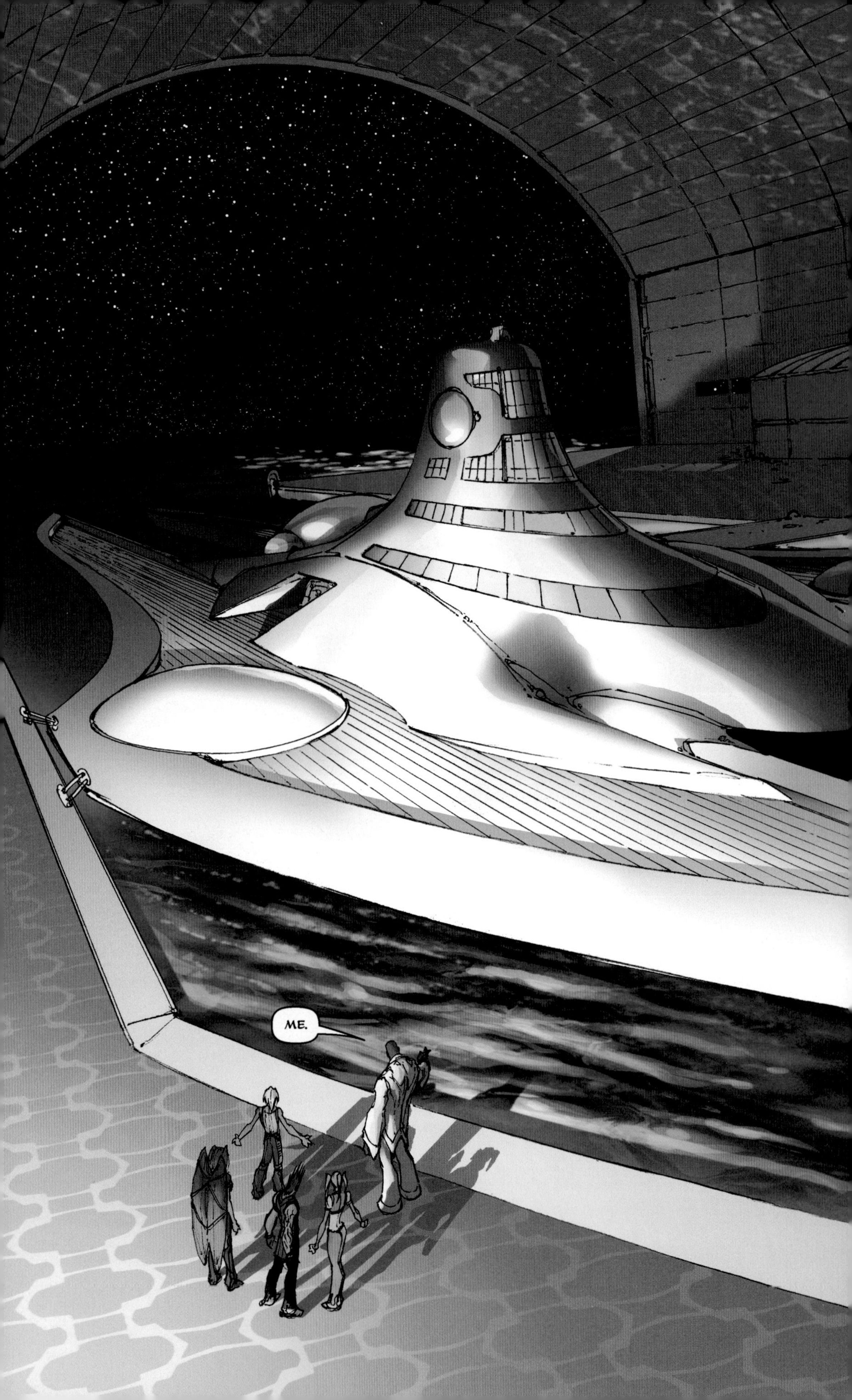
ME.

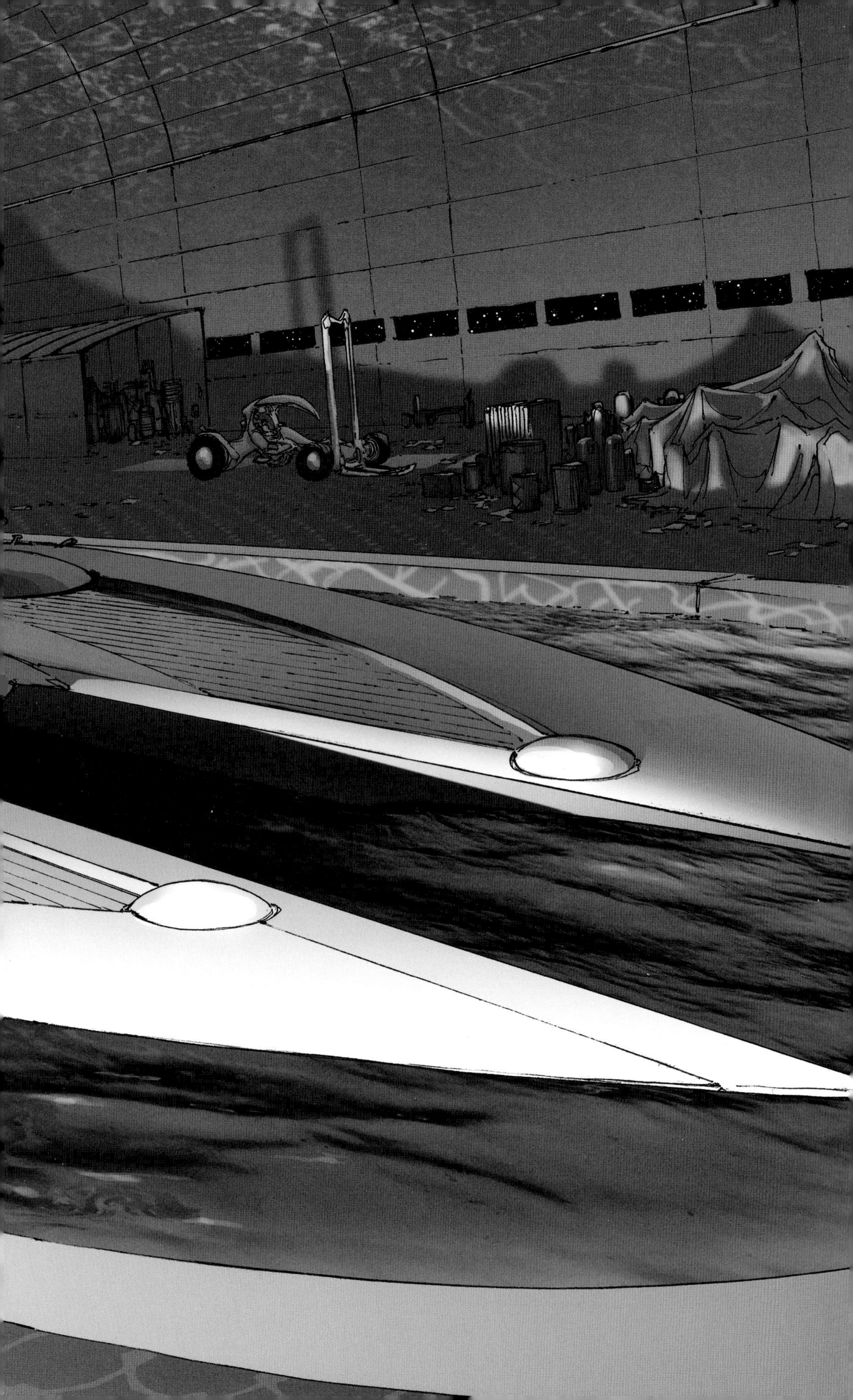

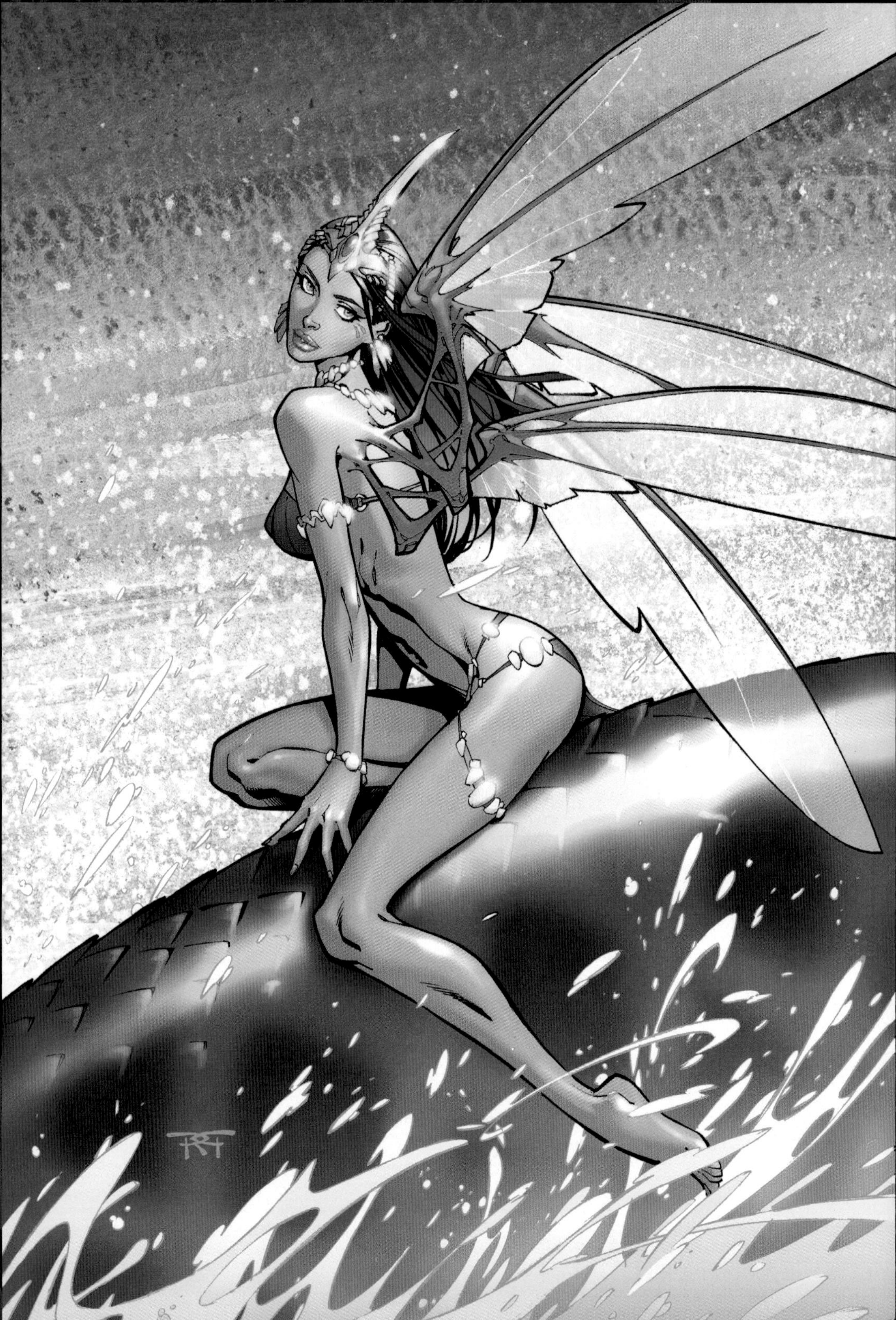
RG

GRACE

· PIN-UP FROM ASPEN SPLASH: 2007 SWIMSUIT SPECTACULAR ·

by

· RANDY GREEN · PETER STEIGERWALD ·

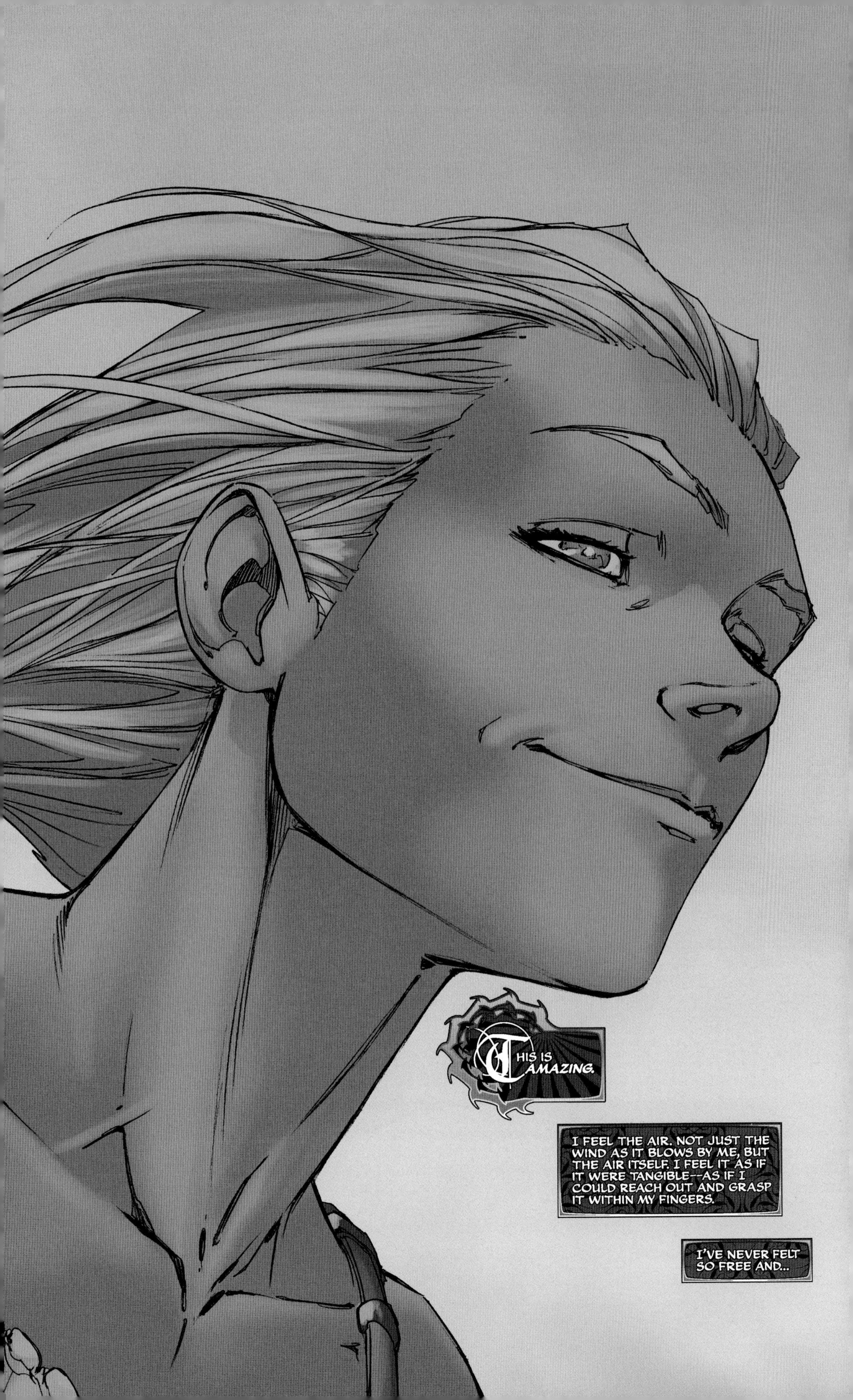
THIS IS AMAZING.
I FEEL THE AIR. NOT JUST THE WIND AS IT BLOWS BY ME, BUT THE AIR ITSELF. I FEEL IT AS IF IT WERE TANGIBLE--AS IF I COULD REACH OUT AND GRASP IT WITHIN MY FINGERS.
I'VE NEVER FELT SO FREE AND...

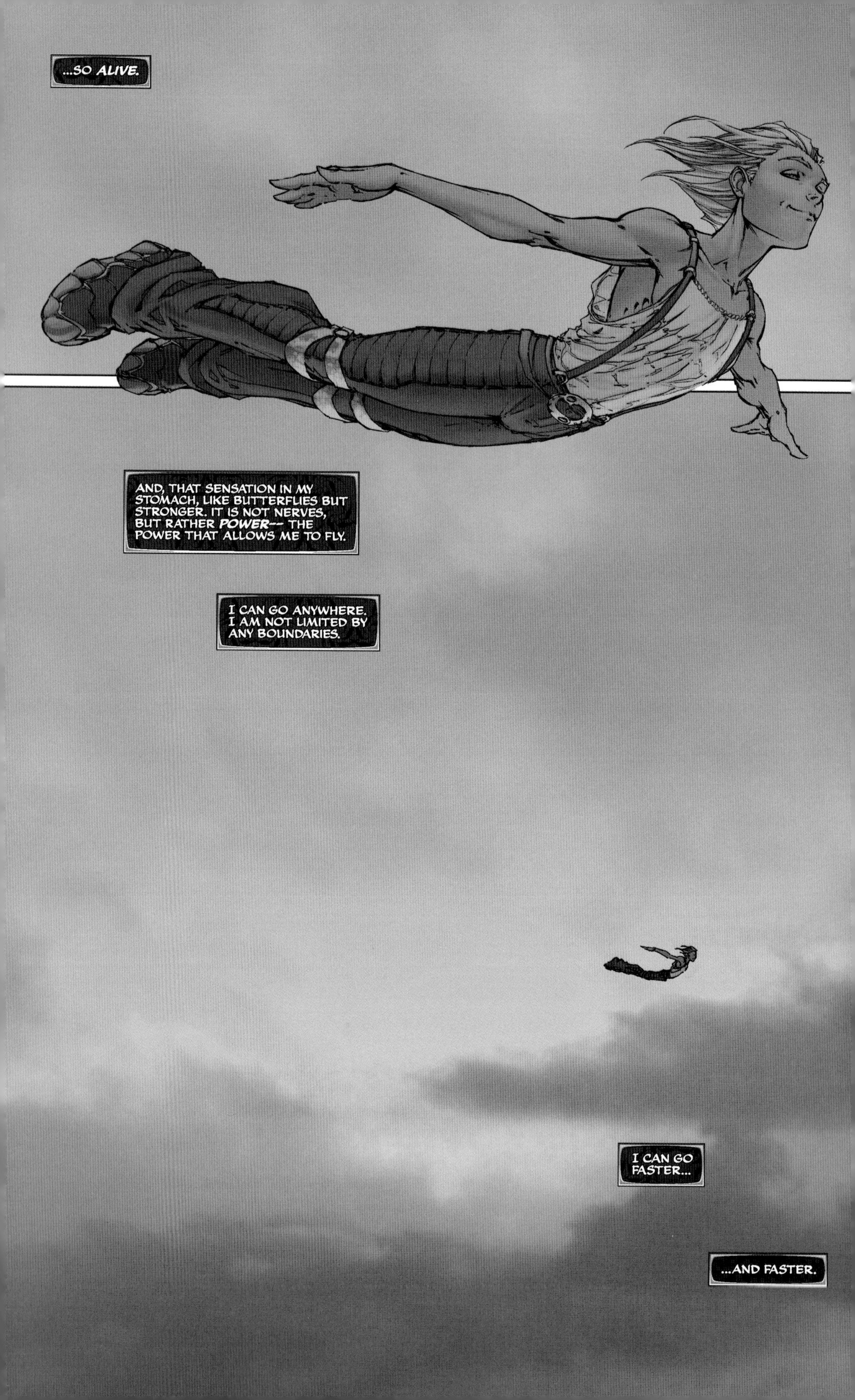
...SO ALIVE.
AND, THAT SENSATION IN MY STOMACH, LIKE BUTTERFLIES BUT STRONGER. IT IS NOT NERVES, BUT RATHER POWER-- THE POWER THAT ALLOWS ME TO FLY.
I CAN GO ANYWHERE. I AM NOT LIMITED BY ANY BOUNDARIES.
I CAN GO FASTER...
...AND FASTER.

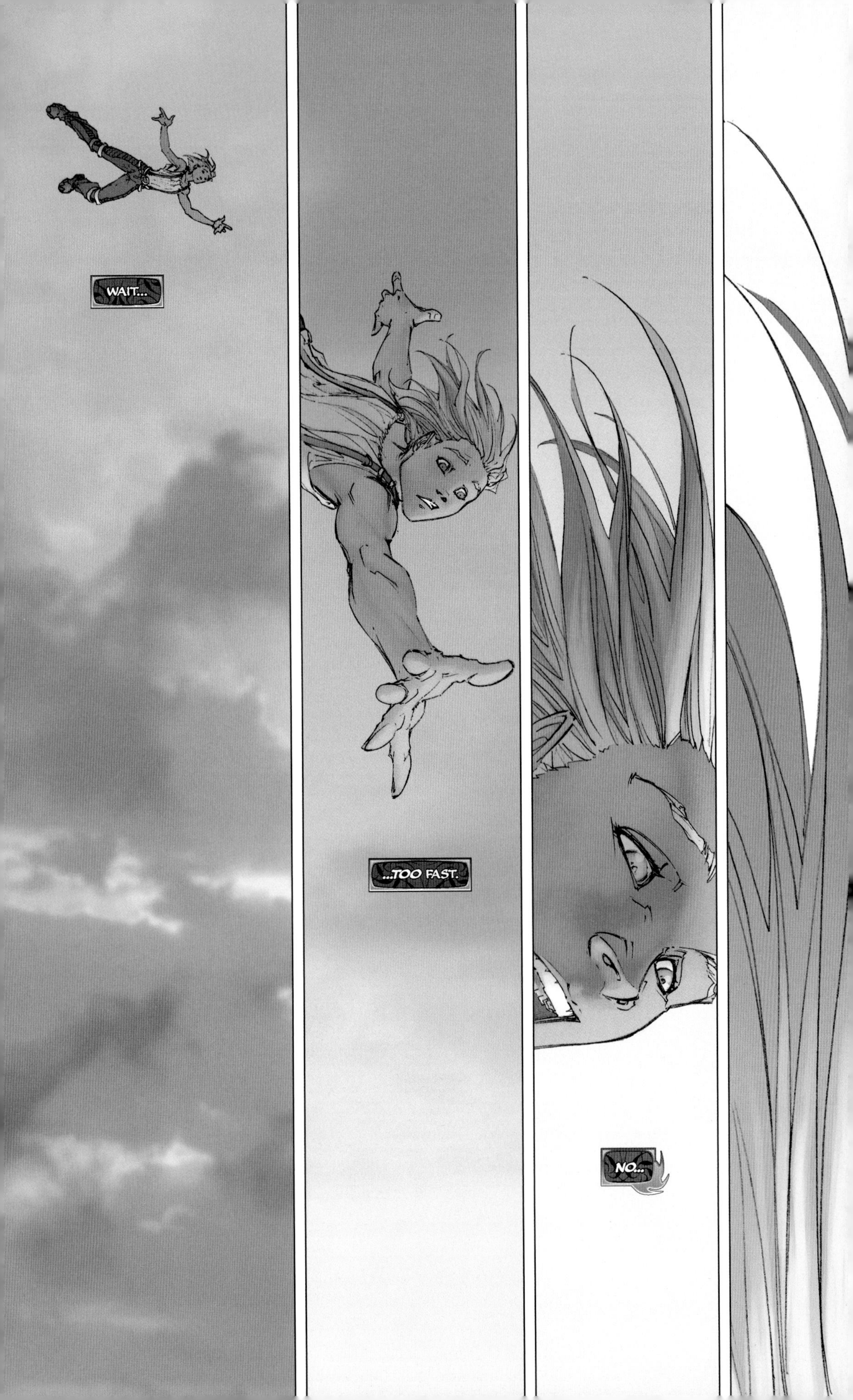
WAIT...
...TOO FAST.
NO...

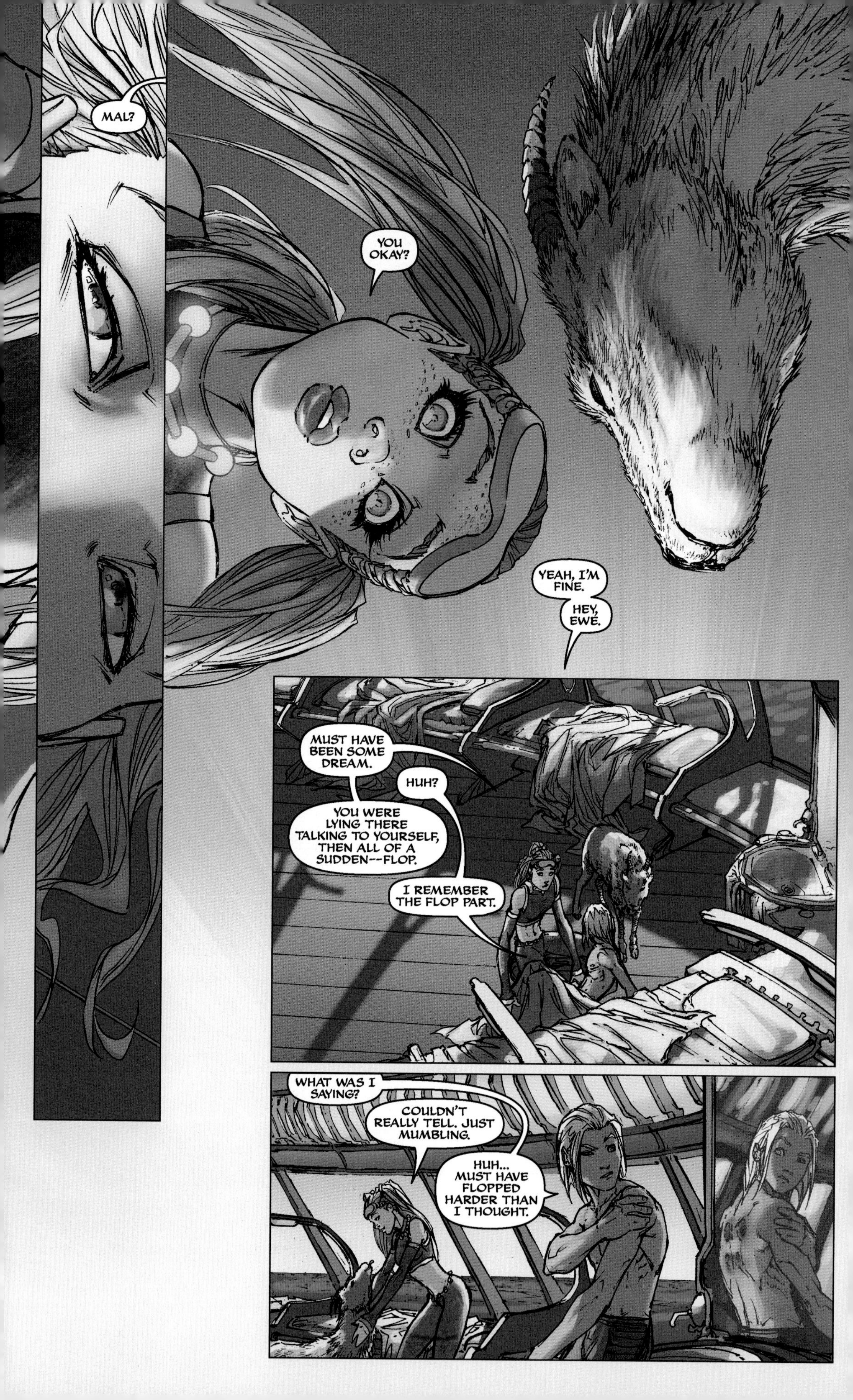
MAL?
YOU OKAY?
YEAH, I'M FINE.
HEY, EWE.
MUST HAVE BEEN SOME DREAM.
HUH?
YOU WERE LYING THERE TALKING TO YOURSELF, THEN ALL OF A SUDDEN--FLOP.
I REMEMBER THE FLOP PART.
WHAT WAS I SAYING?
COULDN'T REALLY TELL. JUST MUMBLING.
HUH... MUST HAVE FLOPPED HARDER THAN I THOUGHT.

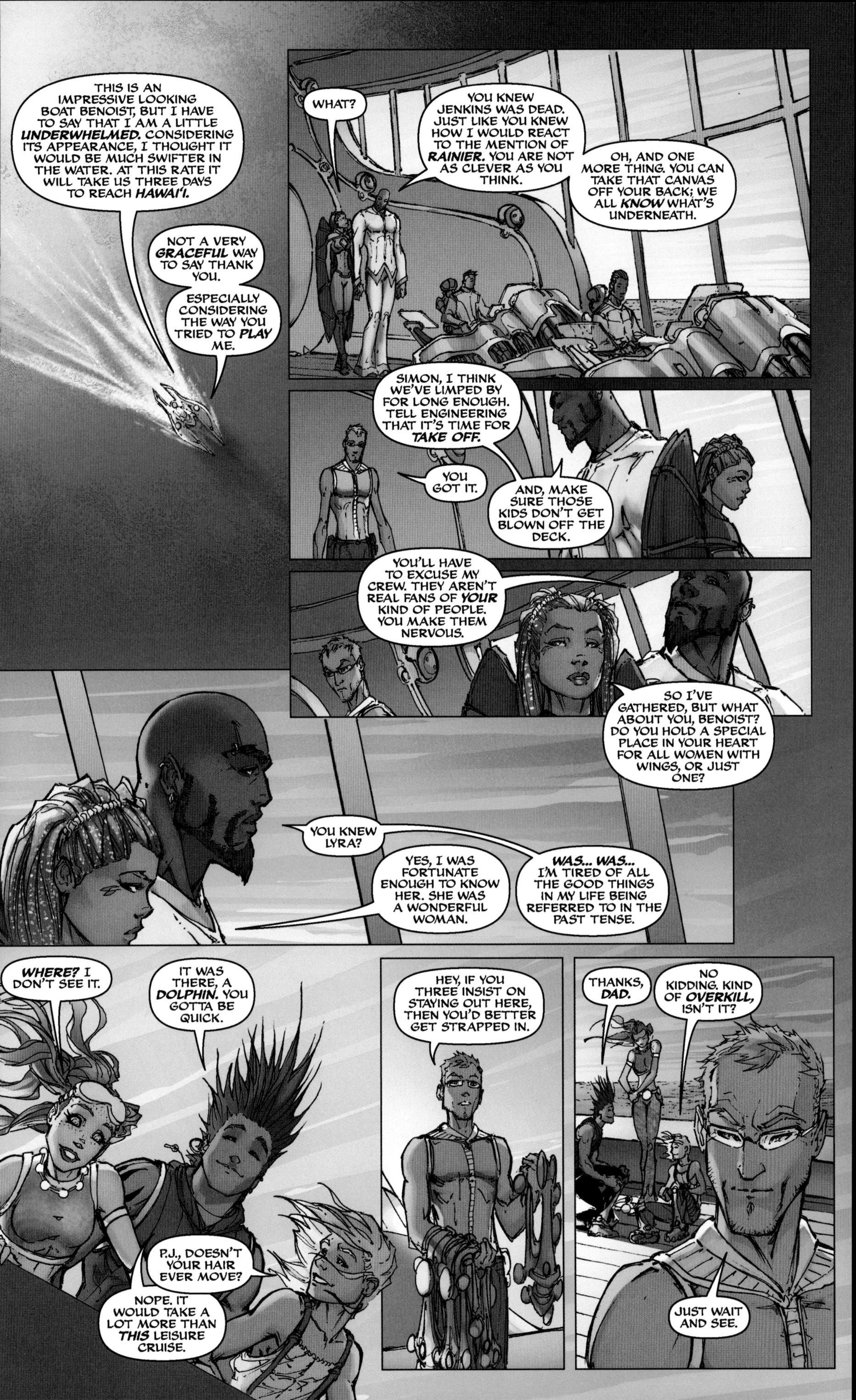
THIS IS AN IMPRESSIVE LOOKING BOAT BENOIST, BUT I HAVE TO SAY THAT I AM A LITTLE UNDERWHELMED. CONSIDERING ITS APPEARANCE, I THOUGHT IT WOULD BE MUCH SWIFTER IN THE WATER. AT THIS RATE IT WILL TAKE US THREE DAYS TO REACH HAWAI'I.
NOT A VERY GRACEFUL WAY TO SAY THANK YOU.
ESPECIALLY CONSIDERING THE WAY YOU TRIED TO PLAY ME.
WHAT?
YOU KNEW JENKINS WAS DEAD. JUST LIKE YOU KNEW HOW I WOULD REACT TO THE MENTION OF RAINIER. YOU ARE NOT AS CLEVER AS YOU THINK.
OH, AND ONE MORE THING. YOU CAN TAKE THAT CANVAS OFF YOUR BACK; WE ALL KNOW WHAT'S UNDERNEATH.
SIMON, I THINK WE'VE LIMPED BY FOR LONG ENOUGH. TELL ENGINEERING THAT IT'S TIME FOR TAKE OFF.
YOU GOT IT.
AND, MAKE SURE THOSE KIDS DON'T GET BLOWN OFF THE DECK.
YOU'LL HAVE TO EXCUSE MY CREW. THEY AREN'T REAL FANS OF YOUR KIND OF PEOPLE. YOU MAKE THEM NERVOUS.
SO I'VE GATHERED, BUT WHAT ABOUT YOU, BENOIST? DO YOU HOLD A SPECIAL PLACE IN YOUR HEART FOR ALL WOMEN WITH WINGS, OR JUST ONE?
YOU KNEW LYRA?
YES, I WAS FORTUNATE ENOUGH TO KNOW HER. SHE WAS A WONDERFUL WOMAN.
WAS... WAS... I'M TIRED OF ALL THE GOOD THINGS IN MY LIFE BEING REFERRED TO IN THE PAST TENSE.
WHERE? I DON'T SEE IT.
IT WAS THERE, A DOLPHIN. YOU GOTTA BE QUICK.
P.J., DOESN'T YOUR HAIR EVER MOVE?
NOPE. IT WOULD TAKE A LOT MORE THAN THIS LEISURE CRUISE.
HEY, IF YOU THREE INSIST ON STAYING OUT HERE, THEN YOU'D BETTER GET STRAPPED IN.
THANKS, DAD.
NO KIDDING. KIND OF OVERKILL, ISN'T IT?
JUST WAIT AND SEE.

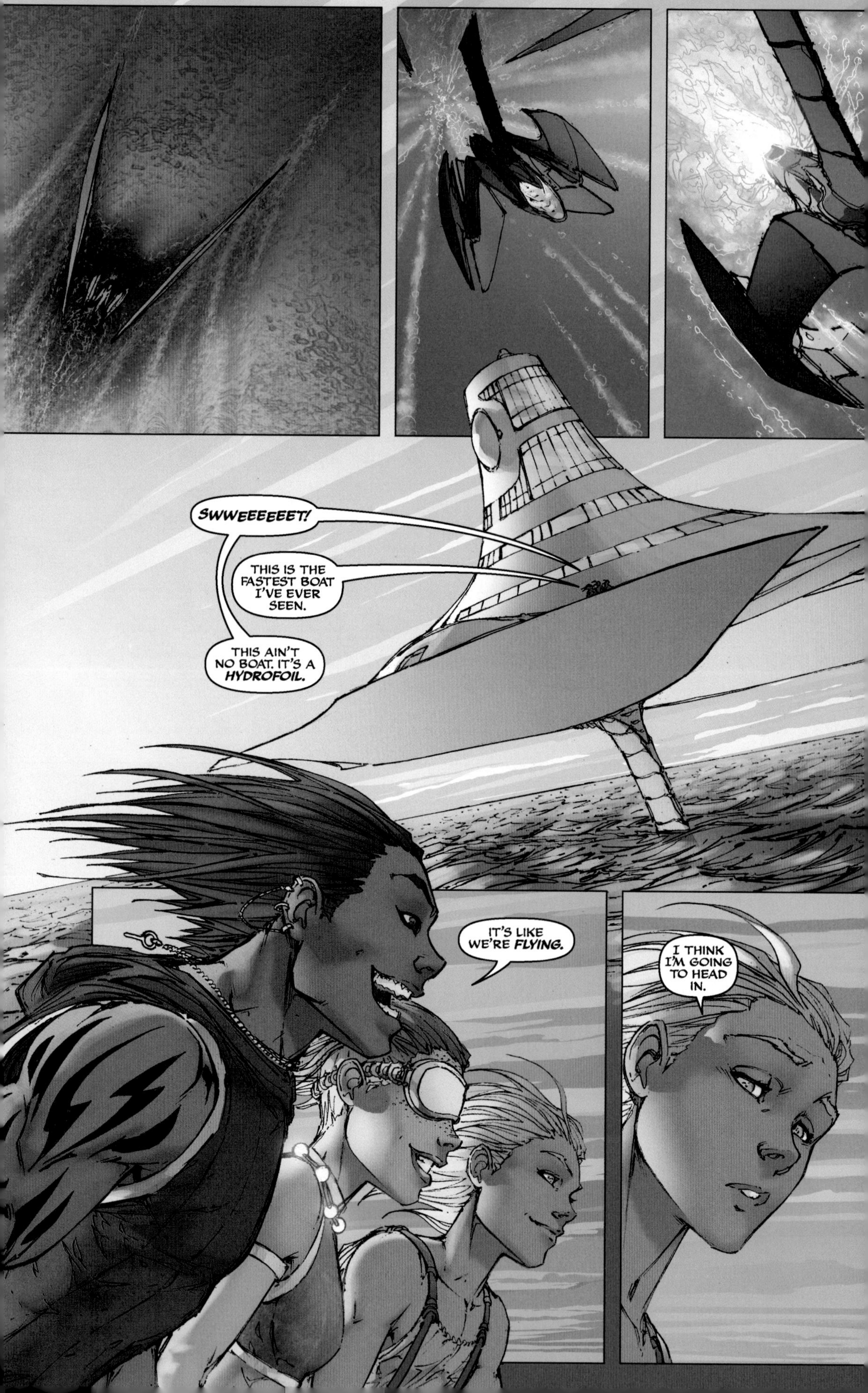
SWWEEEEEET!
THIS IS THE FASTEST BOAT I'VE EVER SEEN.
THIS AIN'T NO BOAT. IT'S A HYDROFOIL.
IT'S LIKE WE'RE FLYING.
I THINK I'M GOING TO HEAD IN.

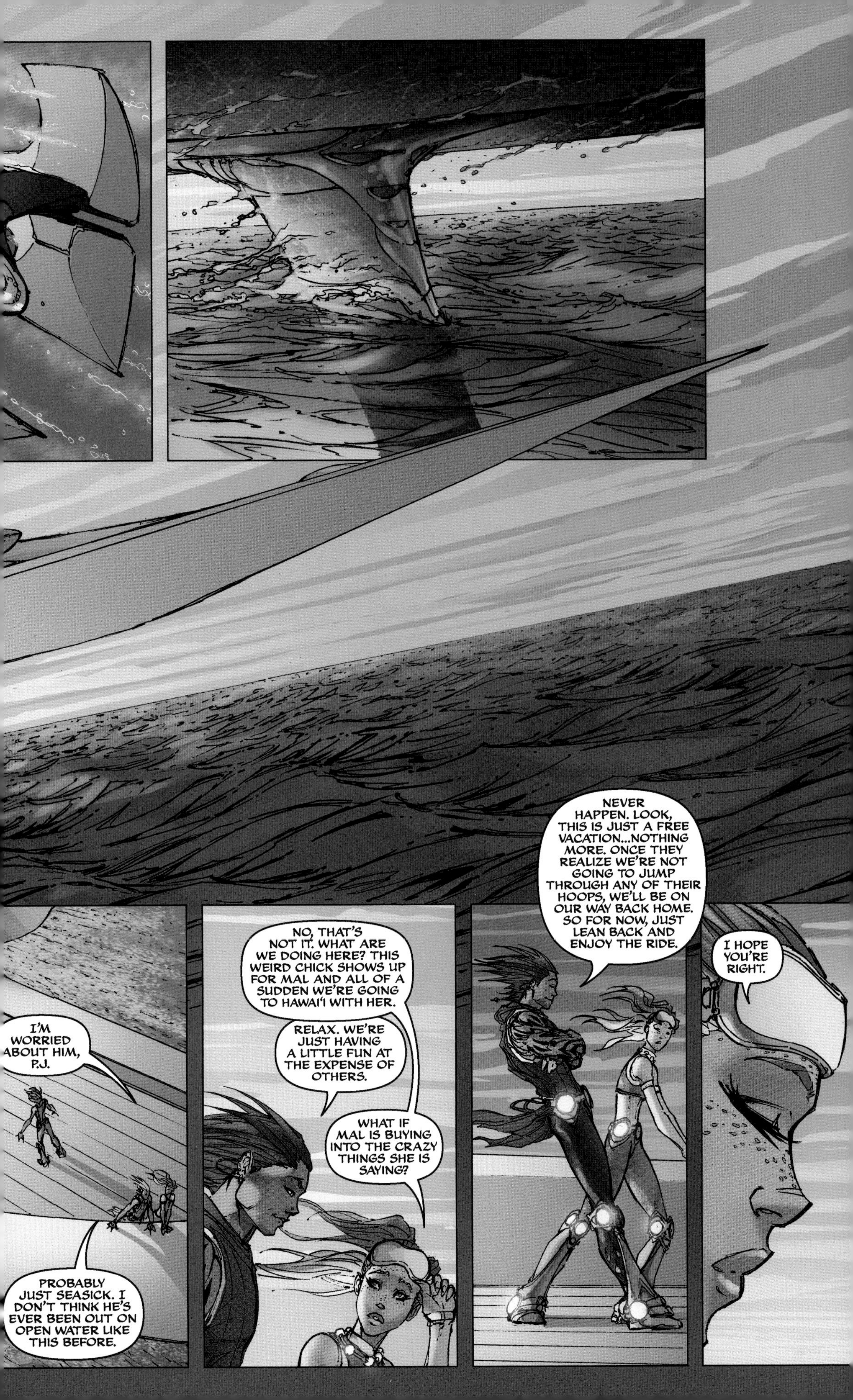
I'M WORRIED ABOUT HIM, P.J.
PROBABLY JUST SEASICK. I DON'T THINK HE'S EVER BEEN OUT ON OPEN WATER LIKE THIS BEFORE.
NO, THAT'S NOT IT. WHAT ARE WE DOING HERE? THIS WEIRD CHICK SHOWS UP FOR MAL AND ALL OF A SUDDEN WE'RE GOING TO HAWAI'I WITH HER.
RELAX. WE'RE JUST HAVING A LITTLE FUN AT THE EXPENSE OF OTHERS.
WHAT IF MAL IS BUYING INTO THE CRAZY THINGS SHE IS SAYING?
NEVER HAPPEN. LOOK, THIS IS JUST A FREE VACATION...NOTHING MORE. ONCE THEY REALIZE WE'RE NOT GOING TO JUMP THROUGH ANY OF THEIR HOOPS, WE'LL BE ON OUR WAY BACK HOME. SO FOR NOW, JUST LEAN BACK AND ENJOY THE RIDE.
I HOPE YOU'RE RIGHT.

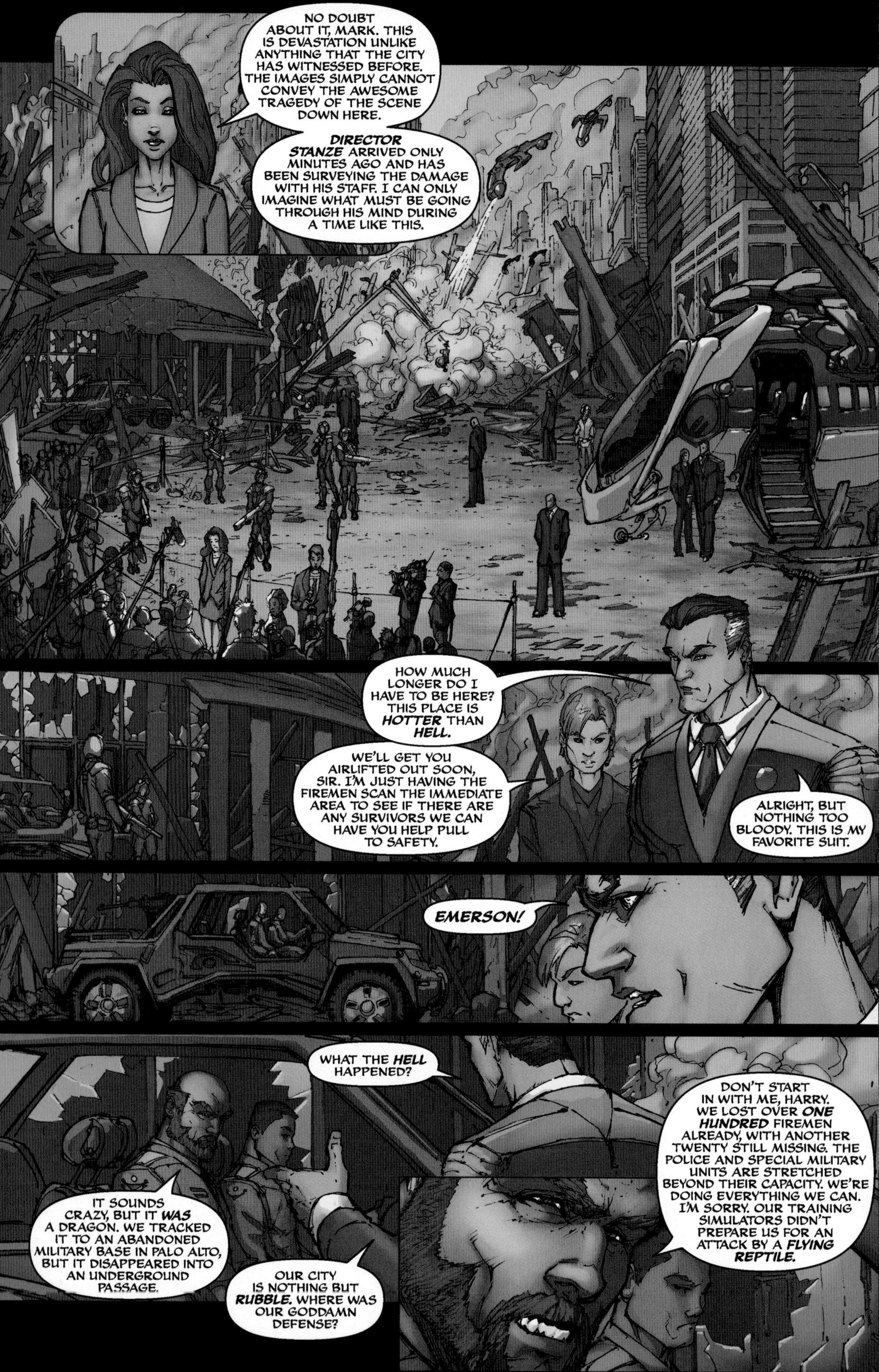
NO DOUBT ABOUT IT, MARK. THIS IS DEVASTATION UNLIKE ANYTHING THAT THE CITY HAS WITNESSED BEFORE. THE IMAGES SIMPLY CANNOT CONVEY THE AWESOME TRAGEDY OF THE SCENE DOWN HERE.
DIRECTOR STANZE ARRIVED ONLY MINUTES AGO AND HAS BEEN SURVEYING THE DAMAGE WITH HIS STAFF. I CAN ONLY IMAGINE WHAT MUST BE GOING THROUGH HIS MIND DURING A TIME LIKE THIS.
HOW MUCH LONGER DO I HAVE TO BE HERE? THIS PLACE IS HOTTER THAN HELL.
WE'LL GET YOU AIRLIFTED OUT SOON, SIR. I'M JUST HAVING THE FIREMEN SCAN THE IMMEDIATE AREA TO SEE IF THERE ARE ANY SURVIVORS WE CAN HAVE YOU HELP PULL TO SAFETY.
ALRIGHT, BUT NOTHING TOO BLOODY. THIS IS MY FAVORITE SUIT.
EMERSON!
WHAT THE HELL HAPPENED?
DON'T START IN WITH ME, HARRY. WE LOST OVER ONE HUNDRED FIREMEN ALREADY, WITH ANOTHER TWENTY STILL MISSING. THE POLICE AND SPECIAL MILITARY UNITS ARE STRETCHED BEYOND THEIR CAPACITY. WE'RE DOING EVERYTHING WE CAN. I'M SORRY. OUR TRAINING SIMULATORS DIDN'T PREPARE US FOR AN ATTACK BY A FLYING REPTILE.
IT SOUNDS CRAZY, BUT IT WAS A DRAGON. WE TRACKED IT TO AN ABANDONED MILITARY BASE IN PALO ALTO, BUT IT DISAPPEARED INTO AN UNDERGROUND PASSAGE.
OUR CITY IS NOTHING BUT RUBBLE. WHERE WAS OUR GODDAMN DEFENSE?

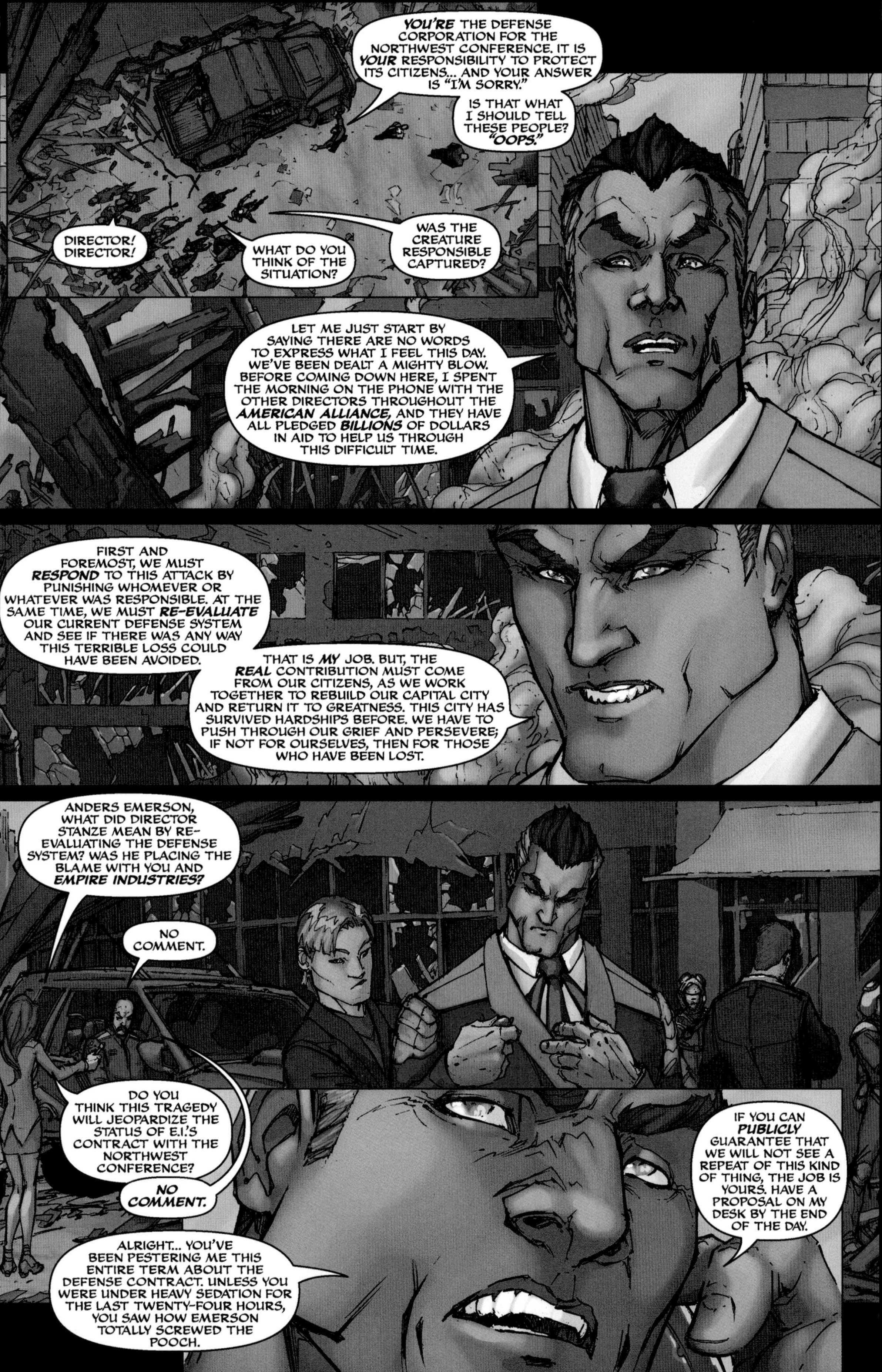

YOU'RE THE DEFENSE CORPORATION FOR THE NORTHWEST CONFERENCE. IT IS YOUR RESPONSIBILITY TO PROTECT ITS CITIZENS... AND YOUR ANSWER IS "I'M SORRY."
IS THAT WHAT I SHOULD TELL THESE PEOPLE? "OOPS."
DIRECTOR! DIRECTOR!
WHAT DO YOU THINK OF THE SITUATION?
WAS THE CREATURE RESPONSIBLE CAPTURED?
LET ME JUST START BY SAYING THERE ARE NO WORDS TO EXPRESS WHAT I FEEL THIS DAY. WE'VE BEEN DEALT A MIGHTY BLOW. BEFORE COMING DOWN HERE, I SPENT THE MORNING ON THE PHONE WITH THE OTHER DIRECTORS THROUGHOUT THE AMERICAN ALLIANCE, AND THEY HAVE ALL PLEDGED BILLIONS OF DOLLARS IN AID TO HELP US THROUGH THIS DIFFICULT TIME.
FIRST AND FOREMOST, WE MUST RESPOND TO THIS ATTACK BY PUNISHING WHOMEVER OR WHATEVER WAS RESPONSIBLE. AT THE SAME TIME, WE MUST RE-EVALUATE OUR CURRENT DEFENSE SYSTEM AND SEE IF THERE WAS ANY WAY THIS TERRIBLE LOSS COULD HAVE BEEN AVOIDED.
THAT IS MY JOB. BUT, THE REAL CONTRIBUTION MUST COME FROM OUR CITIZENS, AS WE WORK TOGETHER TO REBUILD OUR CAPITAL CITY AND RETURN IT TO GREATNESS. THIS CITY HAS SURVIVED HARDSHIPS BEFORE. WE HAVE TO PUSH THROUGH OUR GRIEF AND PERSEVERE; IF NOT FOR OURSELVES, THEN FOR THOSE WHO HAVE BEEN LOST.
ANDERS EMERSON, WHAT DID DIRECTOR STANZE MEAN BY RE-EVALUATING THE DEFENSE SYSTEM? WAS HE PLACING THE BLAME WITH YOU AND EMPIRE INDUSTRIES?
NO COMMENT.
DO YOU THINK THIS TRAGEDY WILL JEOPARDIZE THE STATUS OF E.I.'S CONTRACT WITH THE NORTHWEST CONFERENCE?
NO COMMENT.
ALRIGHT... YOU'VE BEEN PESTERING ME THIS ENTIRE TERM ABOUT THE DEFENSE CONTRACT. UNLESS YOU WERE UNDER HEAVY SEDATION FOR THE LAST TWENTY-FOUR HOURS, YOU SAW HOW EMERSON TOTALLY SCREWED THE POOCH.
IF YOU CAN PUBLICLY GUARANTEE THAT WE WILL NOT SEE A REPEAT OF THIS KIND OF THING, THE JOB IS YOURS. HAVE A PROPOSAL ON MY DESK BY THE END OF THE DAY.

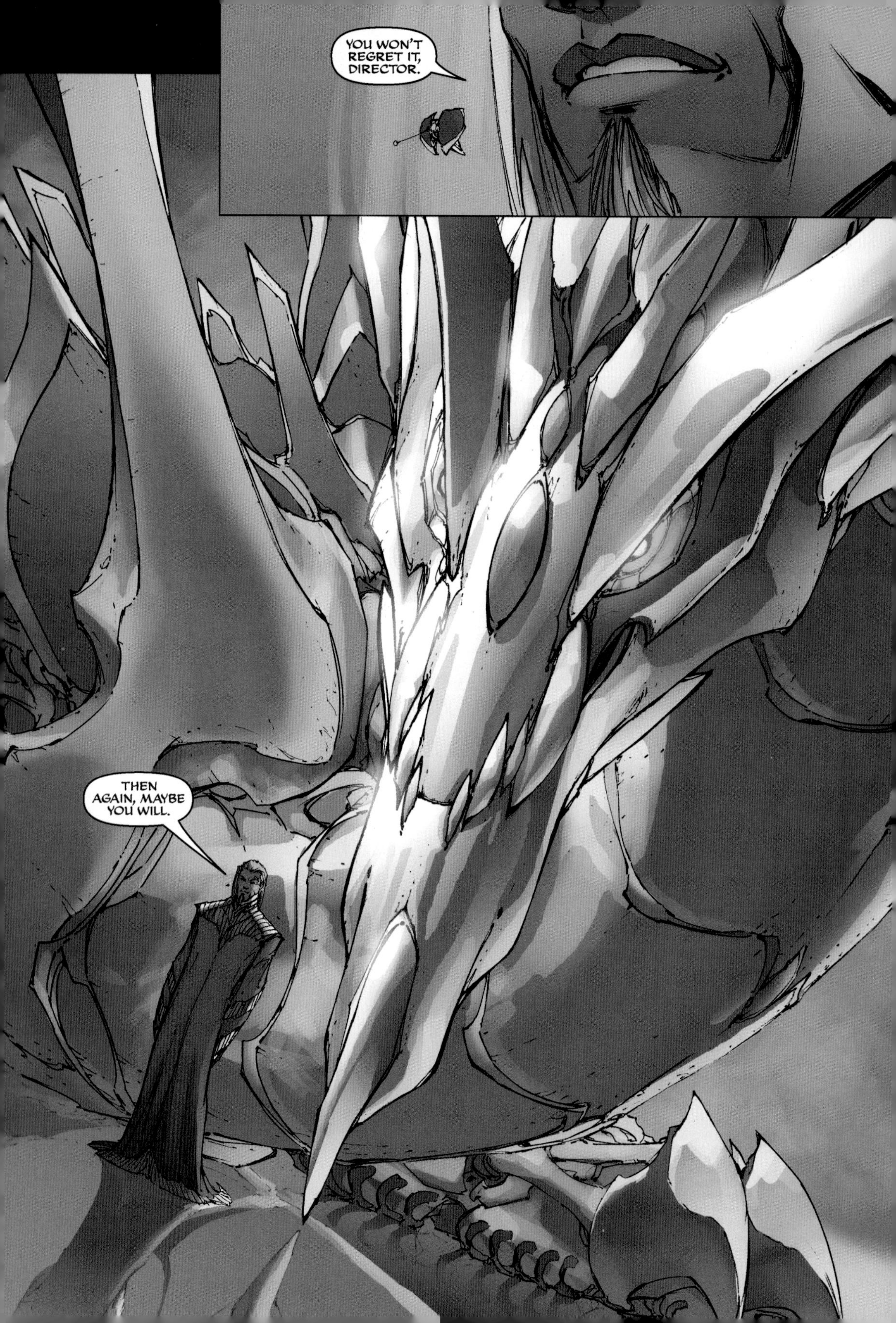
YOU WON'T REGRET IT, DIRECTOR.
THEN AGAIN, MAYBE YOU WILL.

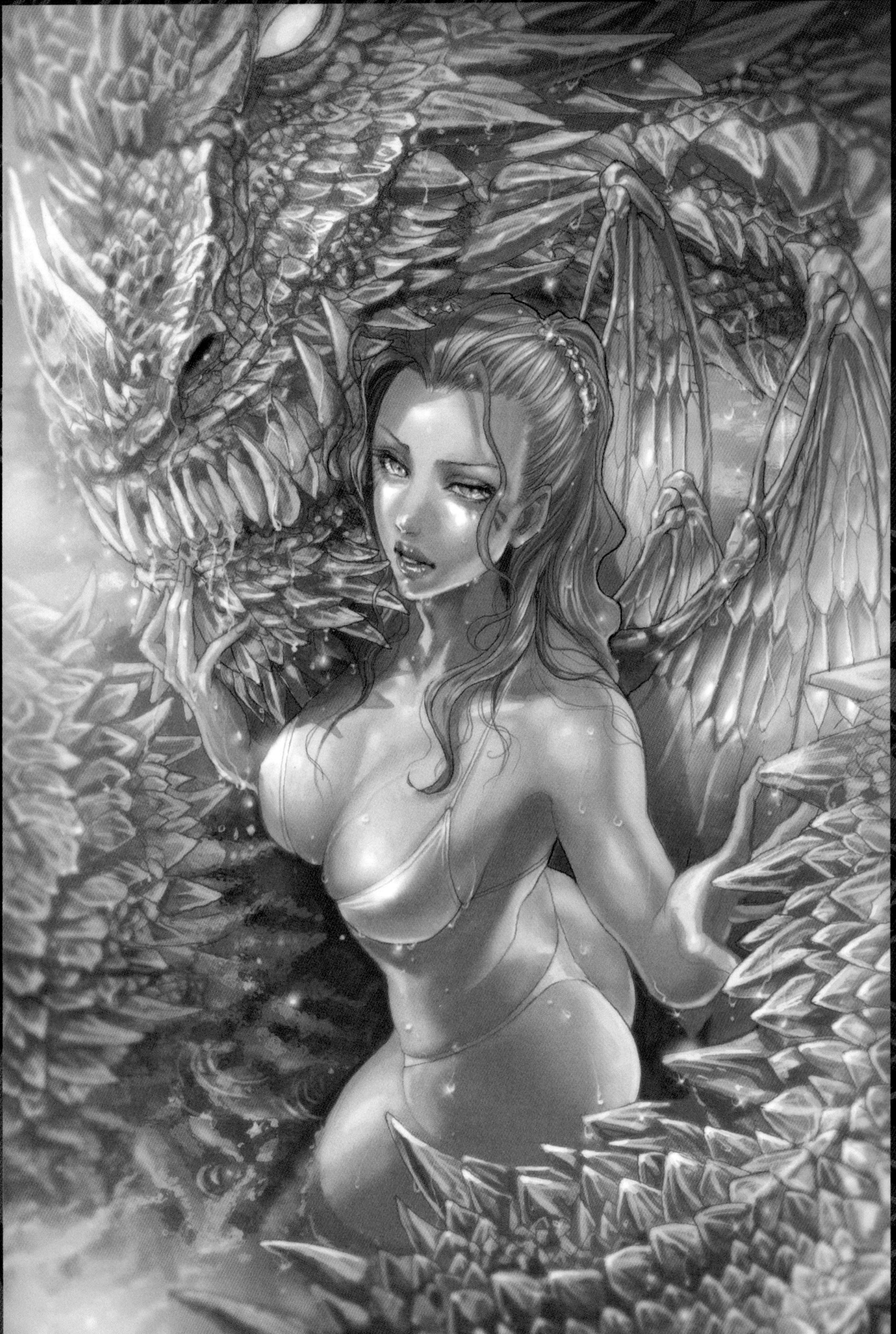

GRACE

· PIN-UP FROM ASPEN SPLASH: 2008 SWIMSUIT SPECTACULAR ·

by

· SANA TAKEDA ·

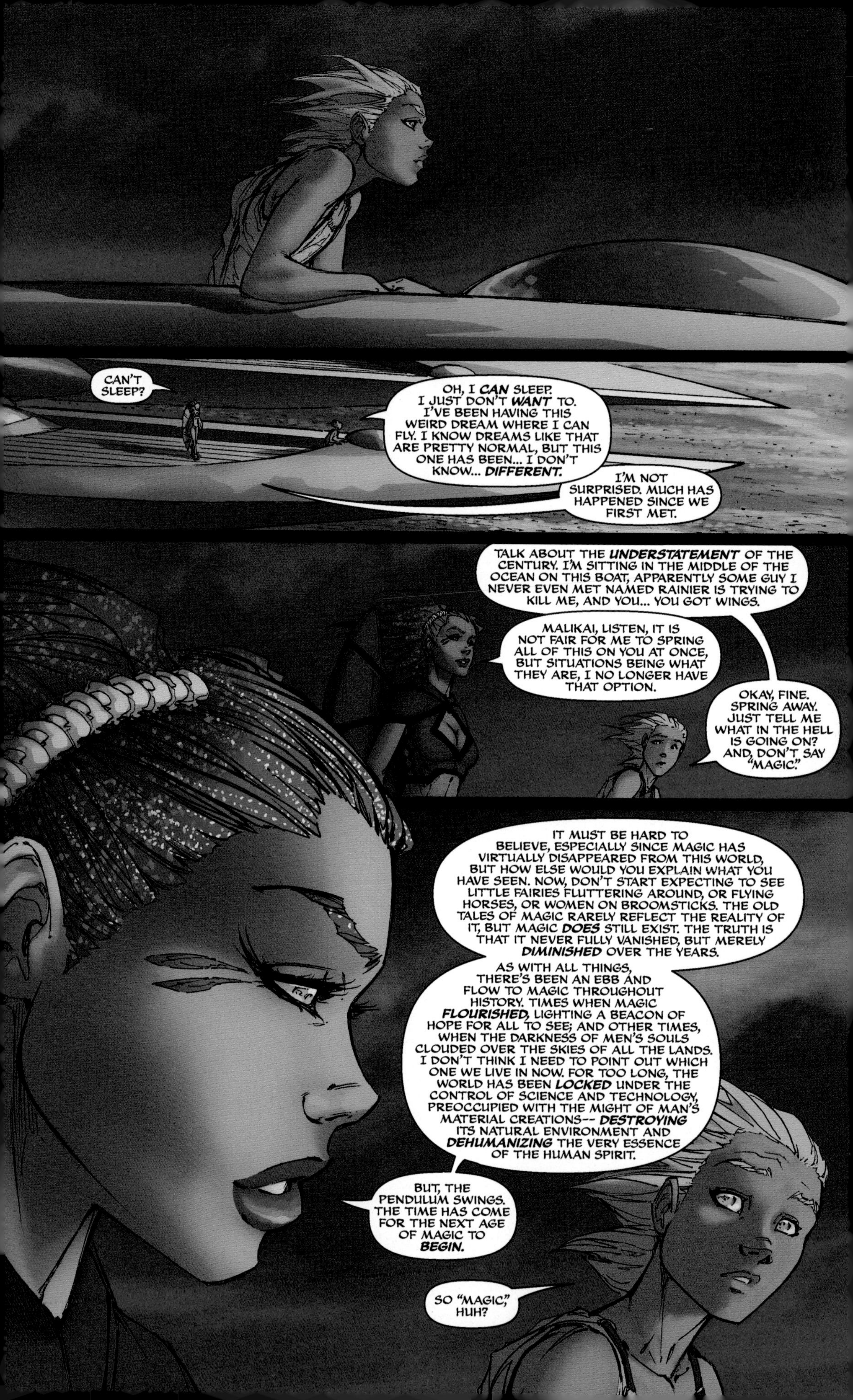
CAN'T SLEEP?
OH, I CAN SLEEP. I JUST DON'T WANT TO. I'VE BEEN HAVING THIS WEIRD DREAM WHERE I CAN FLY. I KNOW DREAMS LIKE THAT ARE PRETTY NORMAL, BUT THIS ONE HAS BEEN... I DON'T KNOW... DIFFERENT.
I'M NOT SURPRISED. MUCH HAS HAPPENED SINCE WE FIRST MET.
TALK ABOUT THE UNDERSTATEMENT OF THE CENTURY. I'M SITTING IN THE MIDDLE OF THE OCEAN ON THIS BOAT, APPARENTLY SOME GUY I NEVER EVEN MET NAMED RAINIER IS TRYING TO KILL ME, AND YOU... YOU GOT WINGS.
MALIKAI, LISTEN, IT IS NOT FAIR FOR ME TO SPRING ALL OF THIS ON YOU AT ONCE, BUT SITUATIONS BEING WHAT THEY ARE, I NO LONGER HAVE THAT OPTION.
OKAY, FINE. SPRING AWAY. JUST TELL ME WHAT IN THE HELL IS GOING ON? AND, DON'T SAY "MAGIC."
IT MUST BE HARD TO BELIEVE, ESPECIALLY SINCE MAGIC HAS VIRTUALLY DISAPPEARED FROM THIS WORLD, BUT HOW ELSE WOULD YOU EXPLAIN WHAT YOU HAVE SEEN. NOW, DON'T START EXPECTING TO SEE LITTLE FAIRIES FLUTTERING AROUND, OR FLYING HORSES, OR WOMEN ON BROOMSTICKS. THE OLD TALES OF MAGIC RARELY REFLECT THE REALITY OF IT, BUT MAGIC DOES STILL EXIST. THE TRUTH IS THAT IT NEVER FULLY VANISHED, BUT MERELY DIMINISHED OVER THE YEARS.
AS WITH ALL THINGS, THERE'S BEEN AN EBB AND FLOW TO MAGIC THROUGHOUT HISTORY. TIMES WHEN MAGIC FLOURISHED, LIGHTING A BEACON OF HOPE FOR ALL TO SEE; AND OTHER TIMES, WHEN THE DARKNESS OF MEN'S SOULS CLOUDED OVER THE SKIES OF ALL THE LANDS. I DON'T THINK I NEED TO POINT OUT WHICH ONE WE LIVE IN NOW. FOR TOO LONG, THE WORLD HAS BEEN LOCKED UNDER THE CONTROL OF SCIENCE AND TECHNOLOGY, PREOCCUPIED WITH THE MIGHT OF MAN'S MATERIAL CREATIONS-- DESTROYING ITS NATURAL ENVIRONMENT AND DEHUMANIZING THE VERY ESSENCE OF THE HUMAN SPIRIT.
BUT, THE PENDULUM SWINGS. THE TIME HAS COME FOR THE NEXT AGE OF MAGIC TO BEGIN.
SO "MAGIC," HUH?

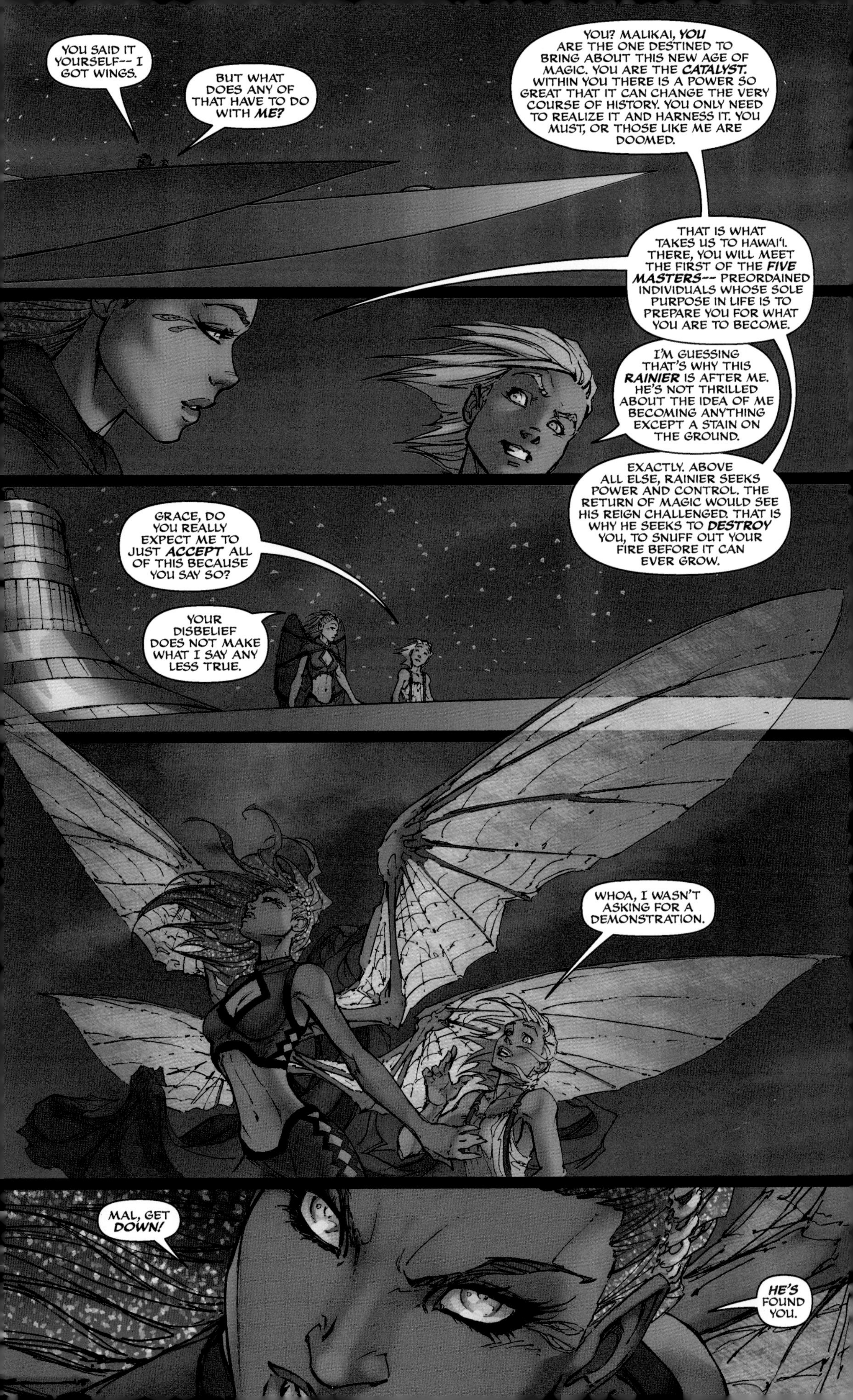
YOU SAID IT YOURSELF-- I GOT WINGS.
BUT WHAT DOES ANY OF THAT HAVE TO DO WITH ME?
YOU? MALIKAI, YOU ARE THE ONE DESTINED TO BRING ABOUT THIS NEW AGE OF MAGIC. YOU ARE THE CATALYST. WITHIN YOU THERE IS A POWER SO GREAT THAT IT CAN CHANGE THE VERY COURSE OF HISTORY. YOU ONLY NEED TO REALIZE IT AND HARNESS IT. YOU MUST, OR THOSE LIKE ME ARE DOOMED.
THAT IS WHAT TAKES US TO HAWAI'I. THERE, YOU WILL MEET THE FIRST OF THE FIVE MASTERS-- PREORDAINED INDIVIDUALS WHOSE SOLE PURPOSE IN LIFE IS TO PREPARE YOU FOR WHAT YOU ARE TO BECOME.
I'M GUESSING THAT'S WHY THIS RAINIER IS AFTER ME. HE'S NOT THRILLED ABOUT THE IDEA OF ME BECOMING ANYTHING EXCEPT A STAIN ON THE GROUND.
EXACTLY. ABOVE ALL ELSE, RAINIER SEEKS POWER AND CONTROL. THE RETURN OF MAGIC WOULD SEE HIS REIGN CHALLENGED. THAT IS WHY HE SEEKS TO DESTROY YOU, TO SNUFF OUT YOUR FIRE BEFORE IT CAN EVER GROW.
GRACE, DO YOU REALLY EXPECT ME TO JUST ACCEPT ALL OF THIS BECAUSE YOU SAY SO?
YOUR DISBELIEF DOES NOT MAKE WHAT I SAY ANY LESS TRUE.
WHOA, I WASN'T ASKING FOR A DEMONSTRATION.
MAL, GET DOWN!
HE'S FOUND YOU.

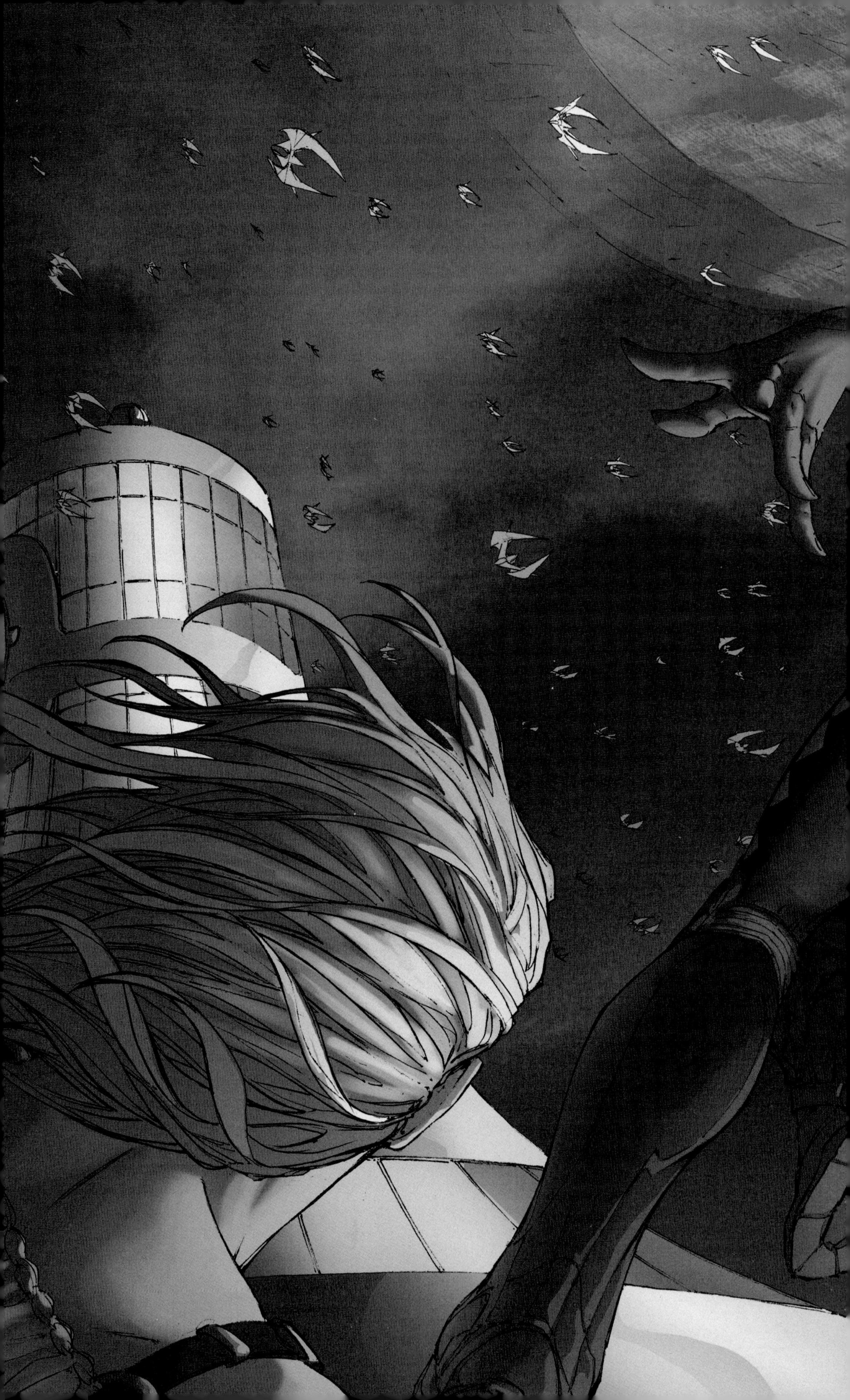

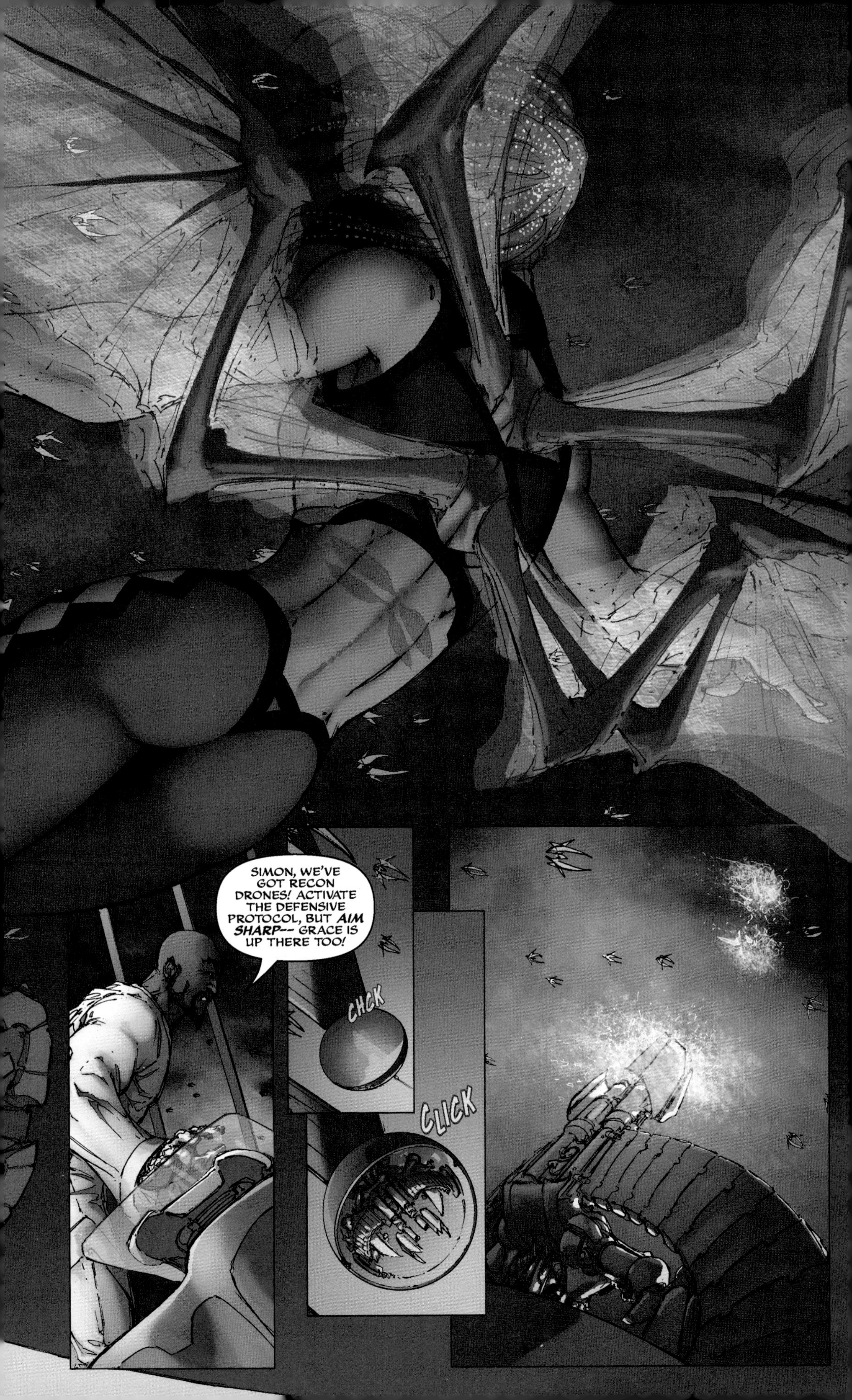
SIMON, WE'VE GOT RECON DRONES! ACTIVATE THE DEFENSIVE PROTOCOL, BUT *AIM SHARP*-- GRACE IS UP THERE TOO!
CHCK
CLICK

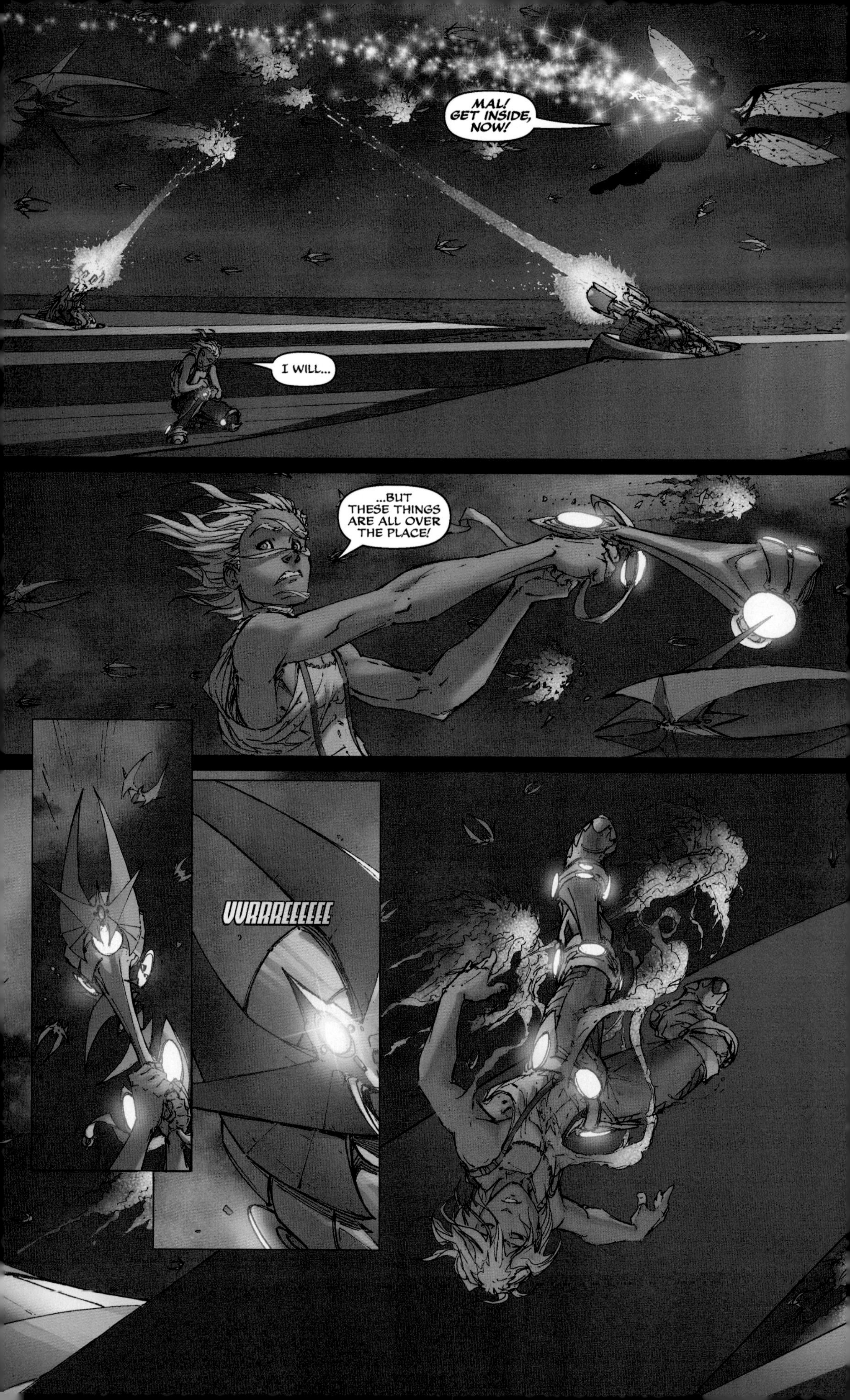
MAL! GET INSIDE, NOW!
I WILL...
...BUT THESE THINGS ARE ALL OVER THE PLACE!
VVRRREEEEEE

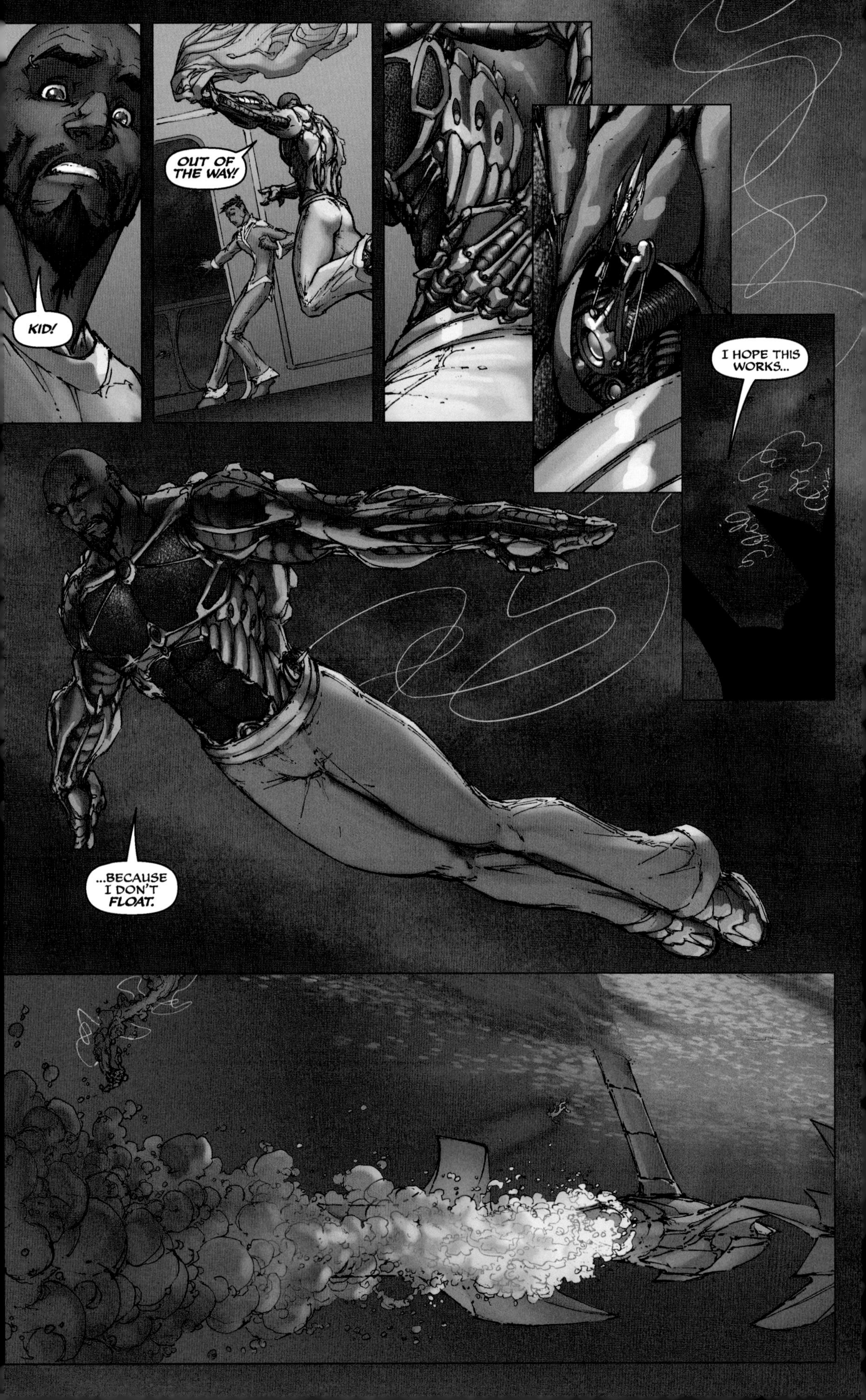
KID!
OUT OF THE WAY!
I HOPE THIS WORKS...
...BECAUSE I DON'T FLOAT.

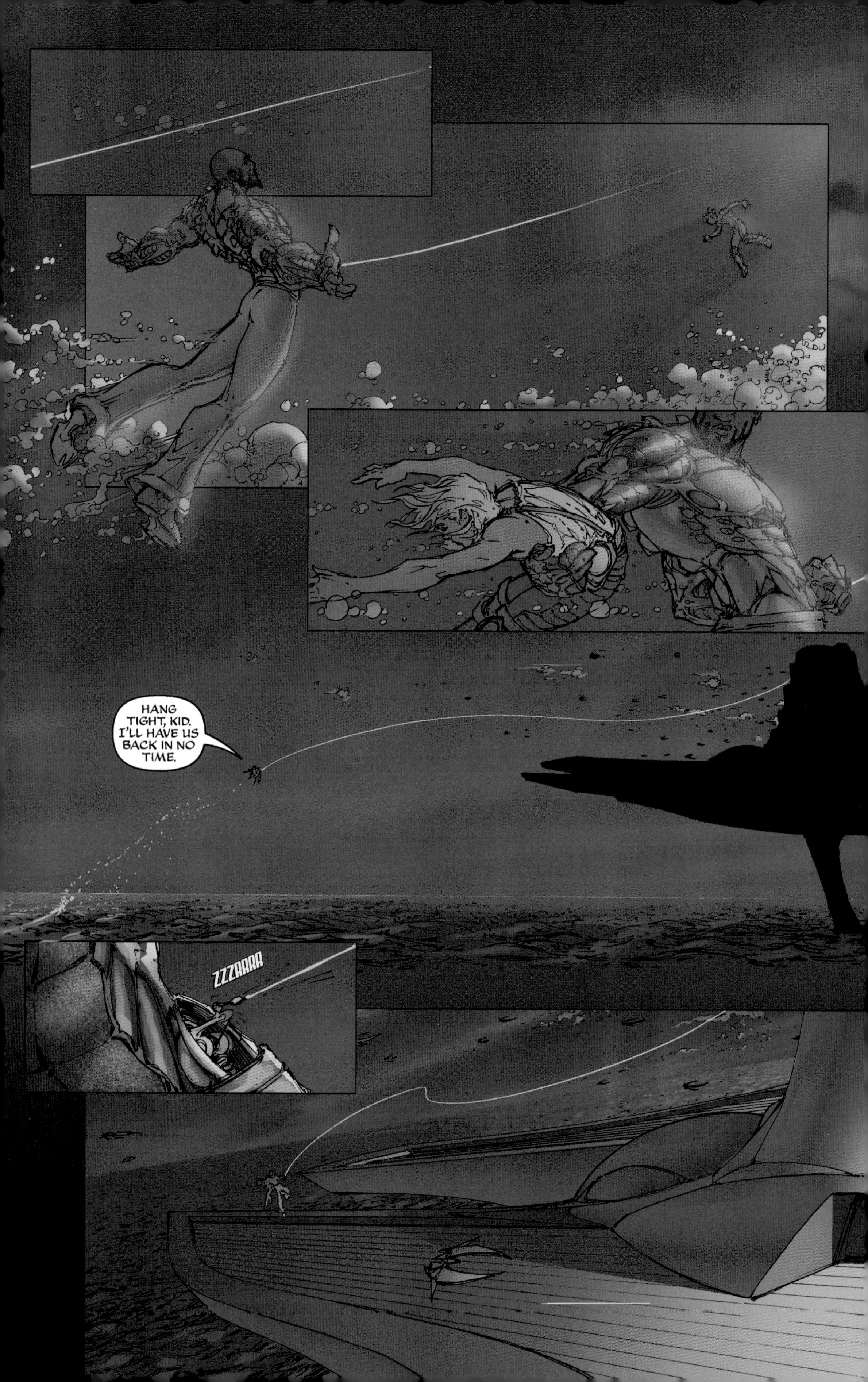
HANG TIGHT, KID. I'LL HAVE US BACK IN NO TIME.
ZZZRRRR

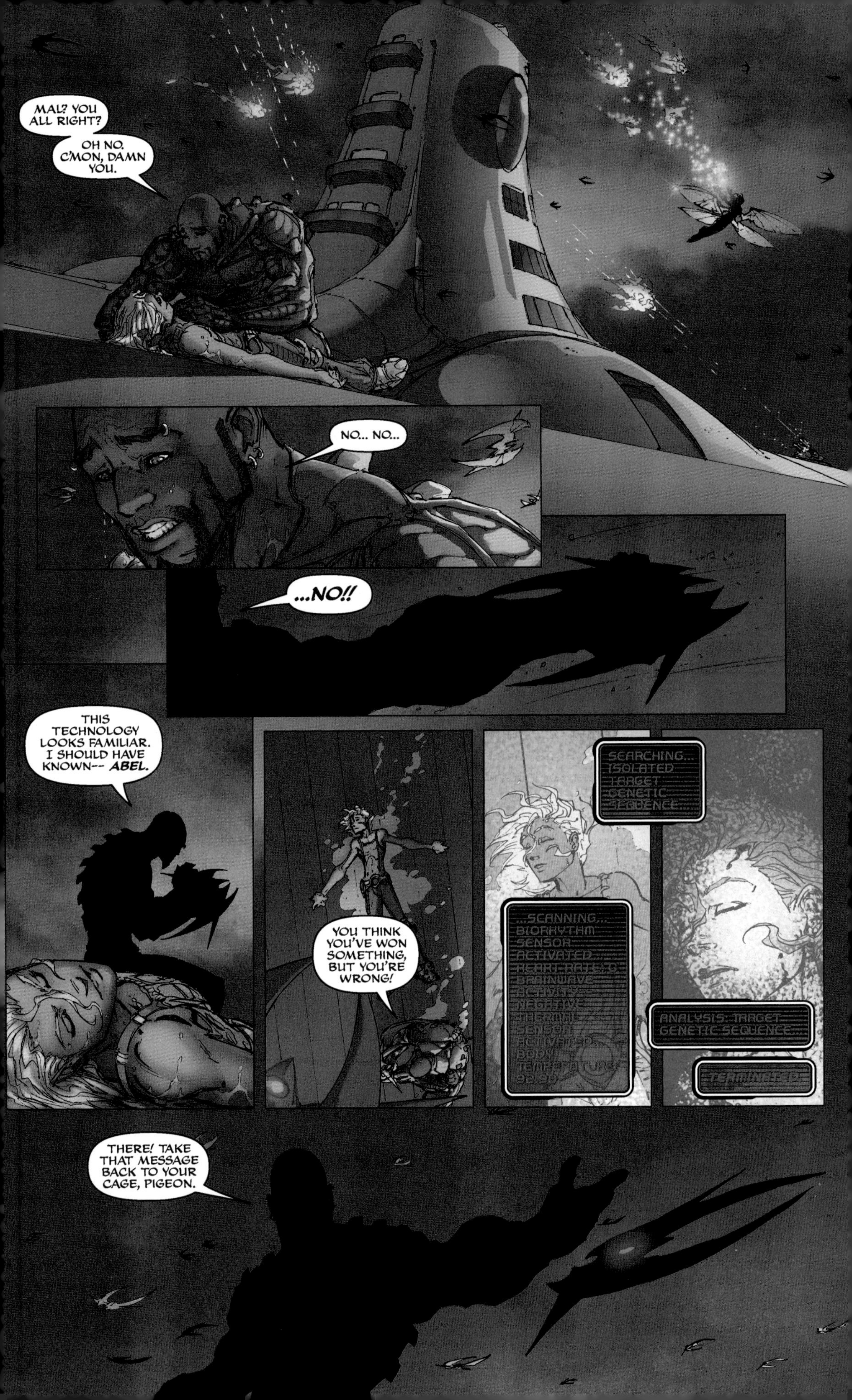
MAL? YOU ALL RIGHT?
OH NO. C'MON, DAMN YOU.
NO... NO...
...NO!!
THIS TECHNOLOGY LOOKS FAMILIAR. I SHOULD HAVE KNOWN-- ABEL.
YOU THINK YOU'VE WON SOMETHING, BUT YOU'RE WRONG!
SEARCHING... ISOLATED TARGET GENETIC SEQUENCE...
...SCANNING... BIORHYTHM SENSOR ACTIVATED... HEART RATE: 0 BRAINWAVE ACTIVITY NEGATIVE
ANALYSIS: TARGET GENETIC SEQUENCE...
TERMINATED.
THERE! TAKE THAT MESSAGE BACK TO YOUR CAGE, PIGEON.

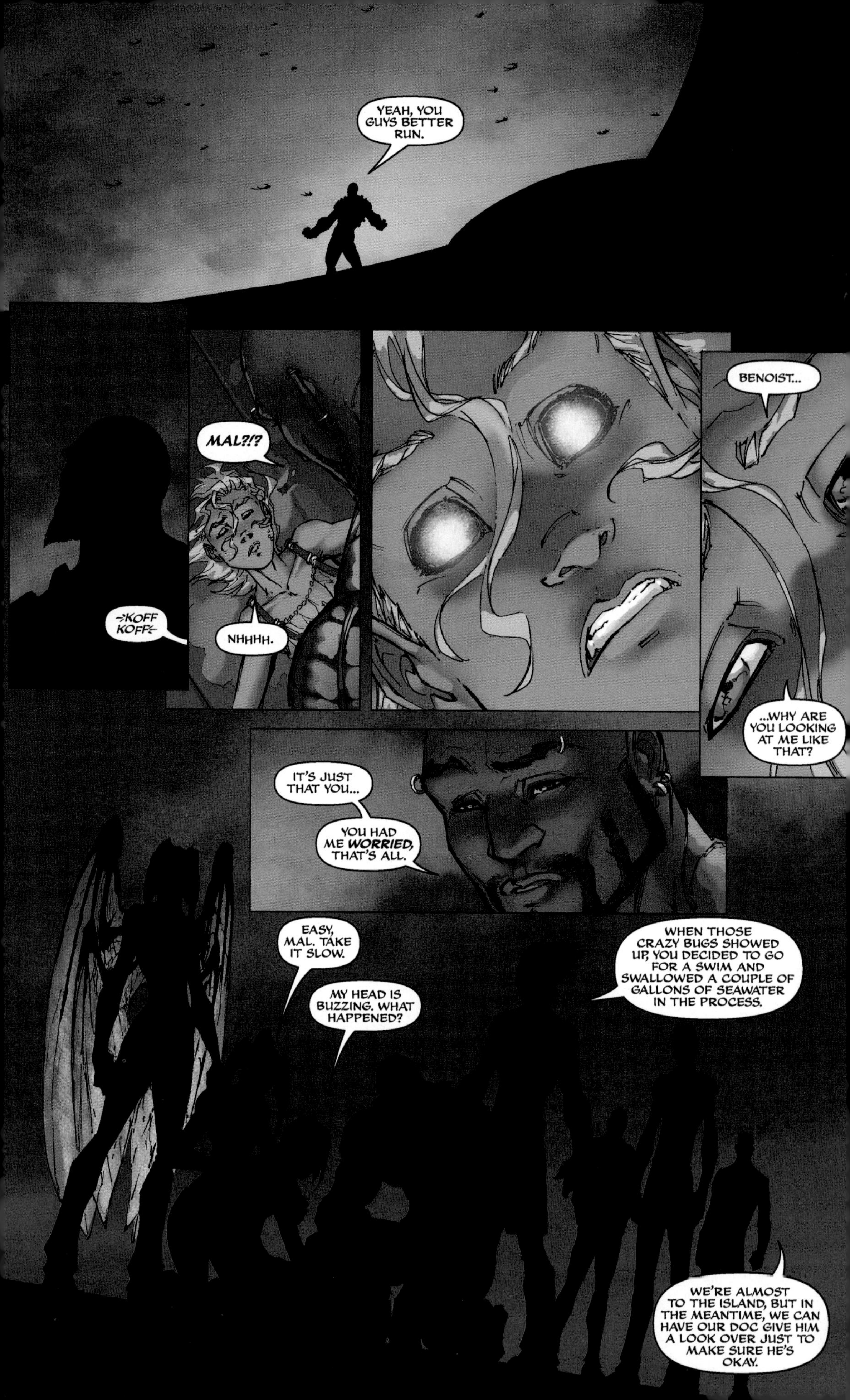
YEAH, YOU GUYS BETTER RUN.
MAL?!?
-KOFF KOFF-
NHHHH.
BENOIST...
...WHY ARE YOU LOOKING AT ME LIKE THAT?
IT'S JUST THAT YOU...
YOU HAD ME WORRIED, THAT'S ALL.
EASY, MAL. TAKE IT SLOW.
MY HEAD IS BUZZING. WHAT HAPPENED?
WHEN THOSE CRAZY BUGS SHOWED UP, YOU DECIDED TO GO FOR A SWIM AND SWALLOWED A COUPLE OF GALLONS OF SEAWATER IN THE PROCESS.
WE'RE ALMOST TO THE ISLAND, BUT IN THE MEANTIME, WE CAN HAVE OUR DOC GIVE HIM A LOOK OVER JUST TO MAKE SURE HE'S OKAY.

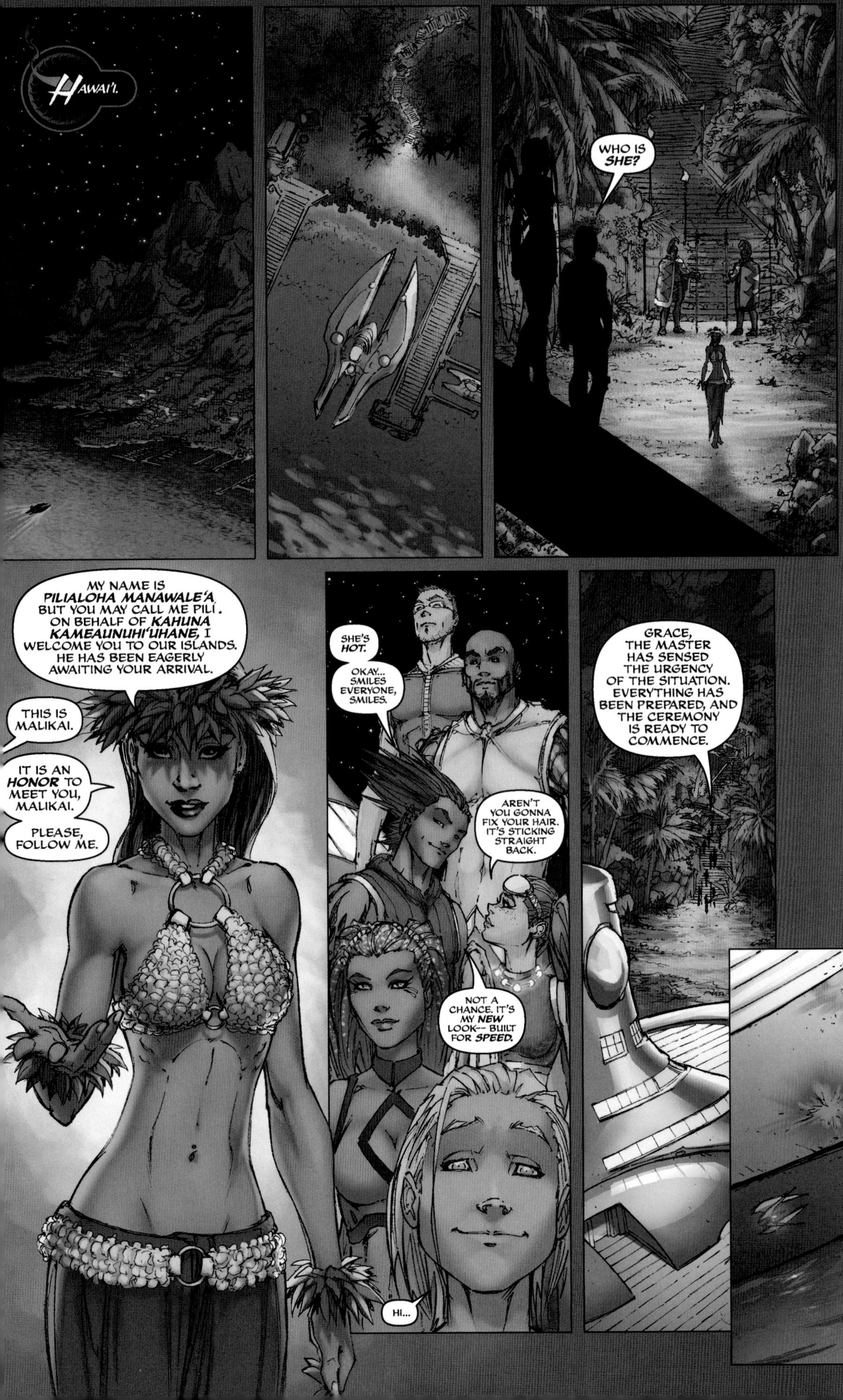
HAWAI'I.
WHO IS SHE?
MY NAME IS PILIALOHA MANAWALE'A, BUT YOU MAY CALL ME PILI. ON BEHALF OF KAHUNA KAMEAUNUHI'UHANE, I WELCOME YOU TO OUR ISLANDS. HE HAS BEEN EAGERLY AWAITING YOUR ARRIVAL.
THIS IS MALIKAI.
IT IS AN HONOR TO MEET YOU, MALIKAI.
PLEASE, FOLLOW ME.
SHE'S HOT.
OKAY... SMILES EVERYONE, SMILES.
AREN'T YOU GONNA FIX YOUR HAIR. IT'S STICKING STRAIGHT BACK.
NOT A CHANCE. IT'S MY NEW LOOK-- BUILT FOR SPEED.
HI...
GRACE, THE MASTER HAS SENSED THE URGENCY OF THE SITUATION. EVERYTHING HAS BEEN PREPARED, AND THE CEREMONY IS READY TO COMMENCE.

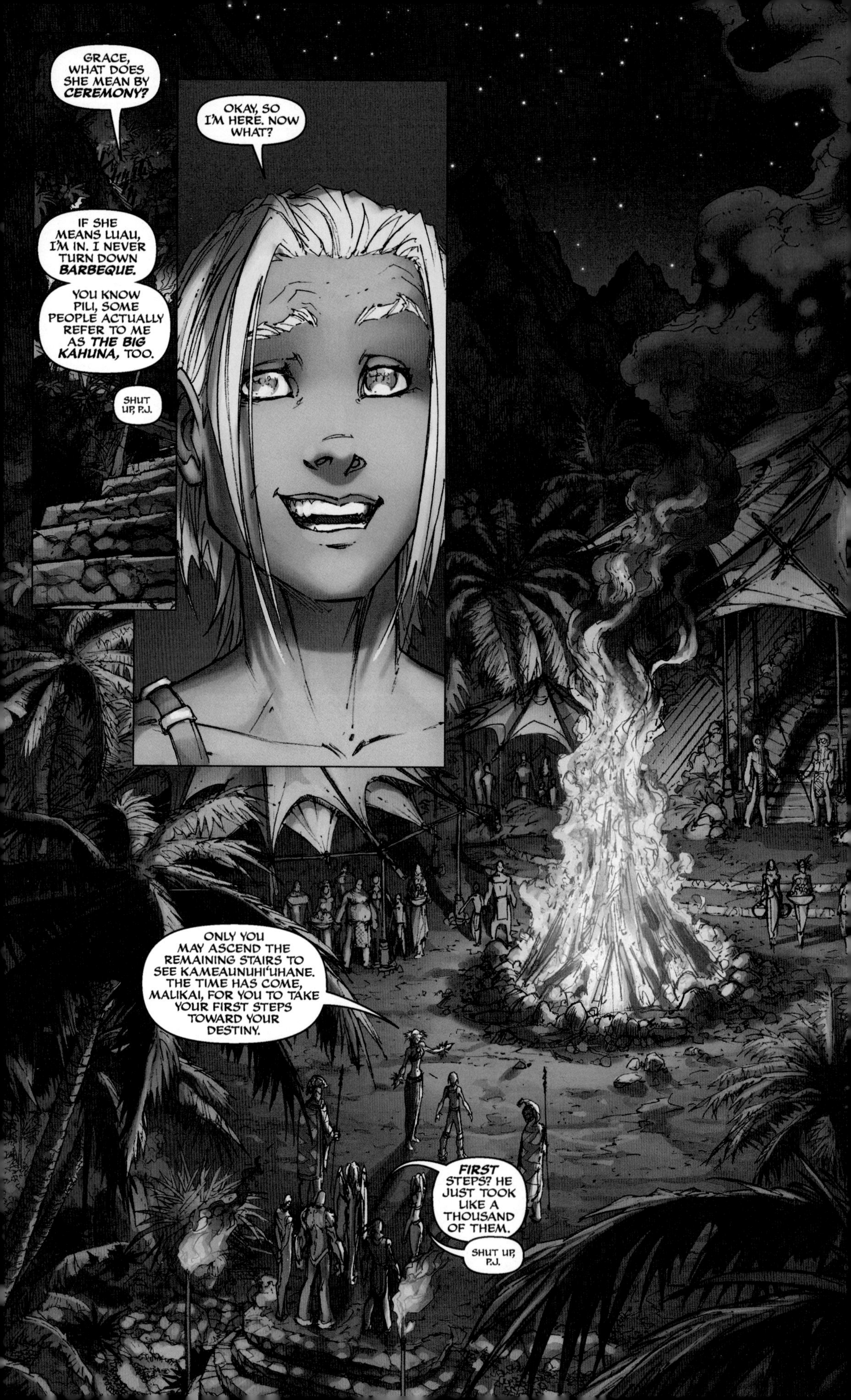
GRACE, WHAT DOES SHE MEAN BY CEREMONY?
OKAY, SO I'M HERE. NOW WHAT?
IF SHE MEANS LUAU, I'M IN. I NEVER TURN DOWN BARBEQUE.
YOU KNOW PILI, SOME PEOPLE ACTUALLY REFER TO ME AS THE BIG KAHUNA, TOO.
SHUT UP, P.J.
ONLY YOU MAY ASCEND THE REMAINING STAIRS TO SEE KAMEAUNUHI'UHANE. THE TIME HAS COME, MALIKAI, FOR YOU TO TAKE YOUR FIRST STEPS TOWARD YOUR DESTINY.
FIRST STEPS? HE JUST TOOK LIKE A THOUSAND OF THEM.
SHUT UP, P.J.

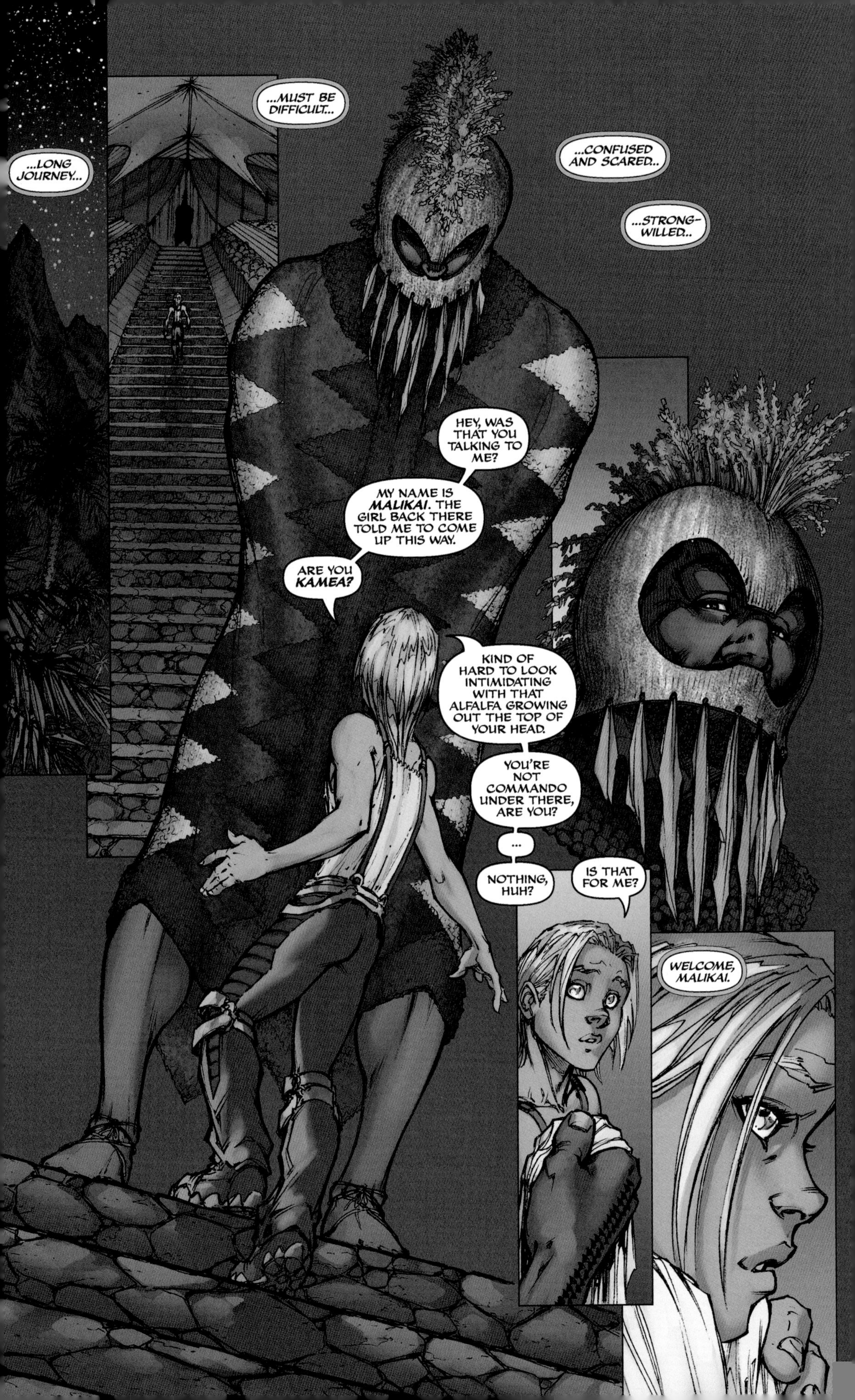

...LONG JOURNEY...
...MUST BE DIFFICULT...
...CONFUSED AND SCARED...
...STRONG-WILLED...
HEY, WAS THAT YOU TALKING TO ME?
MY NAME IS MALIKAI. THE GIRL BACK THERE TOLD ME TO COME UP THIS WAY.
ARE YOU KAMEA?
KIND OF HARD TO LOOK INTIMIDATING WITH THAT ALFALFA GROWING OUT THE TOP OF YOUR HEAD.
YOU'RE NOT COMMANDO UNDER THERE, ARE YOU?
...
NOTHING, HUH?
IS THAT FOR ME?
WELCOME, MALIKAI.

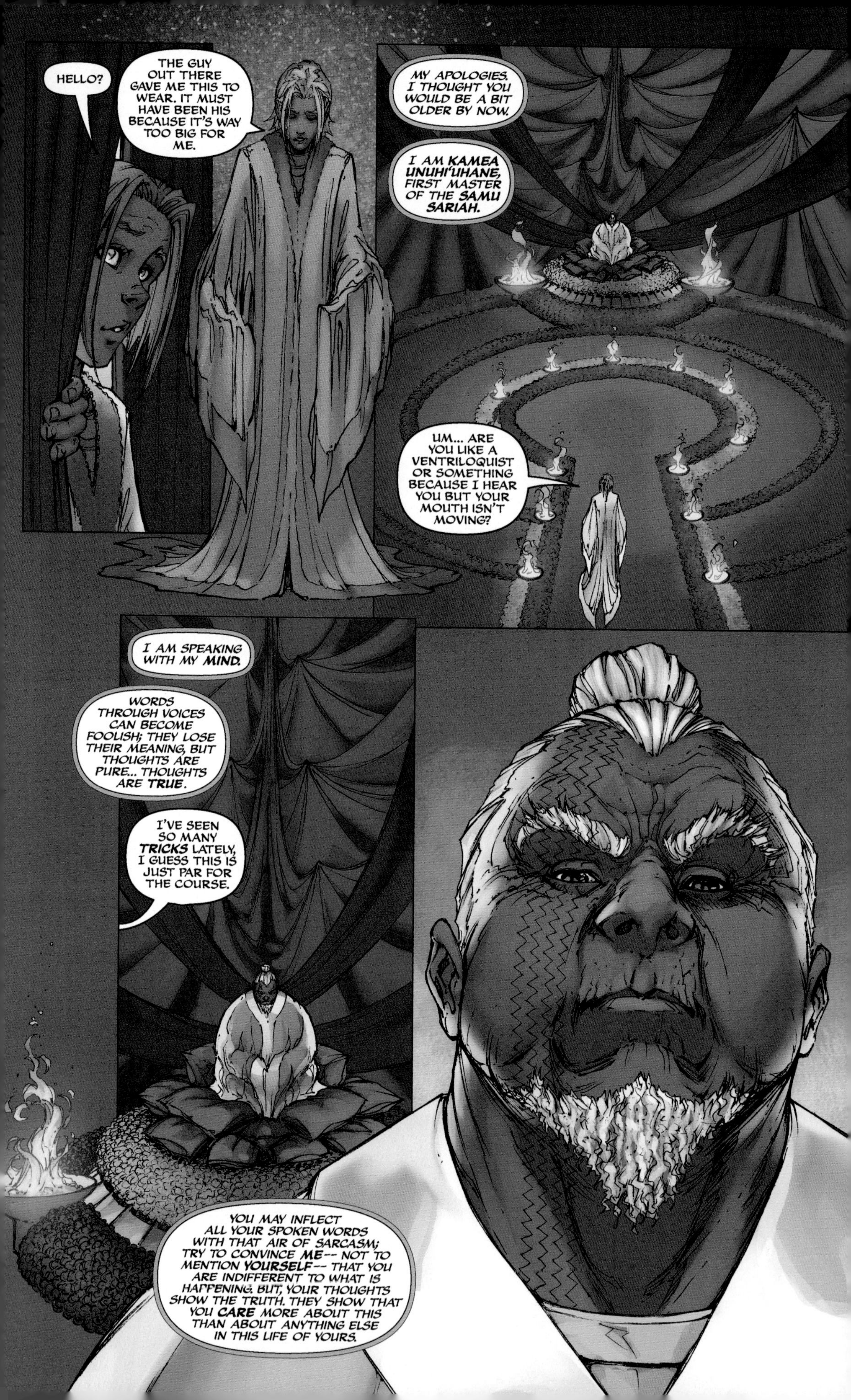
HELLO?
THE GUY OUT THERE GAVE ME THIS TO WEAR. IT MUST HAVE BEEN HIS BECAUSE IT'S WAY TOO BIG FOR ME.
MY APOLOGIES. I THOUGHT YOU WOULD BE A BIT OLDER BY NOW.
I AM KAMEA UNUHI'UHANE, FIRST MASTER OF THE SAMU SARIAH.
UM... ARE YOU LIKE A VENTRILOQUIST OR SOMETHING BECAUSE I HEAR YOU BUT YOUR MOUTH ISN'T MOVING?
I AM SPEAKING WITH MY MIND.
WORDS THROUGH VOICES CAN BECOME FOOLISH; THEY LOSE THEIR MEANING, BUT THOUGHTS ARE PURE... THOUGHTS ARE TRUE.
I'VE SEEN SO MANY TRICKS LATELY, I GUESS THIS IS JUST PAR FOR THE COURSE.
YOU MAY INFLECT ALL YOUR SPOKEN WORDS WITH THAT AIR OF SARCASM; TRY TO CONVINCE ME-- NOT TO MENTION YOURSELF-- THAT YOU ARE INDIFFERENT TO WHAT IS HAPPENING. BUT, YOUR THOUGHTS SHOW THE TRUTH. THEY SHOW THAT YOU CARE MORE ABOUT THIS THAN ABOUT ANYTHING ELSE IN THIS LIFE OF YOURS.

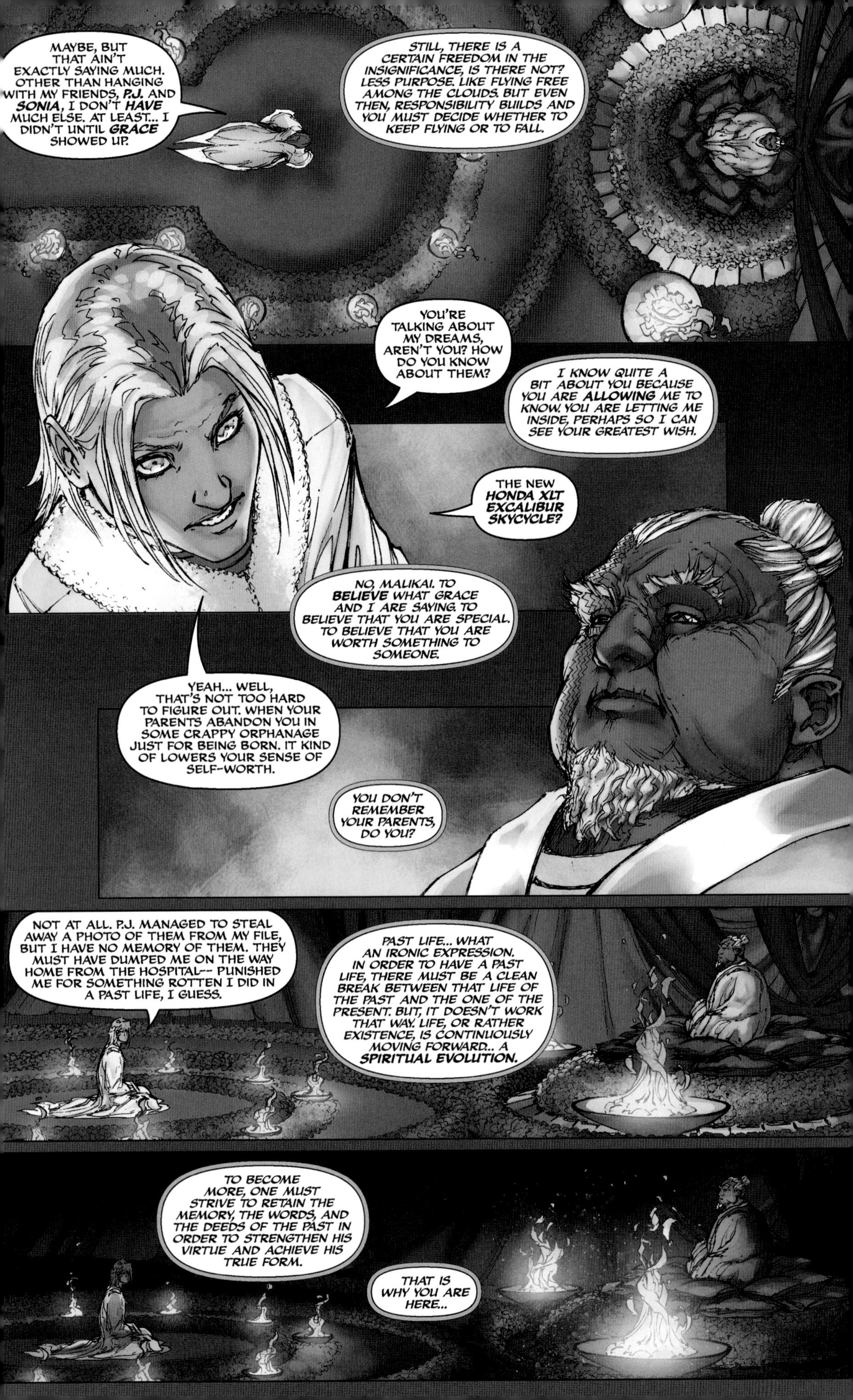
MAYBE, BUT THAT AIN'T EXACTLY SAYING MUCH. OTHER THAN HANGING WITH MY FRIENDS, **P.J.** AND **SONIA**, I DON'T **HAVE** MUCH ELSE. AT LEAST... I DIDN'T UNTIL **GRACE** SHOWED UP.
STILL, THERE IS A CERTAIN FREEDOM IN THE INSIGNIFICANCE, IS THERE NOT? LESS PURPOSE. LIKE FLYING FREE AMONG THE CLOUDS. BUT EVEN THEN, RESPONSIBILITY BUILDS AND YOU MUST DECIDE WHETHER TO KEEP FLYING OR TO FALL.
YOU'RE TALKING ABOUT MY DREAMS, AREN'T YOU? HOW DO YOU KNOW ABOUT THEM?
I KNOW QUITE A BIT ABOUT YOU BECAUSE YOU ARE **ALLOWING** ME TO KNOW. YOU ARE LETTING ME INSIDE, PERHAPS SO I CAN SEE YOUR GREATEST WISH.
THE NEW **HONDA XLT EXCALIBUR SKYCYCLE?**
NO, MALIKAI. TO **BELIEVE** WHAT GRACE AND I ARE SAYING. TO BELIEVE THAT YOU ARE SPECIAL. TO BELIEVE THAT YOU ARE WORTH SOMETHING TO SOMEONE.
YEAH... WELL, THAT'S NOT TOO HARD TO FIGURE OUT. WHEN YOUR PARENTS ABANDON YOU IN SOME CRAPPY ORPHANAGE JUST FOR BEING BORN, IT KIND OF LOWERS YOUR SENSE OF SELF-WORTH.
YOU DON'T REMEMBER YOUR PARENTS, DO YOU?
NOT AT ALL. P.J. MANAGED TO STEAL AWAY A PHOTO OF THEM FROM MY FILE, BUT I HAVE NO MEMORY OF THEM. THEY MUST HAVE DUMPED ME ON THE WAY HOME FROM THE HOSPITAL-- PUNISHED ME FOR SOMETHING ROTTEN I DID IN A PAST LIFE, I GUESS.
PAST LIFE... WHAT AN IRONIC EXPRESSION. IN ORDER TO HAVE A PAST LIFE, THERE MUST BE A CLEAN BREAK BETWEEN THAT LIFE OF THE PAST AND THE ONE OF THE PRESENT. BUT, IT DOESN'T WORK THAT WAY. LIFE, OR RATHER EXISTENCE, IS CONTINUOUSLY MOVING FORWARD... A **SPIRITUAL EVOLUTION.**
TO BECOME MORE, ONE MUST STRIVE TO RETAIN THE MEMORY, THE WORDS, AND THE DEEDS OF THE PAST IN ORDER TO STRENGTHEN HIS VIRTUE AND ACHIEVE HIS TRUE FORM.
THAT IS WHY YOU ARE HERE...

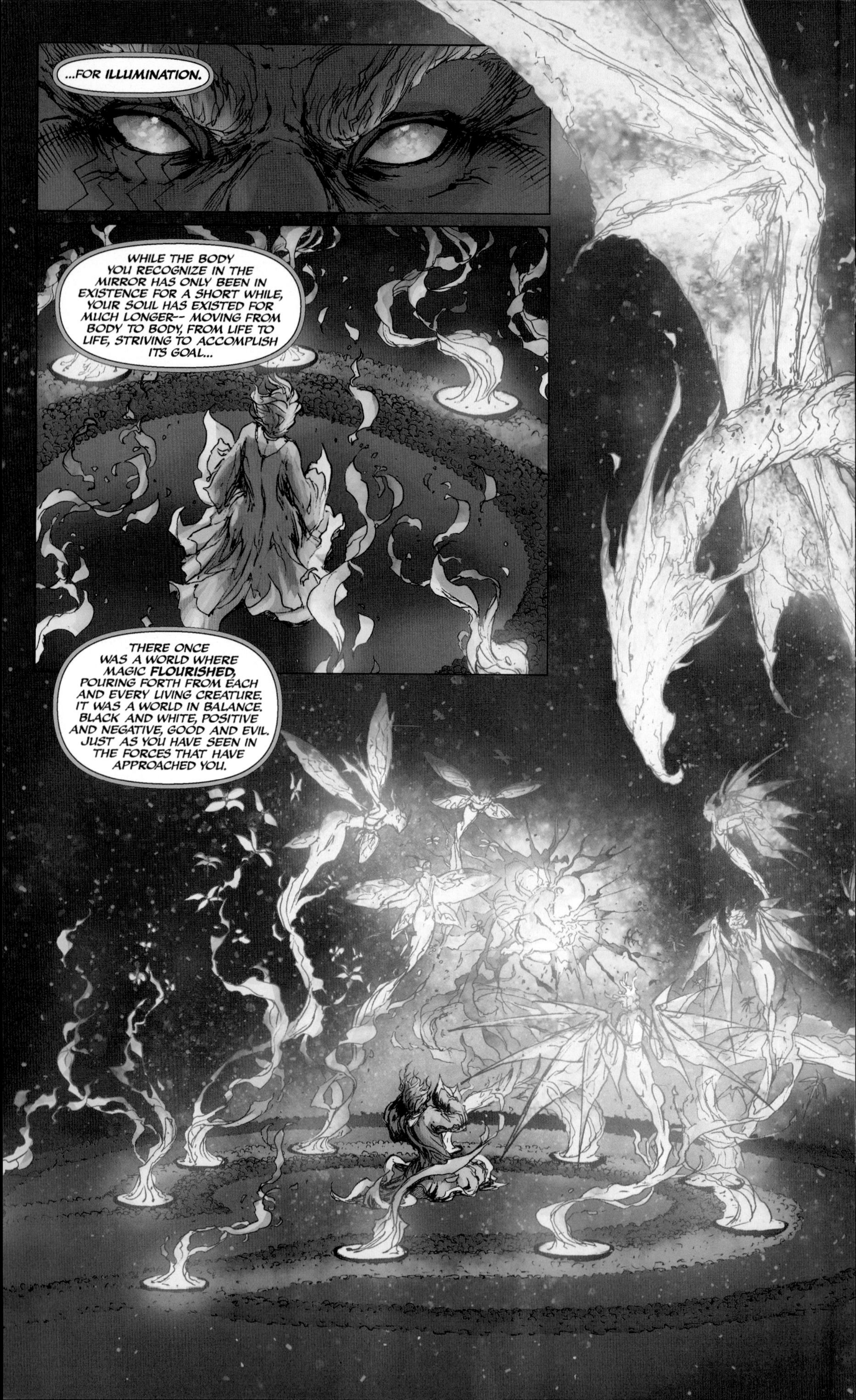
...FOR ILLUMINATION.
WHILE THE BODY YOU RECOGNIZE IN THE MIRROR HAS ONLY BEEN IN EXISTENCE FOR A SHORT WHILE, YOUR SOUL HAS EXISTED FOR MUCH LONGER-- MOVING FROM BODY TO BODY, FROM LIFE TO LIFE, STRIVING TO ACCOMPLISH ITS GOAL...
THERE ONCE WAS A WORLD WHERE MAGIC FLOURISHED, POURING FORTH FROM EACH AND EVERY LIVING CREATURE. IT WAS A WORLD IN BALANCE. BLACK AND WHITE, POSITIVE AND NEGATIVE, GOOD AND EVIL. JUST AS YOU HAVE SEEN IN THE FORCES THAT HAVE APPROACHED YOU.

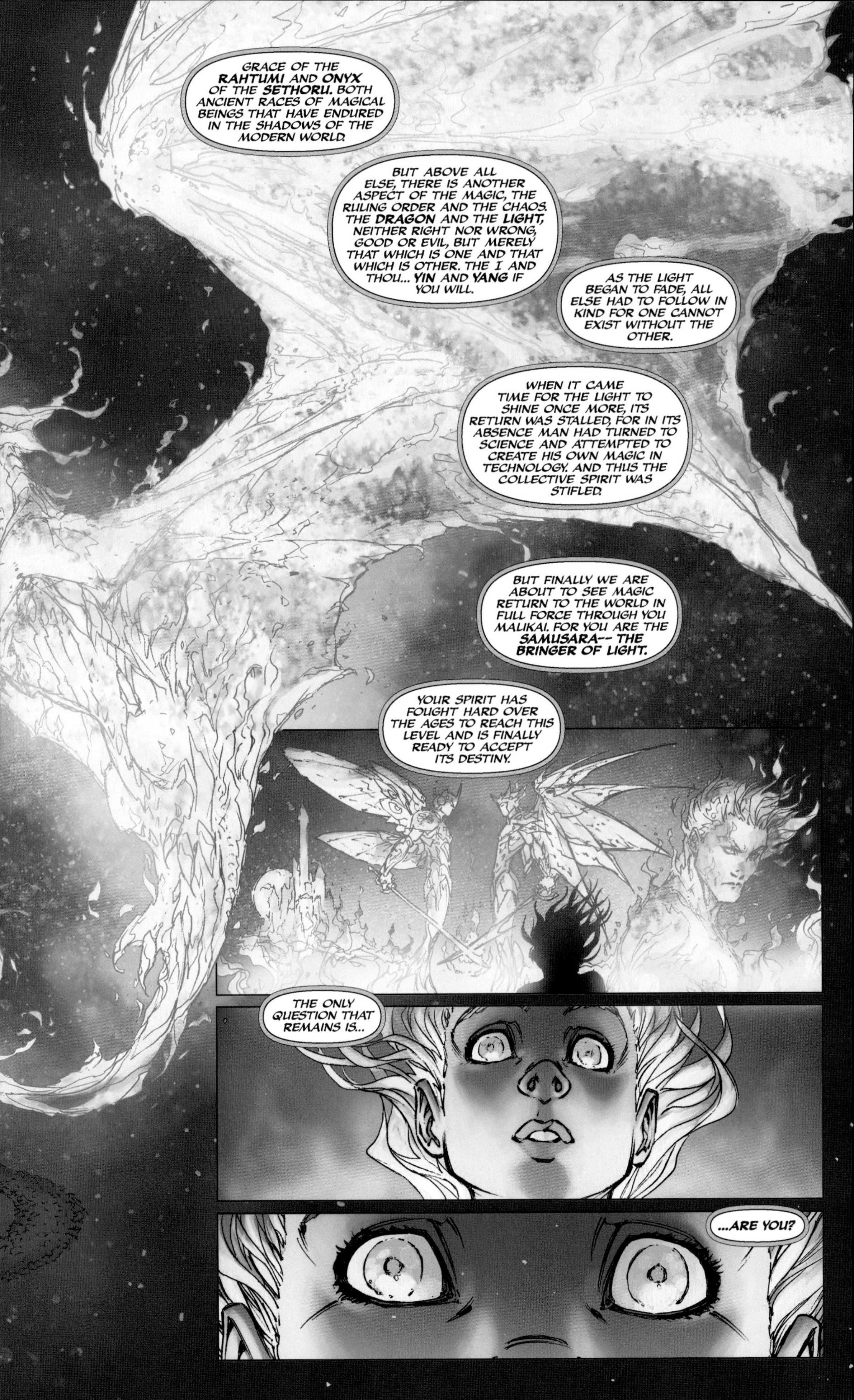
GRACE OF THE RAHTUMI AND ONYX OF THE SETHORU. BOTH ANCIENT RACES OF MAGICAL BEINGS THAT HAVE ENDURED IN THE SHADOWS OF THE MODERN WORLD.
BUT ABOVE ALL ELSE, THERE IS ANOTHER ASPECT OF THE MAGIC, THE RULING ORDER AND THE CHAOS. THE DRAGON AND THE LIGHT, NEITHER RIGHT NOR WRONG, GOOD OR EVIL, BUT MERELY THAT WHICH IS ONE AND THAT WHICH IS OTHER. THE I AND THOU... YIN AND YANG IF YOU WILL.
AS THE LIGHT BEGAN TO FADE, ALL ELSE HAD TO FOLLOW IN KIND FOR ONE CANNOT EXIST WITHOUT THE OTHER.
WHEN IT CAME TIME FOR THE LIGHT TO SHINE ONCE MORE, ITS RETURN WAS STALLED, FOR IN ITS ABSENCE MAN HAD TURNED TO SCIENCE AND ATTEMPTED TO CREATE HIS OWN MAGIC IN TECHNOLOGY. AND THUS THE COLLECTIVE SPIRIT WAS STIFLED.
BUT FINALLY WE ARE ABOUT TO SEE MAGIC RETURN TO THE WORLD IN FULL FORCE THROUGH YOU MALIKAI. FOR YOU ARE THE SAMUSARA-- THE BRINGER OF LIGHT.
YOUR SPIRIT HAS FOUGHT HARD OVER THE AGES TO REACH THIS LEVEL AND IS FINALLY READY TO ACCEPT ITS DESTINY.
THE ONLY QUESTION THAT REMAINS IS...
...ARE YOU?

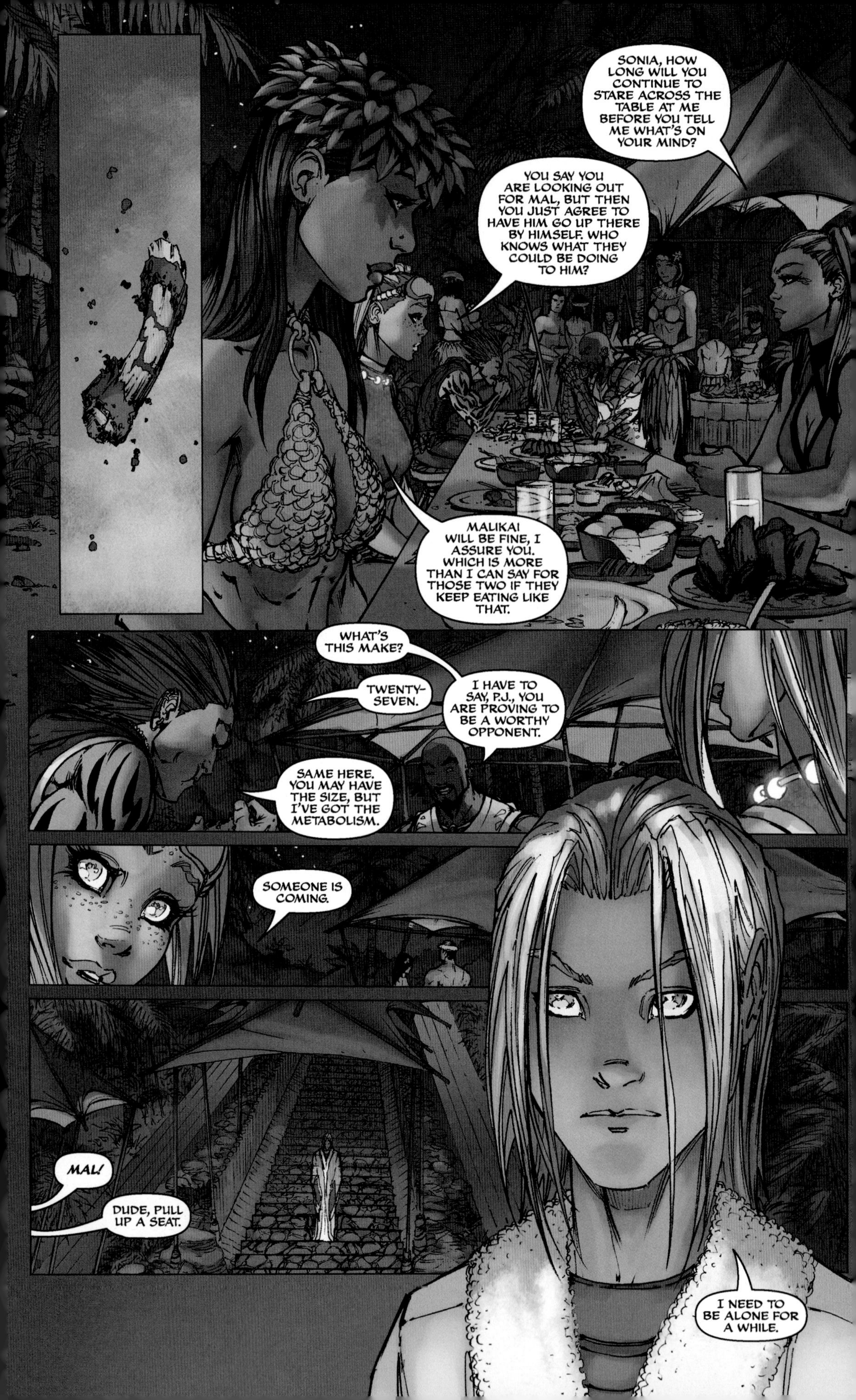
SONIA, HOW LONG WILL YOU CONTINUE TO STARE ACROSS THE TABLE AT ME BEFORE YOU TELL ME WHAT'S ON YOUR MIND?
YOU SAY YOU ARE LOOKING OUT FOR MAL, BUT THEN YOU JUST AGREE TO HAVE HIM GO UP THERE BY HIMSELF. WHO KNOWS WHAT THEY COULD BE DOING TO HIM?
MALIKAI WILL BE FINE, I ASSURE YOU. WHICH IS MORE THAN I CAN SAY FOR THOSE TWO IF THEY KEEP EATING LIKE THAT.
WHAT'S THIS MAKE?
TWENTY-SEVEN.
I HAVE TO SAY, P.J., YOU ARE PROVING TO BE A WORTHY OPPONENT.
SAME HERE. YOU MAY HAVE THE SIZE, BUT I'VE GOT THE METABOLISM.
SOMEONE IS COMING.
MAL!
DUDE, PULL UP A SEAT.
I NEED TO BE ALONE FOR A WHILE.

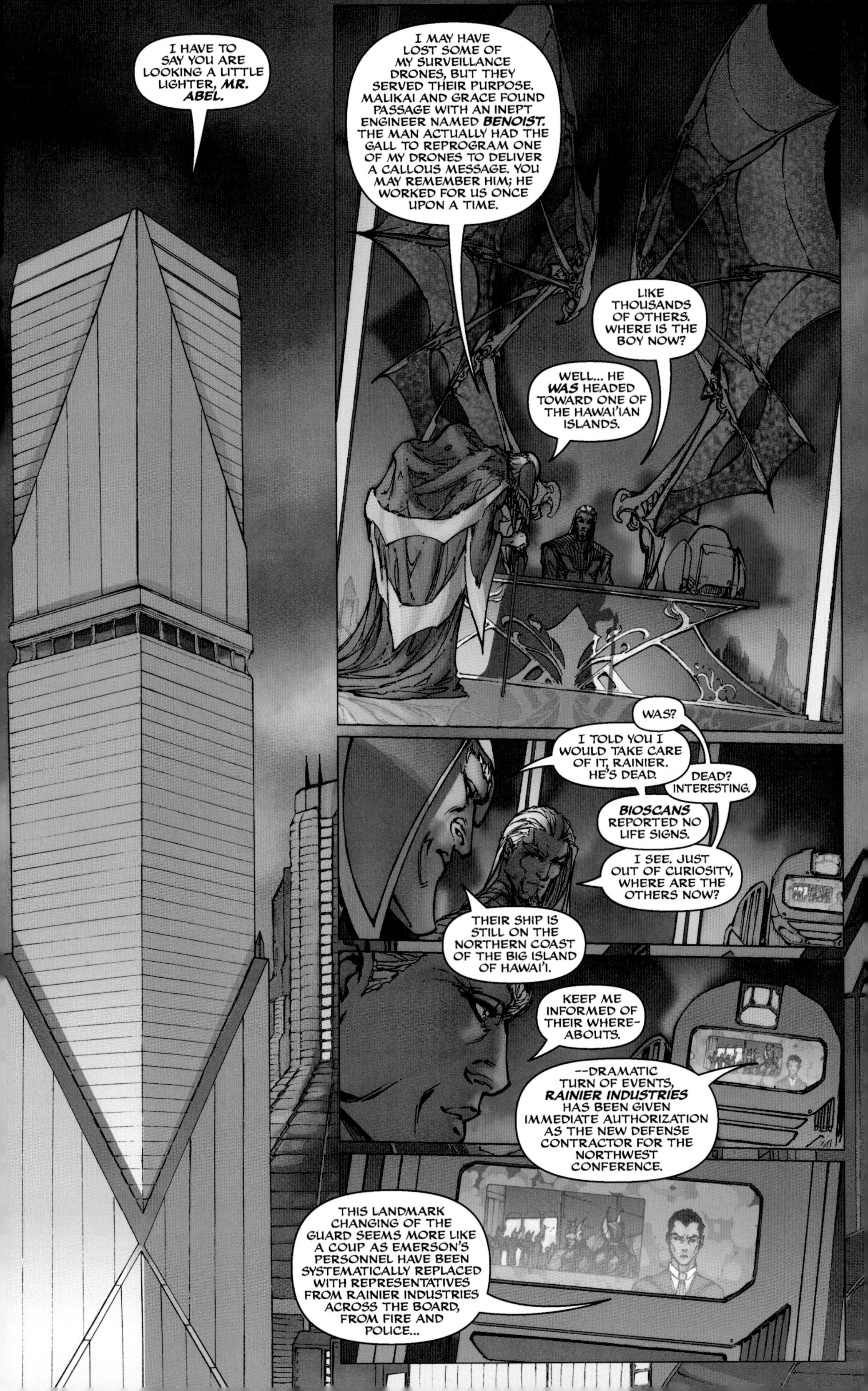
I HAVE TO SAY YOU ARE LOOKING A LITTLE LIGHTER, MR. ABEL.
I MAY HAVE LOST SOME OF MY SURVEILLANCE DRONES, BUT THEY SERVED THEIR PURPOSE. MALIKAI AND GRACE FOUND PASSAGE WITH AN INEPT ENGINEER NAMED BENOIST. THE MAN ACTUALLY HAD THE GALL TO REPROGRAM ONE OF MY DRONES TO DELIVER A CALLOUS MESSAGE. YOU MAY REMEMBER HIM; HE WORKED FOR US ONCE UPON A TIME.
LIKE THOUSANDS OF OTHERS. WHERE IS THE BOY NOW?
WELL... HE WAS HEADED TOWARD ONE OF THE HAWAI'IAN ISLANDS.
WAS?
I TOLD YOU I WOULD TAKE CARE OF IT, RAINIER. HE'S DEAD.
DEAD? INTERESTING.
BIOSCANS REPORTED NO LIFE SIGNS.
I SEE. JUST OUT OF CURIOSITY, WHERE ARE THE OTHERS NOW?
THEIR SHIP IS STILL ON THE NORTHERN COAST OF THE BIG ISLAND OF HAWAI'I.
KEEP ME INFORMED OF THEIR WHERE-ABOUTS.
--DRAMATIC TURN OF EVENTS, RAINIER INDUSTRIES HAS BEEN GIVEN IMMEDIATE AUTHORIZATION AS THE NEW DEFENSE CONTRACTOR FOR THE NORTHWEST CONFERENCE.
THIS LANDMARK CHANGING OF THE GUARD SEEMS MORE LIKE A COUP AS EMERSON'S PERSONNEL HAVE BEEN SYSTEMATICALLY REPLACED WITH REPRESENTATIVES FROM RAINIER INDUSTRIES ACROSS THE BOARD, FROM FIRE AND POLICE...

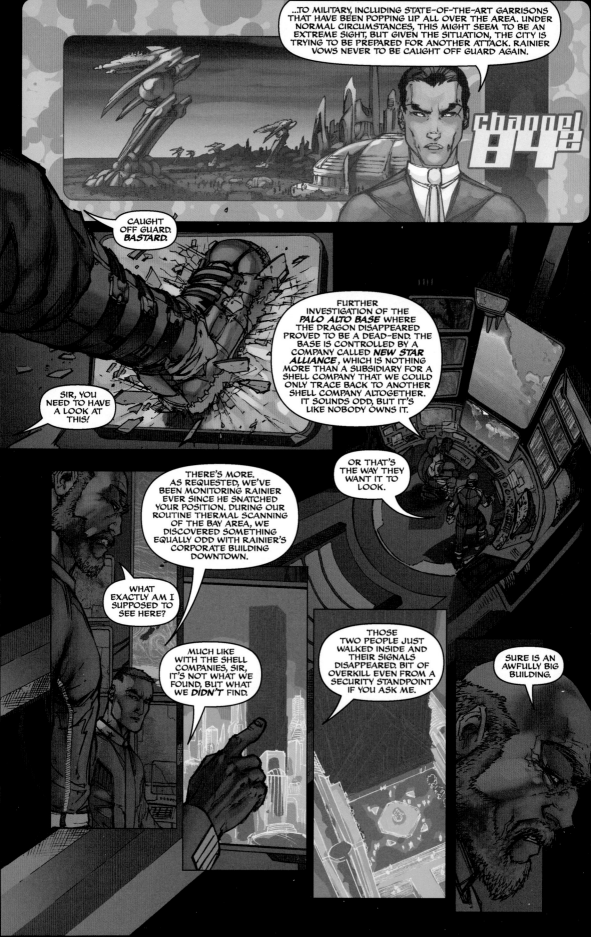

...TO MILITARY, INCLUDING STATE-OF-THE-ART GARRISONS THAT HAVE BEEN POPPING UP ALL OVER THE AREA. UNDER NORMAL CIRCUMSTANCES, THIS MIGHT SEEM TO BE AN EXTREME SIGHT, BUT GIVEN THE SITUATION, THE CITY IS TRYING TO BE PREPARED FOR ANOTHER ATTACK. RAINIER VOWS NEVER TO BE CAUGHT OFF GUARD AGAIN.

channel 84²

CAUGHT OFF GUARD. *BASTARD.*

SIR, YOU NEED TO HAVE A LOOK AT THIS!

FURTHER INVESTIGATION OF THE *PALO ALTO BASE* WHERE THE DRAGON DISAPPEARED PROVED TO BE A DEAD-END. THE BASE IS CONTROLLED BY A COMPANY CALLED *NEW STAR ALLIANCE*, WHICH IS NOTHING MORE THAN A SUBSIDIARY FOR A SHELL COMPANY THAT WE COULD ONLY TRACE BACK TO ANOTHER SHELL COMPANY ALTOGETHER. IT SOUNDS ODD, BUT IT'S LIKE NOBODY OWNS IT.

OR THAT'S THE WAY THEY WANT IT TO LOOK.

THERE'S MORE. AS REQUESTED, WE'VE BEEN MONITORING RAINIER EVER SINCE HE SNATCHED YOUR POSITION. DURING OUR ROUTINE THERMAL SCANNING OF THE BAY AREA, WE DISCOVERED SOMETHING EQUALLY ODD WITH RAINIER'S CORPORATE BUILDING DOWNTOWN.

WHAT EXACTLY AM I SUPPOSED TO SEE HERE?

MUCH LIKE WITH THE SHELL COMPANIES, SIR, IT'S NOT WHAT WE FOUND, BUT WHAT WE *DIDN'T* FIND.

THOSE TWO PEOPLE JUST WALKED INSIDE AND THEIR SIGNALS DISAPPEARED. BIT OF OVERKILL EVEN FROM A SECURITY STANDPOINT IF YOU ASK ME.

SURE IS AN AWFULLY BIG BUILDING.

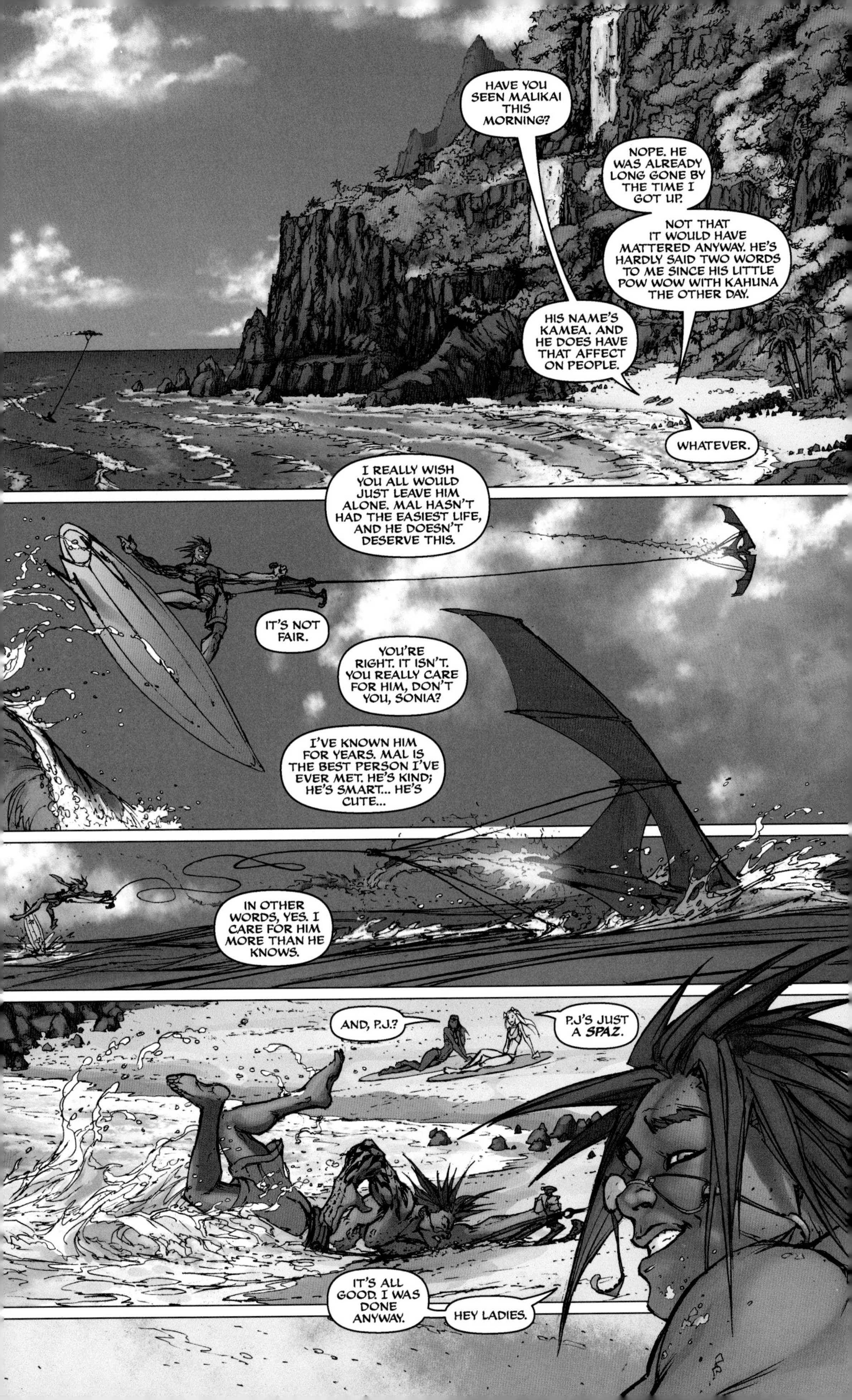
HAVE YOU SEEN MALIKAI THIS MORNING?
NOPE. HE WAS ALREADY LONG GONE BY THE TIME I GOT UP.
NOT THAT IT WOULD HAVE MATTERED ANYWAY. HE'S HARDLY SAID TWO WORDS TO ME SINCE HIS LITTLE POW WOW WITH KAHUNA THE OTHER DAY.
HIS NAME'S KAMEA. AND HE DOES HAVE THAT AFFECT ON PEOPLE.
WHATEVER.
I REALLY WISH YOU ALL WOULD JUST LEAVE HIM ALONE. MAL HASN'T HAD THE EASIEST LIFE, AND HE DOESN'T DESERVE THIS.
IT'S NOT FAIR.
YOU'RE RIGHT. IT ISN'T. YOU REALLY CARE FOR HIM, DON'T YOU, SONIA?
I'VE KNOWN HIM FOR YEARS. MAL IS THE BEST PERSON I'VE EVER MET. HE'S KIND; HE'S SMART... HE'S CUTE...
IN OTHER WORDS, YES. I CARE FOR HIM MORE THAN HE KNOWS.
AND, P.J.?
P.J.'S JUST A *SPAZ*.
IT'S ALL GOOD. I WAS DONE ANYWAY.
HEY LADIES.

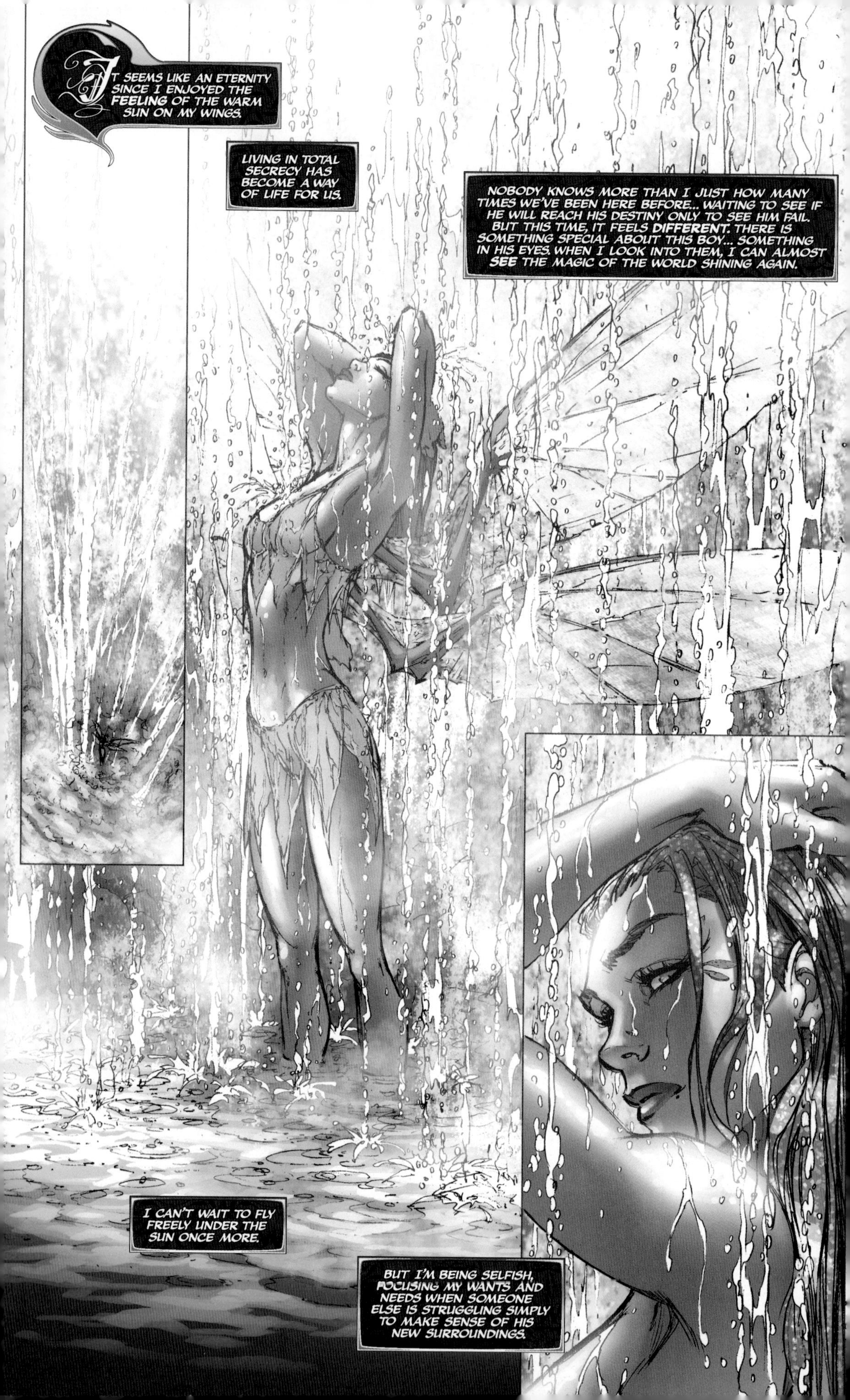
It seems like an eternity since I enjoyed the **FEELING** of the warm sun on my wings.
LIVING IN TOTAL SECRECY HAS BECOME A WAY OF LIFE FOR US.
NOBODY KNOWS MORE THAN I JUST HOW MANY TIMES WE'VE BEEN HERE BEFORE... WAITING TO SEE IF HE WILL REACH HIS DESTINY ONLY TO SEE HIM FAIL. BUT THIS TIME, IT FEELS **DIFFERENT**. THERE IS SOMETHING SPECIAL ABOUT THIS BOY... SOMETHING IN HIS EYES. WHEN I LOOK INTO THEM, I CAN ALMOST **SEE** THE MAGIC OF THE WORLD SHINING AGAIN.
I CAN'T WAIT TO FLY FREELY UNDER THE SUN ONCE MORE.
BUT I'M BEING SELFISH, FOCUSING MY WANTS AND NEEDS WHEN SOMEONE ELSE IS STRUGGLING SIMPLY TO MAKE SENSE OF HIS NEW SURROUNDINGS.

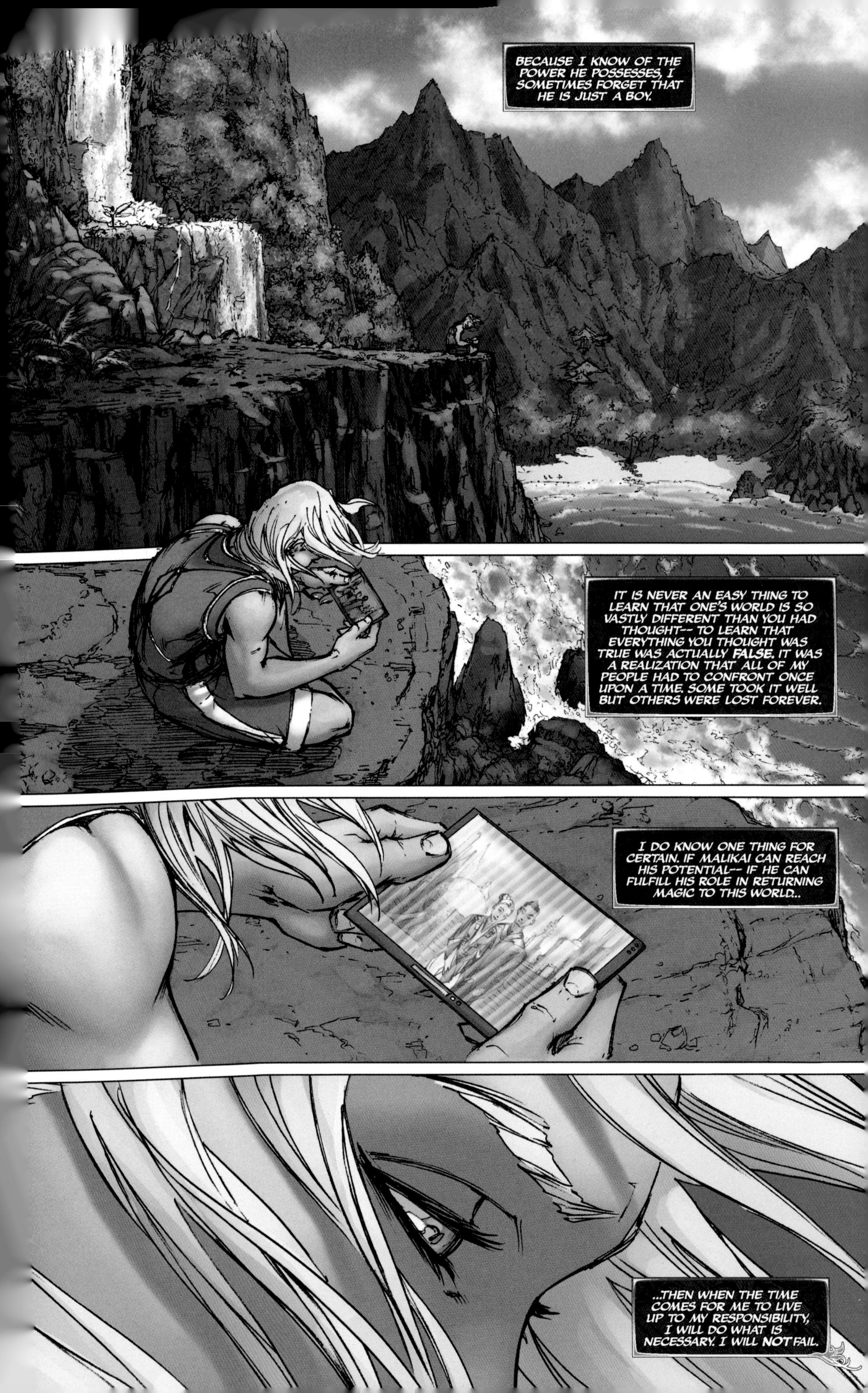
BECAUSE I KNOW OF THE POWER HE POSSESSES, I SOMETIMES FORGET THAT HE IS JUST A BOY.
IT IS NEVER AN EASY THING TO LEARN THAT ONE'S WORLD IS SO VASTLY DIFFERENT THAN YOU HAD THOUGHT-- TO LEARN THAT EVERYTHING YOU THOUGHT WAS TRUE WAS ACTUALLY FALSE. IT WAS A REALIZATION THAT ALL OF MY PEOPLE HAD TO CONFRONT ONCE UPON A TIME. SOME TOOK IT WELL BUT OTHERS WERE LOST FOREVER.
I DO KNOW ONE THING FOR CERTAIN. IF MALIKAI CAN REACH HIS POTENTIAL-- IF HE CAN FULFILL HIS ROLE IN RETURNING MAGIC TO THIS WORLD...
...THEN WHEN THE TIME COMES FOR ME TO LIVE UP TO MY RESPONSIBILITY, I WILL DO WHAT IS NECESSARY. I WILL NOT FAIL.

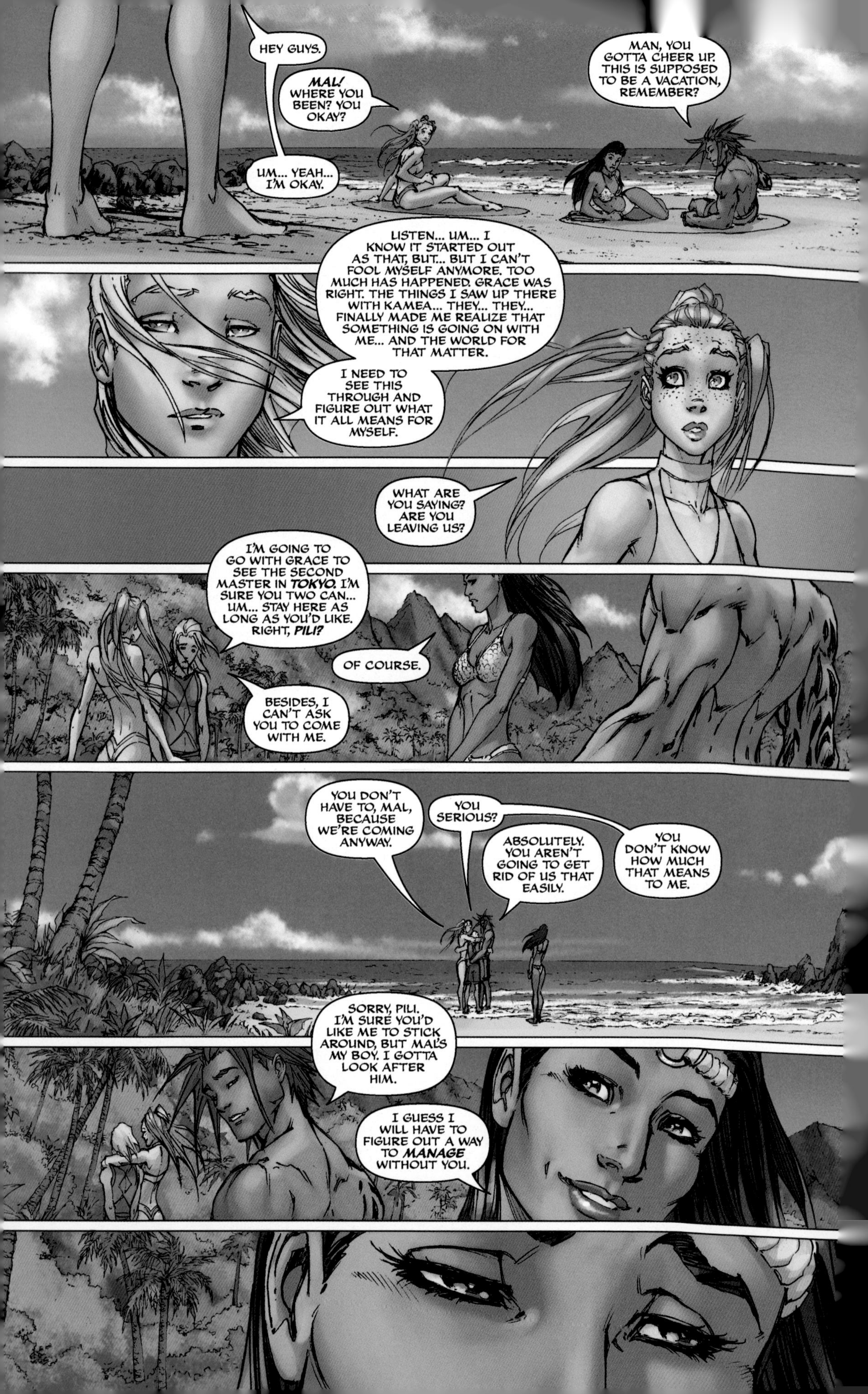
HEY GUYS.
MAL! WHERE YOU BEEN? YOU OKAY?
MAN, YOU GOTTA CHEER UP. THIS IS SUPPOSED TO BE A VACATION, REMEMBER?
UM... YEAH... I'M OKAY.
LISTEN... UM... I KNOW IT STARTED OUT AS THAT, BUT... BUT I CAN'T FOOL MYSELF ANYMORE. TOO MUCH HAS HAPPENED. GRACE WAS RIGHT. THE THINGS I SAW UP THERE WITH KAMEA... THEY... THEY... FINALLY MADE ME REALIZE THAT SOMETHING IS GOING ON WITH ME... AND THE WORLD FOR THAT MATTER.
I NEED TO SEE THIS THROUGH AND FIGURE OUT WHAT IT ALL MEANS FOR MYSELF.
WHAT ARE YOU SAYING? ARE YOU LEAVING US?
I'M GOING TO GO WITH GRACE TO SEE THE SECOND MASTER IN TOKYO. I'M SURE YOU TWO CAN... UM... STAY HERE AS LONG AS YOU'D LIKE. RIGHT, PILI?
OF COURSE.
BESIDES, I CAN'T ASK YOU TO COME WITH ME.
YOU DON'T HAVE TO, MAL, BECAUSE WE'RE COMING ANYWAY.
YOU SERIOUS?
ABSOLUTELY. YOU AREN'T GOING TO GET RID OF US THAT EASILY.
YOU DON'T KNOW HOW MUCH THAT MEANS TO ME.
SORRY, PILI. I'M SURE YOU'D LIKE ME TO STICK AROUND, BUT MAL'S MY BOY. I GOTTA LOOK AFTER HIM.
I GUESS I WILL HAVE TO FIGURE OUT A WAY TO MANAGE WITHOUT YOU.

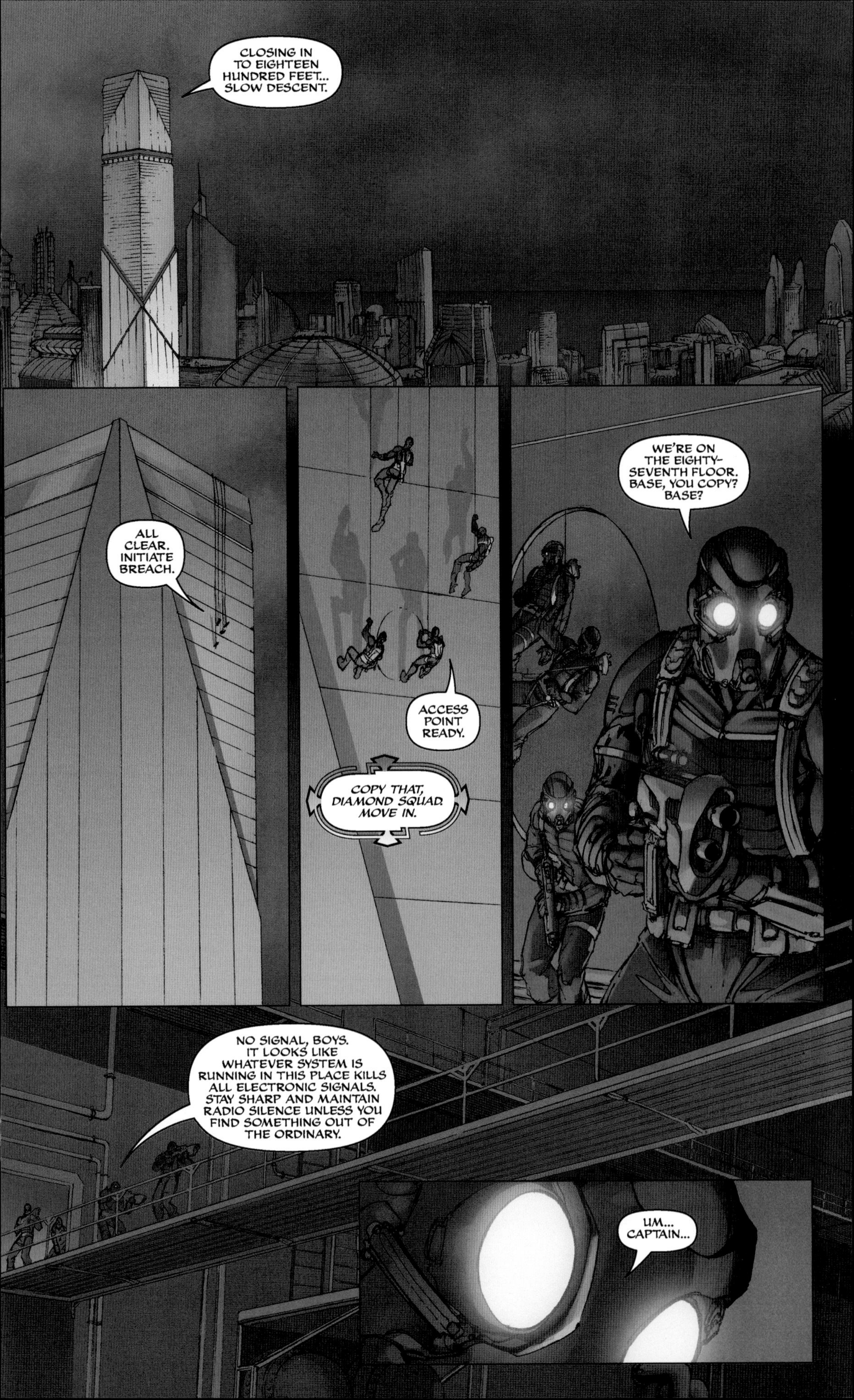
CLOSING IN TO EIGHTEEN HUNDRED FEET... SLOW DESCENT.
ALL CLEAR. INITIATE BREACH.
ACCESS POINT READY.
COPY THAT, DIAMOND SQUAD. MOVE IN.
WE'RE ON THE EIGHTY-SEVENTH FLOOR. BASE, YOU COPY? BASE?
NO SIGNAL, BOYS. IT LOOKS LIKE WHATEVER SYSTEM IS RUNNING IN THIS PLACE KILLS ALL ELECTRONIC SIGNALS. STAY SHARP AND MAINTAIN RADIO SILENCE UNLESS YOU FIND SOMETHING OUT OF THE ORDINARY.
UM... CAPTAIN...

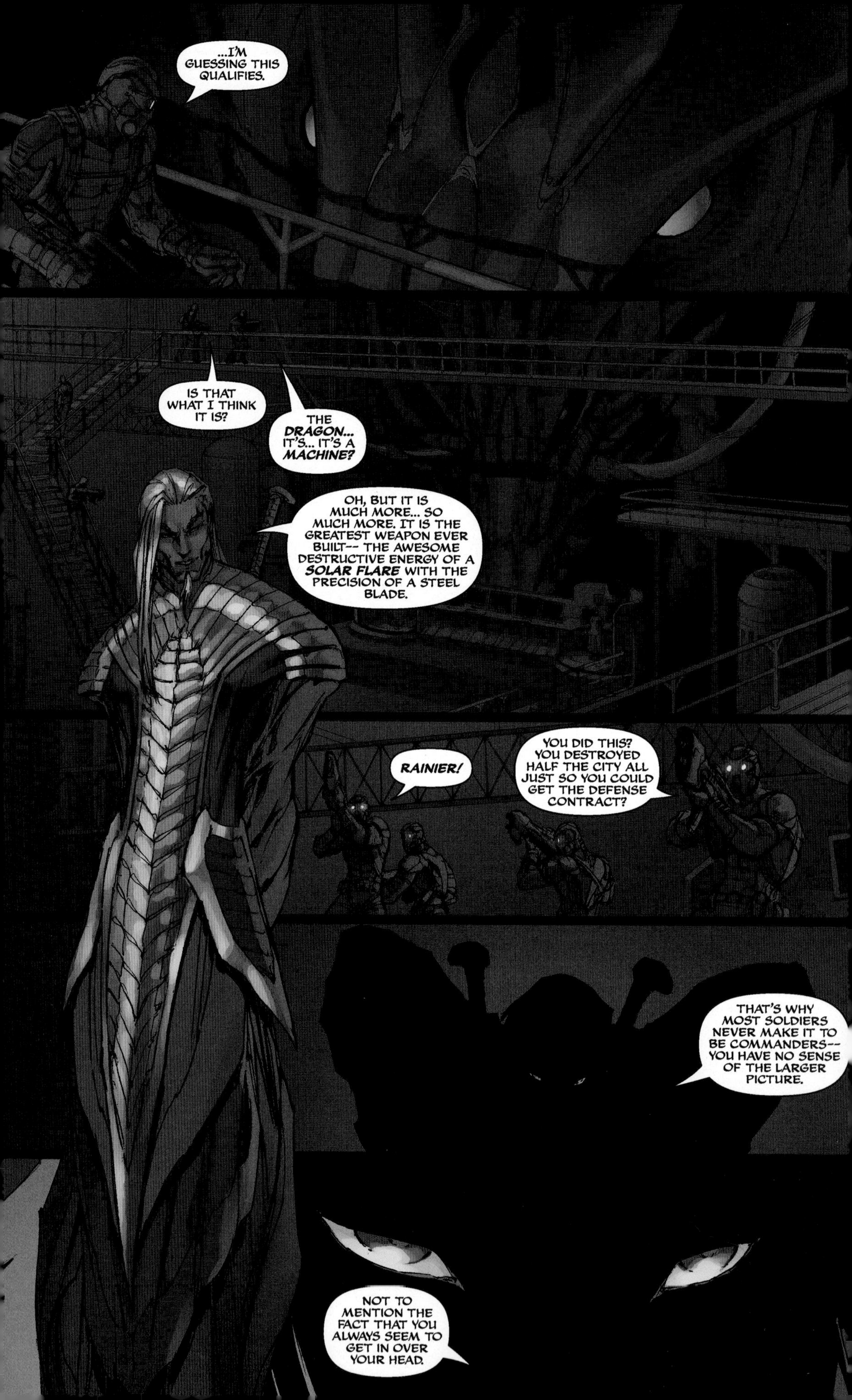
...I'M GUESSING THIS QUALIFIES.
IS THAT WHAT I THINK IT IS?
THE DRAGON... IT'S... IT'S A MACHINE?
OH, BUT IT IS MUCH MORE... SO MUCH MORE. IT IS THE GREATEST WEAPON EVER BUILT-- THE AWESOME DESTRUCTIVE ENERGY OF A SOLAR FLARE WITH THE PRECISION OF A STEEL BLADE.
RAINIER!
YOU DID THIS? YOU DESTROYED HALF THE CITY ALL JUST SO YOU COULD GET THE DEFENSE CONTRACT?
THAT'S WHY MOST SOLDIERS NEVER MAKE IT TO BE COMMANDERS-- YOU HAVE NO SENSE OF THE LARGER PICTURE.
NOT TO MENTION THE FACT THAT YOU ALWAYS SEEM TO GET IN OVER YOUR HEAD.

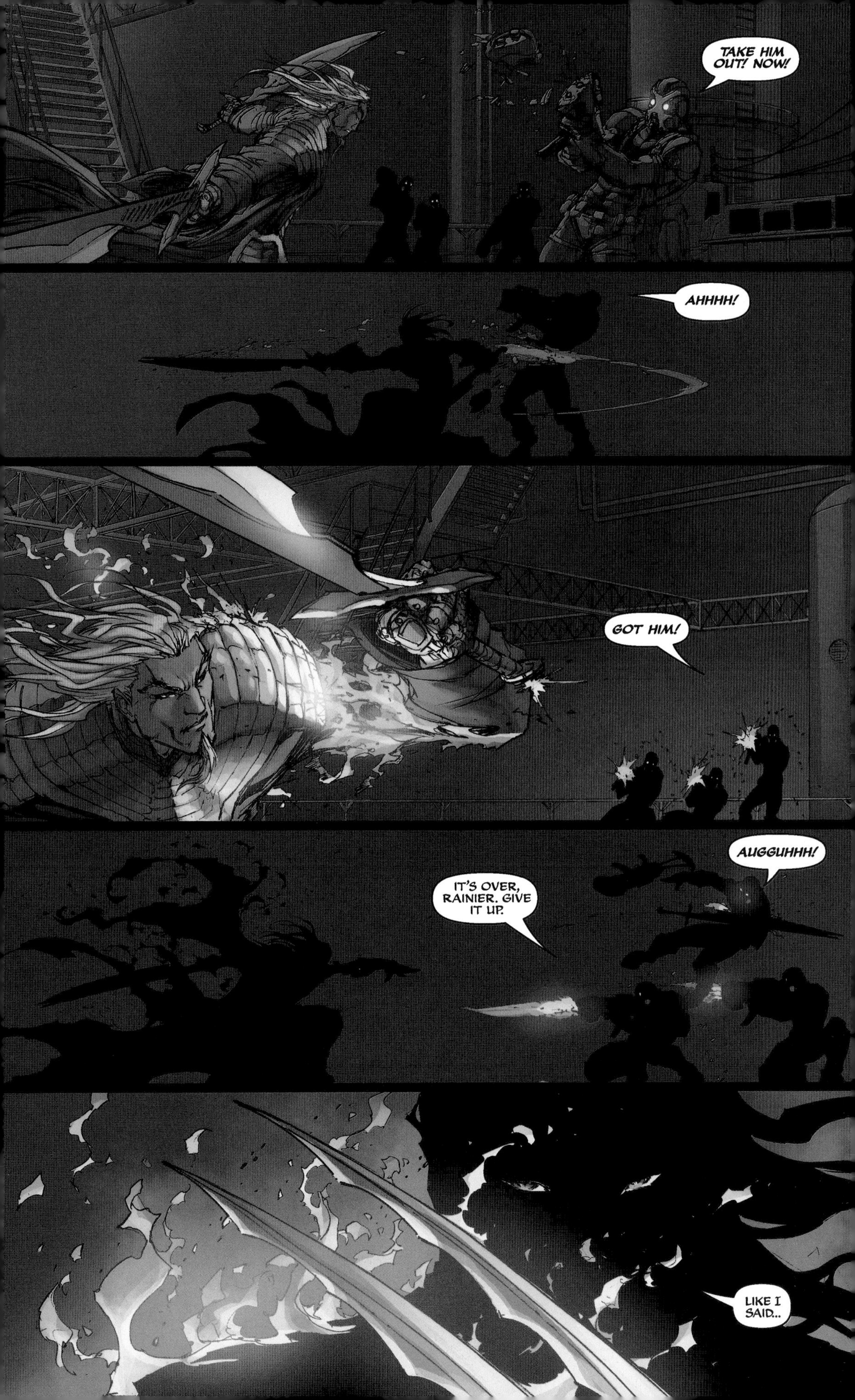
TAKE HIM OUT! NOW!
AHHHH!
GOT HIM!
AUGGUHHH!
IT'S OVER, RAINIER. GIVE IT UP.
LIKE I SAID...

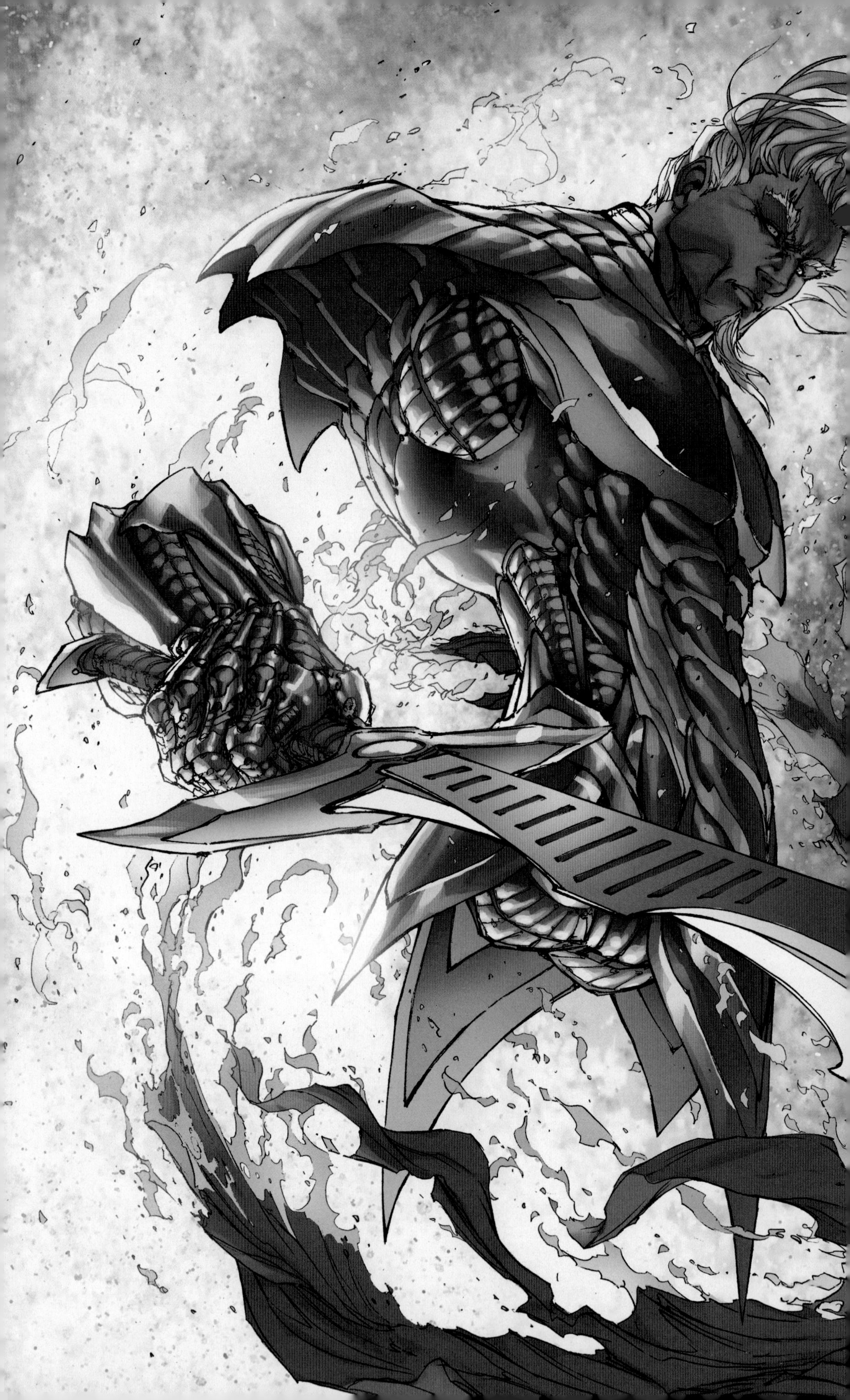

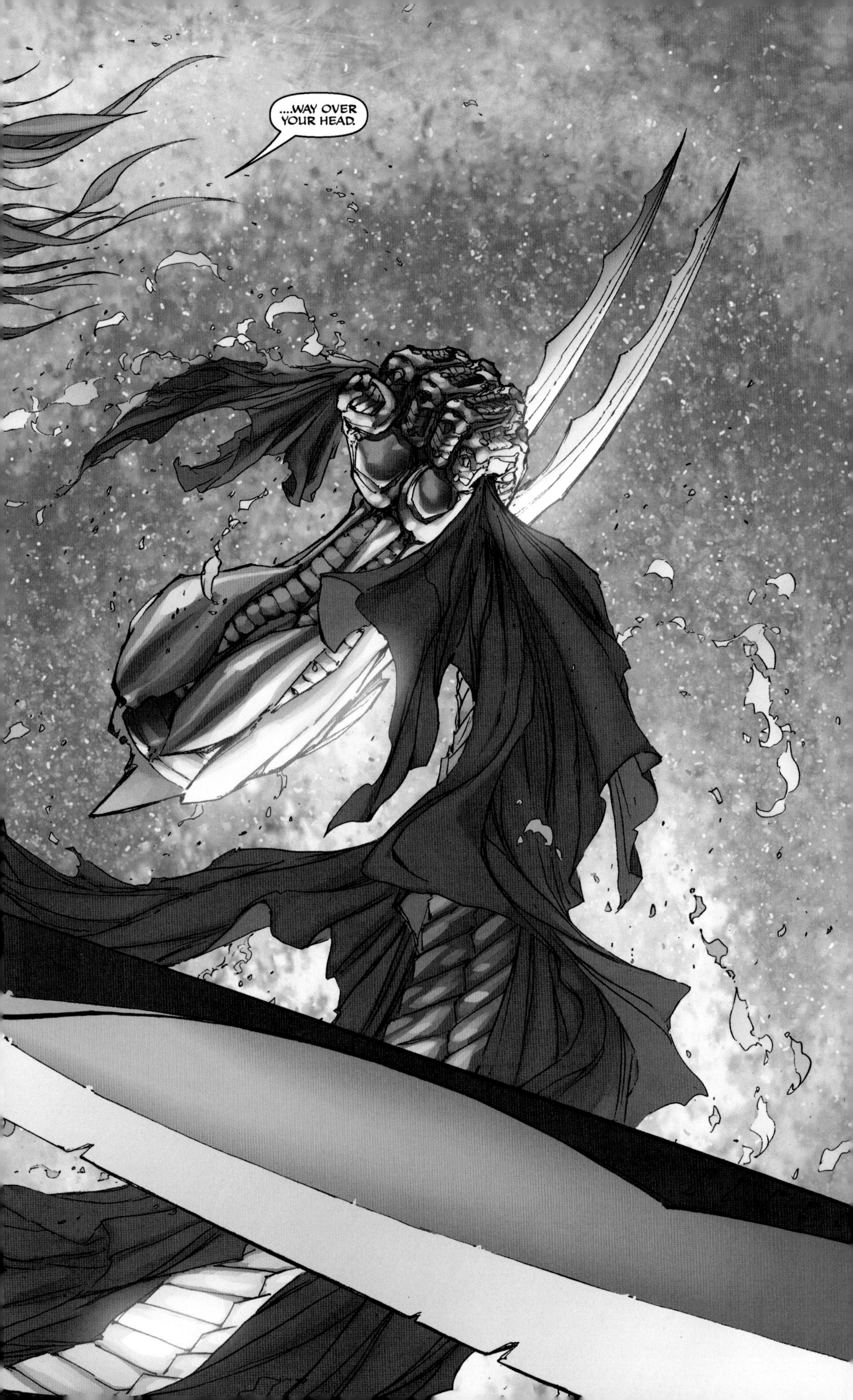
...WAY OVER YOUR HEAD.

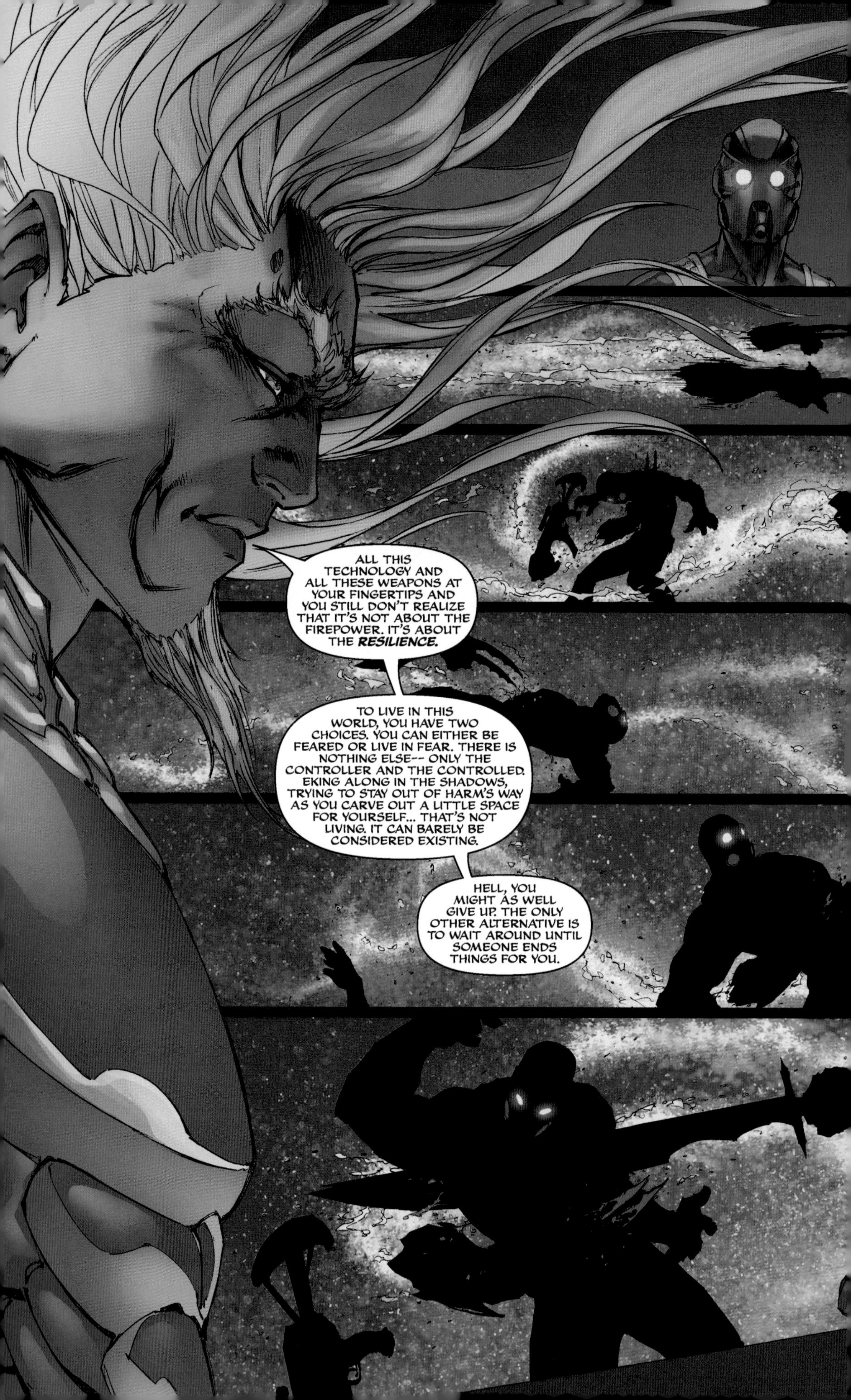
ALL THIS TECHNOLOGY AND ALL THESE WEAPONS AT YOUR FINGERTIPS AND YOU STILL DON'T REALIZE THAT IT'S NOT ABOUT THE FIREPOWER. IT'S ABOUT THE ***RESILIENCE.***
TO LIVE IN THIS WORLD, YOU HAVE TWO CHOICES. YOU CAN EITHER BE FEARED OR LIVE IN FEAR. THERE IS NOTHING ELSE-- ONLY THE CONTROLLER AND THE CONTROLLED. EKING ALONG IN THE SHADOWS, TRYING TO STAY OUT OF HARM'S WAY AS YOU CARVE OUT A LITTLE SPACE FOR YOURSELF... THAT'S NOT LIVING. IT CAN BARELY BE CONSIDERED EXISTING.
HELL, YOU MIGHT AS WELL GIVE UP. THE ONLY OTHER ALTERNATIVE IS TO WAIT AROUND UNTIL SOMEONE ENDS THINGS FOR YOU.

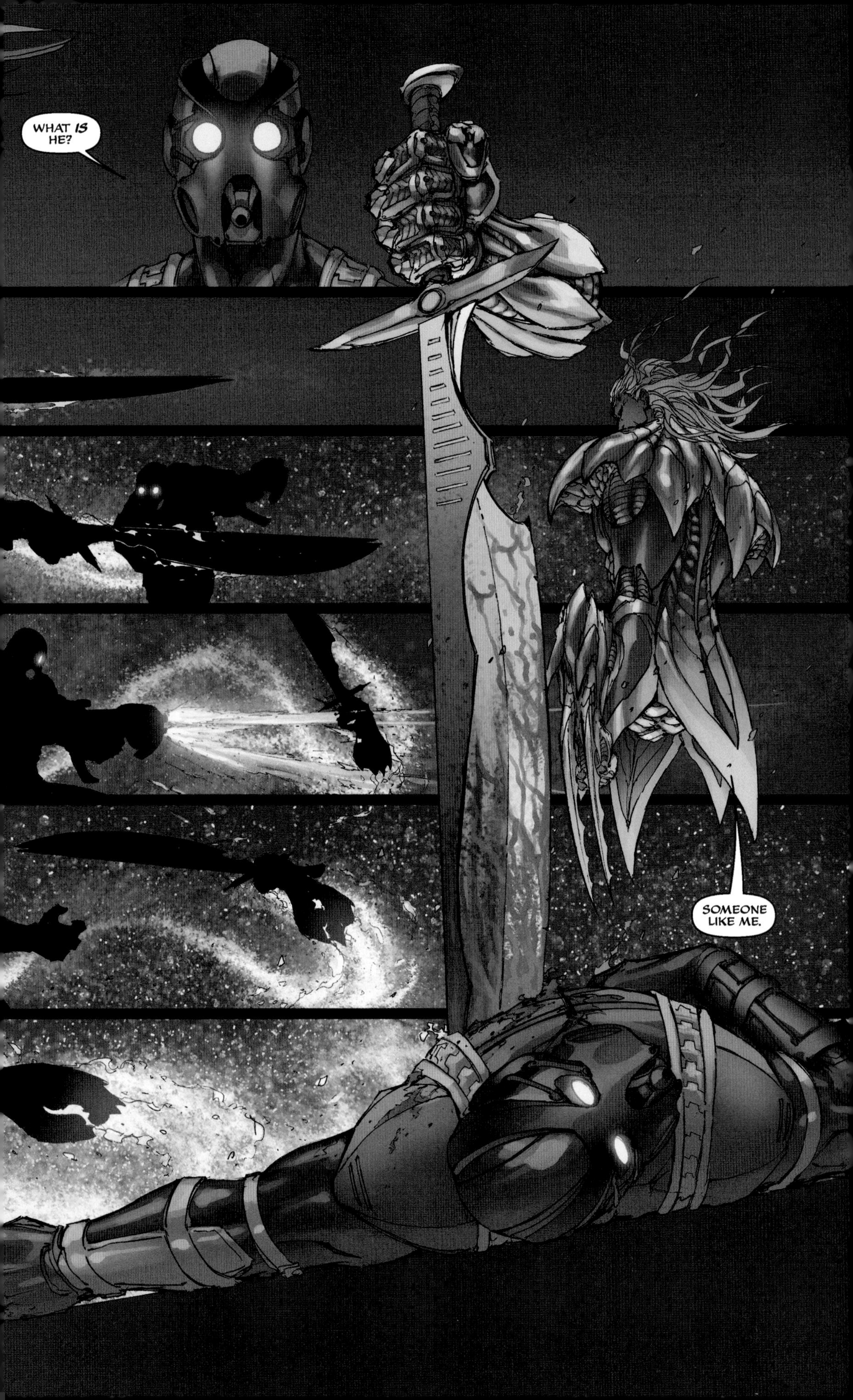
WHAT IS HE?
SOMEONE LIKE ME.

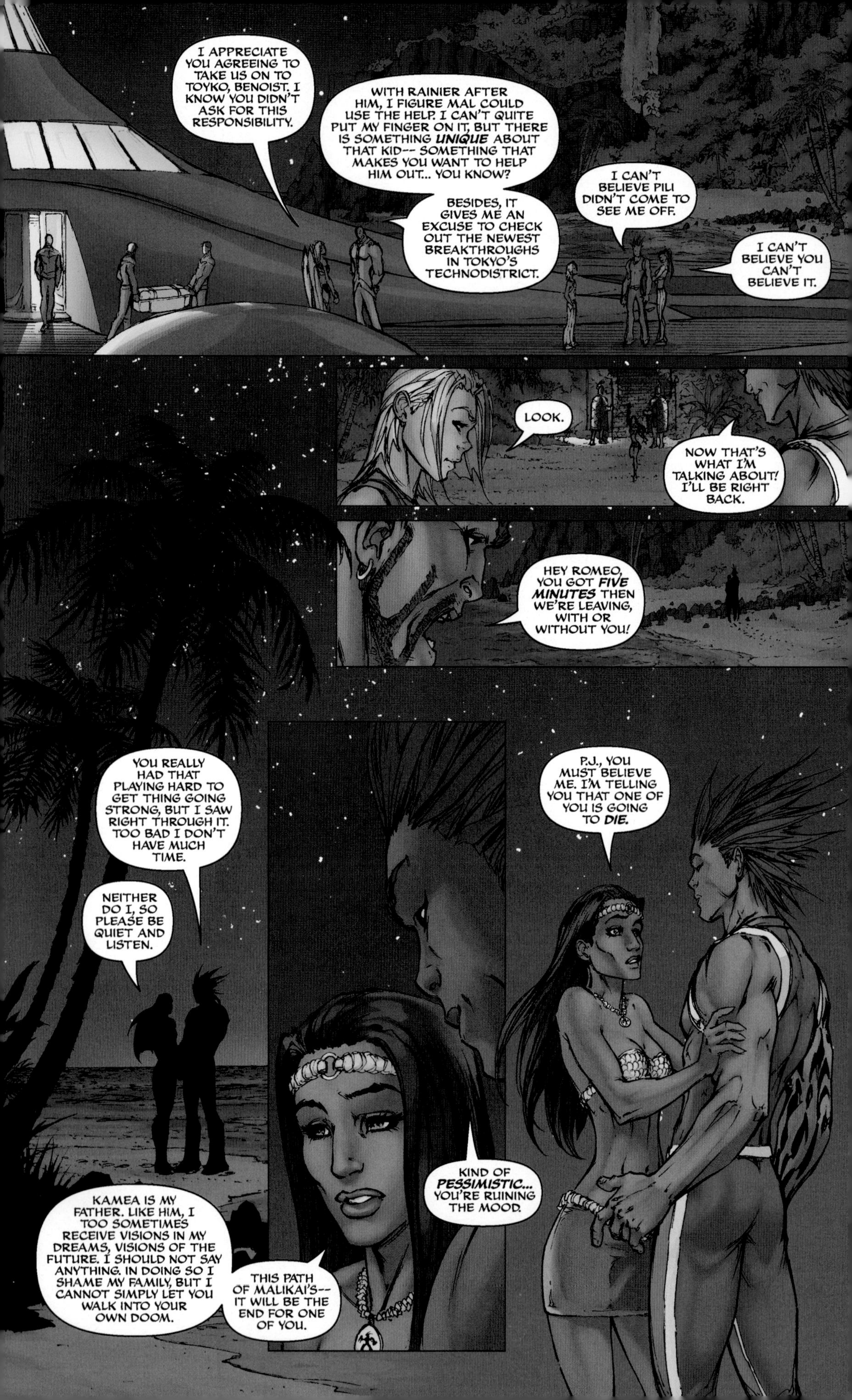
I APPRECIATE YOU AGREEING TO TAKE US ON TO TOYKO, BENOIST. I KNOW YOU DIDN'T ASK FOR THIS RESPONSIBILITY.
WITH RAINIER AFTER HIM, I FIGURE MAL COULD USE THE HELP. I CAN'T QUITE PUT MY FINGER ON IT, BUT THERE IS SOMETHING UNIQUE ABOUT THAT KID-- SOMETHING THAT MAKES YOU WANT TO HELP HIM OUT... YOU KNOW?
BESIDES, IT GIVES ME AN EXCUSE TO CHECK OUT THE NEWEST BREAKTHROUGHS IN TOKYO'S TECHNODISTRICT.
I CAN'T BELIEVE PILI DIDN'T COME TO SEE ME OFF.
I CAN'T BELIEVE YOU CAN'T BELIEVE IT.
LOOK.
NOW THAT'S WHAT I'M TALKING ABOUT! I'LL BE RIGHT BACK.
HEY ROMEO, YOU GOT FIVE MINUTES THEN WE'RE LEAVING, WITH OR WITHOUT YOU!
YOU REALLY HAD THAT PLAYING HARD TO GET THING GOING STRONG, BUT I SAW RIGHT THROUGH IT. TOO BAD I DON'T HAVE MUCH TIME.
NEITHER DO I, SO PLEASE BE QUIET AND LISTEN.
KAMEA IS MY FATHER. LIKE HIM, I TOO SOMETIMES RECEIVE VISIONS IN MY DREAMS, VISIONS OF THE FUTURE. I SHOULD NOT SAY ANYTHING. IN DOING SO I SHAME MY FAMILY, BUT I CANNOT SIMPLY LET YOU WALK INTO YOUR OWN DOOM.
THIS PATH OF MALIKAI'S-- IT WILL BE THE END FOR ONE OF YOU.
KIND OF PESSIMISTIC... YOU'RE RUINING THE MOOD.
P.J., YOU MUST BELIEVE ME. I'M TELLING YOU THAT ONE OF YOU IS GOING TO DIE.

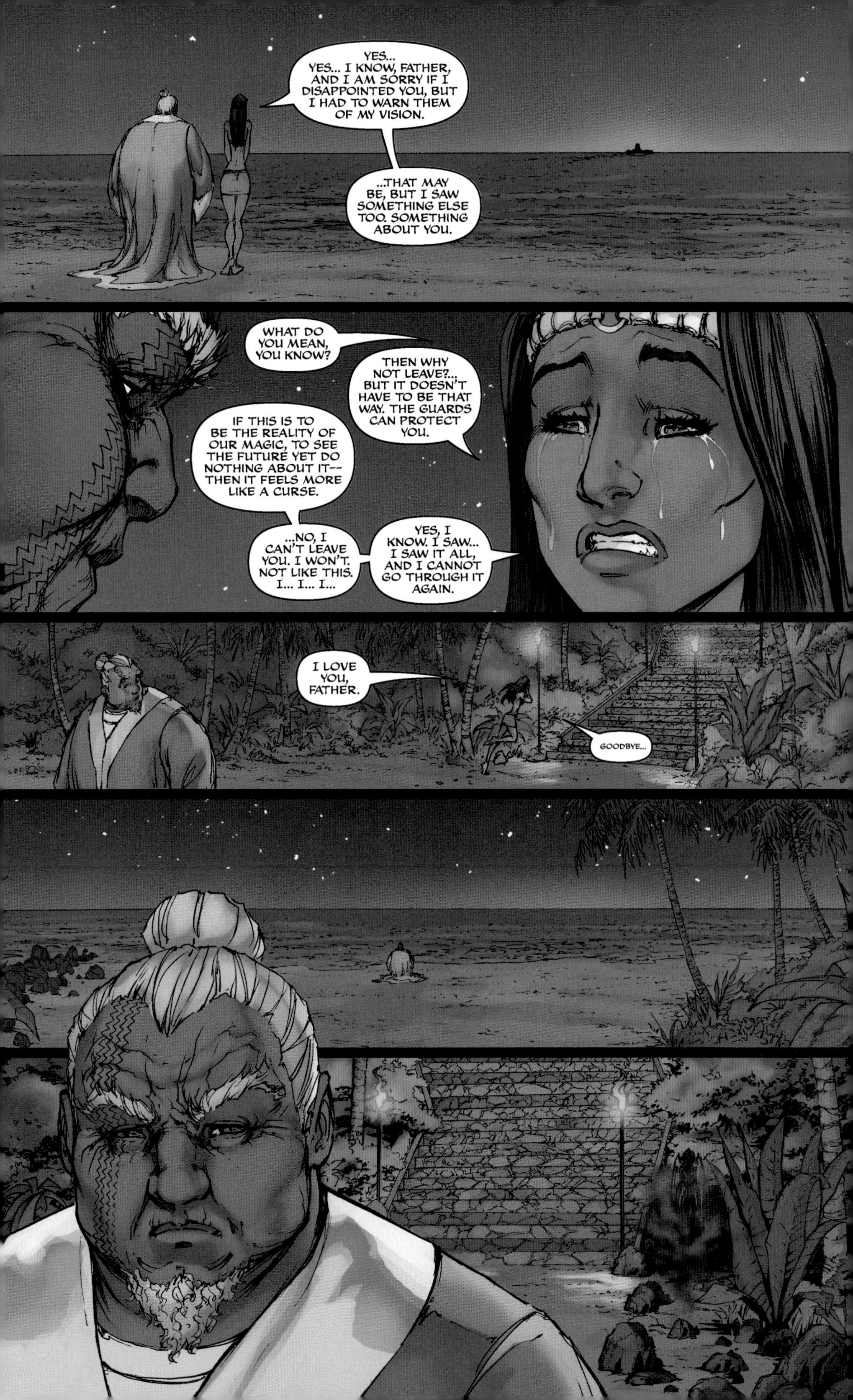
YES...
YES... I KNOW, FATHER, AND I AM SORRY IF I DISAPPOINTED YOU, BUT I HAD TO WARN THEM OF MY VISION.
...THAT MAY BE, BUT I SAW SOMETHING ELSE TOO. SOMETHING ABOUT YOU.
WHAT DO YOU MEAN, YOU KNOW?
THEN WHY NOT LEAVE?... BUT IT DOESN'T HAVE TO BE THAT WAY. THE GUARDS CAN PROTECT YOU.
IF THIS IS TO BE THE REALITY OF OUR MAGIC, TO SEE THE FUTURE YET DO NOTHING ABOUT IT-- THEN IT FEELS MORE LIKE A CURSE.
...NO, I CAN'T LEAVE YOU. I WON'T. NOT LIKE THIS. I... I... I...
YES, I KNOW. I SAW... I SAW IT ALL, AND I CANNOT GO THROUGH IT AGAIN.
I LOVE YOU, FATHER.
GOODBYE...

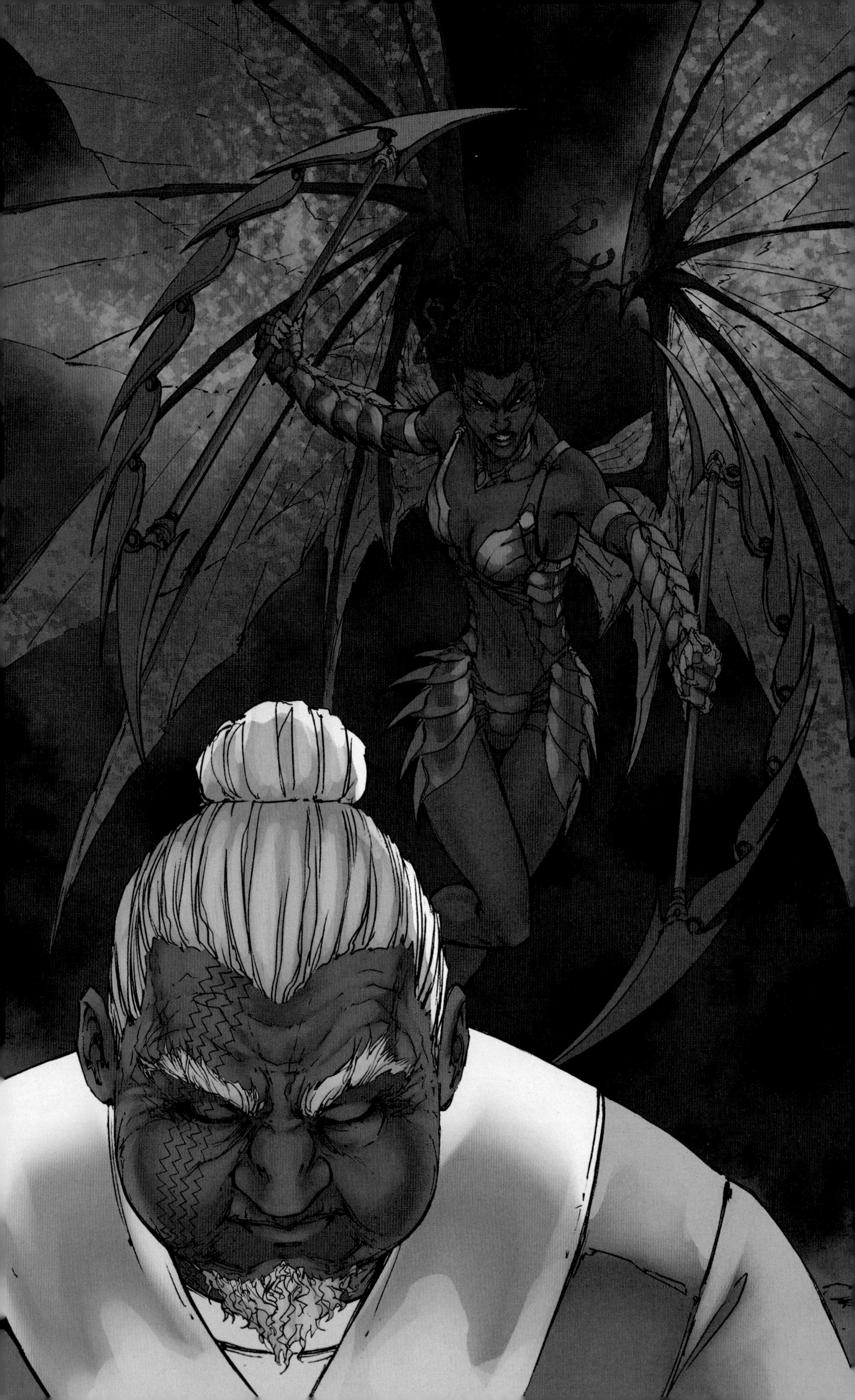

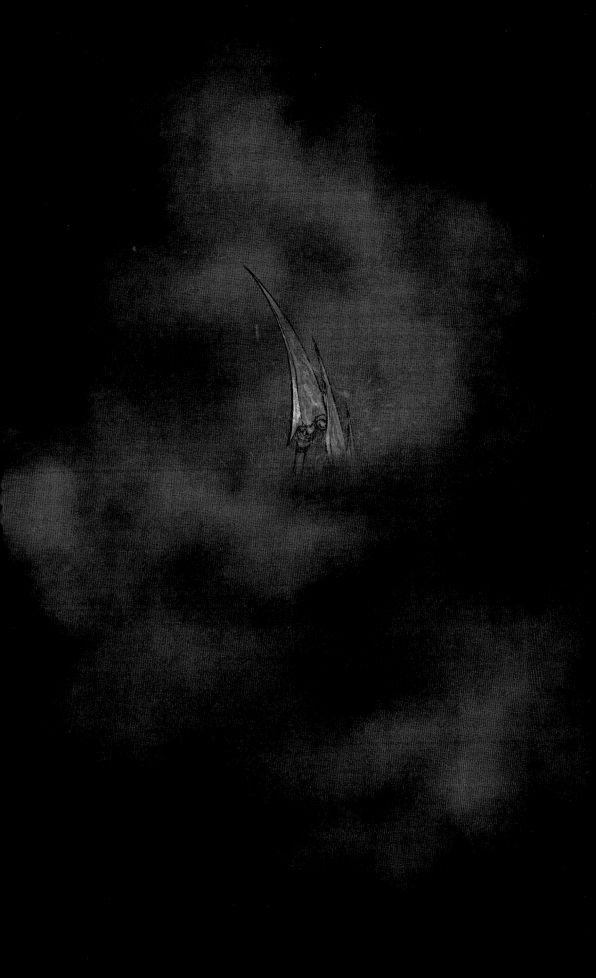

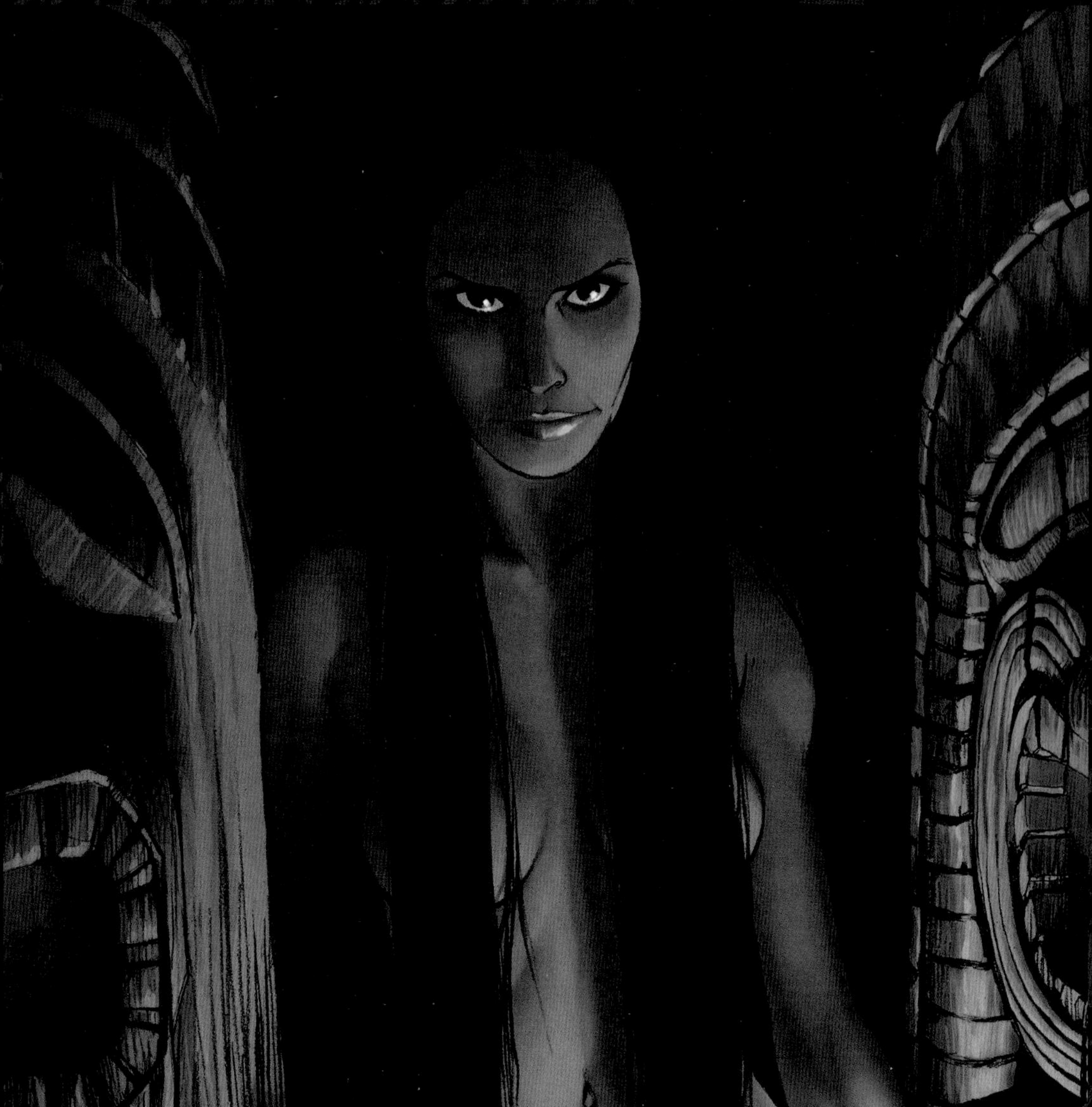

PILI
· PIN-UP FROM ASPEN SPLASH: 2008 SWIMSUIT SPECTACULAR ·
by
· PETER STEIGERWALD ·

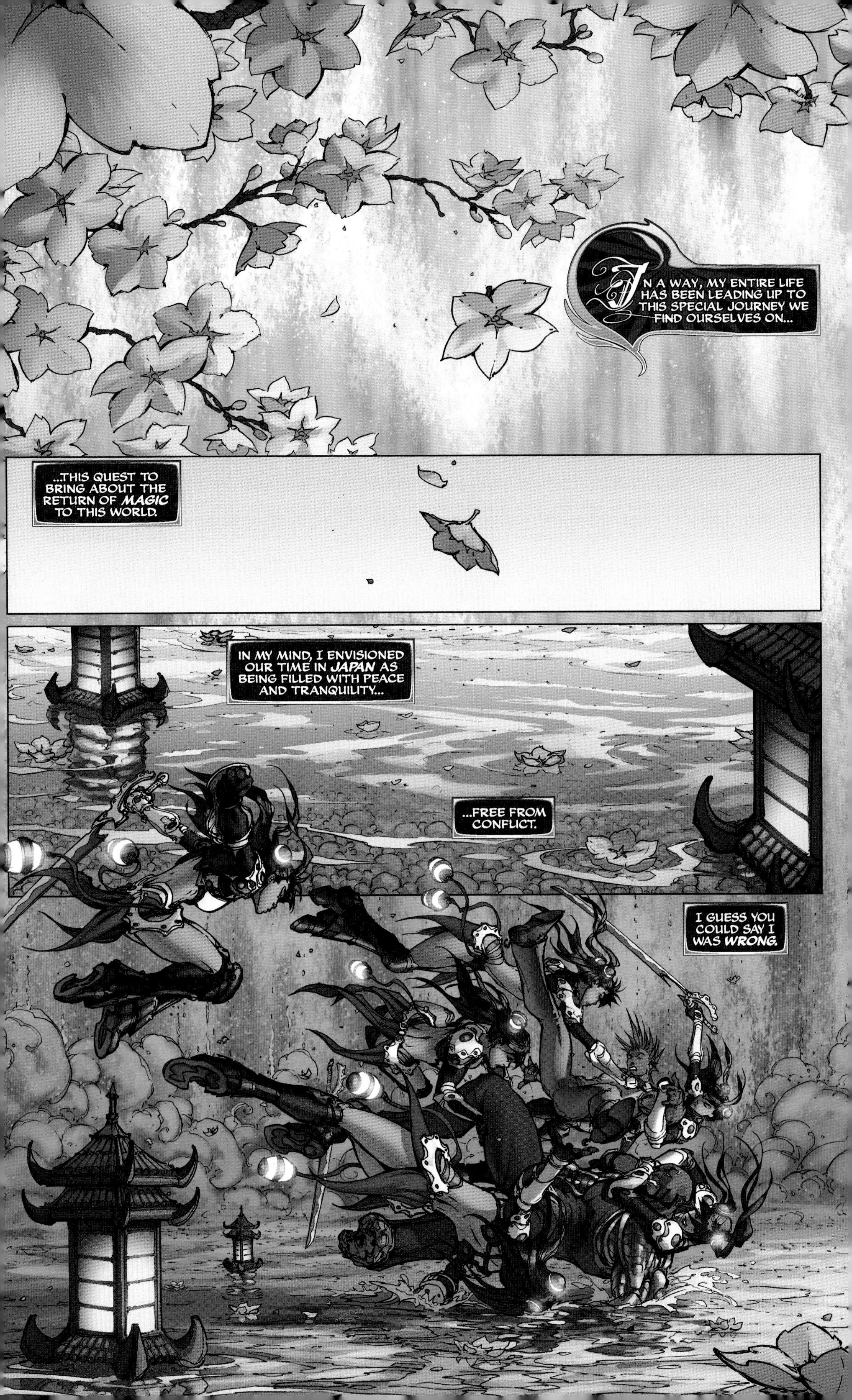
IN A WAY, MY ENTIRE LIFE HAS BEEN LEADING UP TO THIS SPECIAL JOURNEY WE FIND OURSELVES ON...
...THIS QUEST TO BRING ABOUT THE RETURN OF MAGIC TO THIS WORLD.
IN MY MIND, I ENVISIONED OUR TIME IN JAPAN AS BEING FILLED WITH PEACE AND TRANQUILITY...
...FREE FROM CONFLICT.
I GUESS YOU COULD SAY I WAS WRONG.

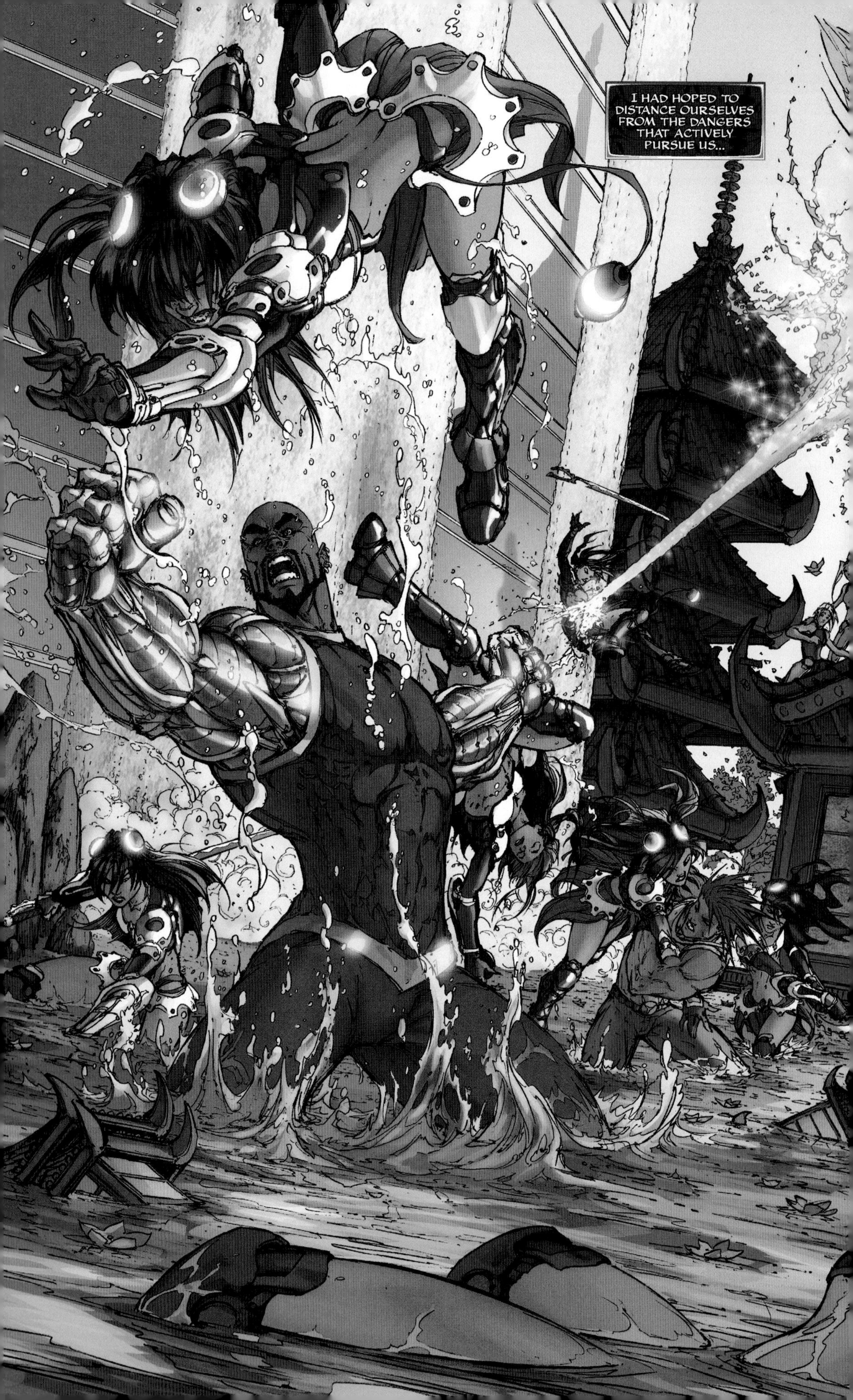
I HAD HOPED TO DISTANCE OURSELVES FROM THE DANGERS THAT ACTIVELY PURSUE US...

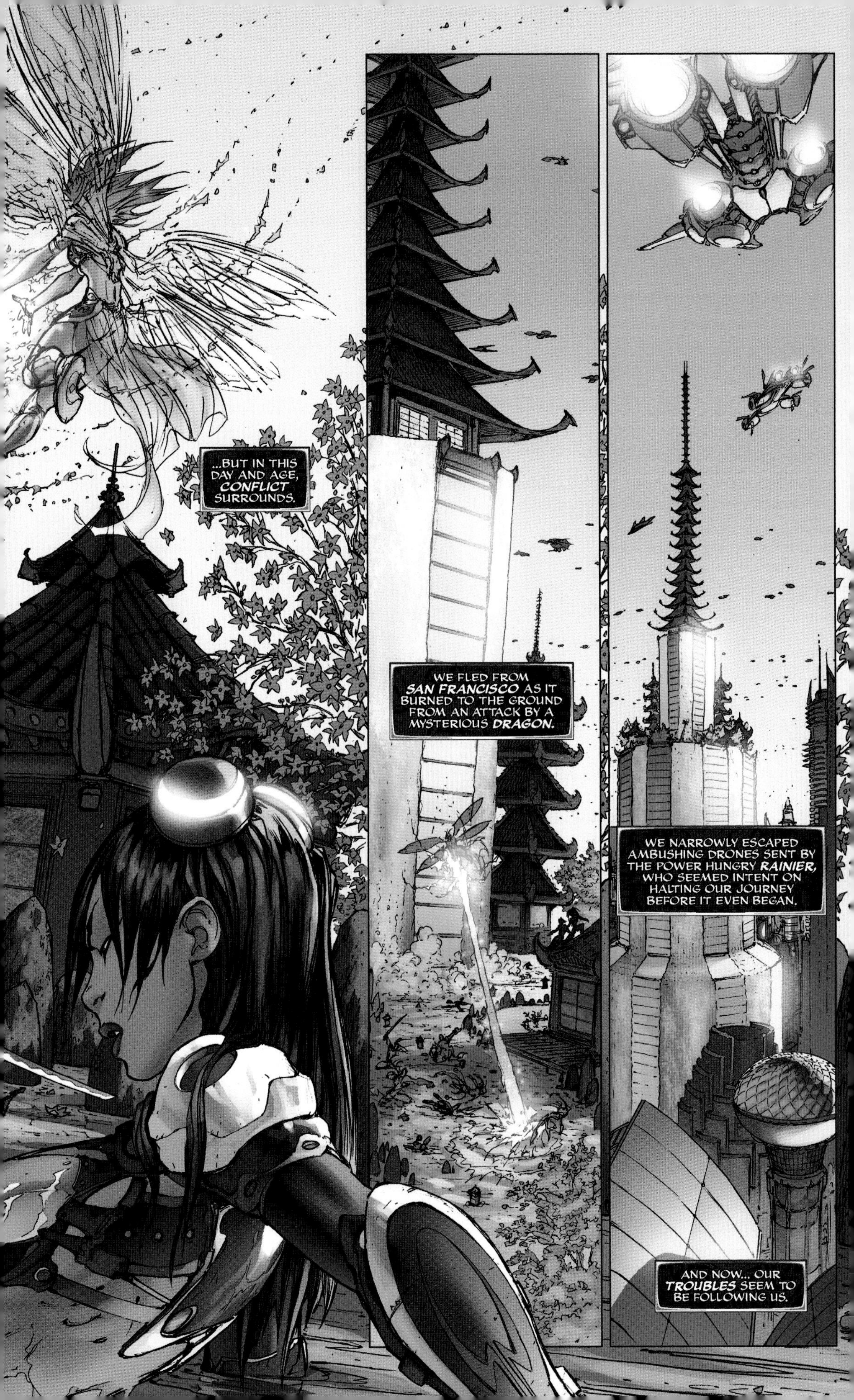
...BUT IN THIS DAY AND AGE, CONFLICT SURROUNDS.
WE FLED FROM SAN FRANCISCO AS IT BURNED TO THE GROUND FROM AN ATTACK BY A MYSTERIOUS DRAGON.
WE NARROWLY ESCAPED AMBUSHING DRONES SENT BY THE POWER HUNGRY RAINIER, WHO SEEMED INTENT ON HALTING OUR JOURNEY BEFORE IT EVEN BEGAN.
AND NOW... OUR TROUBLES SEEM TO BE FOLLOWING US.

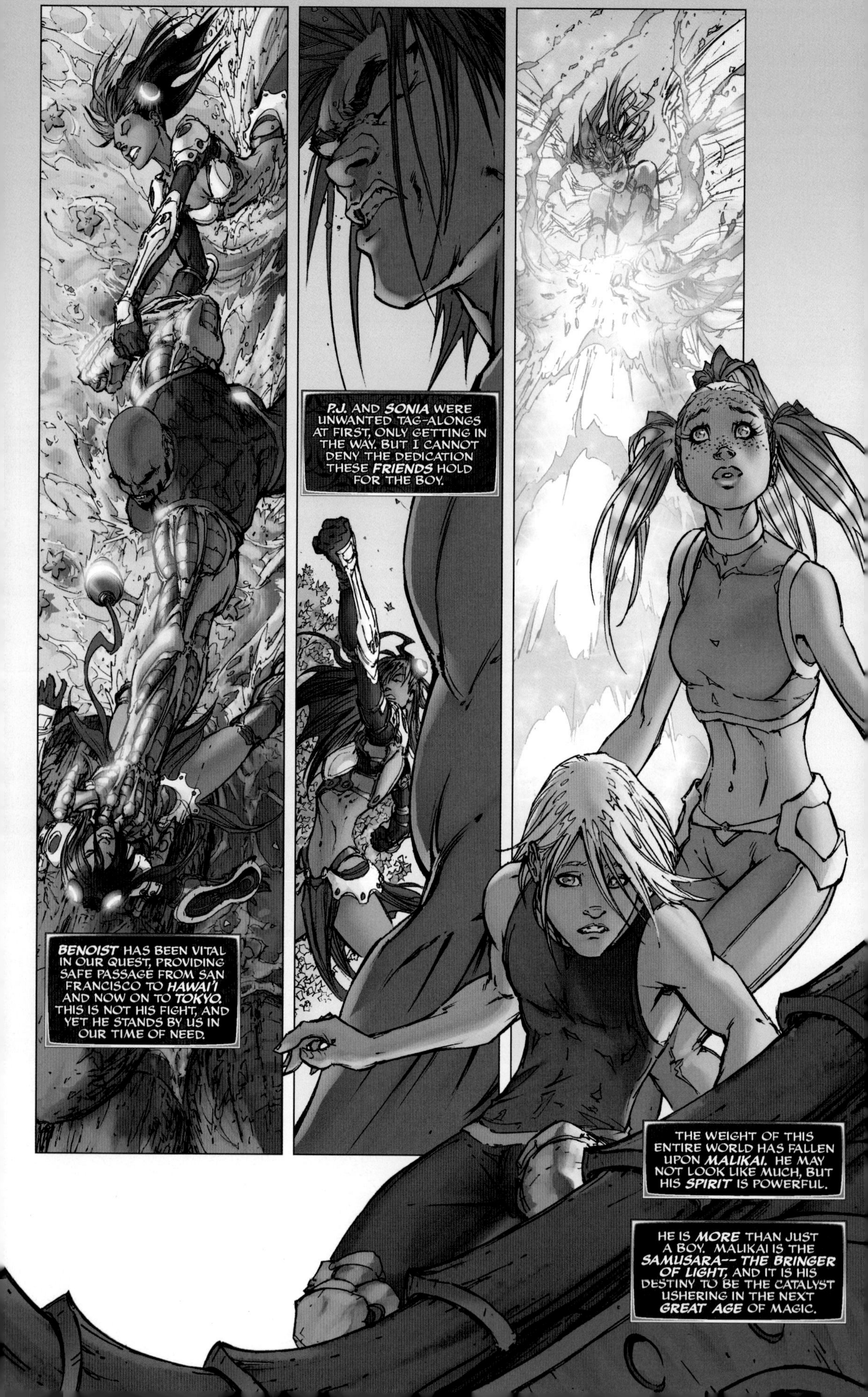

BENOIST HAS BEEN VITAL IN OUR QUEST, PROVIDING SAFE PASSAGE FROM SAN FRANCISCO TO HAWAI'I AND NOW ON TO TOKYO. THIS IS NOT HIS FIGHT, AND YET HE STANDS BY US IN OUR TIME OF NEED.
P.J. AND SONIA WERE UNWANTED TAG-ALONGS AT FIRST, ONLY GETTING IN THE WAY. BUT I CANNOT DENY THE DEDICATION THESE FRIENDS HOLD FOR THE BOY.
THE WEIGHT OF THIS ENTIRE WORLD HAS FALLEN UPON MALIKAI. HE MAY NOT LOOK LIKE MUCH, BUT HIS SPIRIT IS POWERFUL.
HE IS MORE THAN JUST A BOY. MALIKAI IS THE SAMUSARA-- THE BRINGER OF LIGHT, AND IT IS HIS DESTINY TO BE THE CATALYST USHERING IN THE NEXT GREAT AGE OF MAGIC.

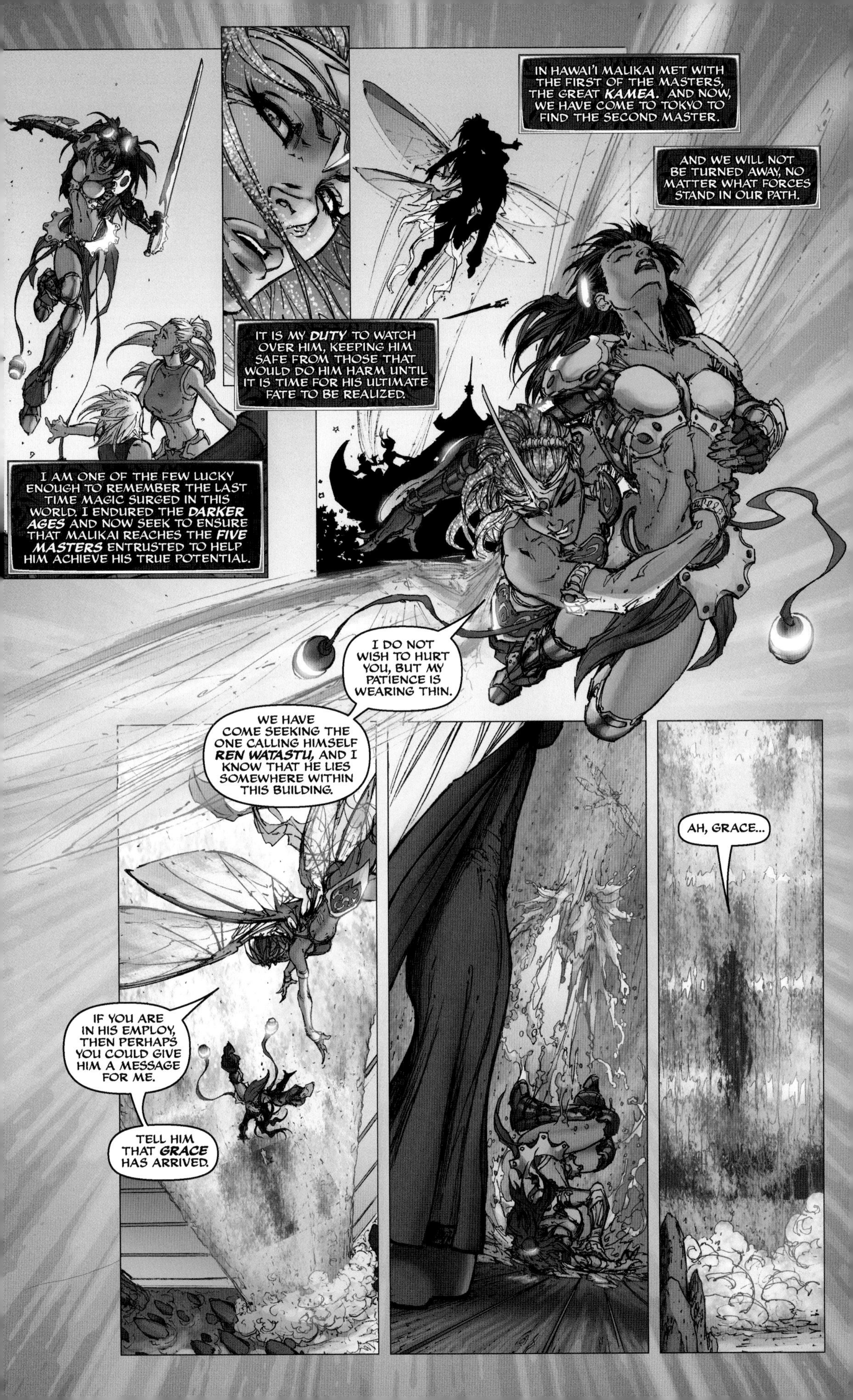
IN HAWAI'I MALIKAI MET WITH THE FIRST OF THE MASTERS, THE GREAT KAMEA. AND NOW, WE HAVE COME TO TOKYO TO FIND THE SECOND MASTER.
AND WE WILL NOT BE TURNED AWAY, NO MATTER WHAT FORCES STAND IN OUR PATH.
IT IS MY DUTY TO WATCH OVER HIM, KEEPING HIM SAFE FROM THOSE THAT WOULD DO HIM HARM UNTIL IT IS TIME FOR HIS ULTIMATE FATE TO BE REALIZED.
I AM ONE OF THE FEW LUCKY ENOUGH TO REMEMBER THE LAST TIME MAGIC SURGED IN THIS WORLD. I ENDURED THE DARKER AGES AND NOW SEEK TO ENSURE THAT MALIKAI REACHES THE FIVE MASTERS ENTRUSTED TO HELP HIM ACHIEVE HIS TRUE POTENTIAL.
I DO NOT WISH TO HURT YOU, BUT MY PATIENCE IS WEARING THIN.
WE HAVE COME SEEKING THE ONE CALLING HIMSELF REN WATASTU, AND I KNOW THAT HE LIES SOMEWHERE WITHIN THIS BUILDING.
IF YOU ARE IN HIS EMPLOY, THEN PERHAPS YOU COULD GIVE HIM A MESSAGE FOR ME.
TELL HIM THAT GRACE HAS ARRIVED.
AH, GRACE...

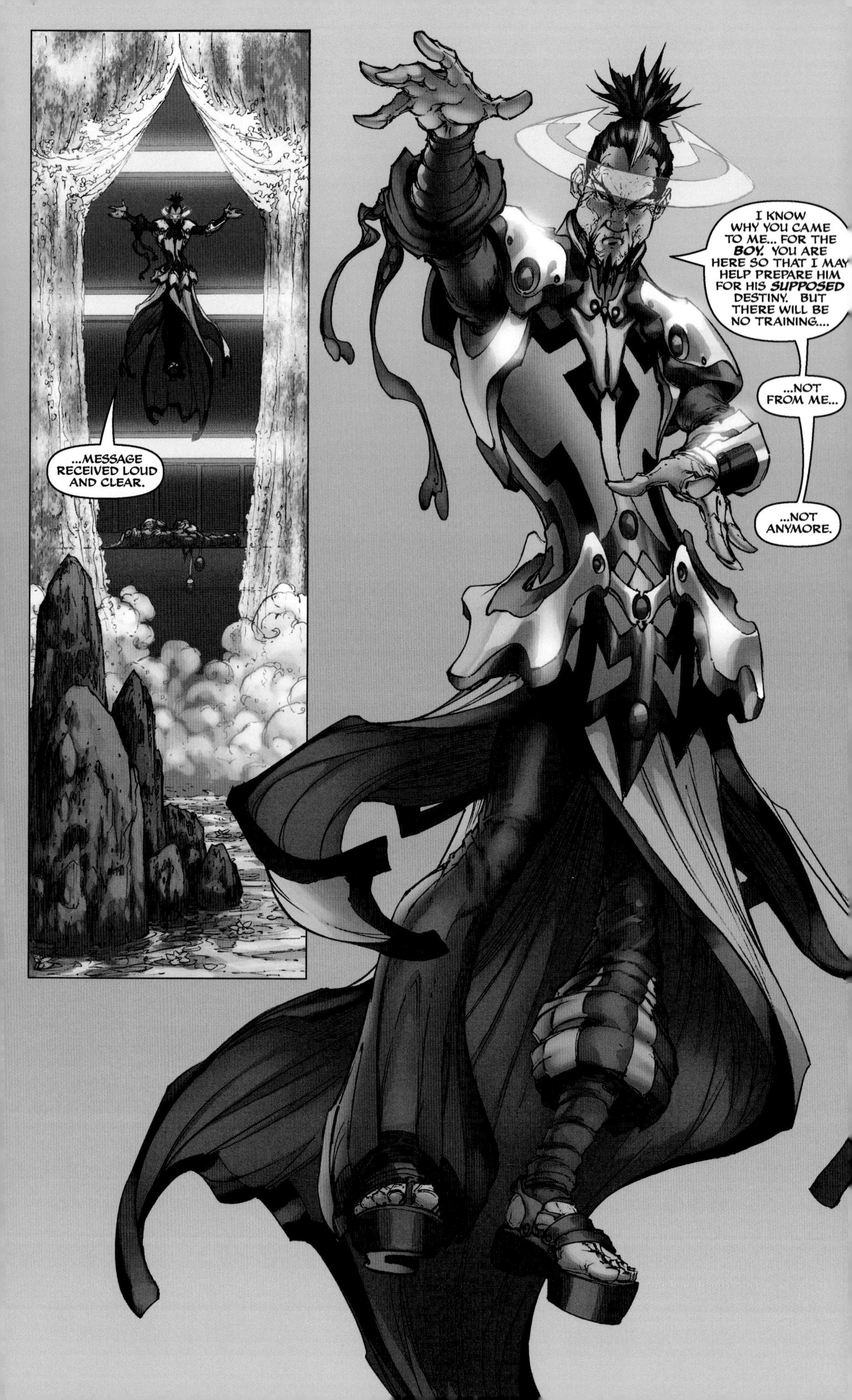
...MESSAGE RECEIVED LOUD AND CLEAR.
I KNOW WHY YOU CAME TO ME... FOR THE BOY. YOU ARE HERE SO THAT I MAY HELP PREPARE HIM FOR HIS SUPPOSED DESTINY. BUT THERE WILL BE NO TRAINING....
...NOT FROM ME...
...NOT ANYMORE.

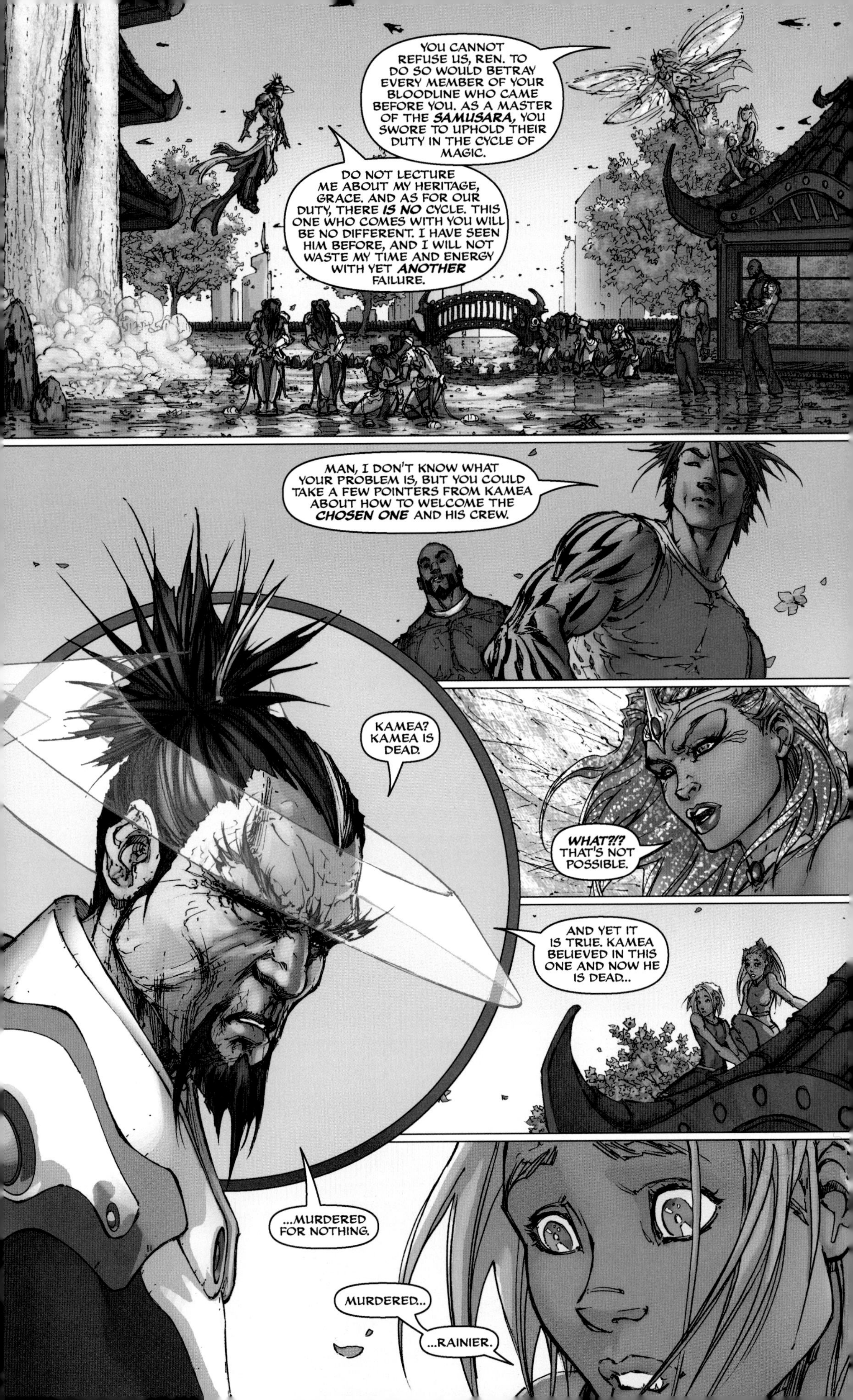
YOU CANNOT REFUSE US, REN. TO DO SO WOULD BETRAY EVERY MEMBER OF YOUR BLOODLINE WHO CAME BEFORE YOU. AS A MASTER OF THE SAMUSARA, YOU SWORE TO UPHOLD THEIR DUTY IN THE CYCLE OF MAGIC.
DO NOT LECTURE ME ABOUT MY HERITAGE, GRACE. AND AS FOR OUR DUTY, THERE IS NO CYCLE. THIS ONE WHO COMES WITH YOU WILL BE NO DIFFERENT. I HAVE SEEN HIM BEFORE, AND I WILL NOT WASTE MY TIME AND ENERGY WITH YET ANOTHER FAILURE.
MAN, I DON'T KNOW WHAT YOUR PROBLEM IS, BUT YOU COULD TAKE A FEW POINTERS FROM KAMEA ABOUT HOW TO WELCOME THE CHOSEN ONE AND HIS CREW.
KAMEA? KAMEA IS DEAD.
WHAT?!? THAT'S NOT POSSIBLE.
AND YET IT IS TRUE. KAMEA BELIEVED IN THIS ONE AND NOW HE IS DEAD...
...MURDERED FOR NOTHING.
MURDERED...
...RAINIER.

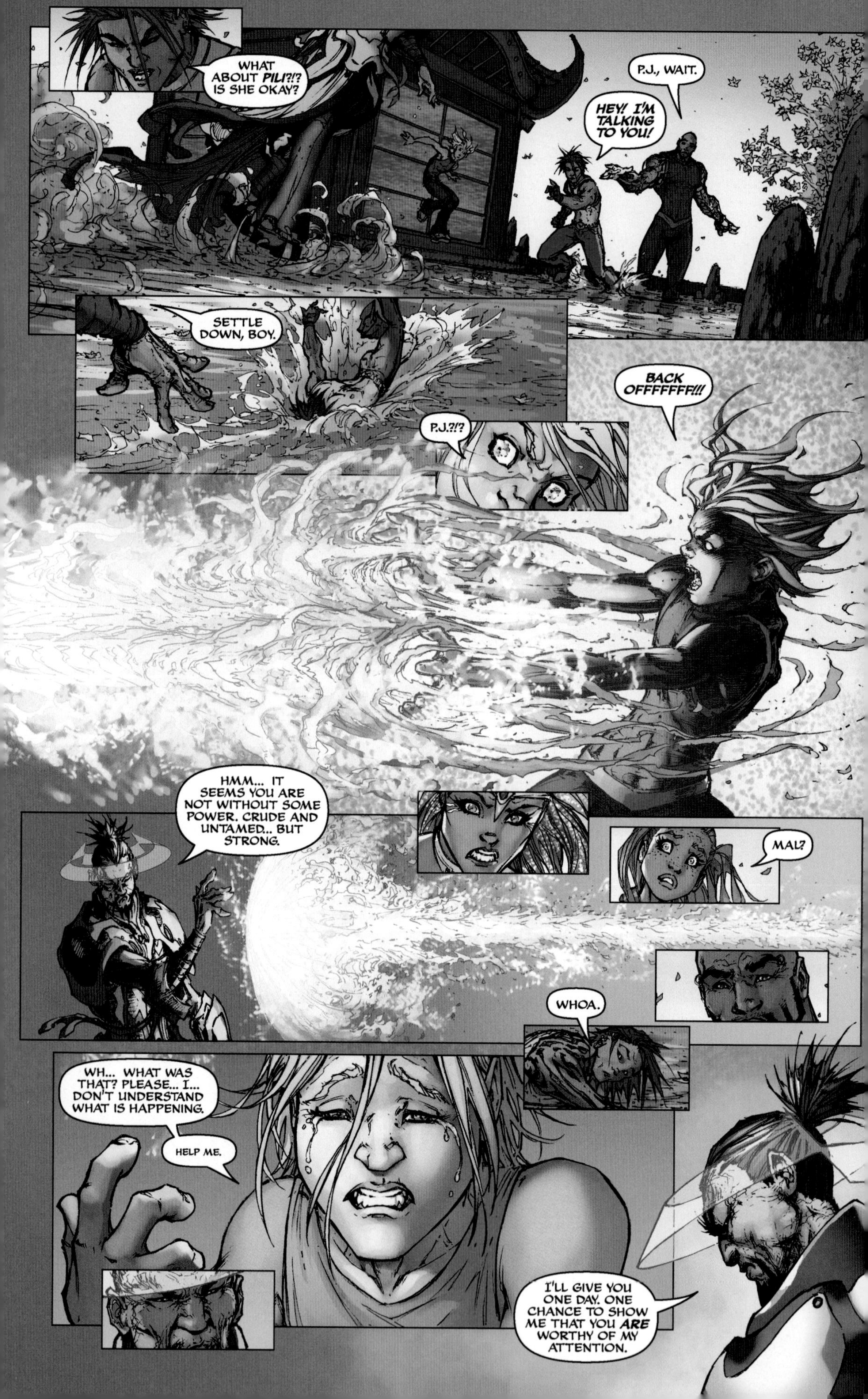
WHAT ABOUT PILI?!? IS SHE OKAY?
P.J., WAIT.
HEY! I'M TALKING TO YOU!
SETTLE DOWN, BOY.
BACK OFFFFFFF!!!
P.J.?!?
HMM... IT SEEMS YOU ARE NOT WITHOUT SOME POWER. CRUDE AND UNTAMED... BUT STRONG.
MAL?
WHOA.
WH... WHAT WAS THAT? PLEASE... I... DON'T UNDERSTAND WHAT IS HAPPENING.
HELP ME.
I'LL GIVE YOU ONE DAY. ONE CHANCE TO SHOW ME THAT YOU ARE WORTHY OF MY ATTENTION.

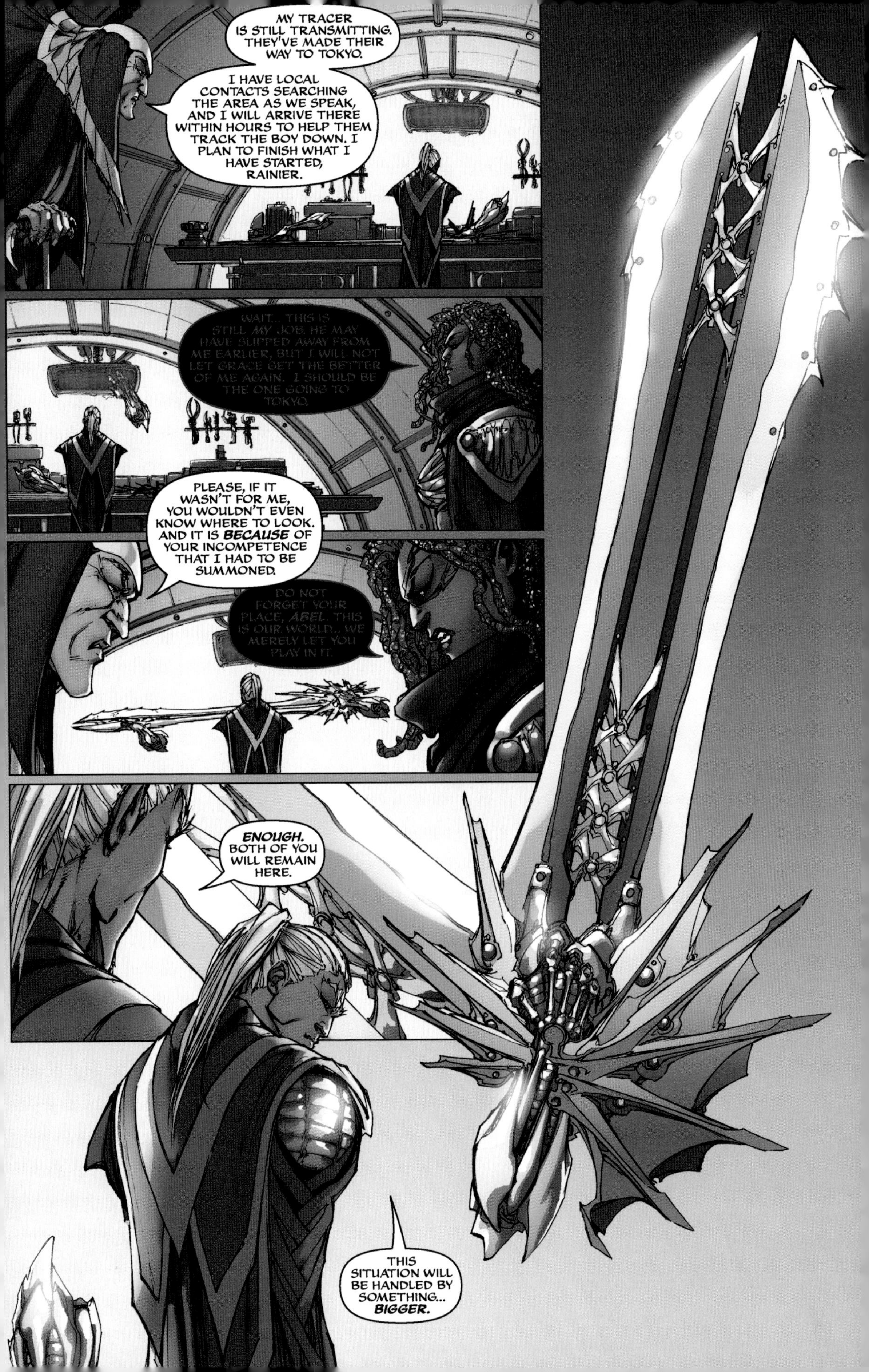
MY TRACER IS STILL TRANSMITTING. THEY'VE MADE THEIR WAY TO TOKYO.
I HAVE LOCAL CONTACTS SEARCHING THE AREA AS WE SPEAK, AND I WILL ARRIVE THERE WITHIN HOURS TO HELP THEM TRACK THE BOY DOWN. I PLAN TO FINISH WHAT I HAVE STARTED, RAINIER.
WAIT... THIS IS STILL MY JOB. HE MAY HAVE SLIPPED AWAY FROM ME EARLIER, BUT I WILL NOT LET GRACE GET THE BETTER OF ME AGAIN. I SHOULD BE THE ONE GOING TO TOKYO.
PLEASE, IF IT WASN'T FOR ME, YOU WOULDN'T EVEN KNOW WHERE TO LOOK. AND IT IS BECAUSE OF YOUR INCOMPETENCE THAT I HAD TO BE SUMMONED.
DO NOT FORGET YOUR PLACE, ABEL. THIS IS OUR WORLD... WE MERELY LET YOU PLAY IN IT.
ENOUGH. BOTH OF YOU WILL REMAIN HERE.
THIS SITUATION WILL BE HANDLED BY SOMETHING... BIGGER.

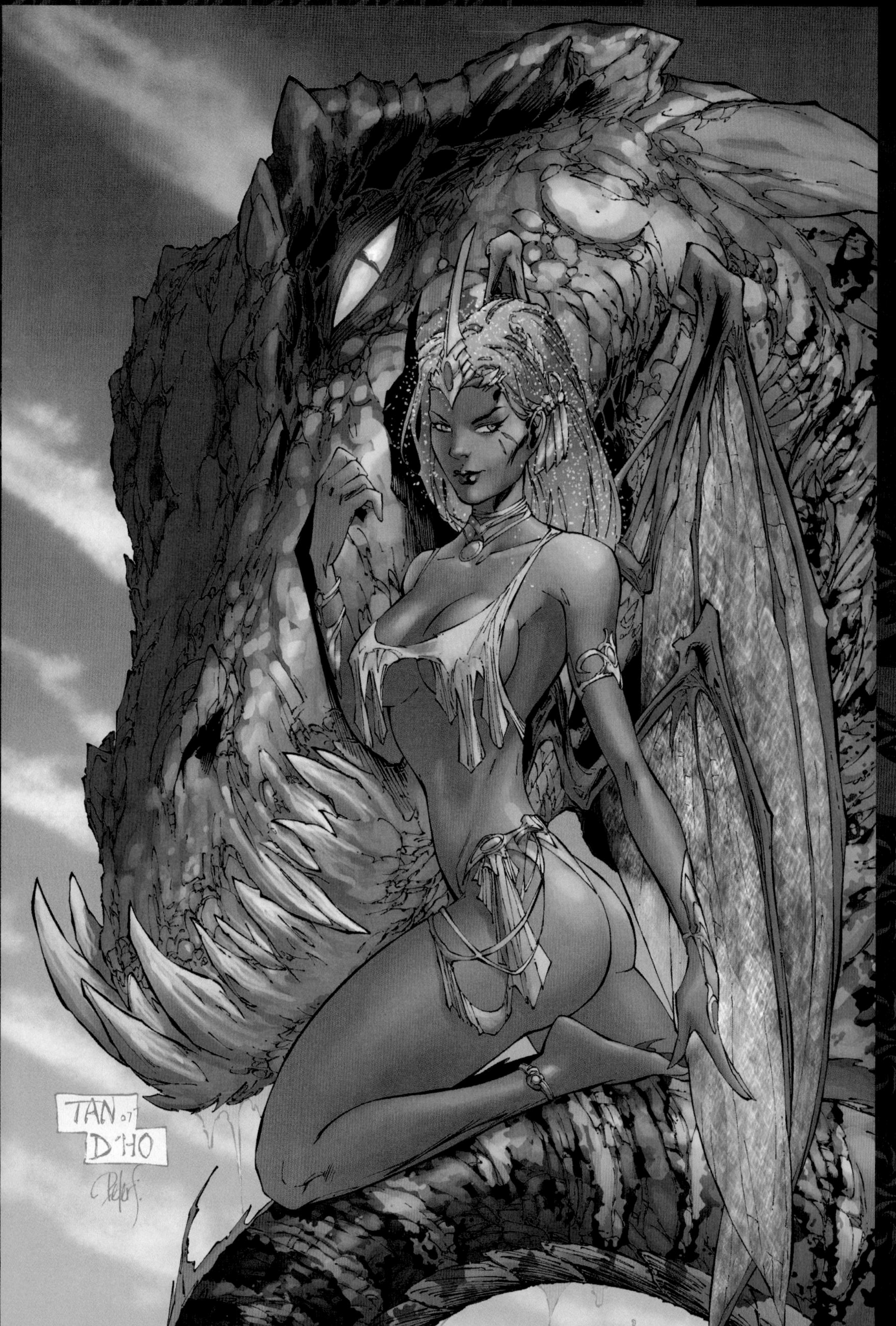
TAN 07
D'HO

GRACE

· PIN-UP FROM ASPEN SPLASH: 2007 SWIMSUIT SPECTACULAR ·

by

· BILLY TAN · DON HO · PETER STEIGERWALD ·

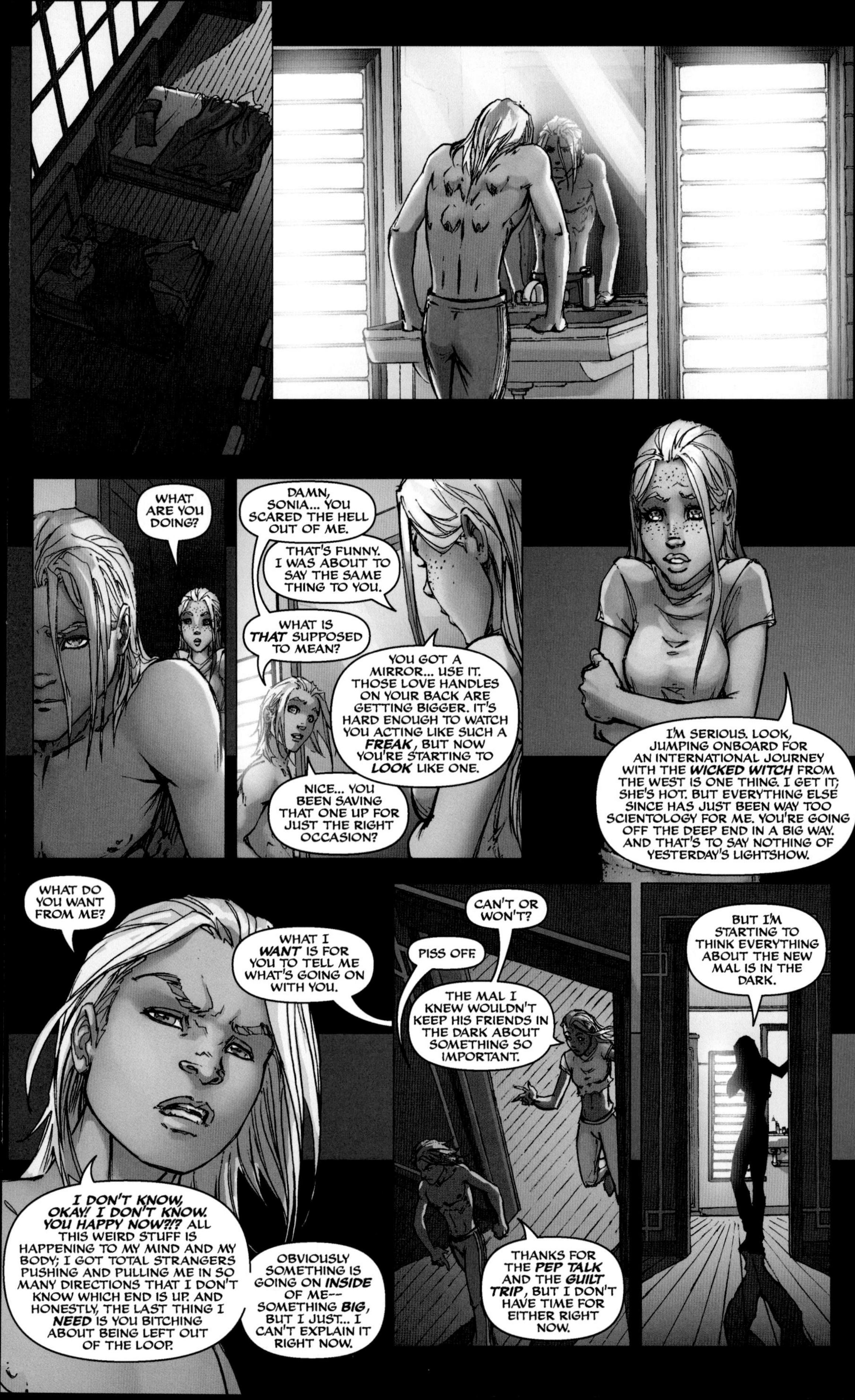
WHAT ARE YOU DOING?
DAMN, SONIA... YOU SCARED THE HELL OUT OF ME.
THAT'S FUNNY. I WAS ABOUT TO SAY THE SAME THING TO YOU.
WHAT IS THAT SUPPOSED TO MEAN?
YOU GOT A MIRROR... USE IT. THOSE LOVE HANDLES ON YOUR BACK ARE GETTING BIGGER. IT'S HARD ENOUGH TO WATCH YOU ACTING LIKE SUCH A FREAK, BUT NOW YOU'RE STARTING TO LOOK LIKE ONE.
NICE... YOU BEEN SAVING THAT ONE UP FOR JUST THE RIGHT OCCASION?
I'M SERIOUS. LOOK, JUMPING ONBOARD FOR AN INTERNATIONAL JOURNEY WITH THE WICKED WITCH FROM THE WEST IS ONE THING. I GET IT; SHE'S HOT. BUT EVERYTHING ELSE SINCE HAS JUST BEEN WAY TOO SCIENTOLOGY FOR ME. YOU'RE GOING OFF THE DEEP END IN A BIG WAY. AND THAT'S TO SAY NOTHING OF YESTERDAY'S LIGHTSHOW.
WHAT DO YOU WANT FROM ME?
WHAT I WANT IS FOR YOU TO TELL ME WHAT'S GOING ON WITH YOU.
I DON'T KNOW, OKAY! I DON'T KNOW. YOU HAPPY NOW?!? ALL THIS WEIRD STUFF IS HAPPENING TO MY MIND AND MY BODY; I GOT TOTAL STRANGERS PUSHING AND PULLING ME IN SO MANY DIRECTIONS THAT I DON'T KNOW WHICH END IS UP. AND HONESTLY, THE LAST THING I NEED IS YOU BITCHING ABOUT BEING LEFT OUT OF THE LOOP.
OBVIOUSLY SOMETHING IS GOING ON INSIDE OF ME-- SOMETHING BIG, BUT I JUST... I CAN'T EXPLAIN IT RIGHT NOW.
CAN'T OR WON'T?
PISS OFF.
THE MAL I KNEW WOULDN'T KEEP HIS FRIENDS IN THE DARK ABOUT SOMETHING SO IMPORTANT.
THANKS FOR THE PEP TALK AND THE GUILT TRIP, BUT I DON'T HAVE TIME FOR EITHER RIGHT NOW.
BUT I'M STARTING TO THINK EVERYTHING ABOUT THE NEW MAL IS IN THE DARK.

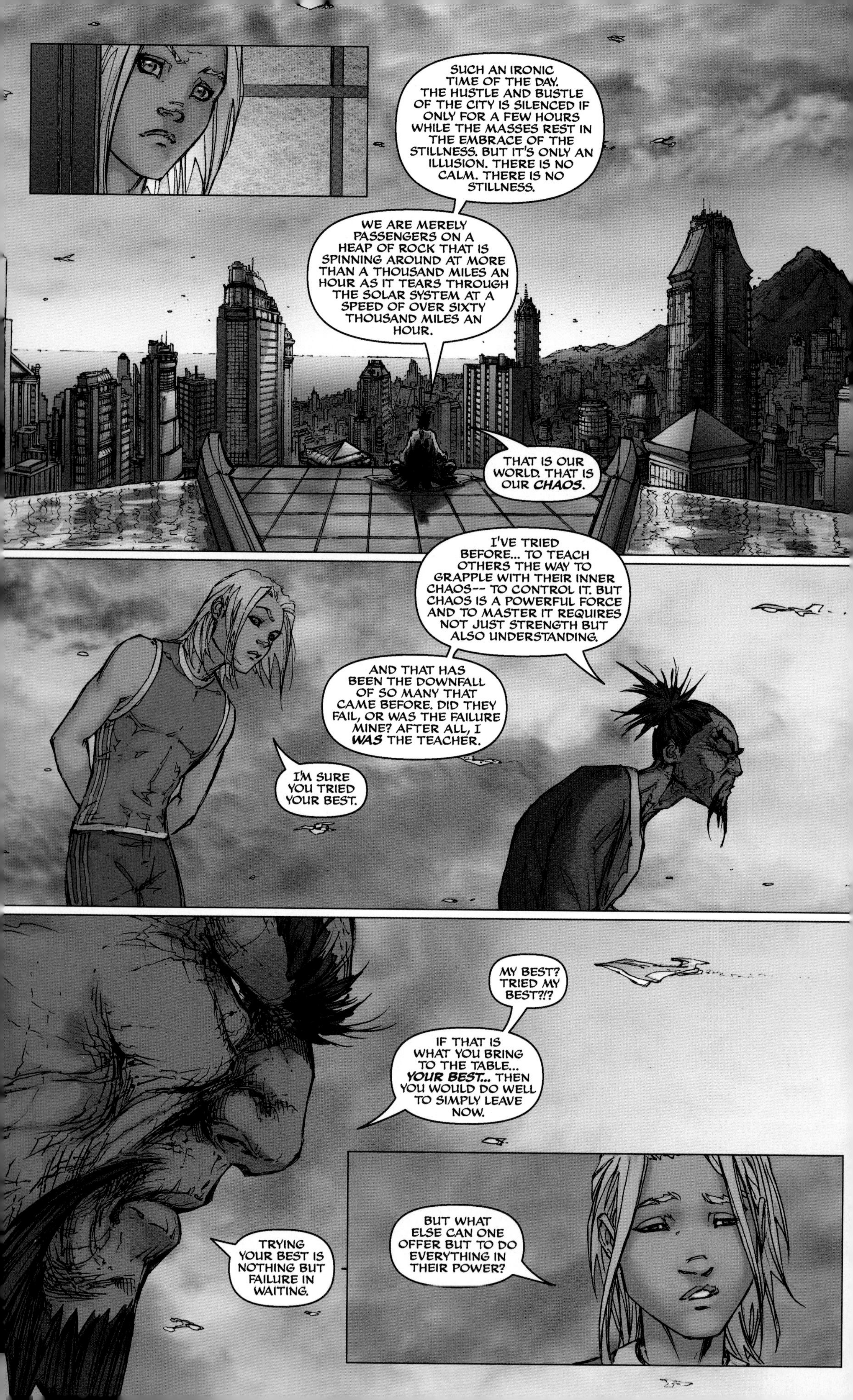
SUCH AN IRONIC TIME OF THE DAY. THE HUSTLE AND BUSTLE OF THE CITY IS SILENCED IF ONLY FOR A FEW HOURS WHILE THE MASSES REST IN THE EMBRACE OF THE STILLNESS. BUT IT'S ONLY AN ILLUSION. THERE IS NO CALM. THERE IS NO STILLNESS.
WE ARE MERELY PASSENGERS ON A HEAP OF ROCK THAT IS SPINNING AROUND AT MORE THAN A THOUSAND MILES AN HOUR AS IT TEARS THROUGH THE SOLAR SYSTEM AT A SPEED OF OVER SIXTY THOUSAND MILES AN HOUR.
THAT IS OUR WORLD. THAT IS OUR *CHAOS*.
I'VE TRIED BEFORE... TO TEACH OTHERS THE WAY TO GRAPPLE WITH THEIR INNER CHAOS-- TO CONTROL IT. BUT CHAOS IS A POWERFUL FORCE AND TO MASTER IT REQUIRES NOT JUST STRENGTH BUT ALSO UNDERSTANDING.
AND THAT HAS BEEN THE DOWNFALL OF SO MANY THAT CAME BEFORE. DID THEY FAIL, OR WAS THE FAILURE MINE? AFTER ALL, I ***WAS*** THE TEACHER.
I'M SURE YOU TRIED YOUR BEST.
MY BEST? TRIED MY BEST?!?
IF THAT IS WHAT YOU BRING TO THE TABLE... ***YOUR BEST...*** THEN YOU WOULD DO WELL TO SIMPLY LEAVE NOW.
TRYING YOUR BEST IS NOTHING BUT FAILURE IN WAITING.
BUT WHAT ELSE CAN ONE OFFER BUT TO DO EVERYTHING IN THEIR POWER?

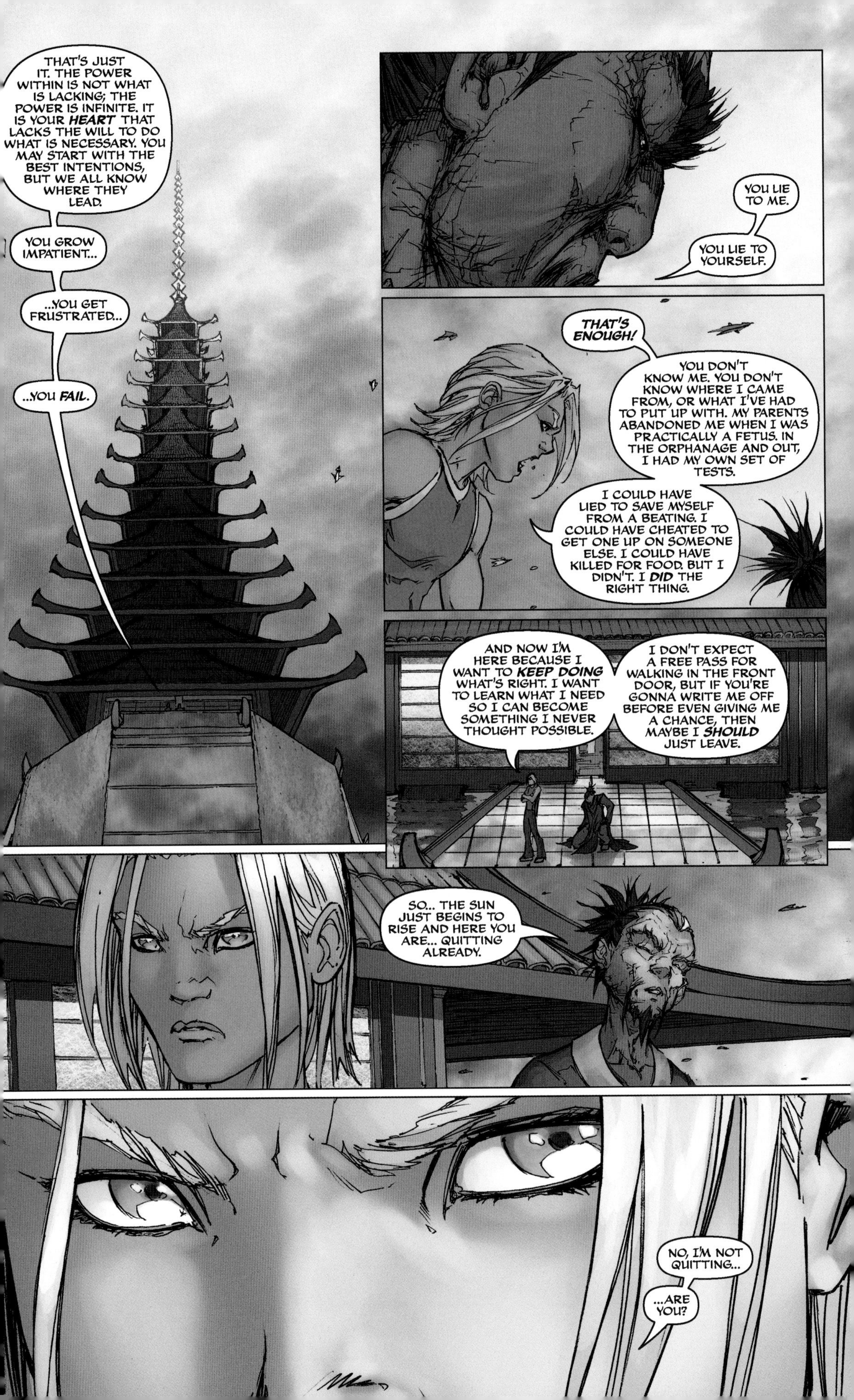
THAT'S JUST IT. THE POWER WITHIN IS NOT WHAT IS LACKING; THE POWER IS INFINITE. IT IS YOUR HEART THAT LACKS THE WILL TO DO WHAT IS NECESSARY. YOU MAY START WITH THE BEST INTENTIONS, BUT WE ALL KNOW WHERE THEY LEAD.
YOU GROW IMPATIENT...
...YOU GET FRUSTRATED...
...YOU FAIL.
YOU LIE TO ME.
YOU LIE TO YOURSELF.
THAT'S ENOUGH!
YOU DON'T KNOW ME. YOU DON'T KNOW WHERE I CAME FROM, OR WHAT I'VE HAD TO PUT UP WITH. MY PARENTS ABANDONED ME WHEN I WAS PRACTICALLY A FETUS. IN THE ORPHANAGE AND OUT, I HAD MY OWN SET OF TESTS.
I COULD HAVE LIED TO SAVE MYSELF FROM A BEATING. I COULD HAVE CHEATED TO GET ONE UP ON SOMEONE ELSE. I COULD HAVE KILLED FOR FOOD. BUT I DIDN'T. I DID THE RIGHT THING.
AND NOW I'M HERE BECAUSE I WANT TO KEEP DOING WHAT'S RIGHT. I WANT TO LEARN WHAT I NEED SO I CAN BECOME SOMETHING I NEVER THOUGHT POSSIBLE.
I DON'T EXPECT A FREE PASS FOR WALKING IN THE FRONT DOOR, BUT IF YOU'RE GONNA WRITE ME OFF BEFORE EVEN GIVING ME A CHANCE, THEN MAYBE I SHOULD JUST LEAVE.
SO... THE SUN JUST BEGINS TO RISE AND HERE YOU ARE... QUITTING ALREADY.
NO, I'M NOT QUITTING...
...ARE YOU?

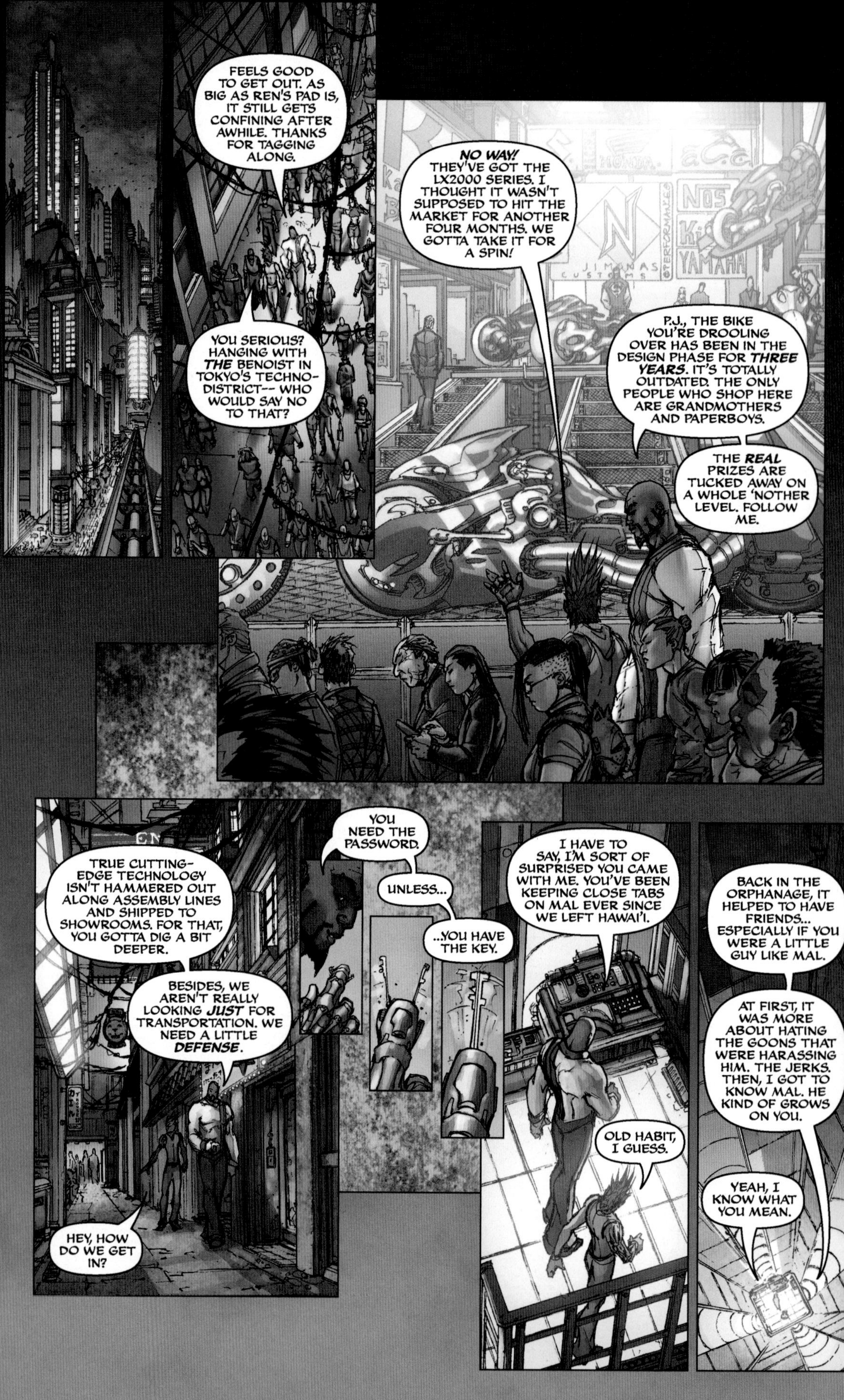
FEELS GOOD TO GET OUT. AS BIG AS REN'S PAD IS, IT STILL GETS CONFINING AFTER AWHILE. THANKS FOR TAGGING ALONG.
YOU SERIOUS? HANGING WITH THE BENOIST IN TOKYO'S TECHNO-DISTRICT-- WHO WOULD SAY NO TO THAT?
NO WAY! THEY'VE GOT THE LX2000 SERIES. I THOUGHT IT WASN'T SUPPOSED TO HIT THE MARKET FOR ANOTHER FOUR MONTHS. WE GOTTA TAKE IT FOR A SPIN!
P.J., THE BIKE YOU'RE DROOLING OVER HAS BEEN IN THE DESIGN PHASE FOR THREE YEARS. IT'S TOTALLY OUTDATED. THE ONLY PEOPLE WHO SHOP HERE ARE GRANDMOTHERS AND PAPERBOYS.
THE REAL PRIZES ARE TUCKED AWAY ON A WHOLE 'NOTHER LEVEL. FOLLOW ME.
HONDA
NOS
YAMAHA
JIMONAS CUSTOMS
TRUE CUTTING-EDGE TECHNOLOGY ISN'T HAMMERED OUT ALONG ASSEMBLY LINES AND SHIPPED TO SHOWROOMS. FOR THAT, YOU GOTTA DIG A BIT DEEPER.
BESIDES, WE AREN'T REALLY LOOKING JUST FOR TRANSPORTATION. WE NEED A LITTLE DEFENSE.
HEY, HOW DO WE GET IN?
YOU NEED THE PASSWORD.
UNLESS...
...YOU HAVE THE KEY.
I HAVE TO SAY, I'M SORT OF SURPRISED YOU CAME WITH ME. YOU'VE BEEN KEEPING CLOSE TABS ON MAL EVER SINCE WE LEFT HAWAI'I.
OLD HABIT, I GUESS.
BACK IN THE ORPHANAGE, IT HELPED TO HAVE FRIENDS... ESPECIALLY IF YOU WERE A LITTLE GUY LIKE MAL.
AT FIRST, IT WAS MORE ABOUT HATING THE GOONS THAT WERE HARASSING HIM. THE JERKS. THEN, I GOT TO KNOW MAL. HE KIND OF GROWS ON YOU.
YEAH, I KNOW WHAT YOU MEAN.

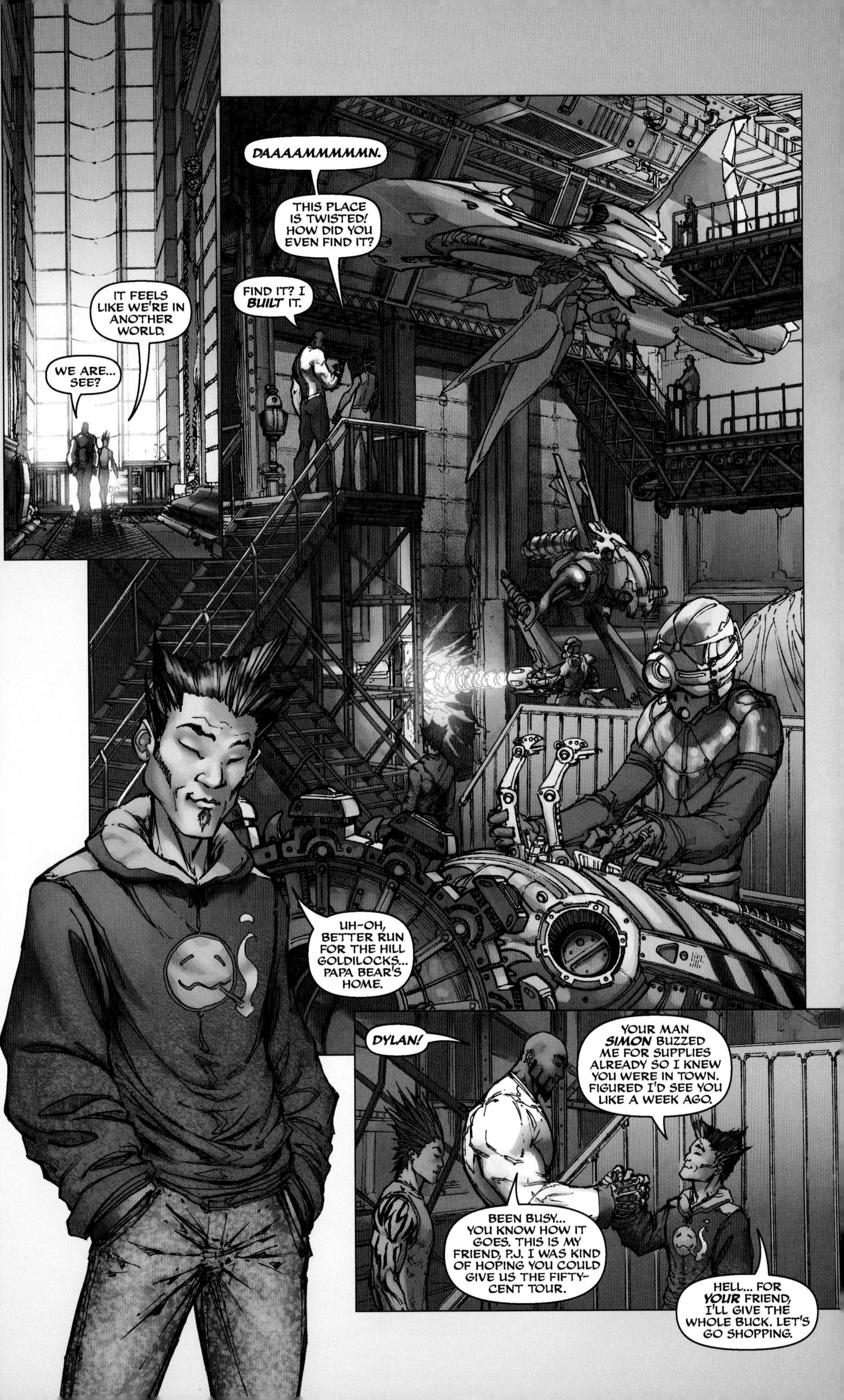
IT FEELS LIKE WE'RE IN ANOTHER WORLD.
WE ARE... SEE?
DAAAAMMMMMN.
THIS PLACE IS TWISTED! HOW DID YOU EVEN FIND IT?
FIND IT? I BUILT IT.
UH-OH, BETTER RUN FOR THE HILL GOLDILOCKS... PAPA BEAR'S HOME.
DYLAN!
YOUR MAN SIMON BUZZED ME FOR SUPPLIES ALREADY SO I KNEW YOU WERE IN TOWN. FIGURED I'D SEE YOU LIKE A WEEK AGO.
BEEN BUSY... YOU KNOW HOW IT GOES. THIS IS MY FRIEND, P.J. I WAS KIND OF HOPING YOU COULD GIVE US THE FIFTY-CENT TOUR.
HELL... FOR YOUR FRIEND, I'LL GIVE THE WHOLE BUCK. LET'S GO SHOPPING.

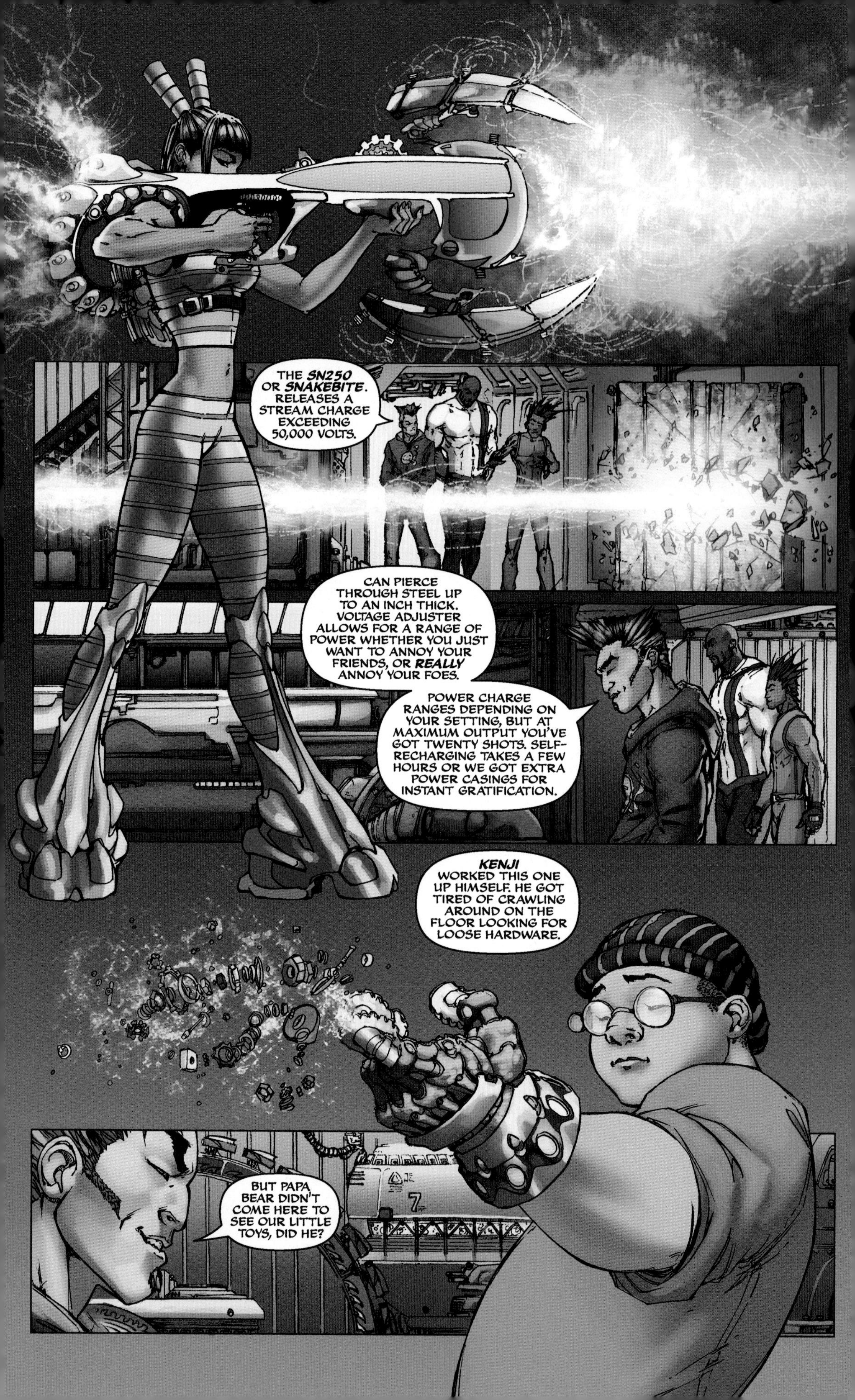
THE SN250 OR SNAKEBITE. RELEASES A STREAM CHARGE EXCEEDING 50,000 VOLTS.
CAN PIERCE THROUGH STEEL UP TO AN INCH THICK. VOLTAGE ADJUSTER ALLOWS FOR A RANGE OF POWER WHETHER YOU JUST WANT TO ANNOY YOUR FRIENDS, OR REALLY ANNOY YOUR FOES.
POWER CHARGE RANGES DEPENDING ON YOUR SETTING, BUT AT MAXIMUM OUTPUT YOU'VE GOT TWENTY SHOTS. SELF-RECHARGING TAKES A FEW HOURS OR WE GOT EXTRA POWER CASINGS FOR INSTANT GRATIFICATION.
KENJI WORKED THIS ONE UP HIMSELF. HE GOT TIRED OF CRAWLING AROUND ON THE FLOOR LOOKING FOR LOOSE HARDWARE.
BUT PAPA BEAR DIDN'T COME HERE TO SEE OUR LITTLE TOYS, DID HE?

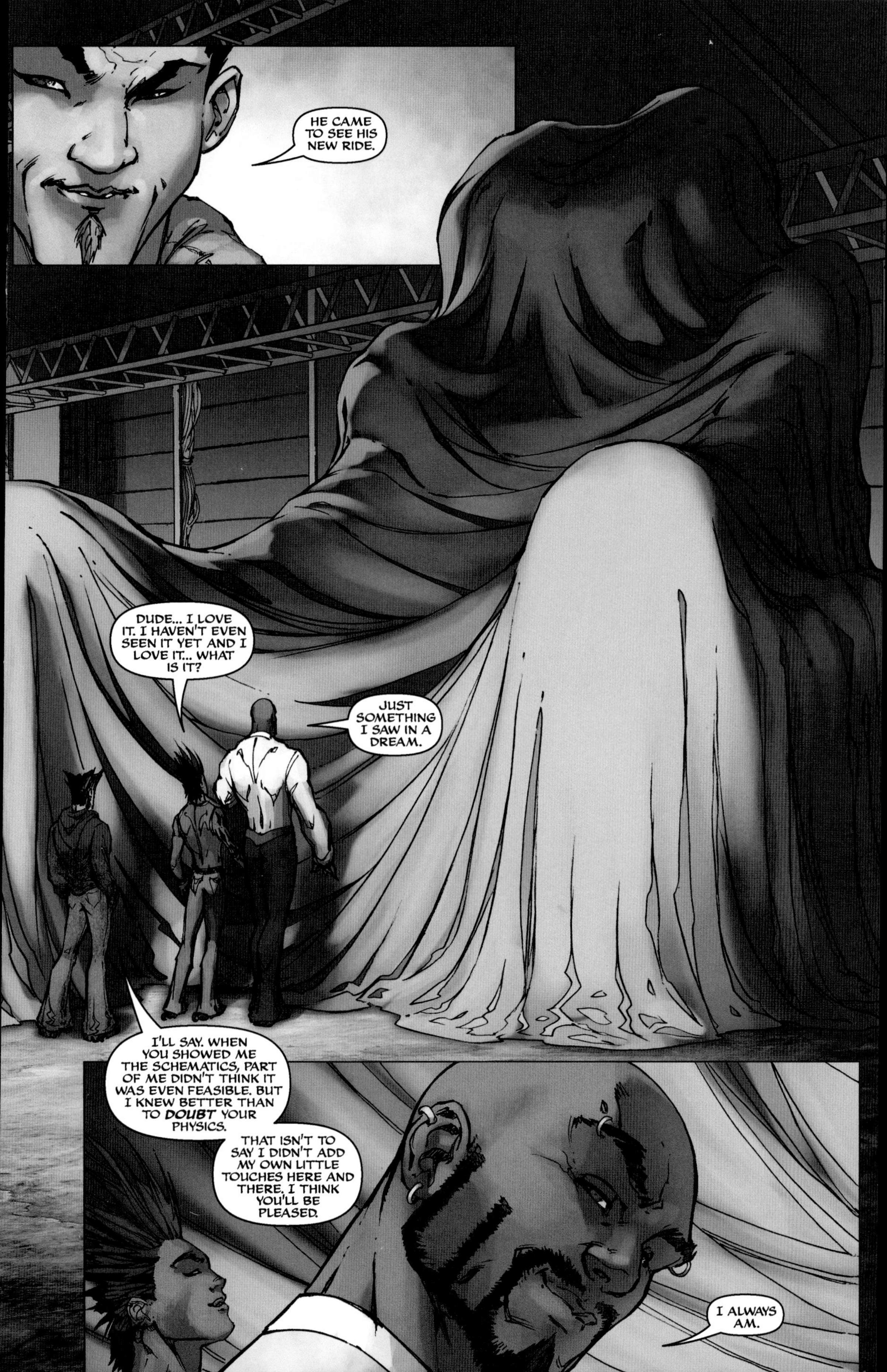
HE CAME TO SEE HIS NEW RIDE.
DUDE... I LOVE IT. I HAVEN'T EVEN SEEN IT YET AND I LOVE IT... WHAT IS IT?
JUST SOMETHING I SAW IN A DREAM.
I'LL SAY. WHEN YOU SHOWED ME THE SCHEMATICS, PART OF ME DIDN'T THINK IT WAS EVEN FEASIBLE. BUT I KNEW BETTER THAN TO *DOUBT* YOUR PHYSICS.
THAT ISN'T TO SAY I DIDN'T ADD MY OWN LITTLE TOUCHES HERE AND THERE. I THINK YOU'LL BE PLEASED.
I ALWAYS AM.

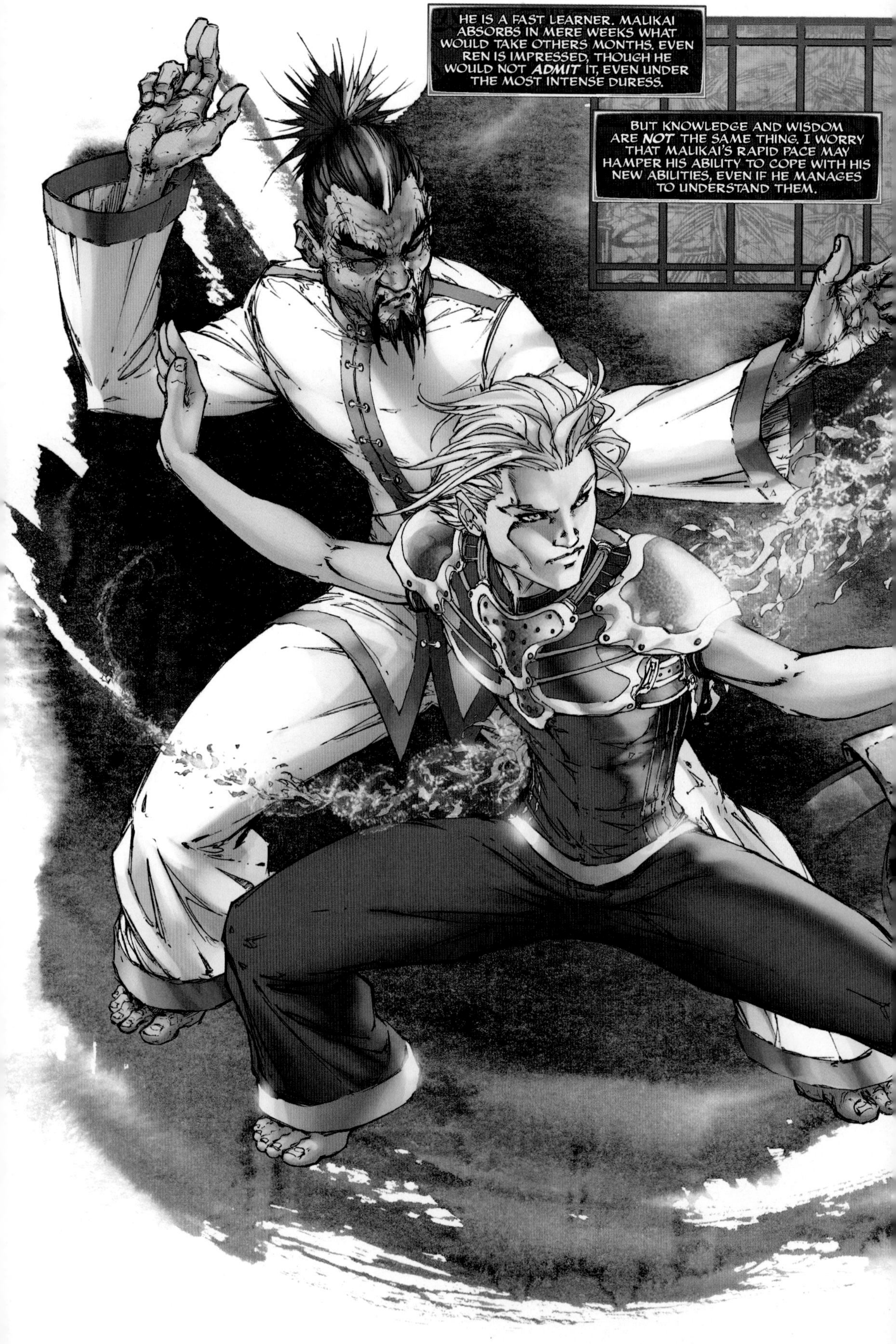
HE IS A FAST LEARNER. MALIKAI ABSORBS IN MERE WEEKS WHAT WOULD TAKE OTHERS MONTHS. EVEN REN IS IMPRESSED, THOUGH HE WOULD NOT ADMIT IT, EVEN UNDER THE MOST INTENSE DURESS.
BUT KNOWLEDGE AND WISDOM ARE NOT THE SAME THING. I WORRY THAT MALIKAI'S RAPID PACE MAY HAMPER HIS ABILITY TO COPE WITH HIS NEW ABILITIES, EVEN IF HE MANAGES TO UNDERSTAND THEM.

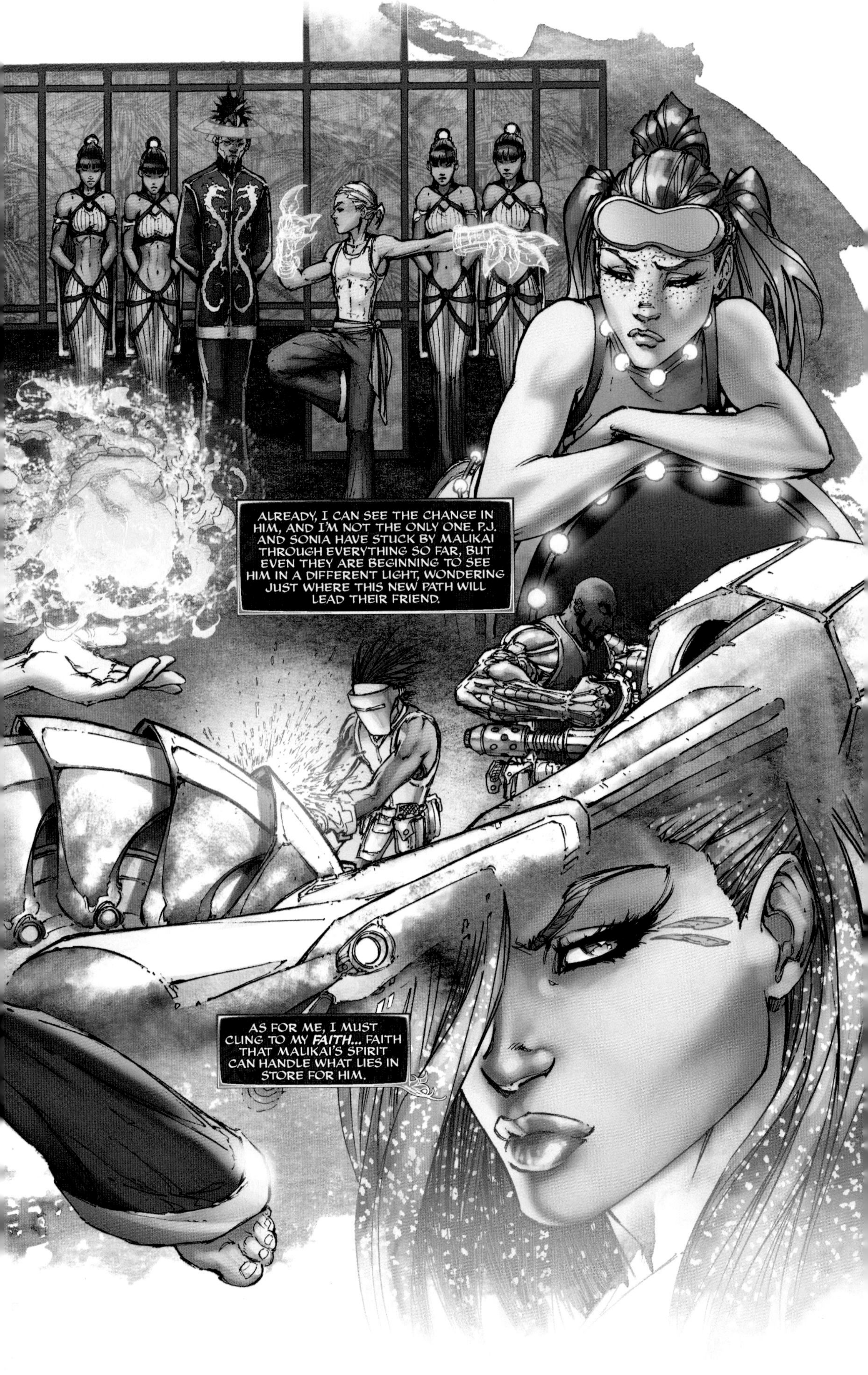
ALREADY, I CAN SEE THE CHANGE IN HIM, AND I'M NOT THE ONLY ONE. P.J. AND SONIA HAVE STUCK BY MALIKAI THROUGH EVERYTHING SO FAR, BUT EVEN THEY ARE BEGINNING TO SEE HIM IN A DIFFERENT LIGHT, WONDERING JUST WHERE THIS NEW PATH WILL LEAD THEIR FRIEND.
AS FOR ME, I MUST CLING TO MY FAITH... FAITH THAT MALIKAI'S SPIRIT CAN HANDLE WHAT LIES IN STORE FOR HIM.

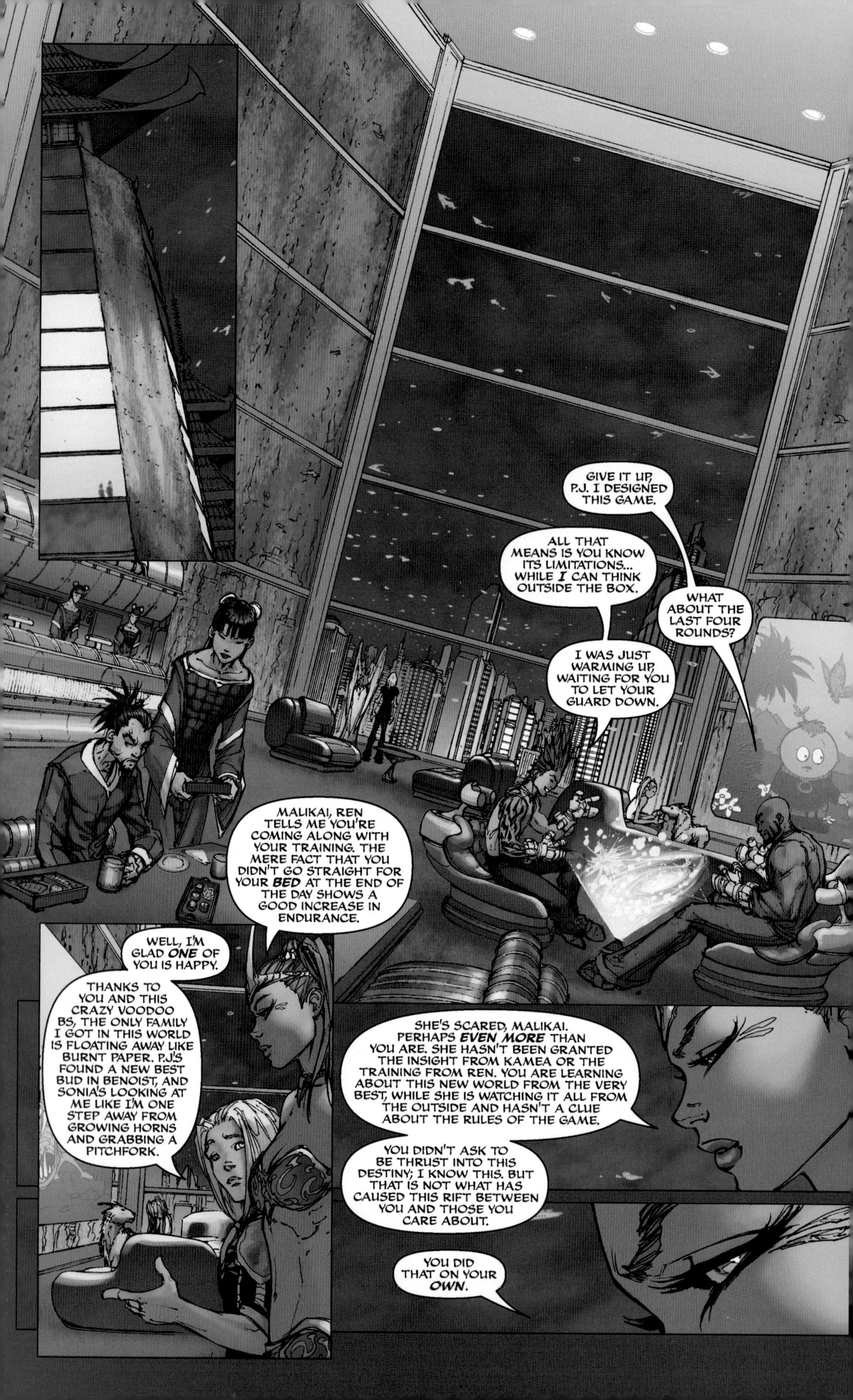
GIVE IT UP, P.J. I DESIGNED THIS GAME.
ALL THAT MEANS IS YOU KNOW ITS LIMITATIONS... WHILE I CAN THINK OUTSIDE THE BOX.
WHAT ABOUT THE LAST FOUR ROUNDS?
I WAS JUST WARMING UP, WAITING FOR YOU TO LET YOUR GUARD DOWN.
MALIKAI, REN TELLS ME YOU'RE COMING ALONG WITH YOUR TRAINING. THE MERE FACT THAT YOU DIDN'T GO STRAIGHT FOR YOUR BED AT THE END OF THE DAY SHOWS A GOOD INCREASE IN ENDURANCE.
WELL, I'M GLAD ONE OF YOU IS HAPPY.
THANKS TO YOU AND THIS CRAZY VOODOO BS, THE ONLY FAMILY I GOT IN THIS WORLD IS FLOATING AWAY LIKE BURNT PAPER. P.J.'S FOUND A NEW BEST BUD IN BENOIST, AND SONIA'S LOOKING AT ME LIKE I'M ONE STEP AWAY FROM GROWING HORNS AND GRABBING A PITCHFORK.
SHE'S SCARED, MALIKAI. PERHAPS EVEN MORE THAN YOU ARE. SHE HASN'T BEEN GRANTED THE INSIGHT FROM KAMEA OR THE TRAINING FROM REN. YOU ARE LEARNING ABOUT THIS NEW WORLD FROM THE VERY BEST, WHILE SHE IS WATCHING IT ALL FROM THE OUTSIDE AND HASN'T A CLUE ABOUT THE RULES OF THE GAME.
YOU DIDN'T ASK TO BE THRUST INTO THIS DESTINY; I KNOW THIS. BUT THAT IS NOT WHAT HAS CAUSED THIS RIFT BETWEEN YOU AND THOSE YOU CARE ABOUT.
YOU DID THAT ON YOUR OWN.

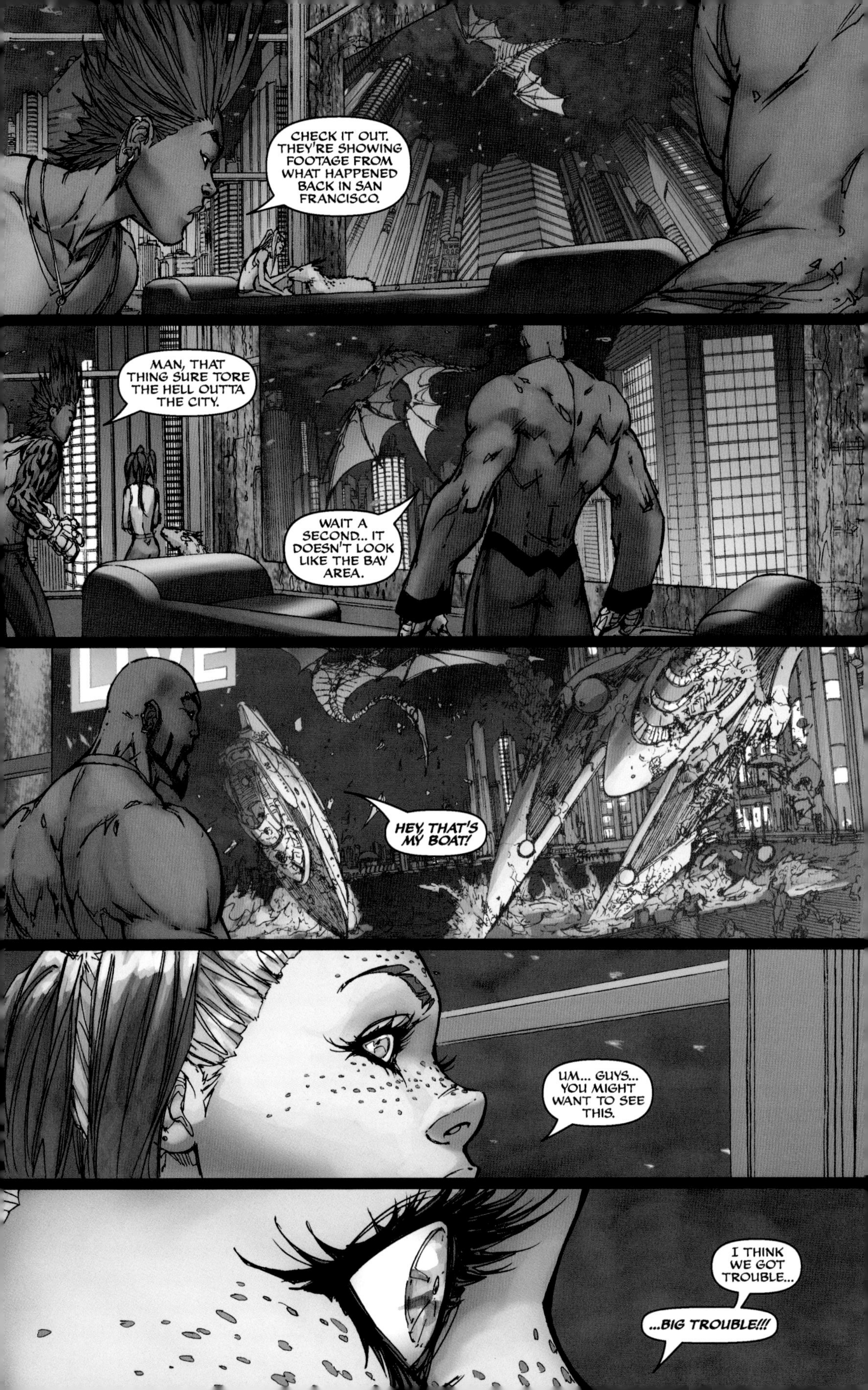
CHECK IT OUT. THEY'RE SHOWING FOOTAGE FROM WHAT HAPPENED BACK IN SAN FRANCISCO.
MAN, THAT THING SURE TORE THE HELL OUTTA THE CITY.
WAIT A SECOND... IT DOESN'T LOOK LIKE THE BAY AREA.
HEY, THAT'S MY BOAT!
UM... GUYS... YOU MIGHT WANT TO SEE THIS.
I THINK WE GOT TROUBLE...
...BIG TROUBLE!!!

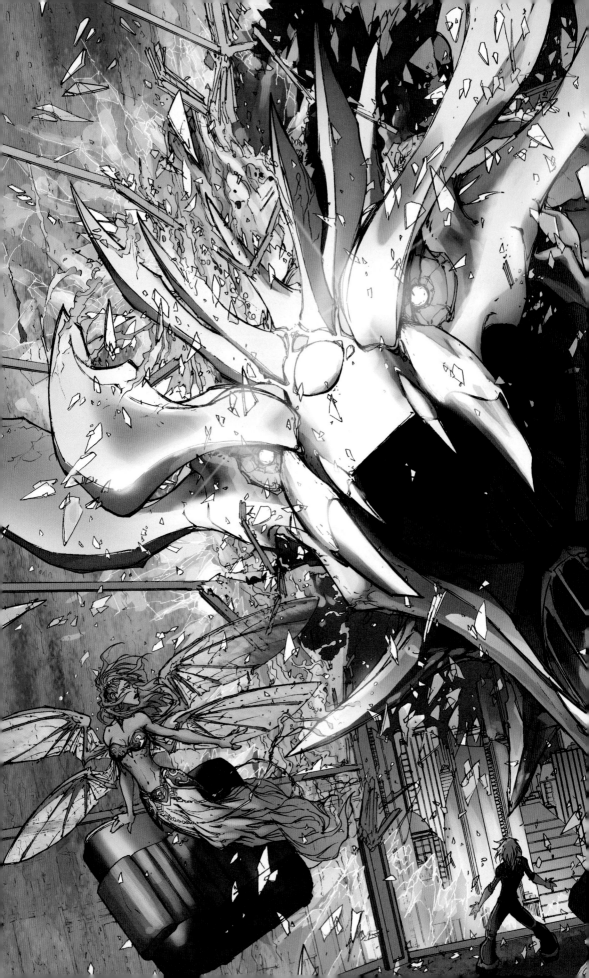

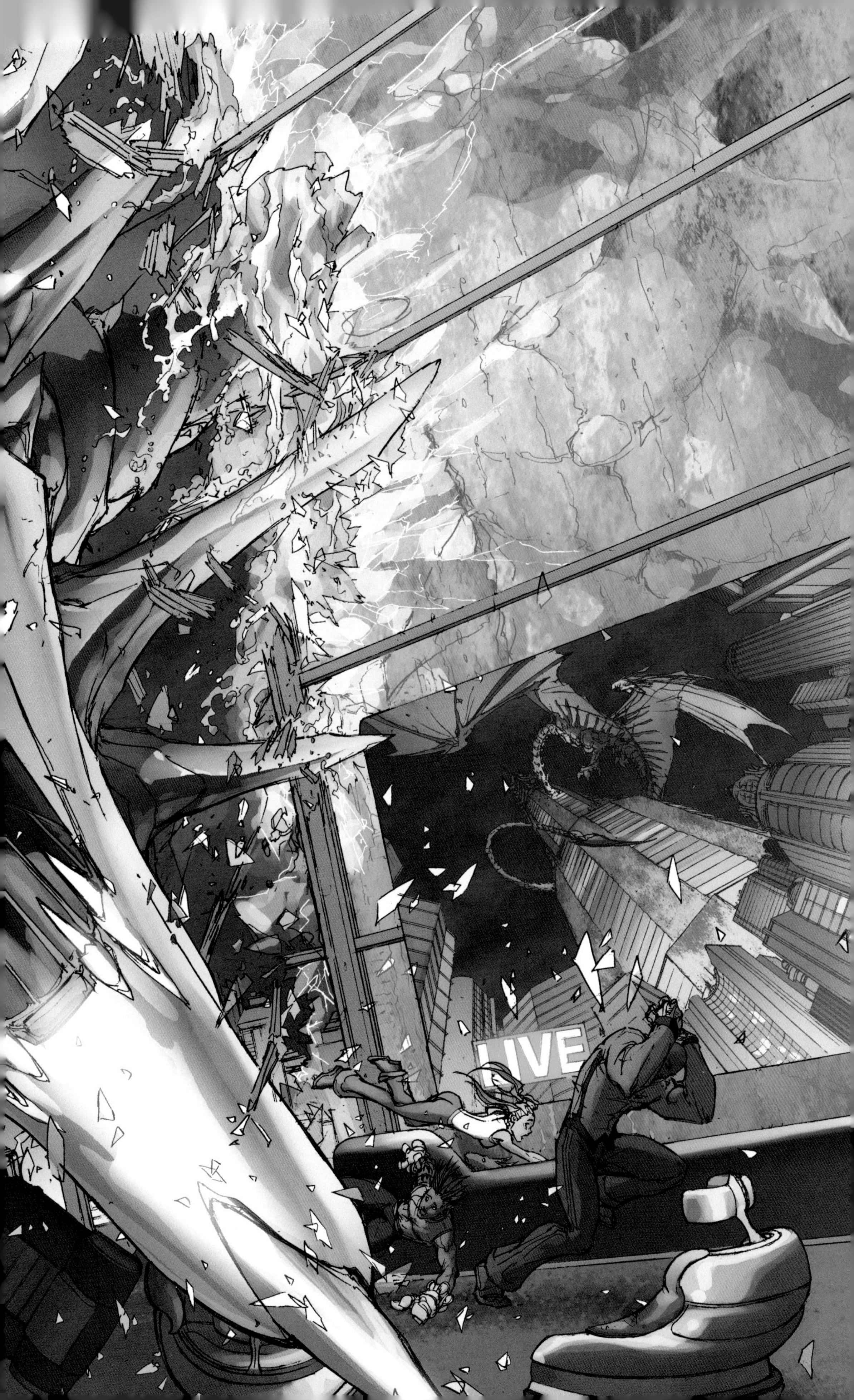
LIVE

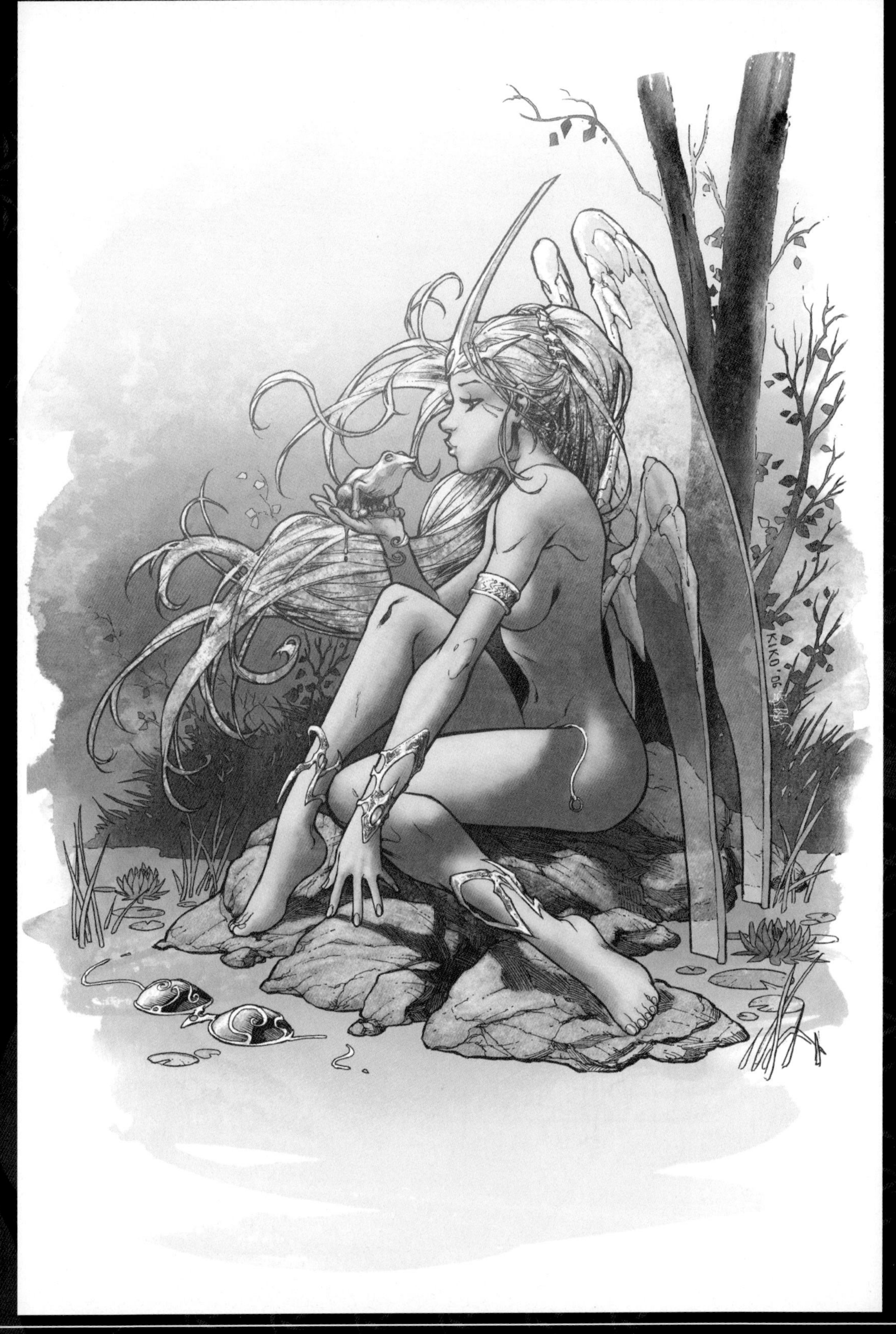
KIKO '06

GRACE

· PIN-UP FROM ASPEN SPLASH: 2006 SWIMSUIT SPECTACULAR ·
by
· Francis MANAPUL ·

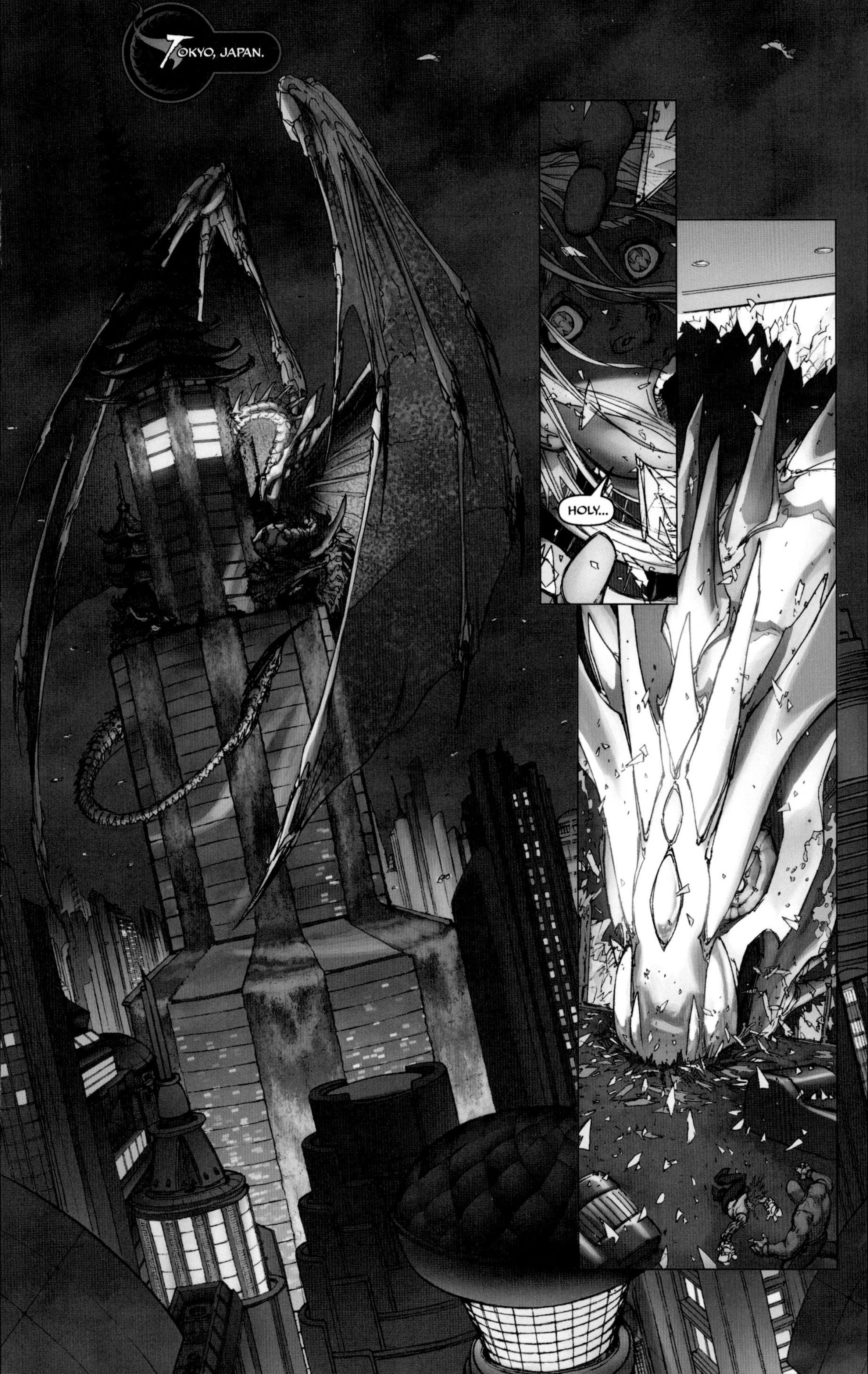
TOKYO, JAPAN.
HOLY...

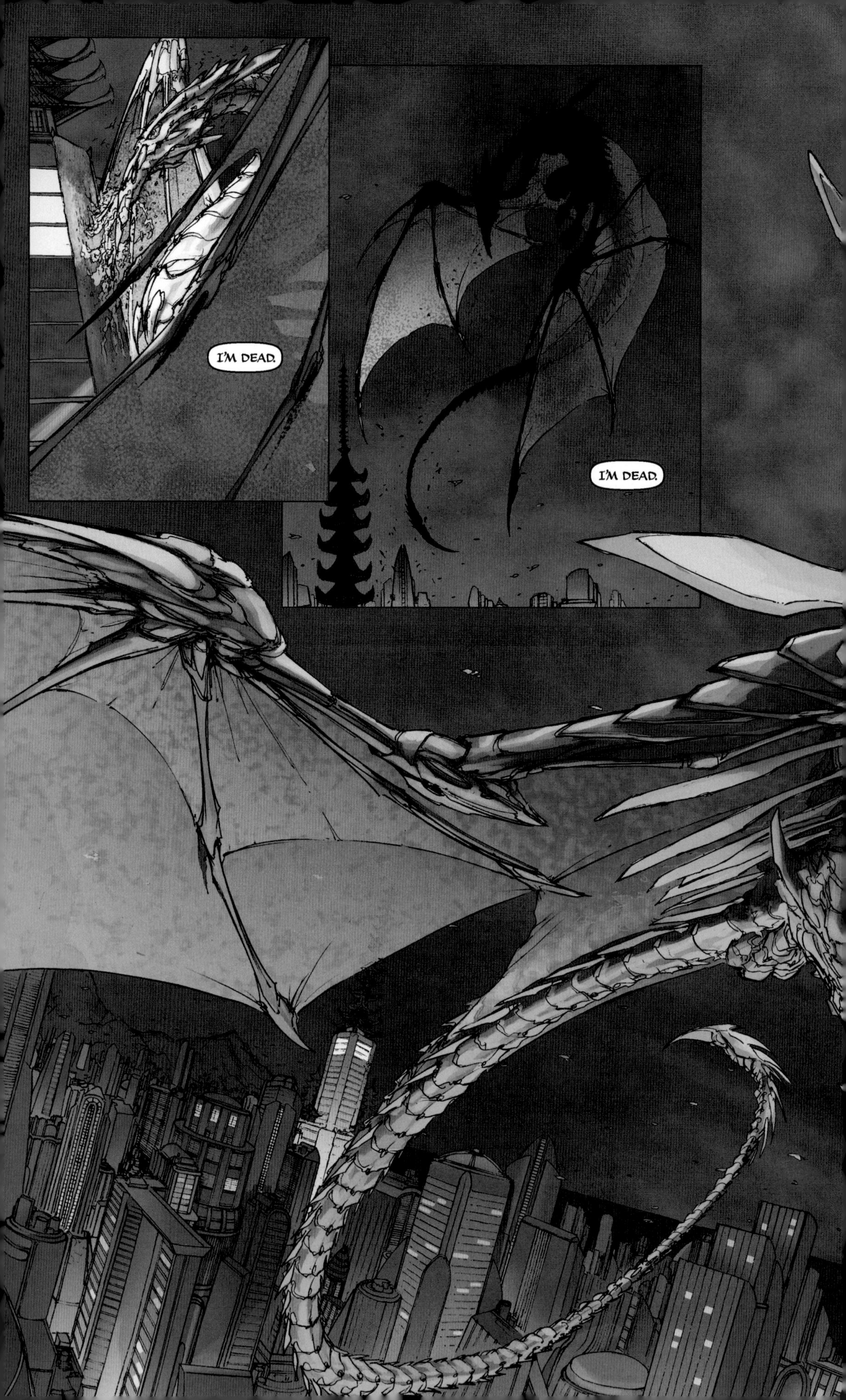
I'M DEAD.
I'M DEAD.

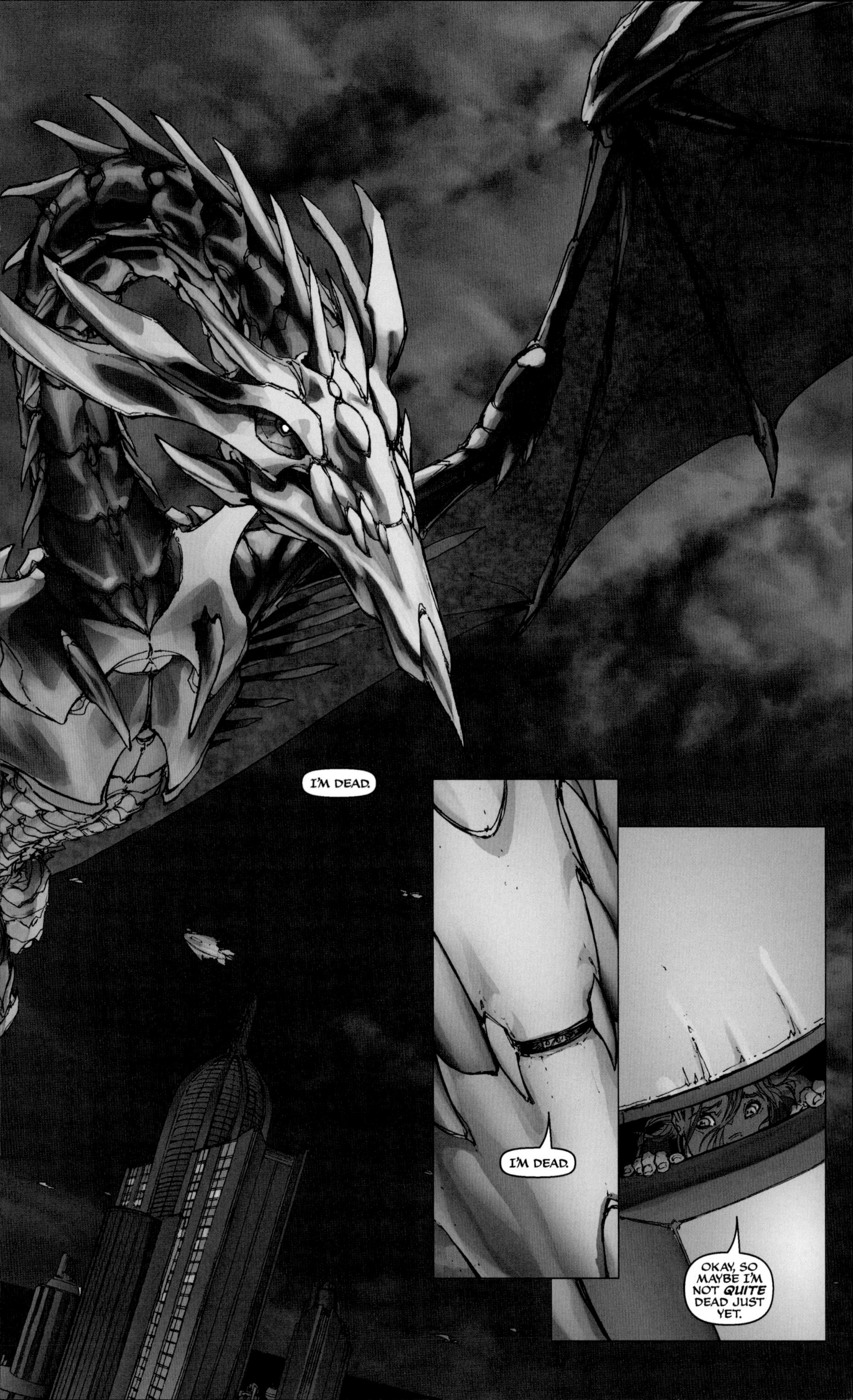
I'M DEAD.
I'M DEAD.
OKAY, SO MAYBE I'M NOT QUITE DEAD JUST YET.

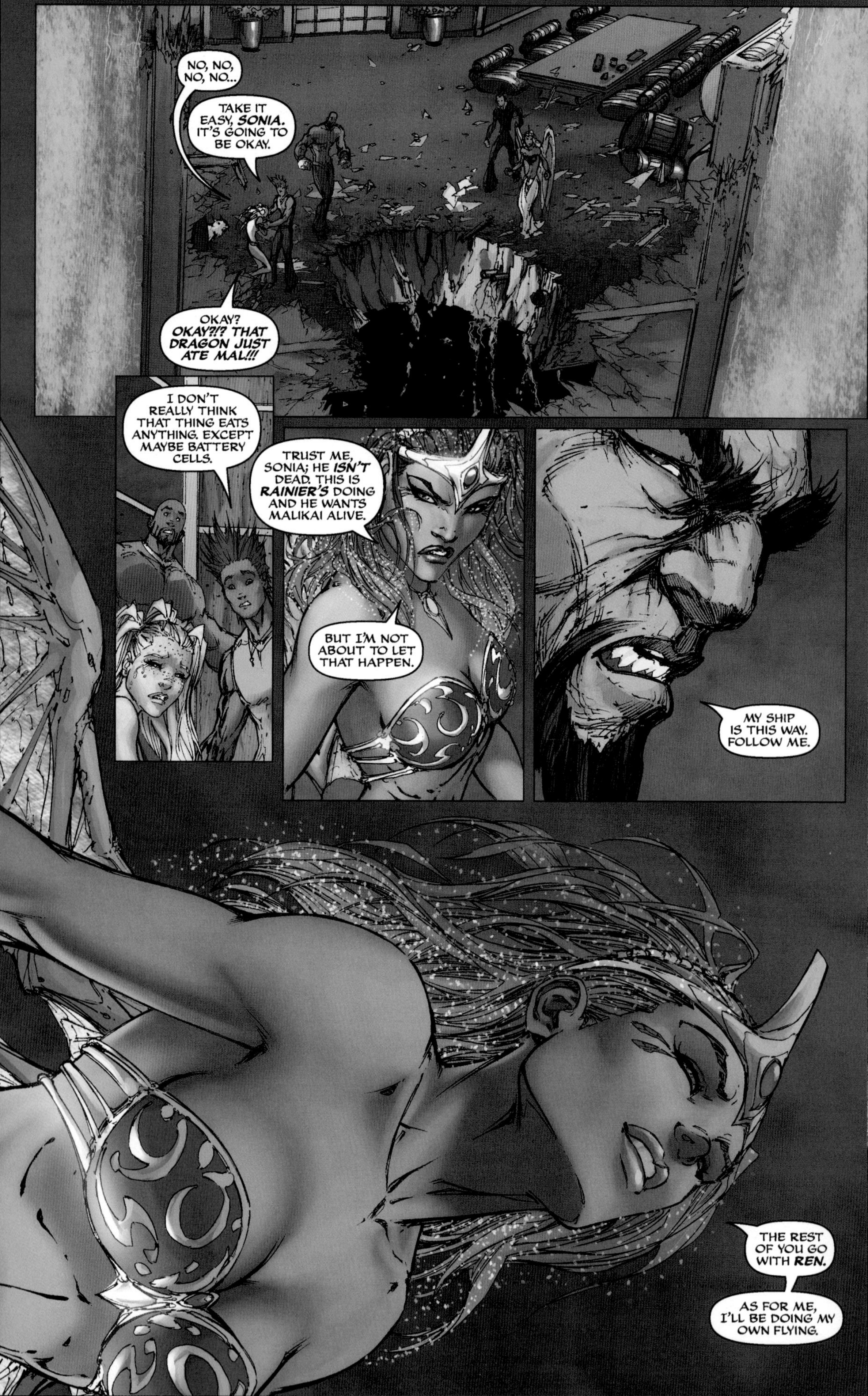
NO, NO, NO, NO...
TAKE IT EASY, SONIA. IT'S GOING TO BE OKAY.
OKAY? OKAY?!? THAT DRAGON JUST ATE MAL!!!
I DON'T REALLY THINK THAT THING EATS ANYTHING. EXCEPT MAYBE BATTERY CELLS.
TRUST ME, SONIA; HE ISN'T DEAD. THIS IS RAINIER'S DOING AND HE WANTS MALIKAI ALIVE.
BUT I'M NOT ABOUT TO LET THAT HAPPEN.
MY SHIP IS THIS WAY. FOLLOW ME.
THE REST OF YOU GO WITH REN.
AS FOR ME, I'LL BE DOING MY OWN FLYING.

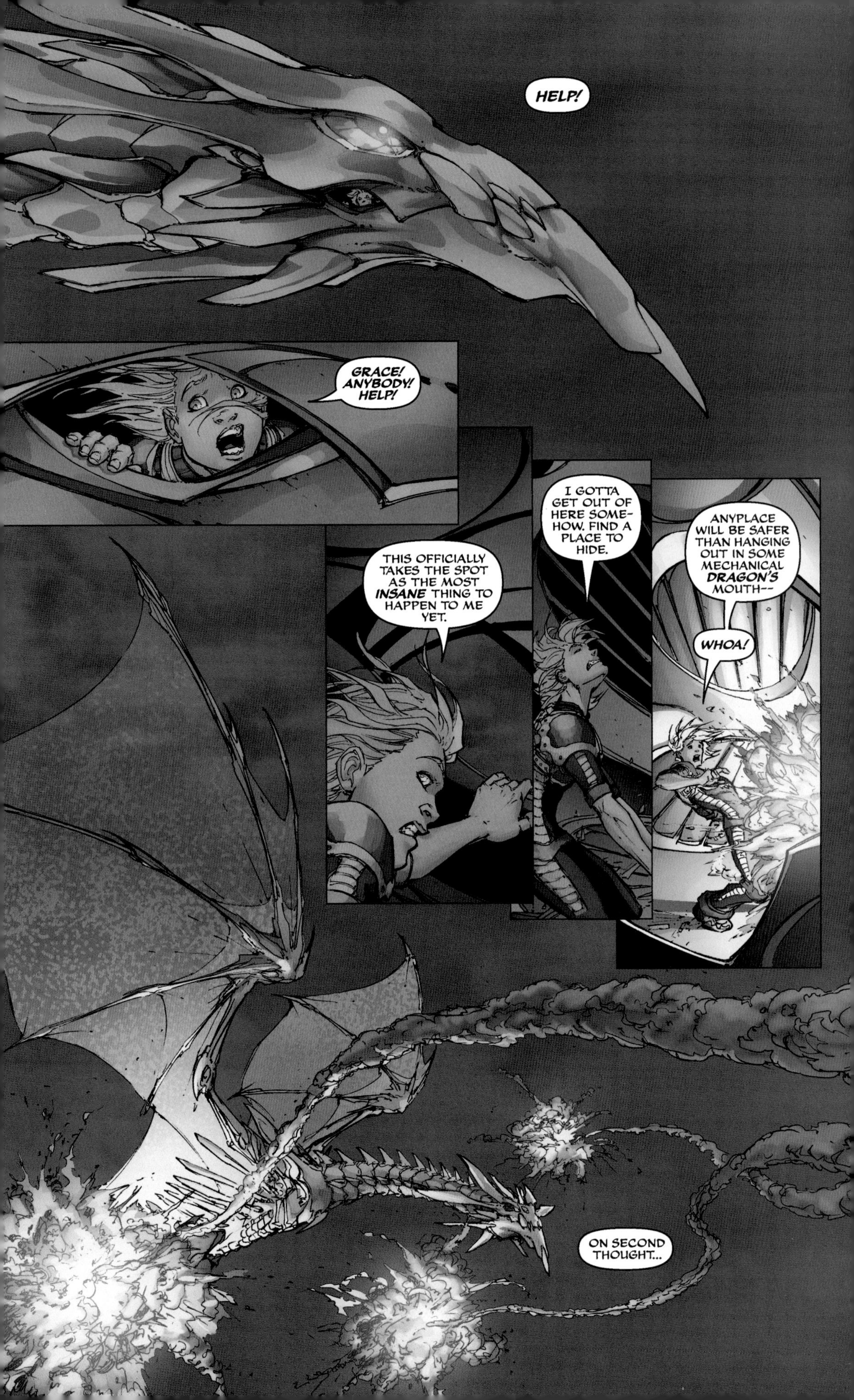
HELP!
GRACE! ANYBODY! HELP!
THIS OFFICIALLY TAKES THE SPOT AS THE MOST INSANE THING TO HAPPEN TO ME YET.
I GOTTA GET OUT OF HERE SOME-HOW. FIND A PLACE TO HIDE.
ANYPLACE WILL BE SAFER THAN HANGING OUT IN SOME MECHANICAL DRAGON'S MOUTH--
WHOA!
ON SECOND THOUGHT...

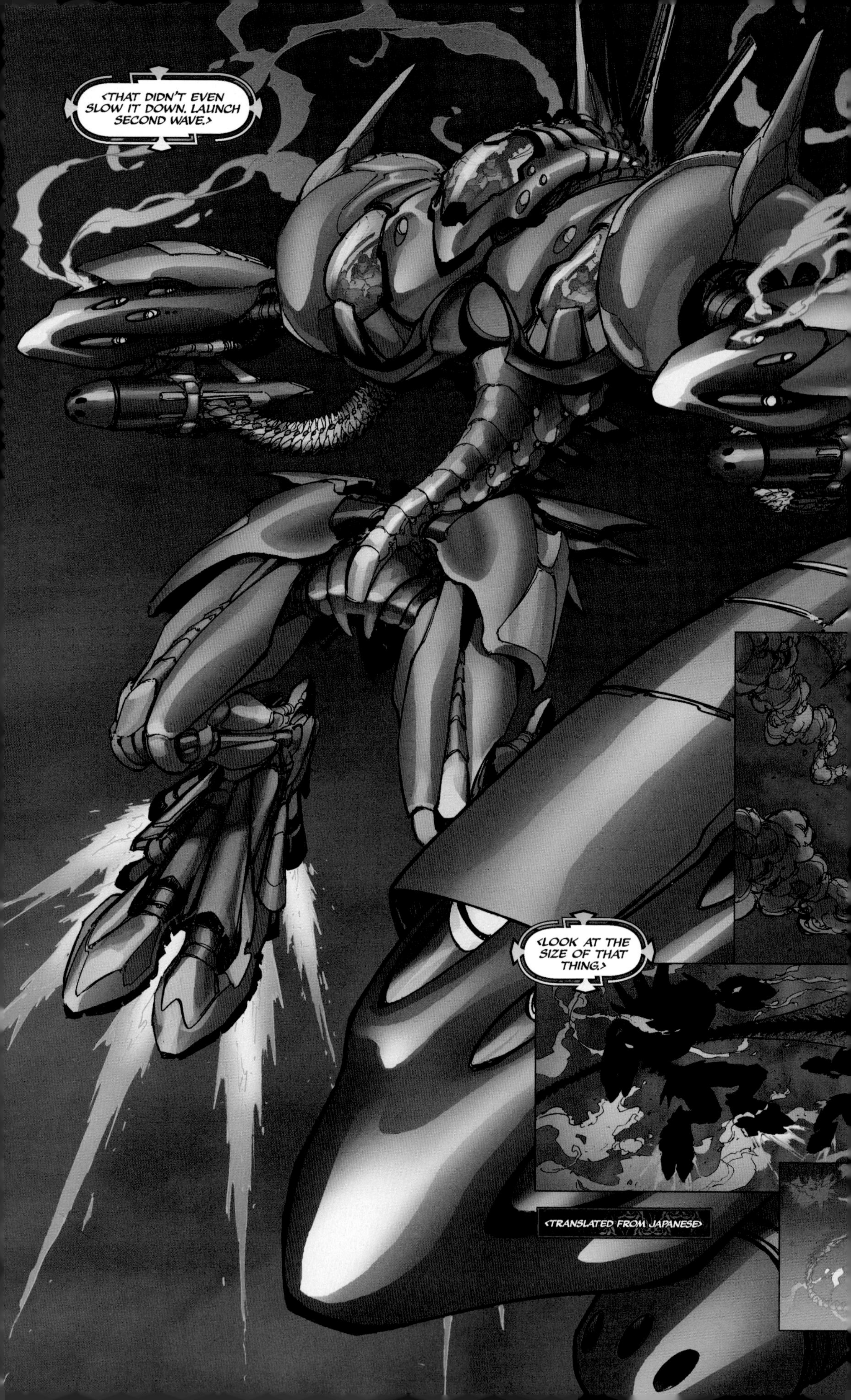
<THAT DIDN'T EVEN SLOW IT DOWN. LAUNCH SECOND WAVE.>
<LOOK AT THE SIZE OF THAT THING.>
<TRANSLATED FROM JAPANESE>

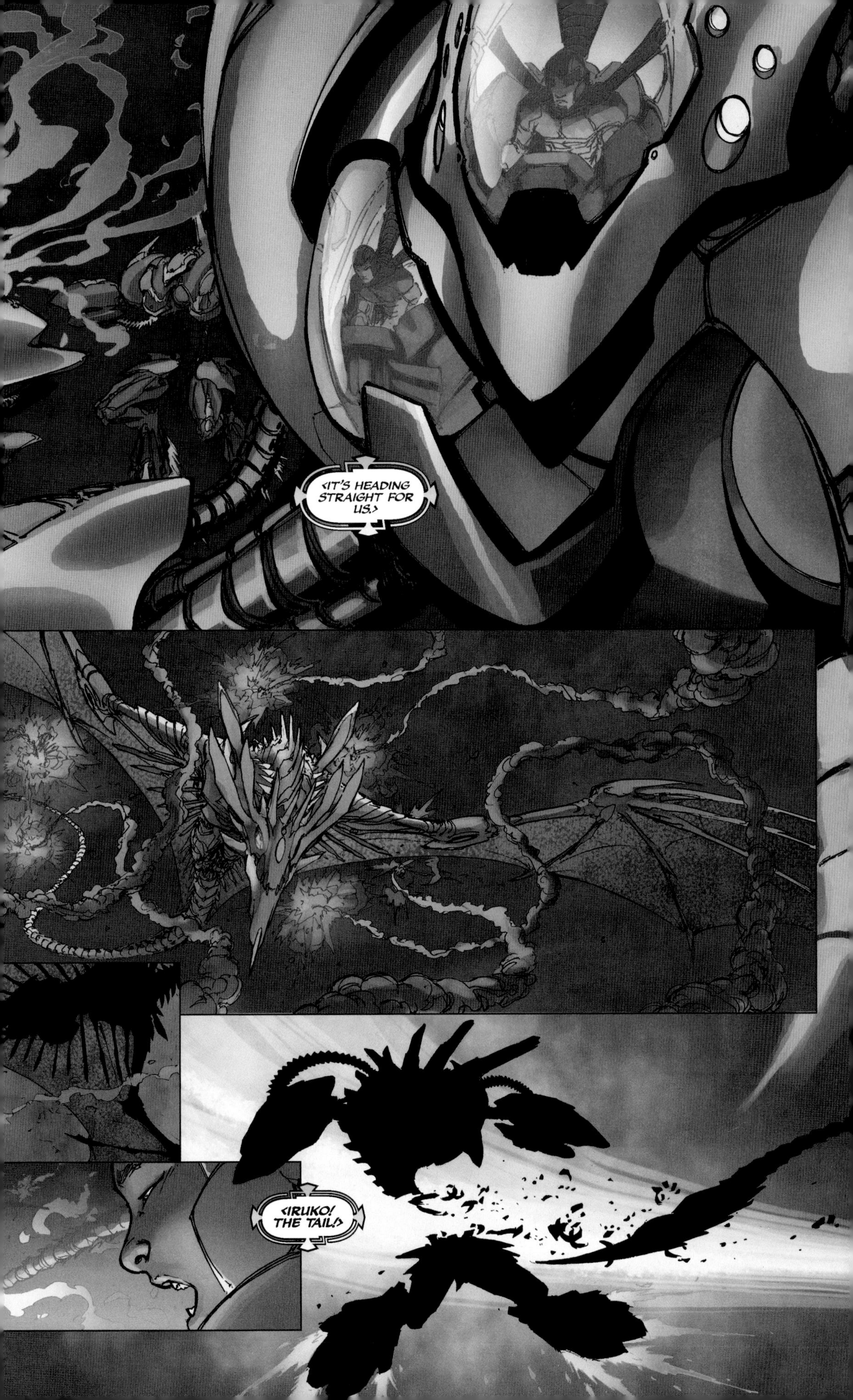
<IT'S HEADING STRAIGHT FOR US.>
<IRUKO! THE TAIL!>

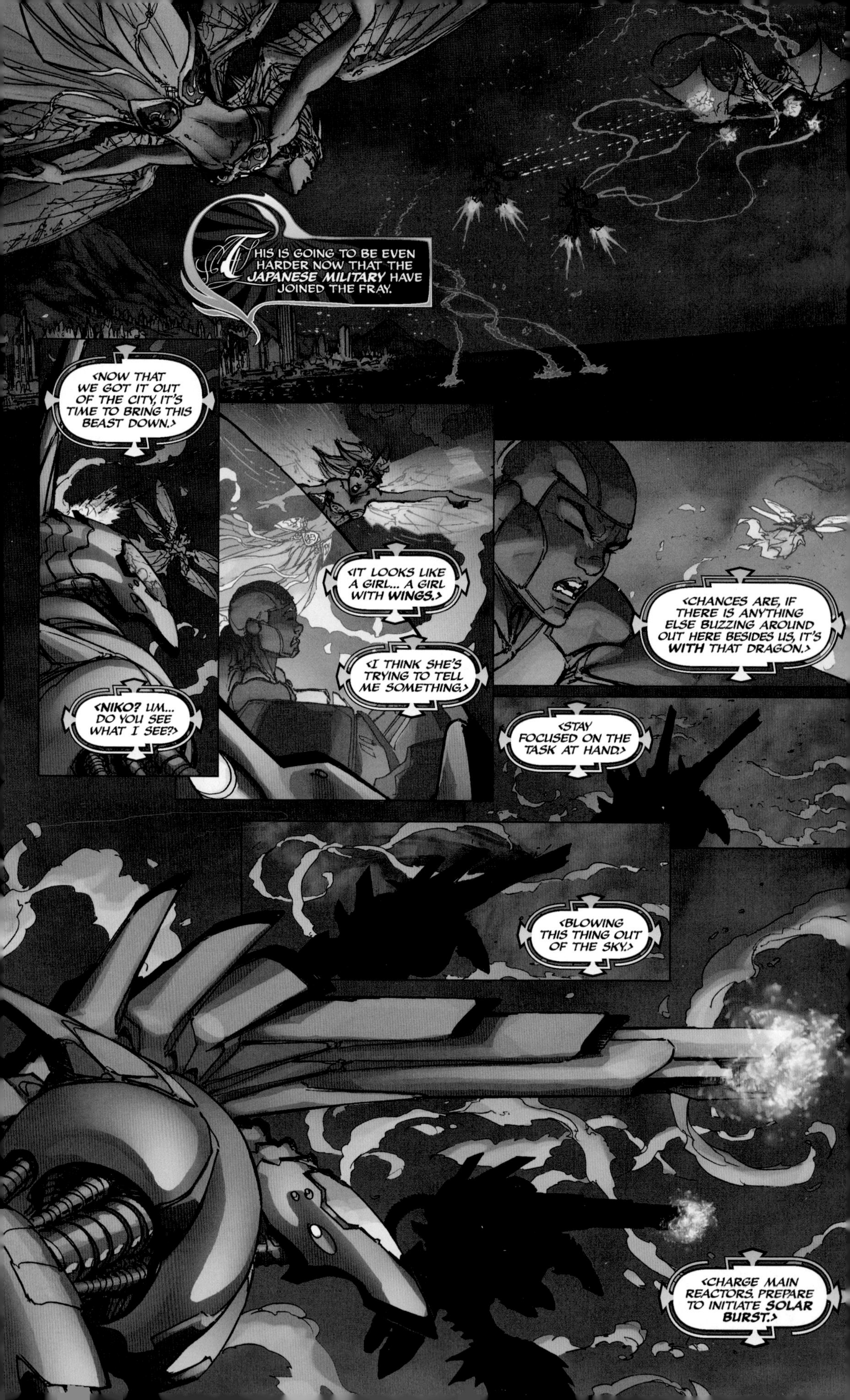
THIS IS GOING TO BE EVEN HARDER NOW THAT THE JAPANESE MILITARY HAVE JOINED THE FRAY.
<NOW THAT WE GOT IT OUT OF THE CITY, IT'S TIME TO BRING THIS BEAST DOWN.>
<NIKO? UM... DO YOU SEE WHAT I SEE?>
<IT LOOKS LIKE A GIRL... A GIRL WITH WINGS.>
<I THINK SHE'S TRYING TO TELL ME SOMETHING.>
<CHANCES ARE, IF THERE IS ANYTHING ELSE BUZZING AROUND OUT HERE BESIDES US, IT'S WITH THAT DRAGON.>
<STAY FOCUSED ON THE TASK AT HAND.>
<BLOWING THIS THING OUT OF THE SKY.>
<CHARGE MAIN REACTORS. PREPARE TO INITIATE SOLAR BURST.>

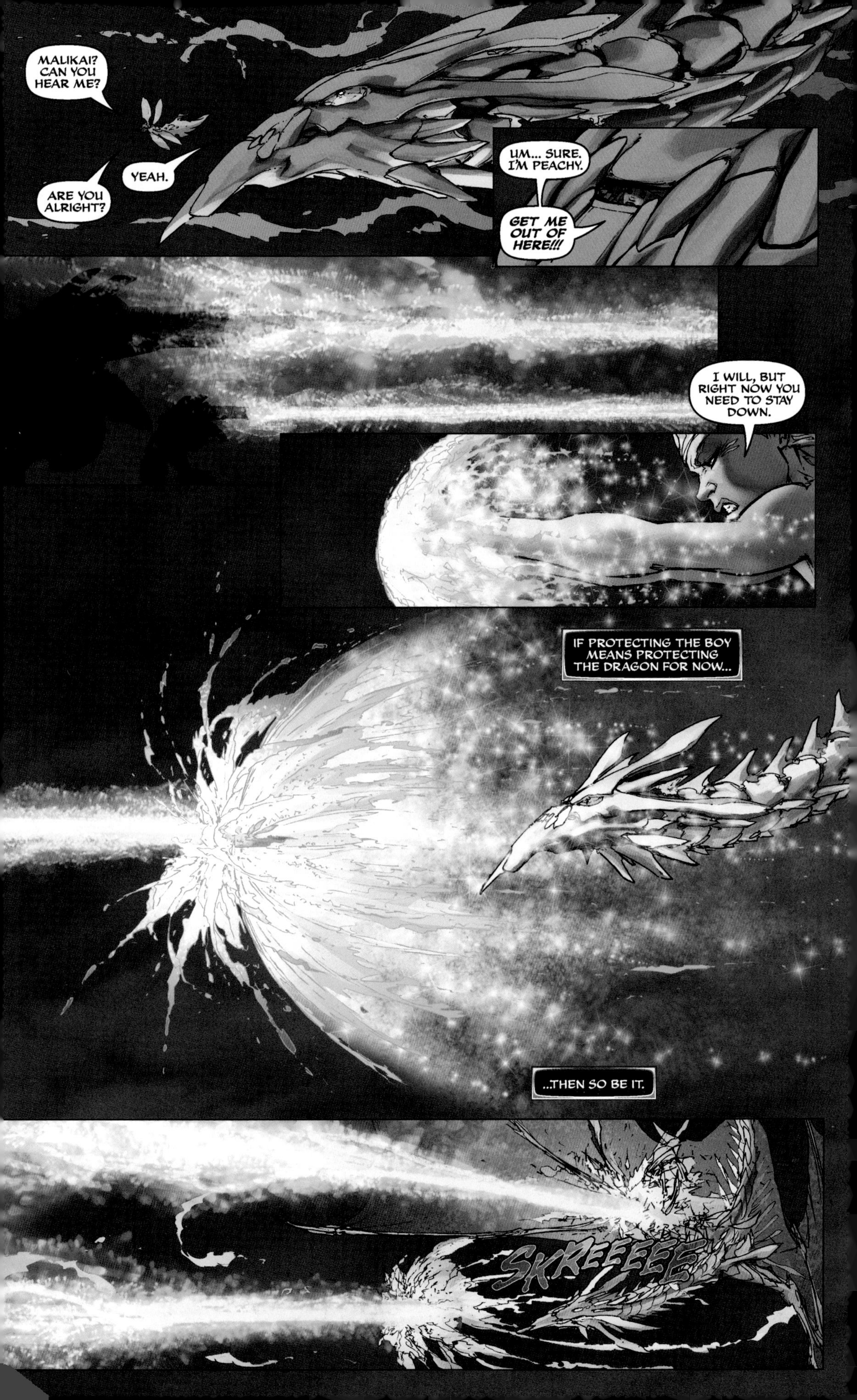
MALIKAI? CAN YOU HEAR ME?
YEAH.
ARE YOU ALRIGHT?
UM... SURE. I'M PEACHY.
GET ME OUT OF HERE!!!
I WILL, BUT RIGHT NOW YOU NEED TO STAY DOWN.
IF PROTECTING THE BOY MEANS PROTECTING THE DRAGON FOR NOW...
..THEN SO BE IT.
SKREEEEEE

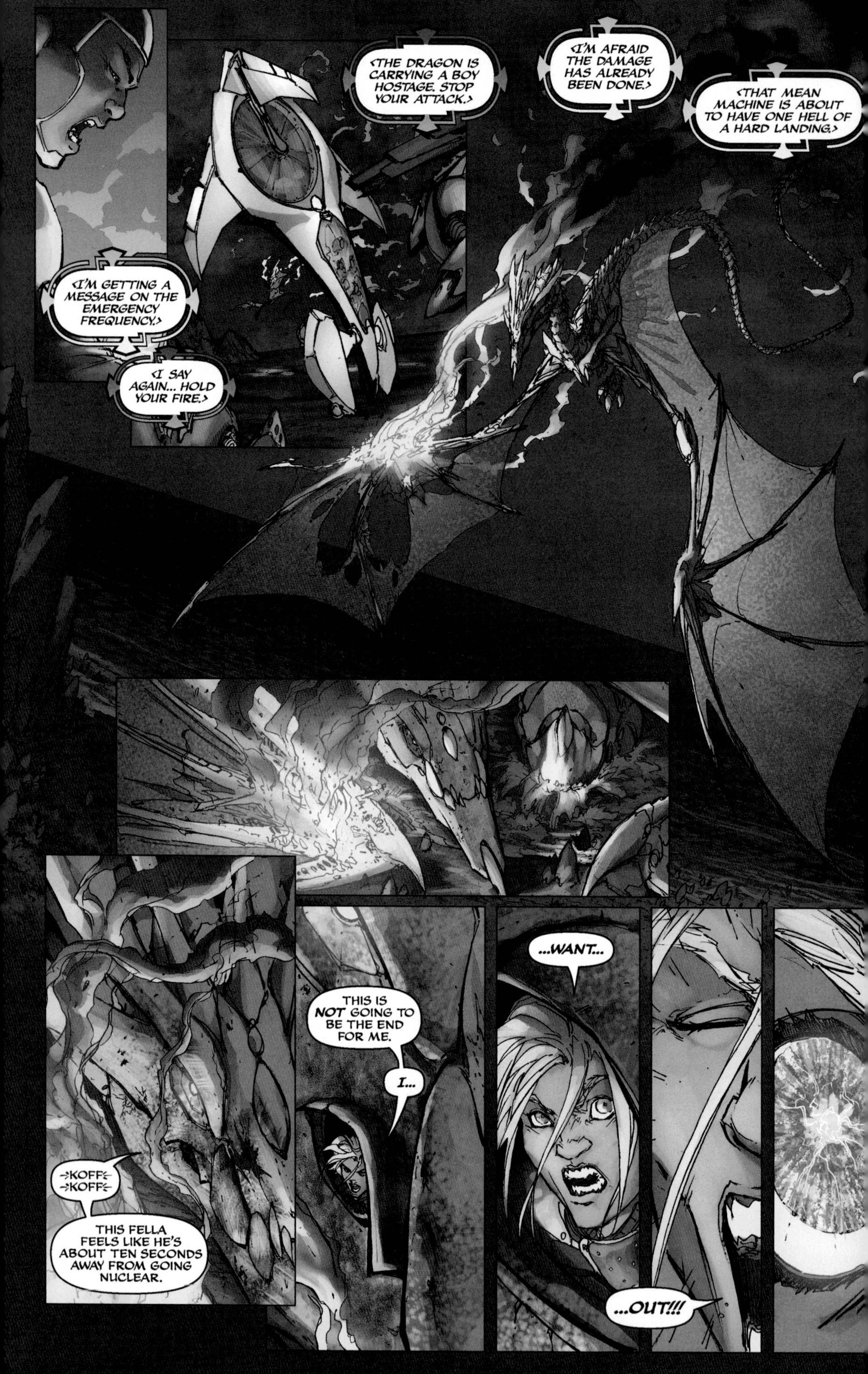
<THE DRAGON IS CARRYING A BOY HOSTAGE. STOP YOUR ATTACK.>
<I'M AFRAID THE DAMAGE HAS ALREADY BEEN DONE.>
<THAT MEAN MACHINE IS ABOUT TO HAVE ONE HELL OF A HARD LANDING.>
<I'M GETTING A MESSAGE ON THE EMERGENCY FREQUENCY.>
<I SAY AGAIN... HOLD YOUR FIRE.>
KOFF KOFF
THIS FELLA FEELS LIKE HE'S ABOUT TEN SECONDS AWAY FROM GOING NUCLEAR.
THIS IS NOT GOING TO BE THE END FOR ME.
I...
...WANT...
...OUT!!!

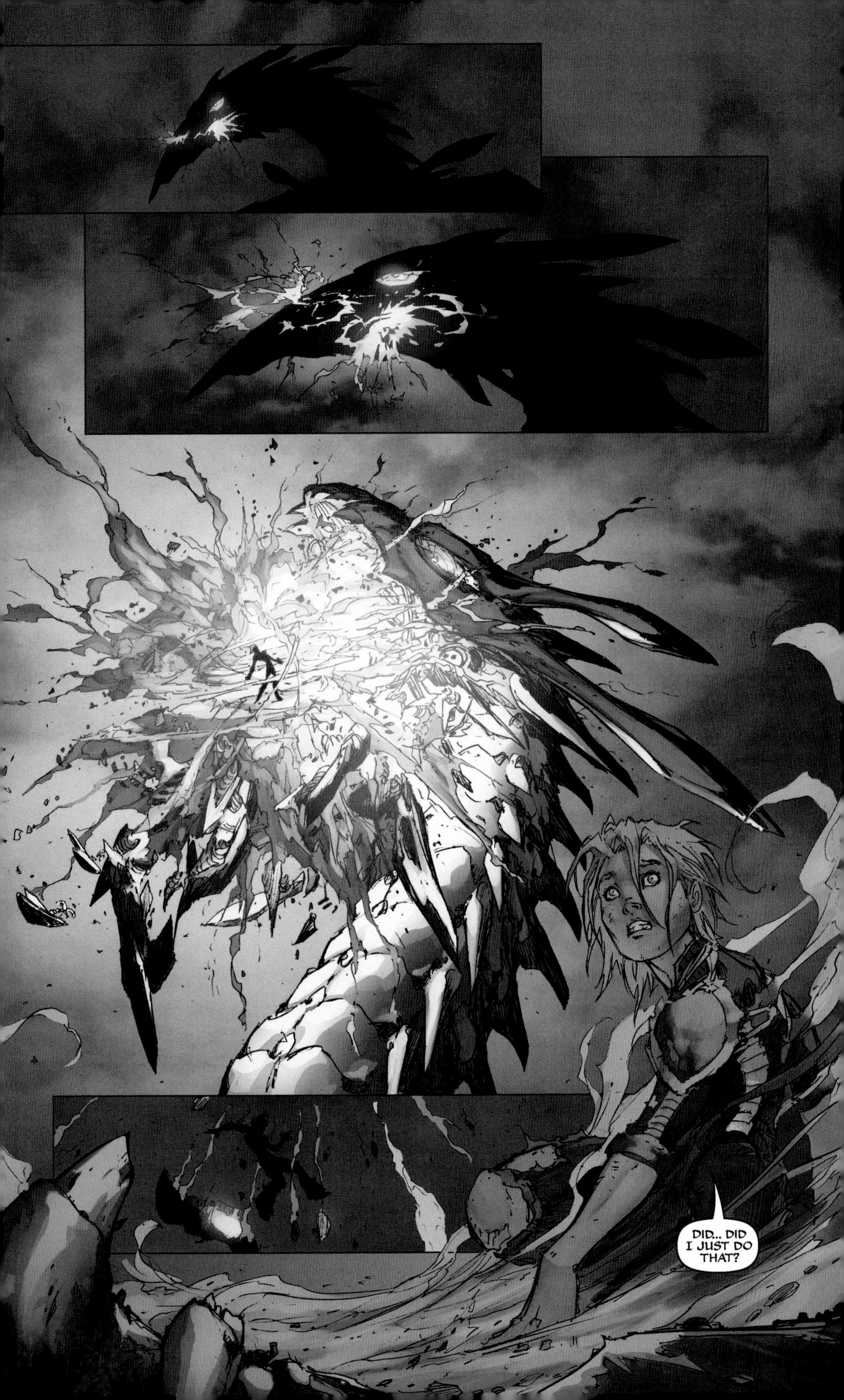
DID... DID I JUST DO THAT?

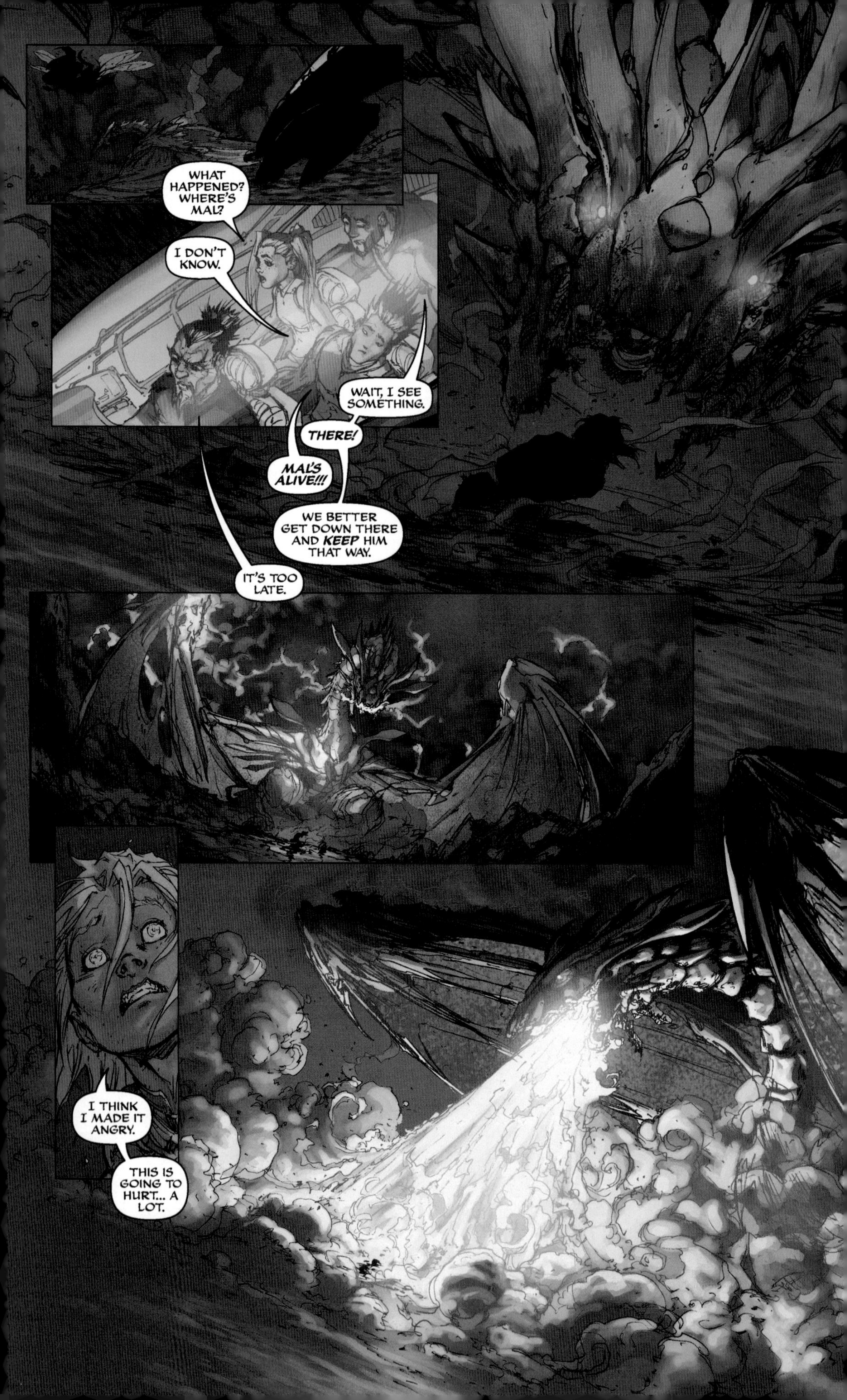
WHAT HAPPENED? WHERE'S MAL?
I DON'T KNOW.
WAIT, I SEE SOMETHING.
THERE!
MAL'S ALIVE!!!
WE BETTER GET DOWN THERE AND KEEP HIM THAT WAY.
IT'S TOO LATE.
I THINK I MADE IT ANGRY.
THIS IS GOING TO HURT... A LOT.

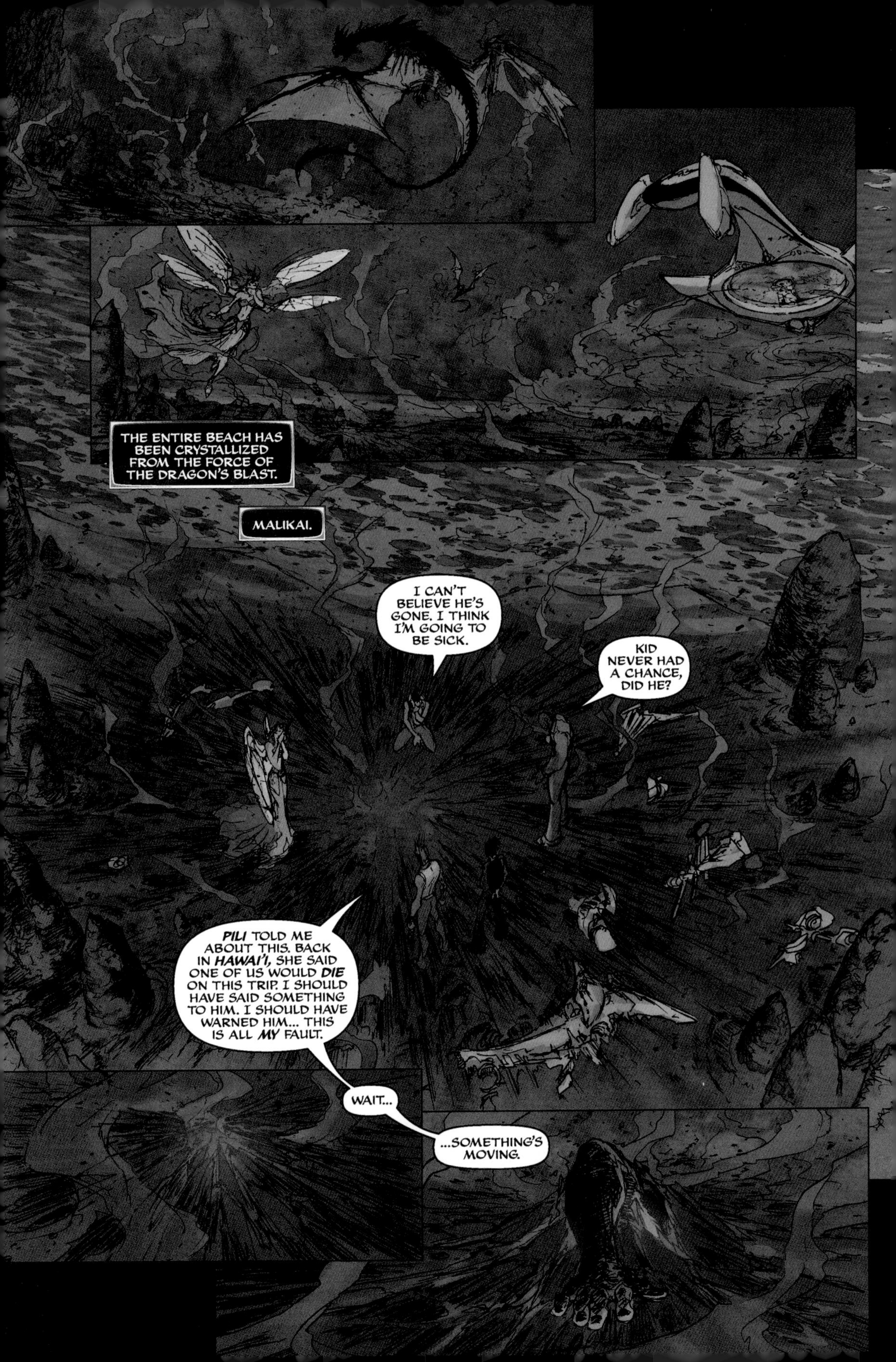
THE ENTIRE BEACH HAS BEEN CRYSTALLIZED FROM THE FORCE OF THE DRAGON'S BLAST.
MALIKAI.
I CAN'T BELIEVE HE'S GONE. I THINK I'M GOING TO BE SICK.
KID NEVER HAD A CHANCE, DID HE?
PILI TOLD ME ABOUT THIS. BACK IN HAWAI'I, SHE SAID ONE OF US WOULD DIE ON THIS TRIP. I SHOULD HAVE SAID SOMETHING TO HIM. I SHOULD HAVE WARNED HIM... THIS IS ALL MY FAULT.
WAIT...
...SOMETHING'S MOVING.

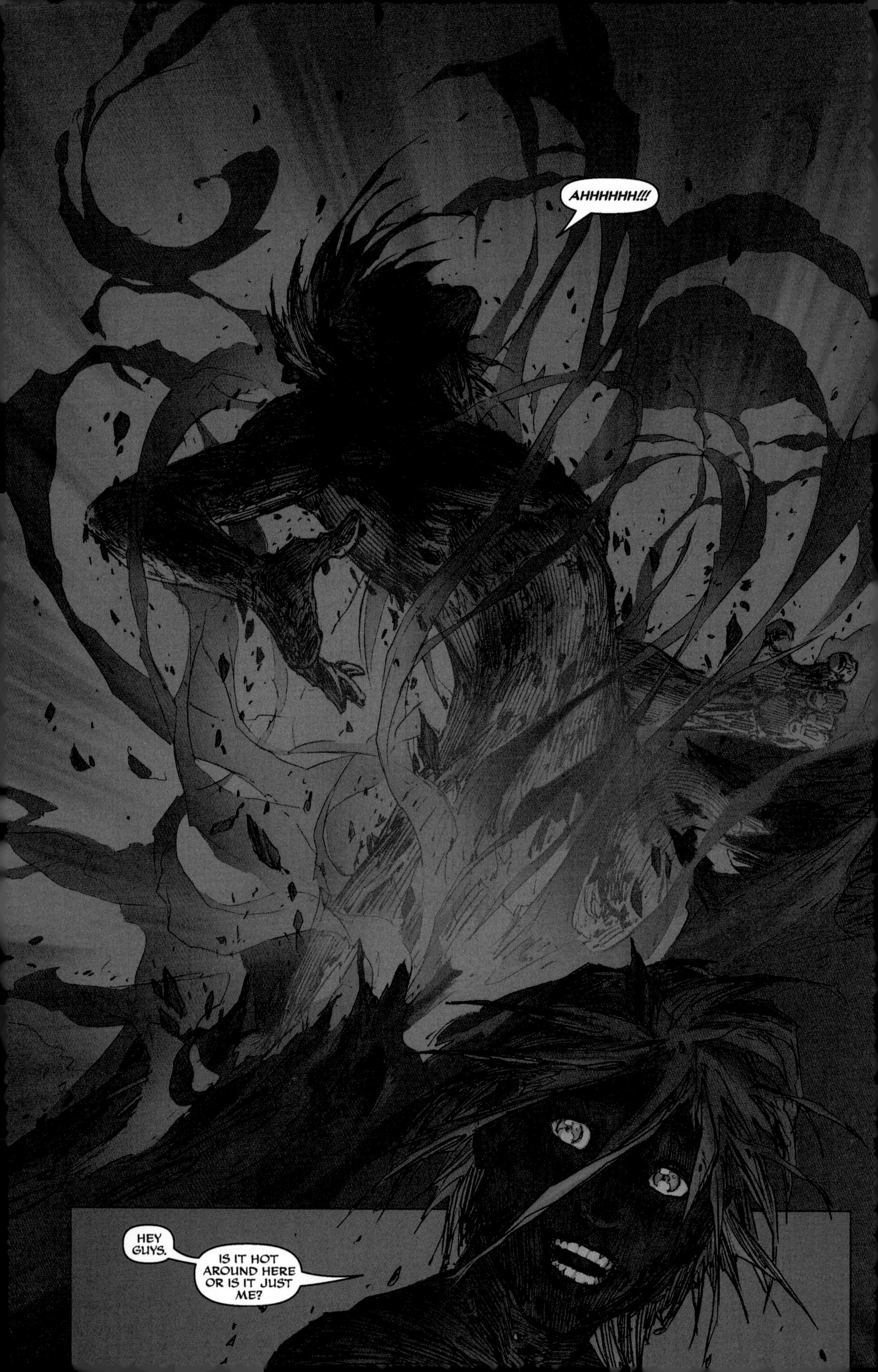
AHHHHHH!!!
HEY GUYS.
IS IT HOT AROUND HERE OR IS IT JUST ME?

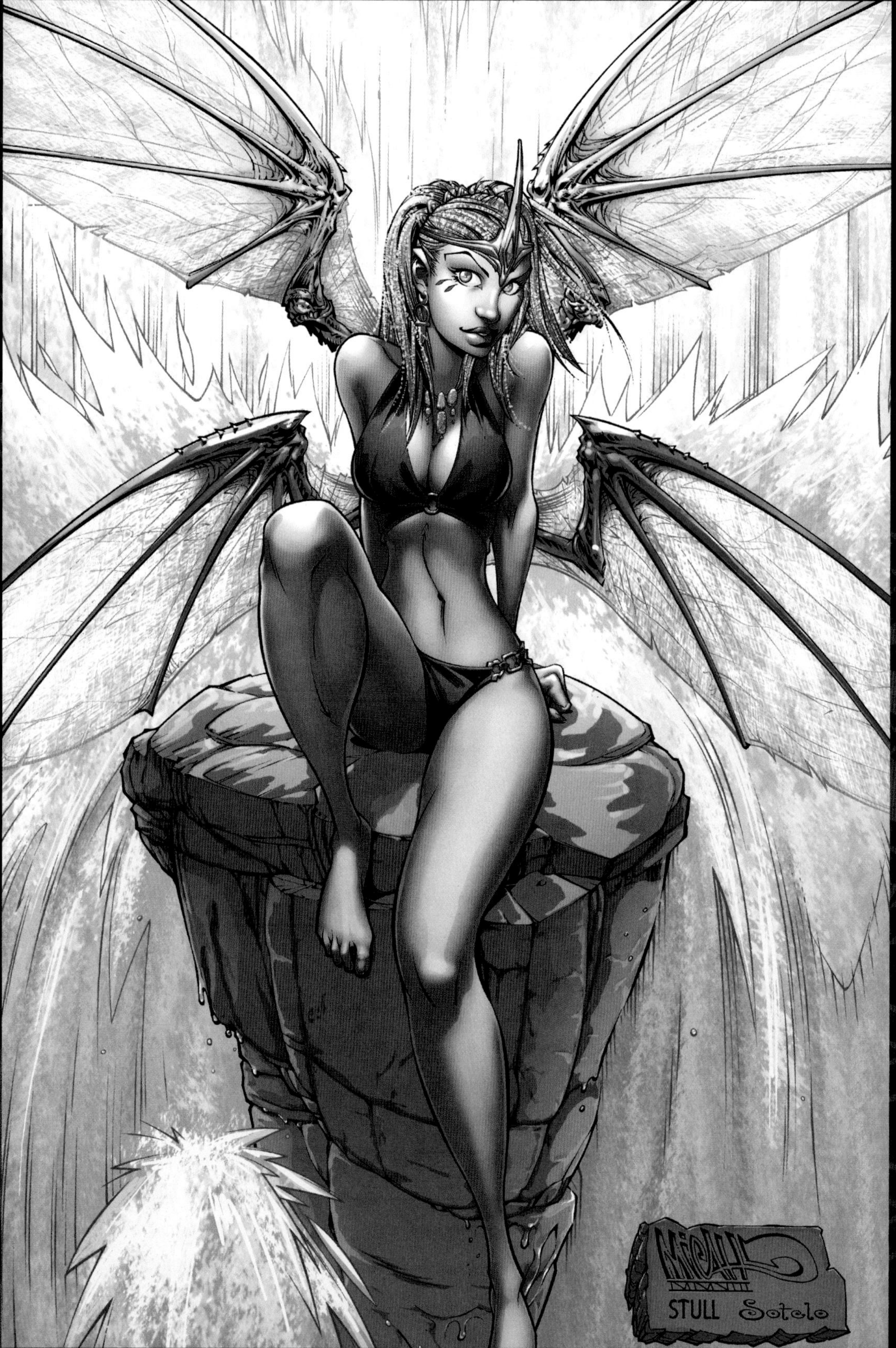
MICAH
STULL Sotelo

GRACE

‧ PIN-UP FROM ASPEN SPLASH: 2008 SWIMSUIT SPECTACULAR ‧

by

‧ MICAH GUNNELL ‧ ROB STULL ‧ BETH SOTELO ‧

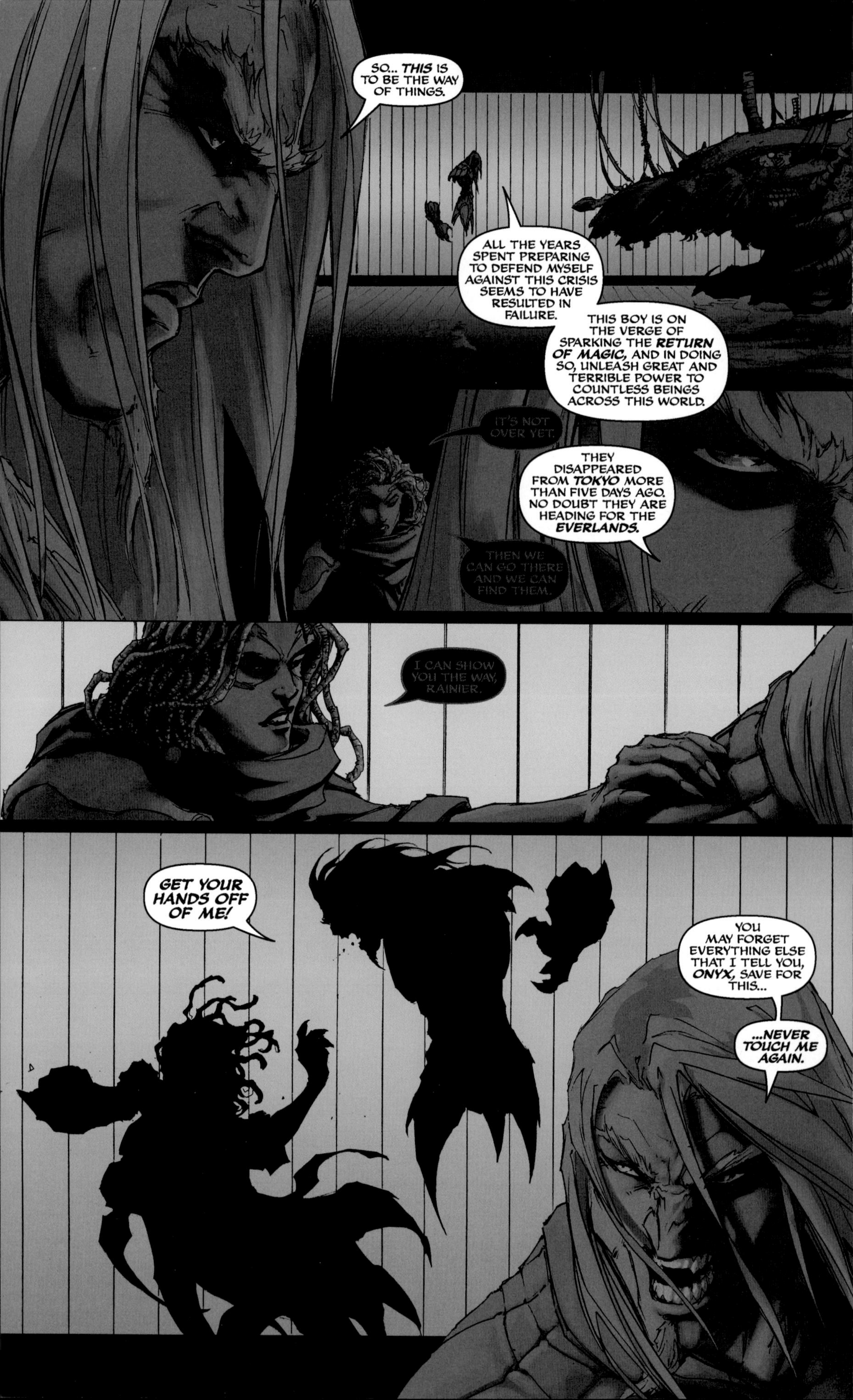
SO... THIS IS TO BE THE WAY OF THINGS.
ALL THE YEARS SPENT PREPARING TO DEFEND MYSELF AGAINST THIS CRISIS SEEMS TO HAVE RESULTED IN FAILURE.
THIS BOY IS ON THE VERGE OF SPARKING THE RETURN OF MAGIC, AND IN DOING SO, UNLEASH GREAT AND TERRIBLE POWER TO COUNTLESS BEINGS ACROSS THIS WORLD.
IT'S NOT OVER YET.
THEY DISAPPEARED FROM TOKYO MORE THAN FIVE DAYS AGO. NO DOUBT THEY ARE HEADING FOR THE EVERLANDS.
THEN WE CAN GO THERE AND WE CAN FIND THEM.
I CAN SHOW YOU THE WAY, RAINIER.
GET YOUR HANDS OFF OF ME!
YOU MAY FORGET EVERYTHING ELSE THAT I TELL YOU, ONYX, SAVE FOR THIS...
...NEVER TOUCH ME AGAIN.

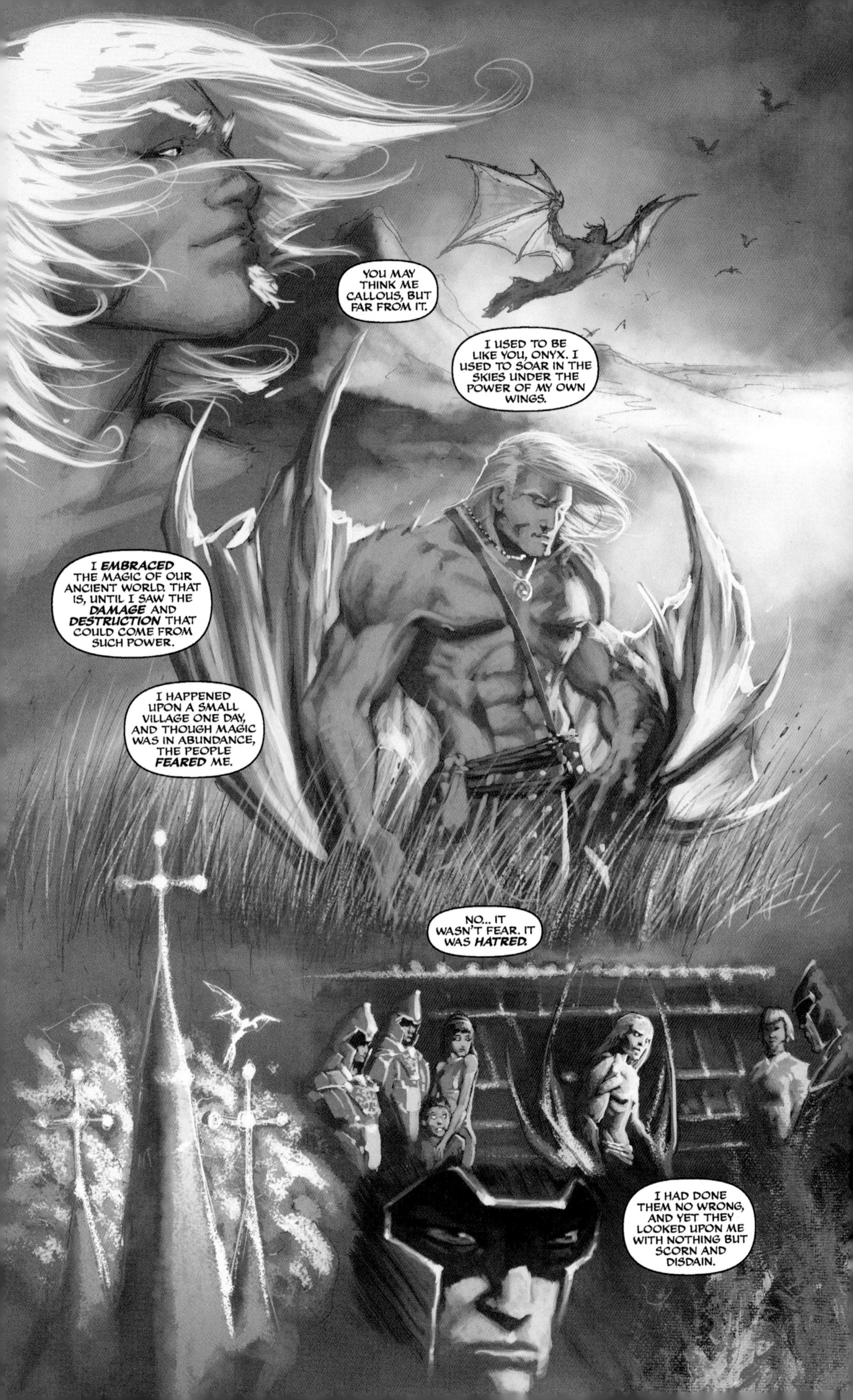
YOU MAY THINK ME CALLOUS, BUT FAR FROM IT.
I USED TO BE LIKE YOU, ONYX. I USED TO SOAR IN THE SKIES UNDER THE POWER OF MY OWN WINGS.
I EMBRACED THE MAGIC OF OUR ANCIENT WORLD. THAT IS, UNTIL I SAW THE DAMAGE AND DESTRUCTION THAT COULD COME FROM SUCH POWER.
I HAPPENED UPON A SMALL VILLAGE ONE DAY, AND THOUGH MAGIC WAS IN ABUNDANCE, THE PEOPLE FEARED ME.
NO... IT WASN'T FEAR. IT WAS HATRED.
I HAD DONE THEM NO WRONG, AND YET THEY LOOKED UPON ME WITH NOTHING BUT SCORN AND DISDAIN.

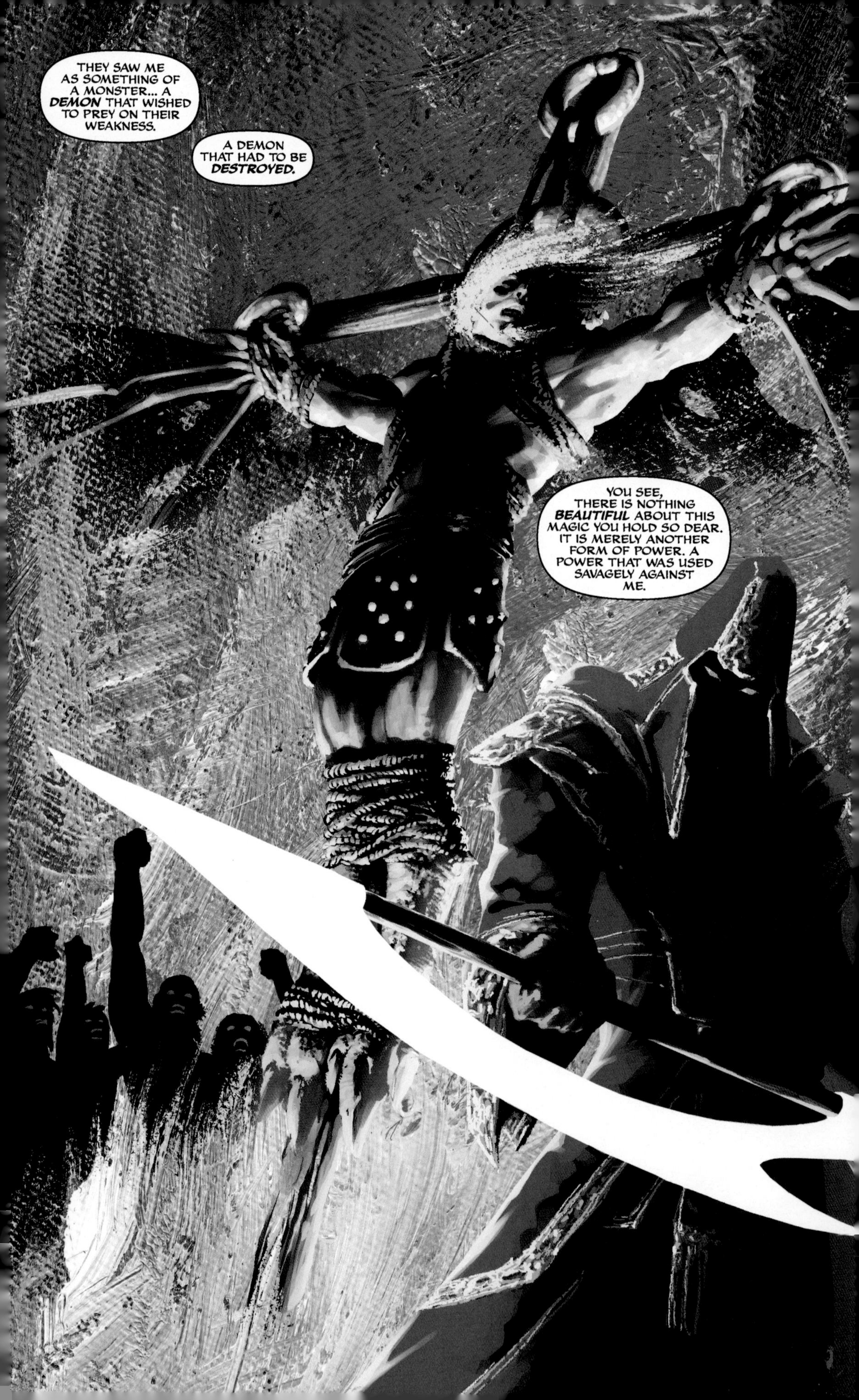
THEY SAW ME AS SOMETHING OF A MONSTER... A DEMON THAT WISHED TO PREY ON THEIR WEAKNESS.
A DEMON THAT HAD TO BE DESTROYED.
YOU SEE, THERE IS NOTHING BEAUTIFUL ABOUT THIS MAGIC YOU HOLD SO DEAR. IT IS MERELY ANOTHER FORM OF POWER. A POWER THAT WAS USED SAVAGELY AGAINST ME.

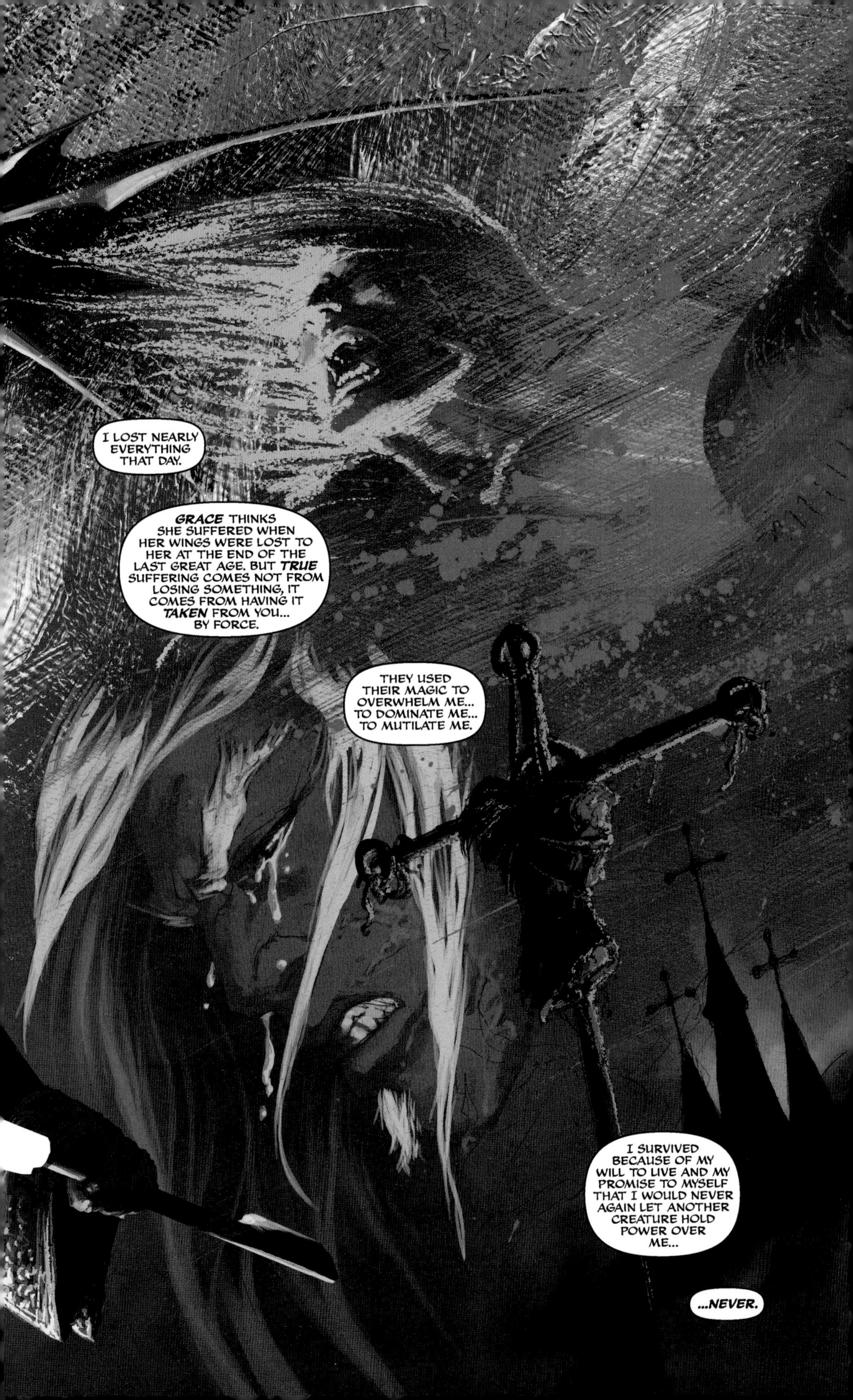
I LOST NEARLY EVERYTHING THAT DAY.
GRACE THINKS SHE SUFFERED WHEN HER WINGS WERE LOST TO HER AT THE END OF THE LAST GREAT AGE. BUT TRUE SUFFERING COMES NOT FROM LOSING SOMETHING, IT COMES FROM HAVING IT TAKEN FROM YOU... BY FORCE.
THEY USED THEIR MAGIC TO OVERWHELM ME... TO DOMINATE ME... TO MUTILATE ME.
I SURVIVED BECAUSE OF MY WILL TO LIVE AND MY PROMISE TO MYSELF THAT I WOULD NEVER AGAIN LET ANOTHER CREATURE HOLD POWER OVER ME...
...NEVER.

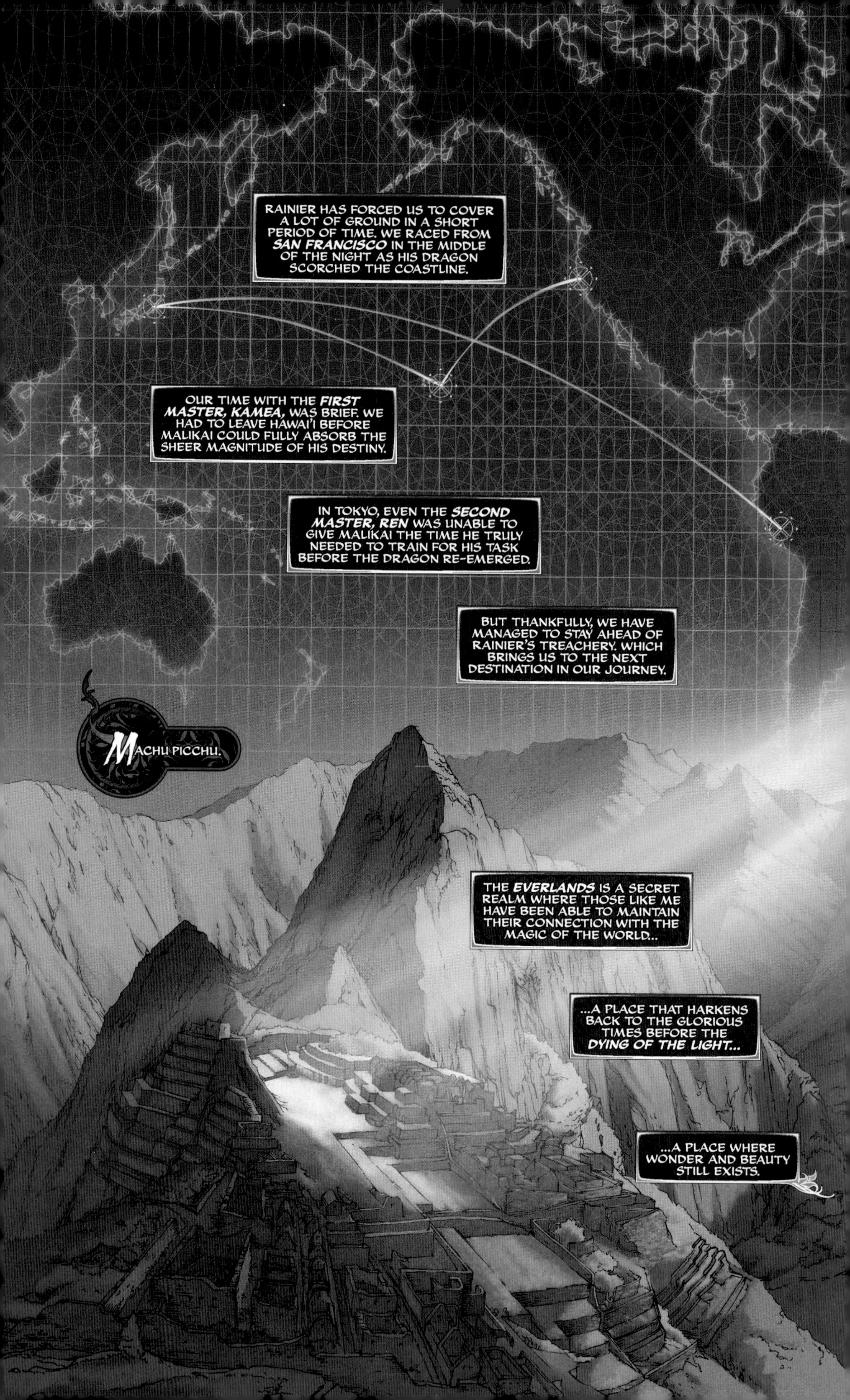
RAINIER HAS FORCED US TO COVER A LOT OF GROUND IN A SHORT PERIOD OF TIME. WE RACED FROM SAN FRANCISCO IN THE MIDDLE OF THE NIGHT AS HIS DRAGON SCORCHED THE COASTLINE.
OUR TIME WITH THE FIRST MASTER, KAMEA, WAS BRIEF. WE HAD TO LEAVE HAWAI'I BEFORE MALIKAI COULD FULLY ABSORB THE SHEER MAGNITUDE OF HIS DESTINY.
IN TOKYO, EVEN THE SECOND MASTER, REN WAS UNABLE TO GIVE MALIKAI THE TIME HE TRULY NEEDED TO TRAIN FOR HIS TASK BEFORE THE DRAGON RE-EMERGED.
BUT THANKFULLY, WE HAVE MANAGED TO STAY AHEAD OF RAINIER'S TREACHERY. WHICH BRINGS US TO THE NEXT DESTINATION IN OUR JOURNEY.
MACHU PICCHU.
THE EVERLANDS IS A SECRET REALM WHERE THOSE LIKE ME HAVE BEEN ABLE TO MAINTAIN THEIR CONNECTION WITH THE MAGIC OF THE WORLD...
...A PLACE THAT HARKENS BACK TO THE GLORIOUS TIMES BEFORE THE DYING OF THE LIGHT...
...A PLACE WHERE WONDER AND BEAUTY STILL EXISTS.

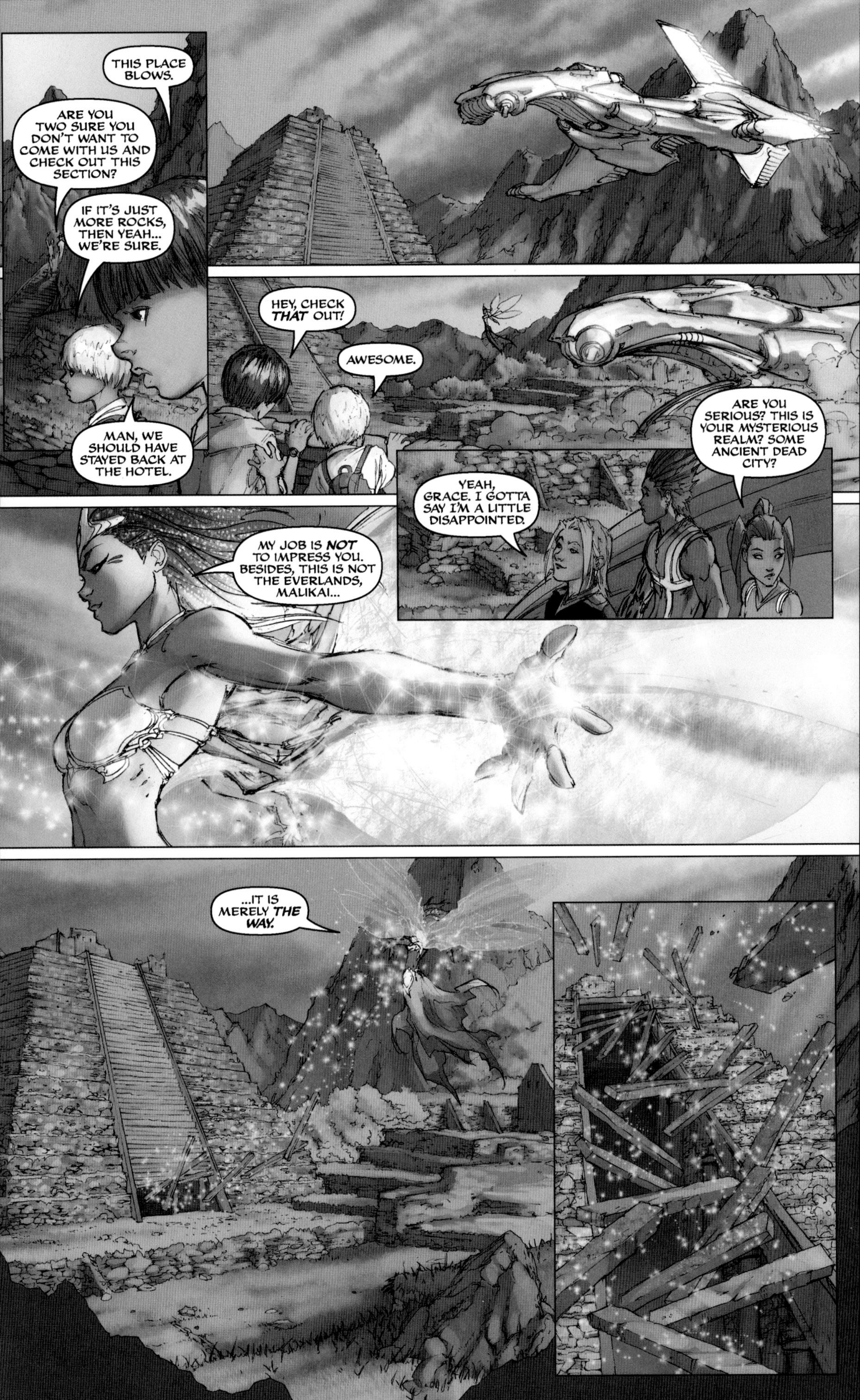
THIS PLACE BLOWS.
ARE YOU TWO SURE YOU DON'T WANT TO COME WITH US AND CHECK OUT THIS SECTION?
IF IT'S JUST MORE ROCKS, THEN YEAH... WE'RE SURE.
MAN, WE SHOULD HAVE STAYED BACK AT THE HOTEL.
HEY, CHECK THAT OUT!
AWESOME.
ARE YOU SERIOUS? THIS IS YOUR MYSTERIOUS REALM? SOME ANCIENT DEAD CITY?
YEAH, GRACE. I GOTTA SAY I'M A LITTLE DISAPPOINTED.
MY JOB IS NOT TO IMPRESS YOU. BESIDES, THIS IS NOT THE EVERLANDS, MALIKAI...
...IT IS MERELY THE WAY.

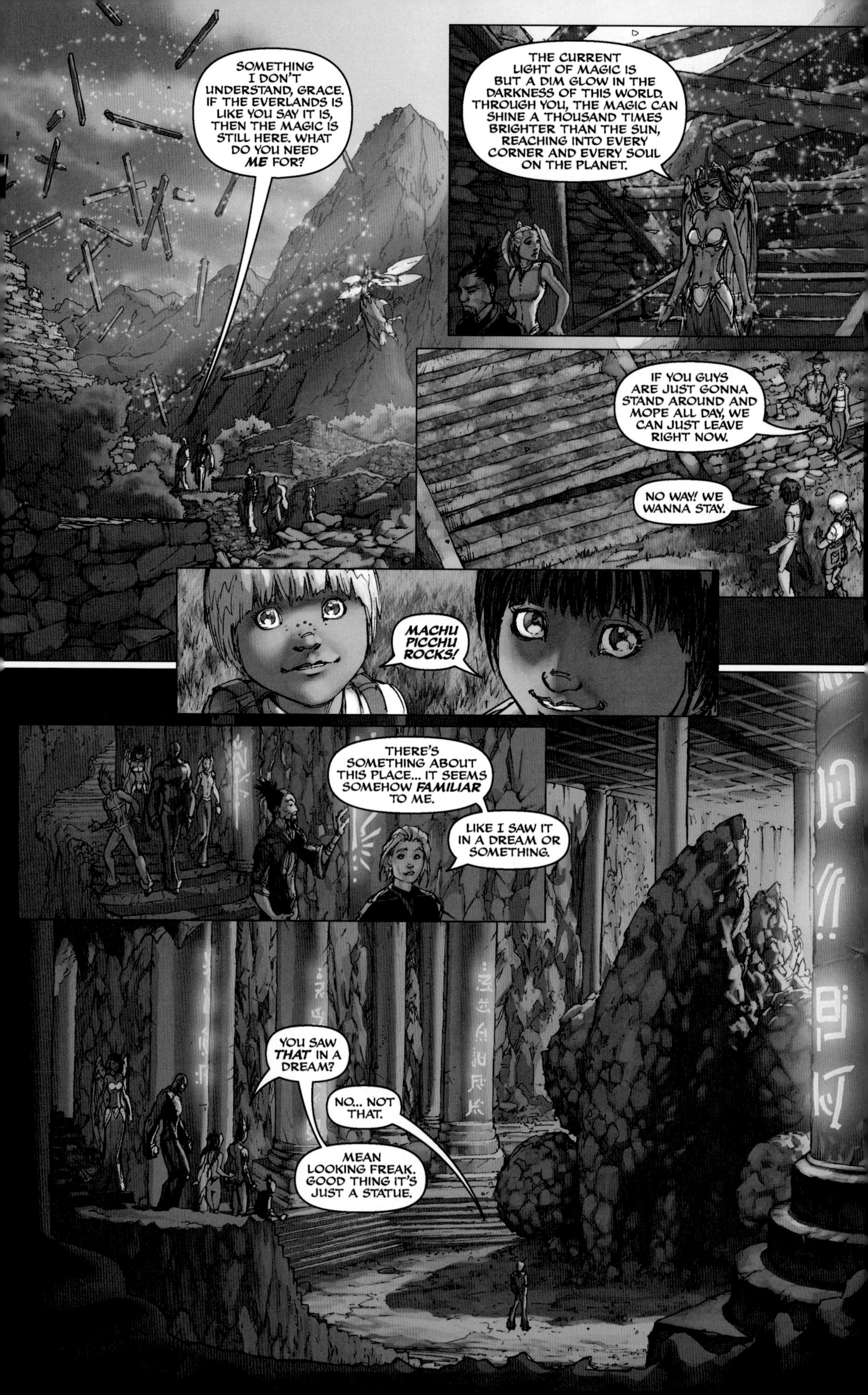
SOMETHING I DON'T UNDERSTAND, GRACE. IF THE EVERLANDS IS LIKE YOU SAY IT IS, THEN THE MAGIC IS STILL HERE. WHAT DO YOU NEED ME FOR?
THE CURRENT LIGHT OF MAGIC IS BUT A DIM GLOW IN THE DARKNESS OF THIS WORLD. THROUGH YOU, THE MAGIC CAN SHINE A THOUSAND TIMES BRIGHTER THAN THE SUN, REACHING INTO EVERY CORNER AND EVERY SOUL ON THE PLANET.
IF YOU GUYS ARE JUST GONNA STAND AROUND AND MOPE ALL DAY, WE CAN JUST LEAVE RIGHT NOW.
NO WAY! WE WANNA STAY.
MACHU PICCHU ROCKS!
THERE'S SOMETHING ABOUT THIS PLACE... IT SEEMS SOMEHOW FAMILIAR TO ME.
LIKE I SAW IT IN A DREAM OR SOMETHING.
YOU SAW THAT IN A DREAM?
NO... NOT THAT.
MEAN LOOKING FREAK. GOOD THING IT'S JUST A STATUE.

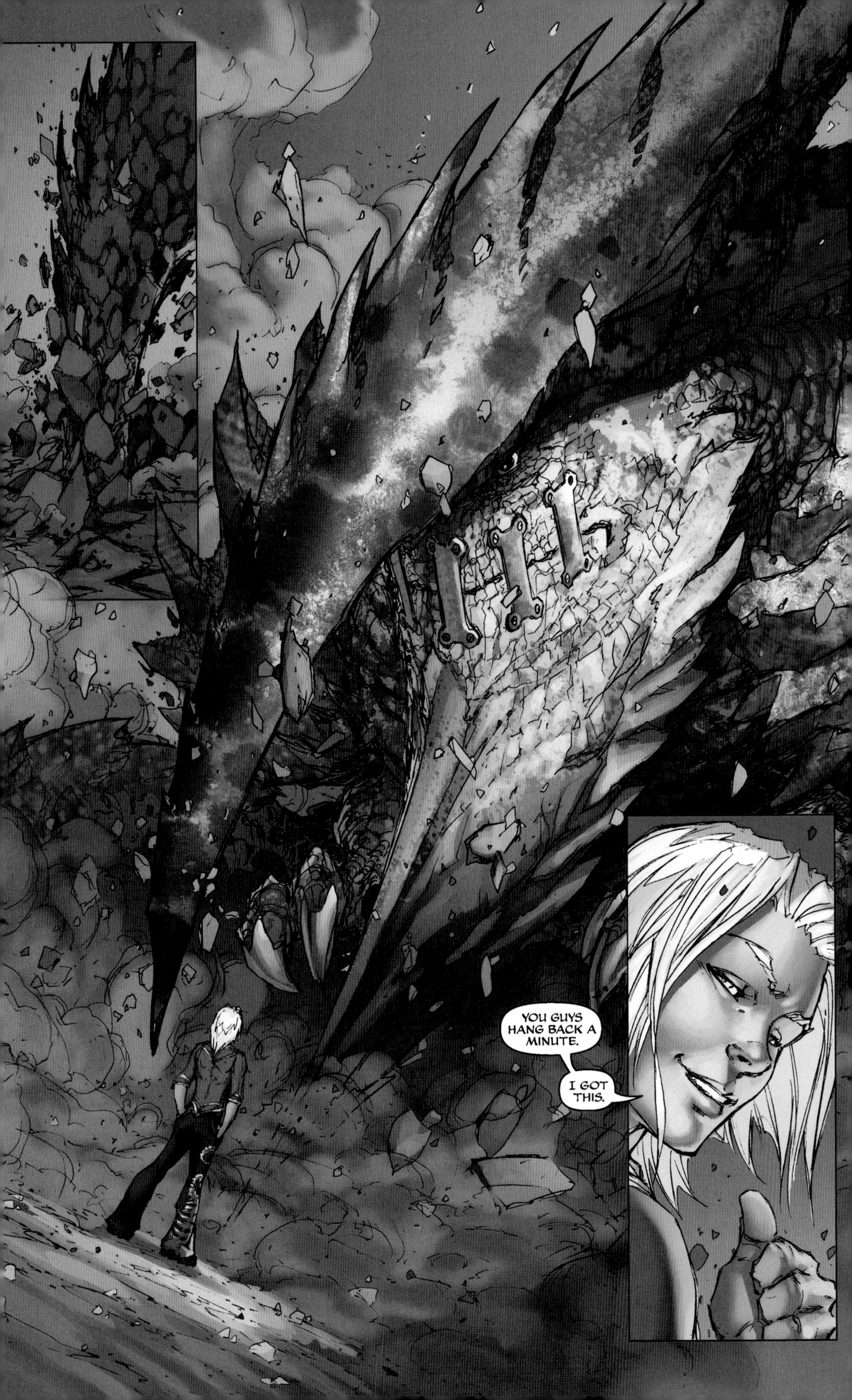
YOU GUYS HANG BACK A MINUTE.
I GOT THIS.

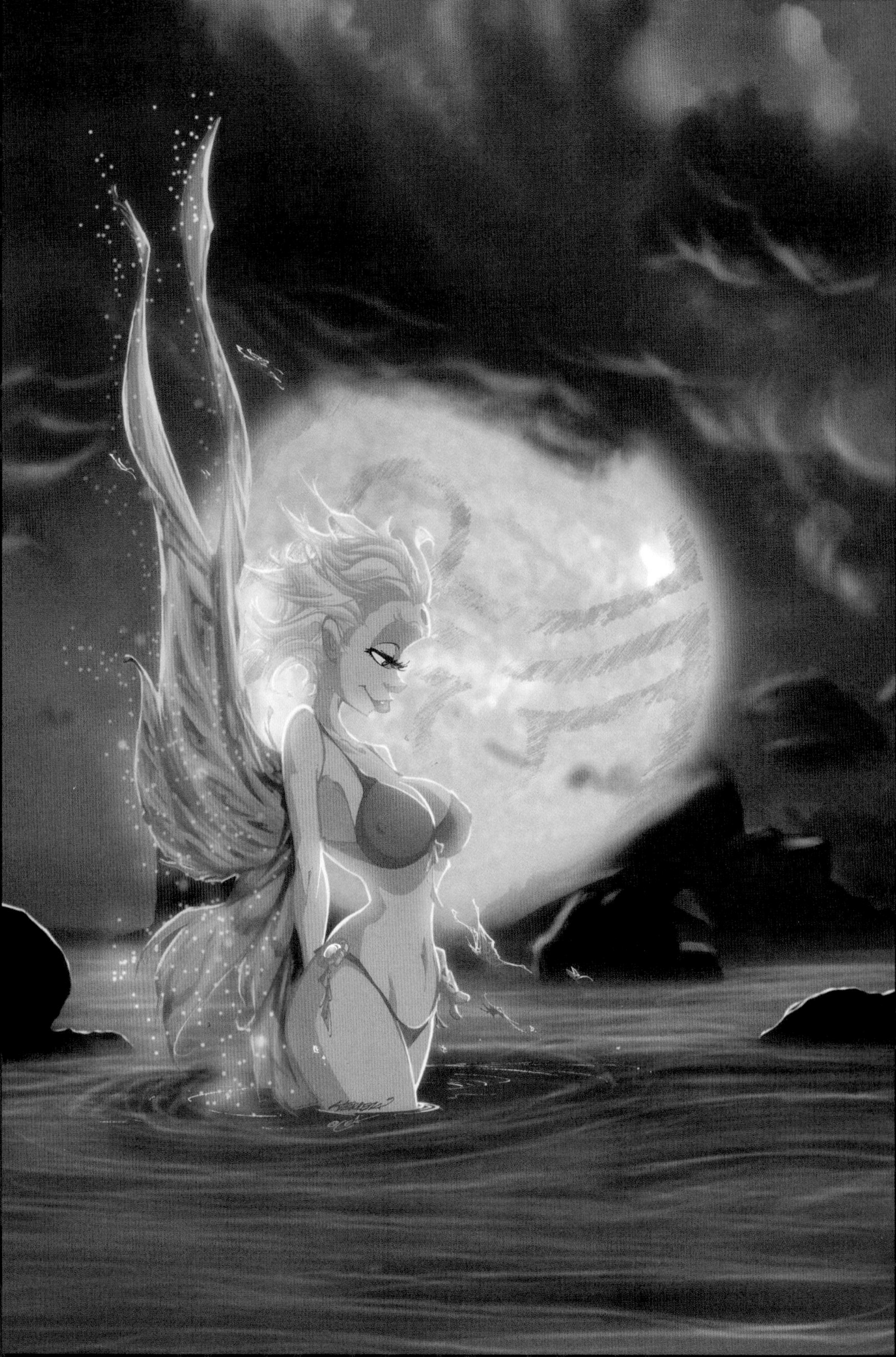

FAYE

· PIN-UP FROM ASPEN SPLASH: 2006 SWIMSUIT SPECTACULAR ·

by

· FRANCISCO HERRERA · LEONARDO OLEA ·

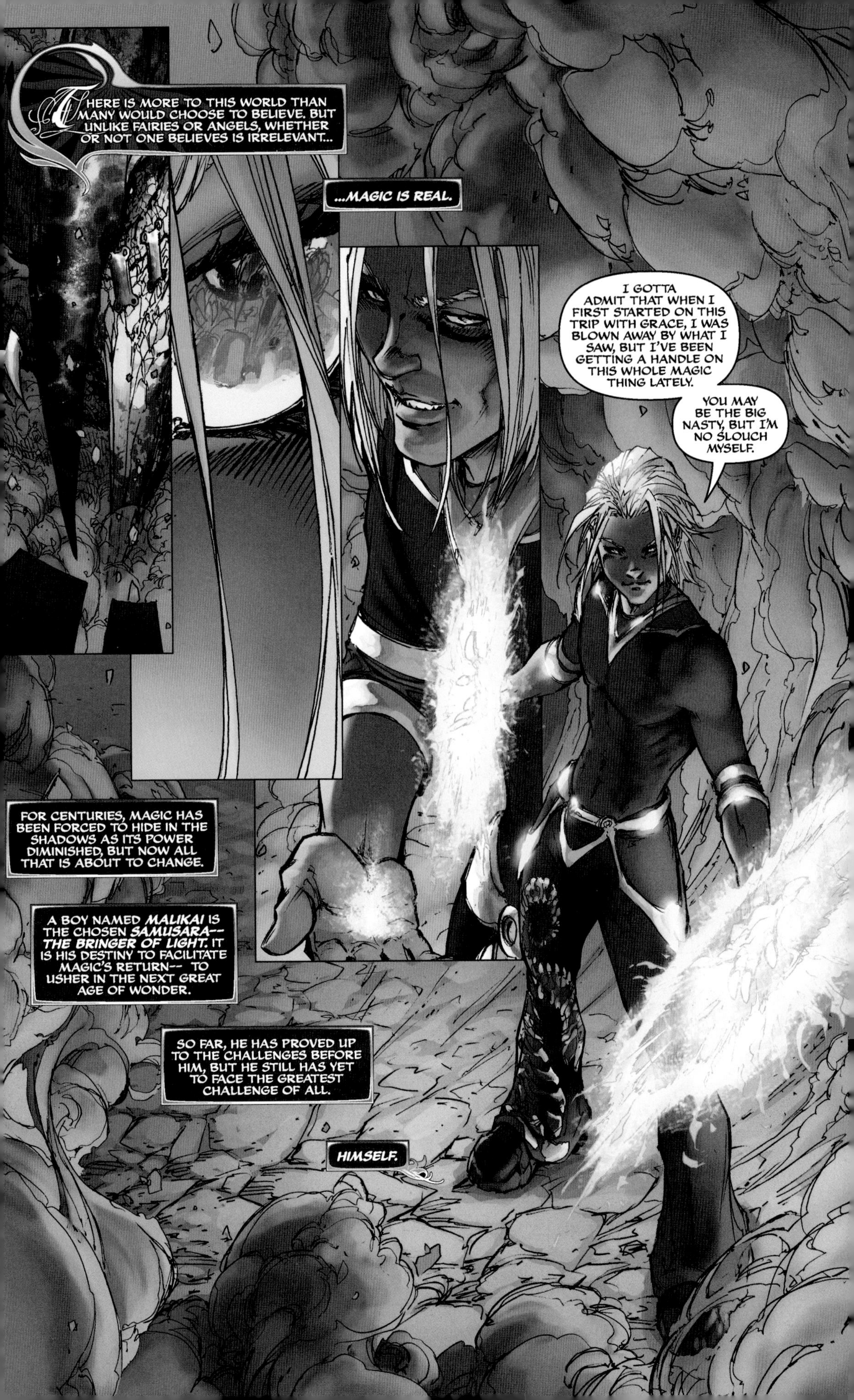
THERE IS MORE TO THIS WORLD THAN MANY WOULD CHOOSE TO BELIEVE. BUT UNLIKE FAIRIES OR ANGELS, WHETHER OR NOT ONE BELIEVES IS IRRELEVANT...
...MAGIC IS REAL.
I GOTTA ADMIT THAT WHEN I FIRST STARTED ON THIS TRIP WITH GRACE, I WAS BLOWN AWAY BY WHAT I SAW, BUT I'VE BEEN GETTING A HANDLE ON THIS WHOLE MAGIC THING LATELY.
YOU MAY BE THE BIG NASTY, BUT I'M NO SLOUCH MYSELF.
FOR CENTURIES, MAGIC HAS BEEN FORCED TO HIDE IN THE SHADOWS AS ITS POWER DIMINISHED, BUT NOW ALL THAT IS ABOUT TO CHANGE.
A BOY NAMED MALIKAI IS THE CHOSEN SAMUSARA-- THE BRINGER OF LIGHT. IT IS HIS DESTINY TO FACILITATE MAGIC'S RETURN-- TO USHER IN THE NEXT GREAT AGE OF WONDER.
SO FAR, HE HAS PROVED UP TO THE CHALLENGES BEFORE HIM, BUT HE STILL HAS YET TO FACE THE GREATEST CHALLENGE OF ALL.
HIMSELF.

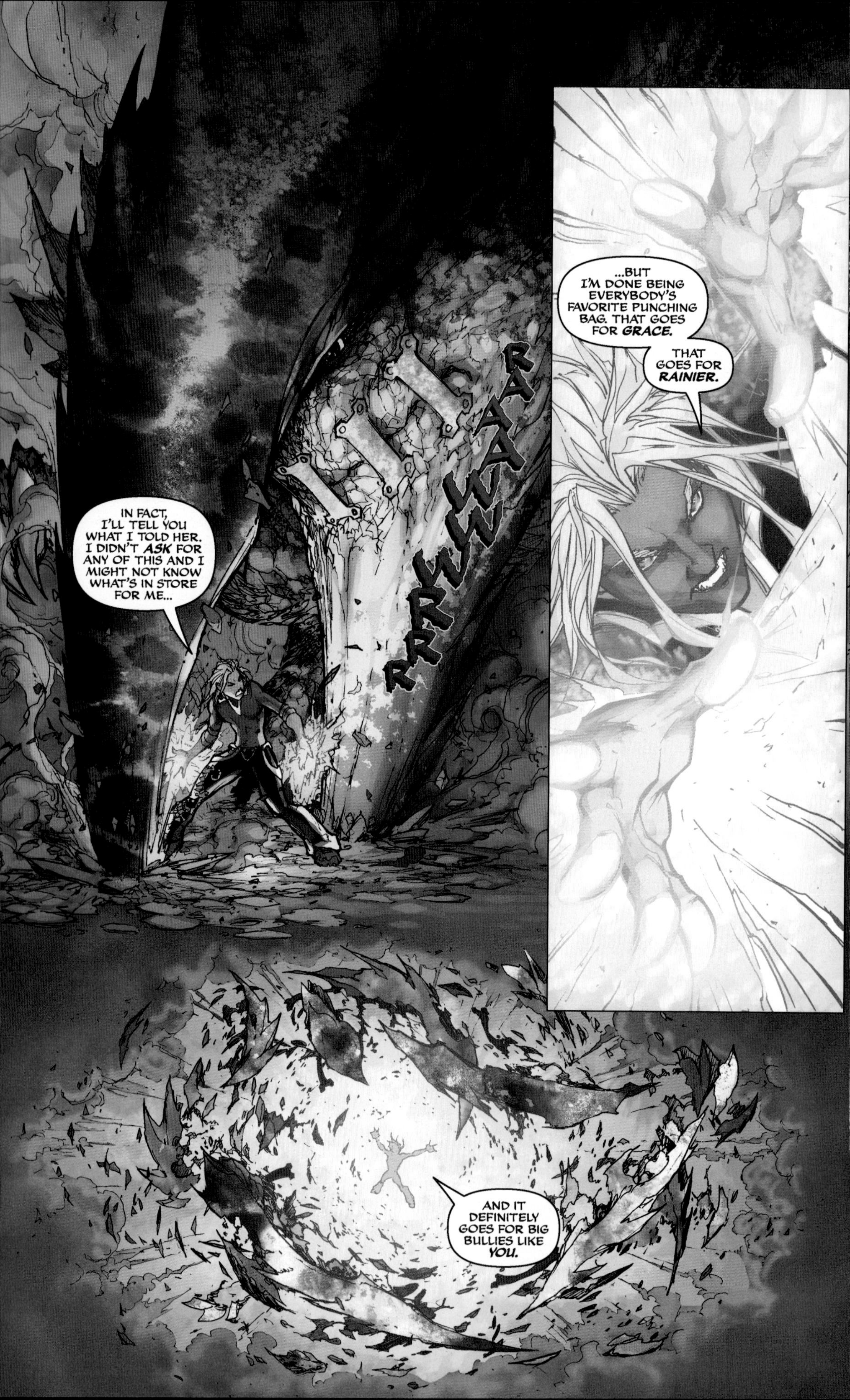
IN FACT, I'LL TELL YOU WHAT I TOLD HER. I DIDN'T ASK FOR ANY OF THIS AND I MIGHT NOT KNOW WHAT'S IN STORE FOR ME...
RRRWWWAAR
...BUT I'M DONE BEING EVERYBODY'S FAVORITE PUNCHING BAG. THAT GOES FOR GRACE.
THAT GOES FOR RAINIER.
AND IT DEFINITELY GOES FOR BIG BULLIES LIKE YOU.

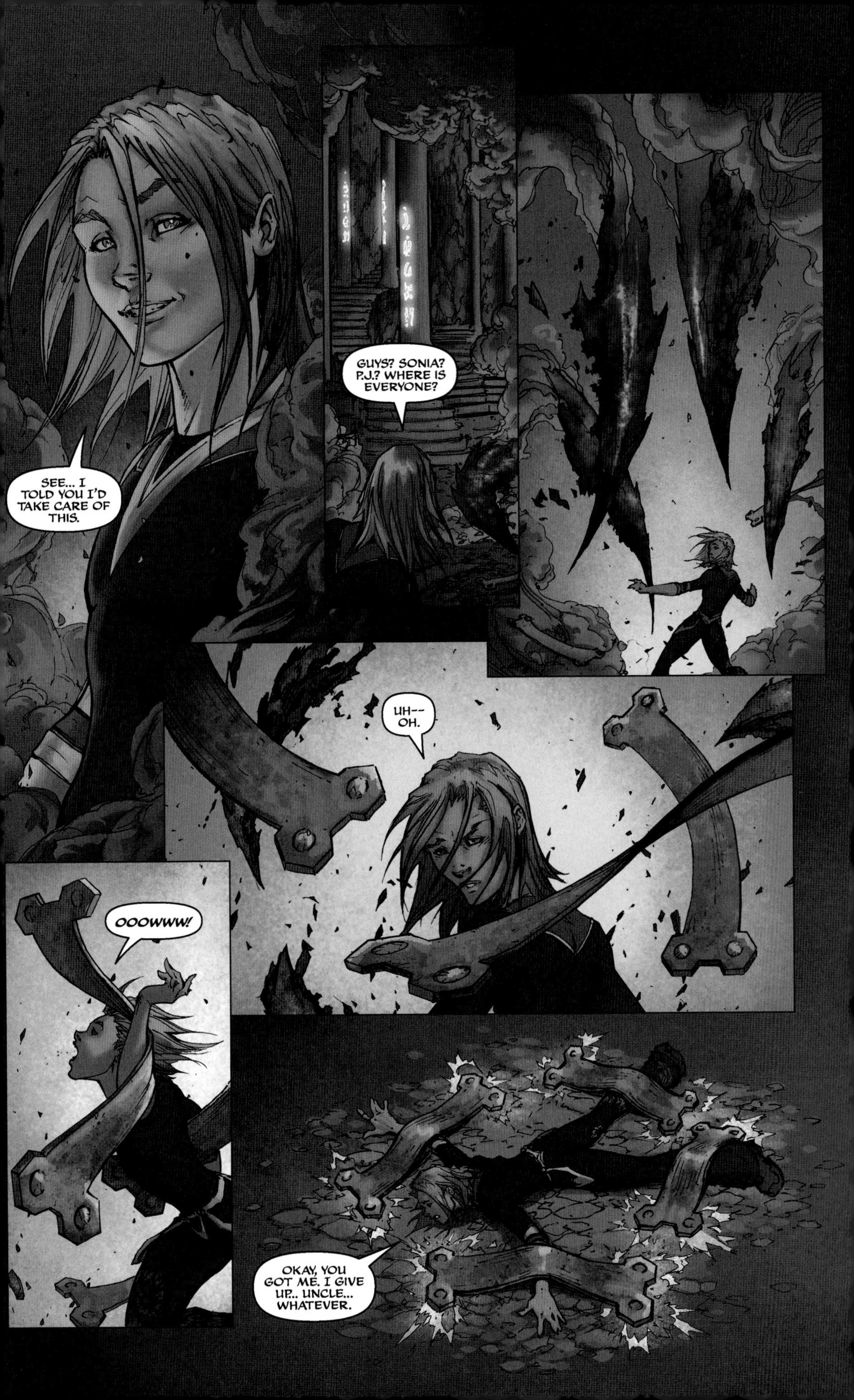
SEE... I TOLD YOU I'D TAKE CARE OF THIS.
GUYS? SONIA? P.J.? WHERE IS EVERYONE?
UH-- OH.
OOOWWW!
OKAY, YOU GOT ME. I GIVE UP... UNCLE... WHATEVER.

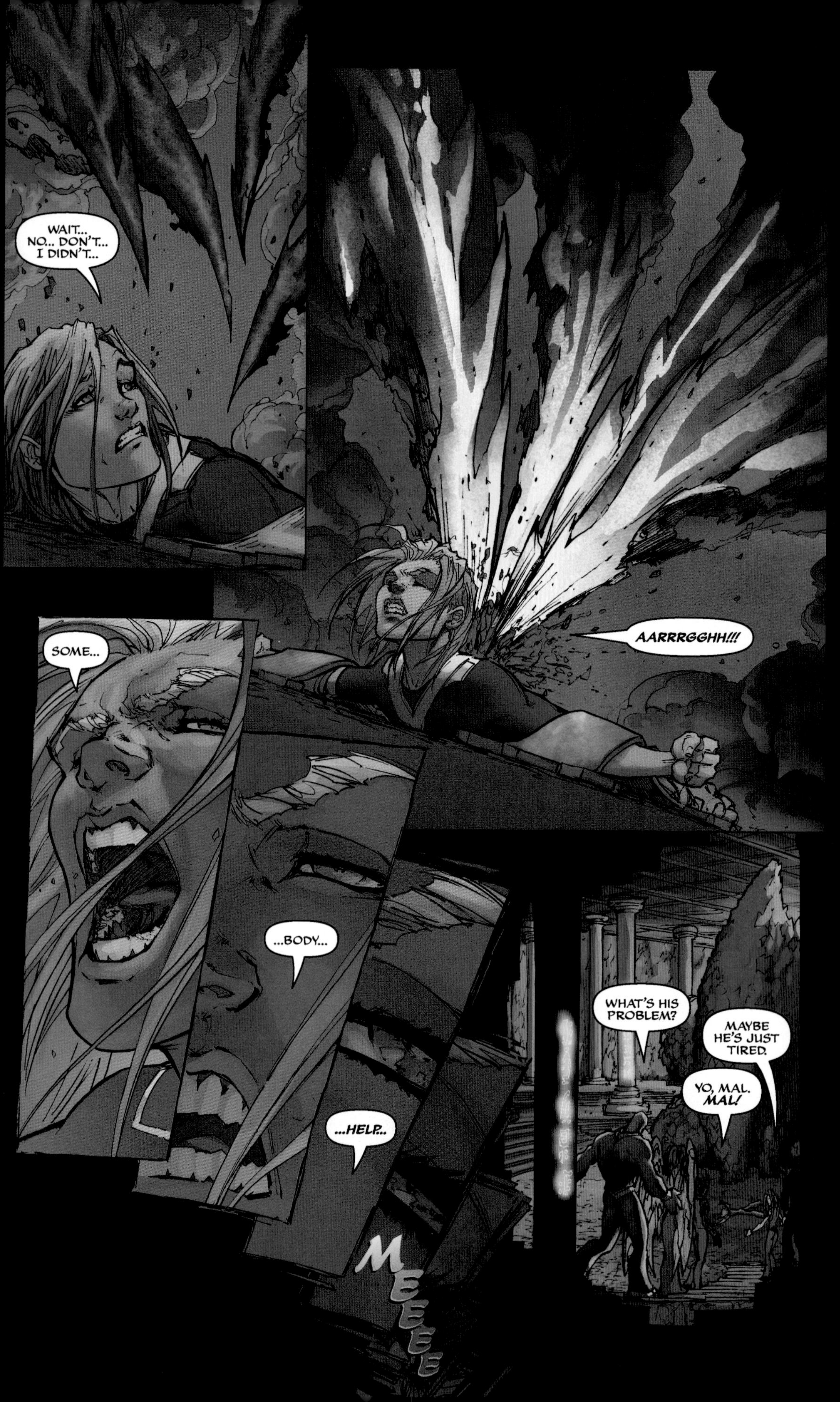
WAIT... NO... DON'T... I DIDN'T...
AARRRGGHH!!!
SOME...
...BODY...
...HELP...
MEEEE
WHAT'S HIS PROBLEM?
MAYBE HE'S JUST TIRED.
YO, MAL. MAL!

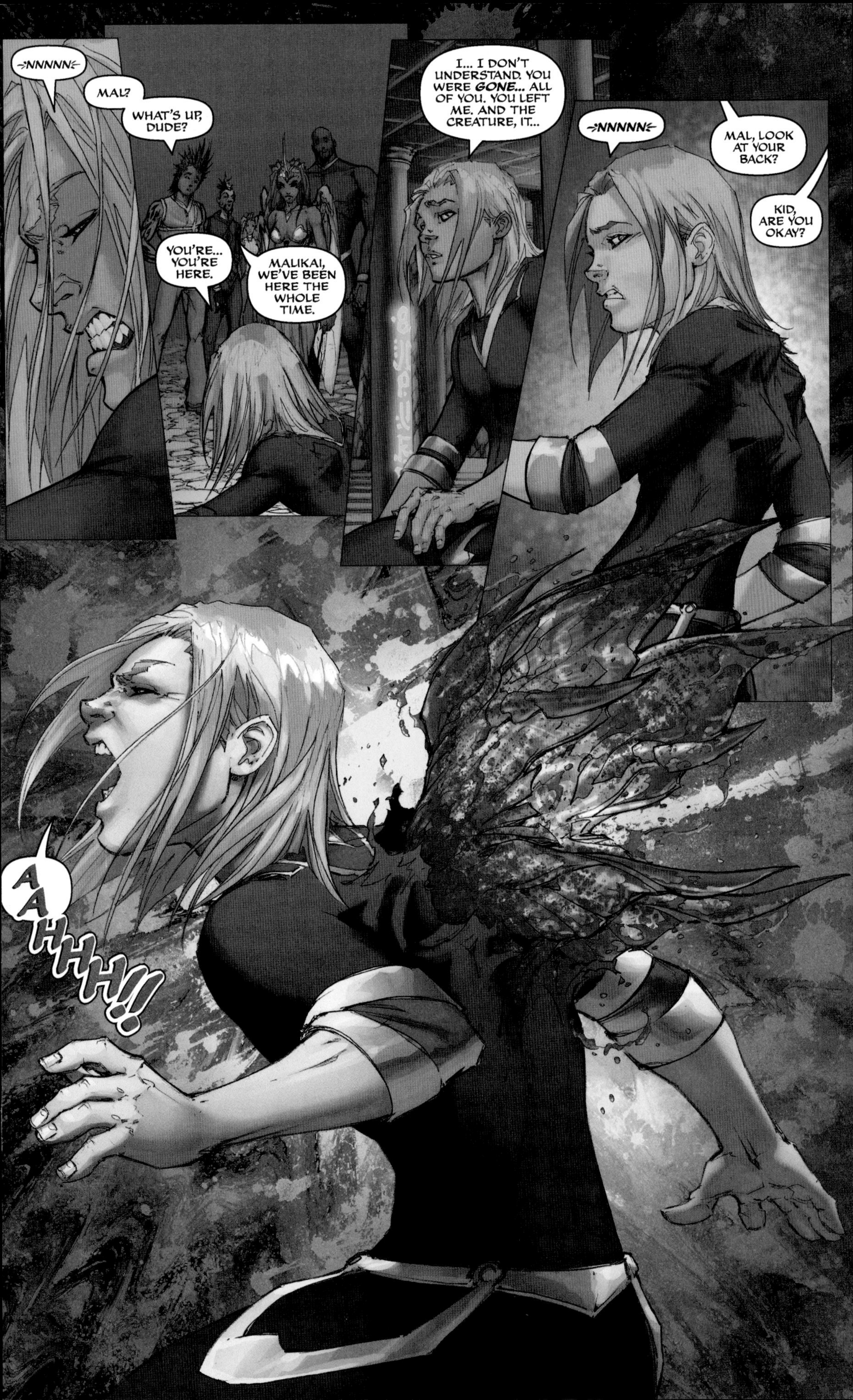
-NNNNN-
MAL?
WHAT'S UP, DUDE?
YOU'RE... YOU'RE HERE.
MALIKAI, WE'VE BEEN HERE THE WHOLE TIME.
I... I DON'T UNDERSTAND. YOU WERE GONE... ALL OF YOU. YOU LEFT ME. AND THE CREATURE, IT...
-NNNNN-
MAL, LOOK AT YOUR BACK?
KID, ARE YOU OKAY?
AAHHHH!!

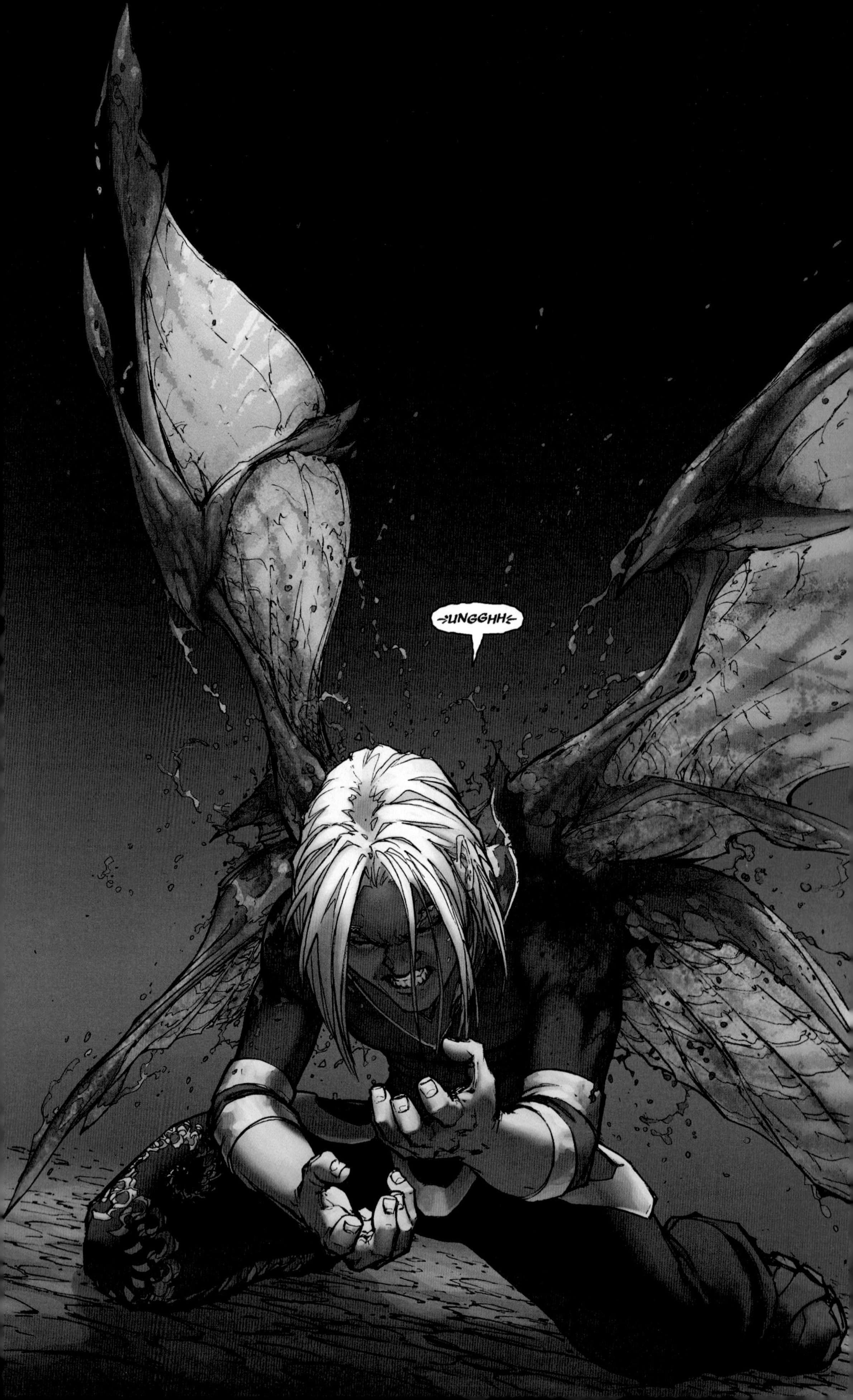
UNGGHH

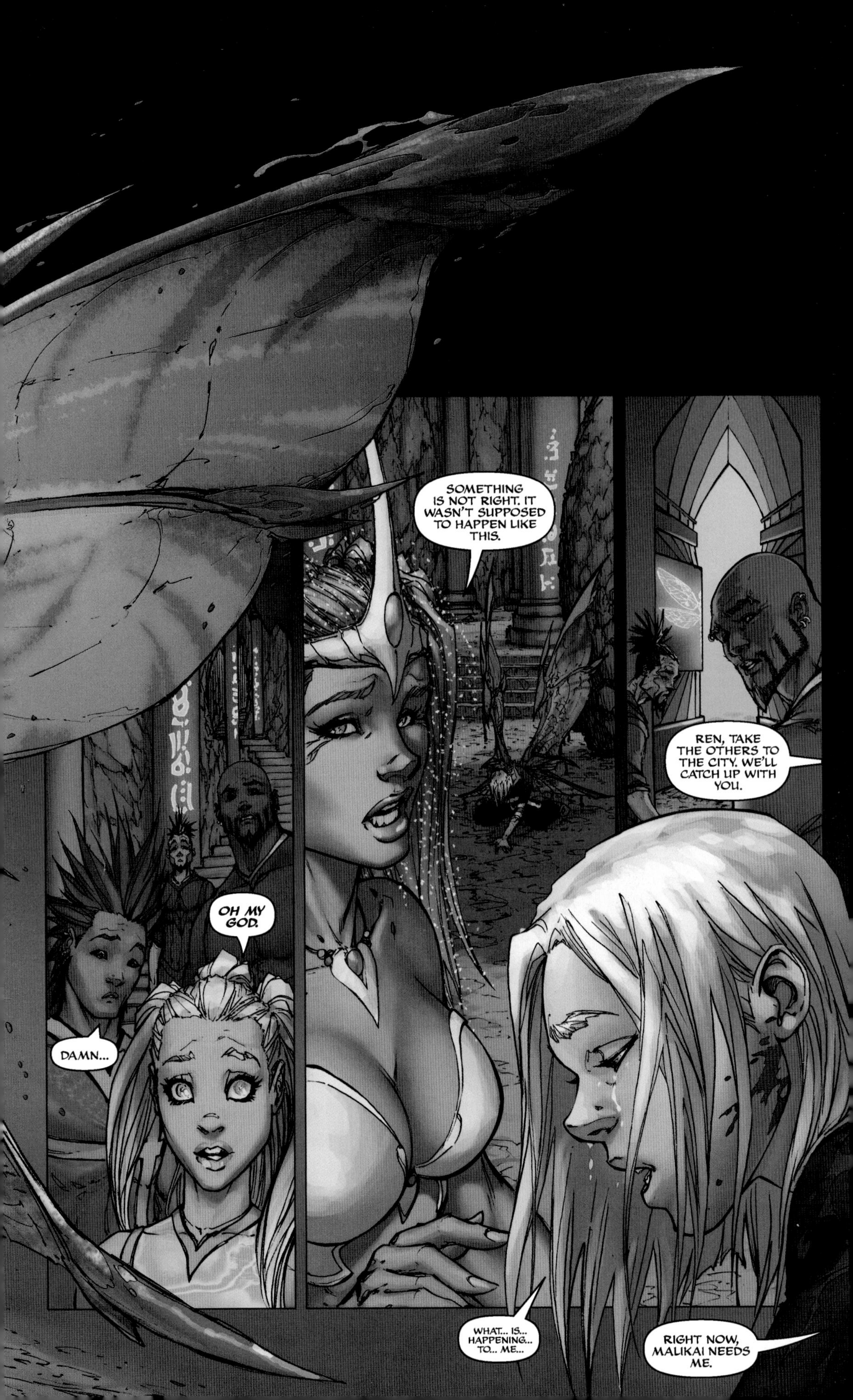
SOMETHING IS NOT RIGHT. IT WASN'T SUPPOSED TO HAPPEN LIKE THIS.
REN, TAKE THE OTHERS TO THE CITY. WE'LL CATCH UP WITH YOU.
OH MY GOD.
DAMN...
WHAT... IS... HAPPENING... TO... ME...
RIGHT NOW, MALIKAI NEEDS ME.

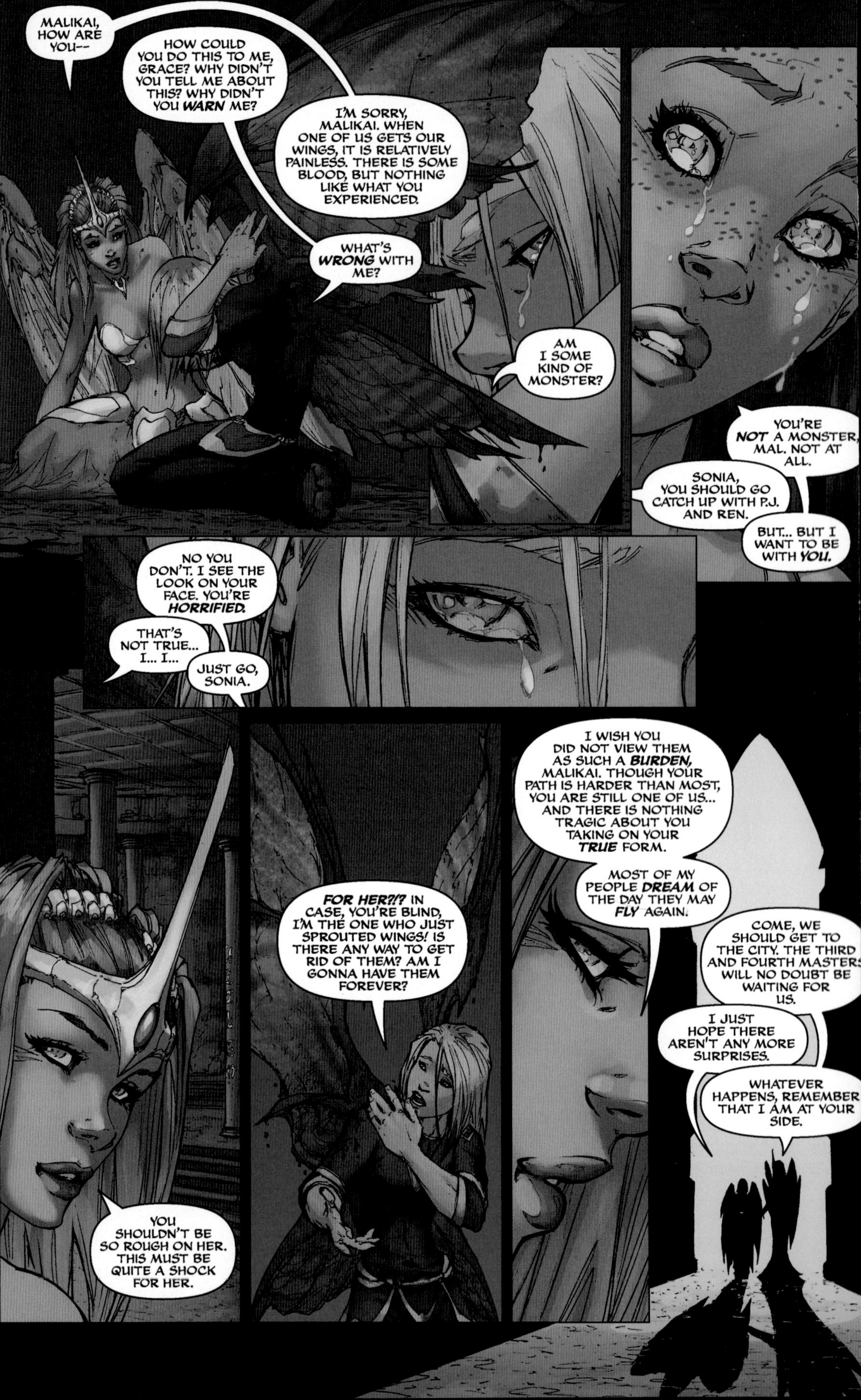
MALIKAI, HOW ARE YOU--
HOW COULD YOU DO THIS TO ME, GRACE? WHY DIDN'T YOU TELL ME ABOUT THIS? WHY DIDN'T YOU WARN ME?
I'M SORRY, MALIKAI. WHEN ONE OF US GETS OUR WINGS, IT IS RELATIVELY PAINLESS. THERE IS SOME BLOOD, BUT NOTHING LIKE WHAT YOU EXPERIENCED.
WHAT'S WRONG WITH ME?
AM I SOME KIND OF MONSTER?
YOU'RE NOT A MONSTER, MAL. NOT AT ALL.
SONIA, YOU SHOULD GO CATCH UP WITH P.J. AND REN.
BUT... BUT I WANT TO BE WITH YOU.
NO YOU DON'T. I SEE THE LOOK ON YOUR FACE. YOU'RE HORRIFIED.
THAT'S NOT TRUE... I... I...
JUST GO, SONIA.
YOU SHOULDN'T BE SO ROUGH ON HER. THIS MUST BE QUITE A SHOCK FOR HER.
FOR HER?!? IN CASE, YOU'RE BLIND, I'M THE ONE WHO JUST SPROUTED WINGS! IS THERE ANY WAY TO GET RID OF THEM? AM I GONNA HAVE THEM FOREVER?
I WISH YOU DID NOT VIEW THEM AS SUCH A BURDEN, MALIKAI. THOUGH YOUR PATH IS HARDER THAN MOST, YOU ARE STILL ONE OF US... AND THERE IS NOTHING TRAGIC ABOUT YOU TAKING ON YOUR TRUE FORM.
MOST OF MY PEOPLE DREAM OF THE DAY THEY MAY FLY AGAIN.
COME, WE SHOULD GET TO THE CITY. THE THIRD AND FOURTH MASTERS WILL NO DOUBT BE WAITING FOR US.
I JUST HOPE THERE AREN'T ANY MORE SURPRISES.
WHATEVER HAPPENS, REMEMBER THAT I AM AT YOUR SIDE.

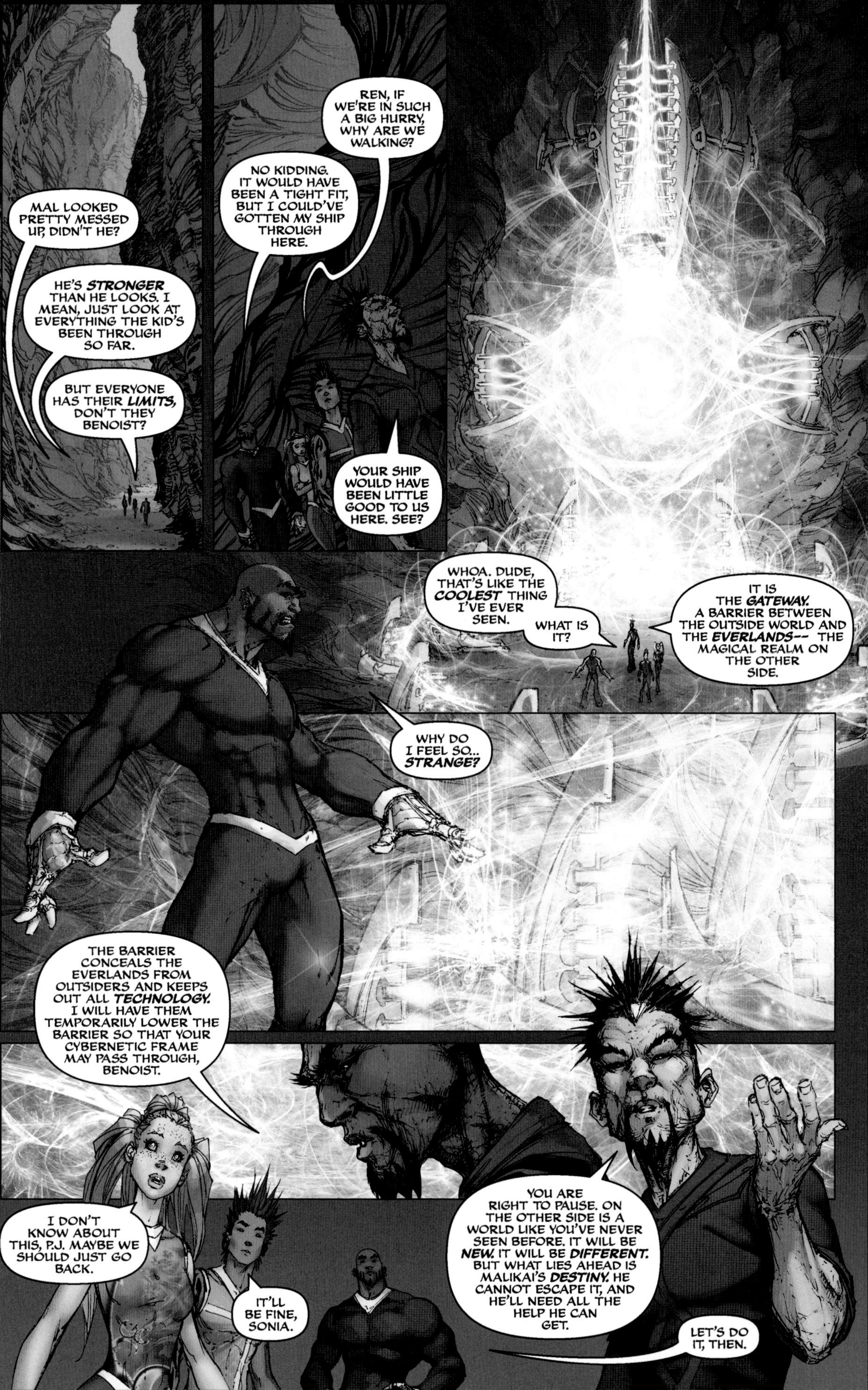
MAL LOOKED PRETTY MESSED UP, DIDN'T HE?
HE'S STRONGER THAN HE LOOKS. I MEAN, JUST LOOK AT EVERYTHING THE KID'S BEEN THROUGH SO FAR.
BUT EVERYONE HAS THEIR LIMITS, DON'T THEY BENOIST?
REN, IF WE'RE IN SUCH A BIG HURRY, WHY ARE WE WALKING?
NO KIDDING. IT WOULD HAVE BEEN A TIGHT FIT, BUT I COULD'VE GOTTEN MY SHIP THROUGH HERE.
YOUR SHIP WOULD HAVE BEEN LITTLE GOOD TO US HERE. SEE?
WHOA. DUDE, THAT'S LIKE THE COOLEST THING I'VE EVER SEEN.
WHAT IS IT?
IT IS THE GATEWAY. A BARRIER BETWEEN THE OUTSIDE WORLD AND THE EVERLANDS-- THE MAGICAL REALM ON THE OTHER SIDE.
WHY DO I FEEL SO... STRANGE?
THE BARRIER CONCEALS THE EVERLANDS FROM OUTSIDERS AND KEEPS OUT ALL TECHNOLOGY. I WILL HAVE THEM TEMPORARILY LOWER THE BARRIER SO THAT YOUR CYBERNETIC FRAME MAY PASS THROUGH, BENOIST.
I DON'T KNOW ABOUT THIS, P.J. MAYBE WE SHOULD JUST GO BACK.
IT'LL BE FINE, SONIA.
YOU ARE RIGHT TO PAUSE. ON THE OTHER SIDE IS A WORLD LIKE YOU'VE NEVER SEEN BEFORE. IT WILL BE NEW. IT WILL BE DIFFERENT. BUT WHAT LIES AHEAD IS MALIKAI'S DESTINY. HE CANNOT ESCAPE IT, AND HE'LL NEED ALL THE HELP HE CAN GET.
LET'S DO IT, THEN.

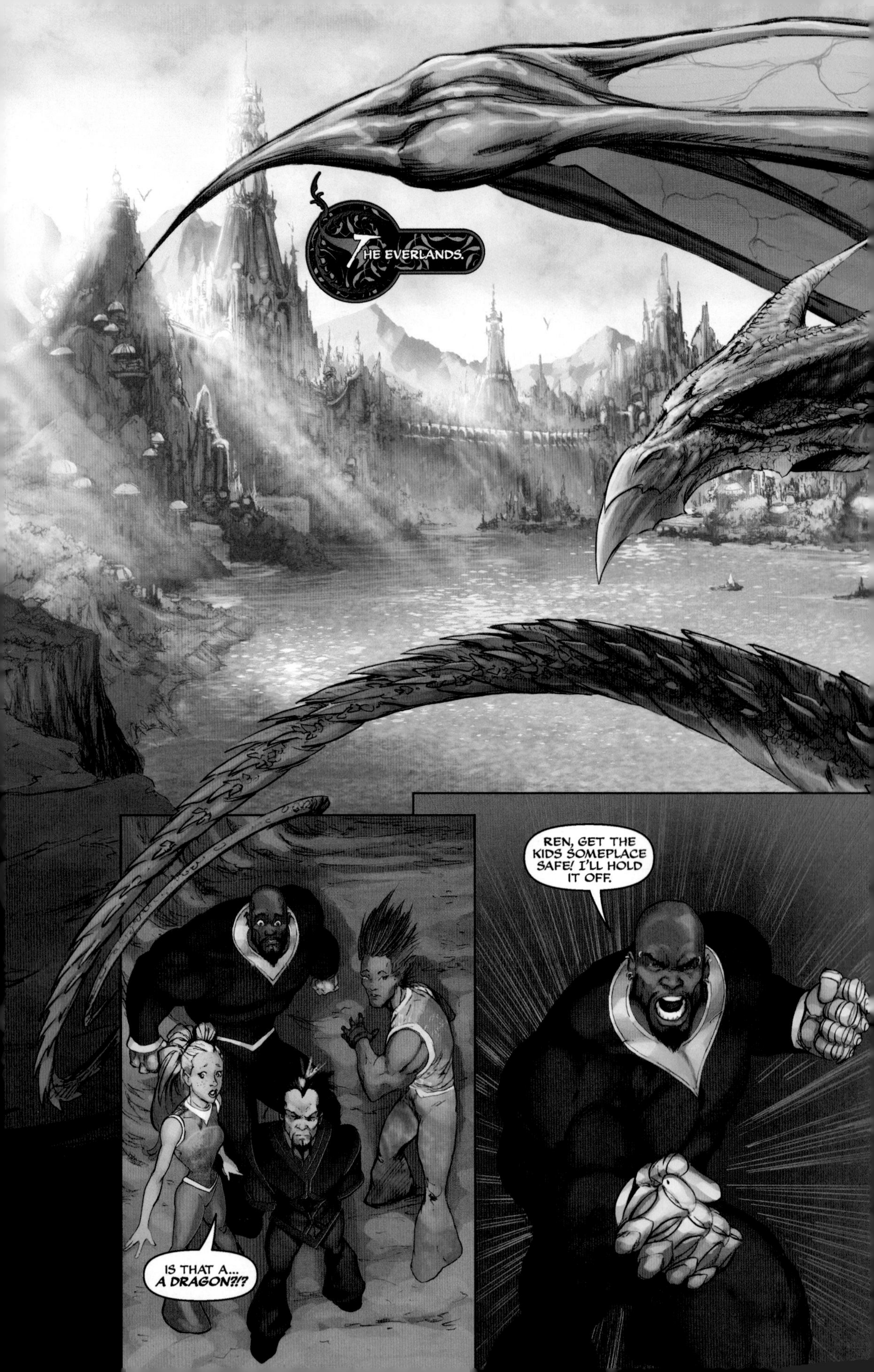
THE EVERLANDS.
IS THAT A... A DRAGON?!?
REN, GET THE KIDS SOMEPLACE SAFE! I'LL HOLD IT OFF.

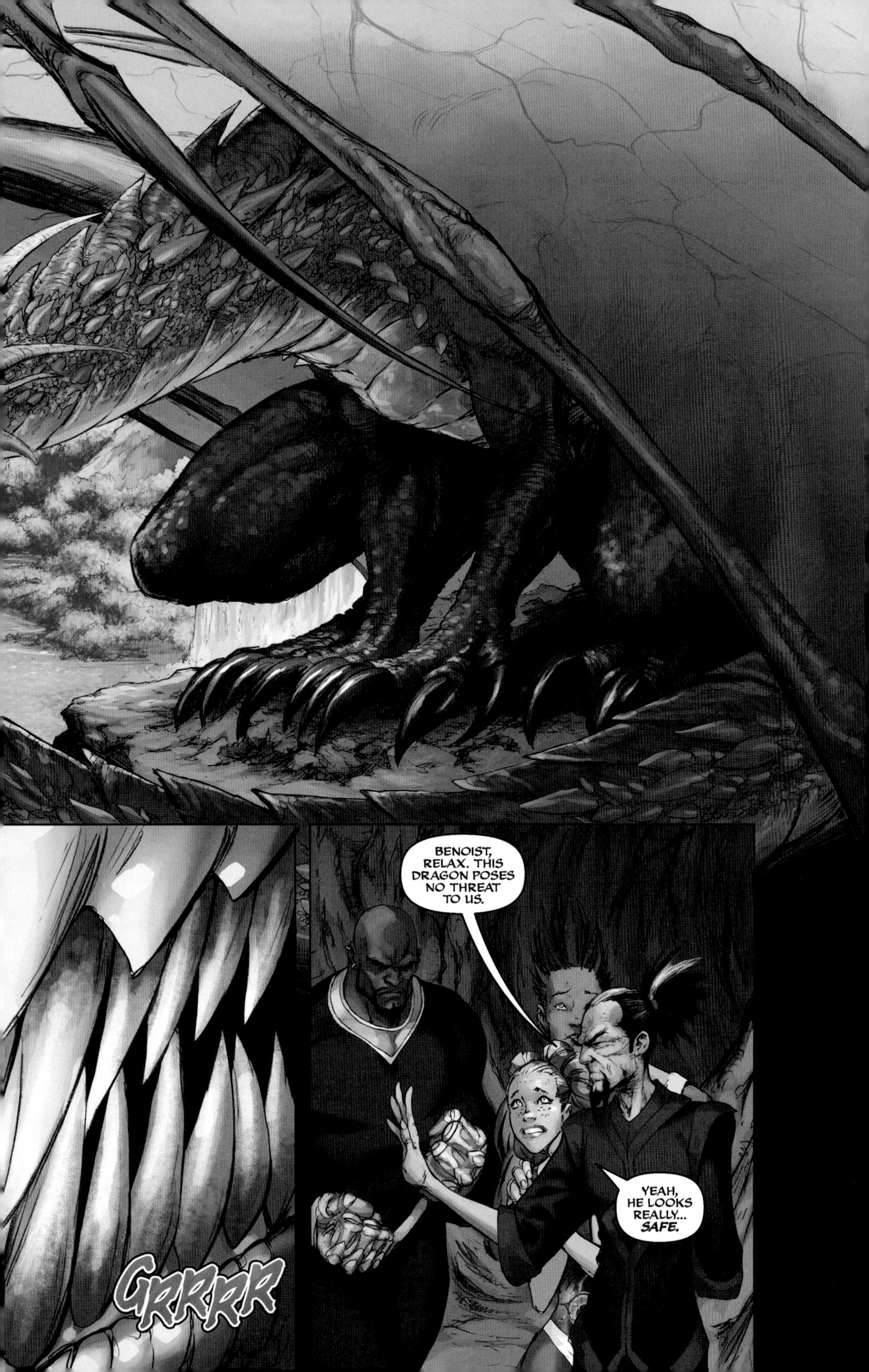
GRRRR
BENOIST, RELAX. THIS DRAGON POSES NO THREAT TO US.
YEAH, HE LOOKS REALLY... SAFE.

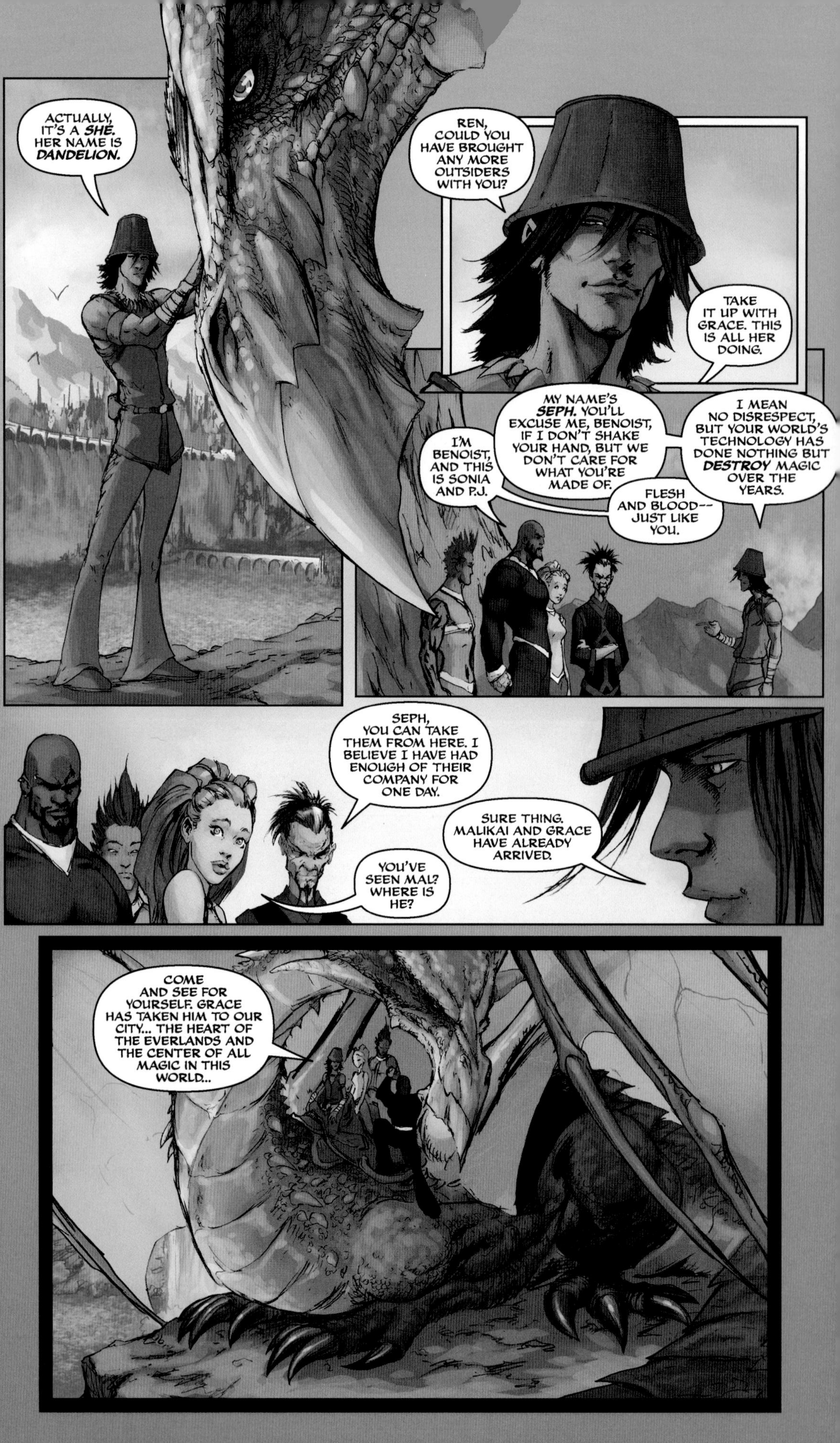
ACTUALLY, IT'S A SHE. HER NAME IS DANDELION.
REN, COULD YOU HAVE BROUGHT ANY MORE OUTSIDERS WITH YOU?
TAKE IT UP WITH GRACE. THIS IS ALL HER DOING.
I'M BENOIST, AND THIS IS SONIA AND P.J.
MY NAME'S SEPH. YOU'LL EXCUSE ME, BENOIST, IF I DON'T SHAKE YOUR HAND, BUT WE DON'T CARE FOR WHAT YOU'RE MADE OF.
FLESH AND BLOOD-- JUST LIKE YOU.
I MEAN NO DISRESPECT, BUT YOUR WORLD'S TECHNOLOGY HAS DONE NOTHING BUT DESTROY MAGIC OVER THE YEARS.
SEPH, YOU CAN TAKE THEM FROM HERE. I BELIEVE I HAVE HAD ENOUGH OF THEIR COMPANY FOR ONE DAY.
SURE THING. MALIKAI AND GRACE HAVE ALREADY ARRIVED.
YOU'VE SEEN MAL? WHERE IS HE?
COME AND SEE FOR YOURSELF. GRACE HAS TAKEN HIM TO OUR CITY... THE HEART OF THE EVERLANDS AND THE CENTER OF ALL MAGIC IN THIS WORLD...

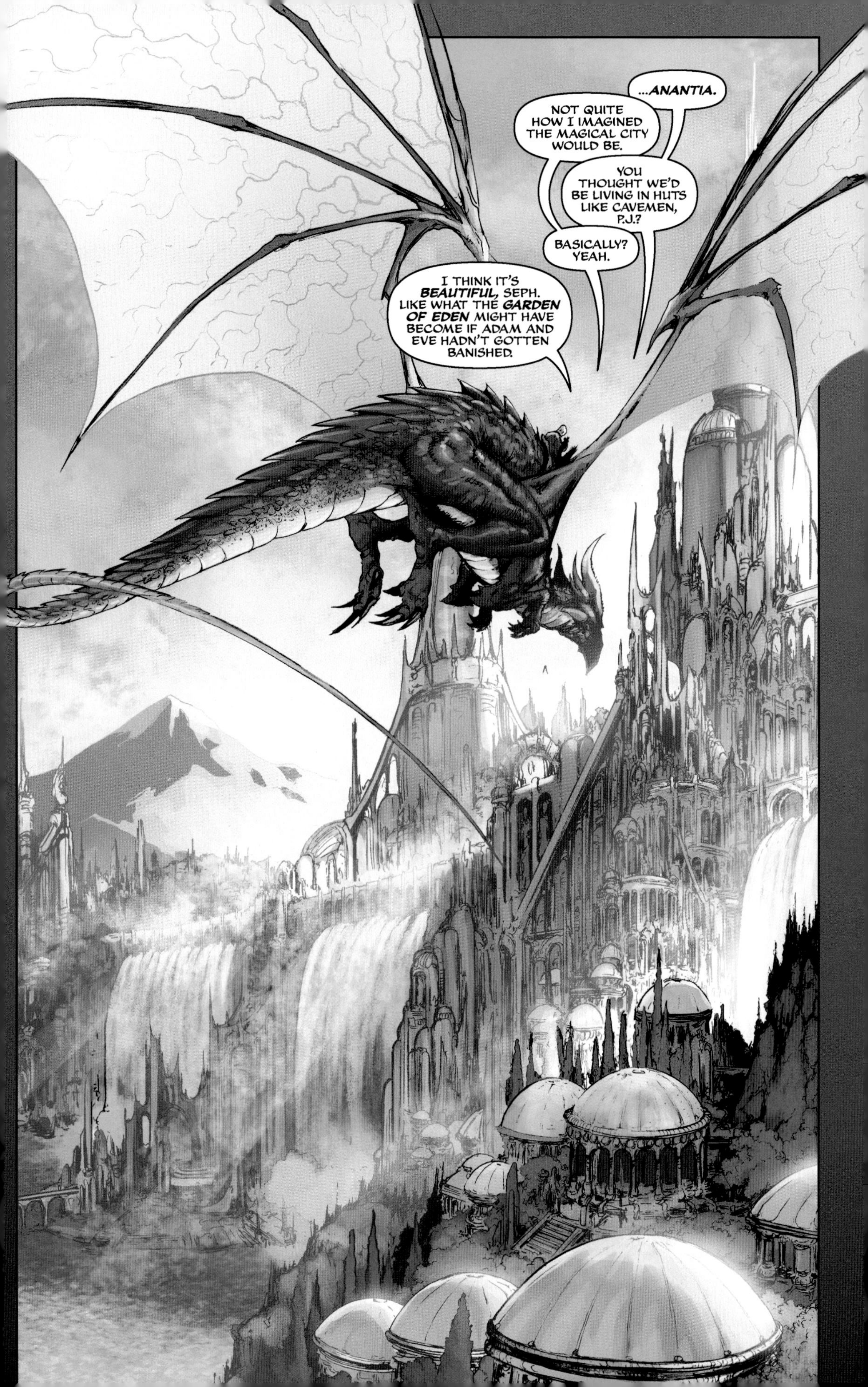

NOT QUITE HOW I IMAGINED THE MAGICAL CITY WOULD BE.
...ANANTIA.
YOU THOUGHT WE'D BE LIVING IN HUTS LIKE CAVEMEN, P.J.?
BASICALLY? YEAH.
I THINK IT'S BEAUTIFUL, SEPH. LIKE WHAT THE GARDEN OF EDEN MIGHT HAVE BECOME IF ADAM AND EVE HADN'T GOTTEN BANISHED.

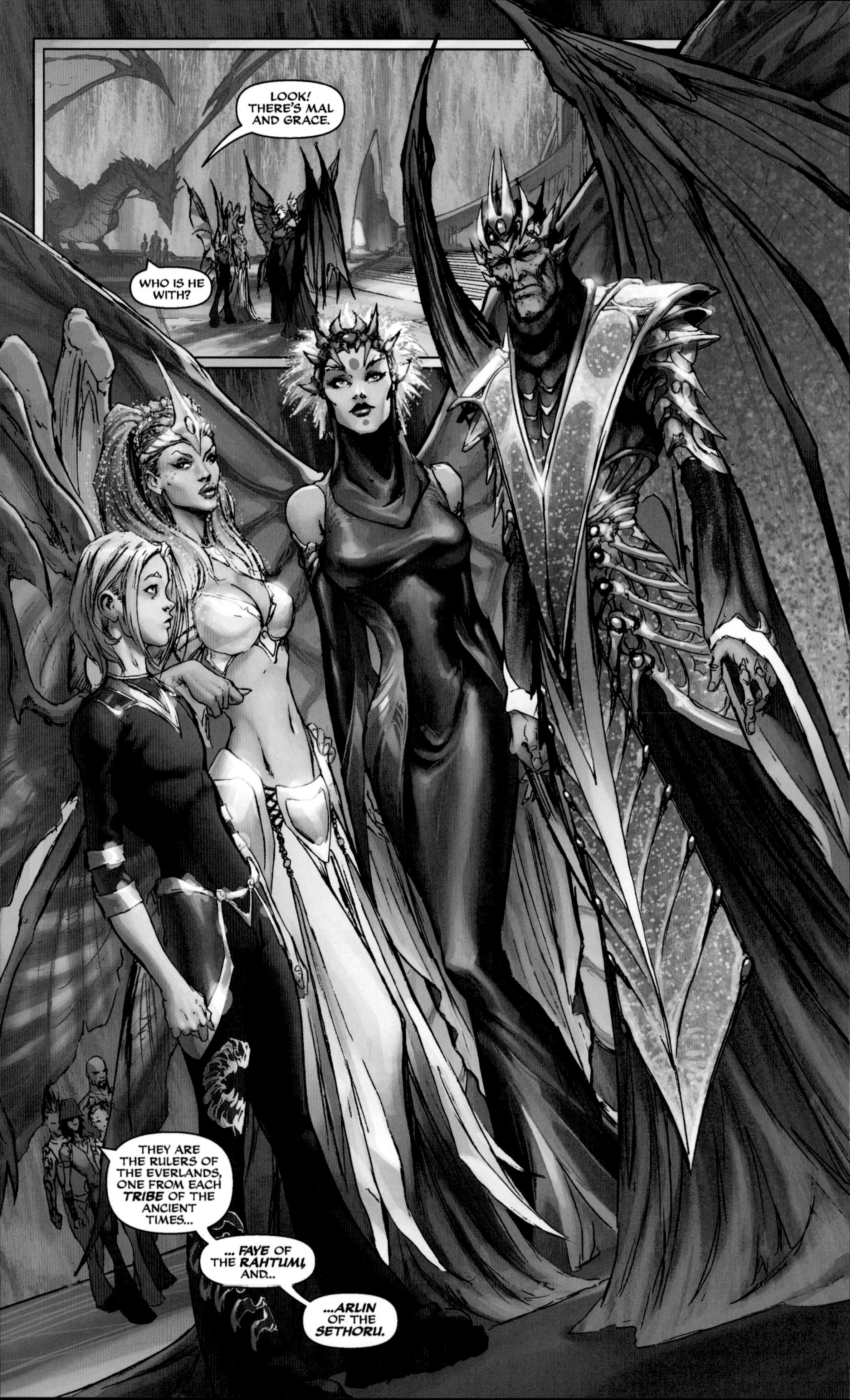

LOOK! THERE'S MAL AND GRACE.
WHO IS HE WITH?
THEY ARE THE RULERS OF THE EVERLANDS, ONE FROM EACH TRIBE OF THE ANCIENT TIMES...
... FAYE OF THE RAHTUMI, AND...
...ARLIN OF THE SETHORU.

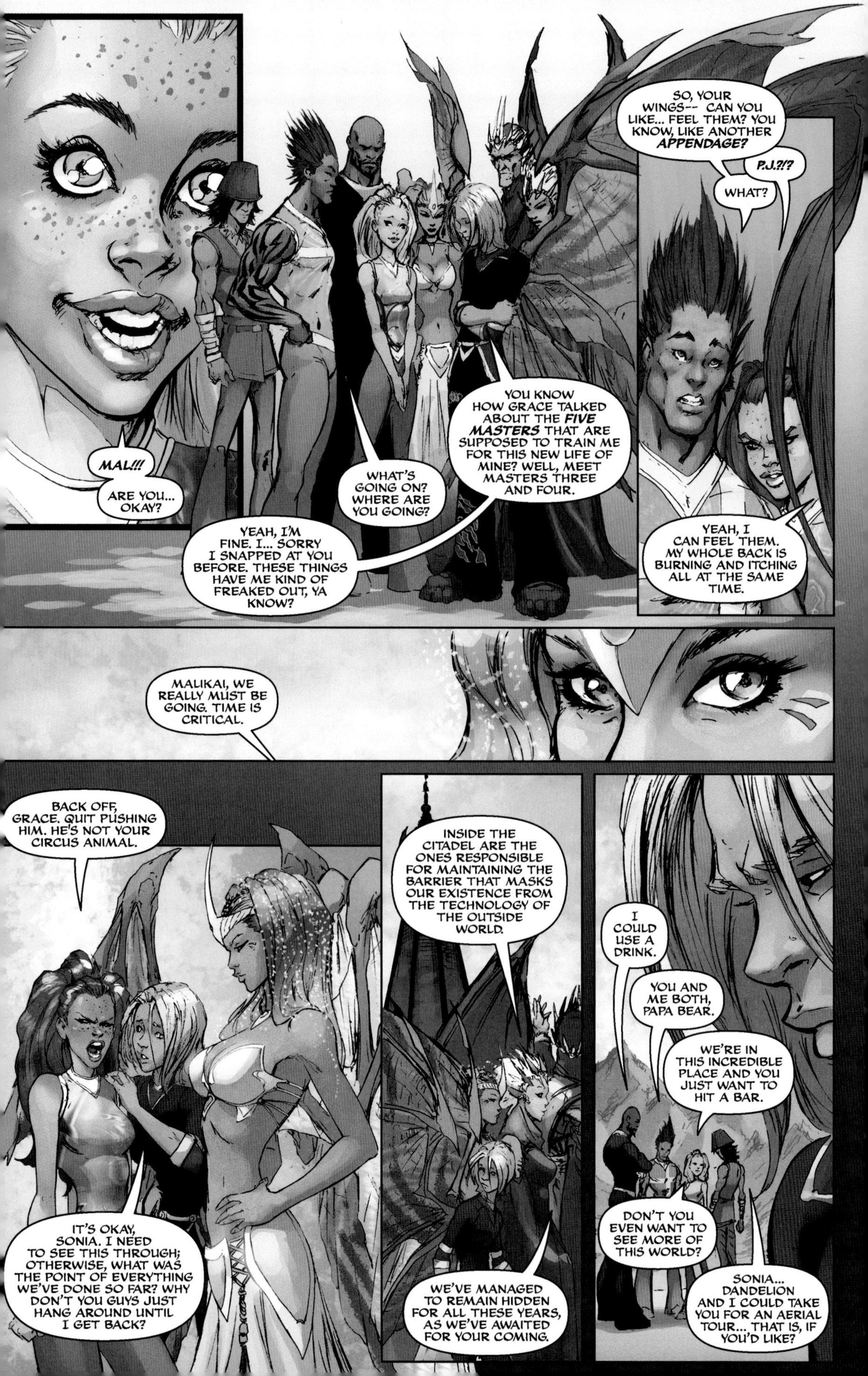

MAL!!!
ARE YOU... OKAY?
WHAT'S GOING ON? WHERE ARE YOU GOING?
YEAH, I'M FINE. I... SORRY I SNAPPED AT YOU BEFORE. THESE THINGS HAVE ME KIND OF FREAKED OUT, YA KNOW?
YOU KNOW HOW GRACE TALKED ABOUT THE FIVE MASTERS THAT ARE SUPPOSED TO TRAIN ME FOR THIS NEW LIFE OF MINE? WELL, MEET MASTERS THREE AND FOUR.
SO, YOUR WINGS-- CAN YOU LIKE... FEEL THEM? YOU KNOW, LIKE ANOTHER APPENDAGE?
P.J.?!?
WHAT?
YEAH, I CAN FEEL THEM. MY WHOLE BACK IS BURNING AND ITCHING ALL AT THE SAME TIME.
MALIKAI, WE REALLY MUST BE GOING. TIME IS CRITICAL.
BACK OFF, GRACE. QUIT PUSHING HIM. HE'S NOT YOUR CIRCUS ANIMAL.
IT'S OKAY, SONIA. I NEED TO SEE THIS THROUGH; OTHERWISE, WHAT WAS THE POINT OF EVERYTHING WE'VE DONE SO FAR? WHY DON'T YOU GUYS JUST HANG AROUND UNTIL I GET BACK?
INSIDE THE CITADEL ARE THE ONES RESPONSIBLE FOR MAINTAINING THE BARRIER THAT MASKS OUR EXISTENCE FROM THE TECHNOLOGY OF THE OUTSIDE WORLD.
WE'VE MANAGED TO REMAIN HIDDEN FOR ALL THESE YEARS, AS WE'VE AWAITED FOR YOUR COMING.
I COULD USE A DRINK.
YOU AND ME BOTH, PAPA BEAR.
WE'RE IN THIS INCREDIBLE PLACE AND YOU JUST WANT TO HIT A BAR.
DON'T YOU EVEN WANT TO SEE MORE OF THIS WORLD?
SONIA... DANDELION AND I COULD TAKE YOU FOR AN AERIAL TOUR... THAT IS, IF YOU'D LIKE?

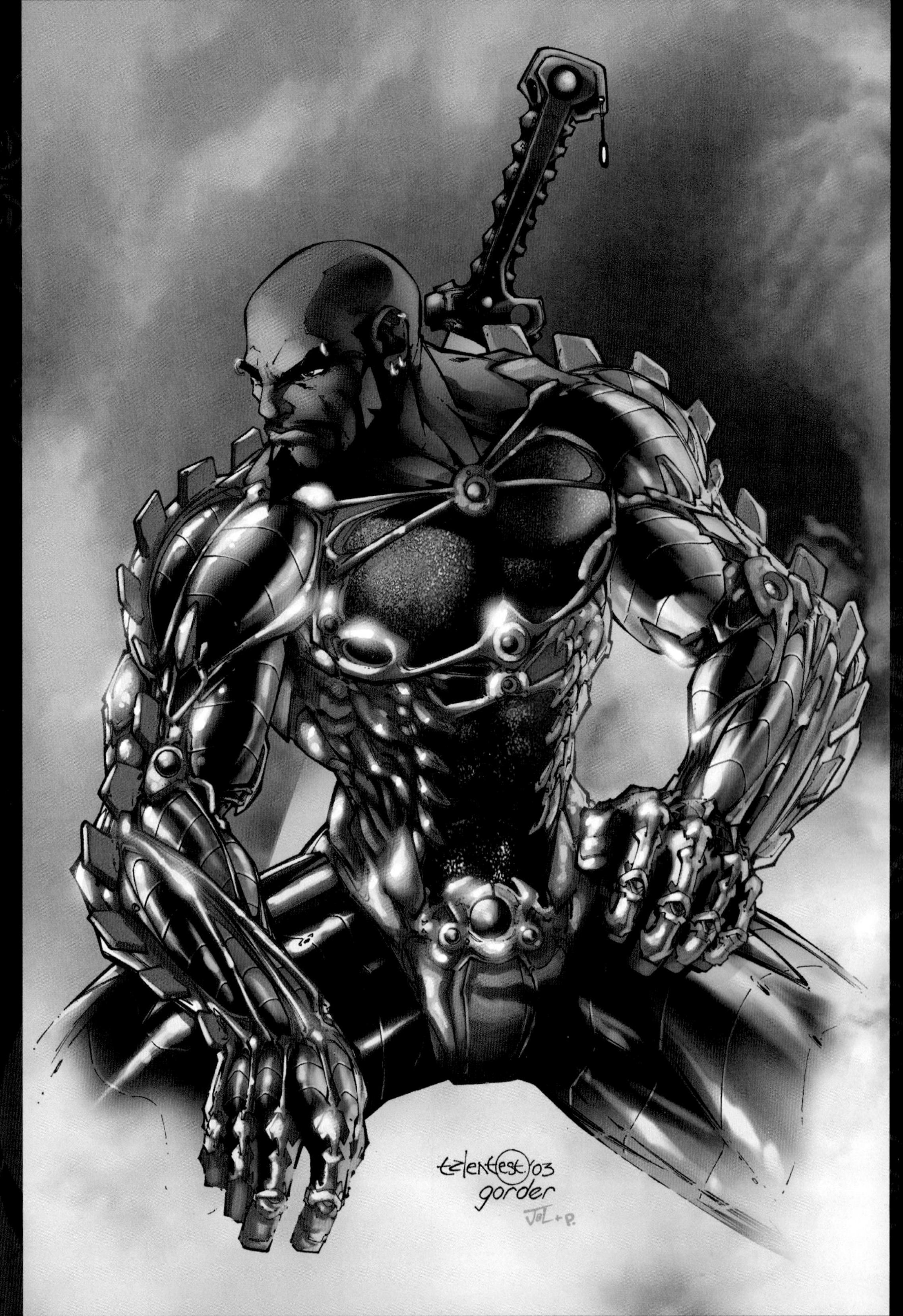

BENOIST

· PIN-UP FROM MICHAEL TURNER PRESENTS: ASPEN 2 ·
by
· Talent CALDWELL · Jason GORDER · Peter STEIGERWALD ·

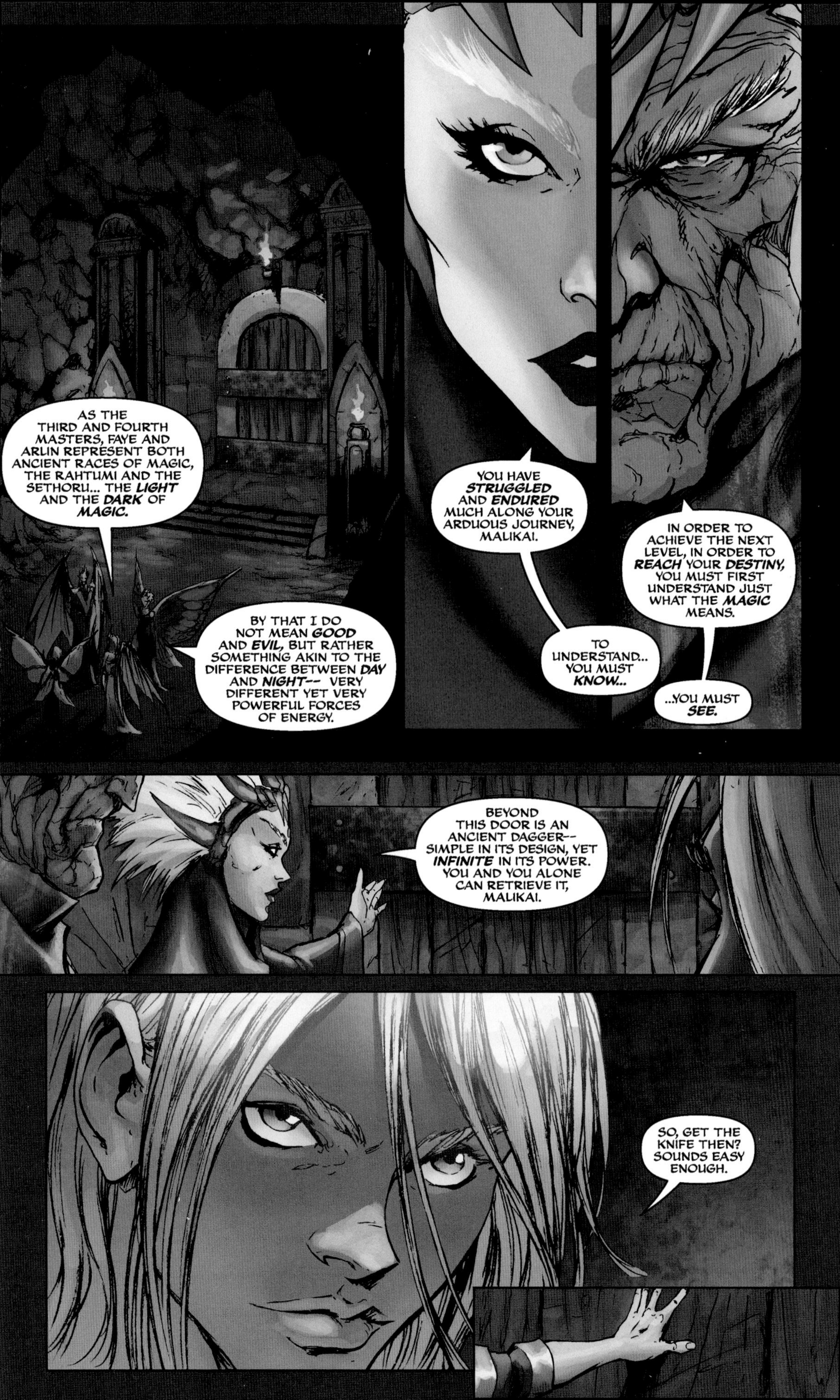
AS THE THIRD AND FOURTH MASTERS, FAYE AND ARLIN REPRESENT BOTH ANCIENT RACES OF MAGIC, THE RAHTUMI AND THE SETHORU... THE *LIGHT* AND THE *DARK* OF *MAGIC.*
BY THAT I DO NOT MEAN *GOOD* AND *EVIL,* BUT RATHER SOMETHING AKIN TO THE DIFFERENCE BETWEEN *DAY* AND *NIGHT*-- VERY DIFFERENT YET VERY POWERFUL FORCES OF ENERGY.
YOU HAVE *STRUGGLED* AND *ENDURED* MUCH ALONG YOUR ARDUOUS JOURNEY, MALIKAI.
TO UNDERSTAND... YOU MUST *KNOW...*
IN ORDER TO ACHIEVE THE NEXT LEVEL, IN ORDER TO *REACH* YOUR *DESTINY,* YOU MUST FIRST UNDERSTAND JUST WHAT THE *MAGIC* MEANS.
...YOU MUST *SEE.*
BEYOND THIS DOOR IS AN ANCIENT DAGGER-- SIMPLE IN ITS DESIGN, YET *INFINITE* IN ITS POWER. YOU AND YOU ALONE CAN RETRIEVE IT, MALIKAI.
SO, GET THE KNIFE THEN? SOUNDS EASY ENOUGH.

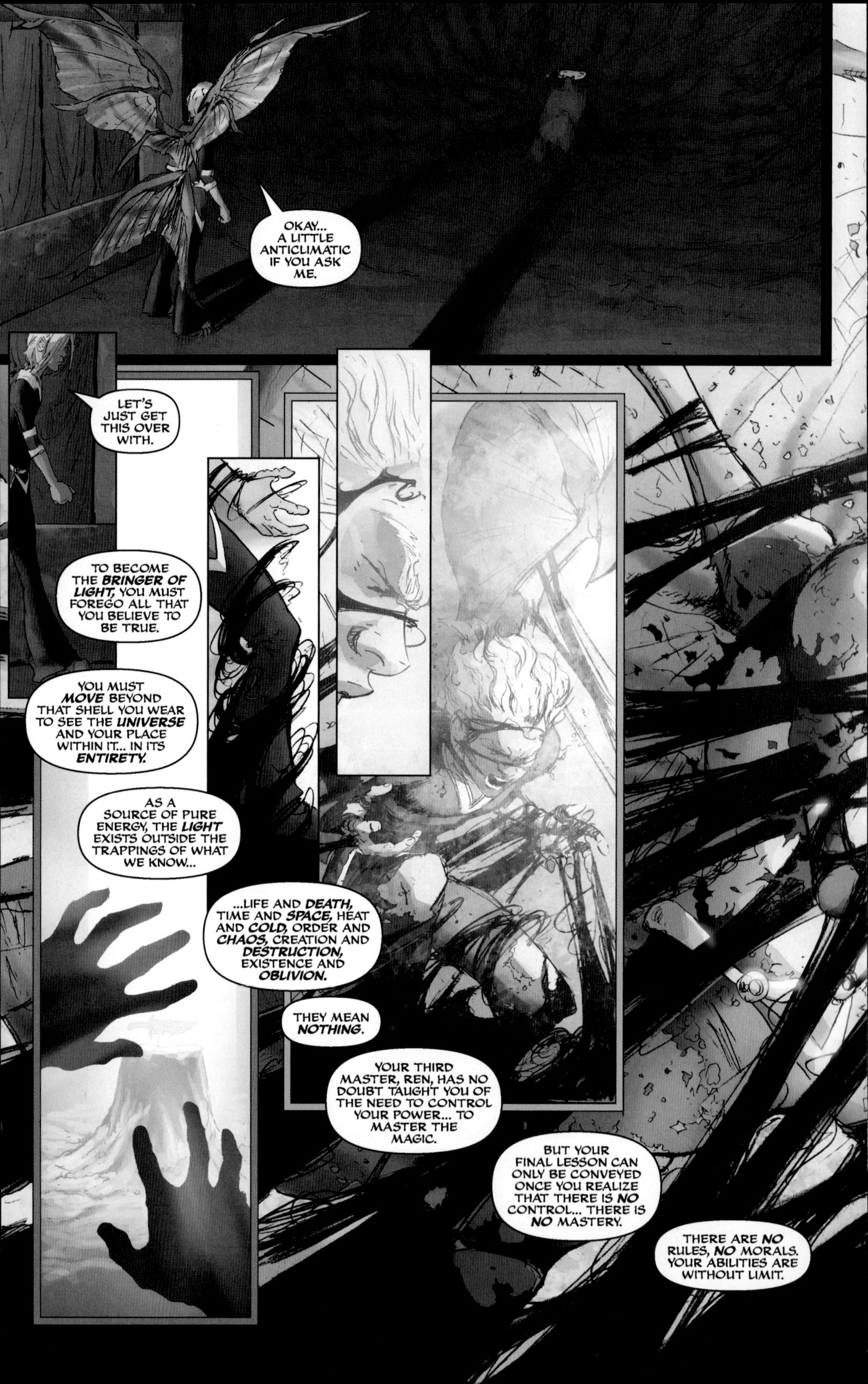
OKAY... A LITTLE ANTICLIMATIC IF YOU ASK ME.
LET'S JUST GET THIS OVER WITH.
TO BECOME THE BRINGER OF LIGHT, YOU MUST FOREGO ALL THAT YOU BELIEVE TO BE TRUE.
YOU MUST MOVE BEYOND THAT SHELL YOU WEAR TO SEE THE UNIVERSE AND YOUR PLACE WITHIN IT... IN ITS ENTIRETY.
AS A SOURCE OF PURE ENERGY, THE LIGHT EXISTS OUTSIDE THE TRAPPINGS OF WHAT WE KNOW...
...LIFE AND DEATH, TIME AND SPACE, HEAT AND COLD, ORDER AND CHAOS, CREATION AND DESTRUCTION, EXISTENCE AND OBLIVION.
THEY MEAN NOTHING.
YOUR THIRD MASTER, REN, HAS NO DOUBT TAUGHT YOU OF THE NEED TO CONTROL YOUR POWER... TO MASTER THE MAGIC.
BUT YOUR FINAL LESSON CAN ONLY BE CONVEYED ONCE YOU REALIZE THAT THERE IS NO CONTROL... THERE IS NO MASTERY.
THERE ARE NO RULES, NO MORALS. YOUR ABILITIES ARE WITHOUT LIMIT.

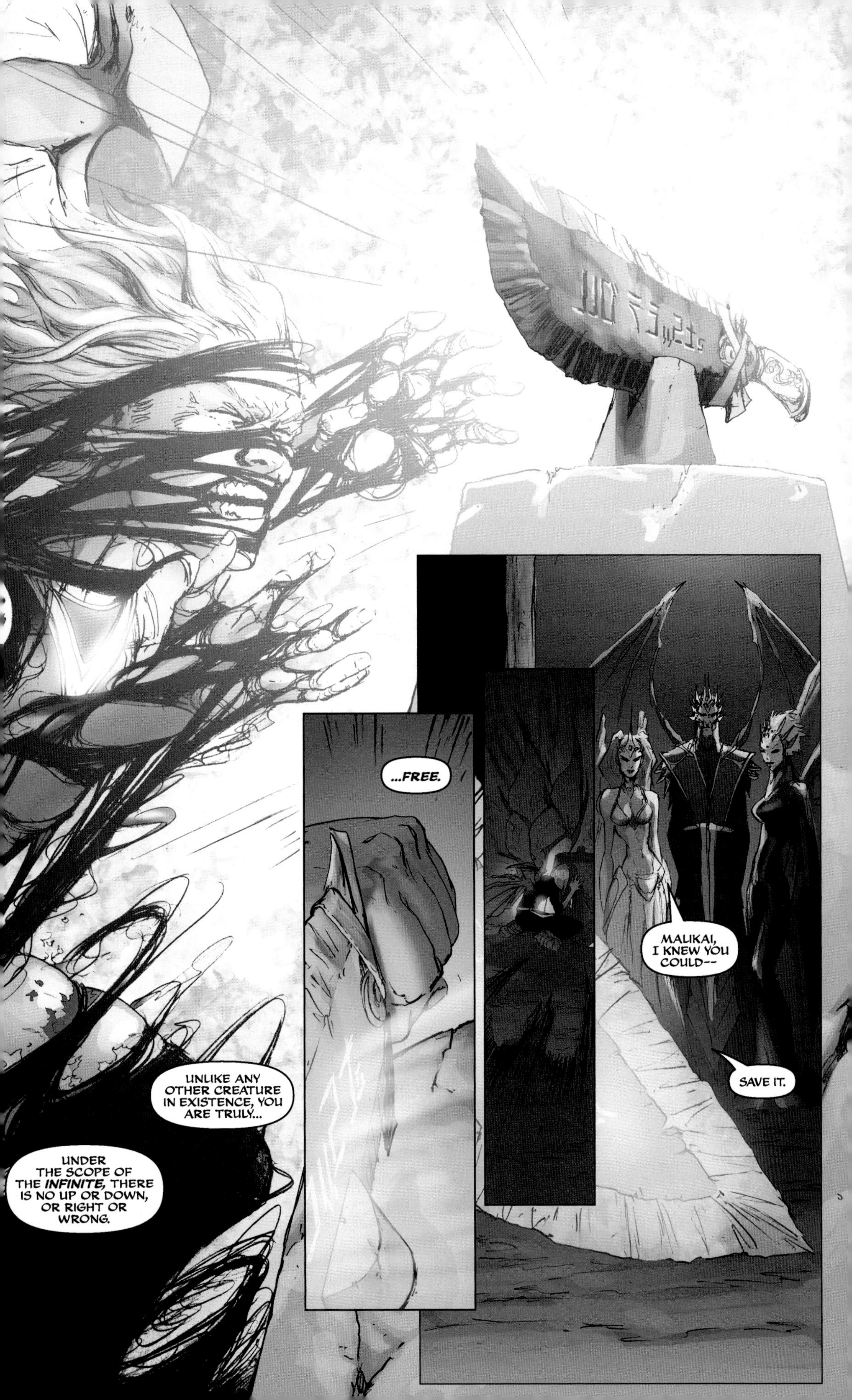
UNDER THE SCOPE OF THE *INFINITE,* THERE IS NO UP OR DOWN, OR RIGHT OR WRONG.
UNLIKE ANY OTHER CREATURE IN EXISTENCE, YOU ARE TRULY...
...FREE.
MALIKAI, I KNEW YOU COULD--
SAVE IT.

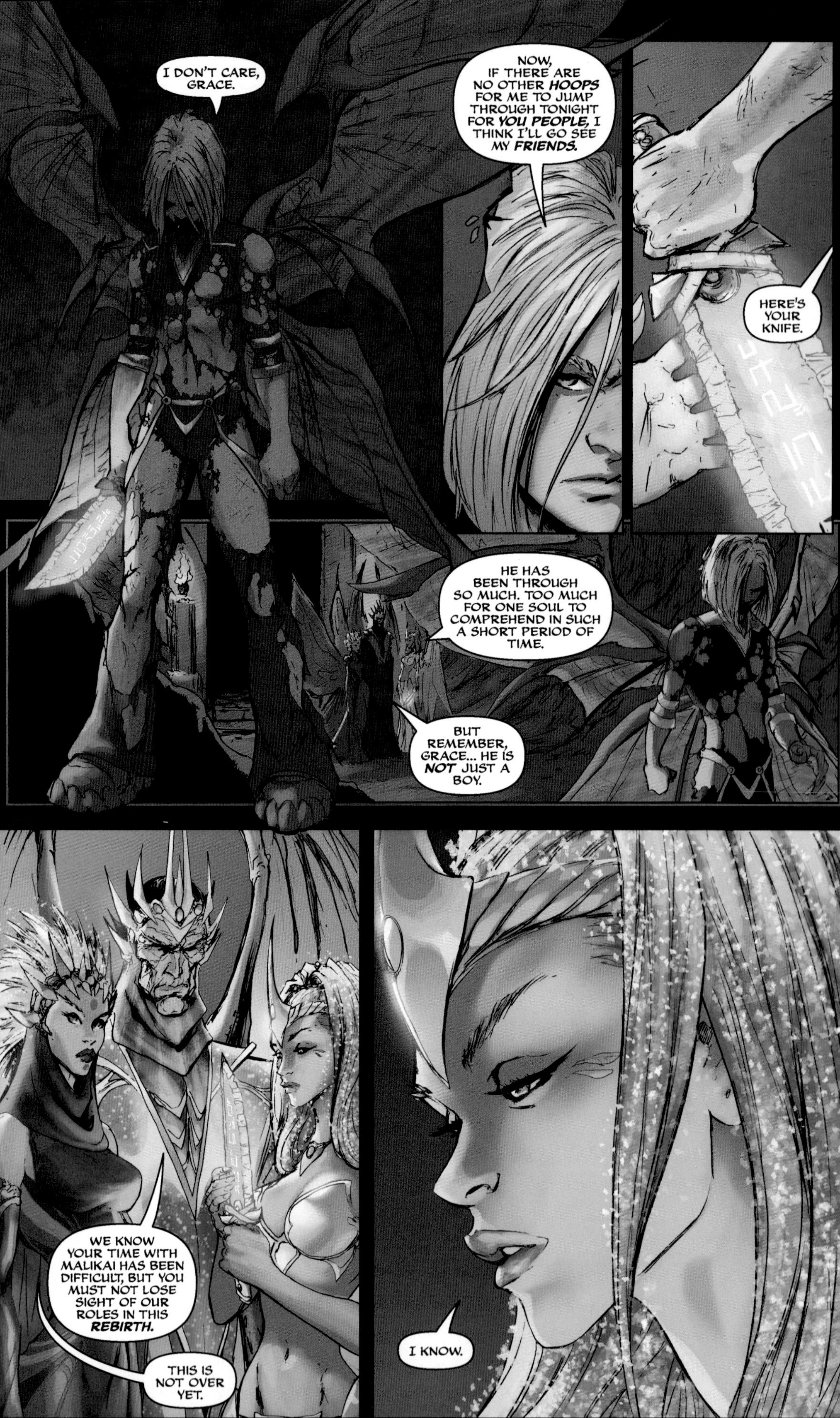

I DON'T CARE, GRACE.
NOW, IF THERE ARE NO OTHER ***HOOPS*** FOR ME TO JUMP THROUGH TONIGHT FOR ***YOU PEOPLE,*** I THINK I'LL GO SEE MY ***FRIENDS.***
HERE'S YOUR KNIFE.
HE HAS BEEN THROUGH SO MUCH. TOO MUCH FOR ONE SOUL TO COMPREHEND IN SUCH A SHORT PERIOD OF TIME.
BUT REMEMBER, GRACE... HE IS ***NOT*** JUST A BOY.
WE KNOW YOUR TIME WITH MALIKAI HAS BEEN DIFFICULT, BUT YOU MUST NOT LOSE SIGHT OF OUR ROLES IN THIS ***REBIRTH.***
THIS IS NOT OVER YET.
I KNOW.

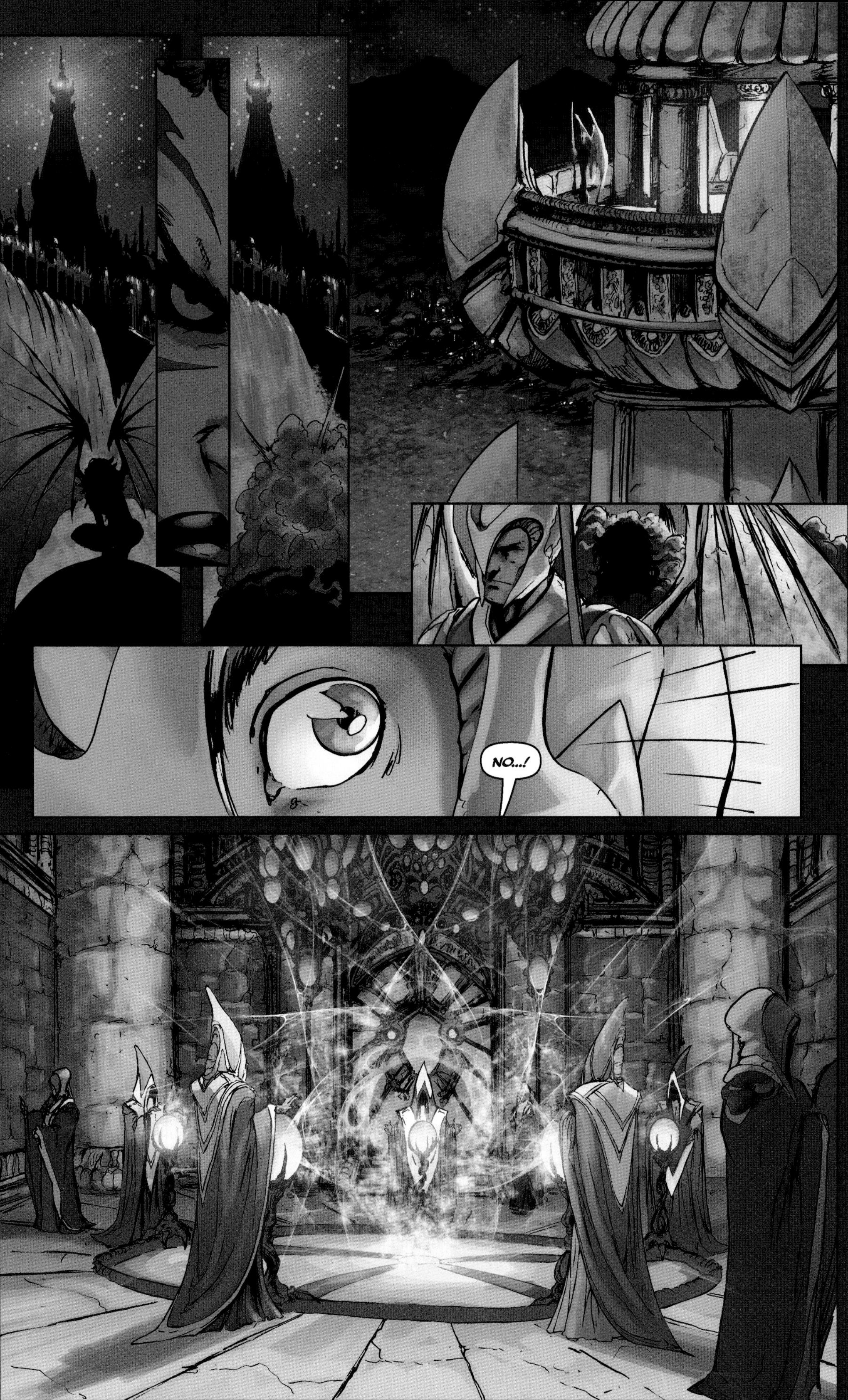
NO...!

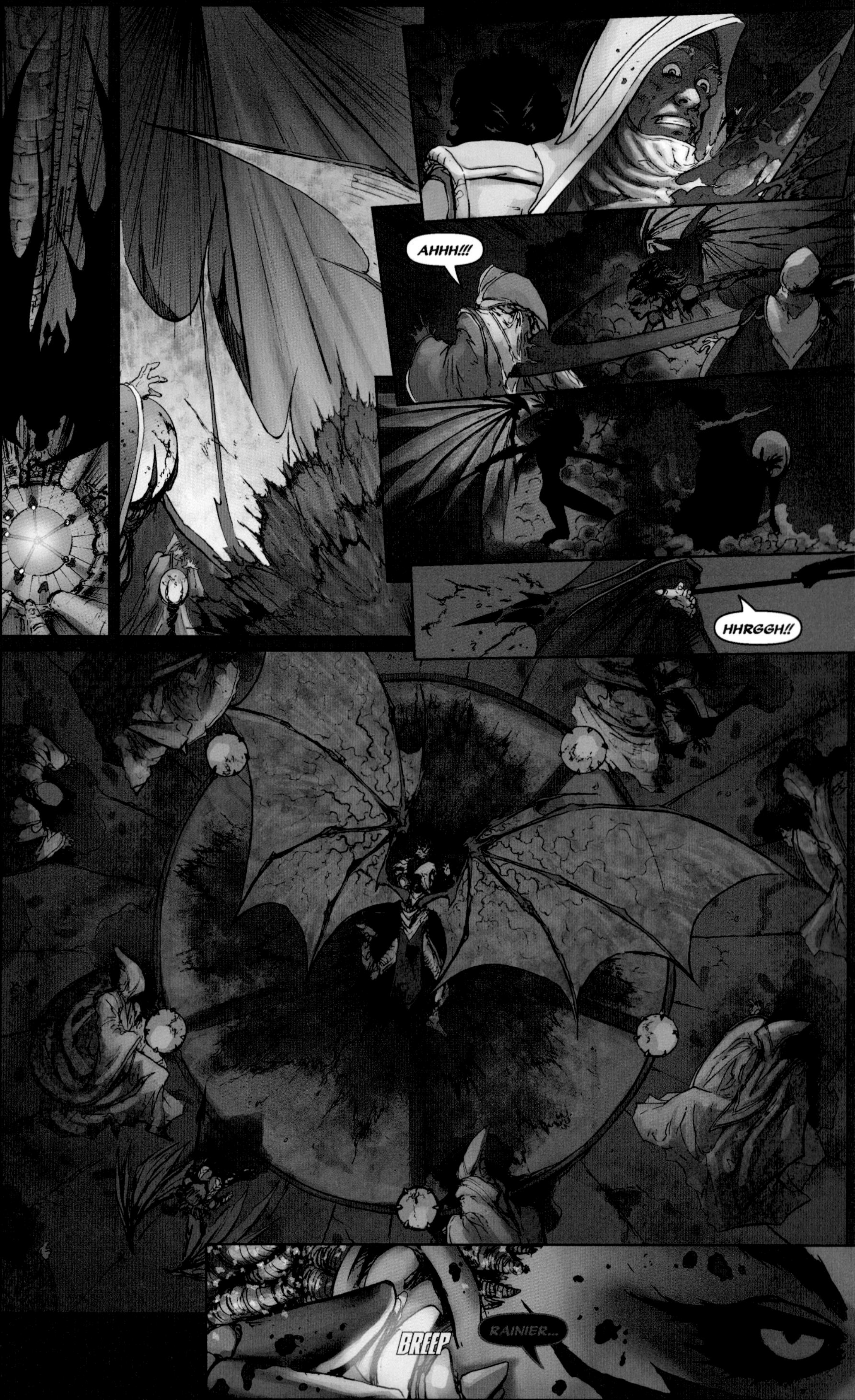
AHHH!!!
HHRGGH!!
BREEP
RAINIER...

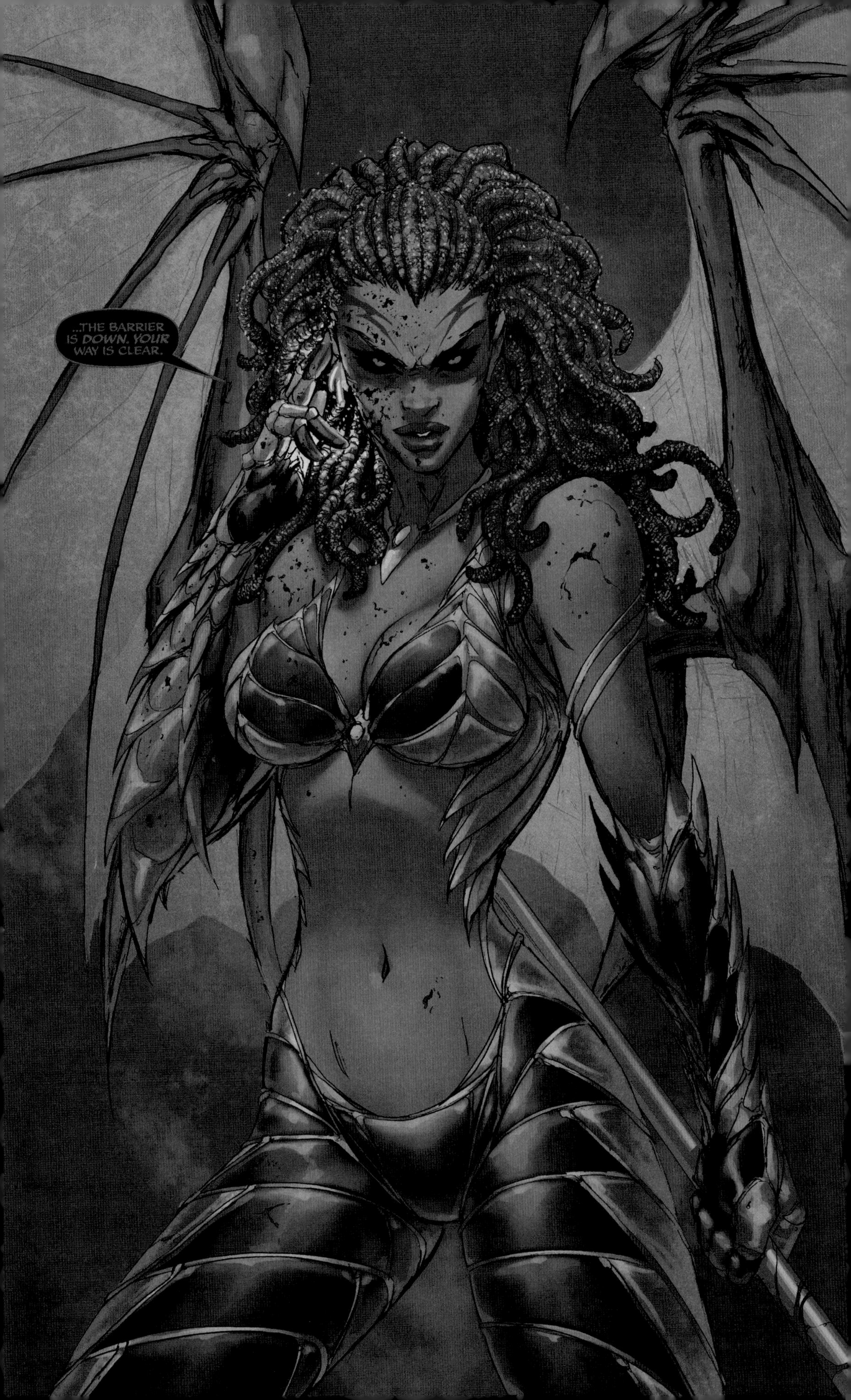
...THE BARRIER IS DOWN. YOUR WAY IS CLEAR.

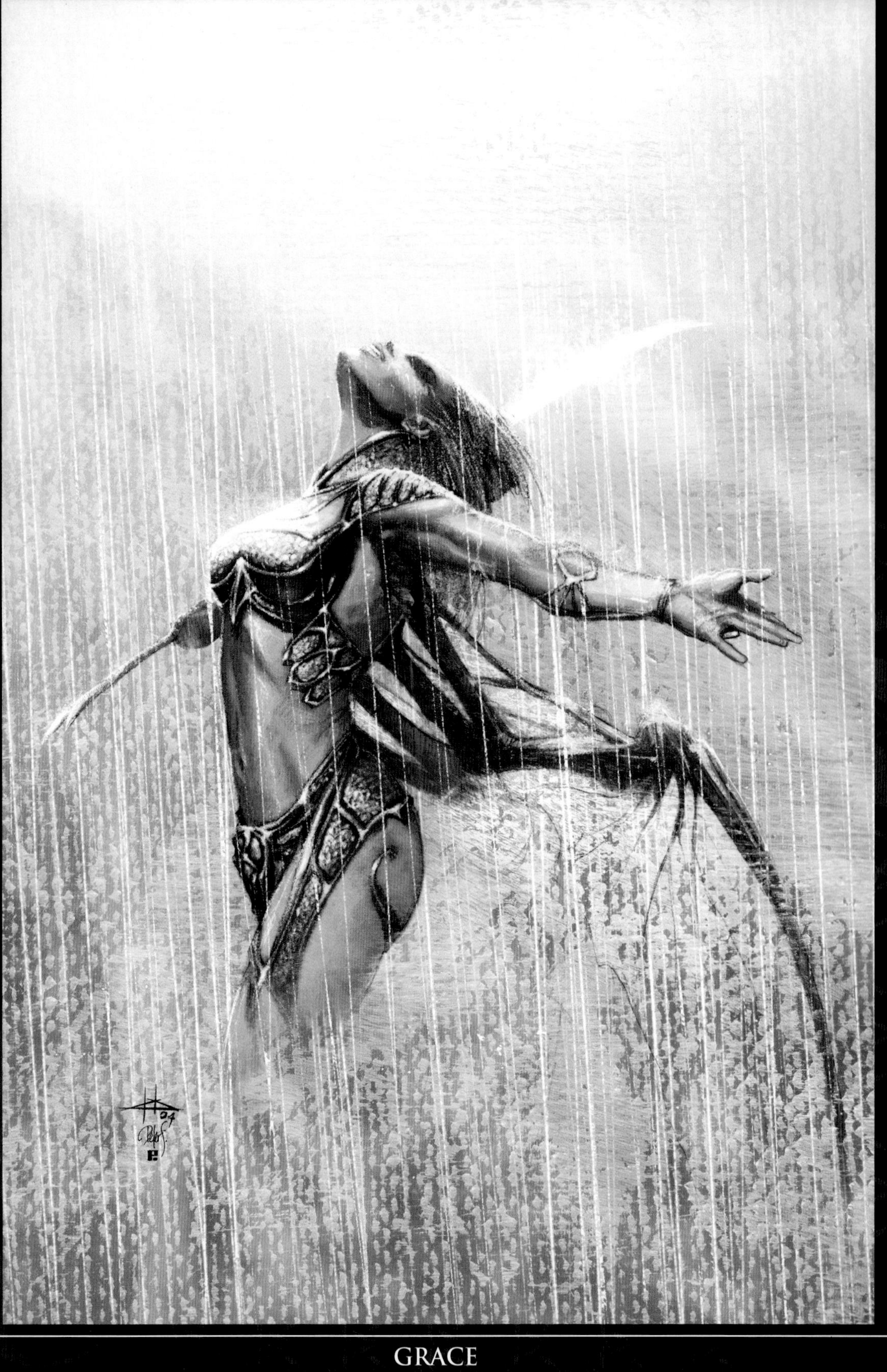

GRACE

· PIN-UP FROM ASPEN SPLASH: 2006 SWIMSUIT SPECTACULAR ·

by

· GABRIELE DELL'OTTO ·

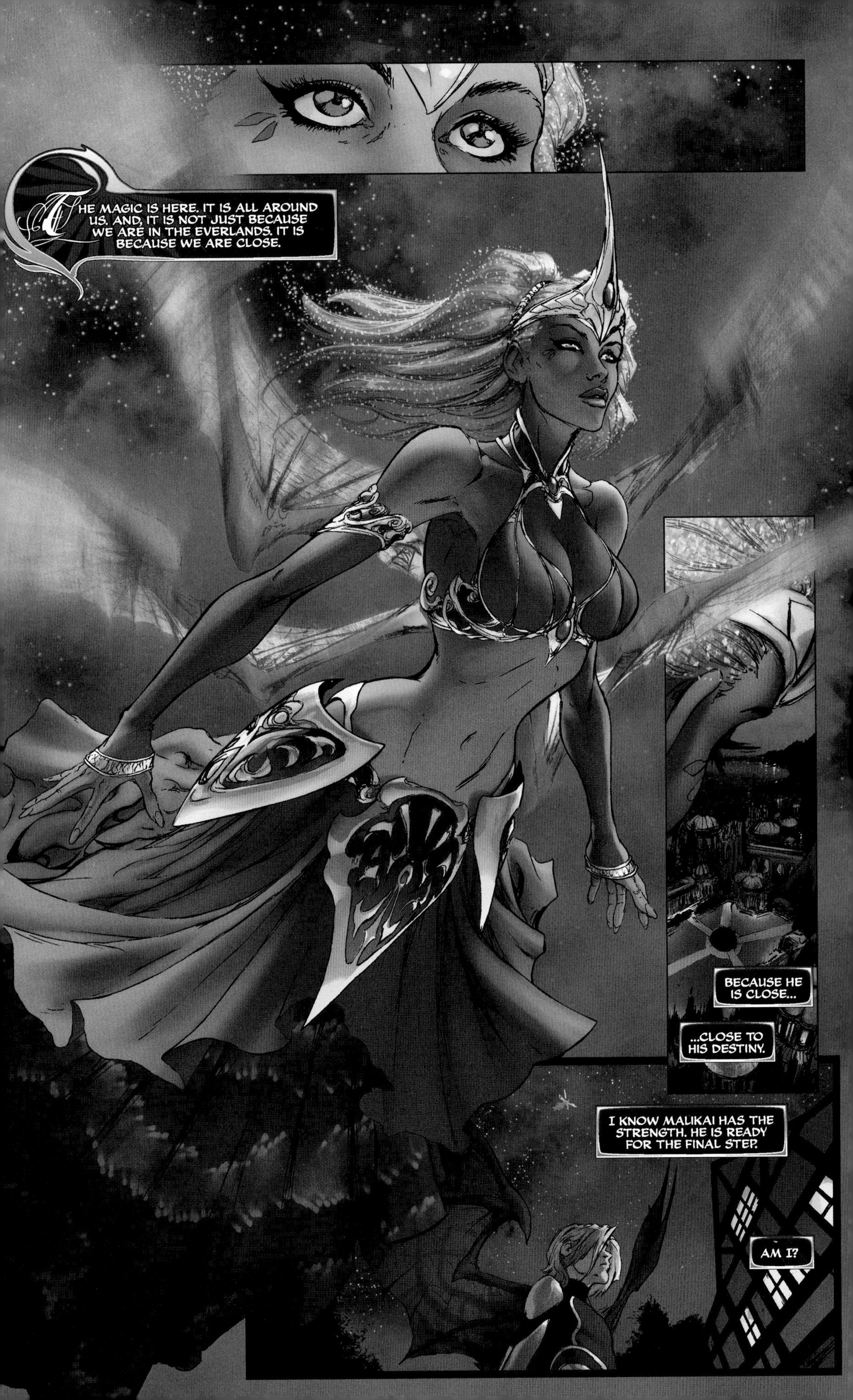
THE MAGIC IS HERE. IT IS ALL AROUND US. AND, IT IS NOT JUST BECAUSE WE ARE IN THE EVERLANDS. IT IS BECAUSE WE ARE CLOSE.
BECAUSE HE IS CLOSE...
...CLOSE TO HIS DESTINY.
I KNOW MALIKAI HAS THE STRENGTH. HE IS READY FOR THE FINAL STEP.
AM I?

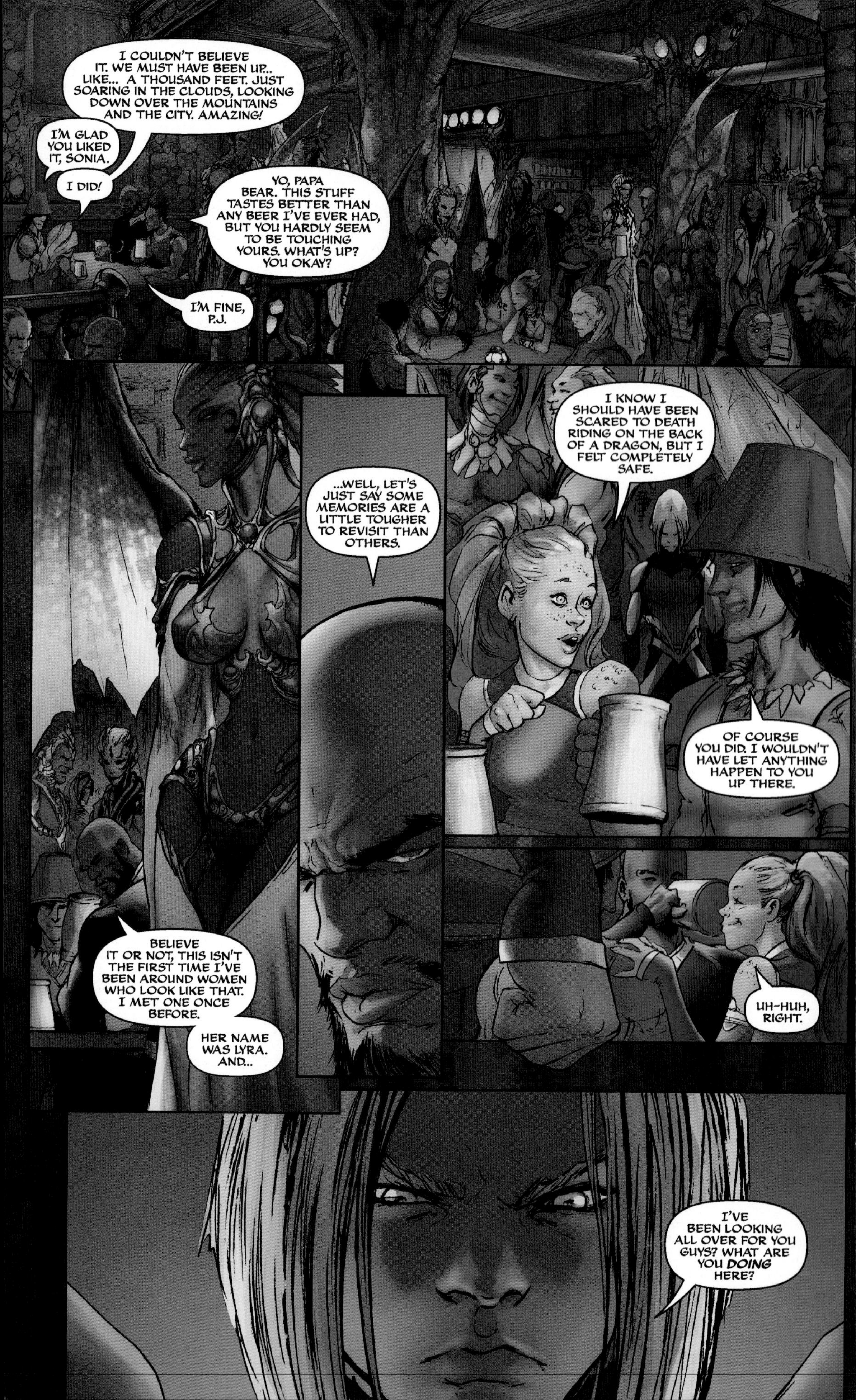

I COULDN'T BELIEVE IT. WE MUST HAVE BEEN UP.. LIKE... A THOUSAND FEET. JUST SOARING IN THE CLOUDS, LOOKING DOWN OVER THE MOUNTAINS AND THE CITY. AMAZING!
I'M GLAD YOU LIKED IT, SONIA.
I DID!
YO, PAPA BEAR. THIS STUFF TASTES BETTER THAN ANY BEER I'VE EVER HAD, BUT YOU HARDLY SEEM TO BE TOUCHING YOURS. WHAT'S UP? YOU OKAY?
I'M FINE, P.J.
BELIEVE IT OR NOT, THIS ISN'T THE FIRST TIME I'VE BEEN AROUND WOMEN WHO LOOK LIKE THAT. I MET ONE ONCE BEFORE.
HER NAME WAS LYRA. AND..
...WELL, LET'S JUST SAY SOME MEMORIES ARE A LITTLE TOUGHER TO REVISIT THAN OTHERS.
I KNOW I SHOULD HAVE BEEN SCARED TO DEATH RIDING ON THE BACK OF A DRAGON, BUT I FELT COMPLETELY SAFE.
OF COURSE YOU DID. I WOULDN'T HAVE LET ANYTHING HAPPEN TO YOU UP THERE.
UH-HUH, RIGHT.
I'VE BEEN LOOKING ALL OVER FOR YOU GUYS? WHAT ARE YOU *DOING* HERE?

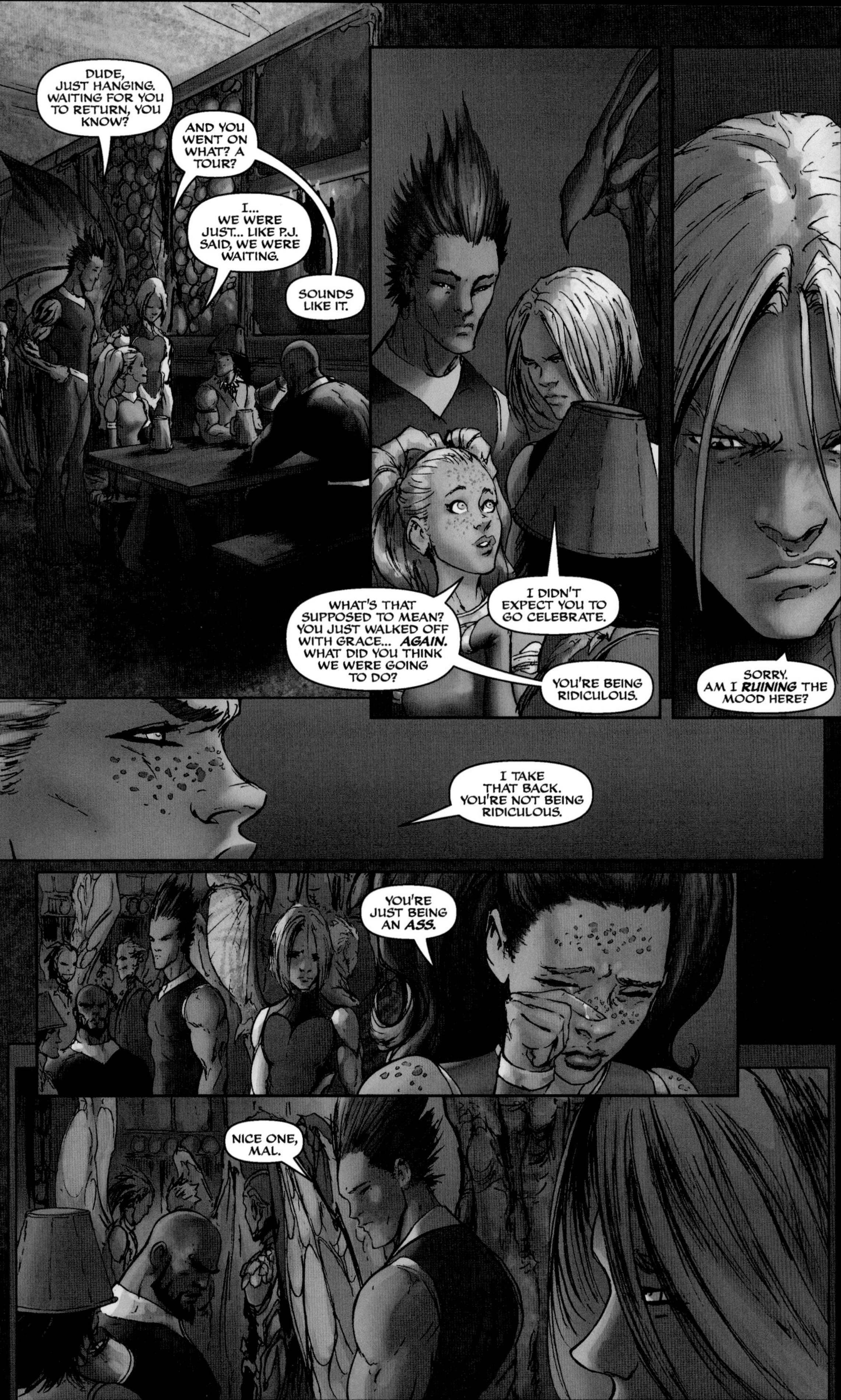

DUDE, JUST HANGING. WAITING FOR YOU TO RETURN, YOU KNOW?
AND YOU WENT ON WHAT? A TOUR?
I... WE WERE JUST... LIKE P.J. SAID, WE WERE WAITING.
SOUNDS LIKE IT.
I DIDN'T EXPECT YOU TO GO CELEBRATE.
WHAT'S THAT SUPPOSED TO MEAN? YOU JUST WALKED OFF WITH GRACE... AGAIN. WHAT DID YOU THINK WE WERE GOING TO DO?
YOU'RE BEING RIDICULOUS.
SORRY. AM I RUINING THE MOOD HERE?
I TAKE THAT BACK. YOU'RE NOT BEING RIDICULOUS.
YOU'RE JUST BEING AN ASS.
NICE ONE, MAL.

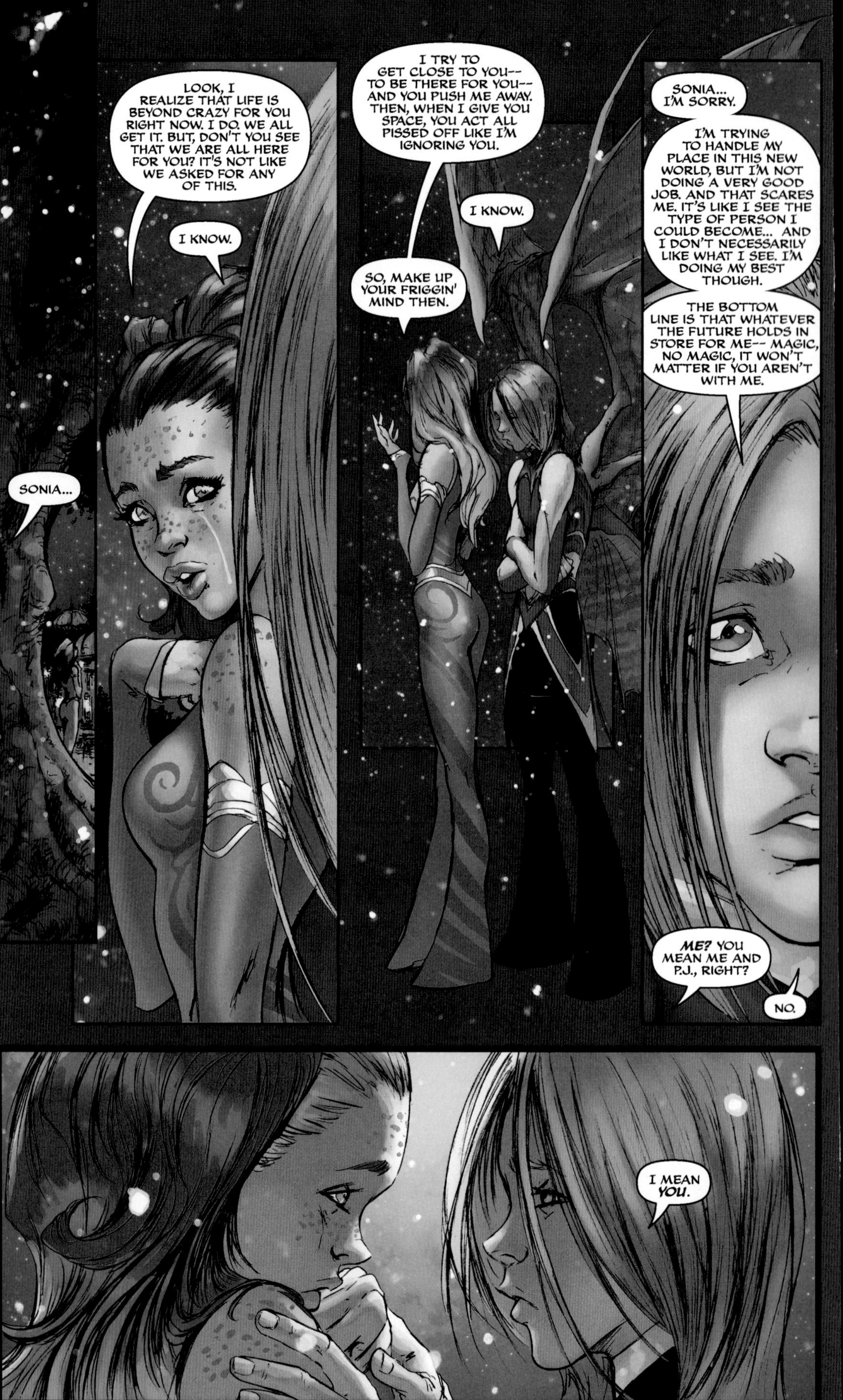
SONIA...
LOOK, I REALIZE THAT LIFE IS BEYOND CRAZY FOR YOU RIGHT NOW. I DO. WE ALL GET IT. BUT, DON'T YOU SEE THAT WE ARE ALL HERE FOR YOU? IT'S NOT LIKE WE ASKED FOR ANY OF THIS.
I KNOW.
I TRY TO GET CLOSE TO YOU-- TO BE THERE FOR YOU-- AND YOU PUSH ME AWAY. THEN, WHEN I GIVE YOU SPACE, YOU ACT ALL PISSED OFF LIKE I'M IGNORING YOU.
I KNOW.
SO, MAKE UP YOUR FRIGGIN' MIND THEN.
SONIA... I'M SORRY.
I'M TRYING TO HANDLE MY PLACE IN THIS NEW WORLD, BUT I'M NOT DOING A VERY GOOD JOB. AND THAT SCARES ME. IT'S LIKE I SEE THE TYPE OF PERSON I COULD BECOME... AND I DON'T NECESSARILY LIKE WHAT I SEE. I'M DOING MY BEST THOUGH.
THE BOTTOM LINE IS THAT WHATEVER THE FUTURE HOLDS IN STORE FOR ME-- MAGIC, NO MAGIC, IT WON'T MATTER IF YOU AREN'T WITH ME.
ME? YOU MEAN ME AND P.J., RIGHT?
NO.
I MEAN YOU.

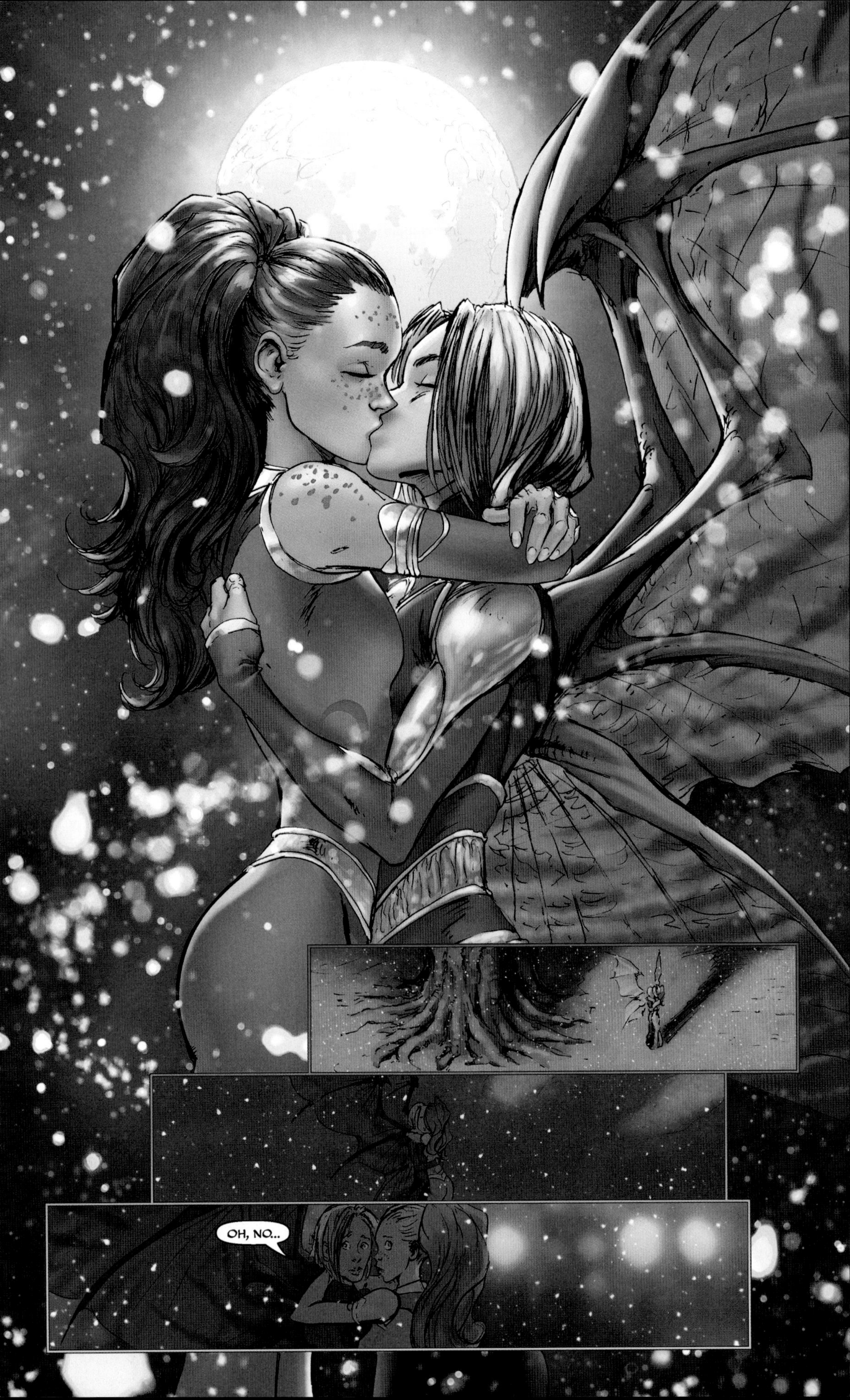
OH, NO...

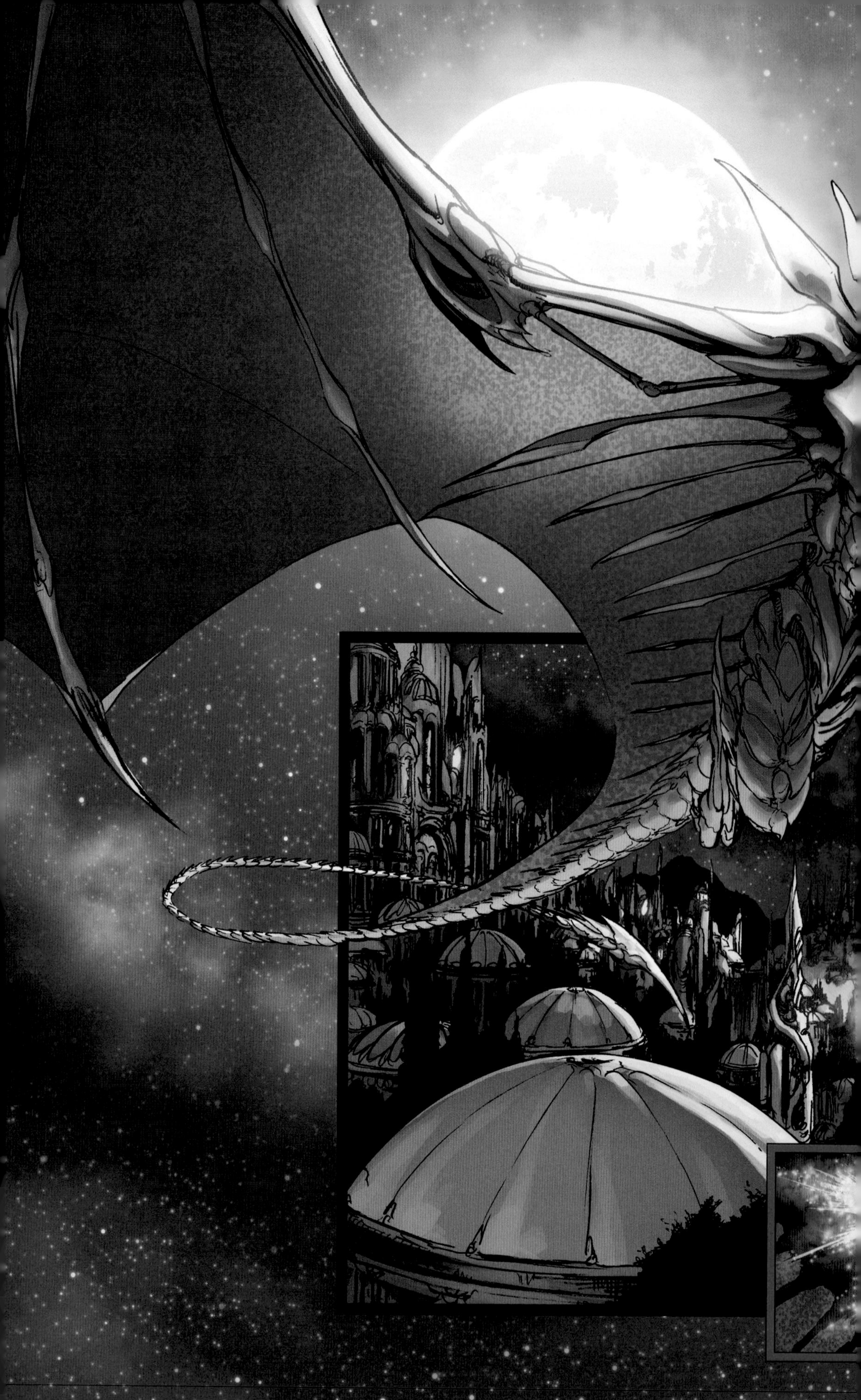

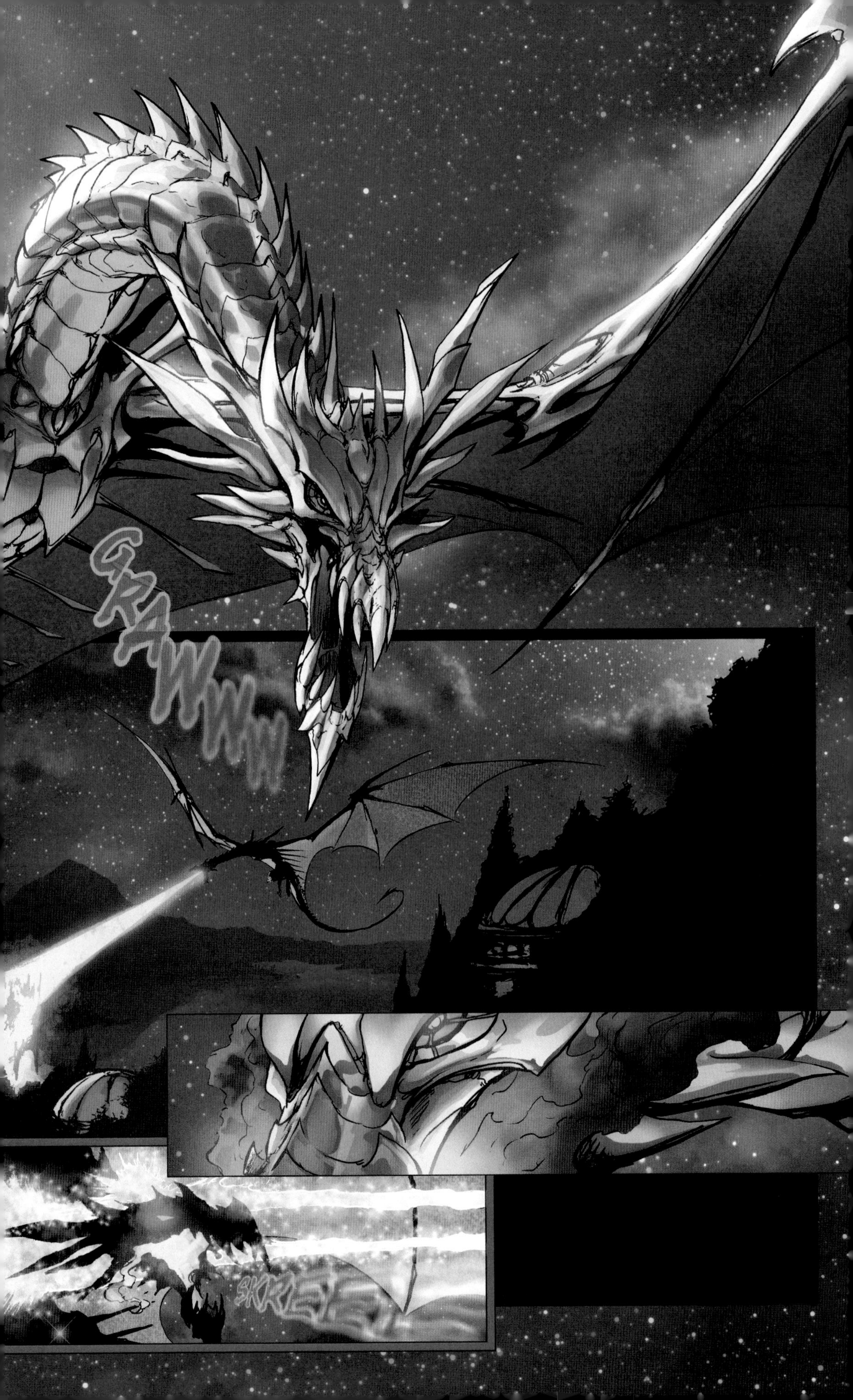
GRAWWWW

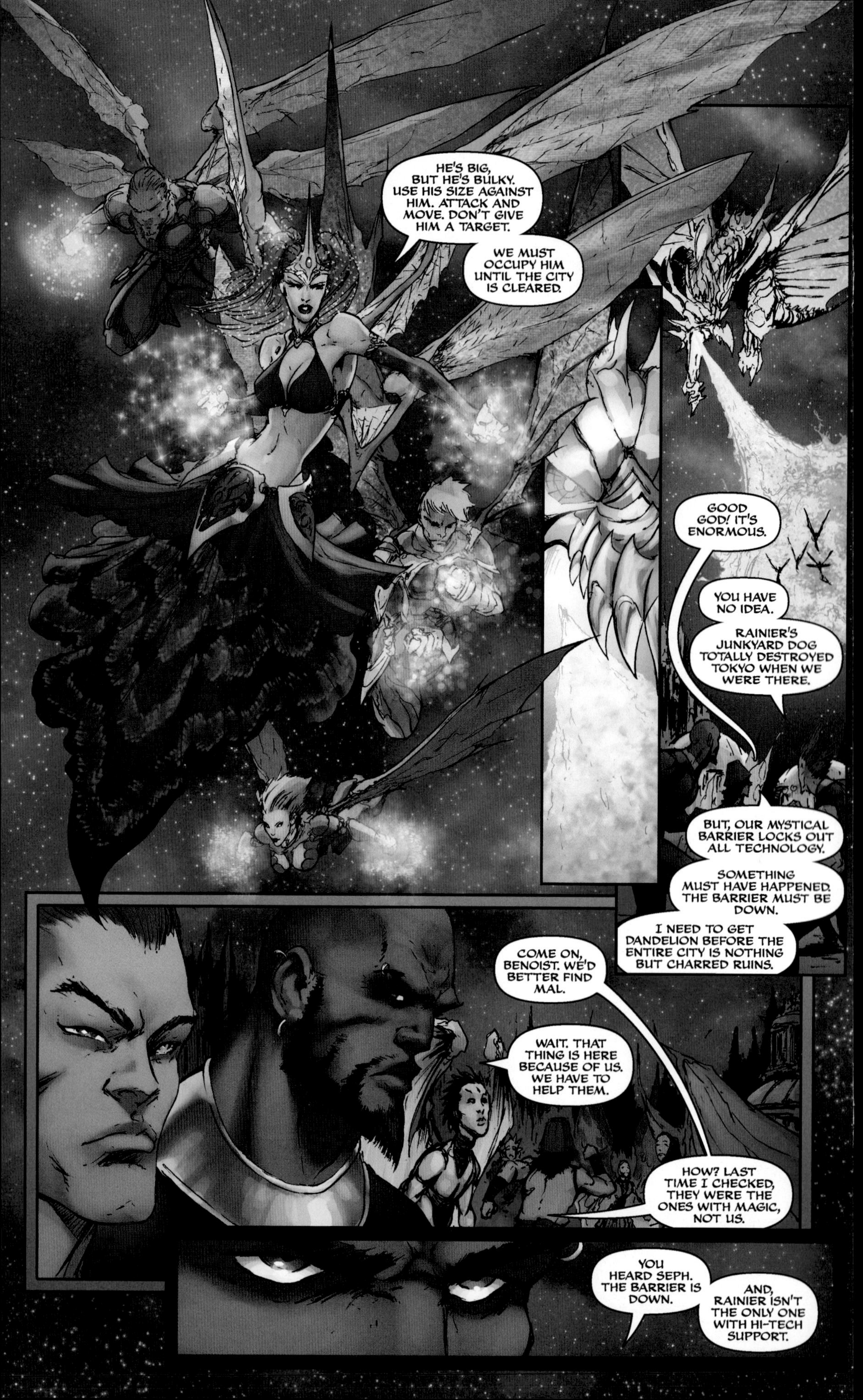
HE'S BIG, BUT HE'S BULKY. USE HIS SIZE AGAINST HIM. ATTACK AND MOVE. DON'T GIVE HIM A TARGET.
WE MUST OCCUPY HIM UNTIL THE CITY IS CLEARED.
GOOD GOD! IT'S ENORMOUS.
YOU HAVE NO IDEA.
RAINIER'S JUNKYARD DOG TOTALLY DESTROYED TOKYO WHEN WE WERE THERE.
BUT, OUR MYSTICAL BARRIER LOCKS OUT ALL TECHNOLOGY.
SOMETHING MUST HAVE HAPPENED. THE BARRIER MUST BE DOWN.
I NEED TO GET DANDELION BEFORE THE ENTIRE CITY IS NOTHING BUT CHARRED RUINS.
COME ON, BENOIST. WE'D BETTER FIND MAL.
WAIT. THAT THING IS HERE BECAUSE OF US. WE HAVE TO HELP THEM.
HOW? LAST TIME I CHECKED, THEY WERE THE ONES WITH MAGIC, NOT US.
YOU HEARD SEPH. THE BARRIER IS DOWN.
AND, RAINIER ISN'T THE ONLY ONE WITH HI-TECH SUPPORT.

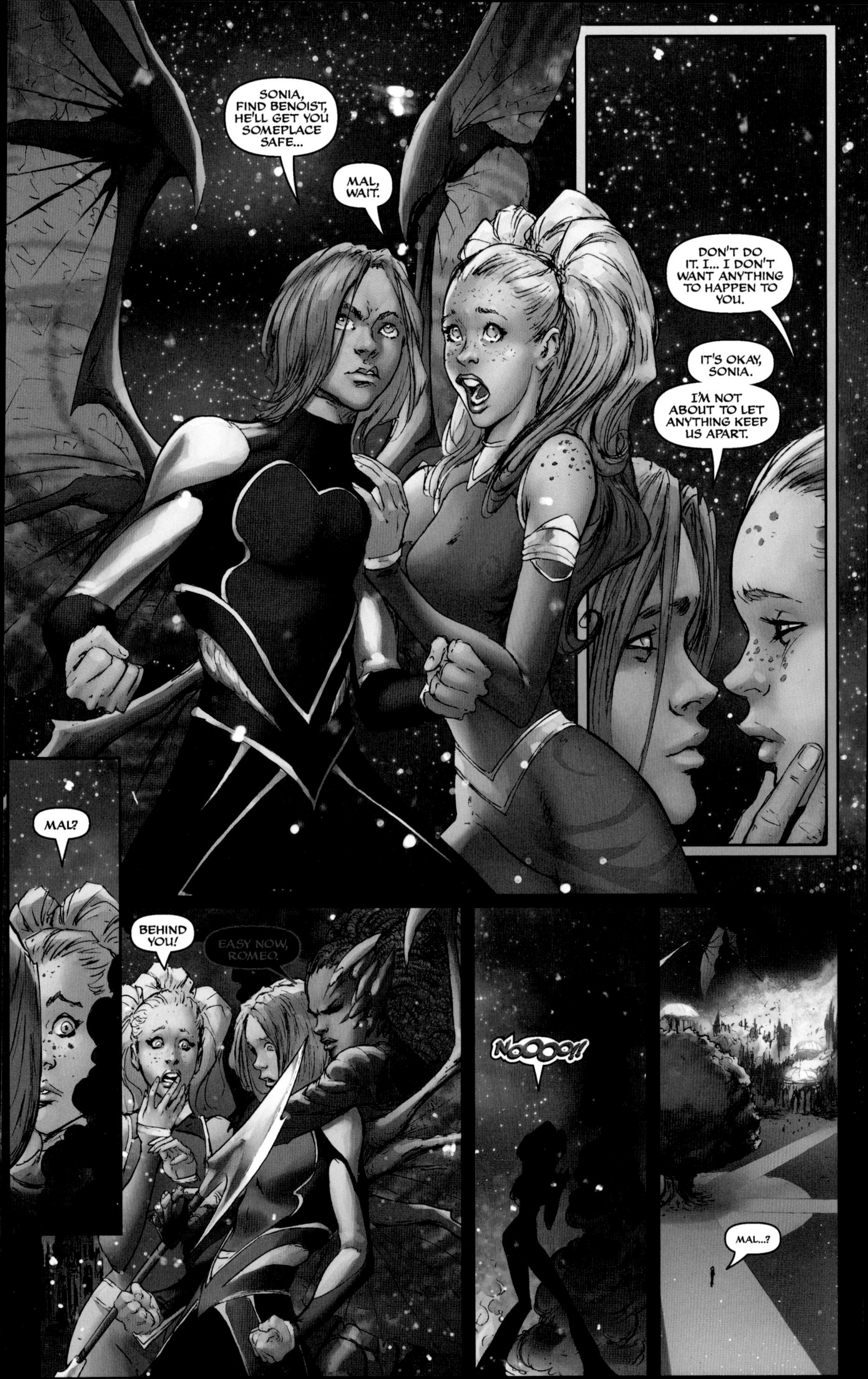
SONIA, FIND BENOIST, HE'LL GET YOU SOMEPLACE SAFE...
MAL, WAIT.
DON'T DO IT. I... I DON'T WANT ANYTHING TO HAPPEN TO YOU.
IT'S OKAY, SONIA.
I'M NOT ABOUT TO LET ANYTHING KEEP US APART.
MAL?
BEHIND YOU!
EASY NOW, ROMEO.
NOOOO!!
MAL...?

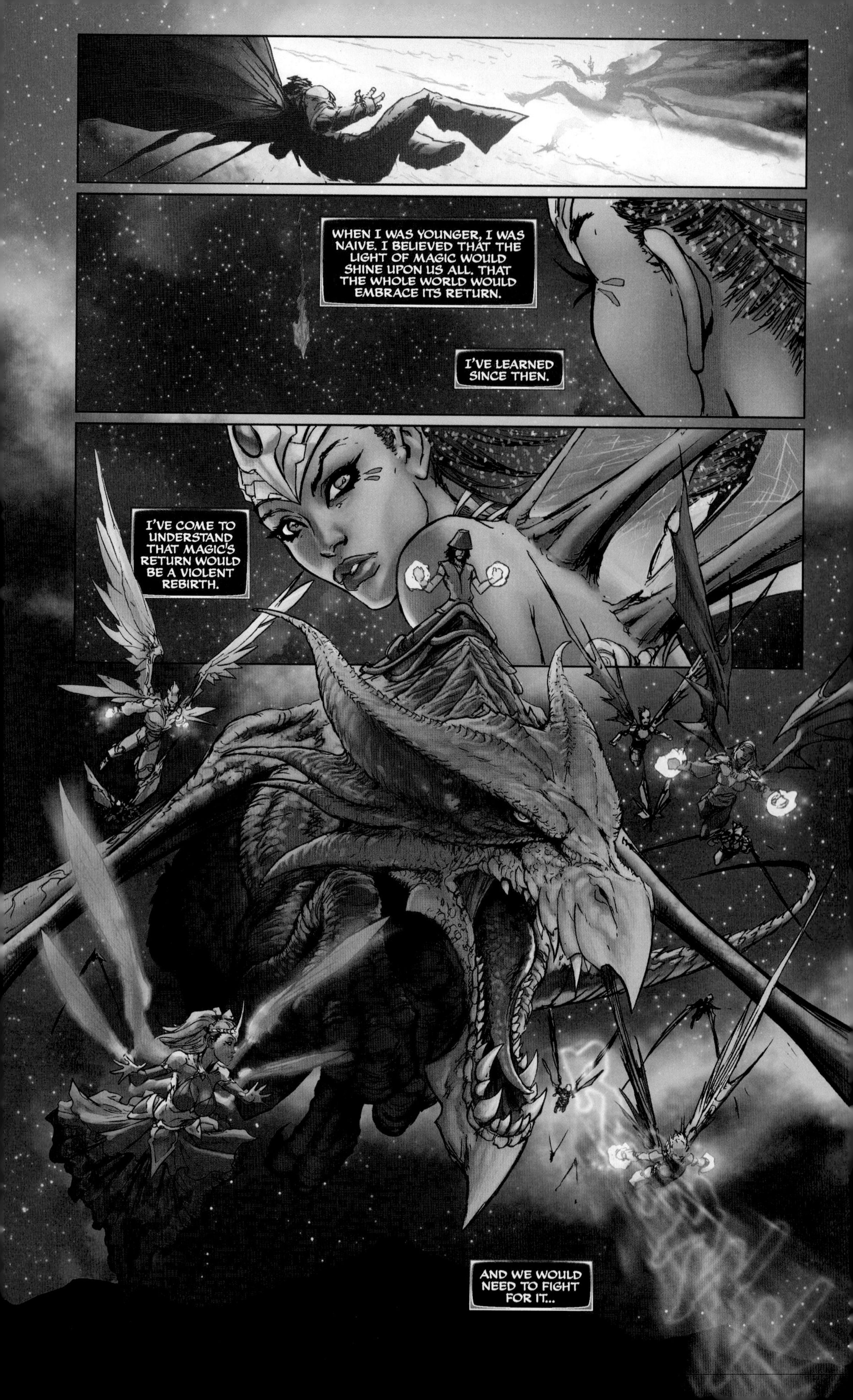
WHEN I WAS YOUNGER, I WAS NAIVE. I BELIEVED THAT THE LIGHT OF MAGIC WOULD SHINE UPON US ALL. THAT THE WHOLE WORLD WOULD EMBRACE ITS RETURN.
I'VE LEARNED SINCE THEN.
I'VE COME TO UNDERSTAND THAT MAGIC'S RETURN WOULD BE A VIOLENT REBIRTH.
AND WE WOULD NEED TO FIGHT FOR IT...

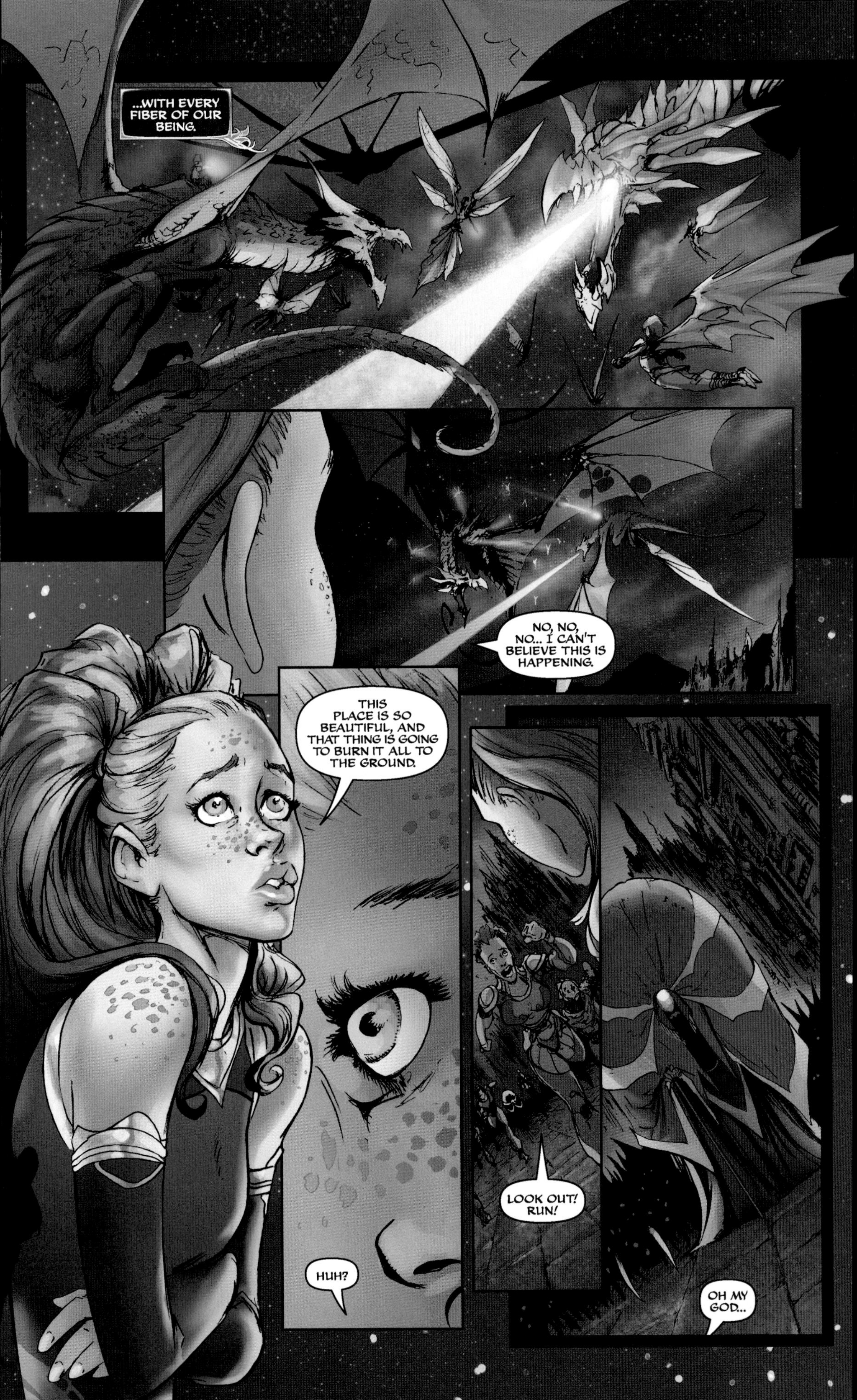
...WITH EVERY FIBER OF OUR BEING.
NO, NO, NO... I CAN'T BELIEVE THIS IS HAPPENING.
THIS PLACE IS SO BEAUTIFUL, AND THAT THING IS GOING TO BURN IT ALL TO THE GROUND.
HUH?
LOOK OUT! RUN!
OH MY GOD...

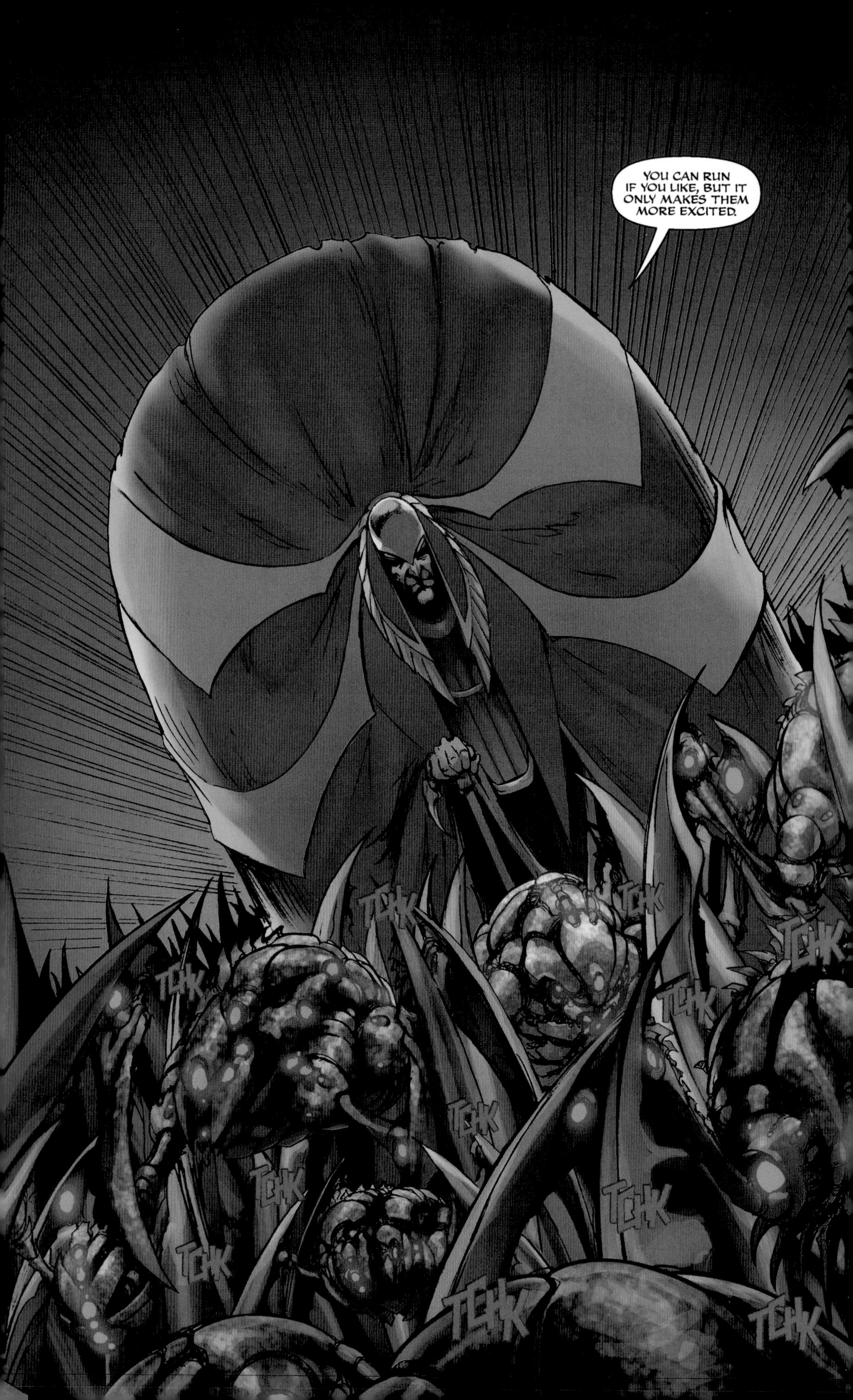
YOU CAN RUN IF YOU LIKE, BUT IT ONLY MAKES THEM MORE EXCITED.
TCHK
TCHK
TCHK
TCHK
TCHK
TCHK
TCHK
TCHK
TCHK
TCHK
TCHK

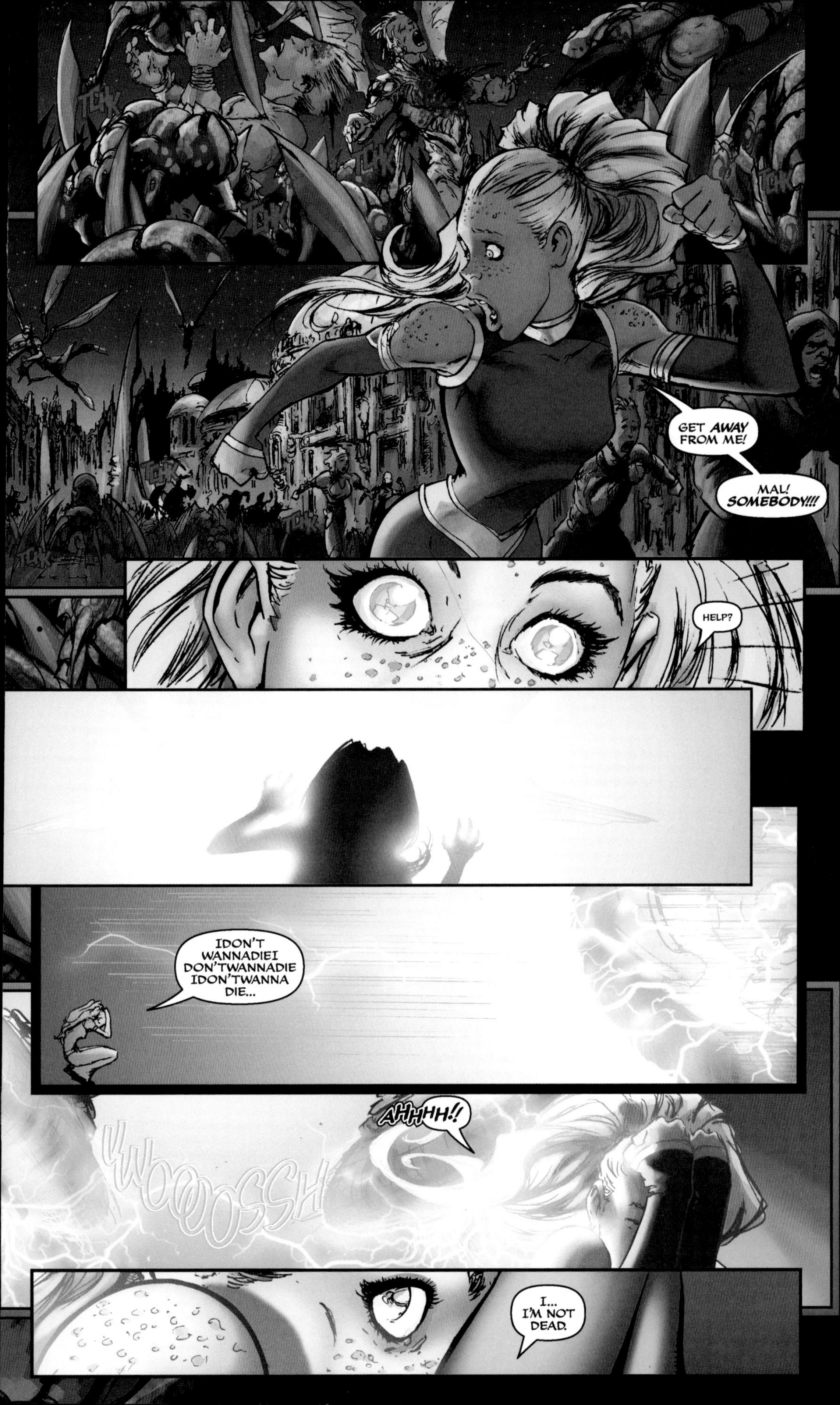
TCHK
TCHK
TCHK
TCHK
GET AWAY FROM ME!
MAL! SOMEBODY!!!
HELP?
IDON'T WANNADIEI DON'TWANNADIE IDON'TWANNA DIE...
AHHHH!!
WOOOOSSH
I... I'M NOT DEAD.

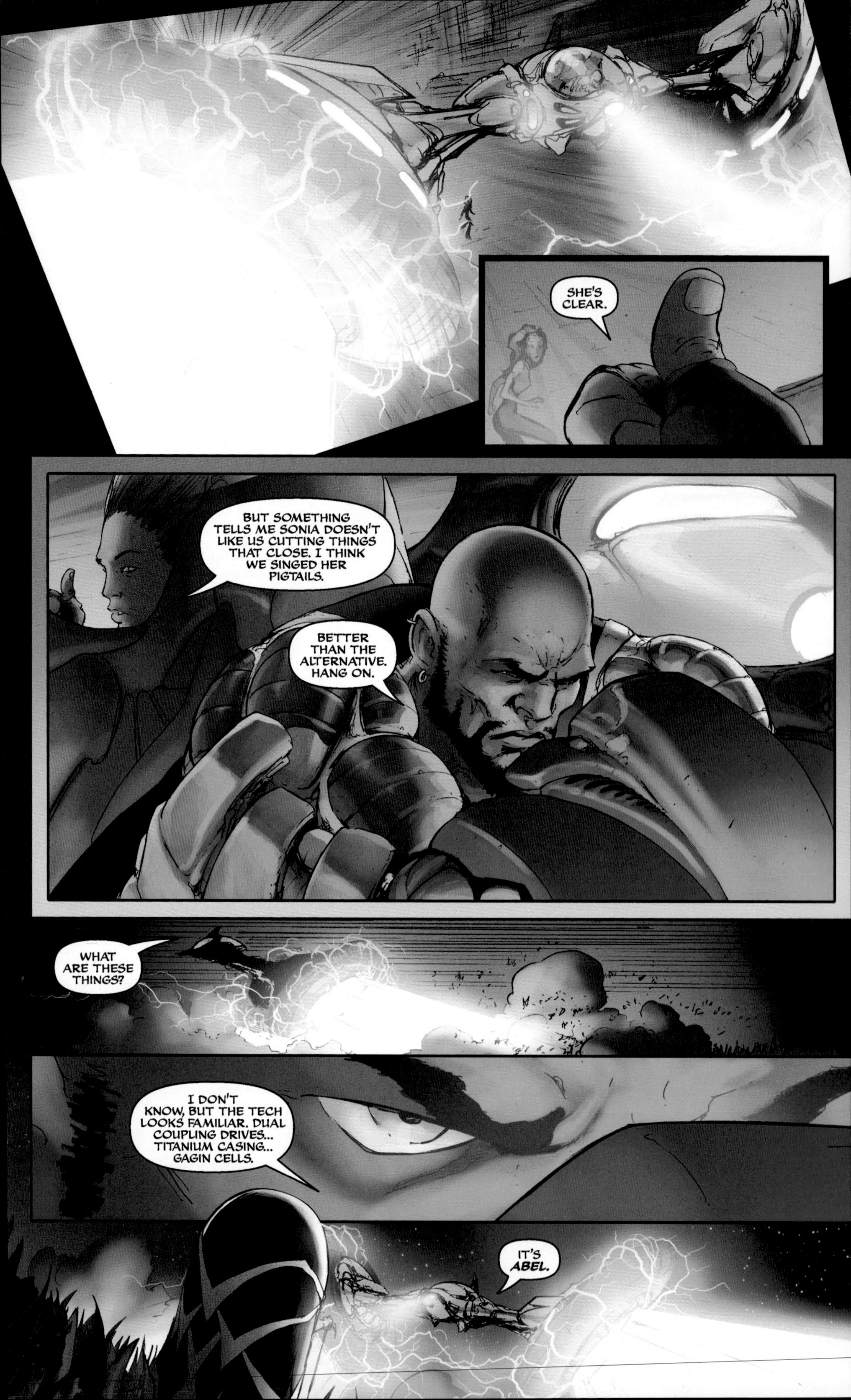
SHE'S CLEAR.
BUT SOMETHING TELLS ME SONIA DOESN'T LIKE US CUTTING THINGS THAT CLOSE. I THINK WE SINGED HER PIGTAILS.
BETTER THAN THE ALTERNATIVE. HANG ON.
WHAT ARE THESE THINGS?
I DON'T KNOW, BUT THE TECH LOOKS FAMILIAR. DUAL COUPLING DRIVES... TITANIUM CASING... GAGIN CELLS.
IT'S ABEL.

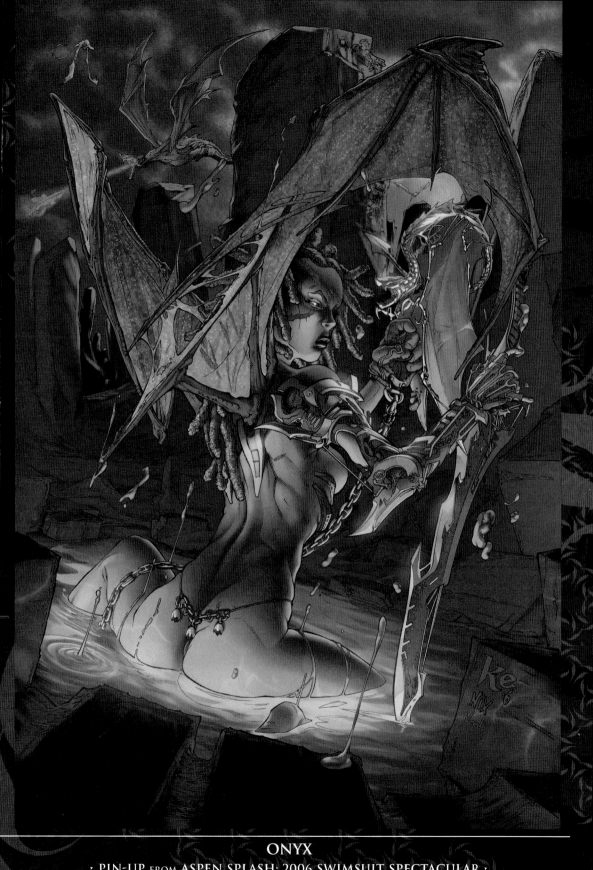

ONYX
· PIN-UP FROM ASPEN SPLASH: 2006 SWIMSUIT SPECTACULAR ·
by
· KHARI EVANS · NICK NIX · DAVID MORÁN ·

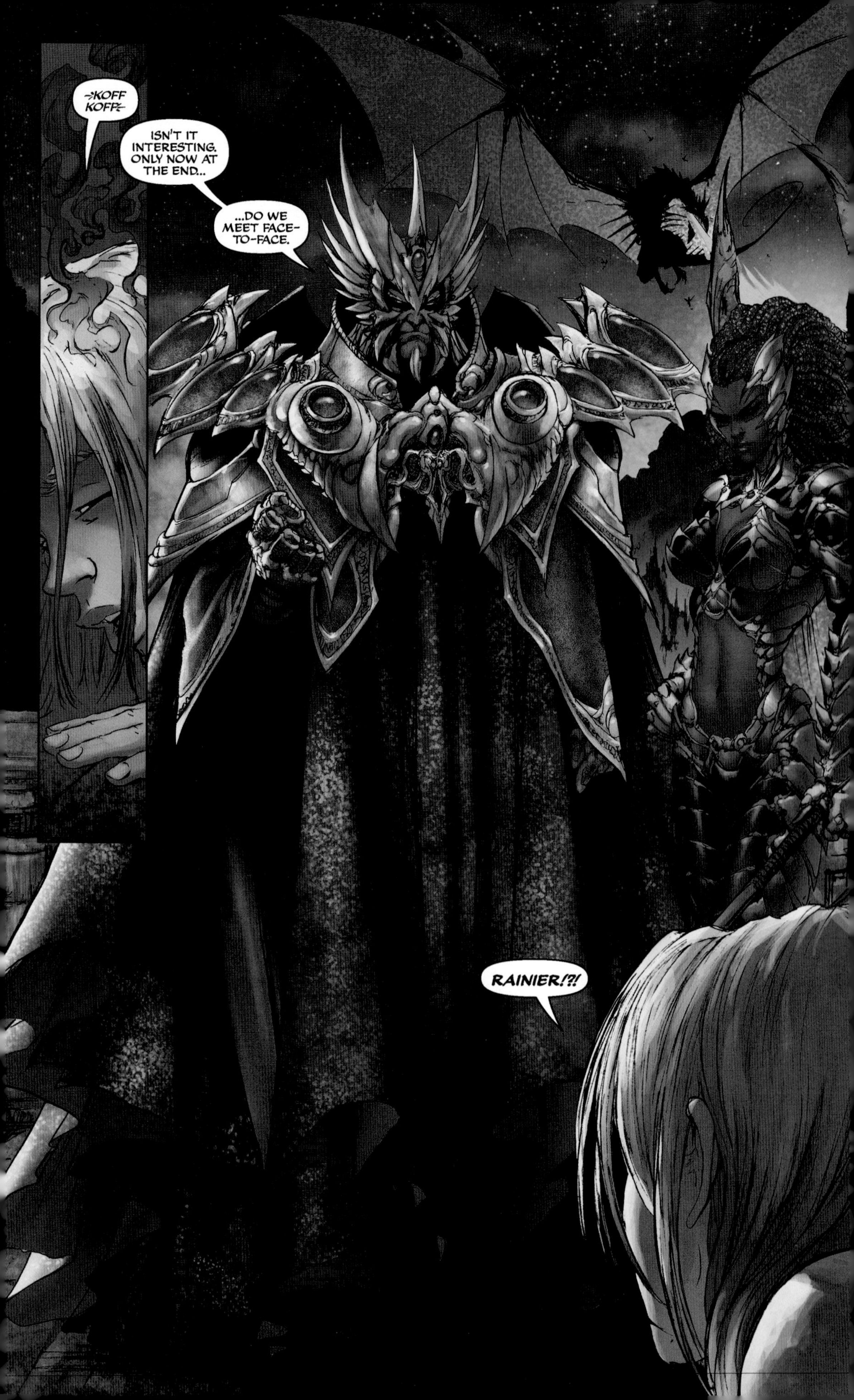

-KOFF KOFF-
ISN'T IT INTERESTING. ONLY NOW AT THE END...
...DO WE MEET FACE-TO-FACE.
RAINIER!?!

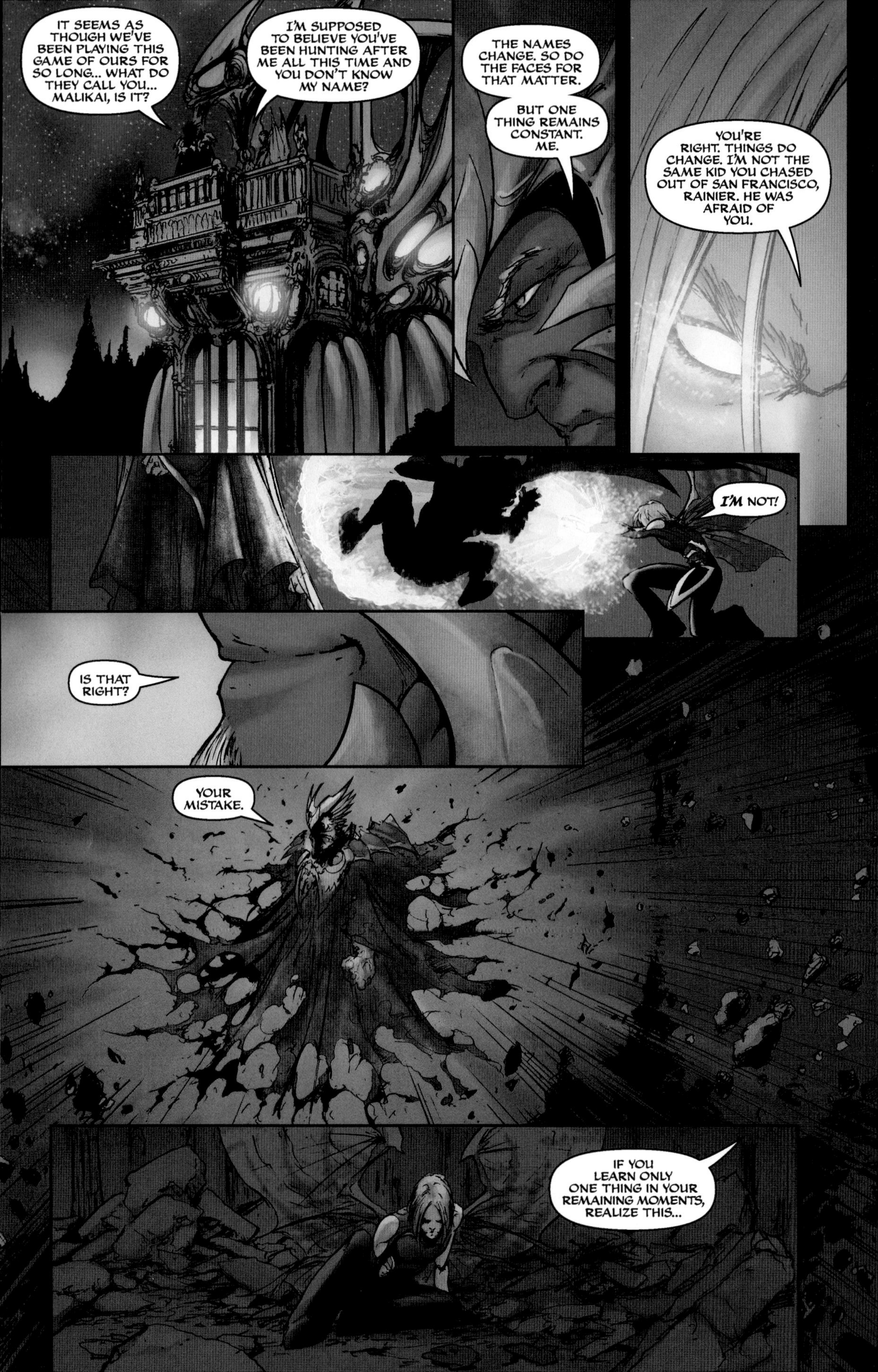
IT SEEMS AS THOUGH WE'VE BEEN PLAYING THIS GAME OF OURS FOR SO LONG... WHAT DO THEY CALL YOU... MALIKAI, IS IT?
I'M SUPPOSED TO BELIEVE YOU'VE BEEN HUNTING AFTER ME ALL THIS TIME AND YOU DON'T KNOW MY NAME?
THE NAMES CHANGE. SO DO THE FACES FOR THAT MATTER.
BUT ONE THING REMAINS CONSTANT. ME.
YOU'RE RIGHT. THINGS DO CHANGE. I'M NOT THE SAME KID YOU CHASED OUT OF SAN FRANCISCO, RAINIER. HE WAS AFRAID OF YOU.
I'M NOT!
IS THAT RIGHT?
YOUR MISTAKE.
IF YOU LEARN ONLY ONE THING IN YOUR REMAINING MOMENTS, REALIZE THIS...

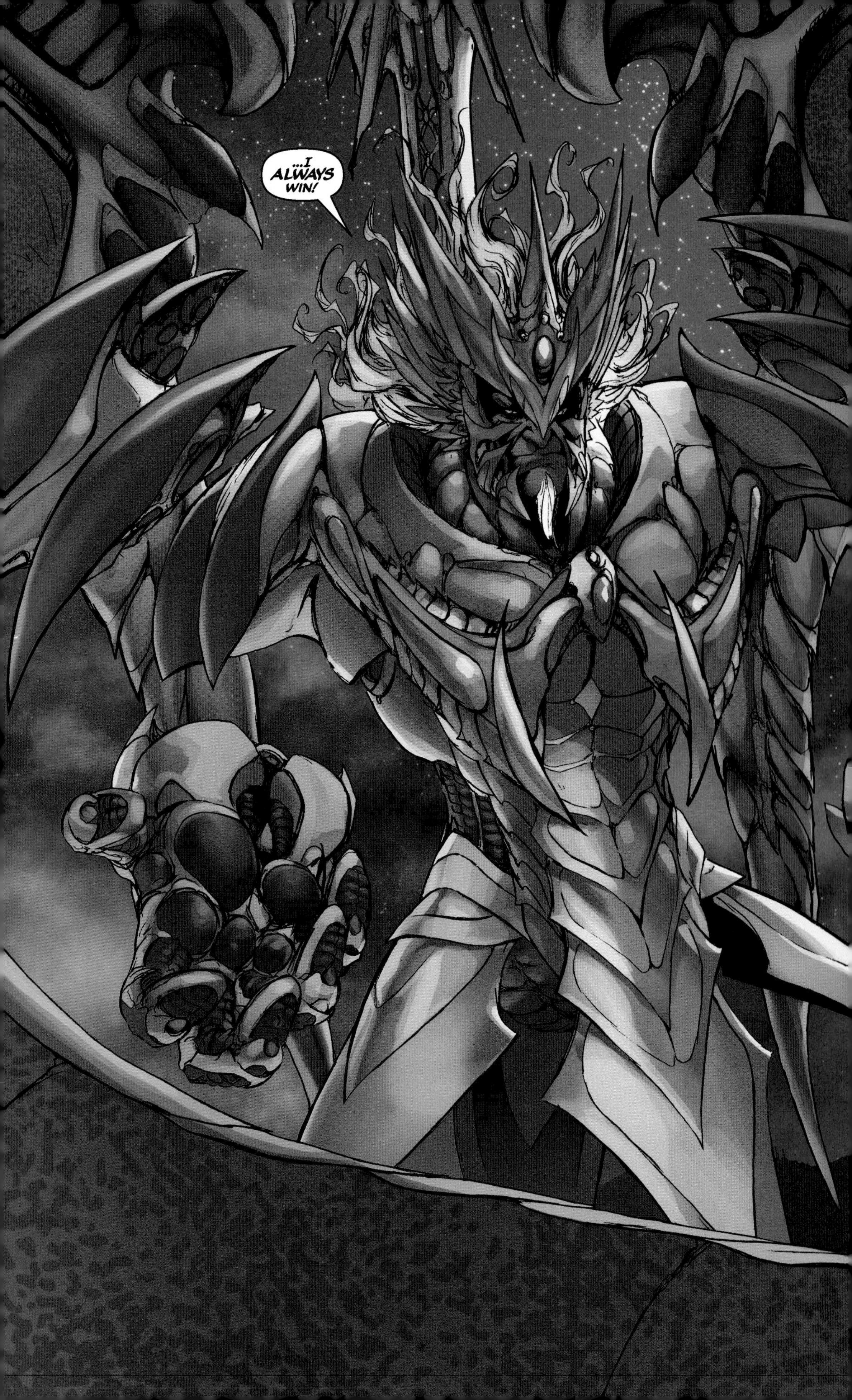
...I ALWAYS WIN!

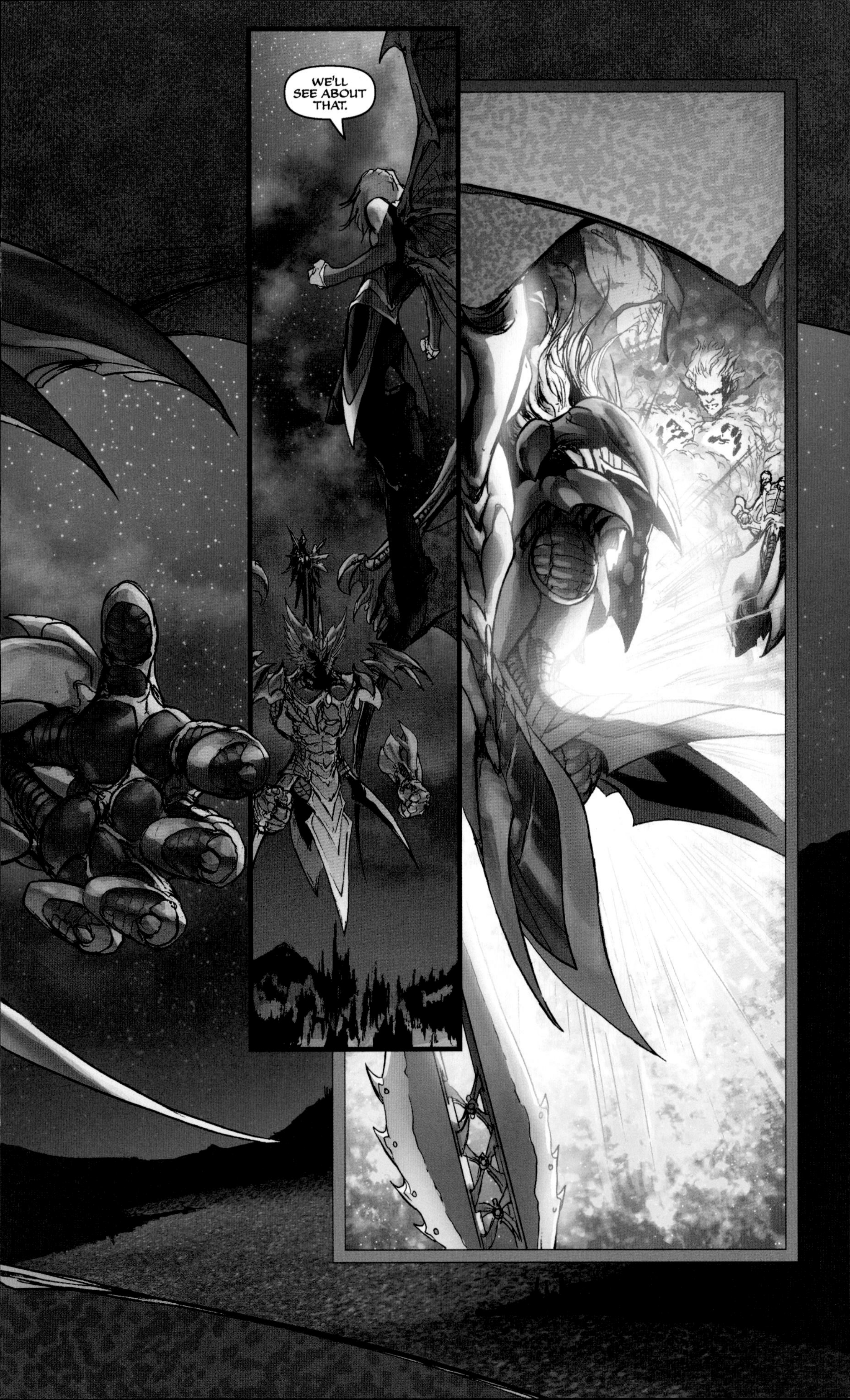
WE'LL SEE ABOUT THAT.

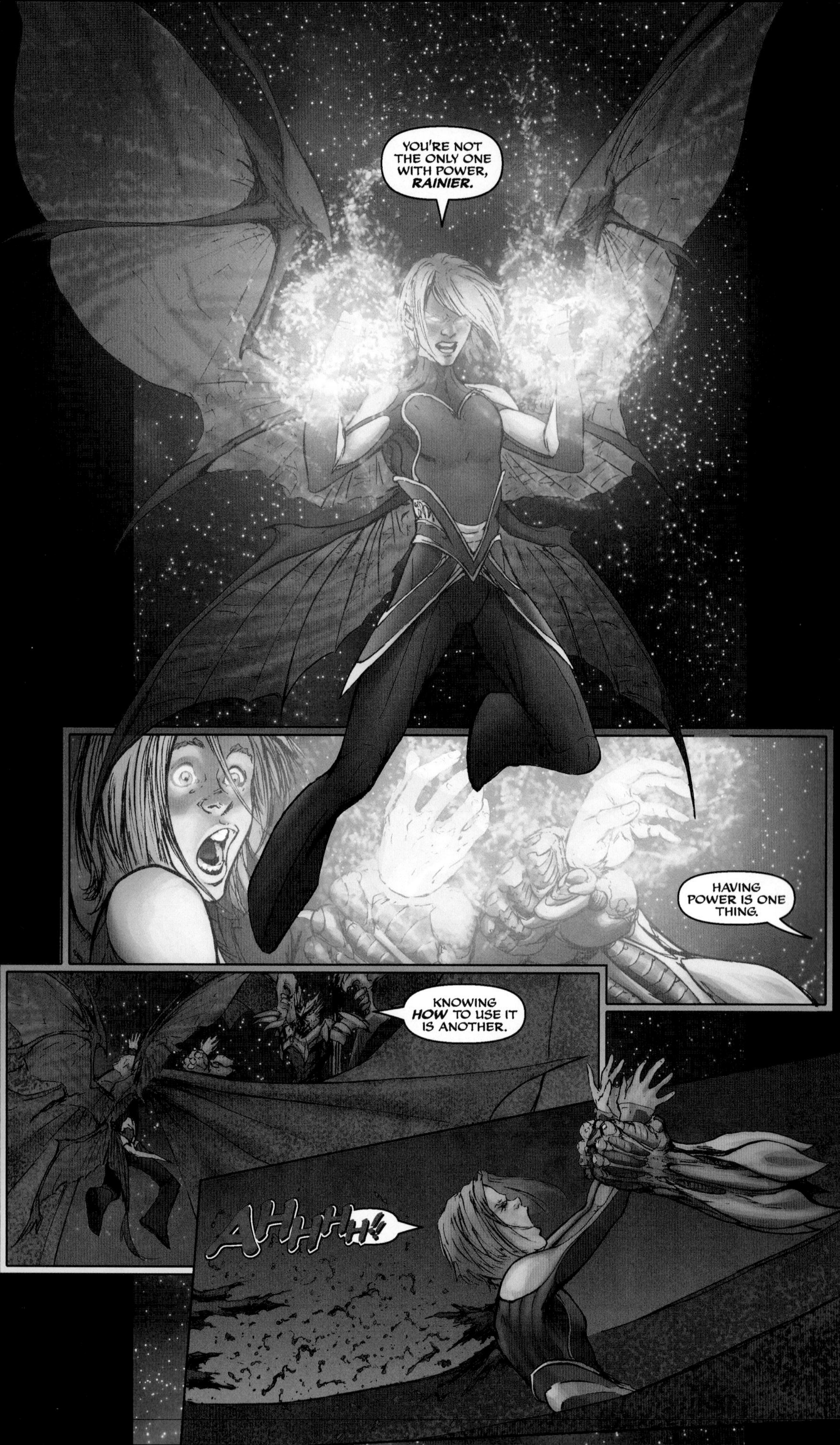

YOU'RE NOT THE ONLY ONE WITH POWER, ***RAINIER.***
HAVING POWER IS ONE THING.
KNOWING ***HOW*** TO USE IT IS ANOTHER.
AHHHH!

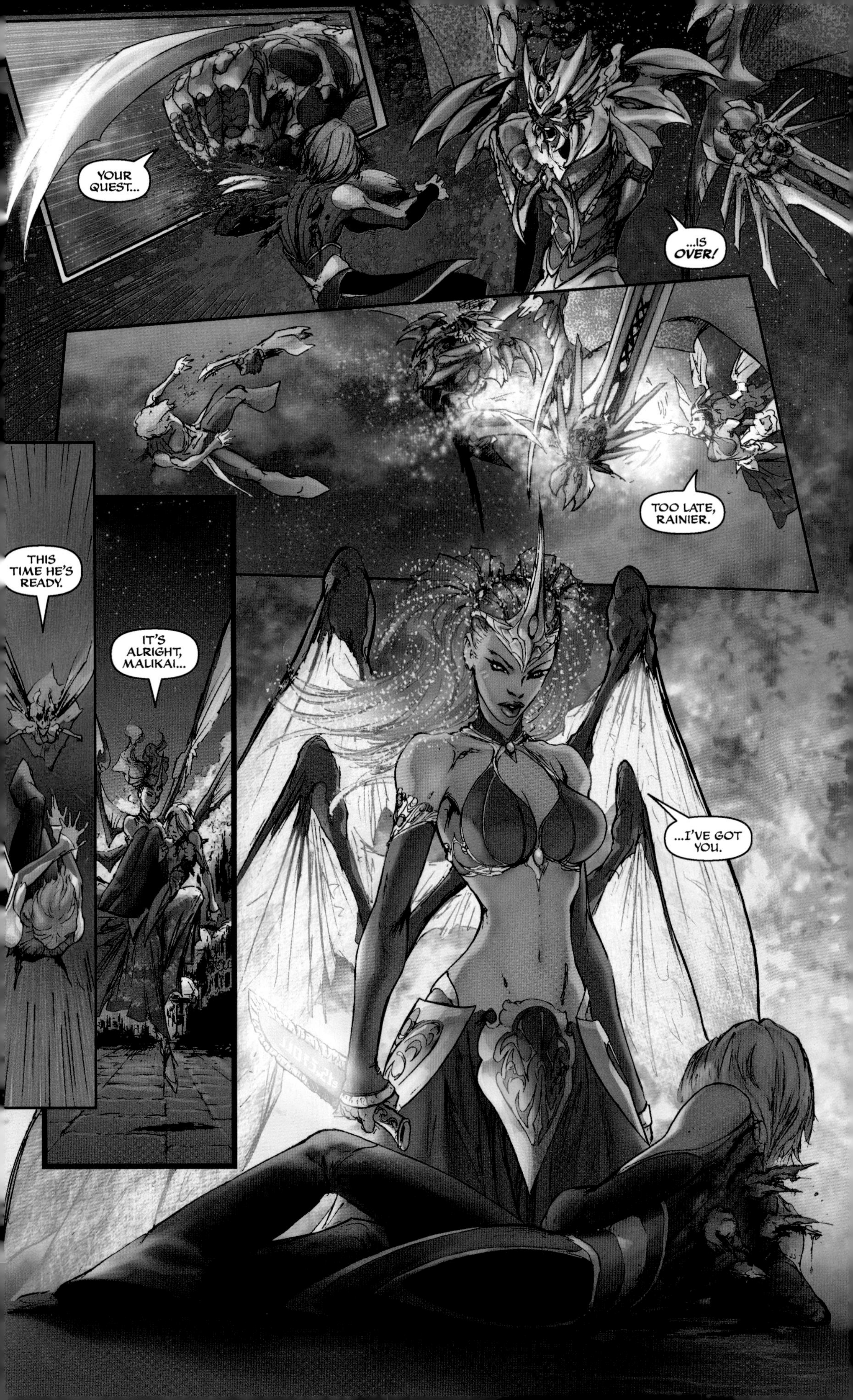
YOUR QUEST...
...IS OVER!
TOO LATE, RAINIER.
THIS TIME HE'S READY.
IT'S ALRIGHT, MALIKAI...
...I'VE GOT YOU.

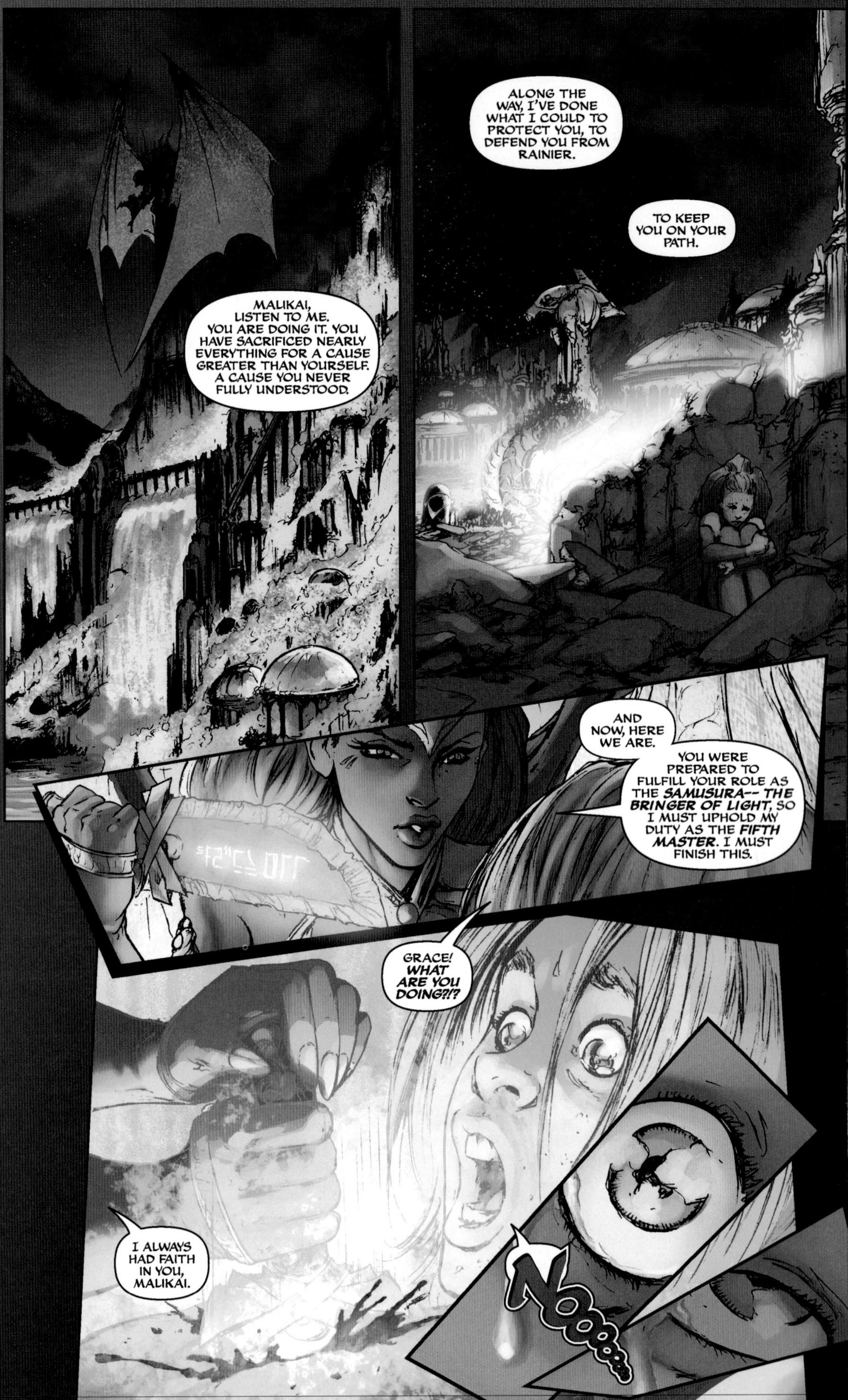
MALIKAI, LISTEN TO ME. YOU ARE DOING IT. YOU HAVE SACRIFICED NEARLY EVERYTHING FOR A CAUSE GREATER THAN YOURSELF. A CAUSE YOU NEVER FULLY UNDERSTOOD.
ALONG THE WAY, I'VE DONE WHAT I COULD TO PROTECT YOU, TO DEFEND YOU FROM RAINIER.
TO KEEP YOU ON YOUR PATH.
AND NOW, HERE WE ARE.
YOU WERE PREPARED TO FULFILL YOUR ROLE AS THE *SAMUSURA-- THE BRINGER OF LIGHT,* SO I MUST UPHOLD MY DUTY AS THE *FIFTH MASTER.* I MUST FINISH THIS.
GRACE! *WHAT ARE YOU DOING?!?*
I ALWAYS HAD FAITH IN YOU, MALIKAI.
NOOOOOO

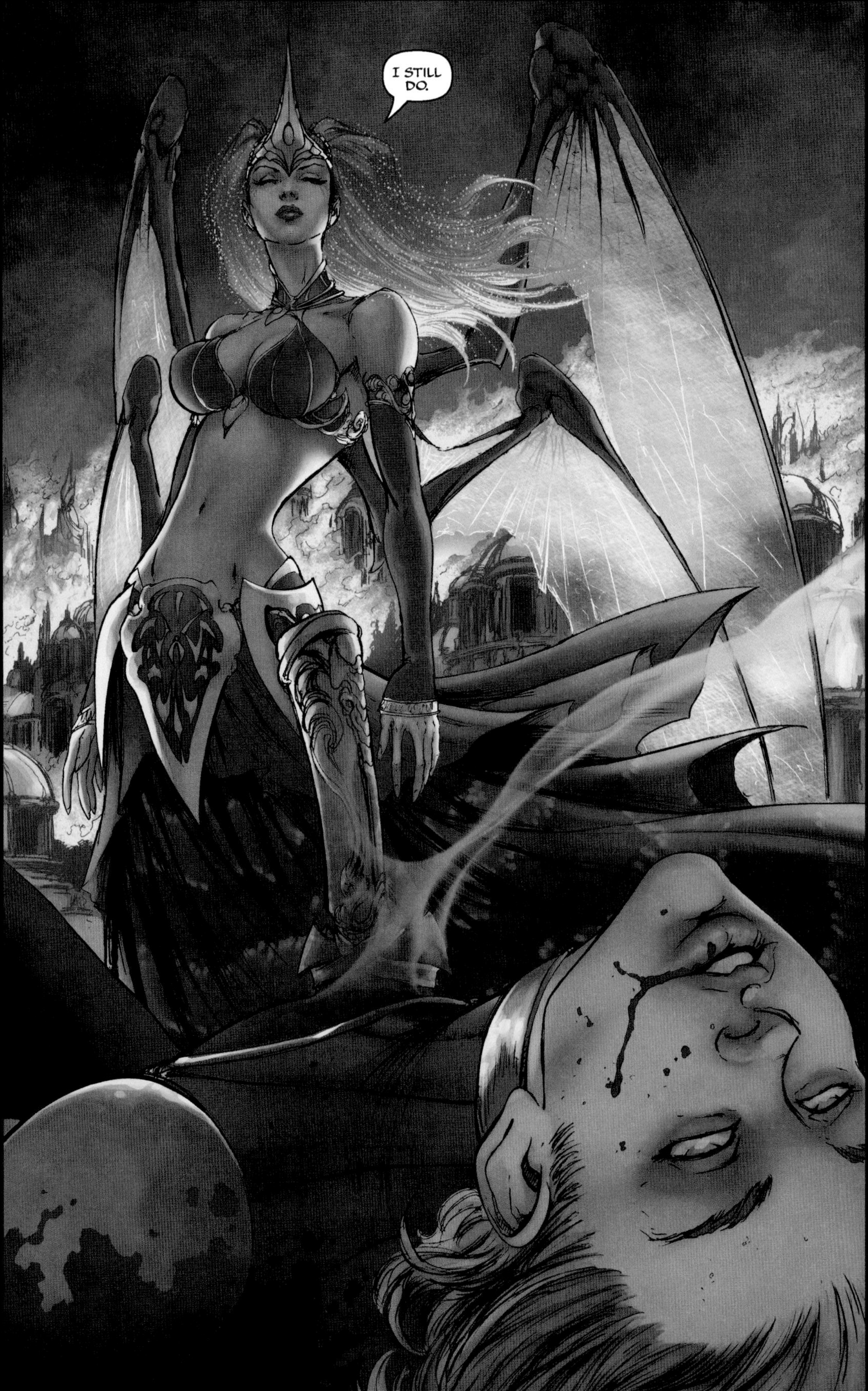
I STILL DO.

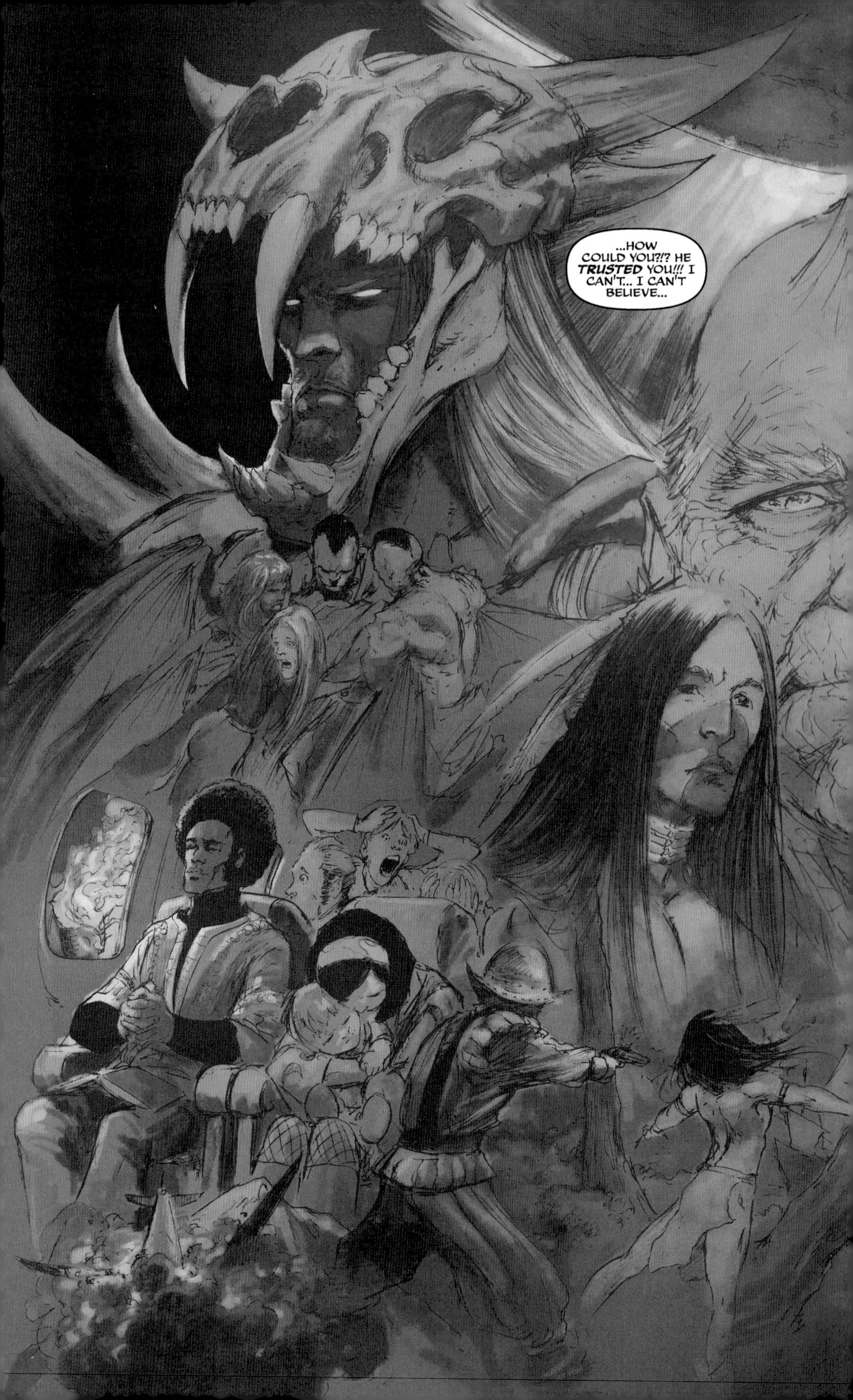
...HOW COULD YOU?!? HE TRUSTED YOU!!! I CAN'T... I CAN'T BELIEVE...

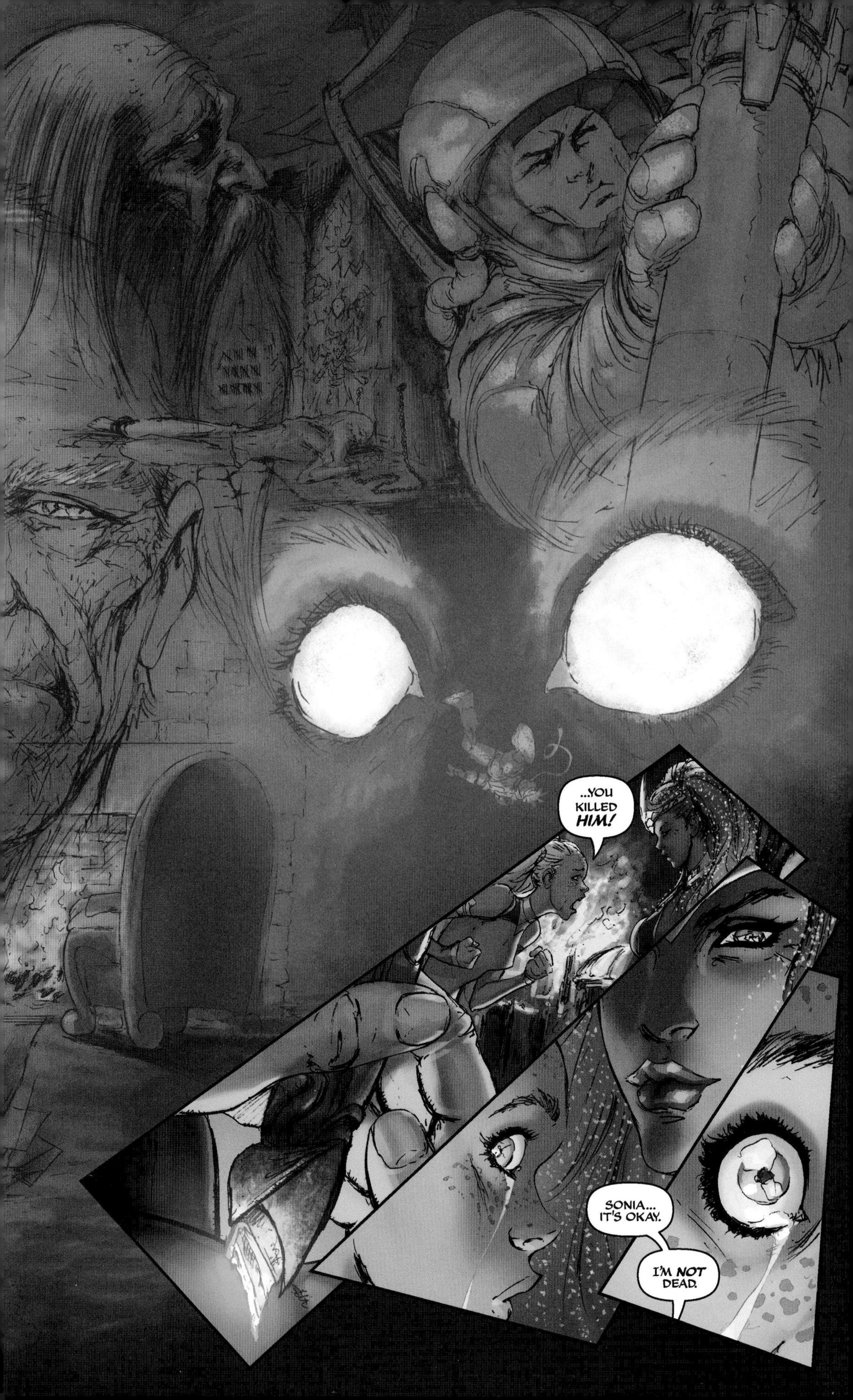
...YOU KILLED HIM!
SONIA... IT'S OKAY.
I'M NOT DEAD.

IN FACT, I'VE NEVER FELT BETTER.
I CAN FEEL IT... THE MAGIC SURGING THROUGH ME, BUILDING IN POWER.
IT'S INTENSE. IT'S AMAZING.

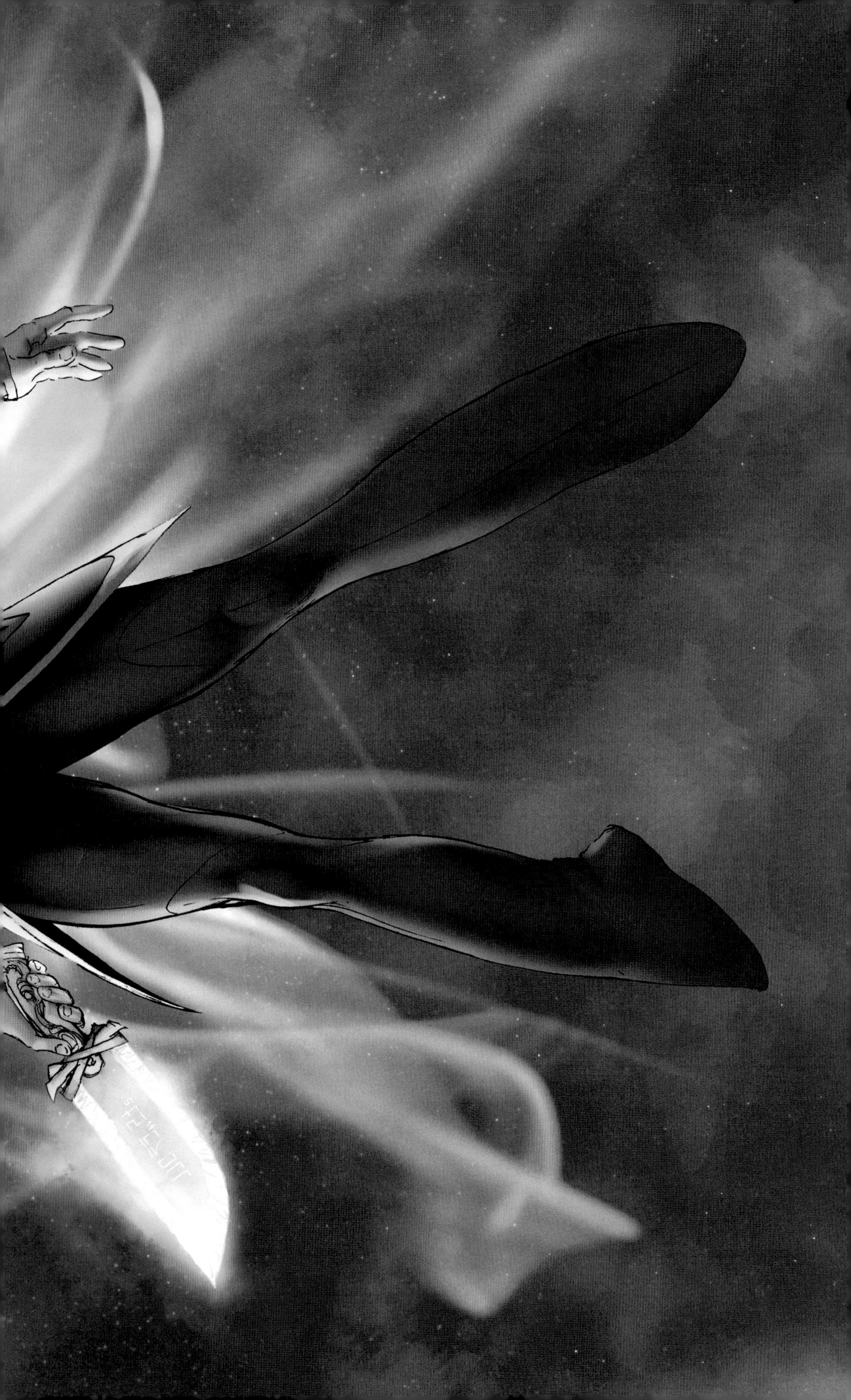

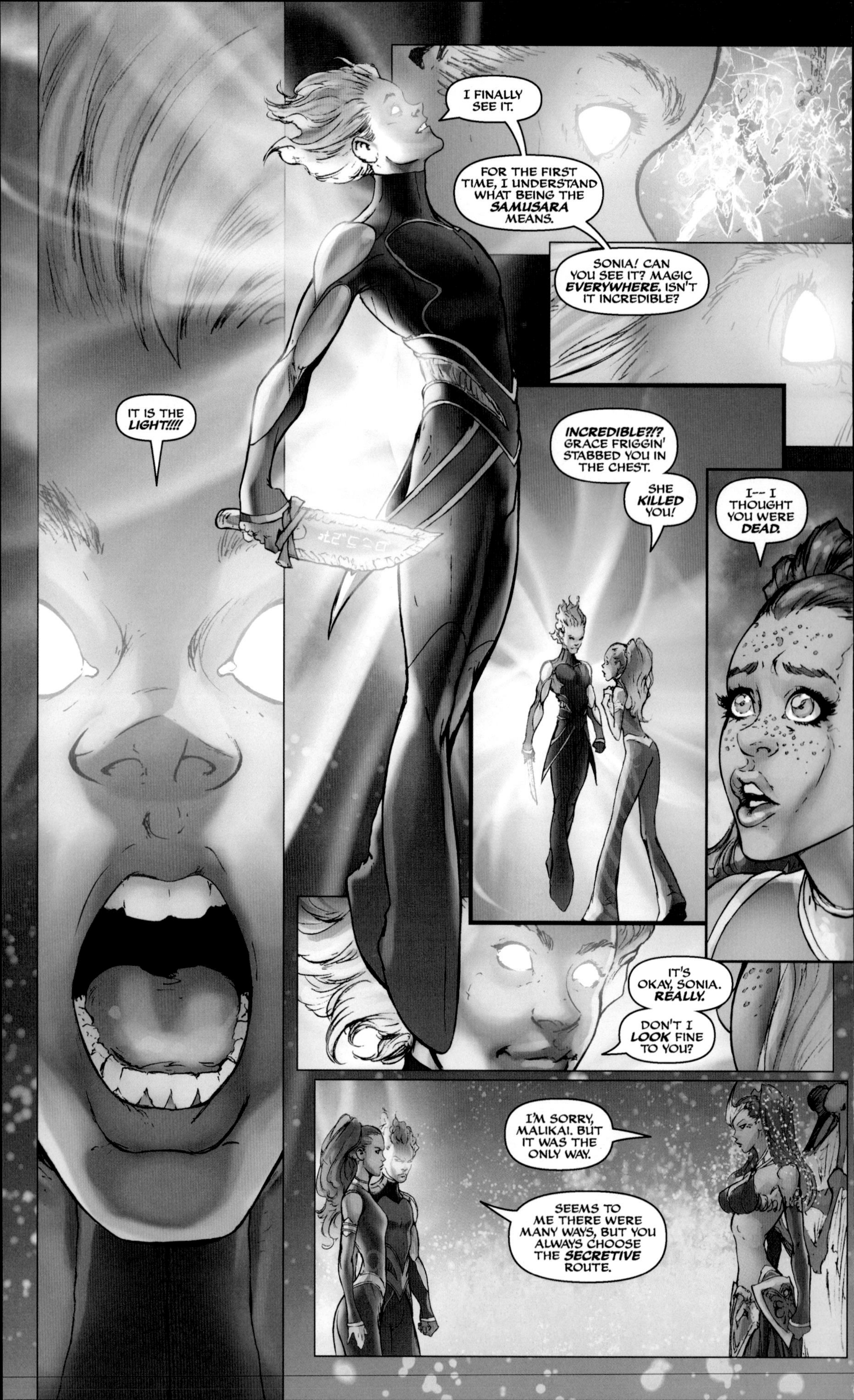

I FINALLY SEE IT.
FOR THE FIRST TIME, I UNDERSTAND WHAT BEING THE SAMUSARA MEANS.
SONIA! CAN YOU SEE IT? MAGIC EVERYWHERE. ISN'T IT INCREDIBLE?
IT IS THE LIGHT!!!!
INCREDIBLE?!? GRACE FRIGGIN' STABBED YOU IN THE CHEST.
SHE KILLED YOU!
I-- I THOUGHT YOU WERE DEAD.
IT'S OKAY, SONIA. REALLY.
DON'T I LOOK FINE TO YOU?
I'M SORRY, MALIKAI. BUT IT WAS THE ONLY WAY.
SEEMS TO ME THERE WERE MANY WAYS, BUT YOU ALWAYS CHOOSE THE SECRETIVE ROUTE.

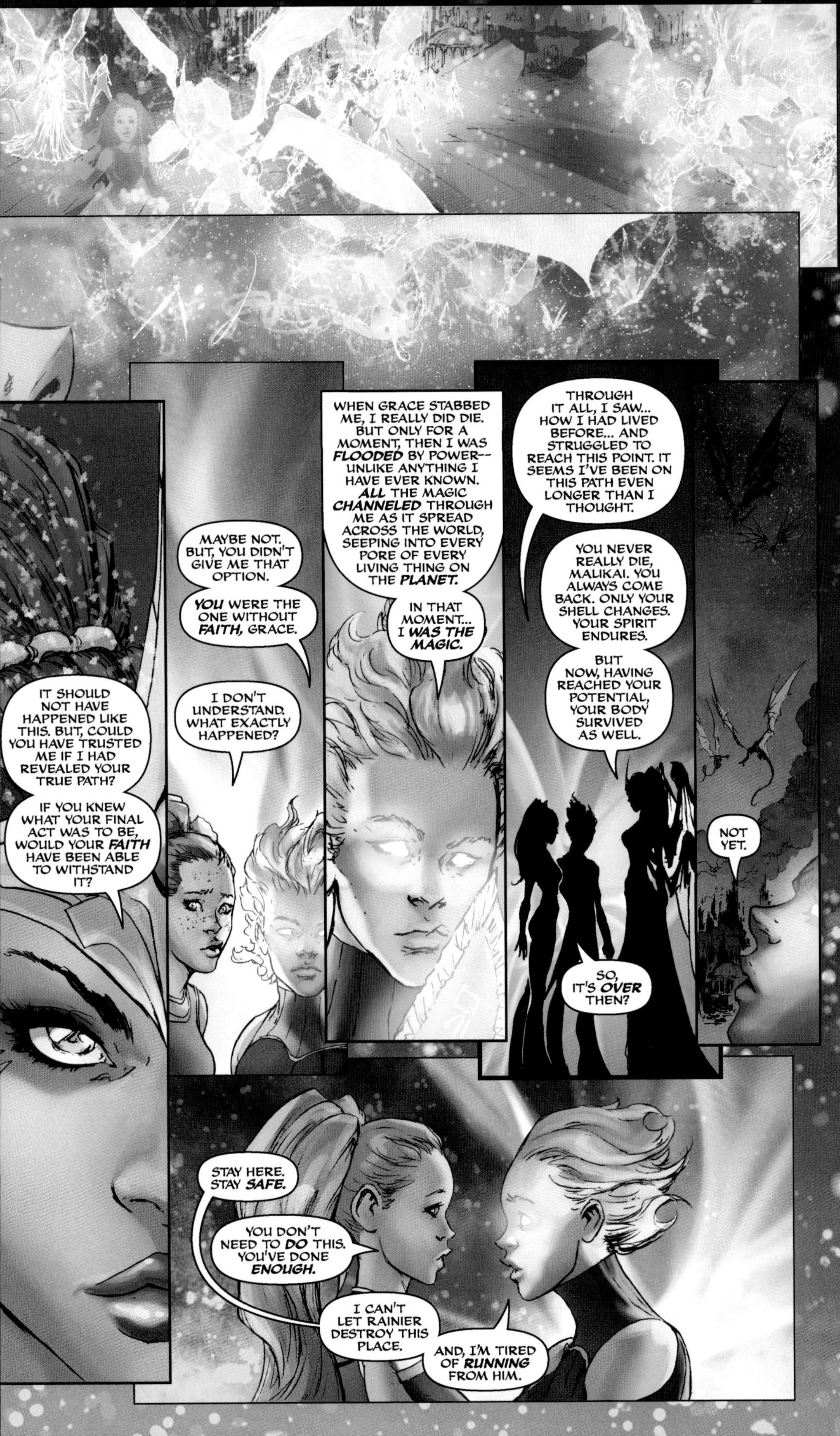

IT SHOULD NOT HAVE HAPPENED LIKE THIS. BUT, COULD YOU HAVE TRUSTED ME IF I HAD REVEALED YOUR TRUE PATH?
IF YOU KNEW WHAT YOUR FINAL ACT WAS TO BE, WOULD YOUR FAITH HAVE BEEN ABLE TO WITHSTAND IT?
MAYBE NOT. BUT, YOU DIDN'T GIVE ME THAT OPTION.
YOU WERE THE ONE WITHOUT FAITH, GRACE.
I DON'T UNDERSTAND. WHAT EXACTLY HAPPENED?
WHEN GRACE STABBED ME, I REALLY DID DIE. BUT ONLY FOR A MOMENT, THEN I WAS FLOODED BY POWER-- UNLIKE ANYTHING I HAVE EVER KNOWN. ALL THE MAGIC CHANNELED THROUGH ME AS IT SPREAD ACROSS THE WORLD, SEEPING INTO EVERY PORE OF EVERY LIVING THING ON THE PLANET.
IN THAT MOMENT... I WAS THE MAGIC.
THROUGH IT ALL, I SAW... HOW I HAD LIVED BEFORE... AND STRUGGLED TO REACH THIS POINT. IT SEEMS I'VE BEEN ON THIS PATH EVEN LONGER THAN I THOUGHT.
YOU NEVER REALLY DIE, MALIKAI. YOU ALWAYS COME BACK. ONLY YOUR SHELL CHANGES. YOUR SPIRIT ENDURES.
BUT NOW, HAVING REACHED YOUR POTENTIAL, YOUR BODY SURVIVED AS WELL.
SO, IT'S OVER THEN?
NOT YET.
STAY HERE. STAY SAFE.
YOU DON'T NEED TO DO THIS. YOU'VE DONE ENOUGH.
I CAN'T LET RAINIER DESTROY THIS PLACE.
AND, I'M TIRED OF RUNNING FROM HIM.

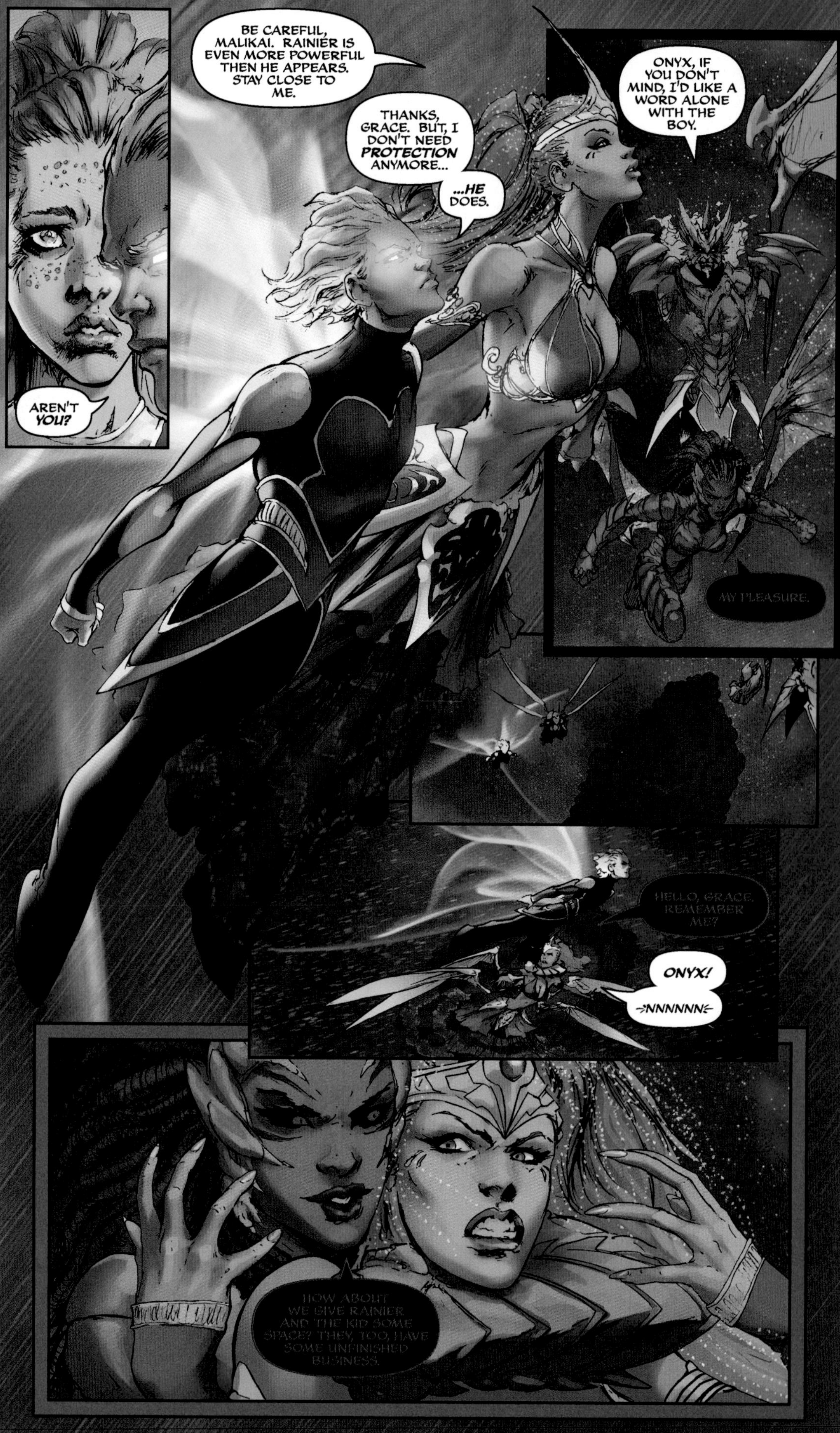
BE CAREFUL, MALIKAI. RAINIER IS EVEN MORE POWERFUL THEN HE APPEARS. STAY CLOSE TO ME.
THANKS, GRACE. BUT, I DON'T NEED PROTECTION ANYMORE...
...HE DOES.
AREN'T YOU?
ONYX, IF YOU DON'T MIND, I'D LIKE A WORD ALONE WITH THE BOY.
MY PLEASURE.
HELLO, GRACE. REMEMBER ME?
ONYX!
NNNNNN
HOW ABOUT WE GIVE RAINIER AND THE KID SOME SPACE? THEY, TOO, HAVE SOME UNFINISHED BUSINESS.

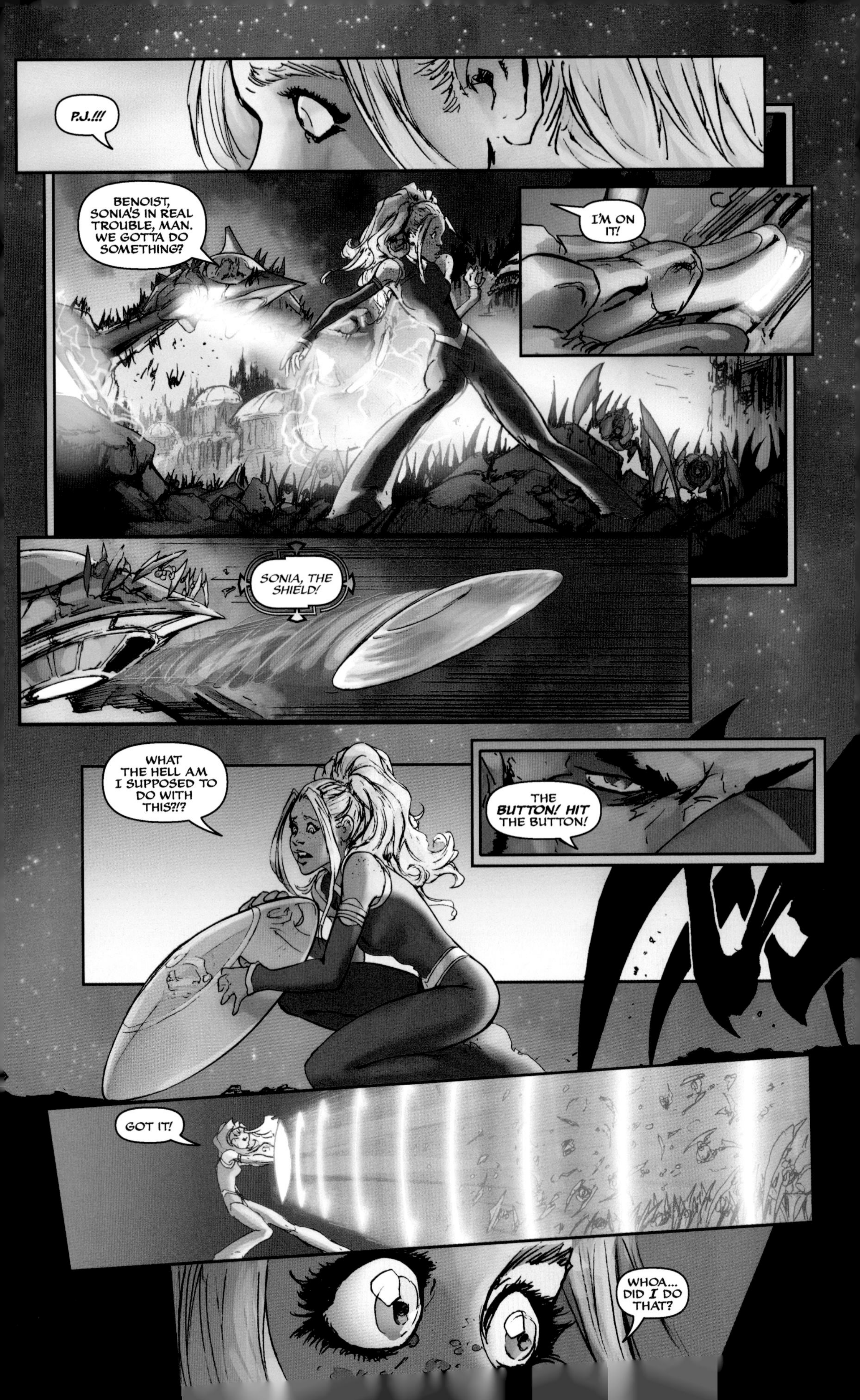
P.J.!!!
BENOIST, SONIA'S IN REAL TROUBLE, MAN. WE GOTTA DO SOMETHING?
I'M ON IT!
SONIA, THE SHIELD!
WHAT THE HELL AM I SUPPOSED TO DO WITH THIS?!?
THE BUTTON! HIT THE BUTTON!
GOT IT!
WHOA... DID I DO THAT?

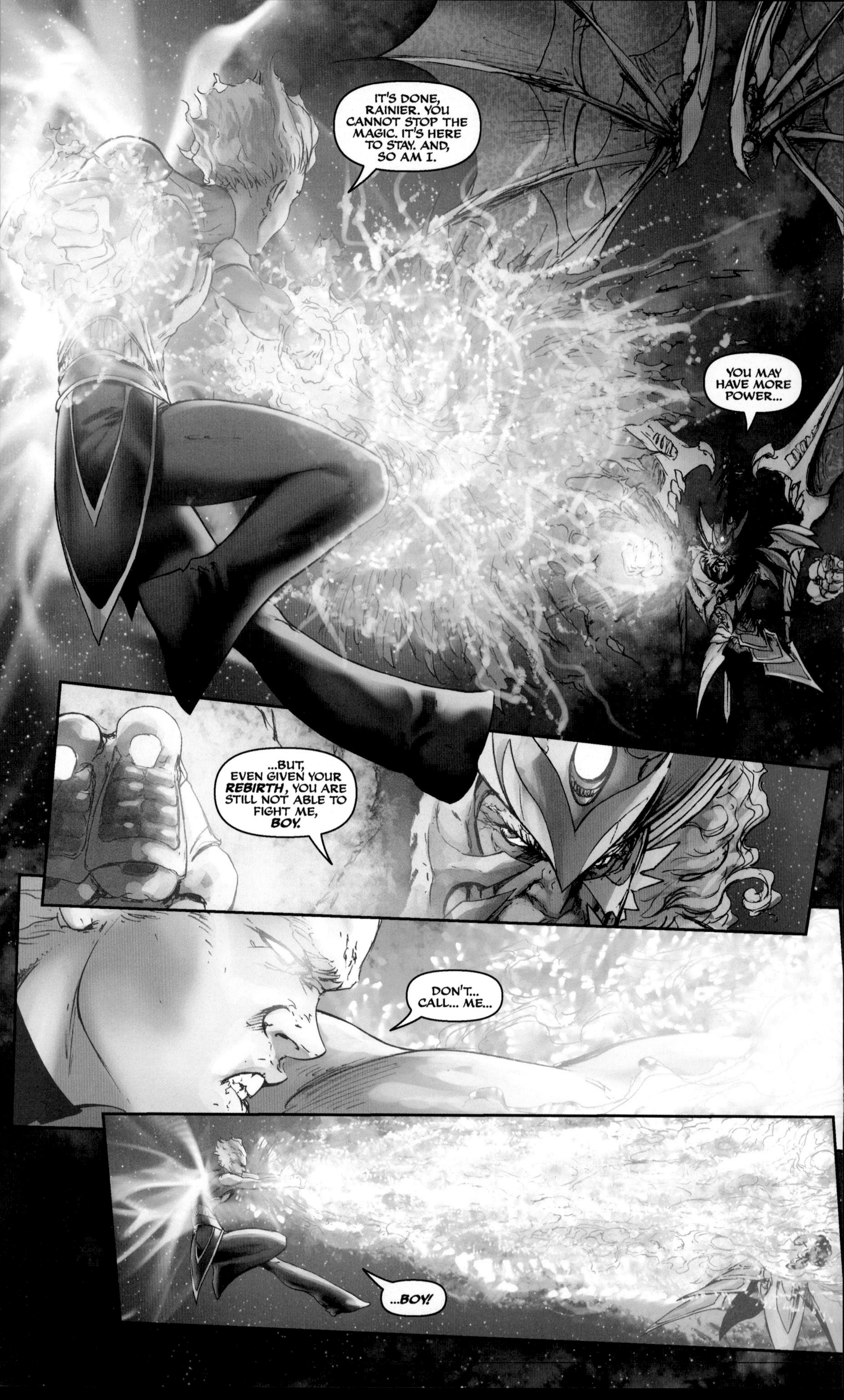
IT'S DONE, RAINIER. YOU CANNOT STOP THE MAGIC. IT'S HERE TO STAY. AND, SO AM I.
YOU MAY HAVE MORE POWER...
...BUT, EVEN GIVEN YOUR REBIRTH, YOU ARE STILL NOT ABLE TO FIGHT ME, BOY.
DON'T... CALL... ME...
...BOY!

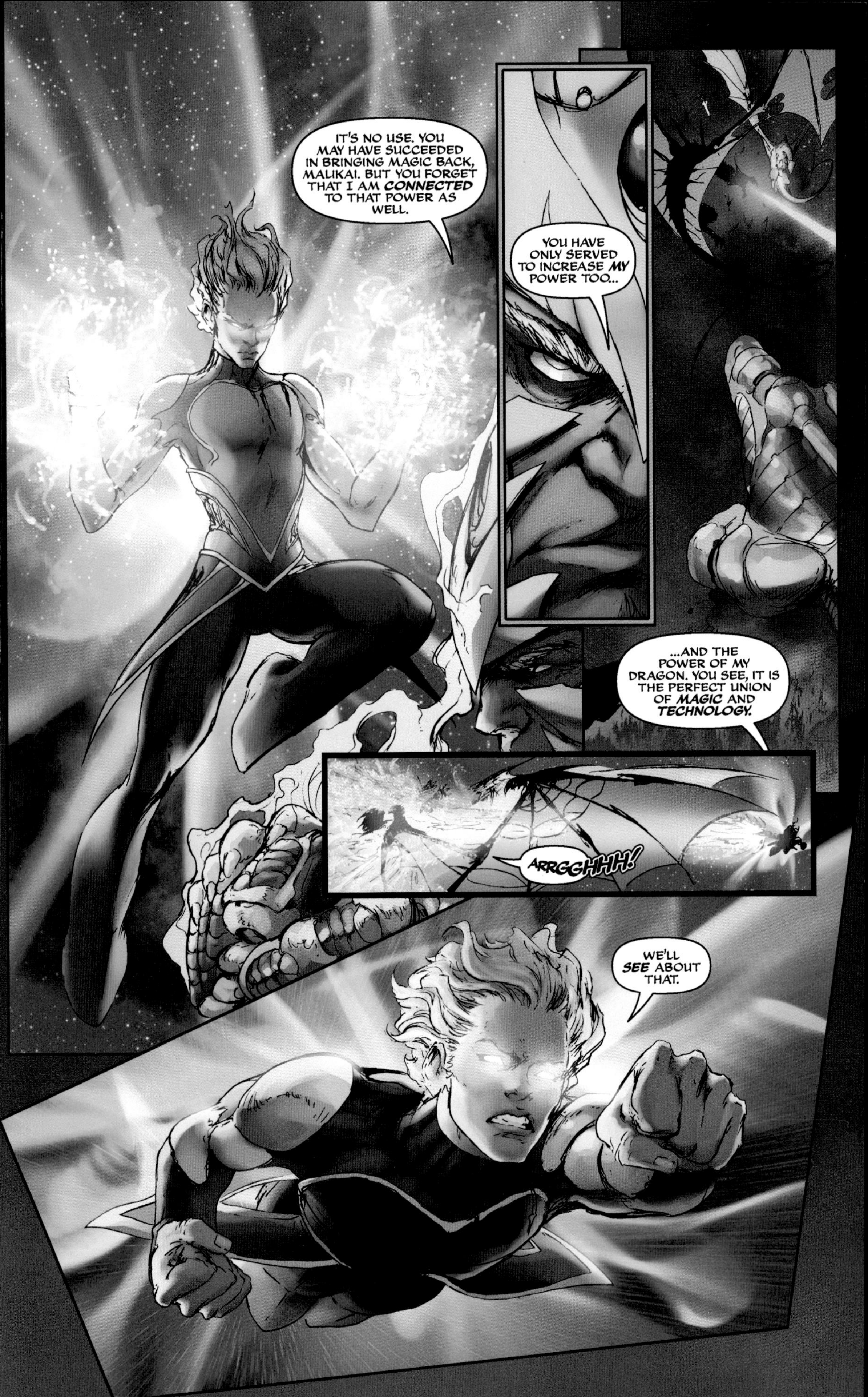
IT'S NO USE. YOU MAY HAVE SUCCEEDED IN BRINGING MAGIC BACK, MALIKAI. BUT YOU FORGET THAT I AM CONNECTED TO THAT POWER AS WELL.
YOU HAVE ONLY SERVED TO INCREASE MY POWER TOO...
...AND THE POWER OF MY DRAGON. YOU SEE, IT IS THE PERFECT UNION OF MAGIC AND TECHNOLOGY.
ARRGGHHH!
WE'LL SEE ABOUT THAT.

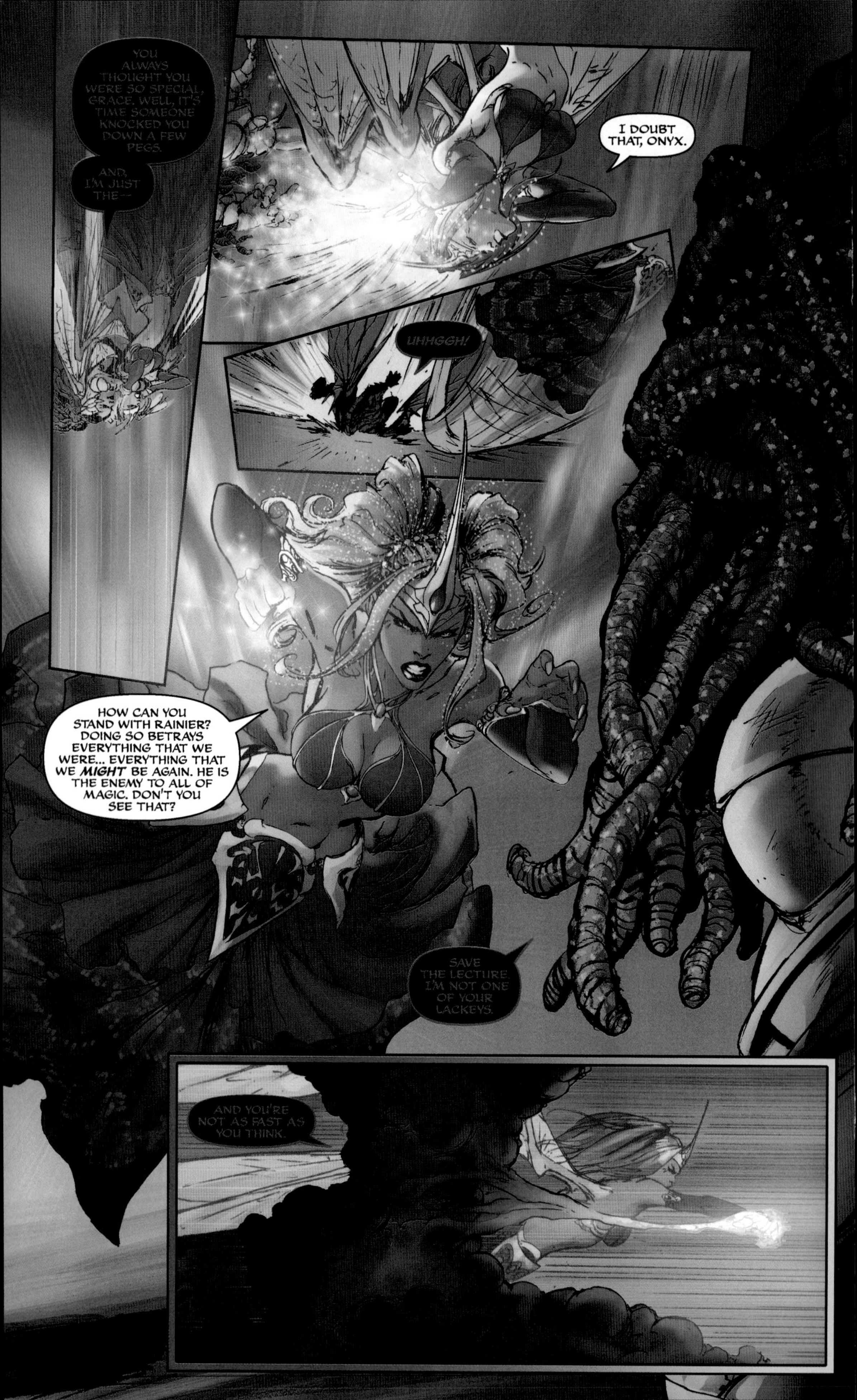
YOU ALWAYS THOUGHT YOU WERE SO SPECIAL, GRACE. WELL, IT'S TIME SOMEONE KNOCKED YOU DOWN A FEW PEGS.
AND, I'M JUST THE--
I DOUBT THAT, ONYX.
UHHGGH!
HOW CAN YOU STAND WITH RAINIER? DOING SO BETRAYS EVERYTHING THAT WE WERE... EVERYTHING THAT WE MIGHT BE AGAIN. HE IS THE ENEMY TO ALL OF MAGIC. DON'T YOU SEE THAT?
SAVE THE LECTURE. I'M NOT ONE OF YOUR LACKEYS.
AND YOU'RE NOT AS FAST AS YOU THINK.

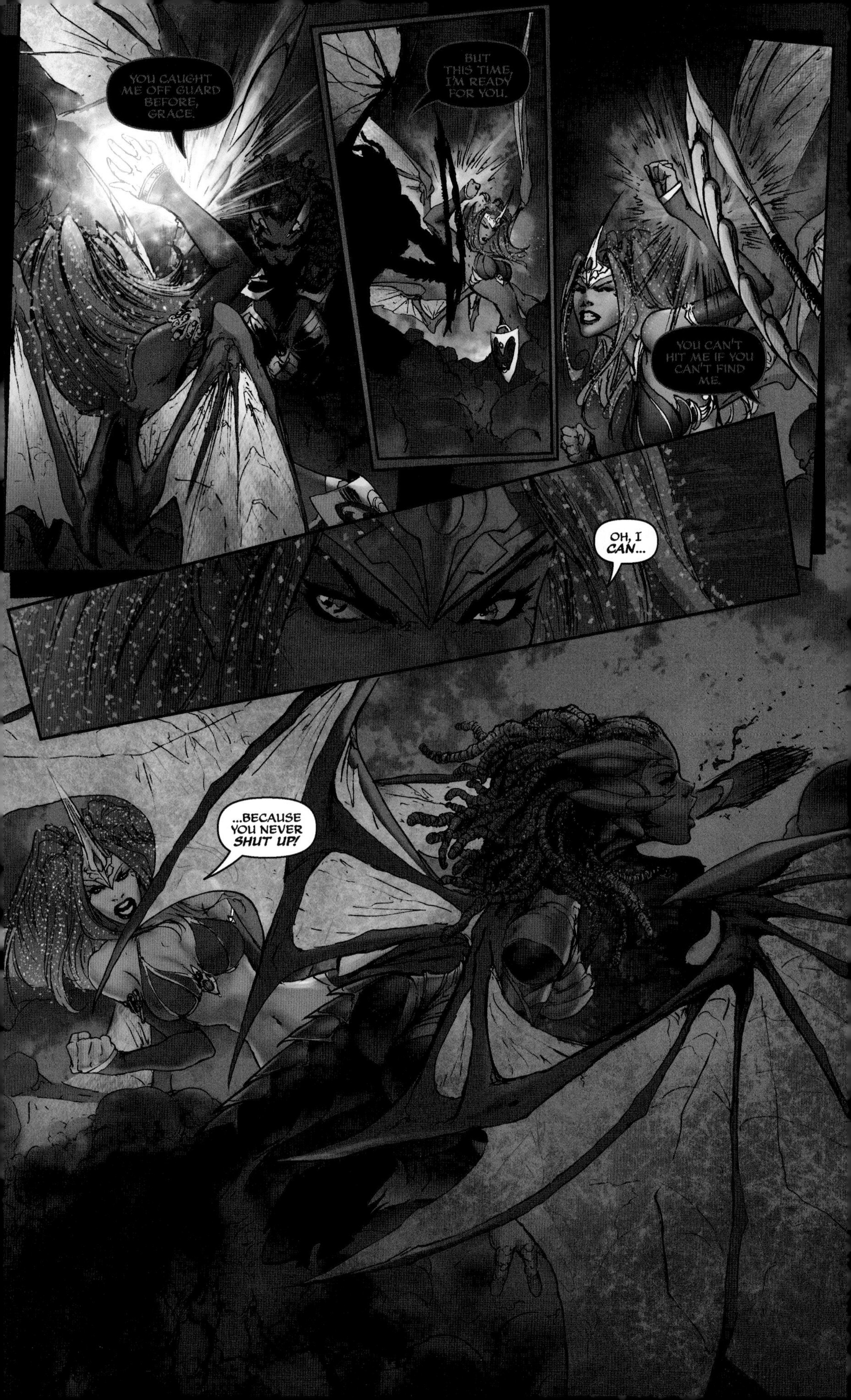
YOU CAUGHT ME OFF GUARD BEFORE, GRACE.
BUT THIS TIME, I'M READY FOR YOU.
YOU CAN'T HIT ME IF YOU CAN'T FIND ME.
OH, I CAN...
...BECAUSE YOU NEVER SHUT UP!

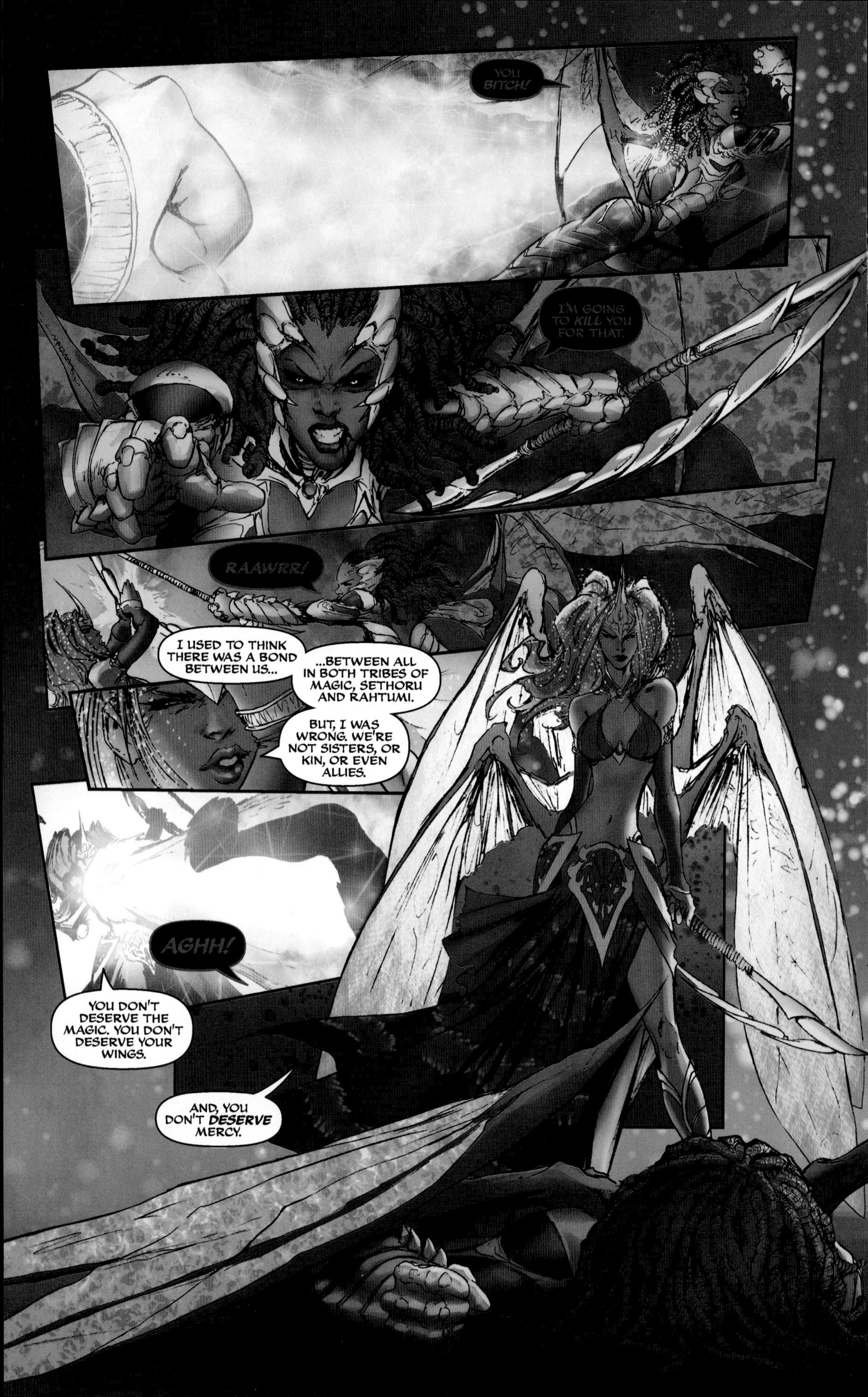
YOU BITCH!
I'M GOING TO KILL YOU FOR THAT.
RAAWRR!
I USED TO THINK THERE WAS A BOND BETWEEN US...
...BETWEEN ALL IN BOTH TRIBES OF MAGIC, SETHORU AND RAHTUMI.
BUT, I WAS WRONG. WE'RE NOT SISTERS, OR KIN, OR EVEN ALLIES.
AGHH!
YOU DON'T DESERVE THE MAGIC. YOU DON'T DESERVE YOUR WINGS.
AND, YOU DON'T DESERVE MERCY.

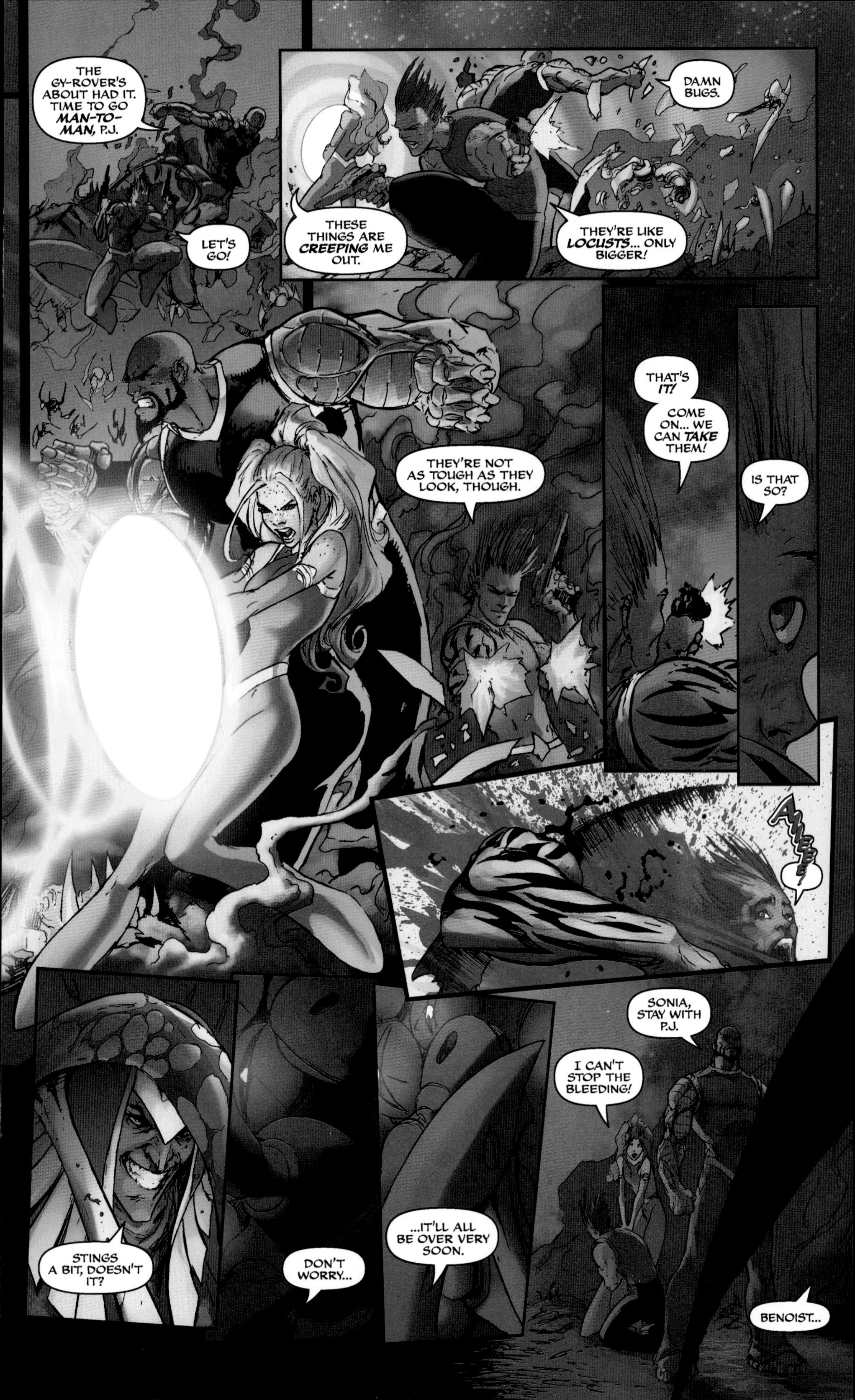
THE GY-ROVER'S ABOUT HAD IT. TIME TO GO MAN-TO-MAN, P.J.
LET'S GO!
DAMN BUGS.
THESE THINGS ARE CREEPING ME OUT.
THEY'RE LIKE LOCUSTS... ONLY BIGGER!
THEY'RE NOT AS TOUGH AS THEY LOOK, THOUGH.
THAT'S IT!
COME ON... WE CAN TAKE THEM!
IS THAT SO?
AIIEEE!
STINGS A BIT, DOESN'T IT?
DON'T WORRY...
...IT'LL ALL BE OVER VERY SOON.
SONIA, STAY WITH P.J.
I CAN'T STOP THE BLEEDING!
BENOIST...

...THIS HAS BEEN A LONG TIME COMING, OLD FRIEND.
YOU KNOW WHAT YOUR PROBLEM IS, ABEL? YOU'RE A SLAVE TO TO YOUR OWN TECHNOLOGY.
LIKE THOSE LITTLE DRONES ON YOUR BACK. THEY'RE THE SAME ONES YOU SENT AFTER THE KID BEFORE. THE ONES WE FOUGHT OFF ON OUR WAY TO HAWAI'I.
SO, I GAVE ONE A MESSAGE TO GIVE TO YOU. I THINK IT'S ABOUT TIME YOU GOT IT.

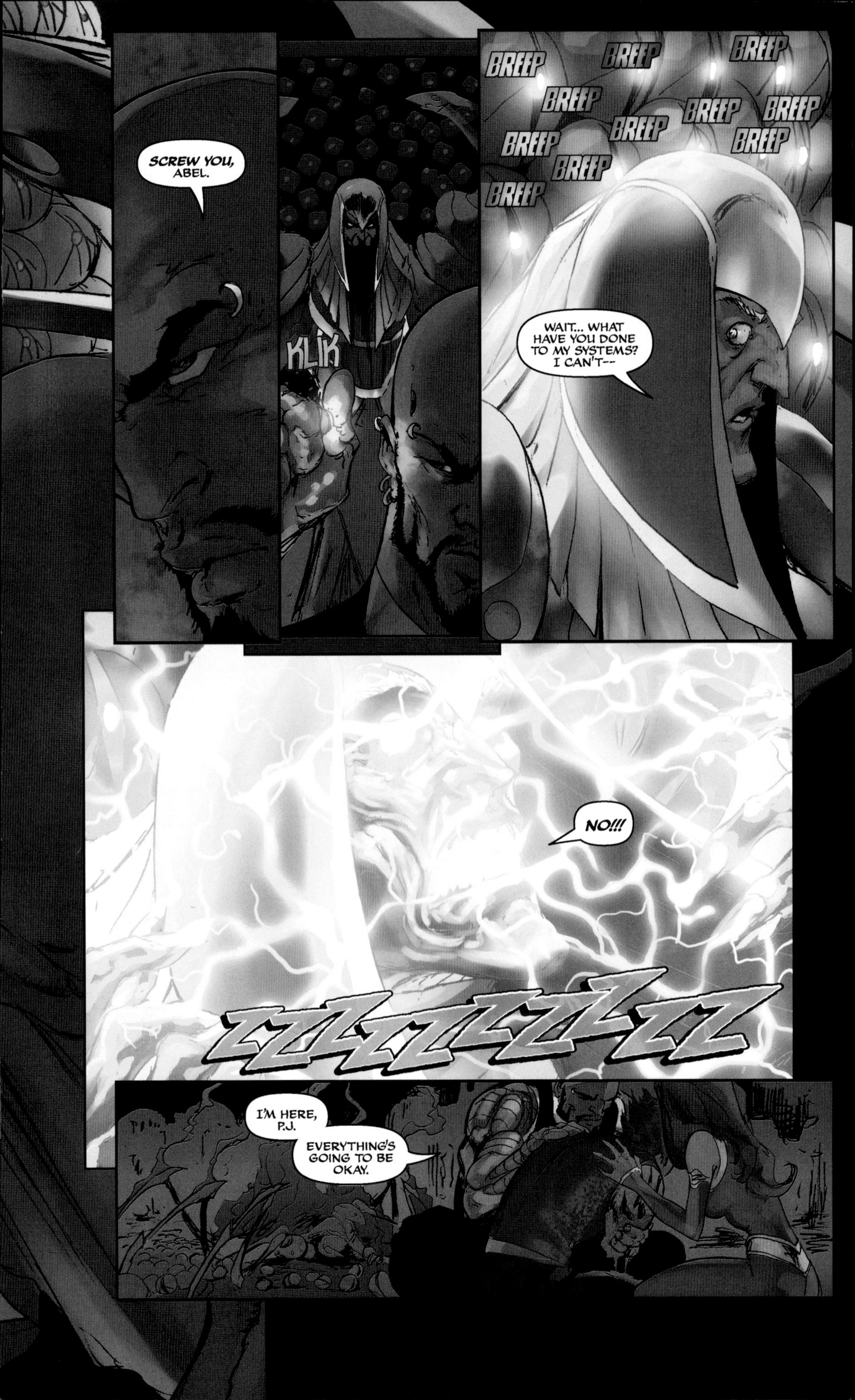
SCREW YOU, ABEL.
BREEP BREEP BREEP BREEP BREEP BREEP BREEP BREEP BREEP BREEP BREEP
WAIT... WHAT HAVE YOU DONE TO MY SYSTEMS? I CAN'T--
NO!!!
ZZZZZZZZZZZZ
I'M HERE, P.J.
EVERYTHING'S GOING TO BE OKAY.

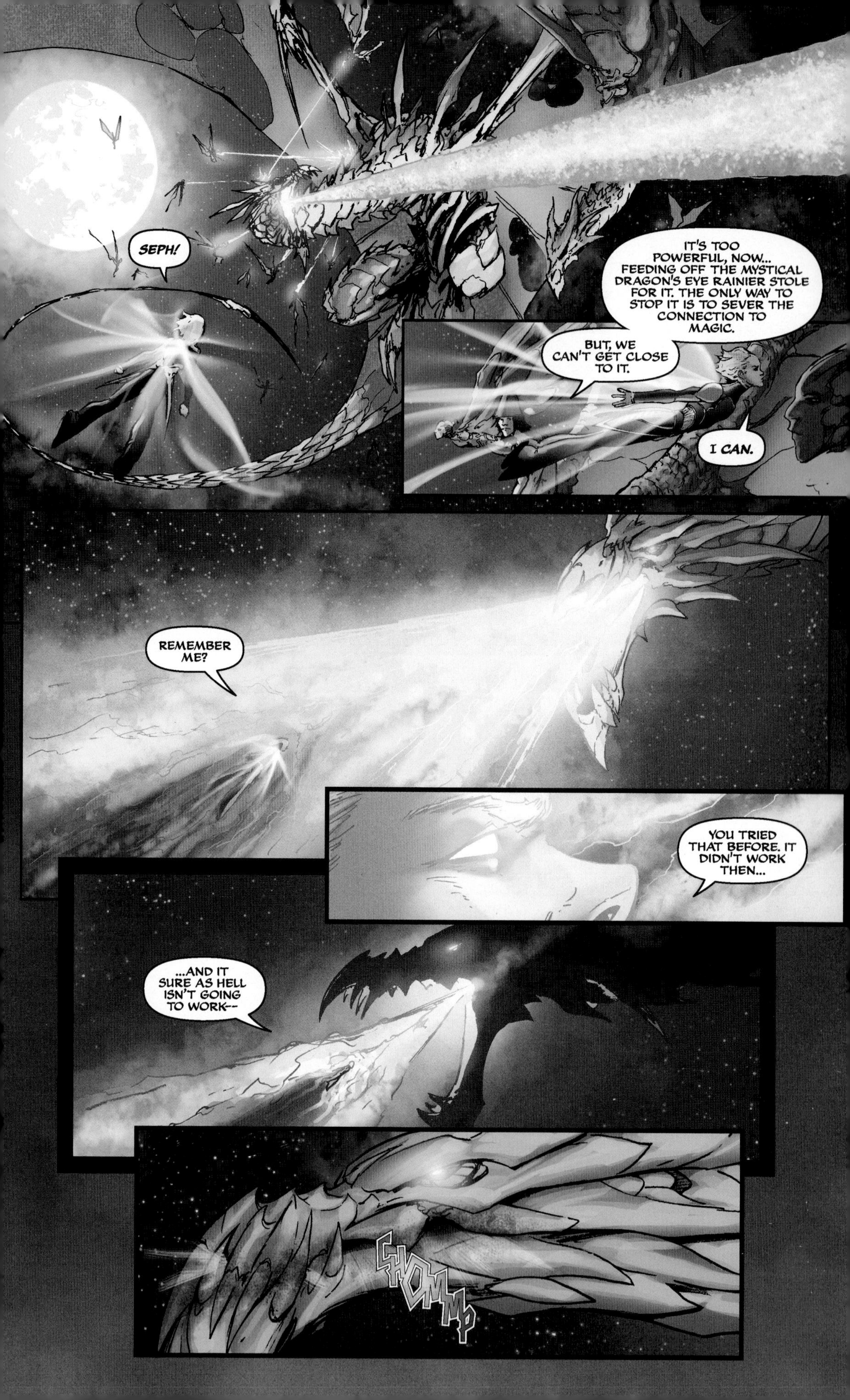
SEPH!
IT'S TOO POWERFUL, NOW... FEEDING OFF THE MYSTICAL DRAGON'S EYE RAINIER STOLE FOR IT. THE ONLY WAY TO STOP IT IS TO SEVER THE CONNECTION TO MAGIC.
BUT, WE CAN'T GET CLOSE TO IT.
I CAN.
REMEMBER ME?
YOU TRIED THAT BEFORE. IT DIDN'T WORK THEN...
...AND IT SURE AS HELL ISN'T GOING TO WORK--
CHOMMP

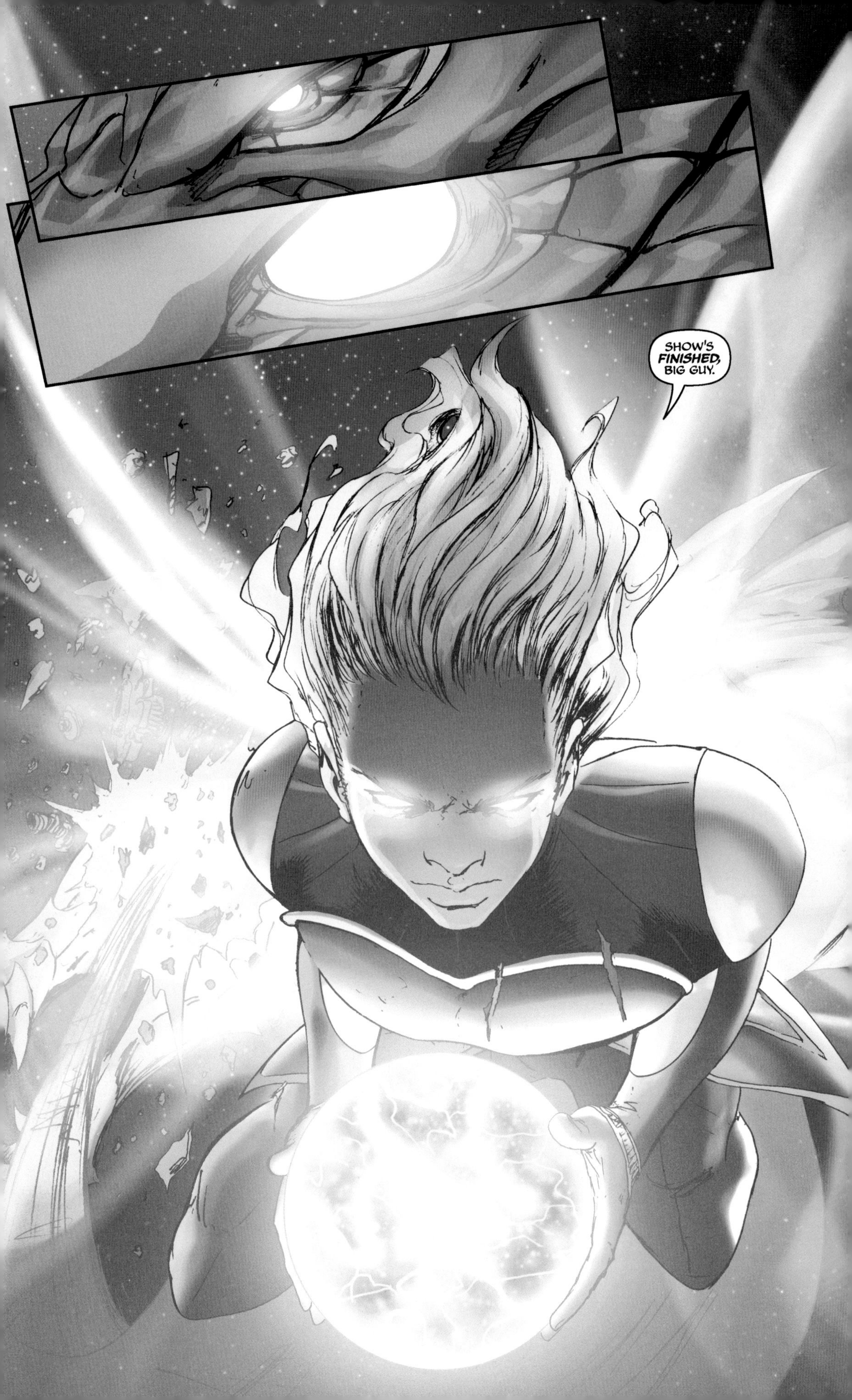
SHOW'S **FINISHED,** BIG GUY.

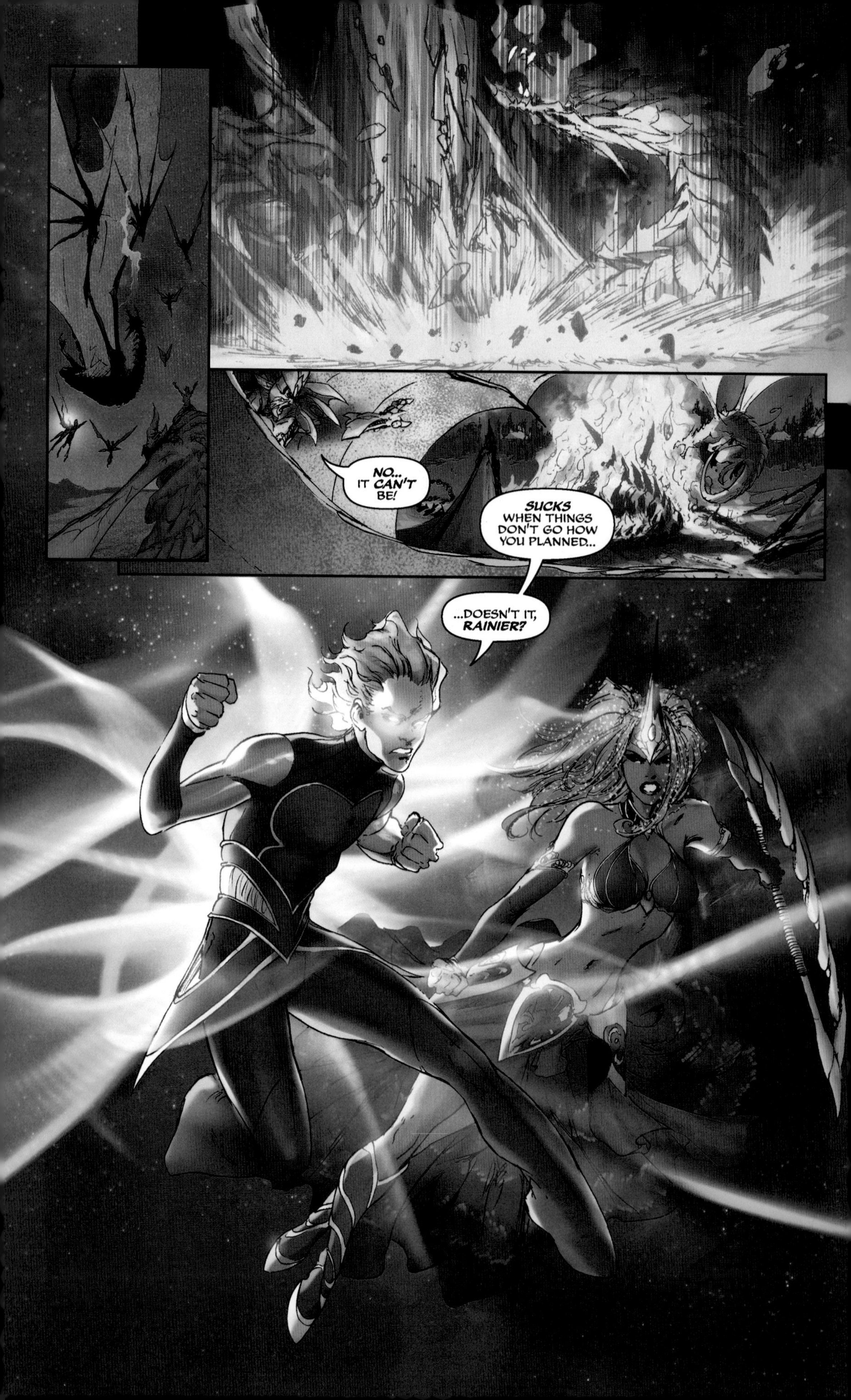
NO... IT CAN'T BE!
SUCKS WHEN THINGS DON'T GO HOW YOU PLANNED...
...DOESN'T IT, RAINIER?

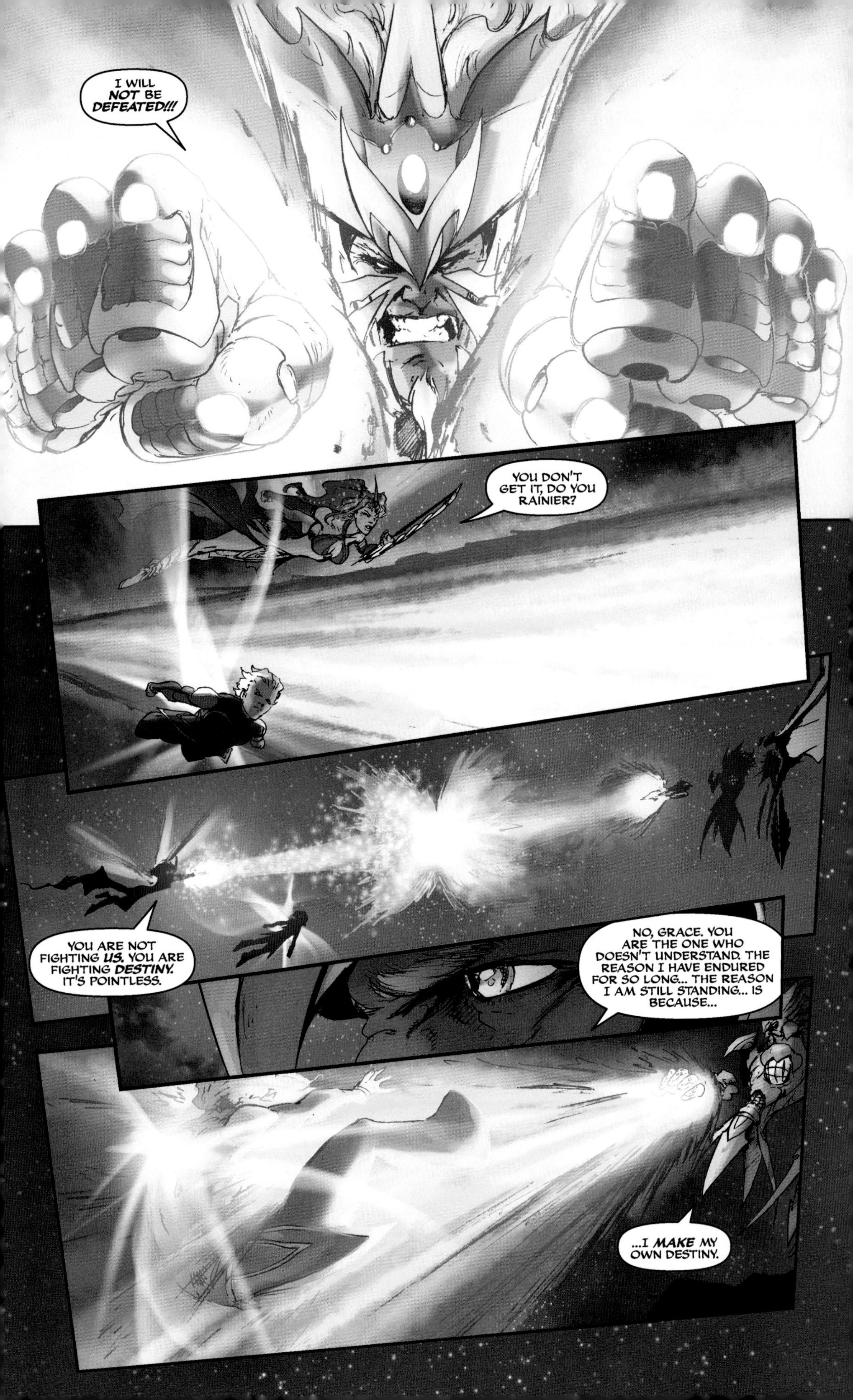
I WILL NOT BE DEFEATED!!!
YOU DON'T GET IT, DO YOU RAINIER?
YOU ARE NOT FIGHTING US. YOU ARE FIGHTING DESTINY. IT'S POINTLESS.
NO, GRACE. YOU ARE THE ONE WHO DOESN'T UNDERSTAND. THE REASON I HAVE ENDURED FOR SO LONG... THE REASON I AM STILL STANDING... IS BECAUSE...
...I MAKE MY OWN DESTINY.

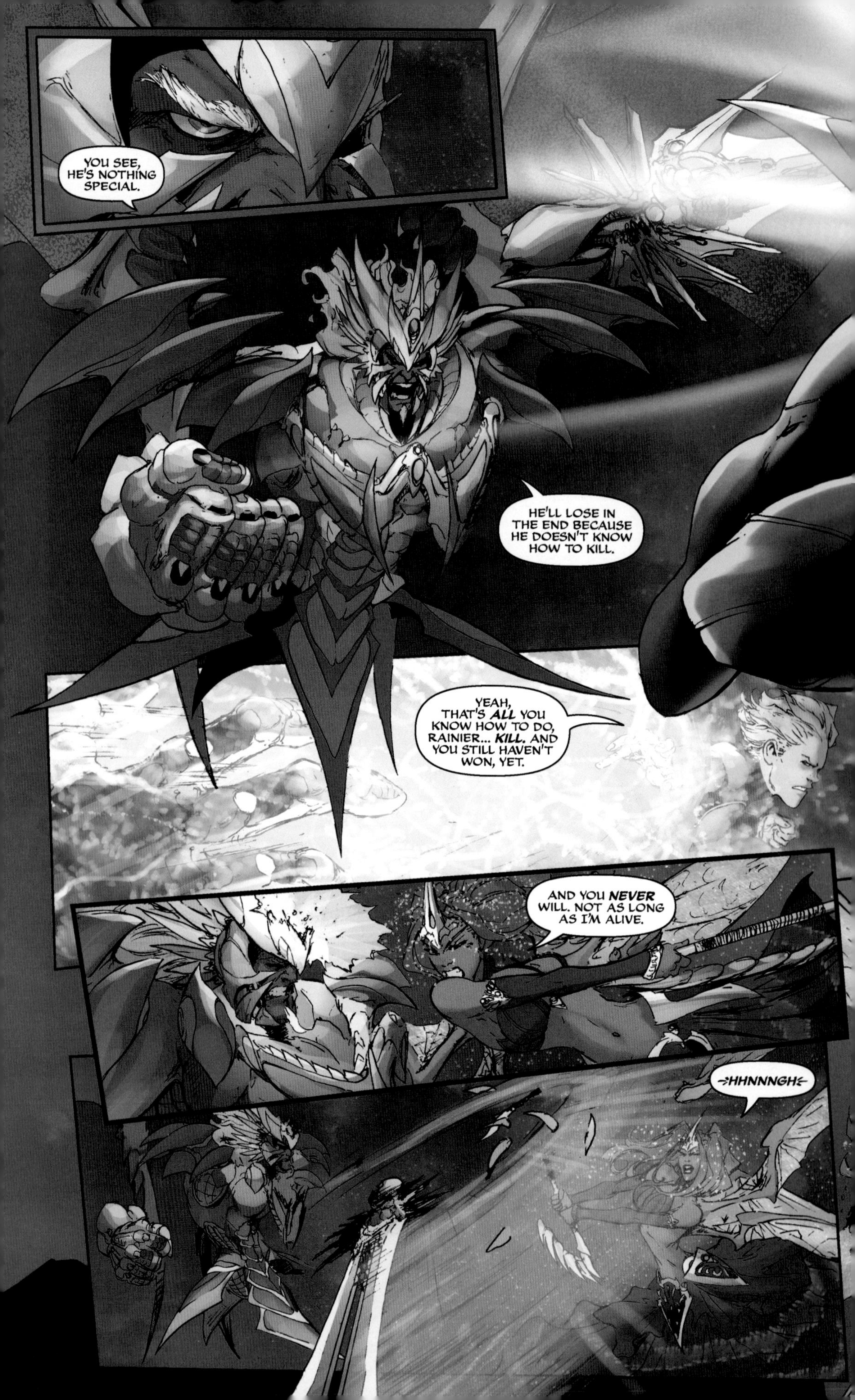
YOU SEE, HE'S NOTHING SPECIAL.
HE'LL LOSE IN THE END BECAUSE HE DOESN'T KNOW HOW TO KILL.
YEAH, THAT'S ALL YOU KNOW HOW TO DO, RAINIER... KILL. AND YOU STILL HAVEN'T WON, YET.
AND YOU NEVER WILL. NOT AS LONG AS I'M ALIVE.
HHNNNGH

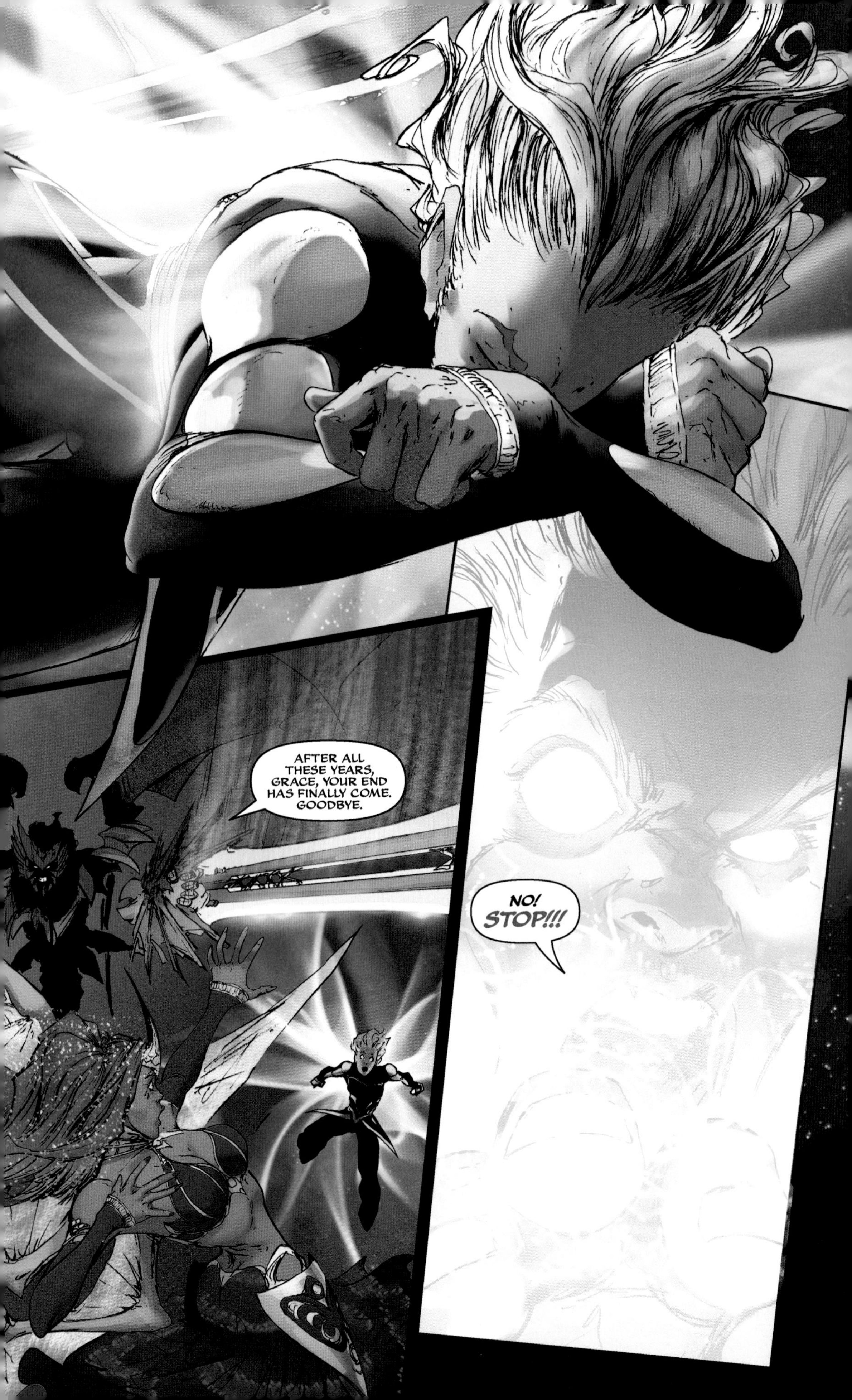
AFTER ALL THESE YEARS, GRACE, YOUR END HAS FINALLY COME. GOODBYE.
NO! STOP!!!

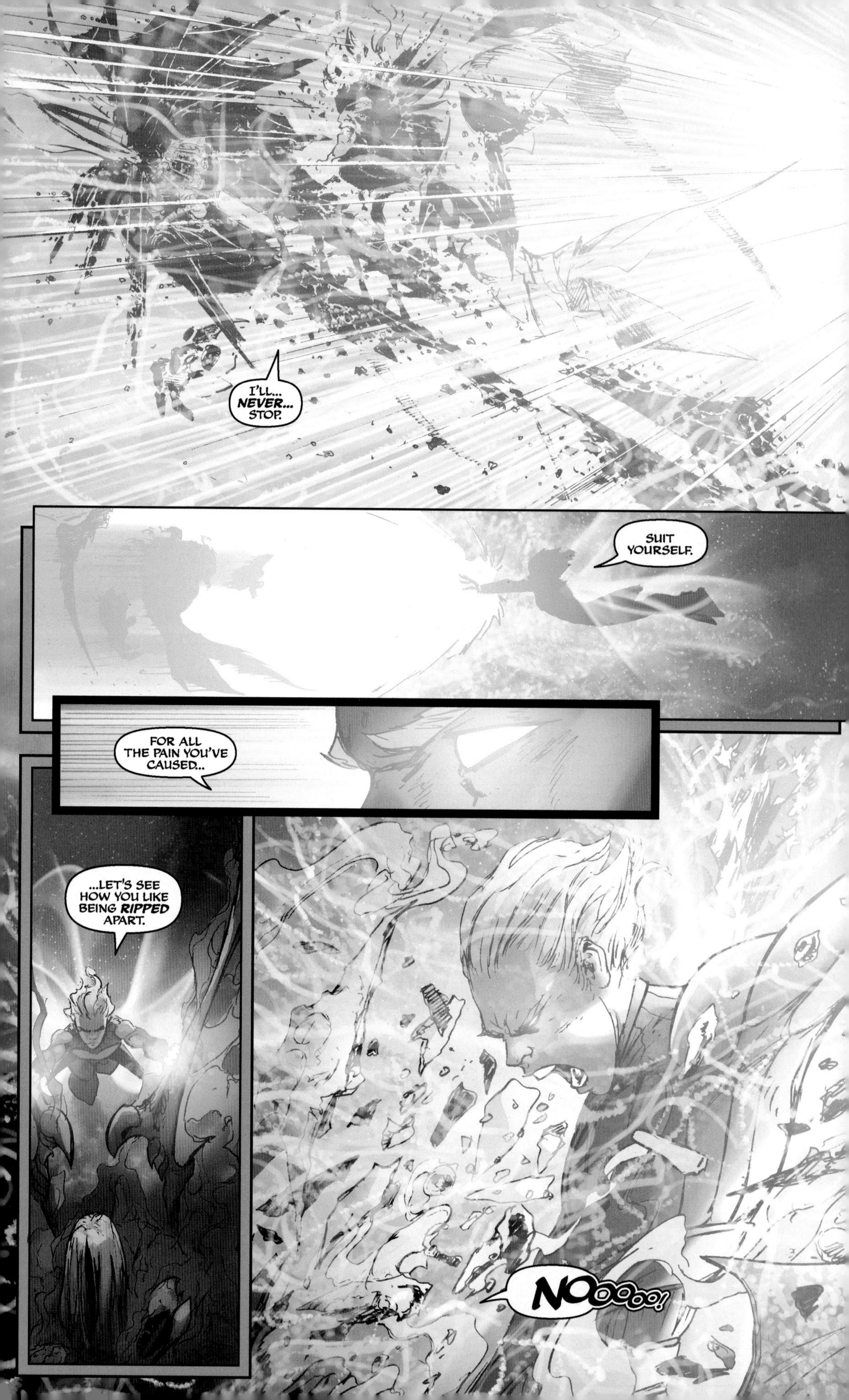
I'LL... NEVER... STOP.
SUIT YOURSELF.
FOR ALL THE PAIN YOU'VE CAUSED...
...LET'S SEE HOW YOU LIKE BEING RIPPED APART.
NOooooo!

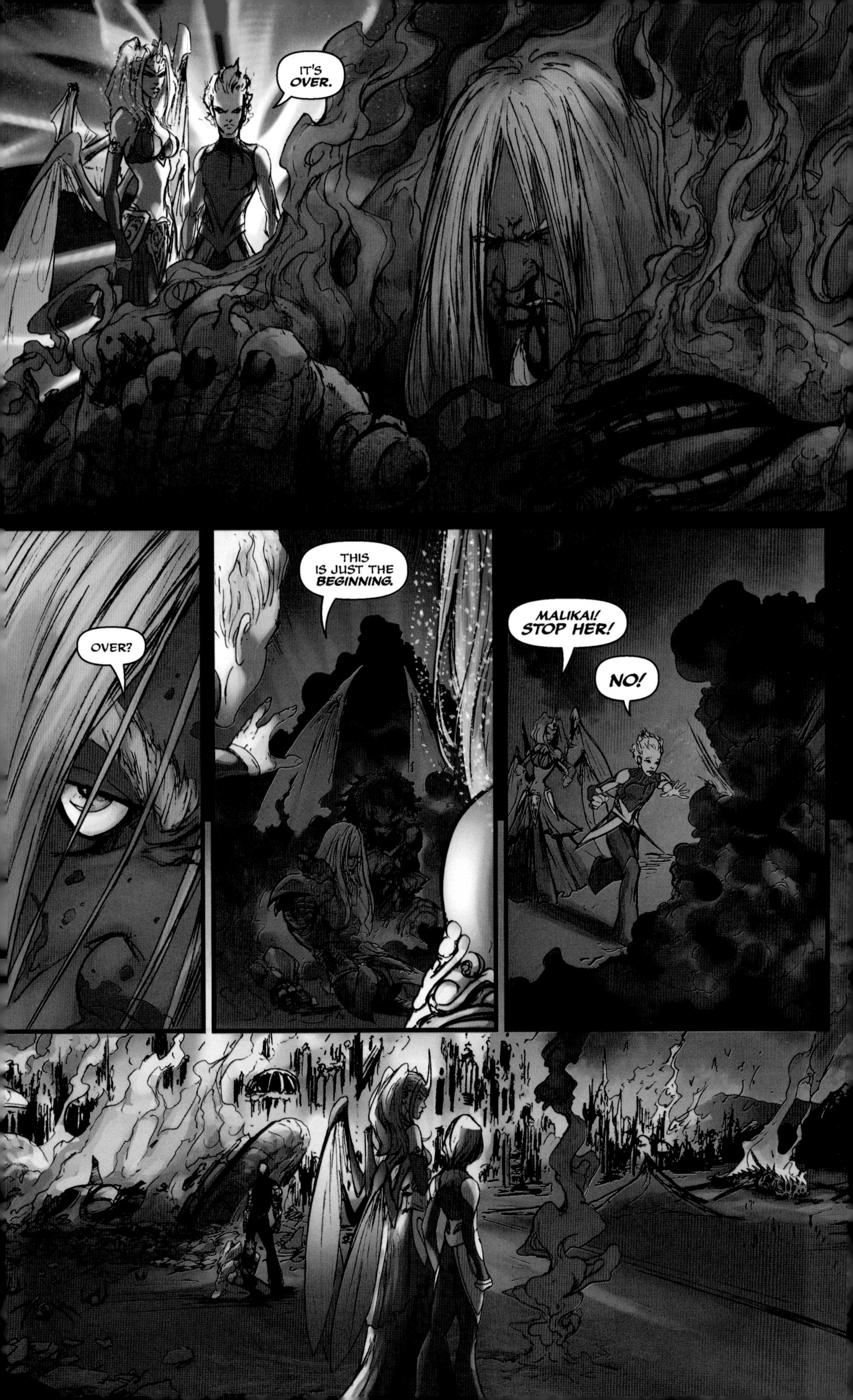
IT'S OVER.
OVER?
THIS IS JUST THE BEGINNING.
MALIKAI! STOP HER!
NO!

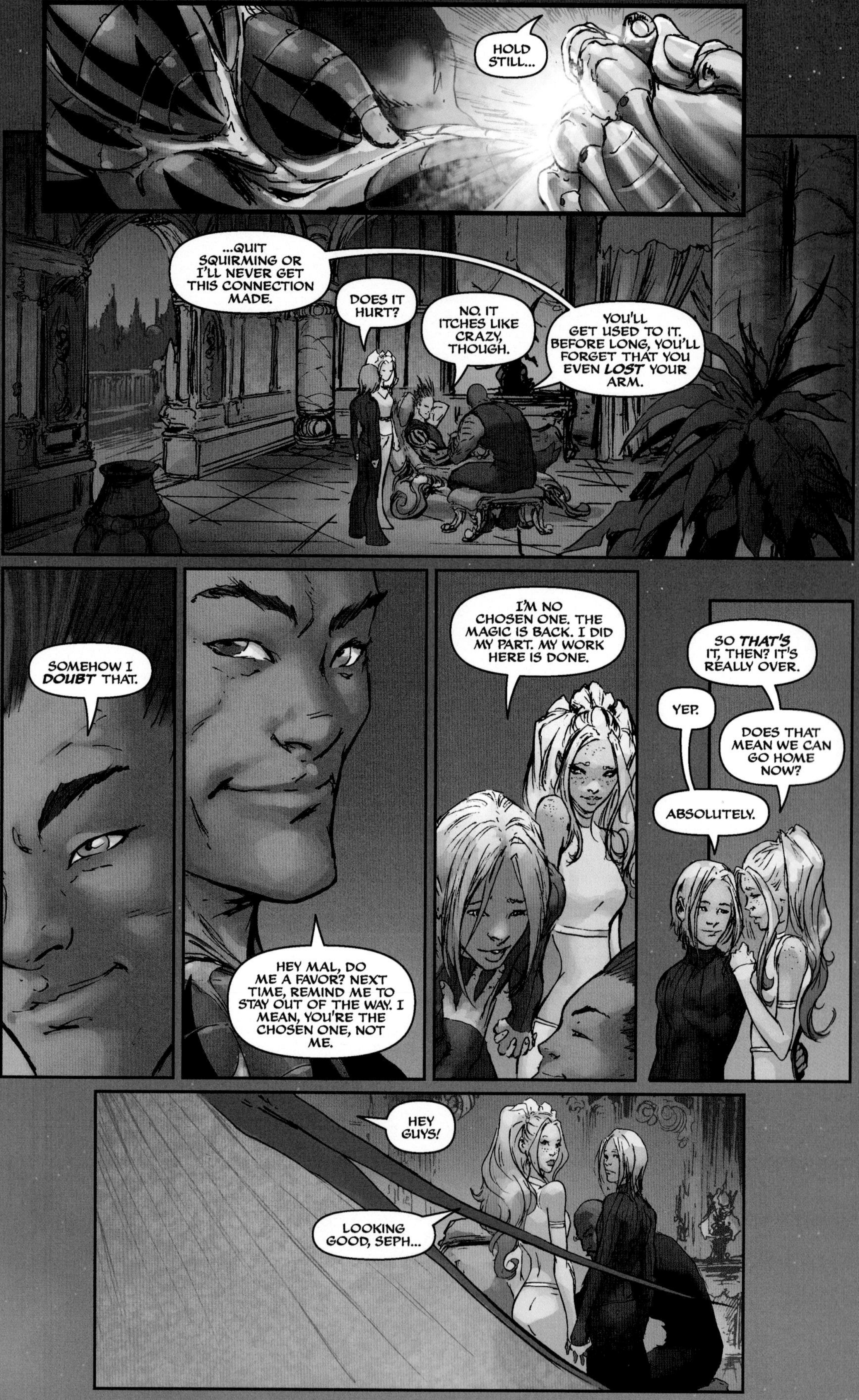
HOLD STILL...
...QUIT SQUIRMING OR I'LL NEVER GET THIS CONNECTION MADE.
DOES IT HURT?
NO, IT ITCHES LIKE CRAZY, THOUGH.
YOU'LL GET USED TO IT. BEFORE LONG, YOU'LL FORGET THAT YOU EVEN LOST YOUR ARM.
SOMEHOW I DOUBT THAT.
HEY MAL, DO ME A FAVOR? NEXT TIME, REMIND ME TO STAY OUT OF THE WAY. I MEAN, YOU'RE THE CHOSEN ONE, NOT ME.
I'M NO CHOSEN ONE. THE MAGIC IS BACK. I DID MY PART. MY WORK HERE IS DONE.
SO THAT'S IT, THEN? IT'S REALLY OVER.
YEP.
DOES THAT MEAN WE CAN GO HOME NOW?
ABSOLUTELY.
HEY GUYS!
LOOKING GOOD, SEPH...

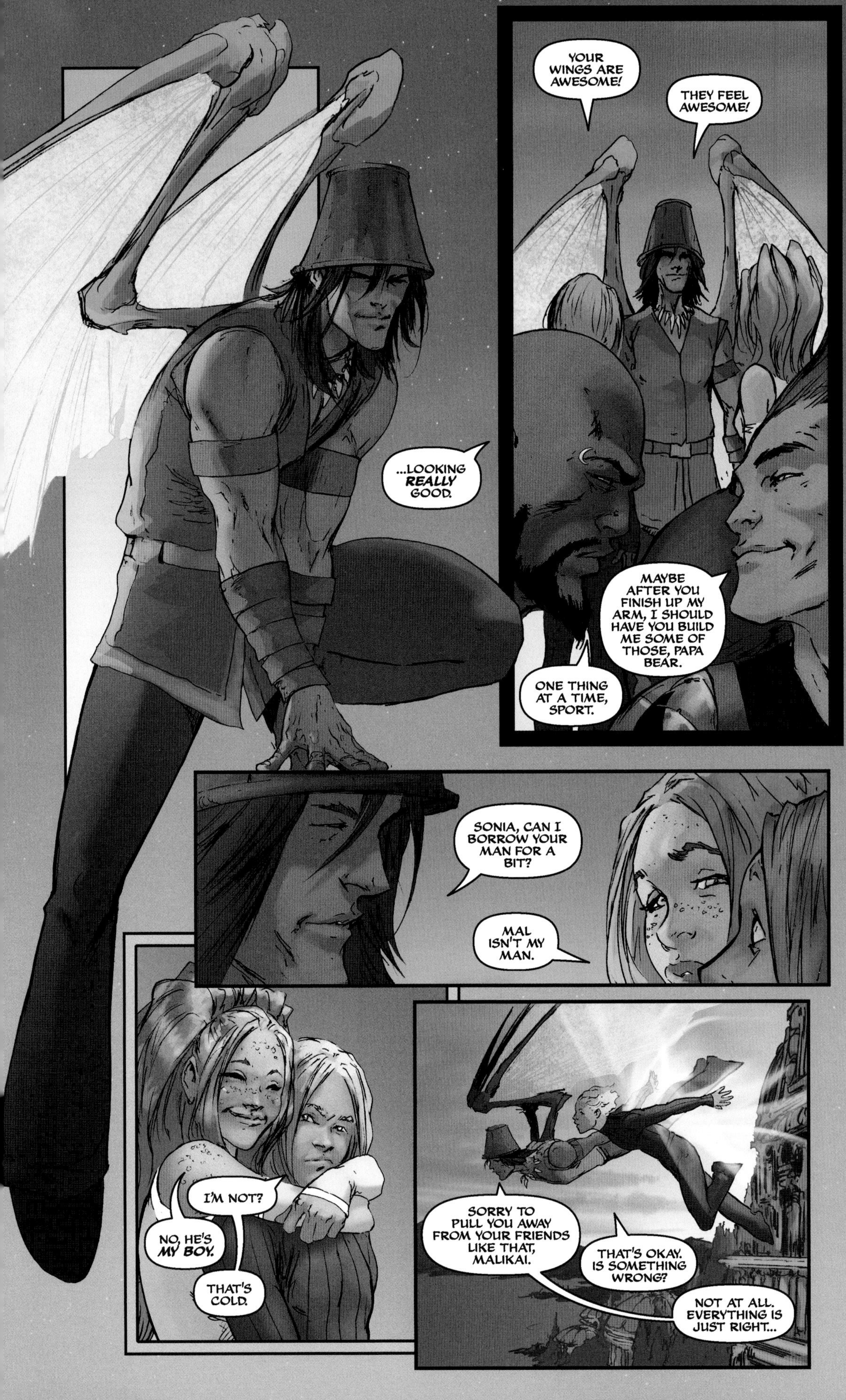
YOUR WINGS ARE AWESOME!
THEY FEEL AWESOME!
...LOOKING *REALLY* GOOD.
MAYBE AFTER YOU FINISH UP MY ARM, I SHOULD HAVE YOU BUILD ME SOME OF THOSE, PAPA BEAR.
ONE THING AT A TIME, SPORT.
SONIA, CAN I BORROW YOUR MAN FOR A BIT?
MAL ISN'T MY MAN.
I'M NOT?
NO, HE'S *MY BOY*.
THAT'S COLD.
SORRY TO PULL YOU AWAY FROM YOUR FRIENDS LIKE THAT, MALIKAI.
THAT'S OKAY. IS SOMETHING WRONG?
NOT AT ALL. EVERYTHING IS JUST RIGHT...

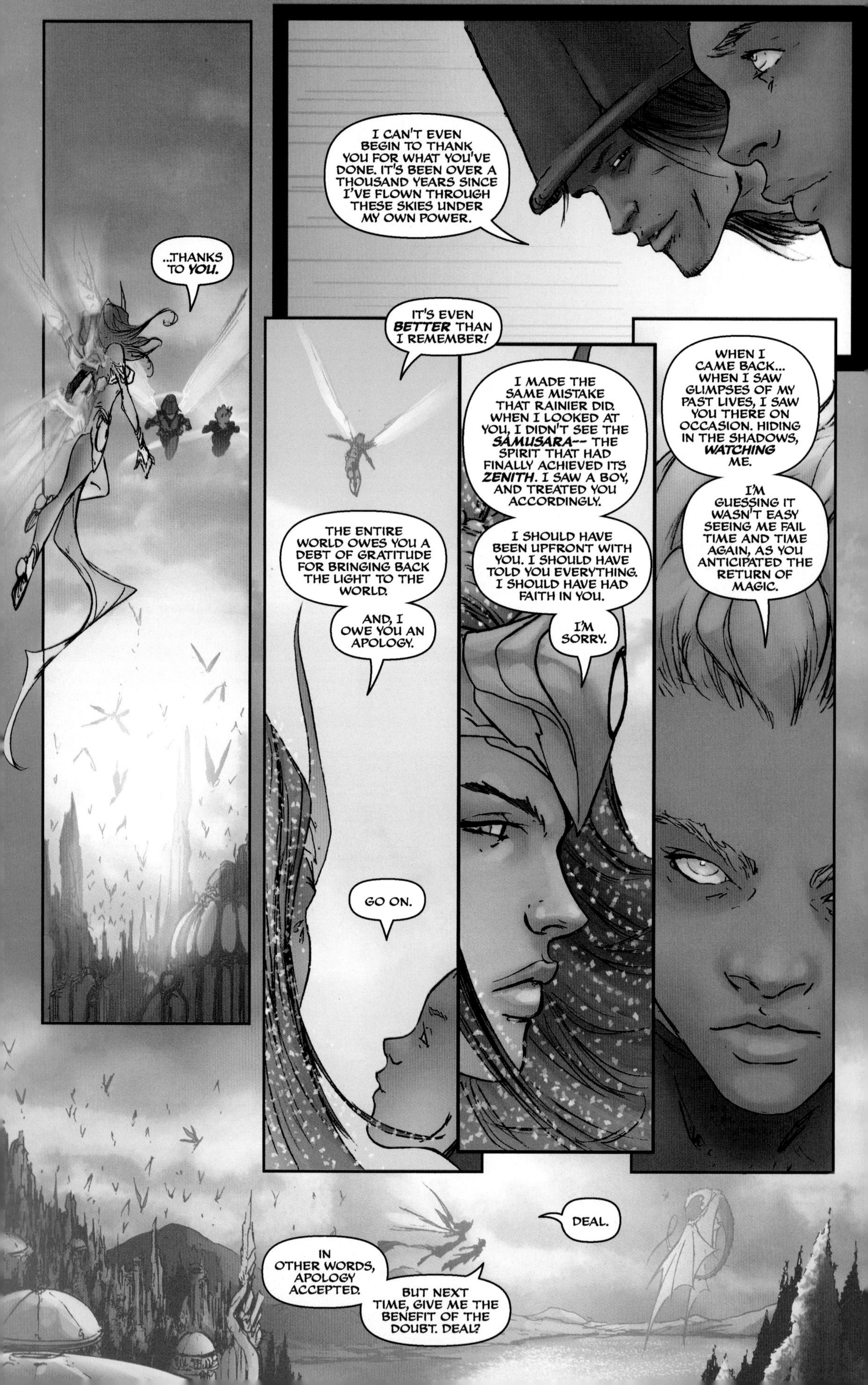
I CAN'T EVEN BEGIN TO THANK YOU FOR WHAT YOU'VE DONE. IT'S BEEN OVER A THOUSAND YEARS SINCE I'VE FLOWN THROUGH THESE SKIES UNDER MY OWN POWER.
...THANKS TO *YOU.*
IT'S EVEN **BETTER** THAN I REMEMBER!
THE ENTIRE WORLD OWES YOU A DEBT OF GRATITUDE FOR BRINGING BACK THE LIGHT TO THE WORLD.
AND, I OWE YOU AN APOLOGY.
I MADE THE SAME MISTAKE THAT RAINIER DID. WHEN I LOOKED AT YOU, I DIDN'T SEE THE ***SAMUSARA***-- THE SPIRIT THAT HAD FINALLY ACHIEVED ITS ***ZENITH***. I SAW A BOY, AND TREATED YOU ACCORDINGLY.
I SHOULD HAVE BEEN UPFRONT WITH YOU. I SHOULD HAVE TOLD YOU EVERYTHING. I SHOULD HAVE HAD FAITH IN YOU.
I'M SORRY.
WHEN I CAME BACK... WHEN I SAW GLIMPSES OF MY PAST LIVES, I SAW YOU THERE ON OCCASION. HIDING IN THE SHADOWS, ***WATCHING*** ME.
I'M GUESSING IT WASN'T EASY SEEING ME FAIL TIME AND TIME AGAIN, AS YOU ANTICIPATED THE RETURN OF MAGIC.
GO ON.
IN OTHER WORDS, APOLOGY ACCEPTED.
BUT NEXT TIME, GIVE ME THE BENEFIT OF THE DOUBT. DEAL?
DEAL.

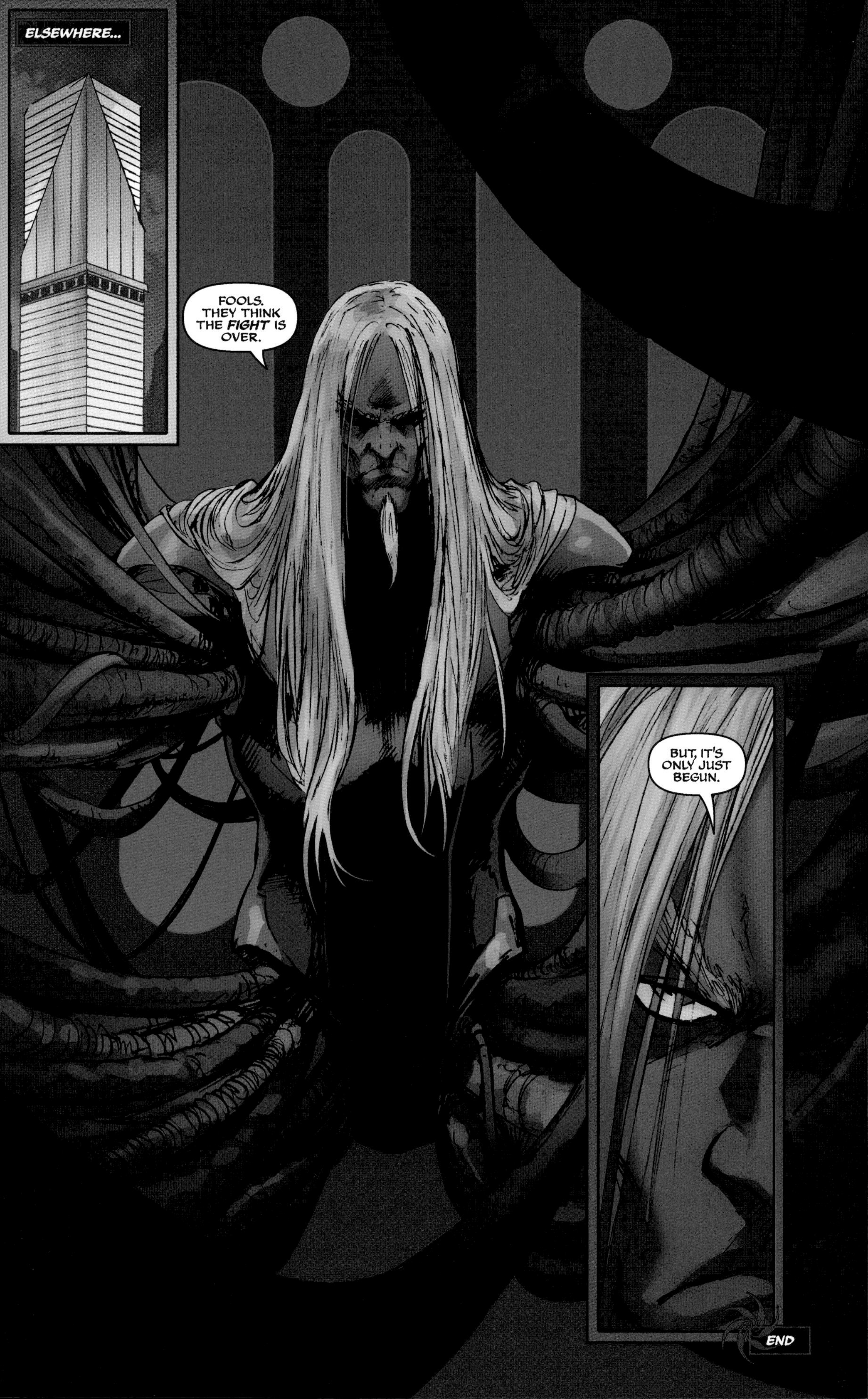
ELSEWHERE...
FOOLS. THEY THINK THE FIGHT IS OVER.
BUT, IT'S ONLY JUST BEGUN.
END

The following short story represents artist Joe Benitez and Peter Steigerwald's first combined foray into the Soulfire universe. After the late Michael Turner's tragic passing, Aspen decided to hand over his art duties on Soulfire to his friend and former colleague, Benitez. Included as the feature story in the Aspen Seasons: Winter 2009 title, "Destiny's Child" heralded the return of magic through the visionary artistic eye of Krul, Benitez and Steigerwald.

story: **J.T. Krul** - *pencils:* **Joe Benitez**
colors: **Peter Steigerwald** - *letters:* **Josh Reed**

SOULFIRE SEASONS
Winter 2009 – "Destiny's Child"

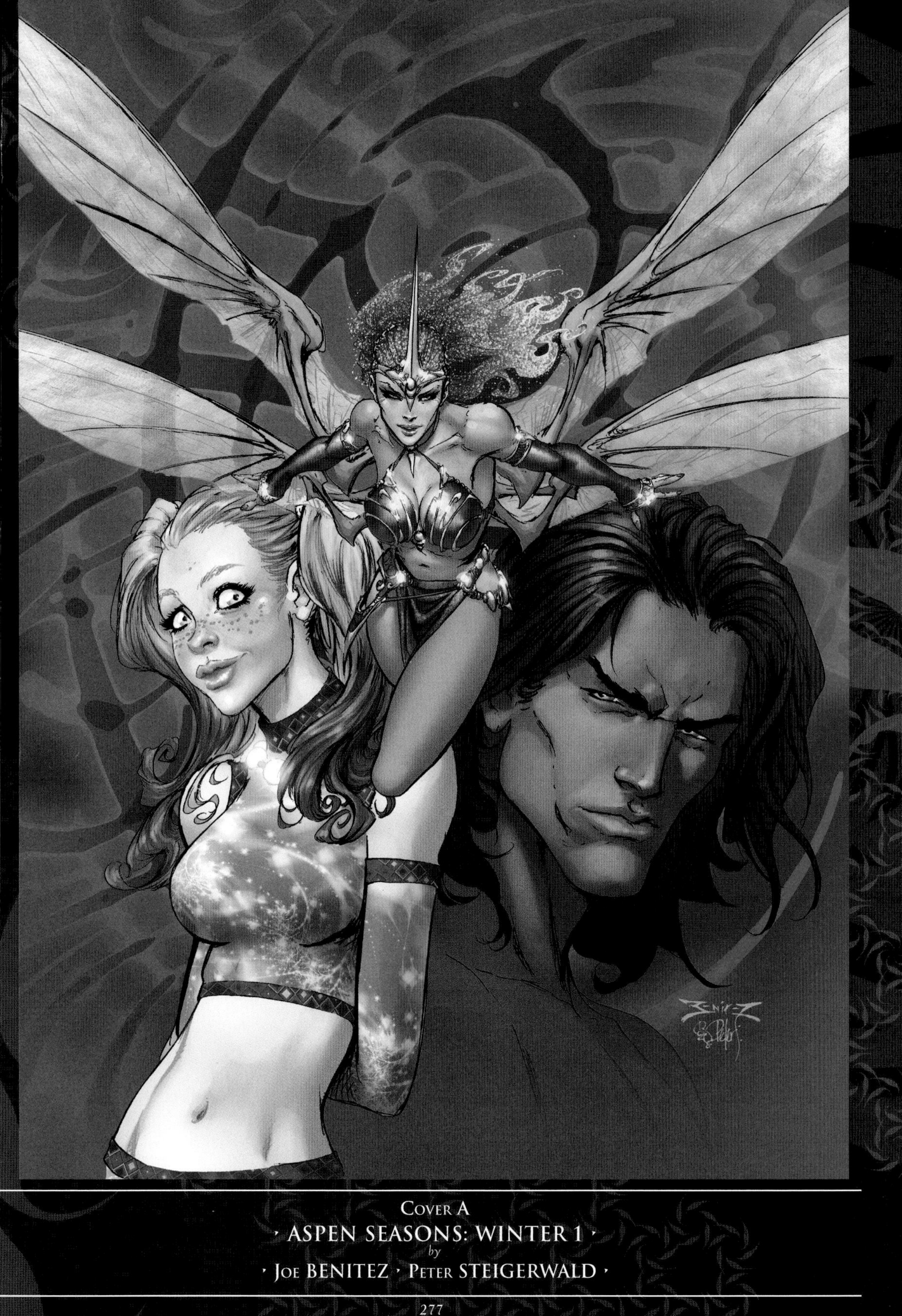

Cover A
‧ ASPEN SEASONS: WINTER 1 ‧
by
‧ Joe BENITEZ ‧ Peter STEIGERWALD ‧

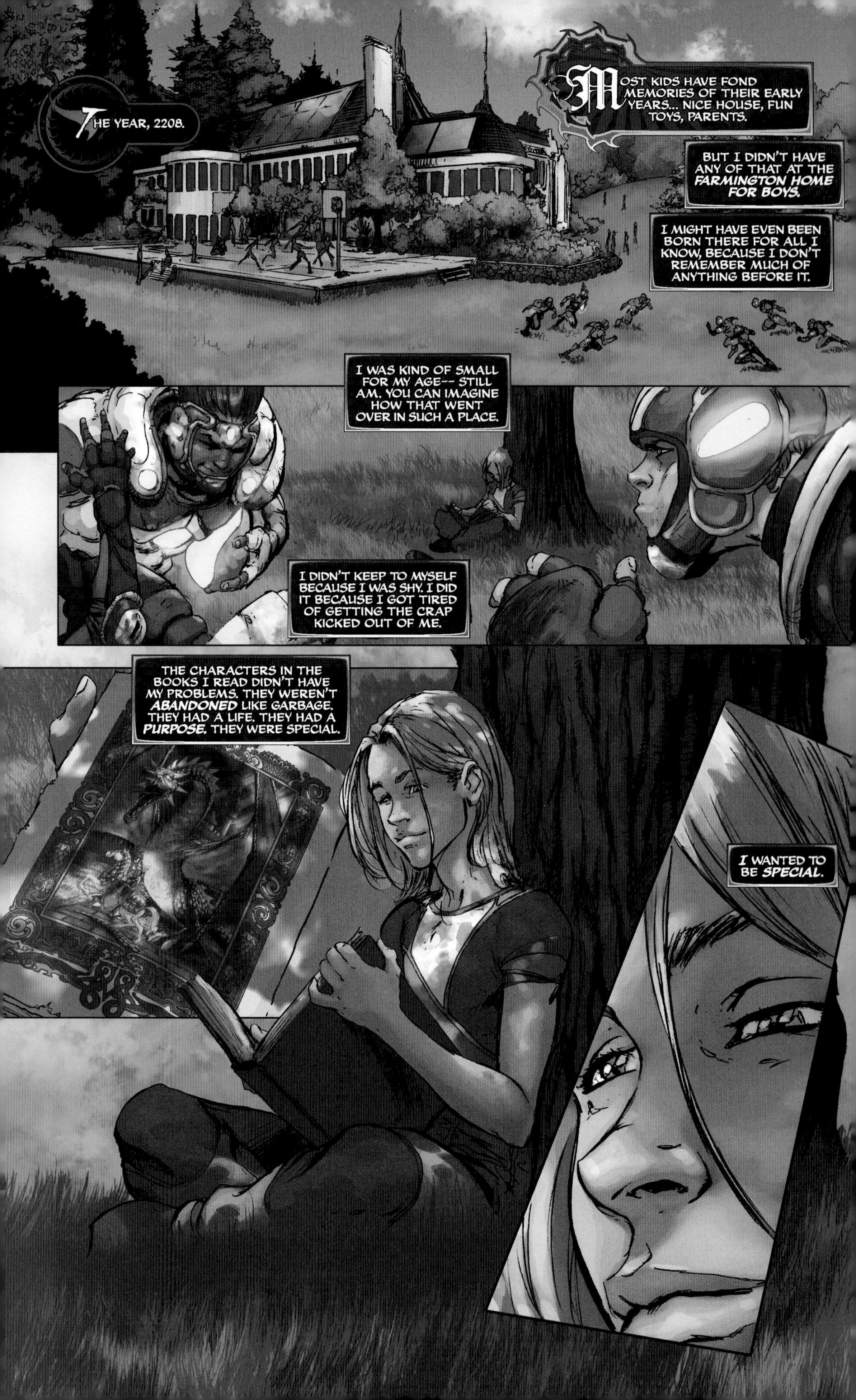
THE YEAR, 2208.
MOST KIDS HAVE FOND MEMORIES OF THEIR EARLY YEARS... NICE HOUSE, FUN TOYS, PARENTS.
BUT I DIDN'T HAVE ANY OF THAT AT THE FARMINGTON HOME FOR BOYS.
I MIGHT HAVE EVEN BEEN BORN THERE FOR ALL I KNOW, BECAUSE I DON'T REMEMBER MUCH OF ANYTHING BEFORE IT.
I WAS KIND OF SMALL FOR MY AGE-- STILL AM. YOU CAN IMAGINE HOW THAT WENT OVER IN SUCH A PLACE.
I DIDN'T KEEP TO MYSELF BECAUSE I WAS SHY. I DID IT BECAUSE I GOT TIRED OF GETTING THE CRAP KICKED OUT OF ME.
THE CHARACTERS IN THE BOOKS I READ DIDN'T HAVE MY PROBLEMS. THEY WEREN'T ABANDONED LIKE GARBAGE. THEY HAD A LIFE. THEY HAD A PURPOSE. THEY WERE SPECIAL.
I WANTED TO BE SPECIAL.

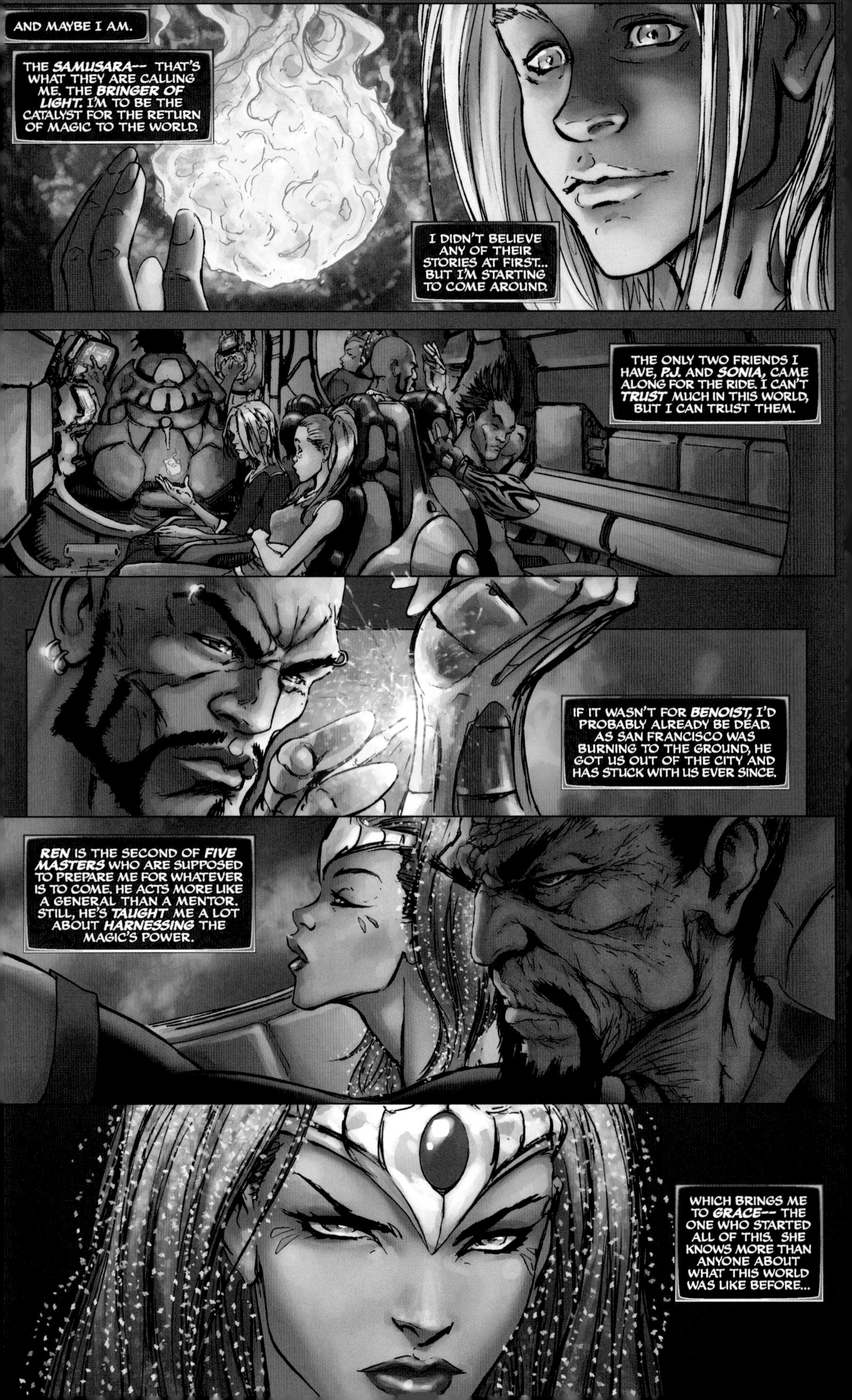
AND MAYBE I AM.
THE SAMUSARA-- THAT'S WHAT THEY ARE CALLING ME. THE BRINGER OF LIGHT. I'M TO BE THE CATALYST FOR THE RETURN OF MAGIC TO THE WORLD.
I DIDN'T BELIEVE ANY OF THEIR STORIES AT FIRST... BUT I'M STARTING TO COME AROUND.
THE ONLY TWO FRIENDS I HAVE, P.J. AND SONIA, CAME ALONG FOR THE RIDE. I CAN'T TRUST MUCH IN THIS WORLD, BUT I CAN TRUST THEM.
IF IT WASN'T FOR BENOIST, I'D PROBABLY ALREADY BE DEAD. AS SAN FRANCISCO WAS BURNING TO THE GROUND, HE GOT US OUT OF THE CITY AND HAS STUCK WITH US EVER SINCE.
REN IS THE SECOND OF FIVE MASTERS WHO ARE SUPPOSED TO PREPARE ME FOR WHATEVER IS TO COME. HE ACTS MORE LIKE A GENERAL THAN A MENTOR. STILL, HE'S TAUGHT ME A LOT ABOUT HARNESSING THE MAGIC'S POWER.
WHICH BRINGS ME TO GRACE-- THE ONE WHO STARTED ALL OF THIS. SHE KNOWS MORE THAN ANYONE ABOUT WHAT THIS WORLD WAS LIKE BEFORE...

...BECAUSE SHE WAS *THERE.*
THOUSANDS OF YEARS AGO, IT WAS A SIMPLER TIME. IT WAS A BRIGHTER TIME.
IT WAS A *MAGICAL* TIME.
WHERE NOBODY WOULD GIVE A SECOND GLANCE AT SEEING PEOPLE SOARING IN THE SKIES.
OR *DRAGONS* FOR THAT MATTER.
GRACE AND HER PEOPLE REVELED IN THE MAGIC OF THEIR AGE, BUT THEY DIDN'T REALIZE THAT THE LIGHT WOULD NOT ENDURE FOREVER.
THAT IT WOULD GROW *DARK.*

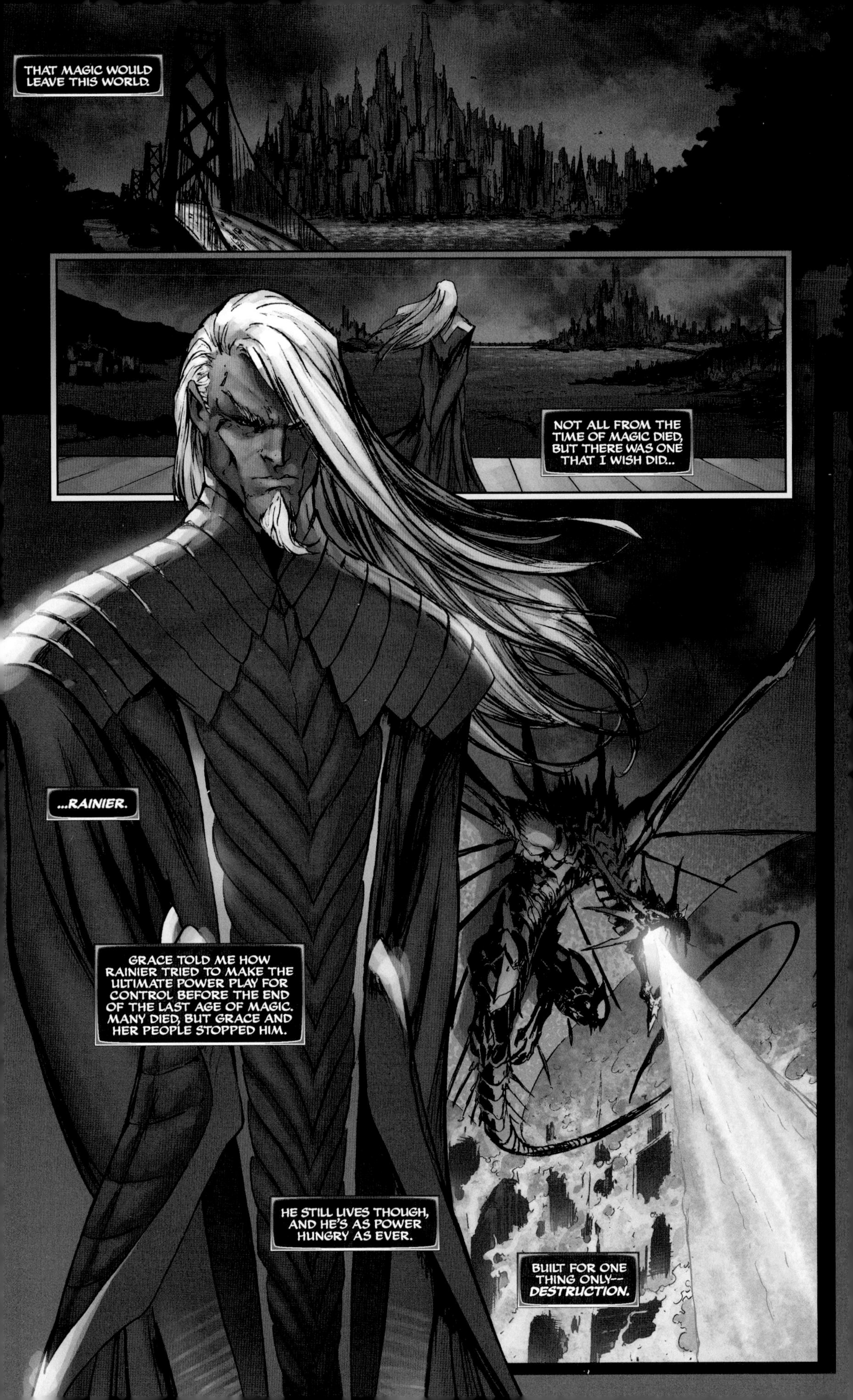
THAT MAGIC WOULD LEAVE THIS WORLD.
NOT ALL FROM THE TIME OF MAGIC DIED, BUT THERE WAS ONE THAT I WISH DID...
...RAINIER.
GRACE TOLD ME HOW RAINIER TRIED TO MAKE THE ULTIMATE POWER PLAY FOR CONTROL BEFORE THE END OF THE LAST AGE OF MAGIC. MANY DIED, BUT GRACE AND HER PEOPLE STOPPED HIM.
HE STILL LIVES THOUGH, AND HE'S AS POWER HUNGRY AS EVER.
BUILT FOR ONE THING ONLY-- DESTRUCTION.

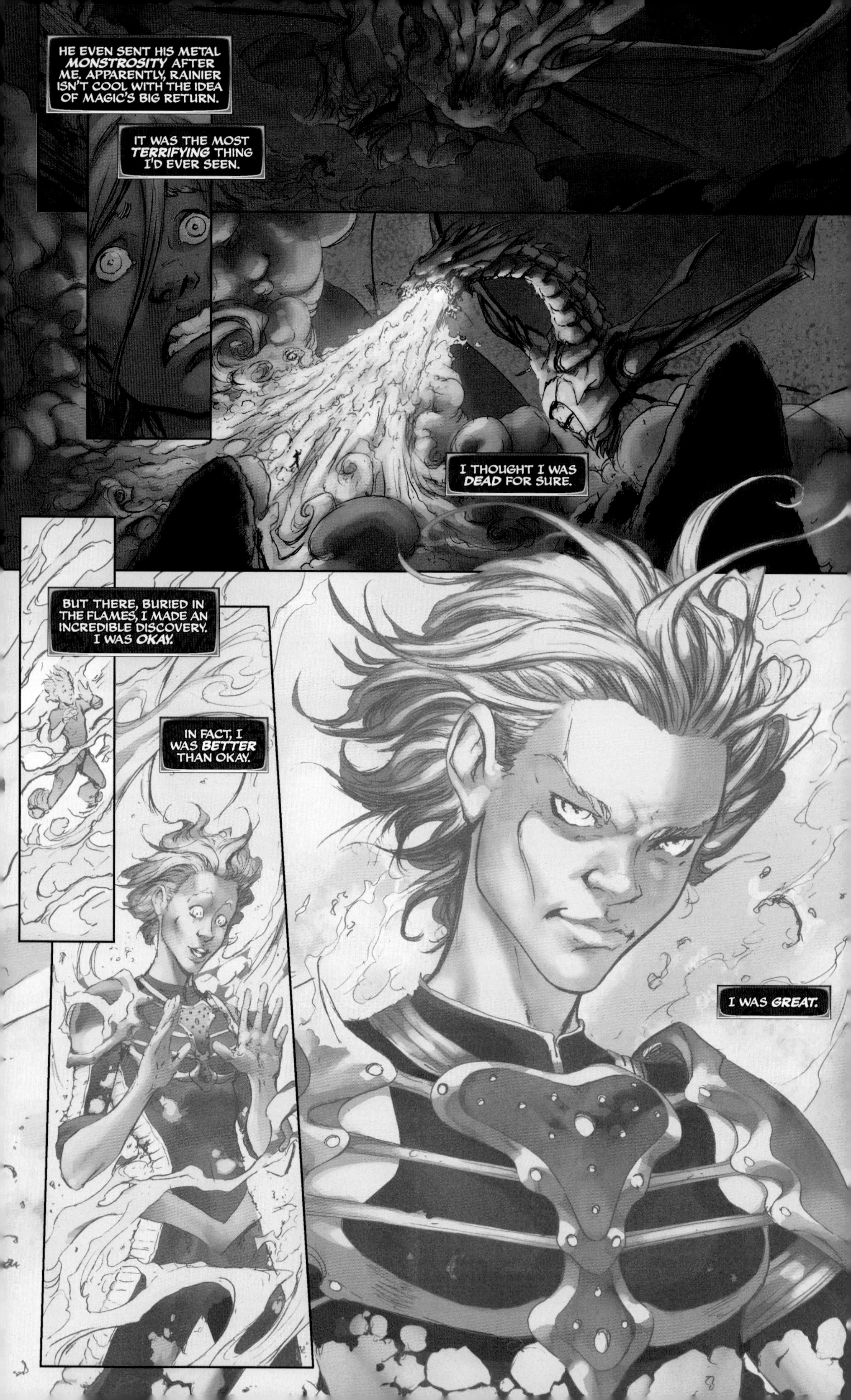
HE EVEN SENT HIS METAL MONSTROSITY AFTER ME. APPARENTLY, RAINIER ISN'T COOL WITH THE IDEA OF MAGIC'S BIG RETURN.
IT WAS THE MOST TERRIFYING THING I'D EVER SEEN.
I THOUGHT I WAS DEAD FOR SURE.
BUT THERE, BURIED IN THE FLAMES, I MADE AN INCREDIBLE DISCOVERY. I WAS OKAY.
IN FACT, I WAS BETTER THAN OKAY.
I WAS GREAT.

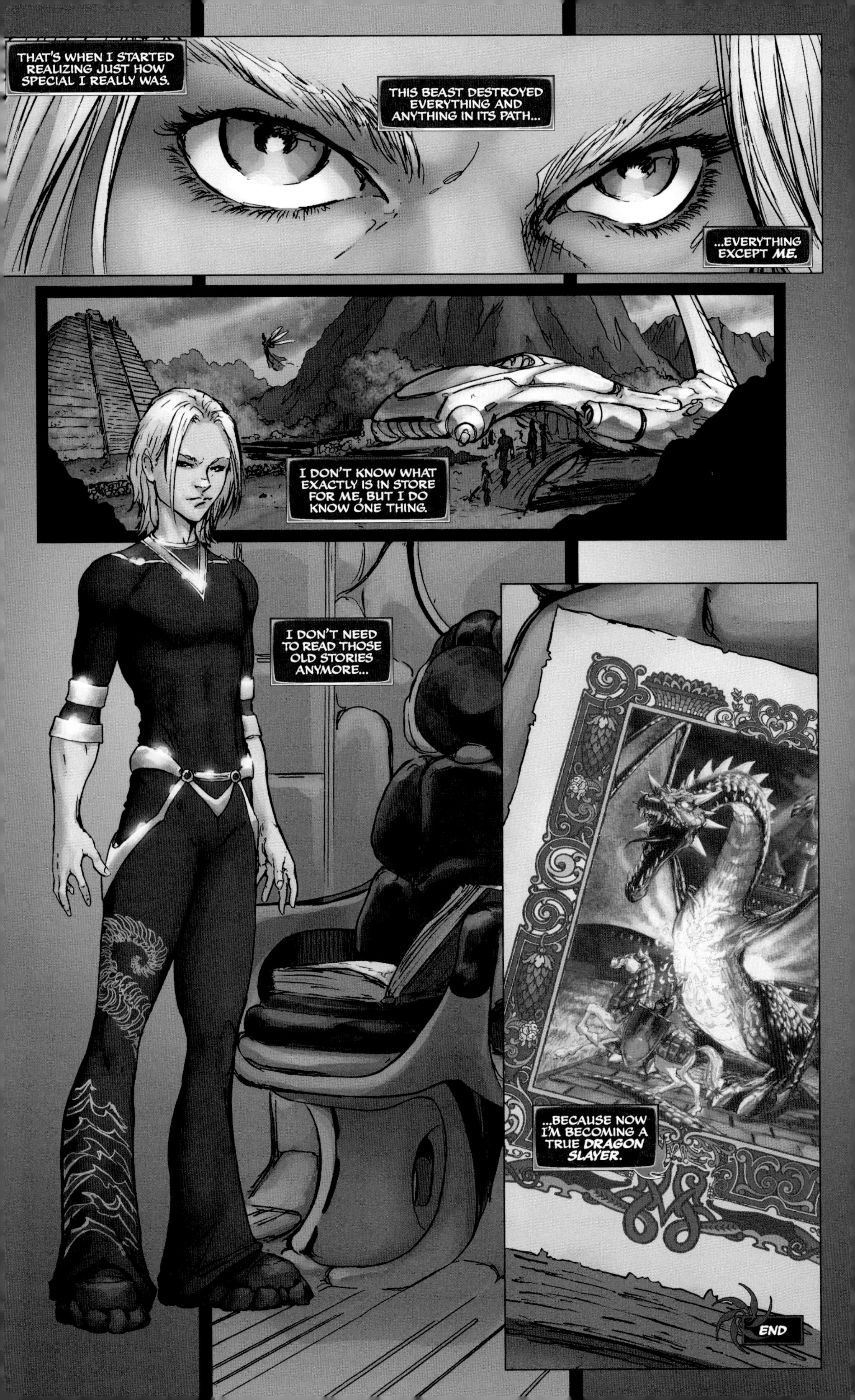
THAT'S WHEN I STARTED REALIZING JUST HOW SPECIAL I REALLY WAS.
THIS BEAST DESTROYED EVERYTHING AND ANYTHING IN ITS PATH...
...EVERYTHING EXCEPT ME.
I DON'T KNOW WHAT EXACTLY IS IN STORE FOR ME, BUT I DO KNOW ONE THING.
I DON'T NEED TO READ THOSE OLD STORIES ANYMORE...
...BECAUSE NOW I'M BECOMING A TRUE DRAGON SLAYER.
END

SOULFIRE COVER GALLERY

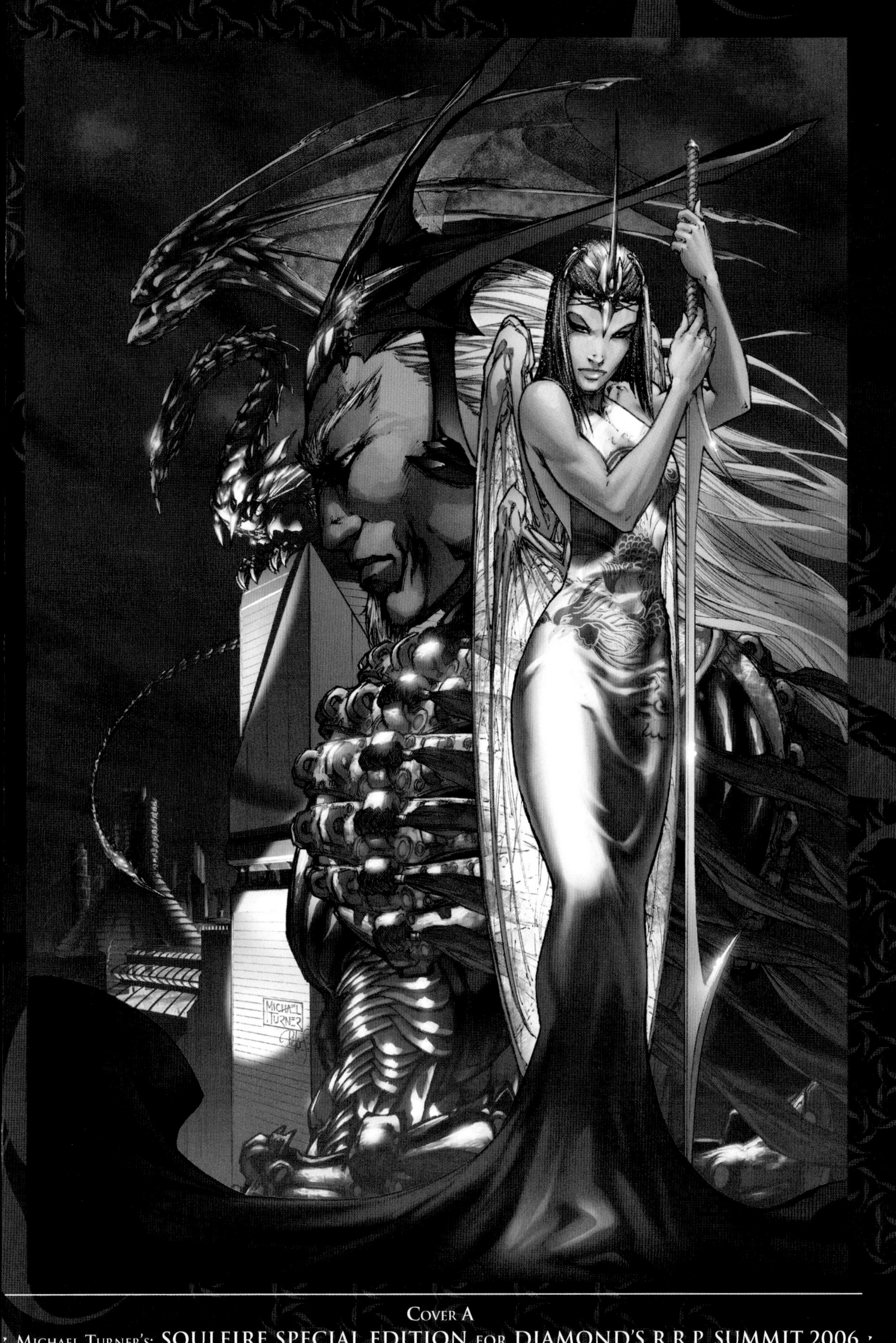
MICHAEL TURNER

Cover A
‣ Michael Turner's: SOULFIRE SPECIAL EDITION for DIAMOND'S R.R.P. SUMMIT 2006 ‣
by
‣ Michael TURNER ‣ Peter STEIGERWALD ‣

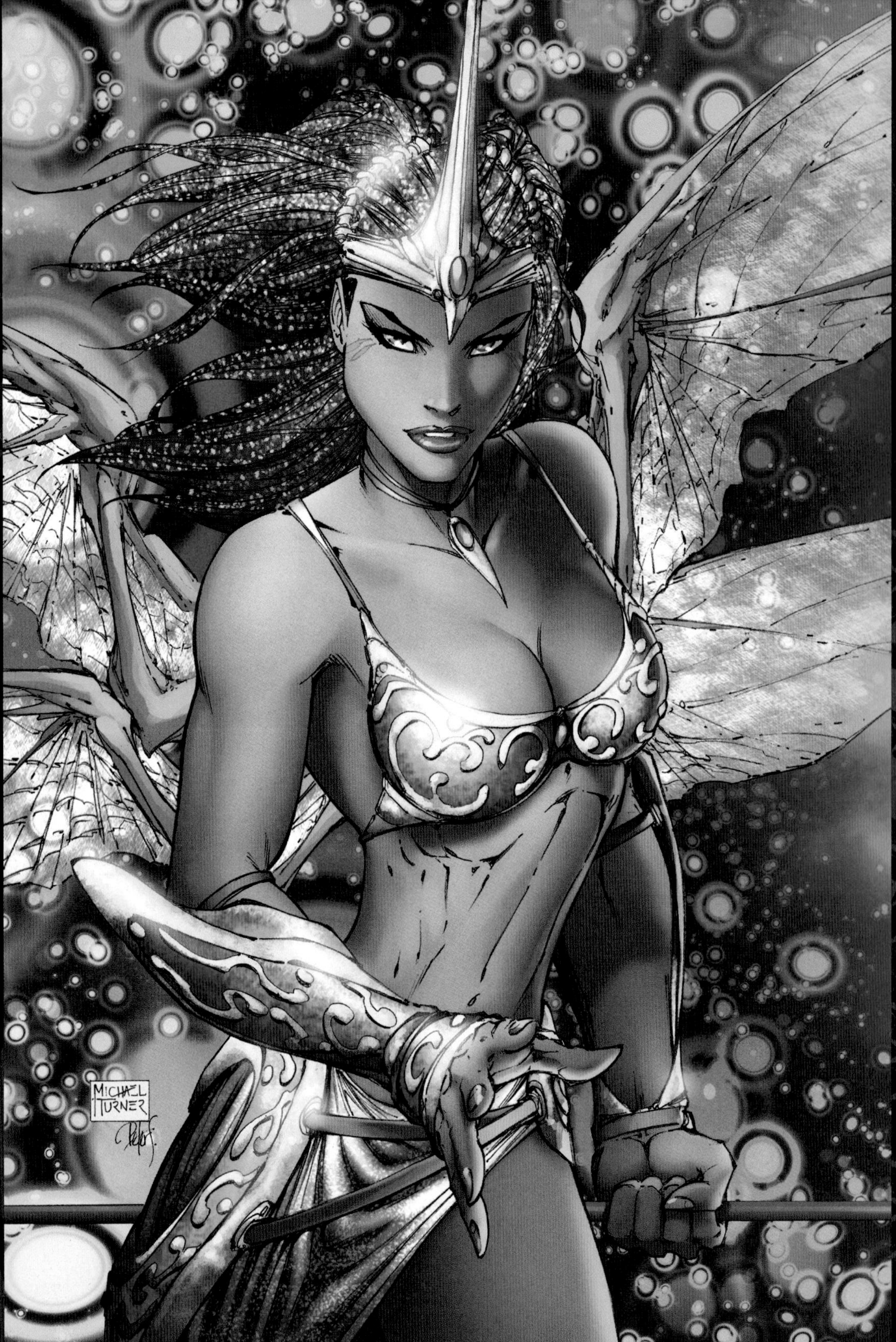
MICHAEL TURNER

DynamicForces.Com "Triumphant" Exclusive Cover C

· Michael Turner's: SOULFIRE 0 ·

by

· Michael TURNER · Peter STEIGERWALD ·

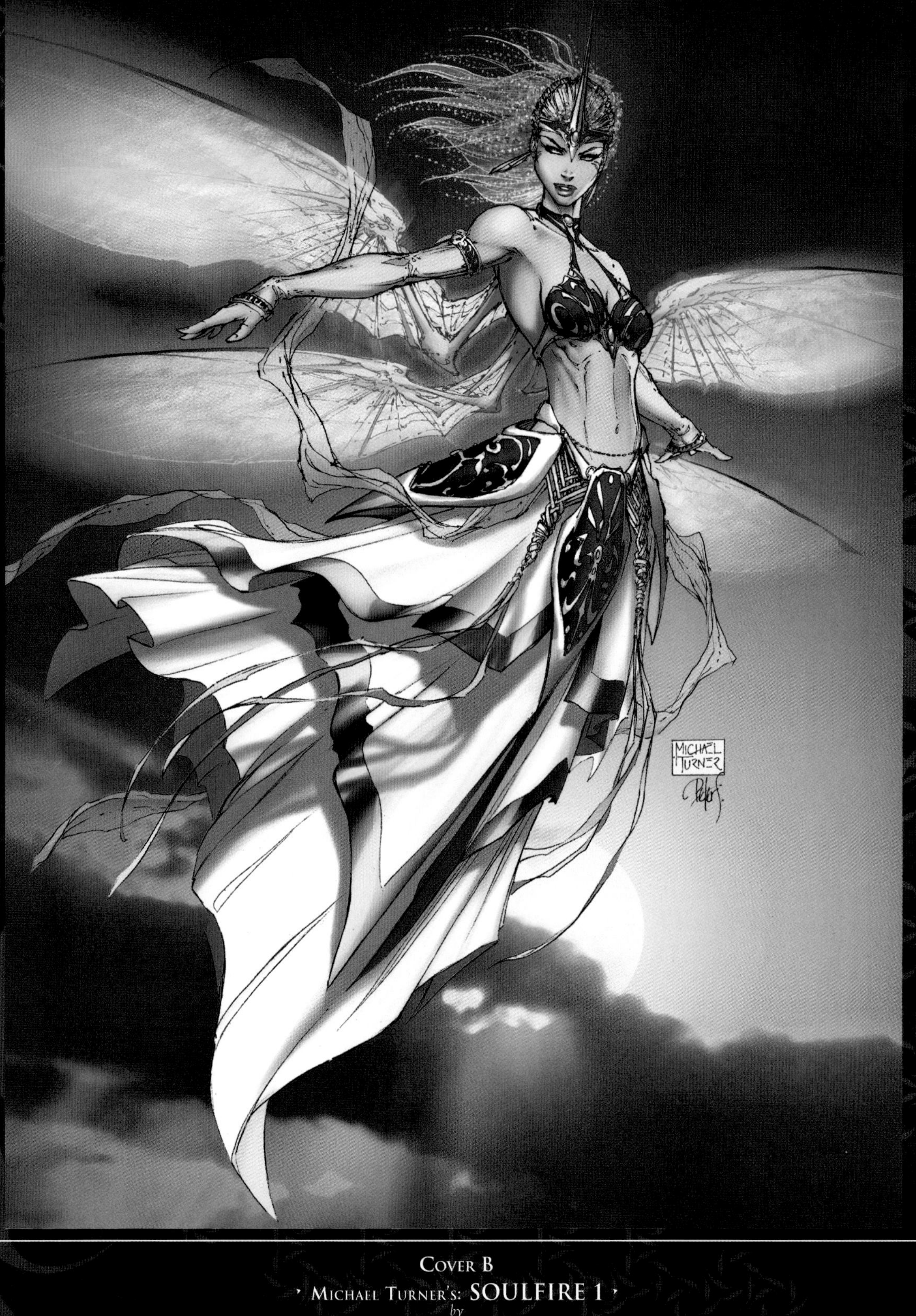
MICHAEL TURNER

COVER B
‧ MICHAEL TURNER'S: SOULFIRE 1 ‧
by
‧ MICHAEL TURNER ‧ PETER STEIGERWALD ‧

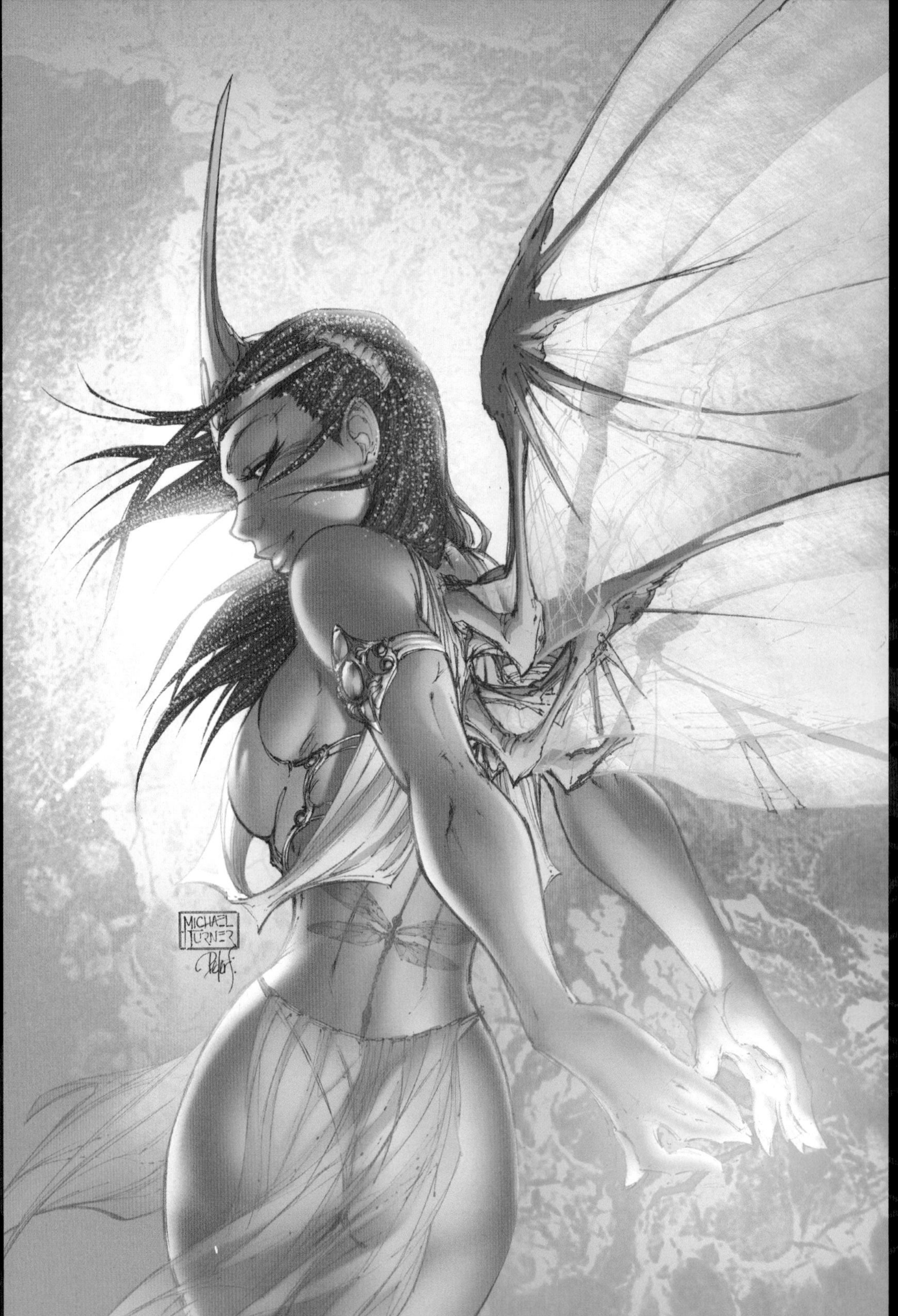
MICHAEL TURNER

Diamond Previews Exclusive Cover C

‣ Michael Turner's: SOULFIRE 1 ‣

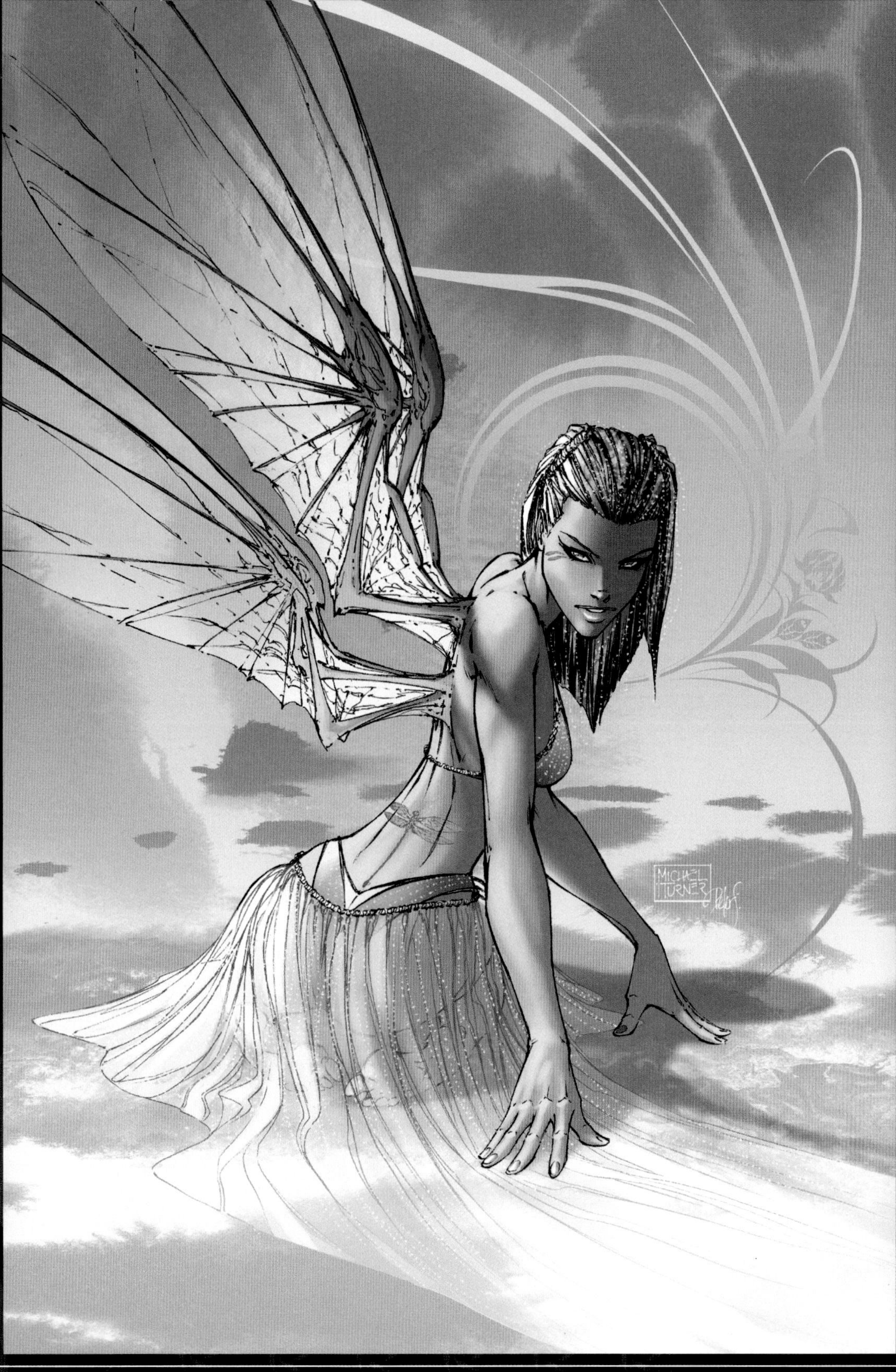
MICHAEL TURNER

Jay Company Comics Exclusive Cover D

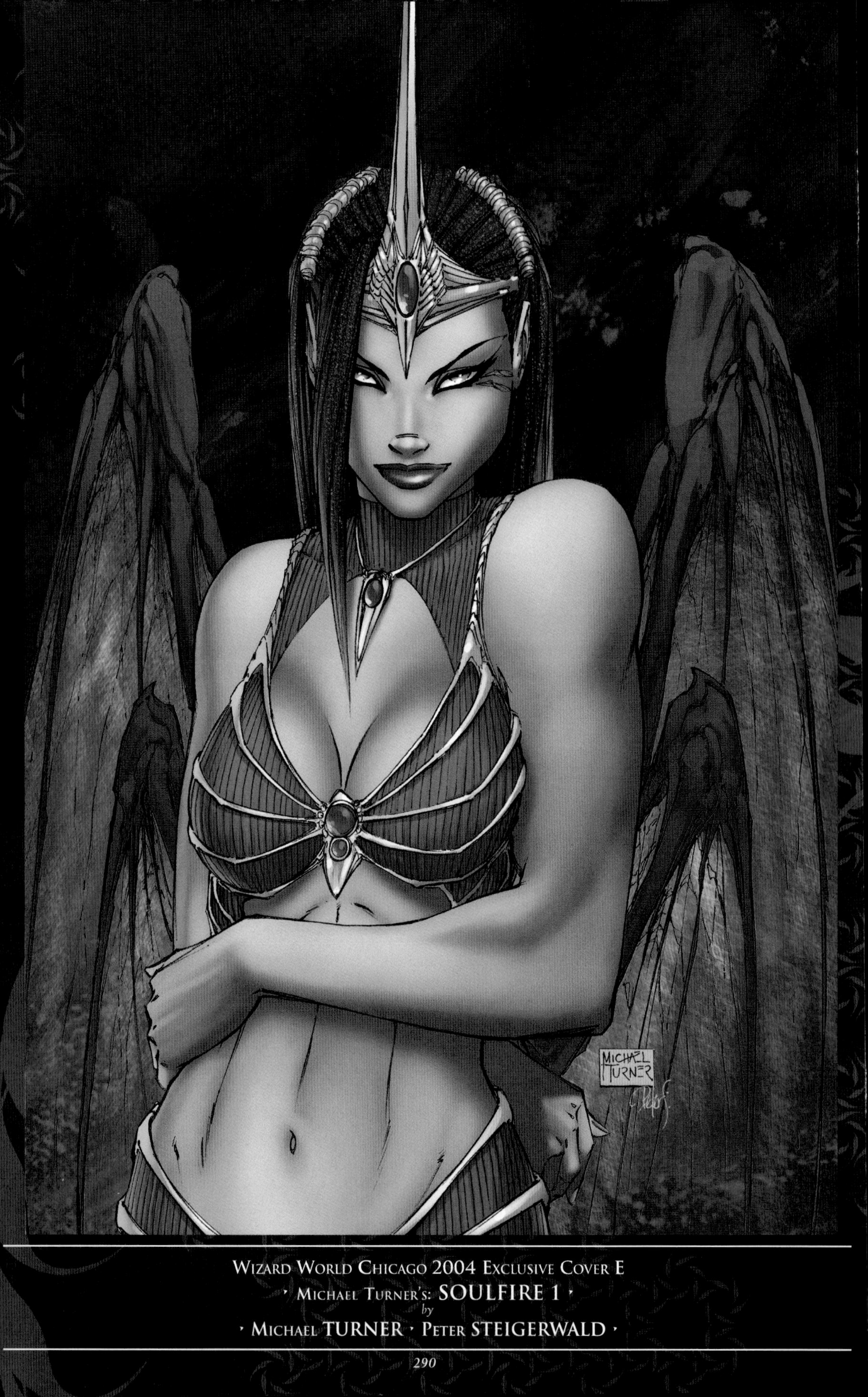
MICHAEL TURNER

Wizard World Chicago 2004 Exclusive Cover E
· Michael Turner's: SOULFIRE 1 ·
by
· Michael TURNER · Peter STEIGERWALD ·

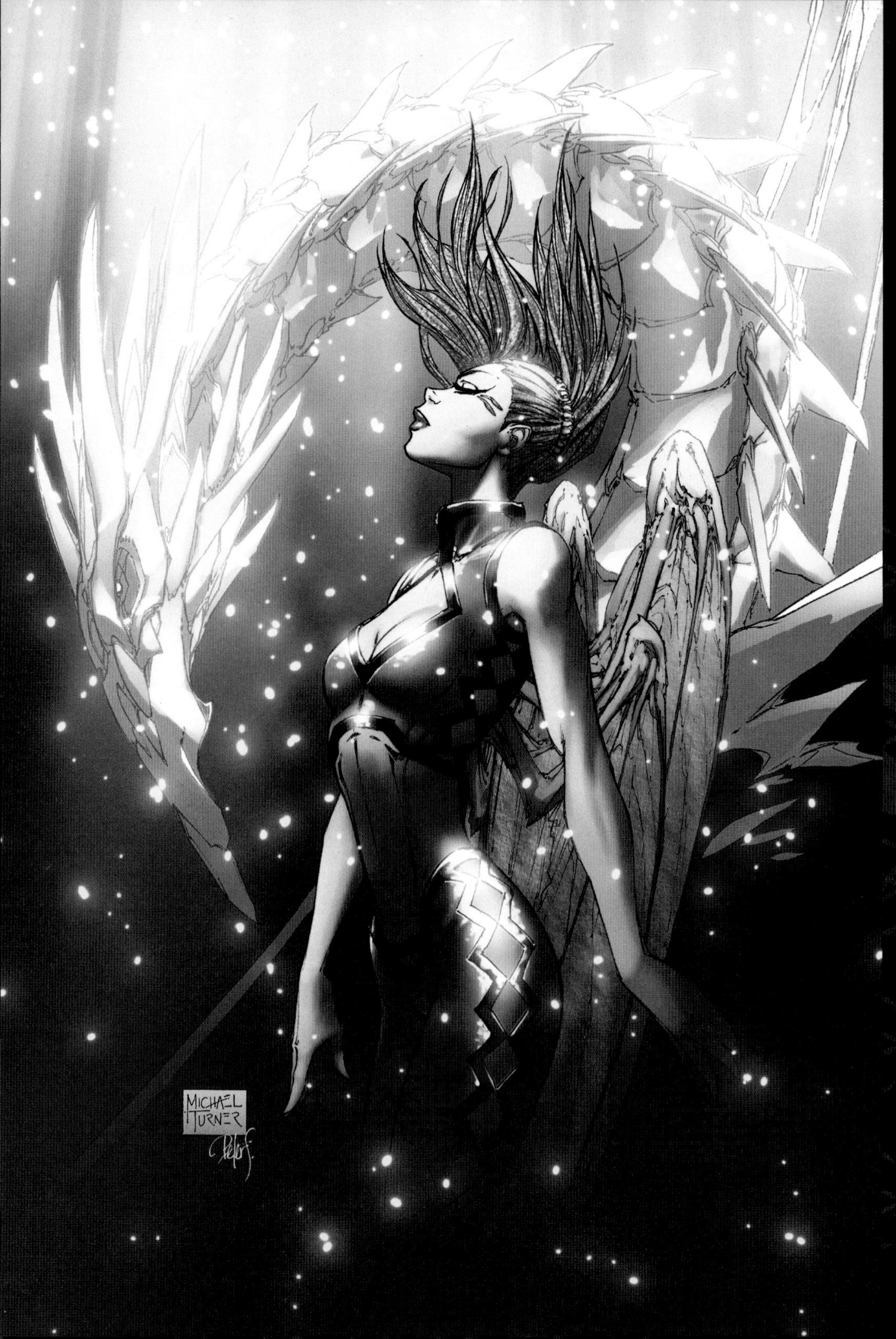
MICHAEL
TURNER

WIZARD WORLD CHICAGO 2004 PREMIERE EXCLUSIVE COVER F
‣ MICHAEL TURNER'S: SOULFIRE 1 ‣
by
‣ MICHAEL TURNER ‣ PETER STEIGERWALD ‣

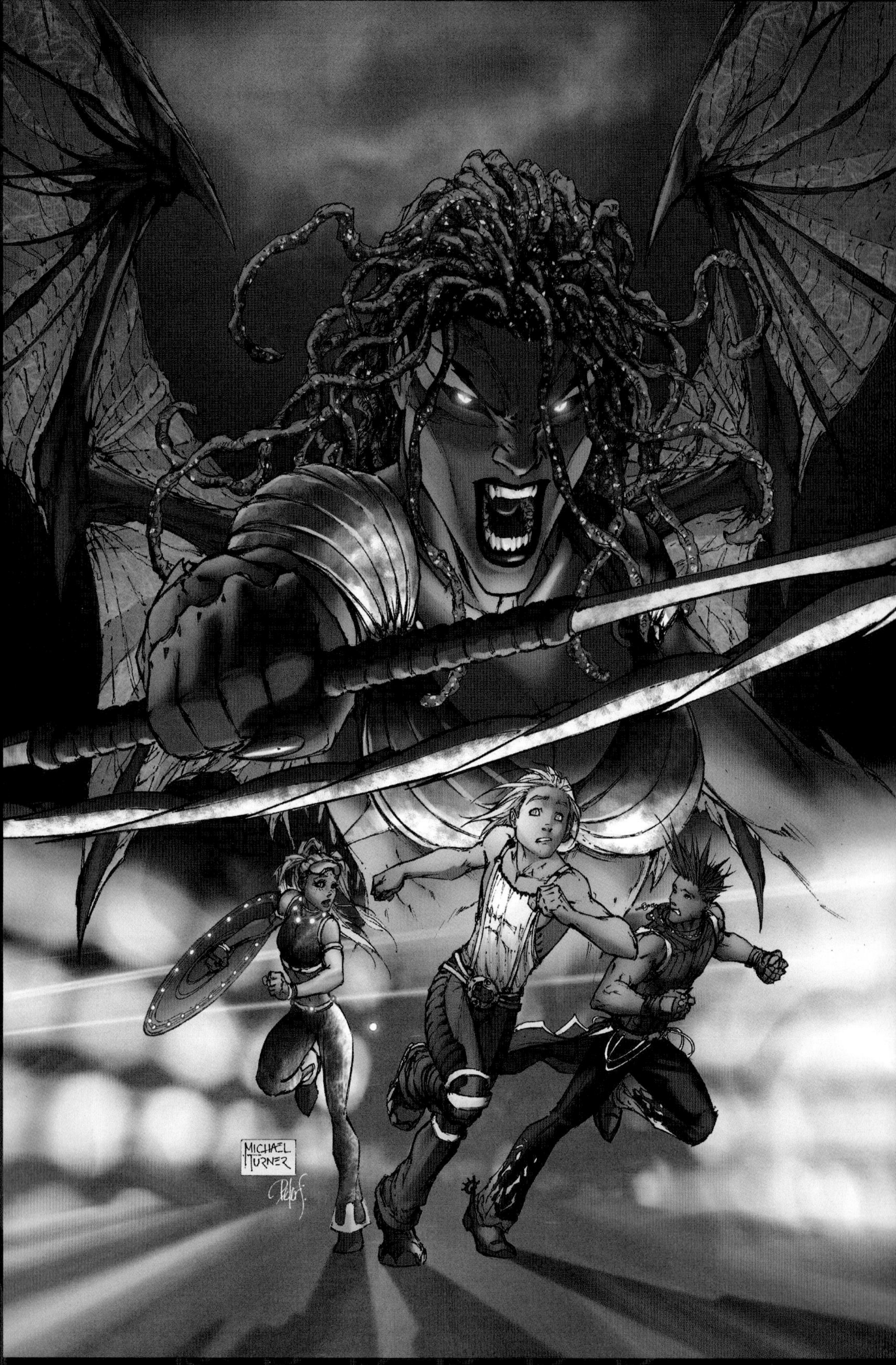
MICHAEL TURNER

Cover A

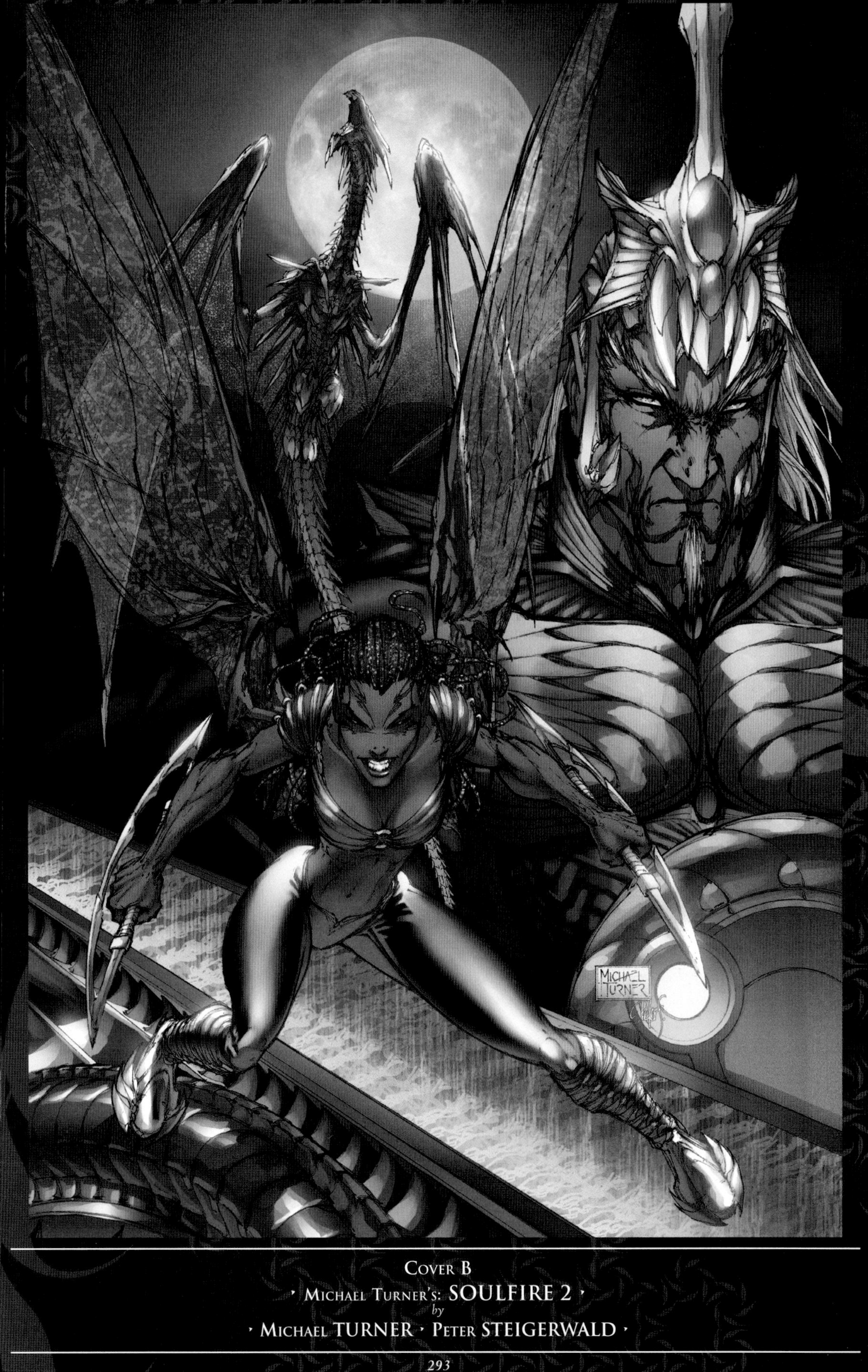
MICHAEL TURNER

Cover B

· Michael Turner's: SOULFIRE 2 ·

by

· Michael TURNER · Peter STEIGERWALD ·

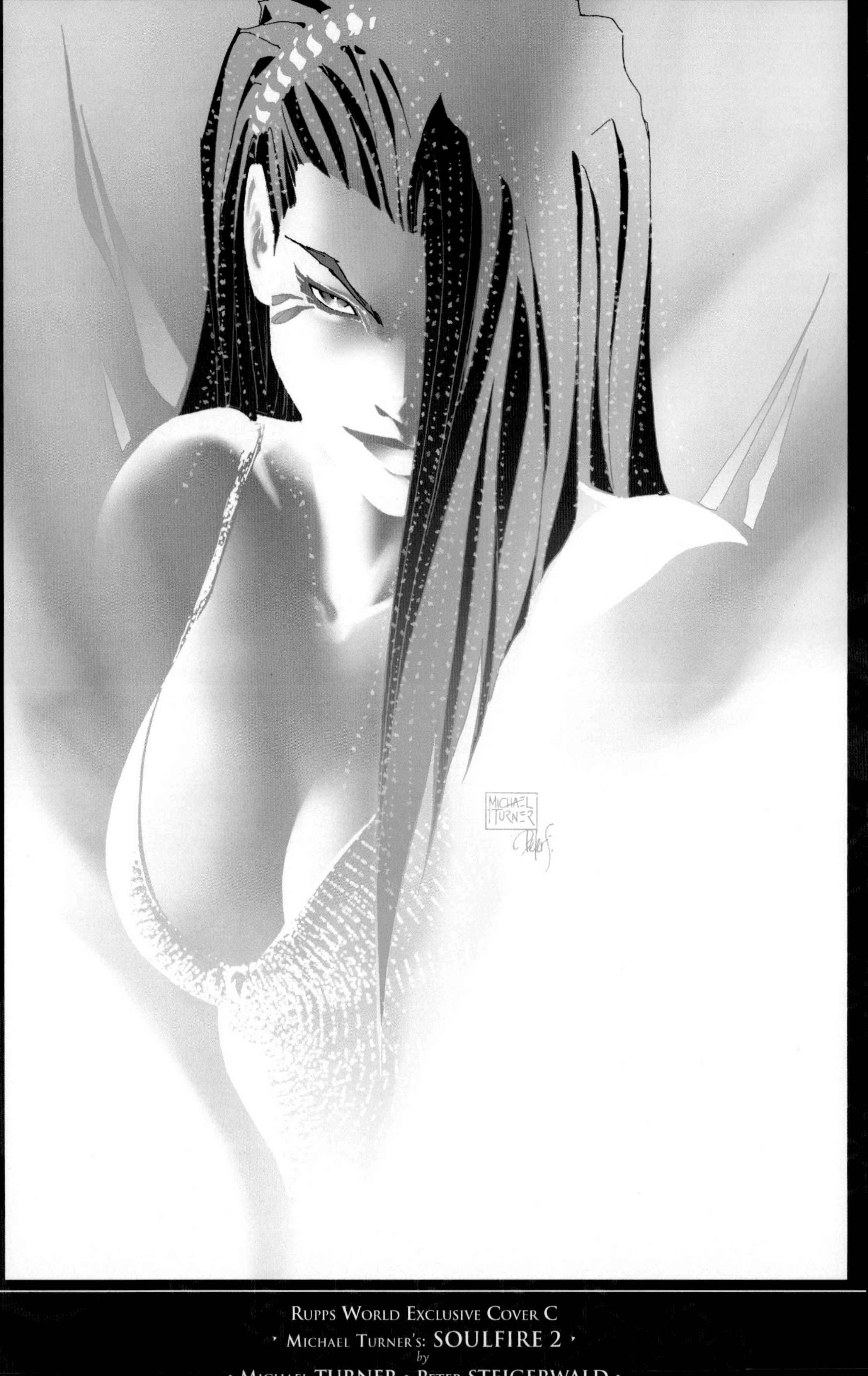
MICHAEL TURNER

Rupps World Exclusive Cover C
· Michael Turner's: SOULFIRE 2 ·
by
· Michael TURNER · Peter STEIGERWALD ·

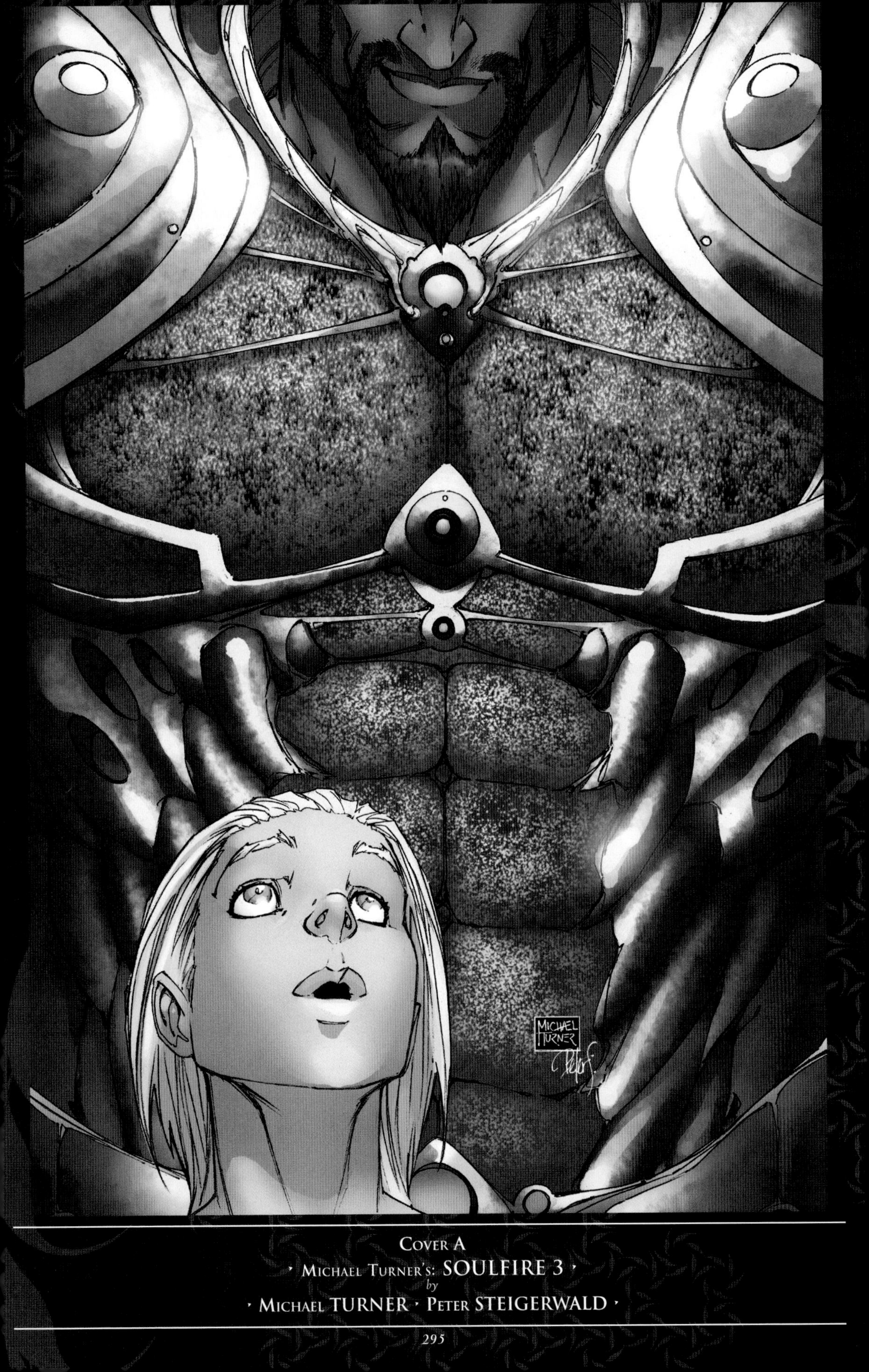
MICHAEL TURNER

Cover A
· Michael Turner's: SOULFIRE 3 ·
by
· Michael TURNER · Peter STEIGERWALD ·

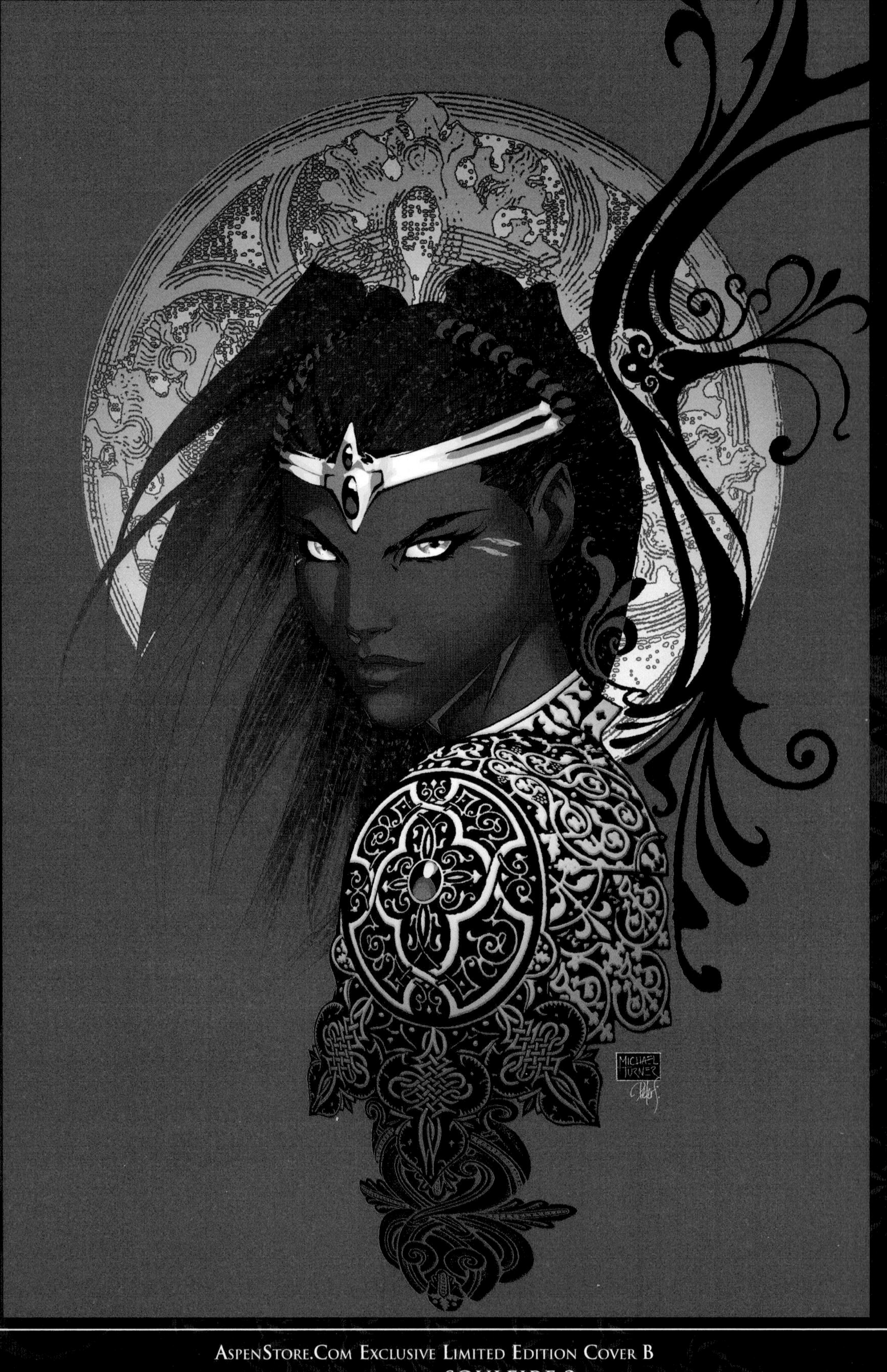
MICHAEL TURNER

AspenStore.Com Exclusive Limited Edition Cover B
· Michael Turner's: SOULFIRE 3 ·
by
· Michael TURNER · Peter STEIGERWALD ·

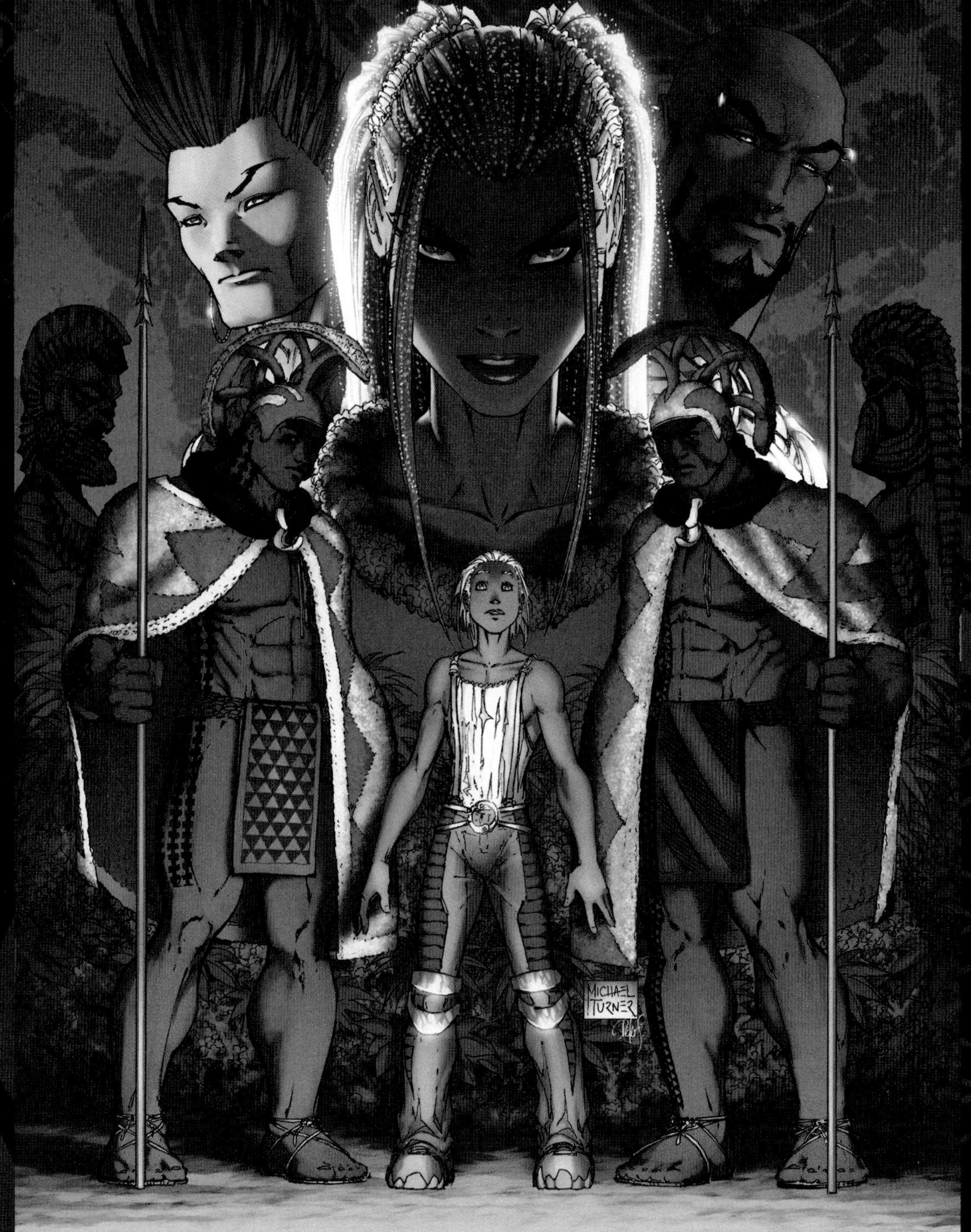
MICHAEL TURNER

Cover A
· Michael Turner's: SOULFIRE 4 ·
by
· Michael TURNER · Peter STEIGERWALD ·

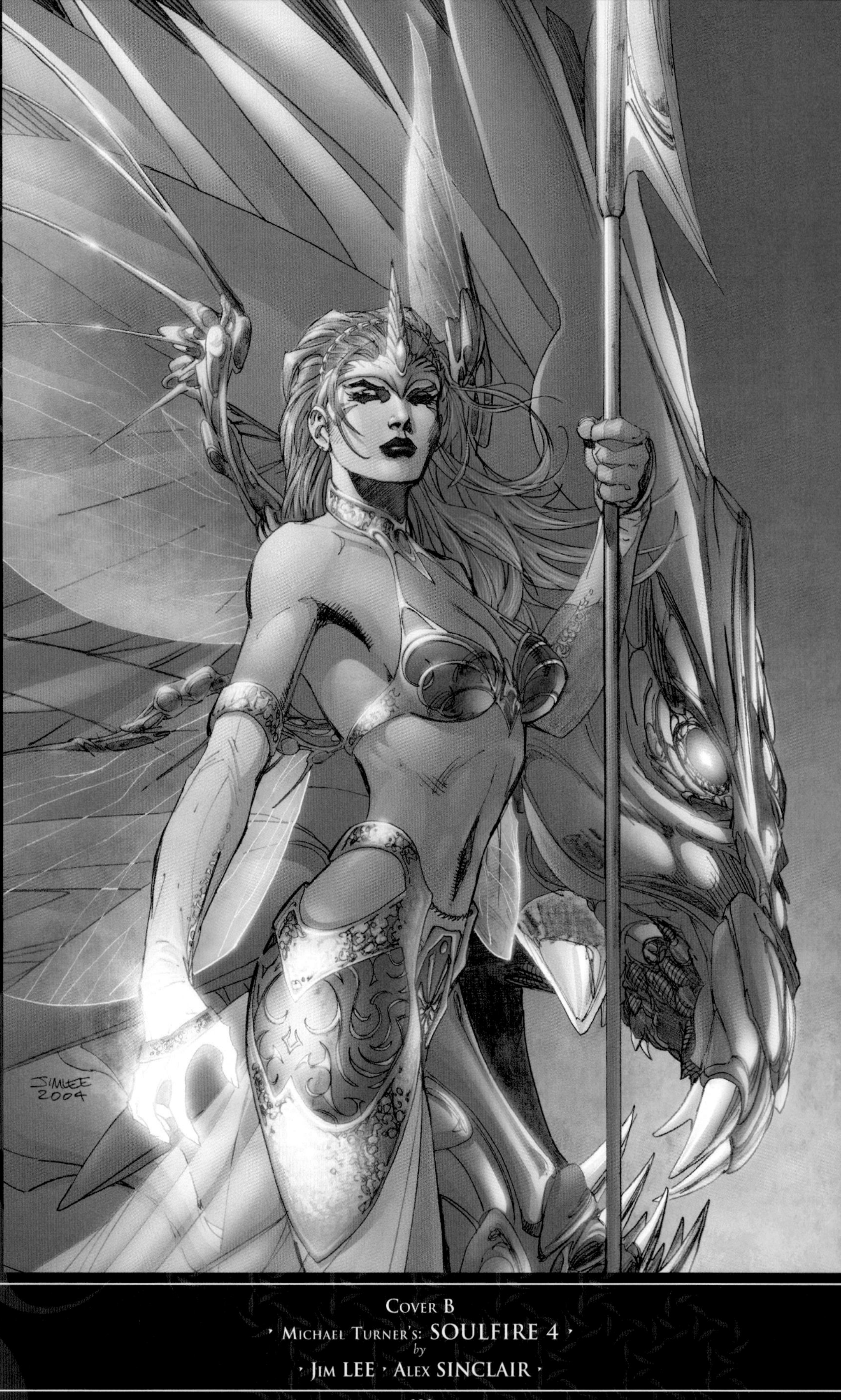

Cover B
‹ Michael Turner's: SOULFIRE 4 ›
by
‹ Jim LEE ‹ Alex SINCLAIR ›

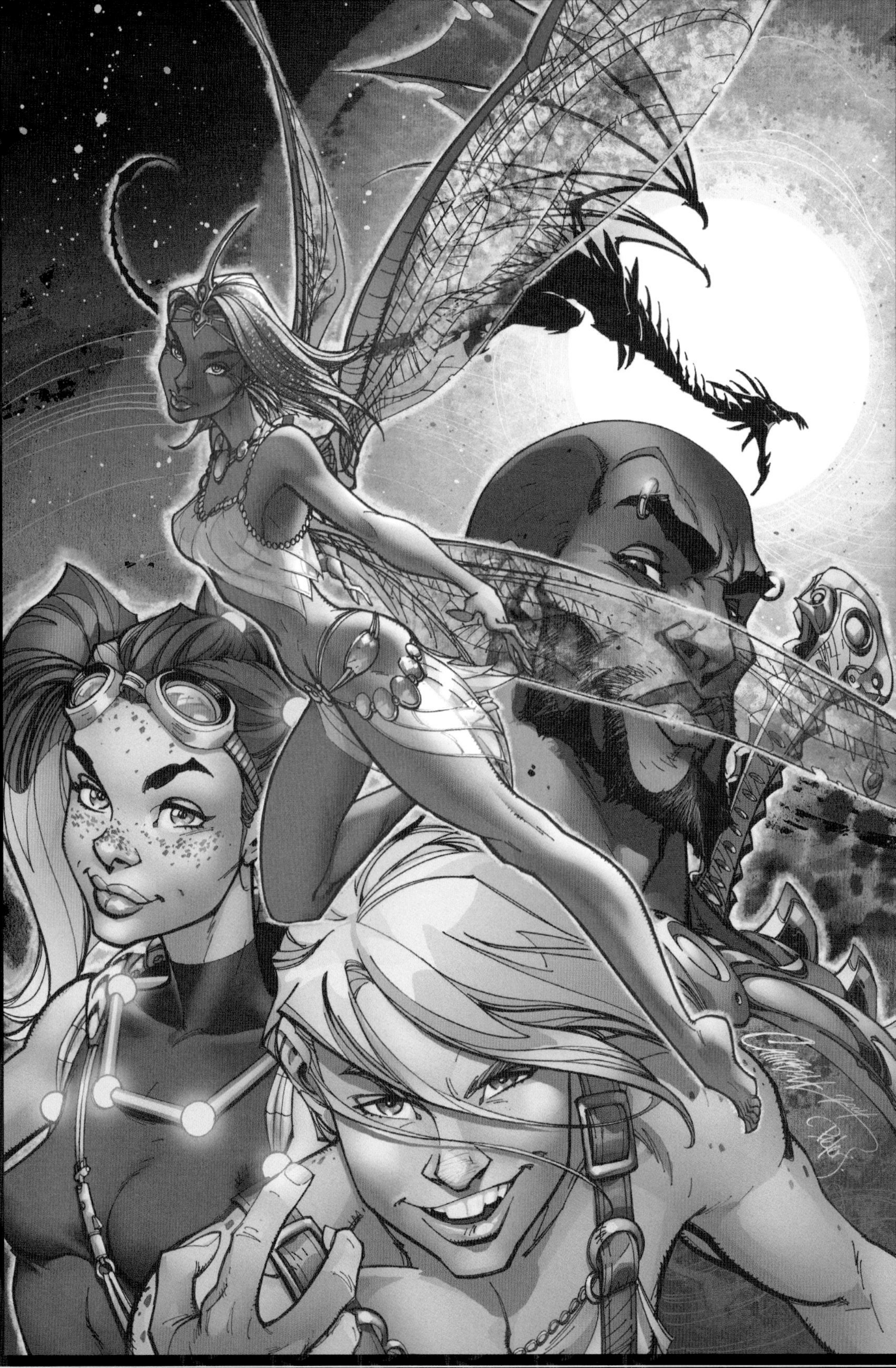

Cover C
· Michael Turner's: SOULFIRE 4 ·
by
· J. Scott CAMPBELL · Peter STEIGERWALD ·

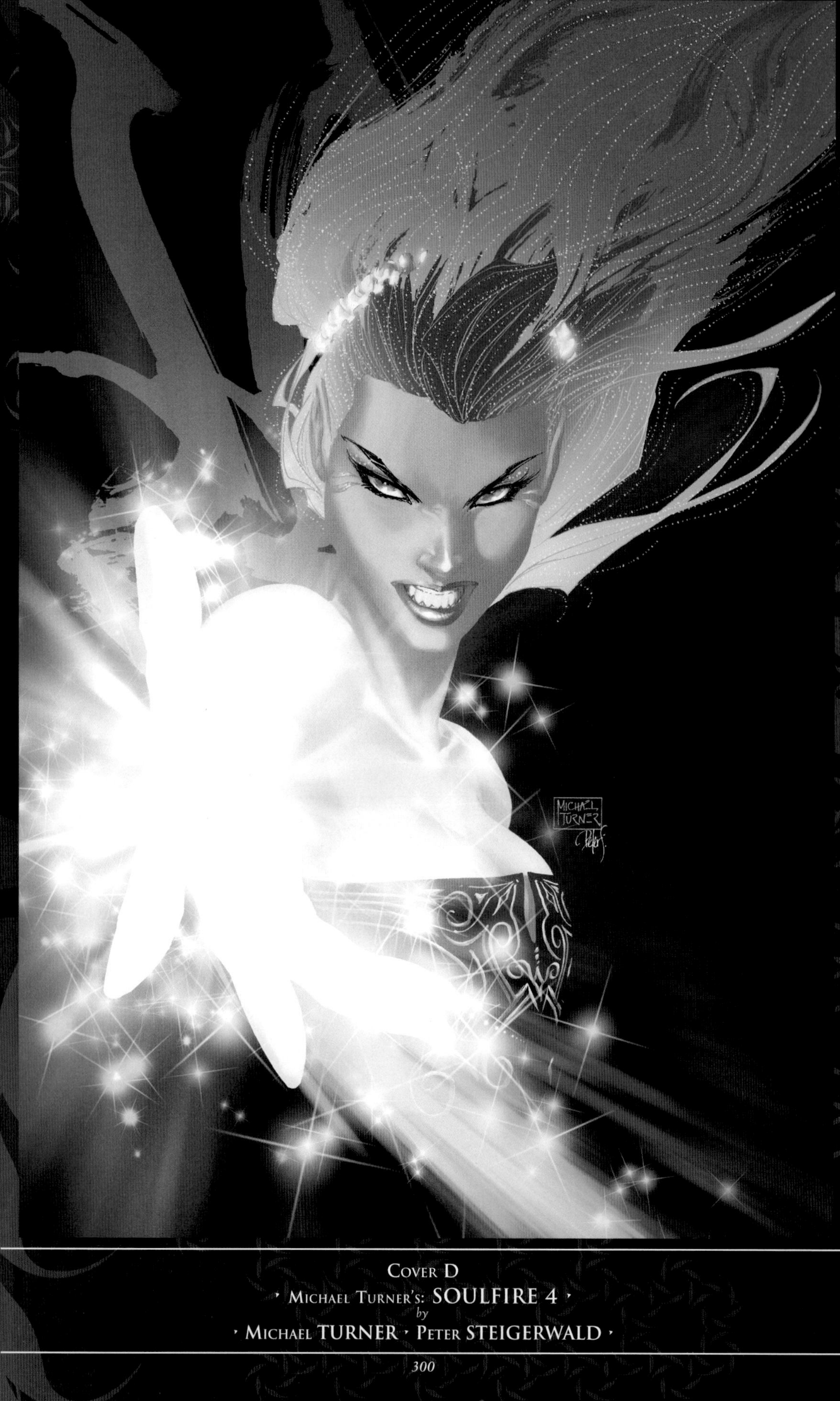
MICHAEL TURNER

Cover D
· Michael Turner's: SOULFIRE 4 ·
by
· Michael TURNER · Peter STEIGERWALD ·

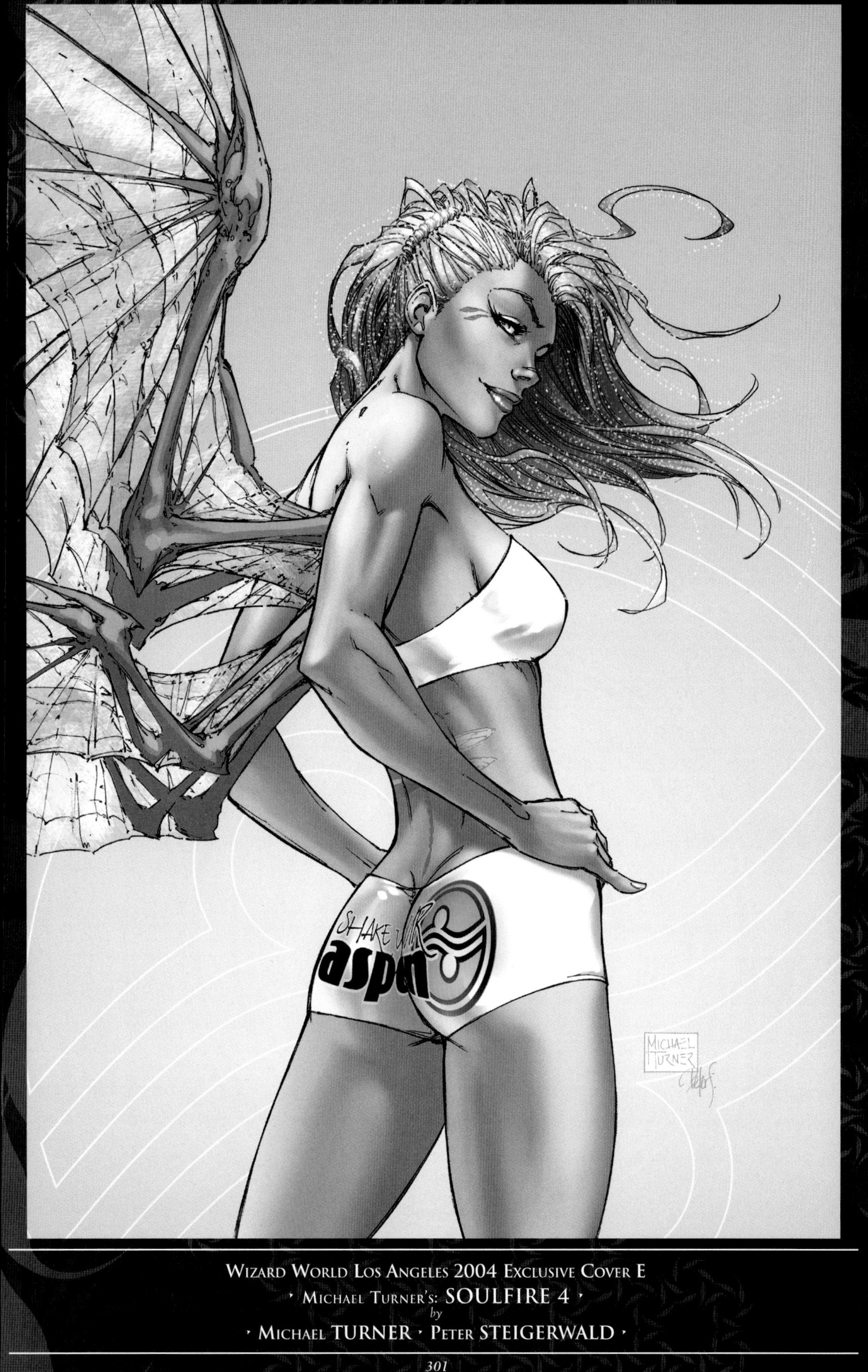
SHAKE YUR
aspen
MICHAEL TURNER

Wizard World Los Angeles 2004 Exclusive Cover E

· Michael Turner's: SOULFIRE 4 ·

by

· Michael TURNER · Peter STEIGERWALD ·

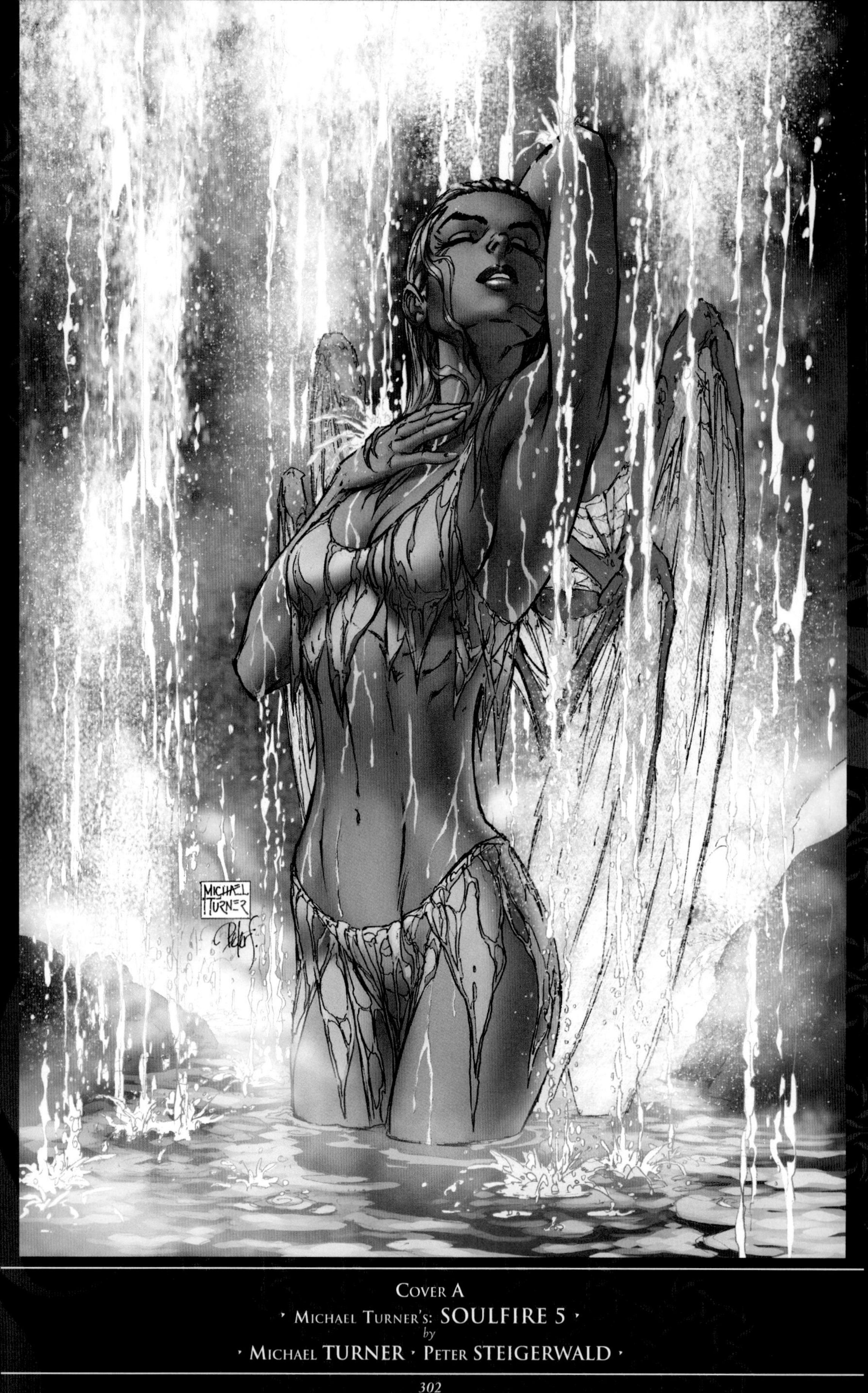
MICHAEL TURNER

Cover A

· Michael Turner's: SOULFIRE 5 ·

by

· Michael TURNER · Peter STEIGERWALD ·

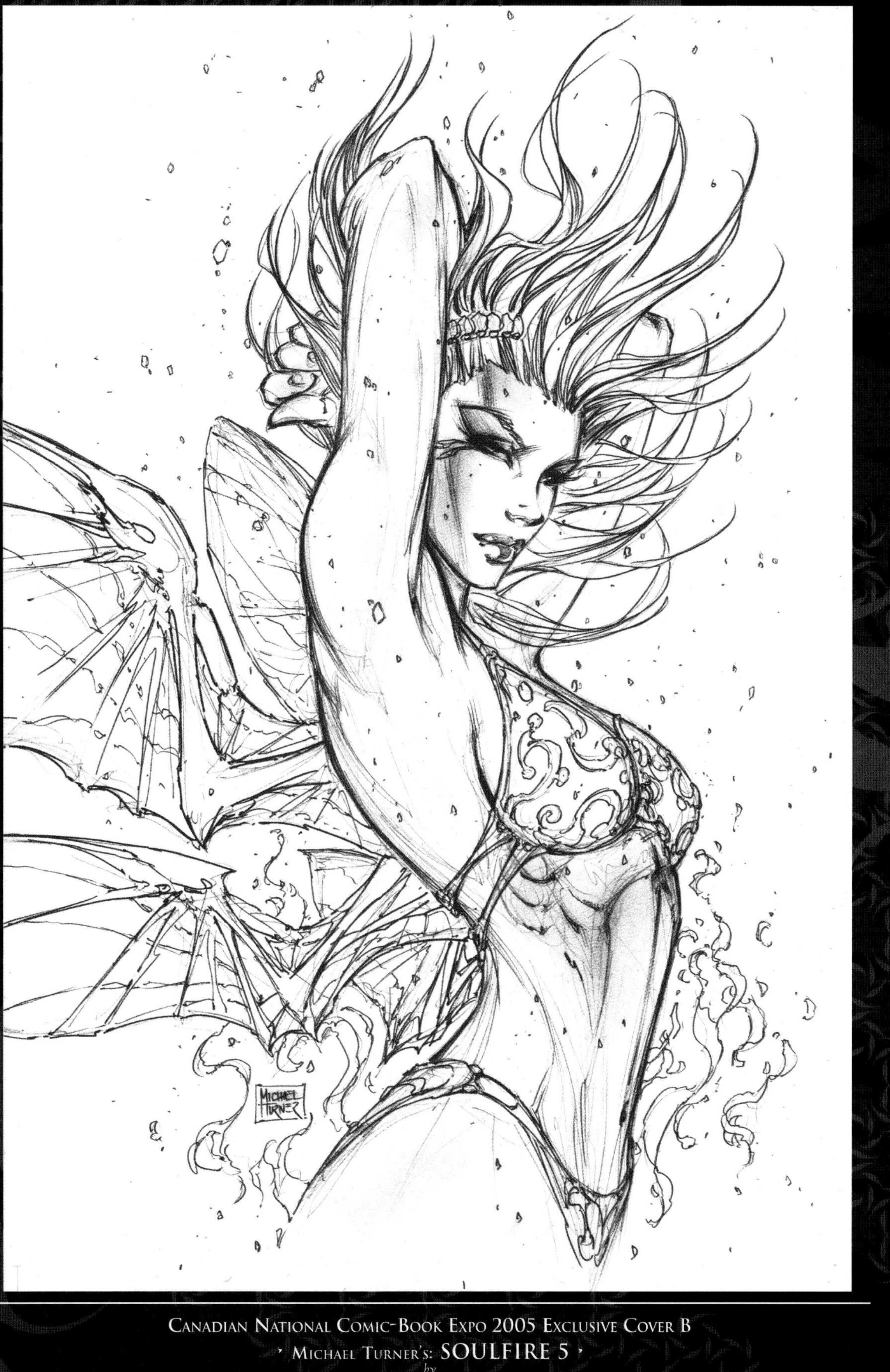

Canadian National Comic-Book Expo 2005 Exclusive Cover B
‹ Michael Turner's: SOULFIRE 5 ›
by
‹ Michael TURNER ›

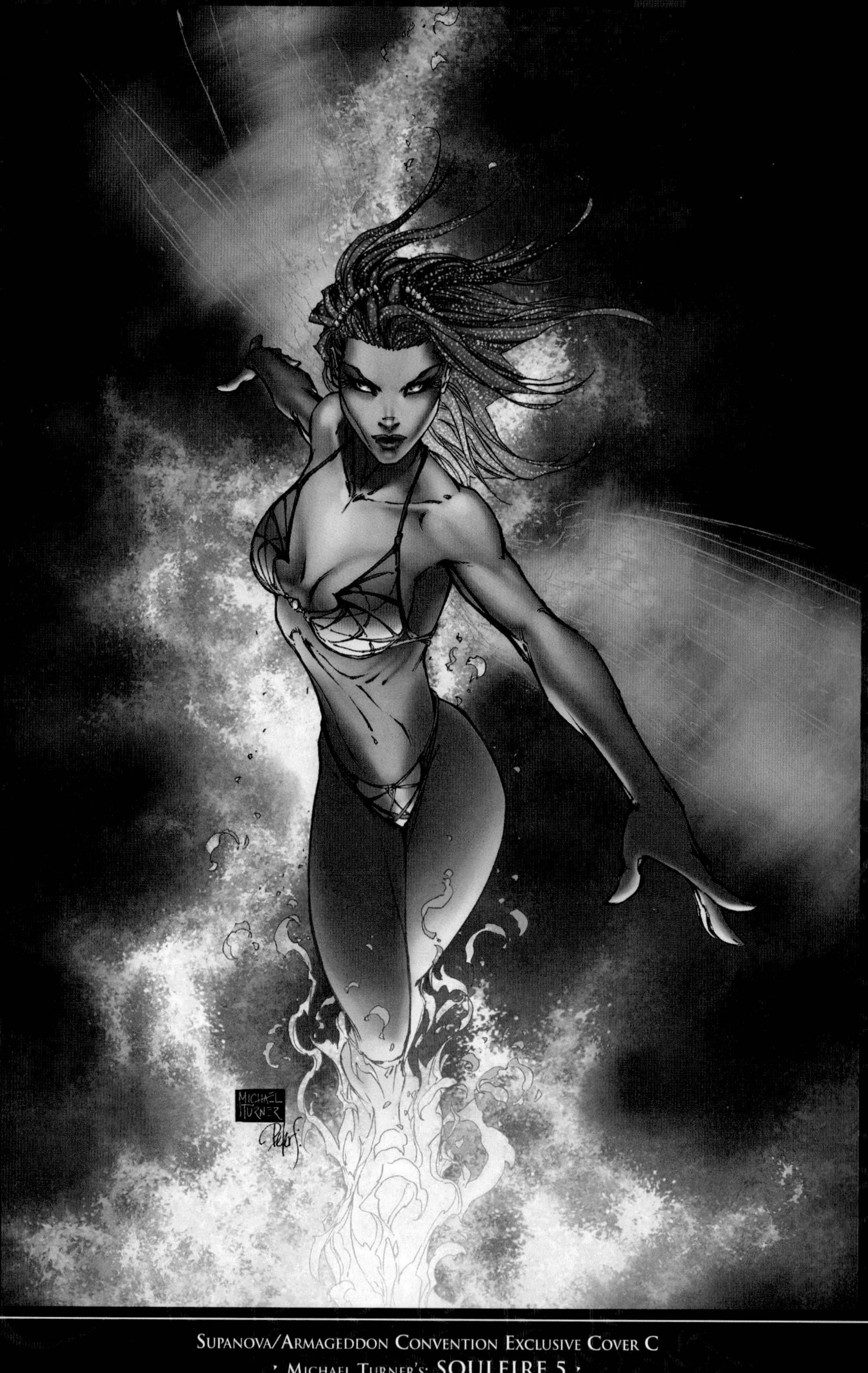
MICHAEL TURNER

SUPANOVA/ARMAGEDDON CONVENTION EXCLUSIVE COVER C
· MICHAEL TURNER'S: SOULFIRE 5 ·
by
· MICHAEL TURNER · PETER STEIGERWALD ·

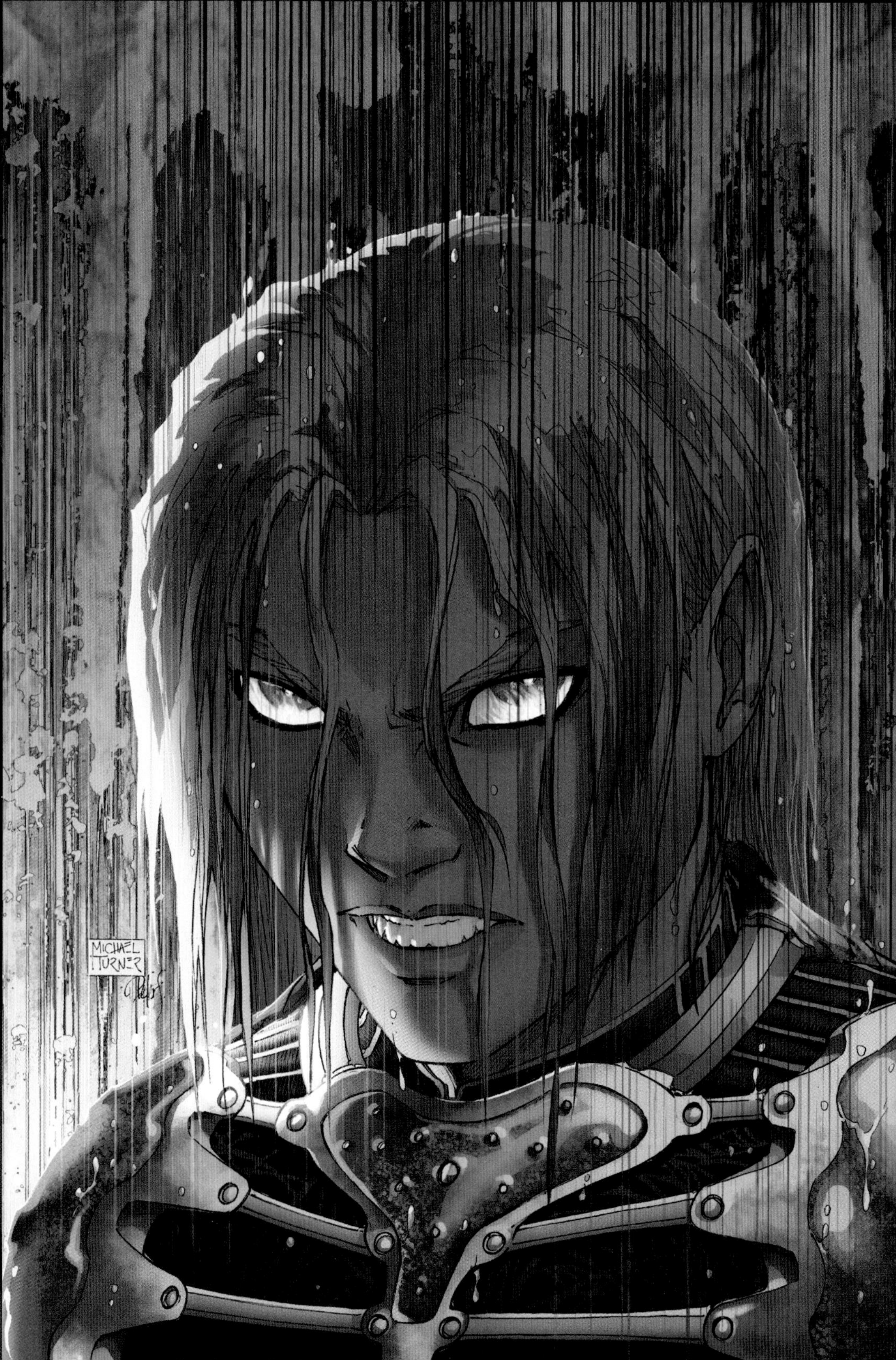
MICHAEL TURNER

Cover A
· Michael Turner's: SOULFIRE 6 ·
by
· Michael TURNER · Peter STEIGERWALD ·

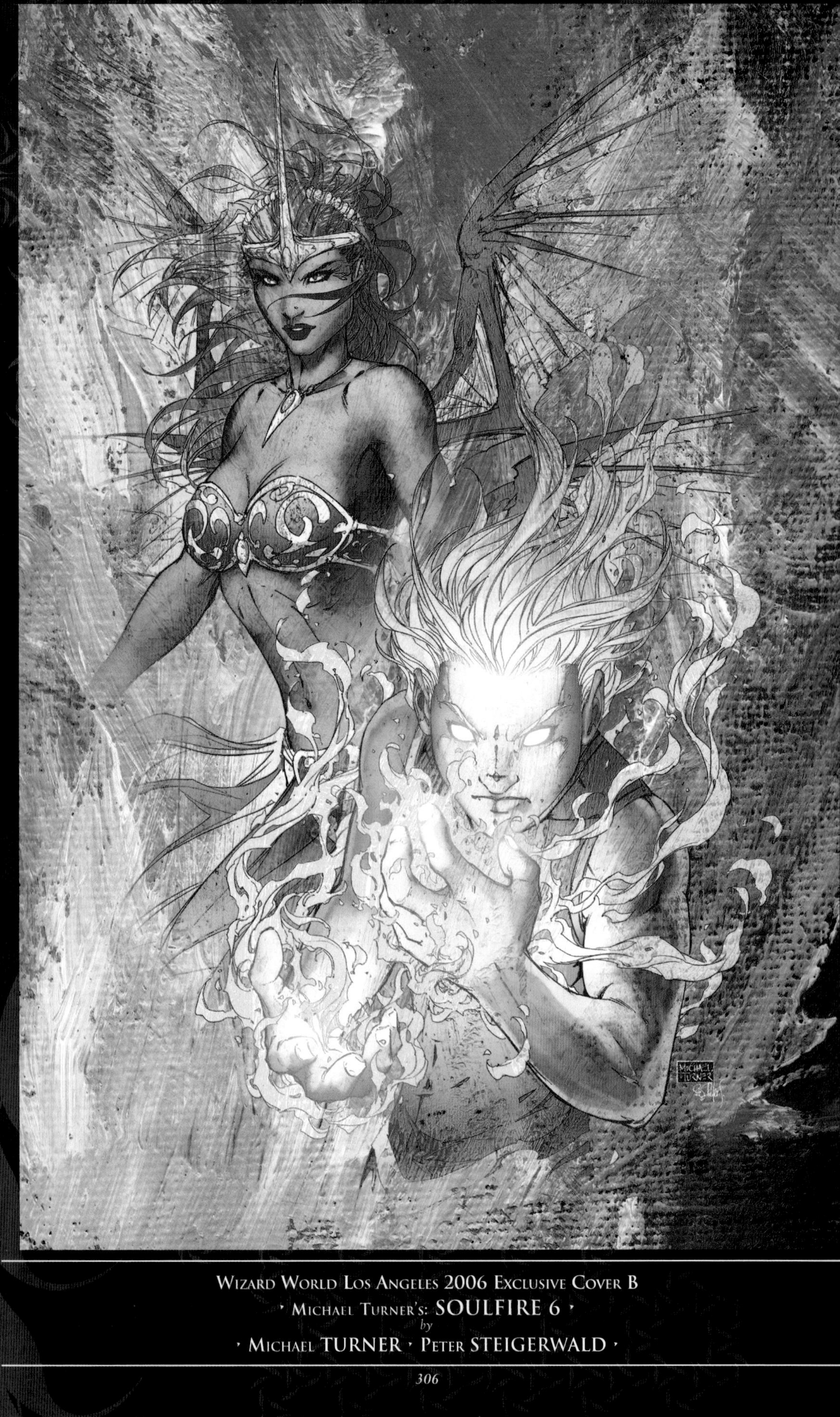
MICHAEL TURNER

Wizard World Los Angeles 2006 Exclusive Cover B
· Michael Turner's: SOULFIRE 6 ·
by
· Michael TURNER · Peter STEIGERWALD ·

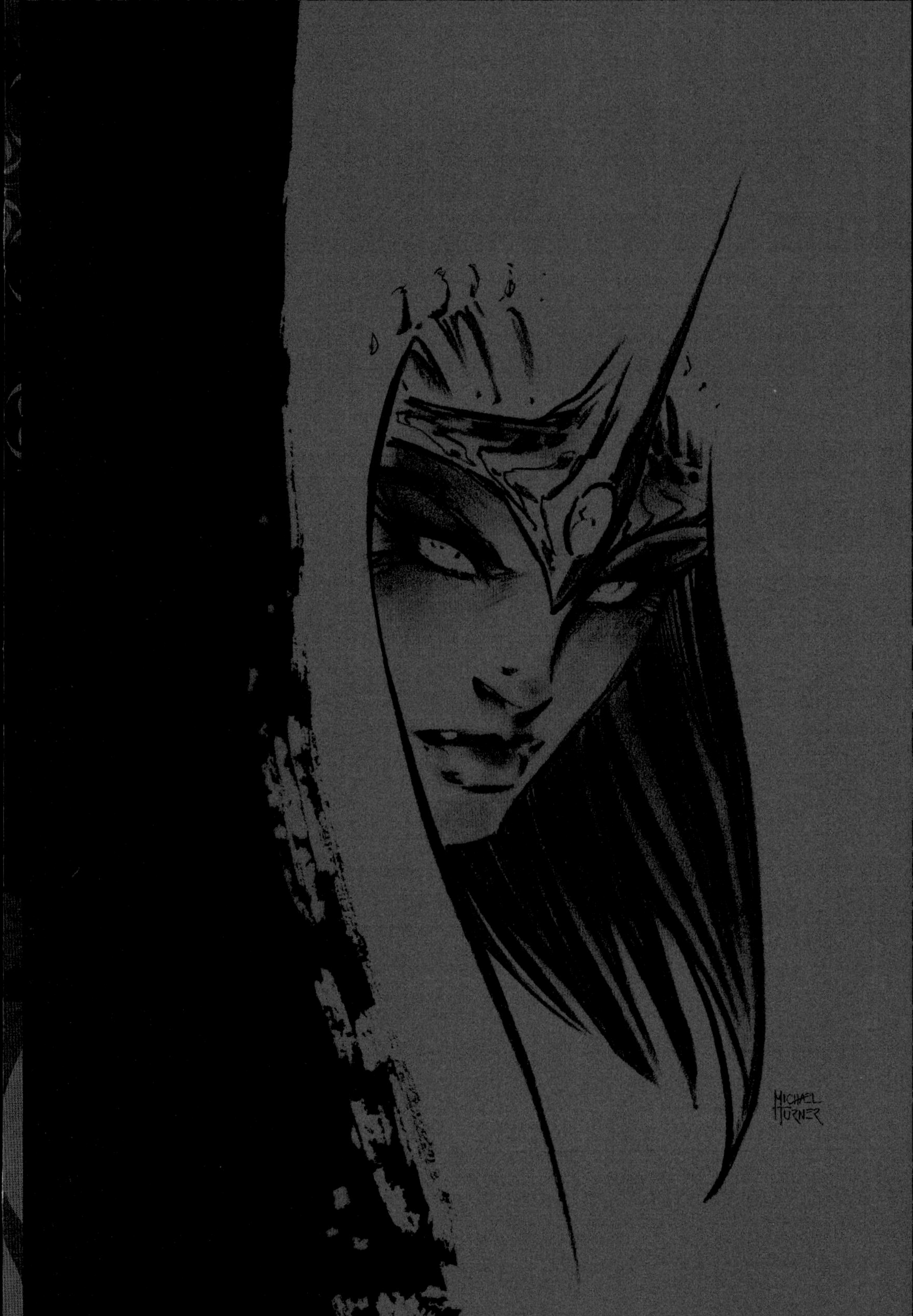
MICHAEL TURNER

Wizard World Los Angeles 2006 V.I.P. Exclusive Cover C
· Michael Turner's: SOULFIRE 6 ·
by
· Michael TURNER ·

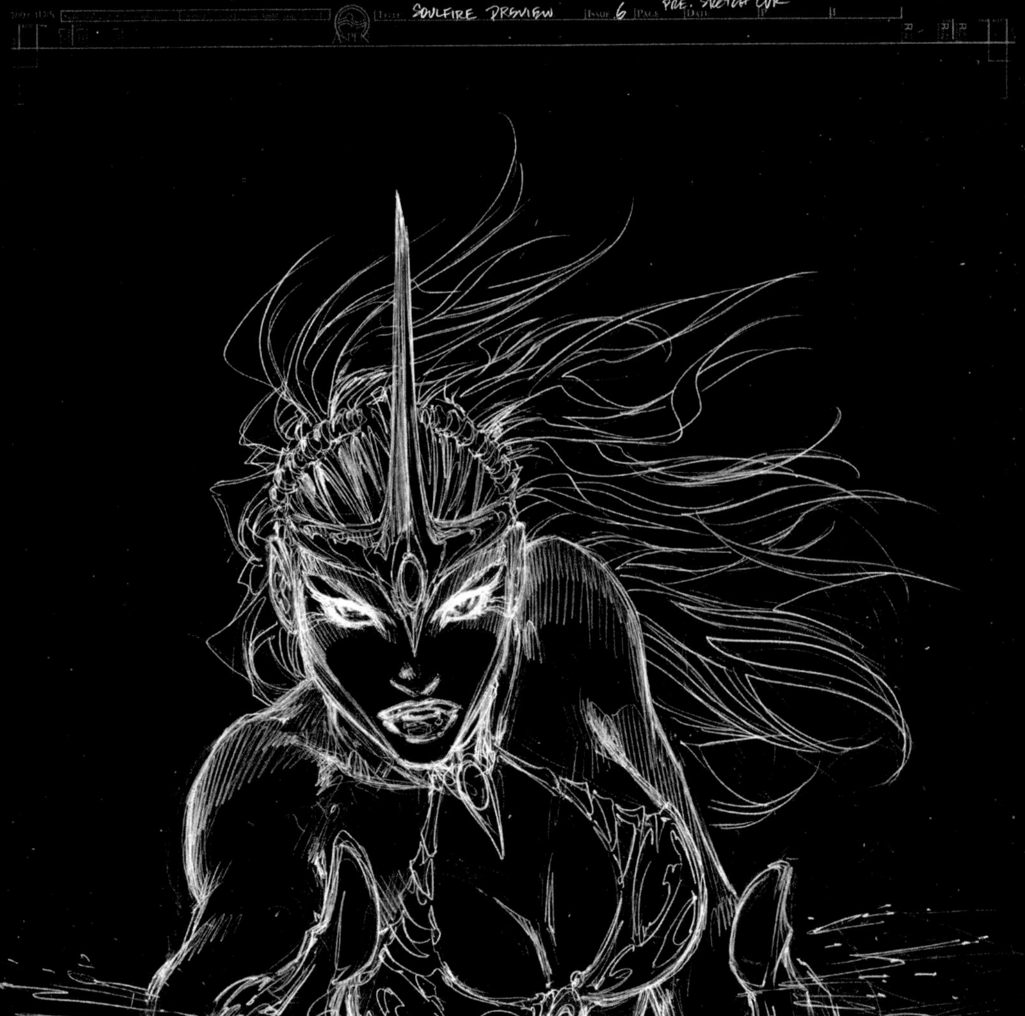
SOULFIRE PREVIEW
ISSUE 6
PRE. SKETCH CVR
MICHAEL TURNER
Printed by Blue Line Pro, WWW.BLUELINEPRO.COM

WIZARD WORLD LOS ANGELES 2006 EXCLUSIVE COVER B

· MICHAEL TURNER'S: SOULFIRE/SHRUGGED PREVIEW ·

by

· MICHAEL TURNER ·

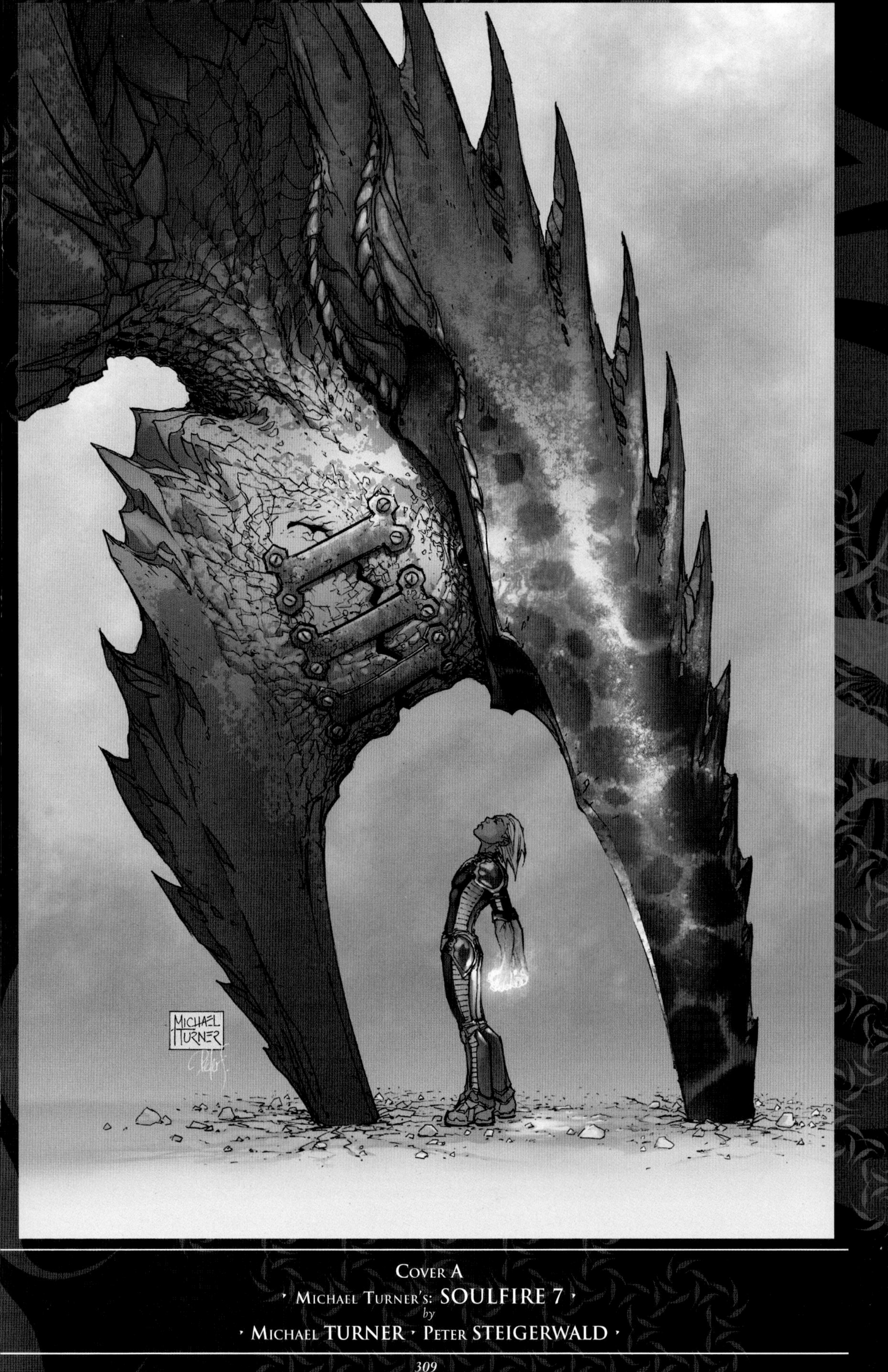
MICHAEL
TURNER

Cover A
‣ Michael Turner's: SOULFIRE 7 ‣
by
‣ Michael TURNER ‣ Peter STEIGERWALD ‣

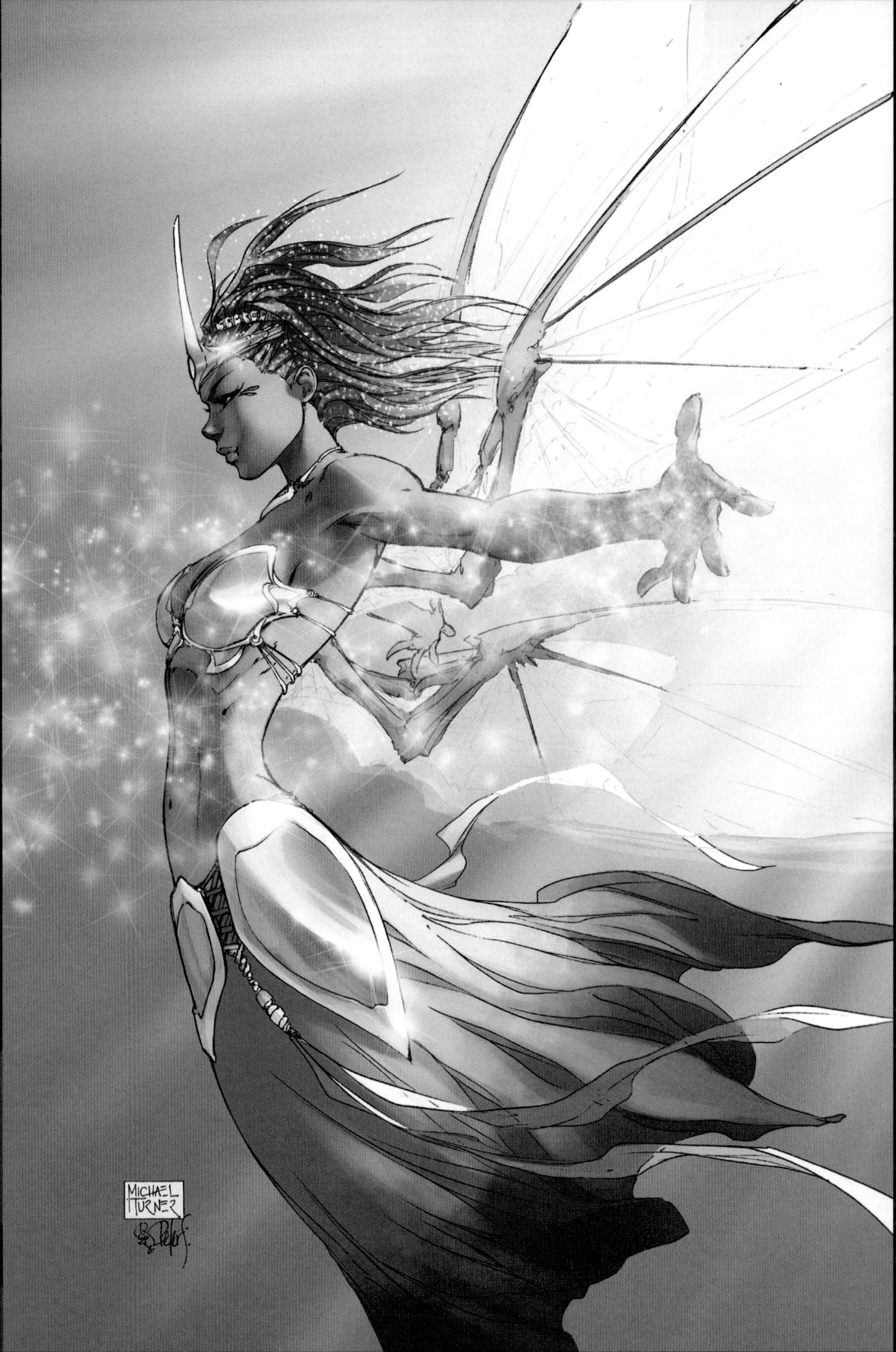
MICHAEL TURNER

Wizard World Philadelphia 2006 Exclusive Cover B
· Michael Turner's: SOULFIRE 7 ·
by
· Michael TURNER · Peter STEIGERWALD ·

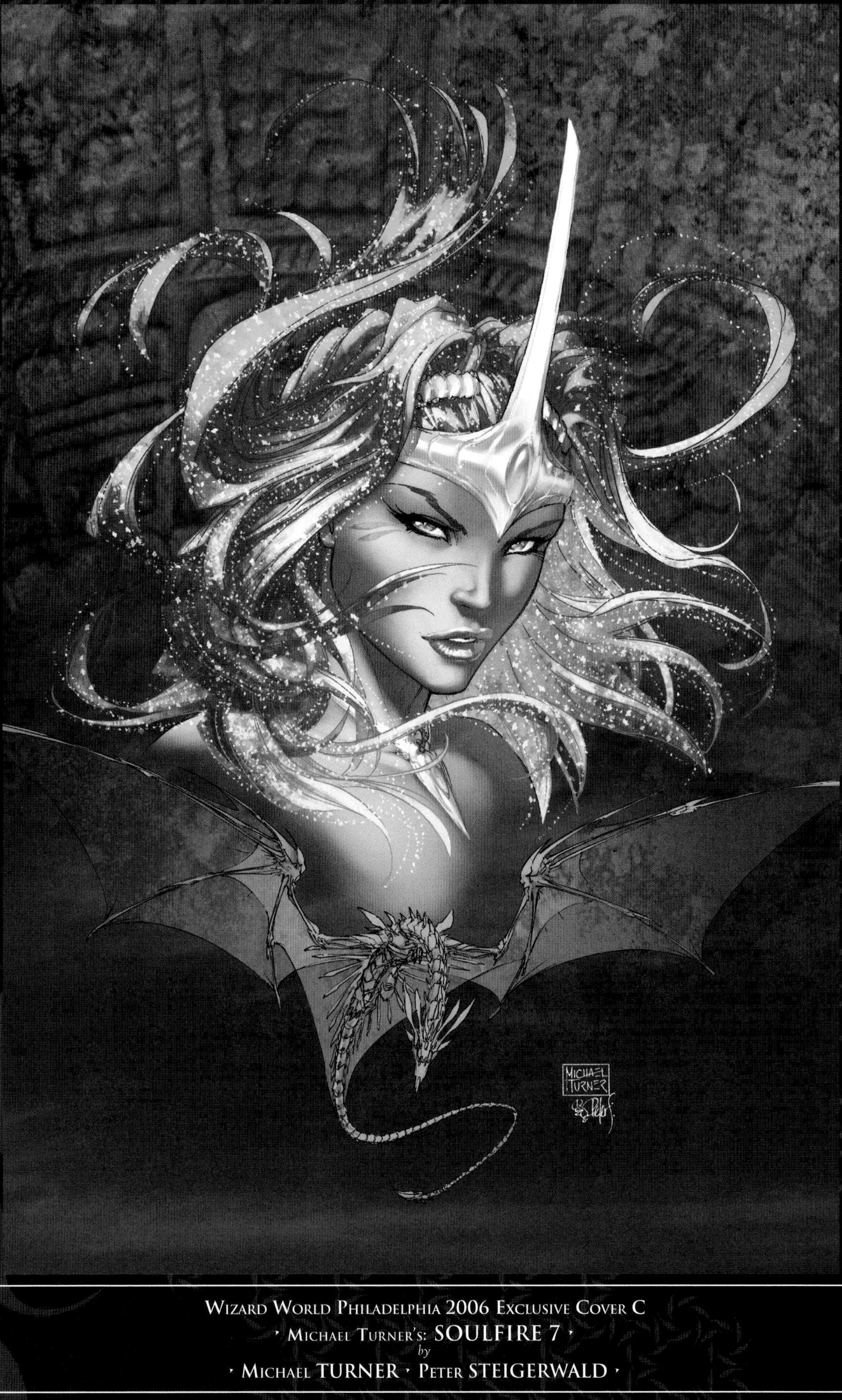
MICHAEL
TURNER

Wizard World Philadelphia 2006 Exclusive Cover C
· Michael Turner's: SOULFIRE 7 ·
by
· Michael TURNER · Peter STEIGERWALD ·

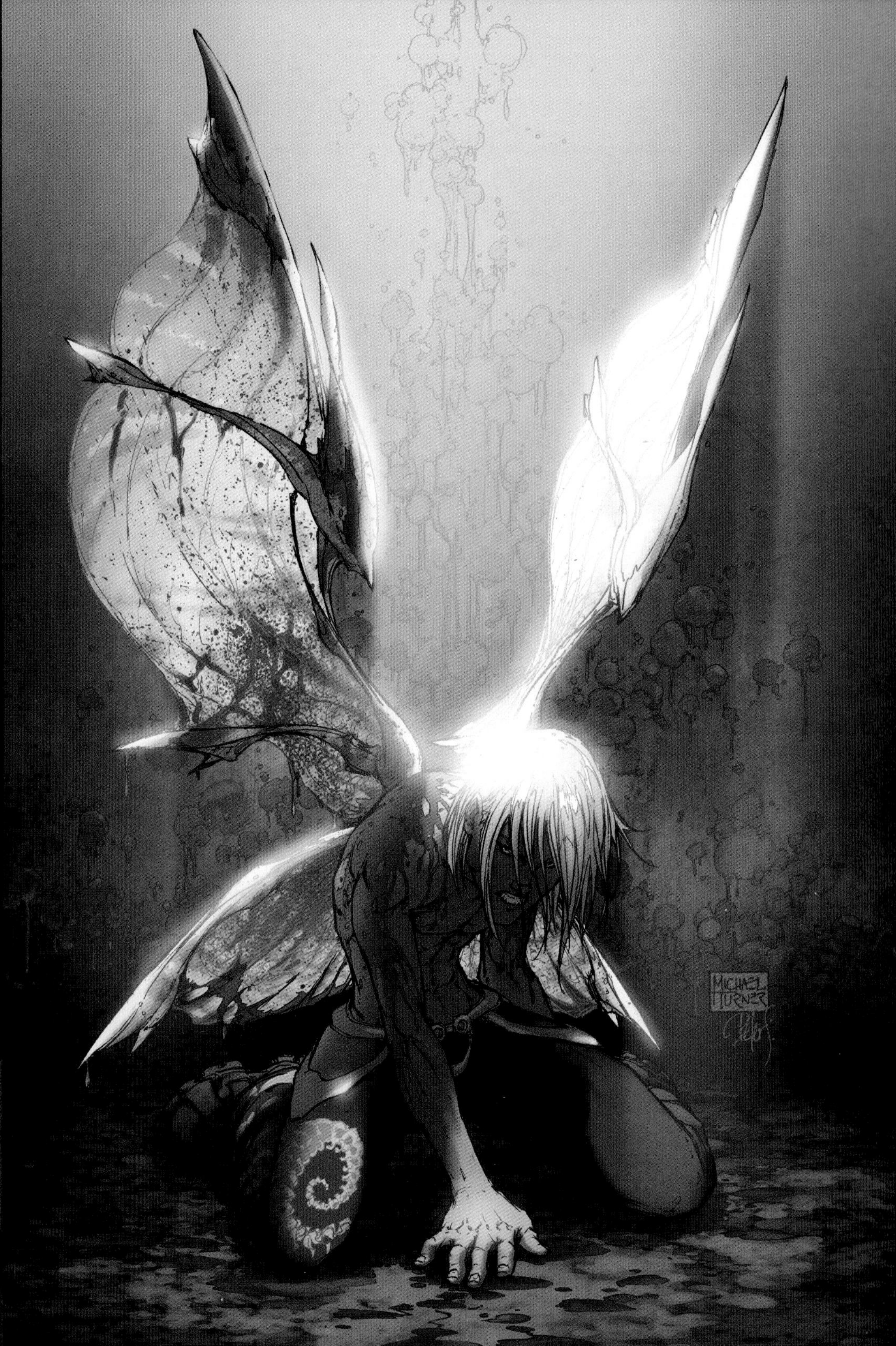
MICHAEL TURNER

Cover A

· Michael Turner's: SOULFIRE 8 ·

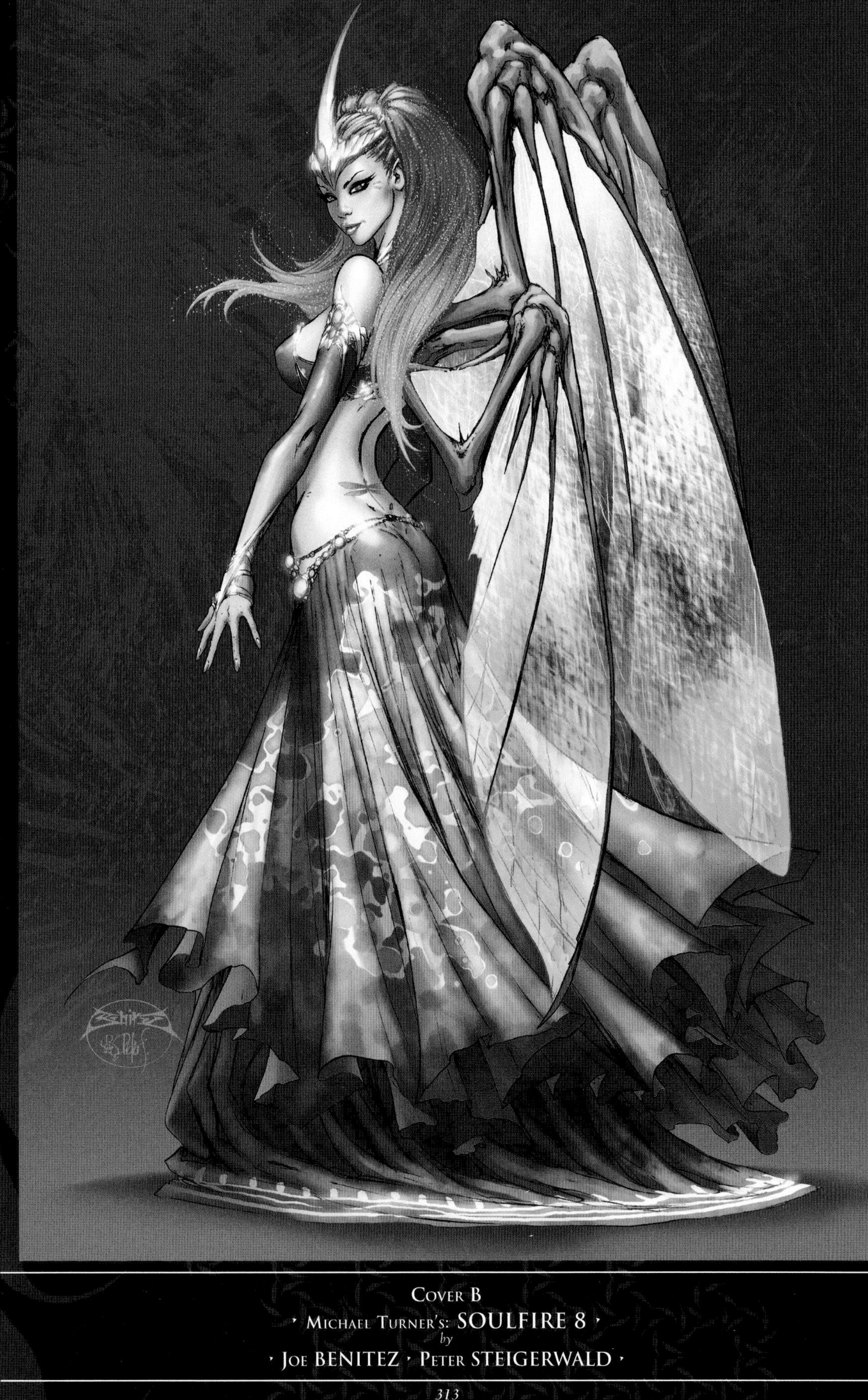

Cover B
· Michael Turner's: SOULFIRE 8 ·
by
· Joe BENITEZ · Peter STEIGERWALD ·

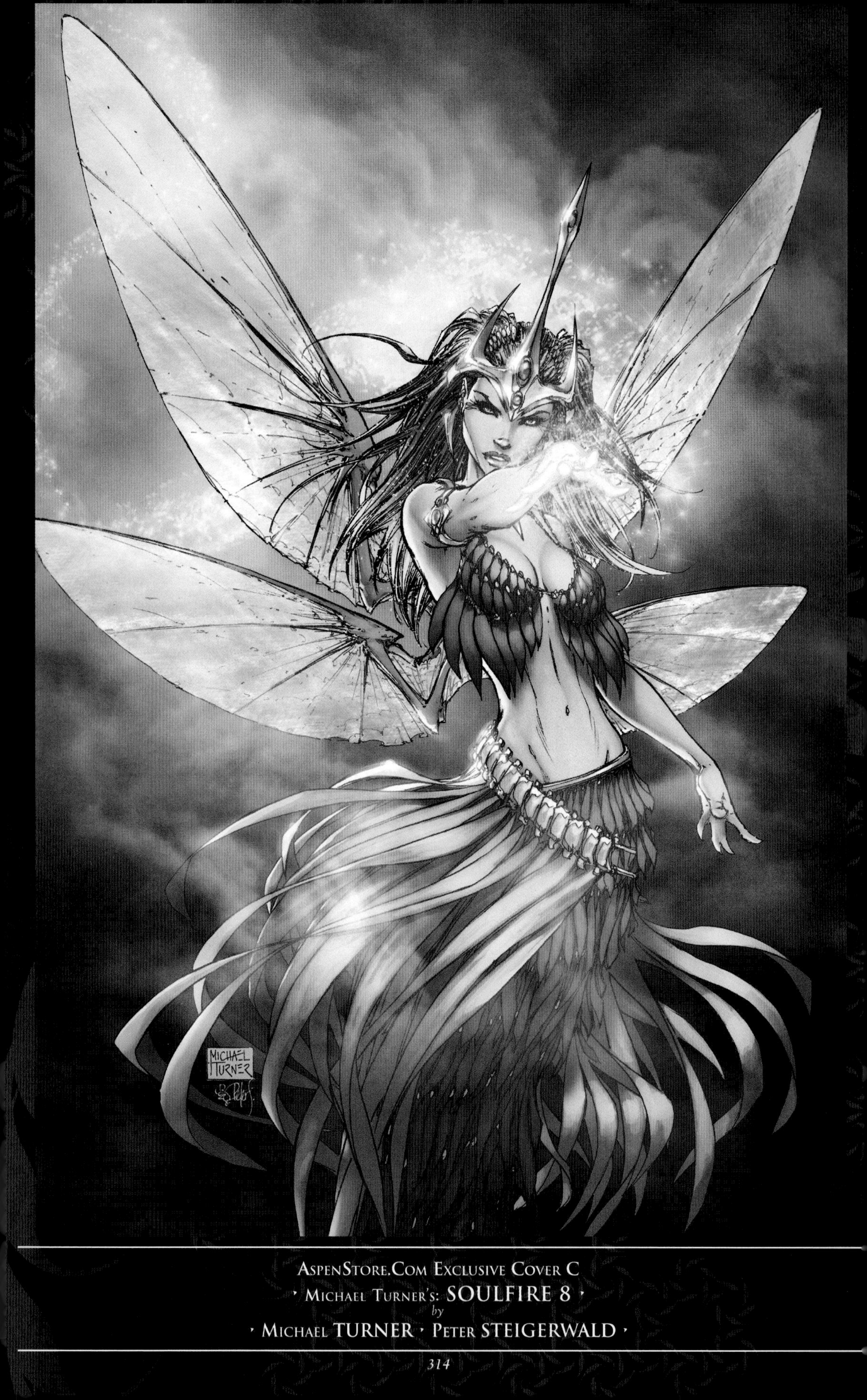
MICHAEL TURNER

AspenStore.Com Exclusive Cover C
· Michael Turner's: SOULFIRE 8 ·
by
· Michael TURNER · Peter STEIGERWALD ·

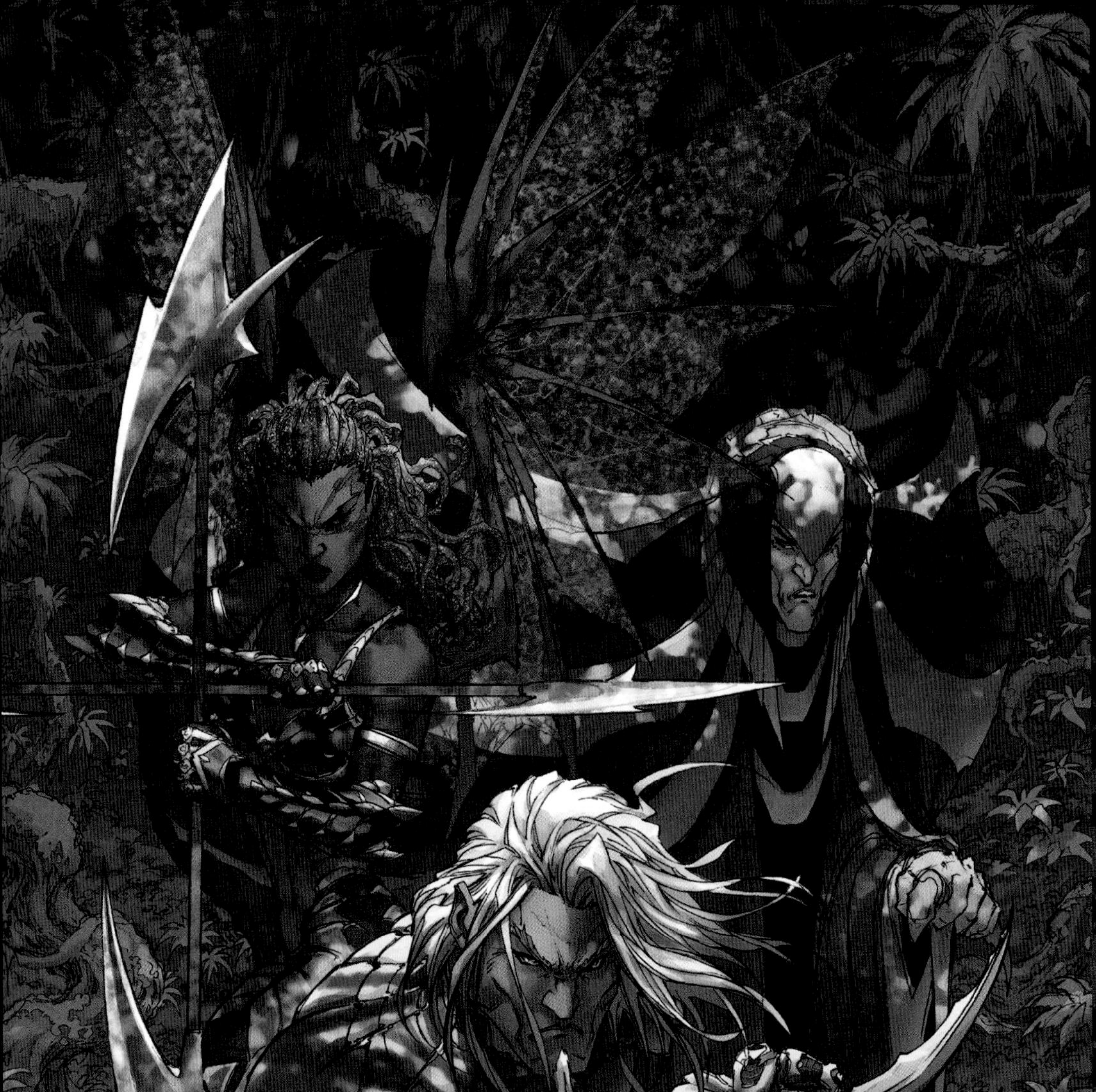
MICHAEL TURNER

Cover A
· Michael Turner's: SOULFIRE 9 ·
by
· Michael TURNER · Peter STEIGERWALD ·

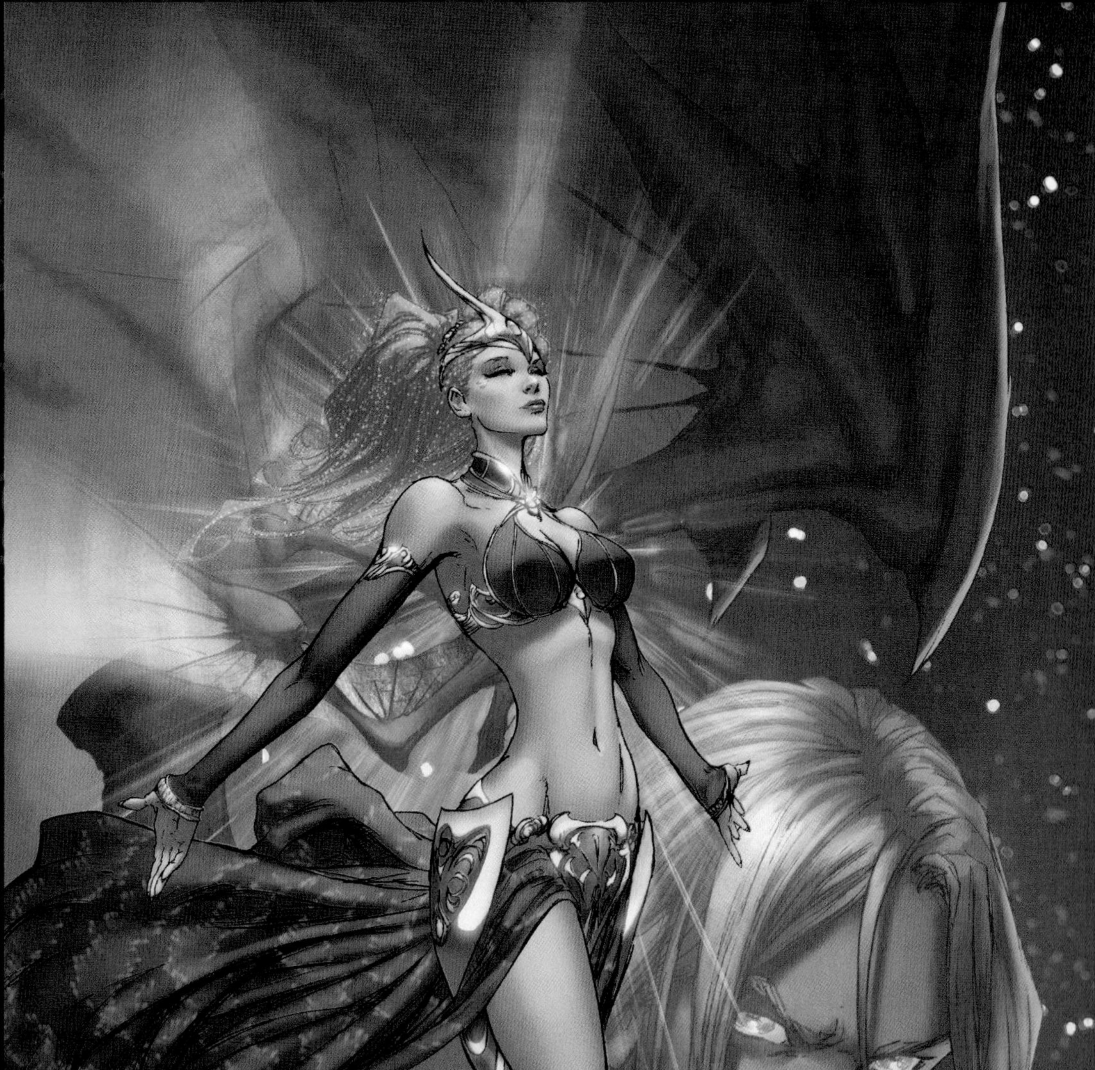

Cover B
· Michael Turner's: SOULFIRE 9 ·
by
· Joe BENITEZ · Peter STEIGERWALD ·

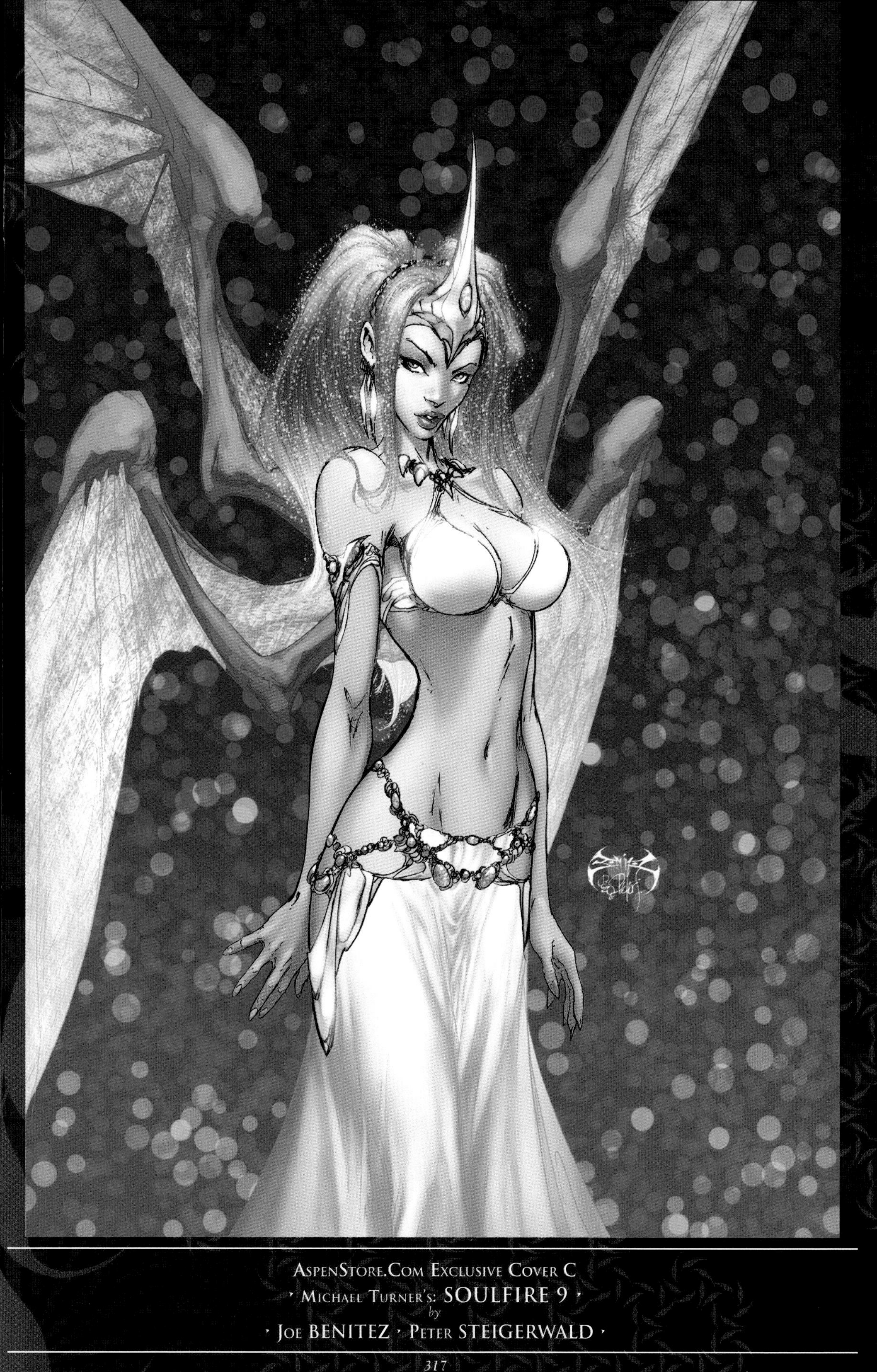

AspenStore.Com Exclusive Cover C
‣ Michael Turner's: SOULFIRE 9 ‣
by
‣ Joe BENITEZ ‣ Peter STEIGERWALD ‣

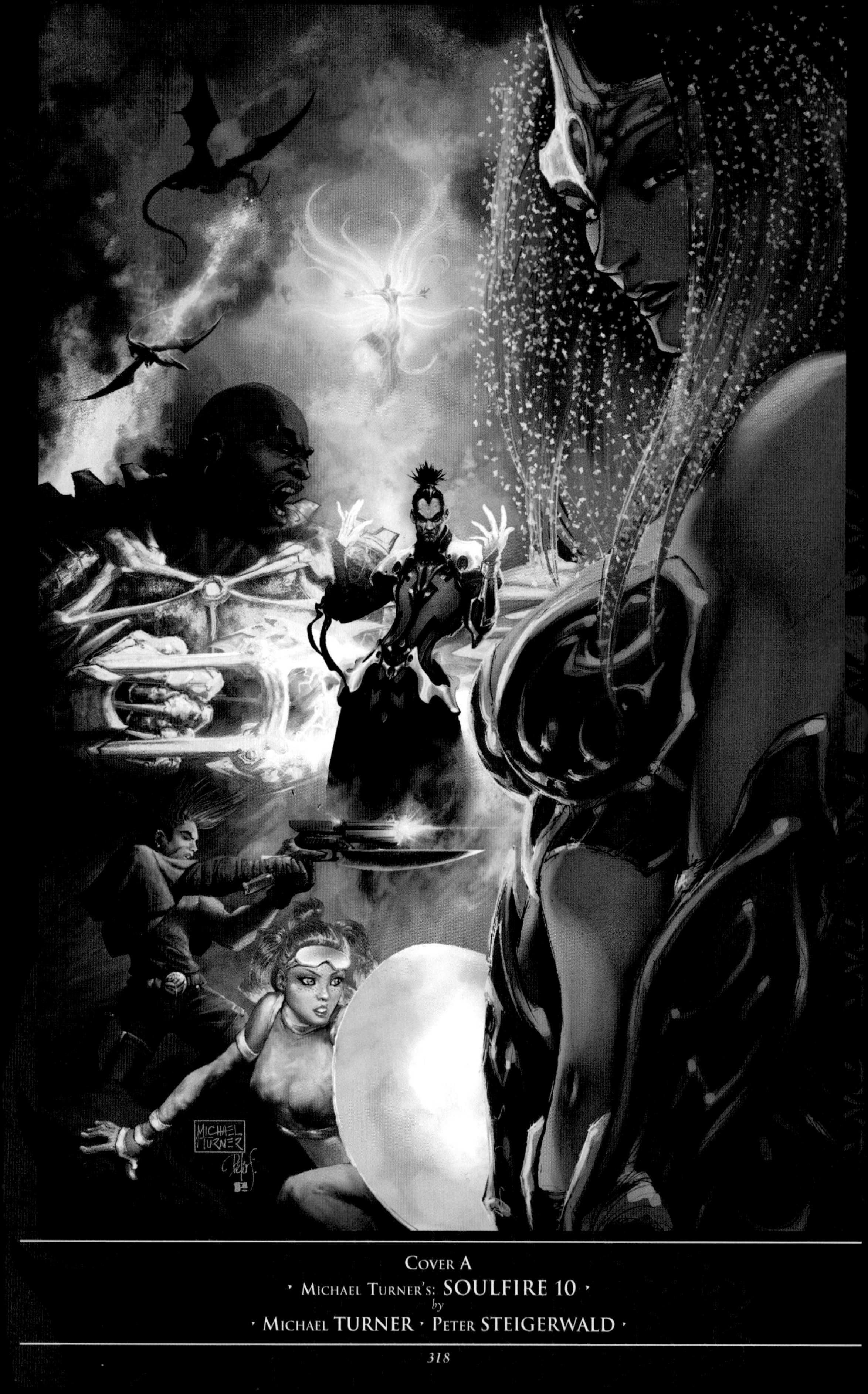
MICHAEL TURNER

Cover A
· Michael Turner's: SOULFIRE 10 ·
by
· Michael TURNER · Peter STEIGERWALD ·

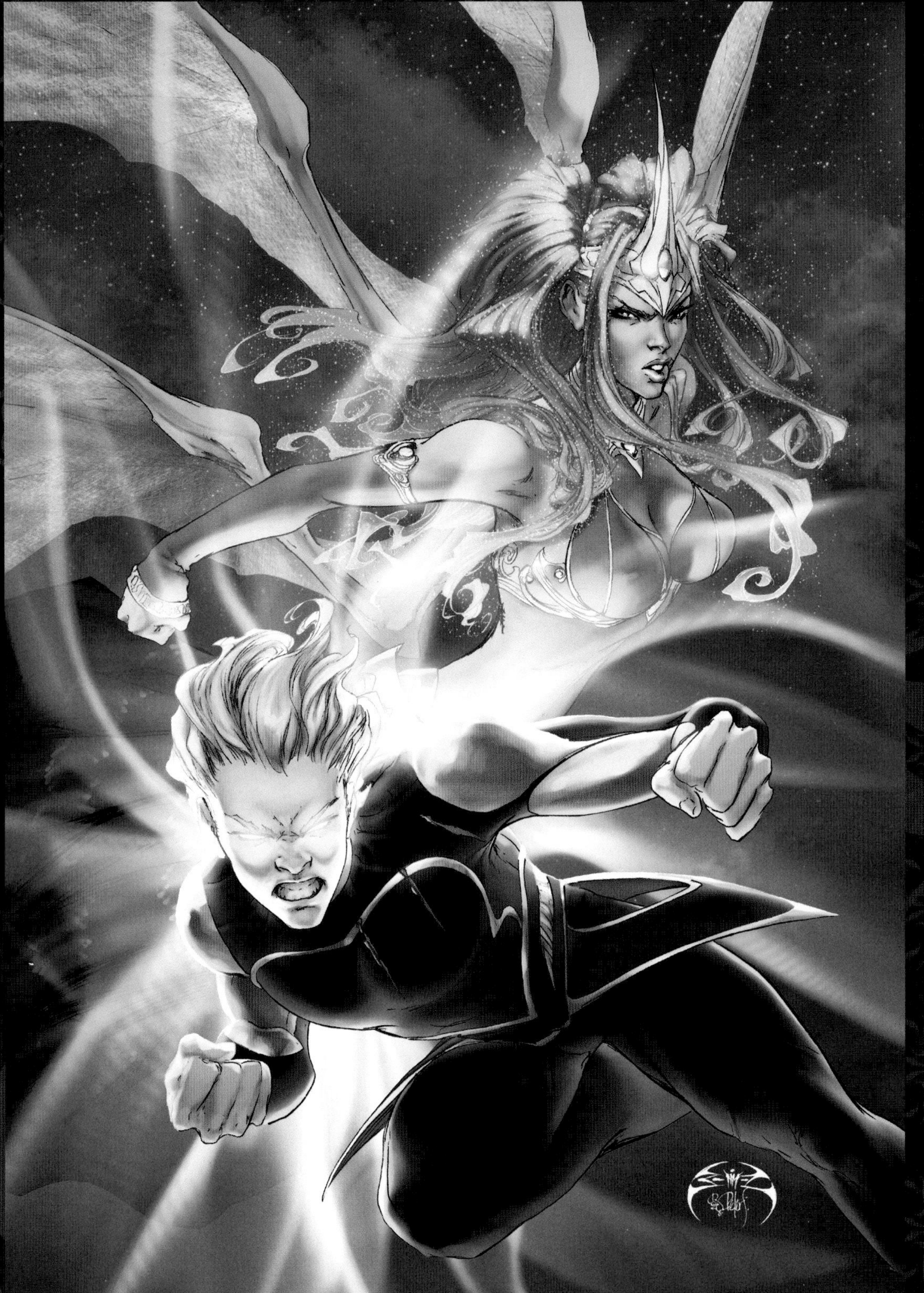

Cover B
‣ Michael Turner's: SOULFIRE 10 ‣
by
‣ Joe BENITEZ ‣ Peter STEIGERWALD ‣

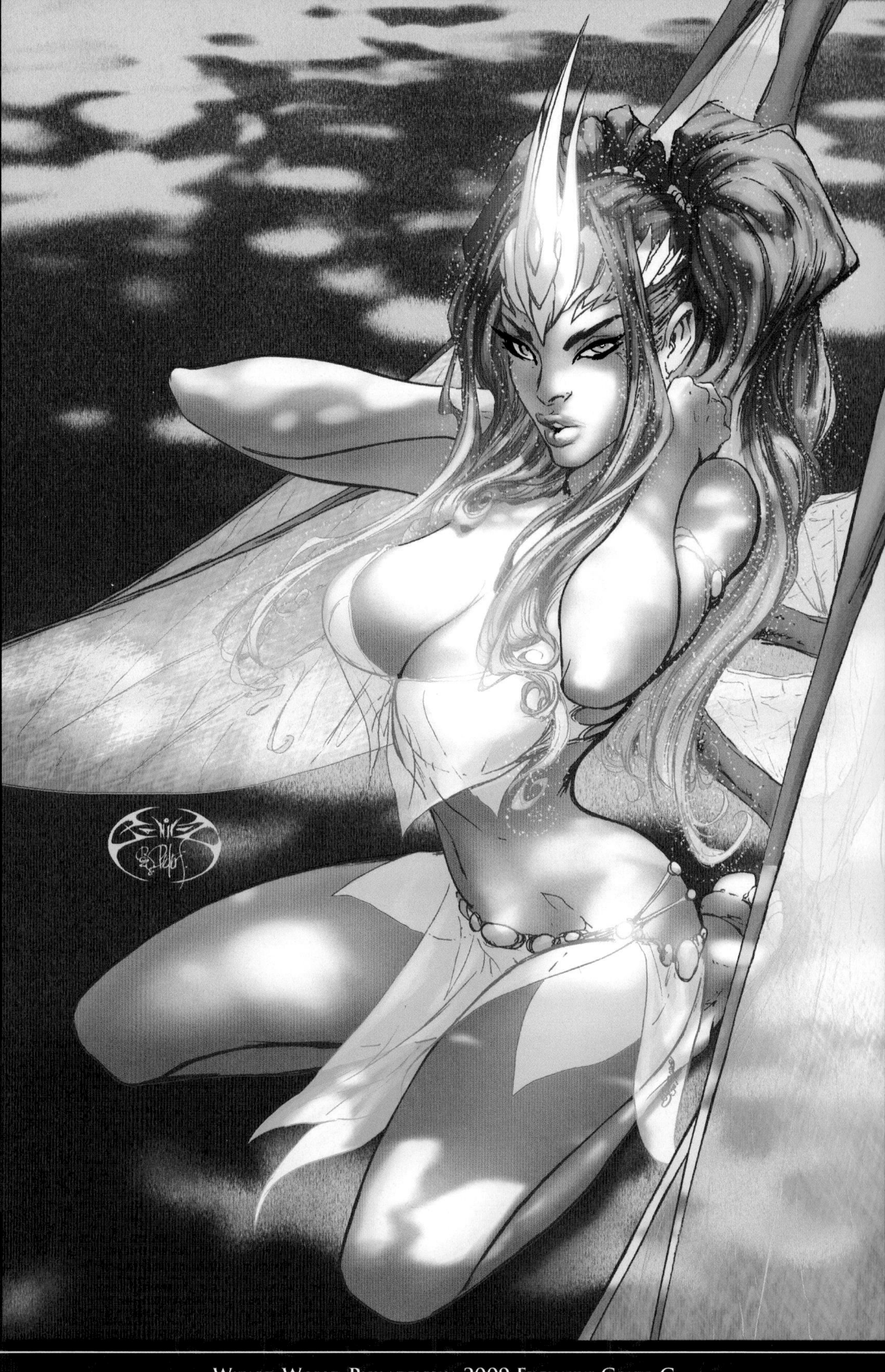

Wizard World Philadelphia 2009 Exclusive Cover C
› Michael Turner's: SOULFIRE 10 ›
by
› Joe BENITEZ › Peter STEIGERWALD ›

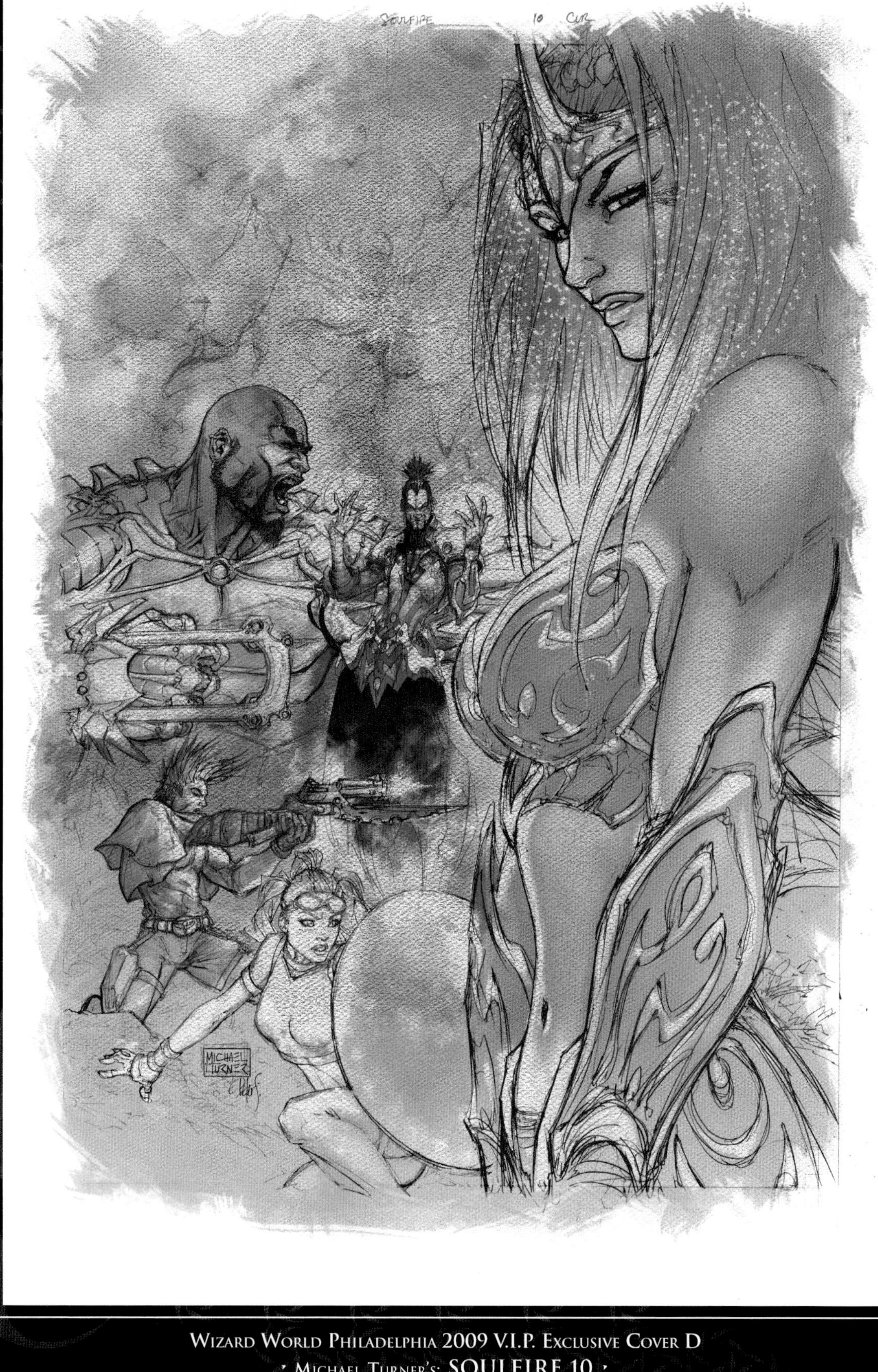
SOULFIRE 10 CVR
MICHAEL TURNER

Wizard World Philadelphia 2009 V.I.P. Exclusive Cover D

· Michael Turner's: SOULFIRE 10 ·

by

· Michael TURNER · Peter STEIGERWALD ·

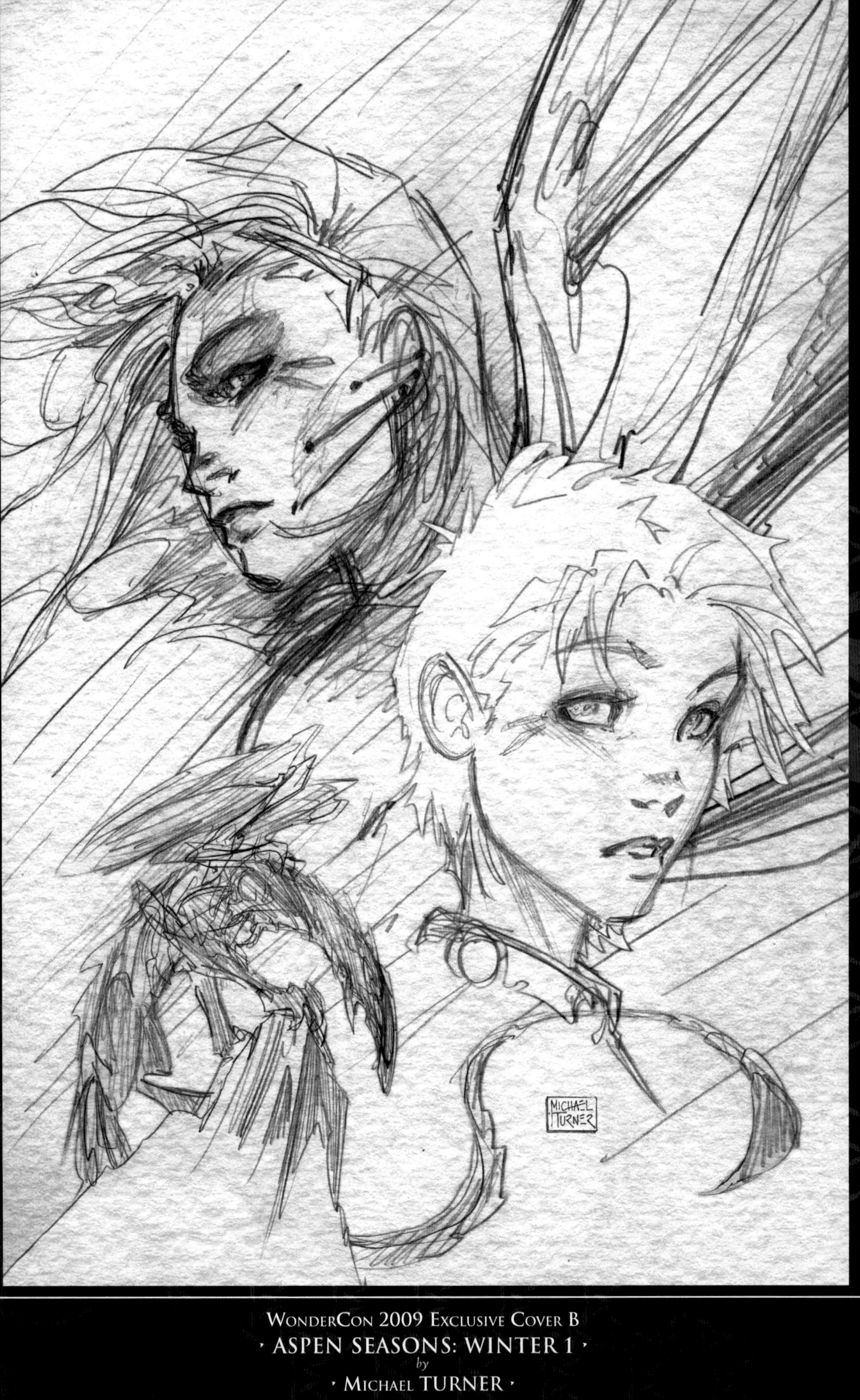
MICHAEL TURNER

WonderCon 2009 Exclusive Cover B
· ASPEN SEASONS: WINTER 1 ·
by
· Michael TURNER ·

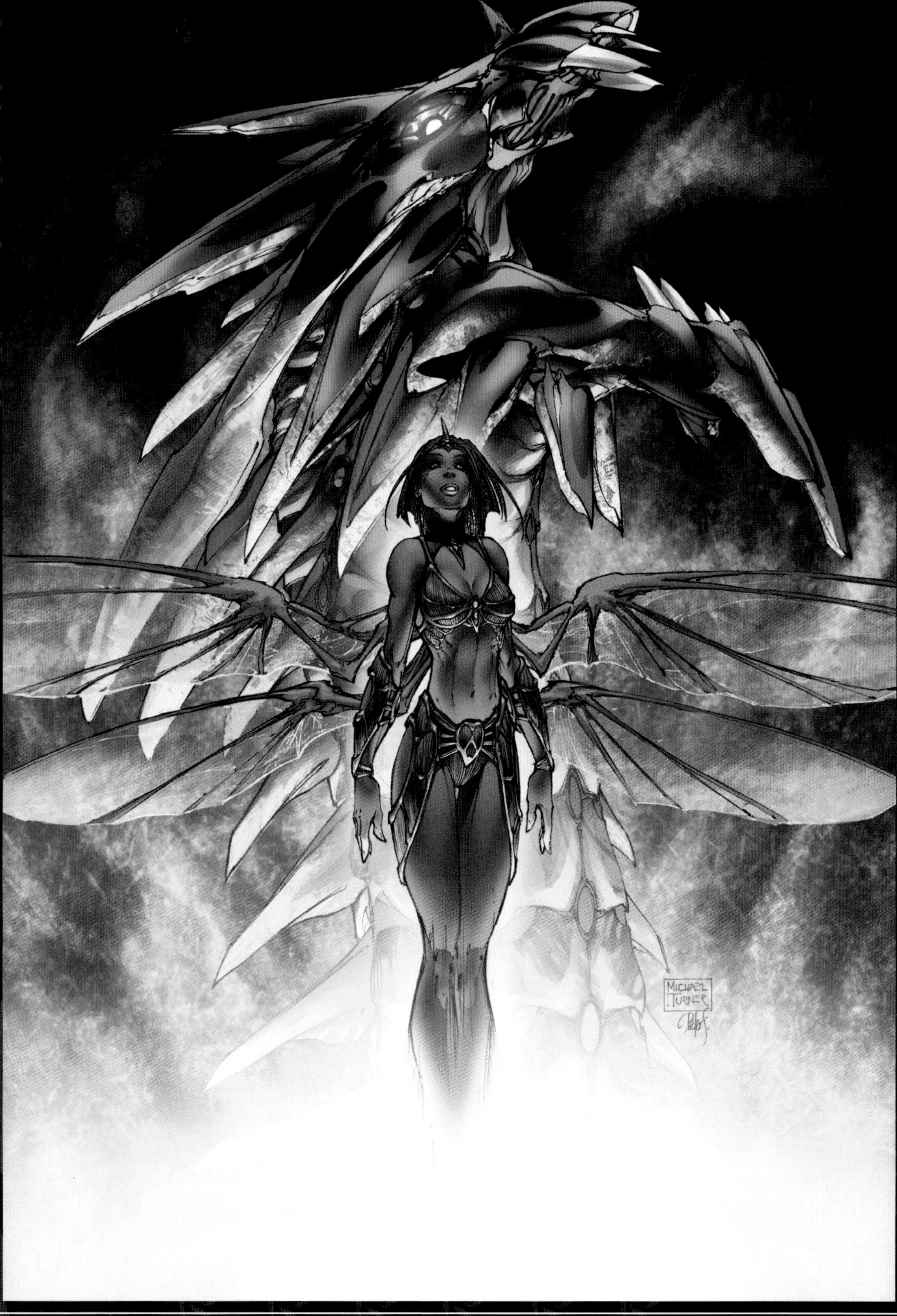
MICHAEL TURNER

1:25 Chase Edition Exclusive Cover B
· MICHAEL TURNER PRESENTS: ASPEN 1 ·
by
· Michael TURNER · Peter STEIGERWALD ·

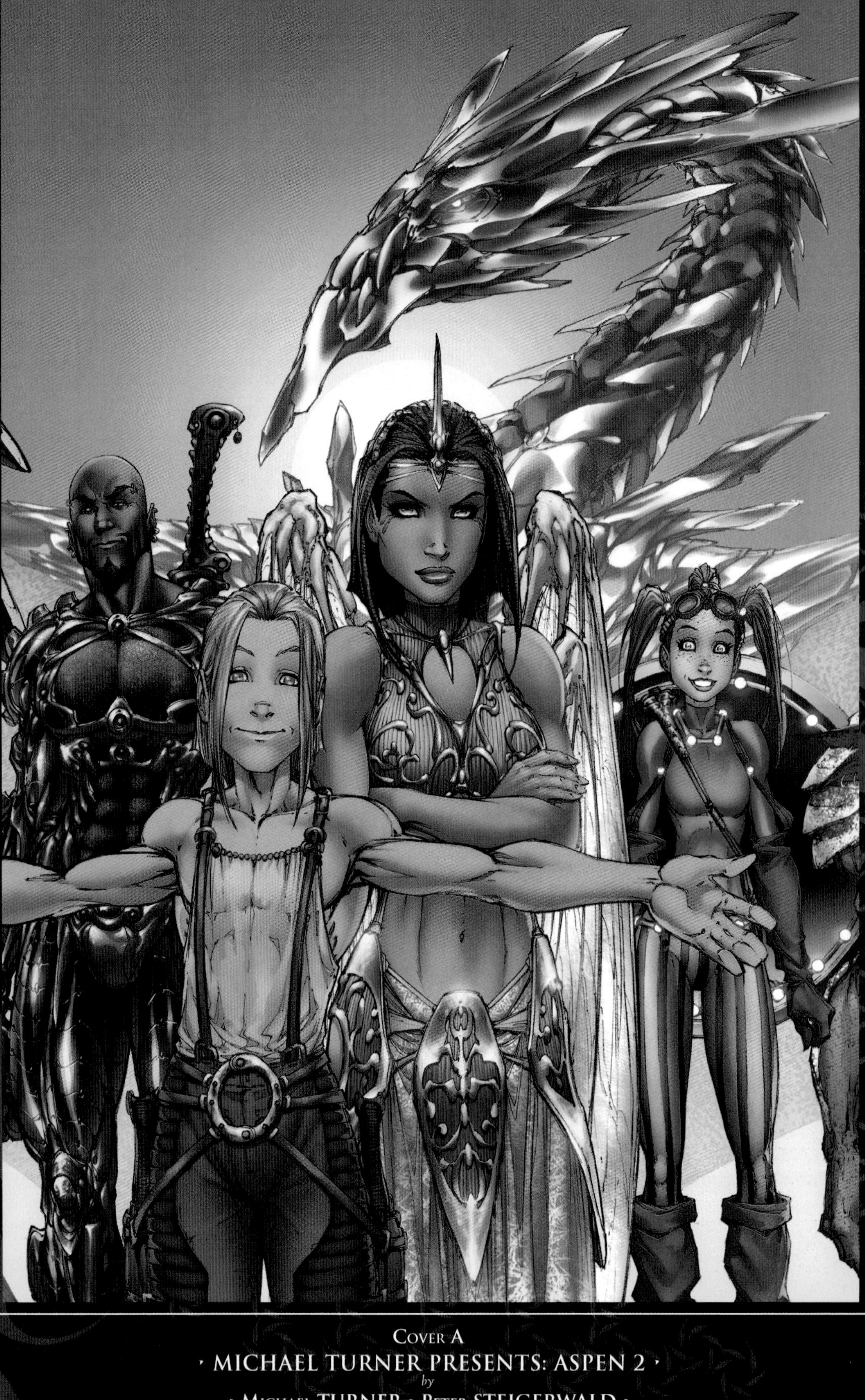

Cover A
· MICHAEL TURNER PRESENTS: ASPEN 2 ·
by
· Michael TURNER · Peter STEIGERWALD ·

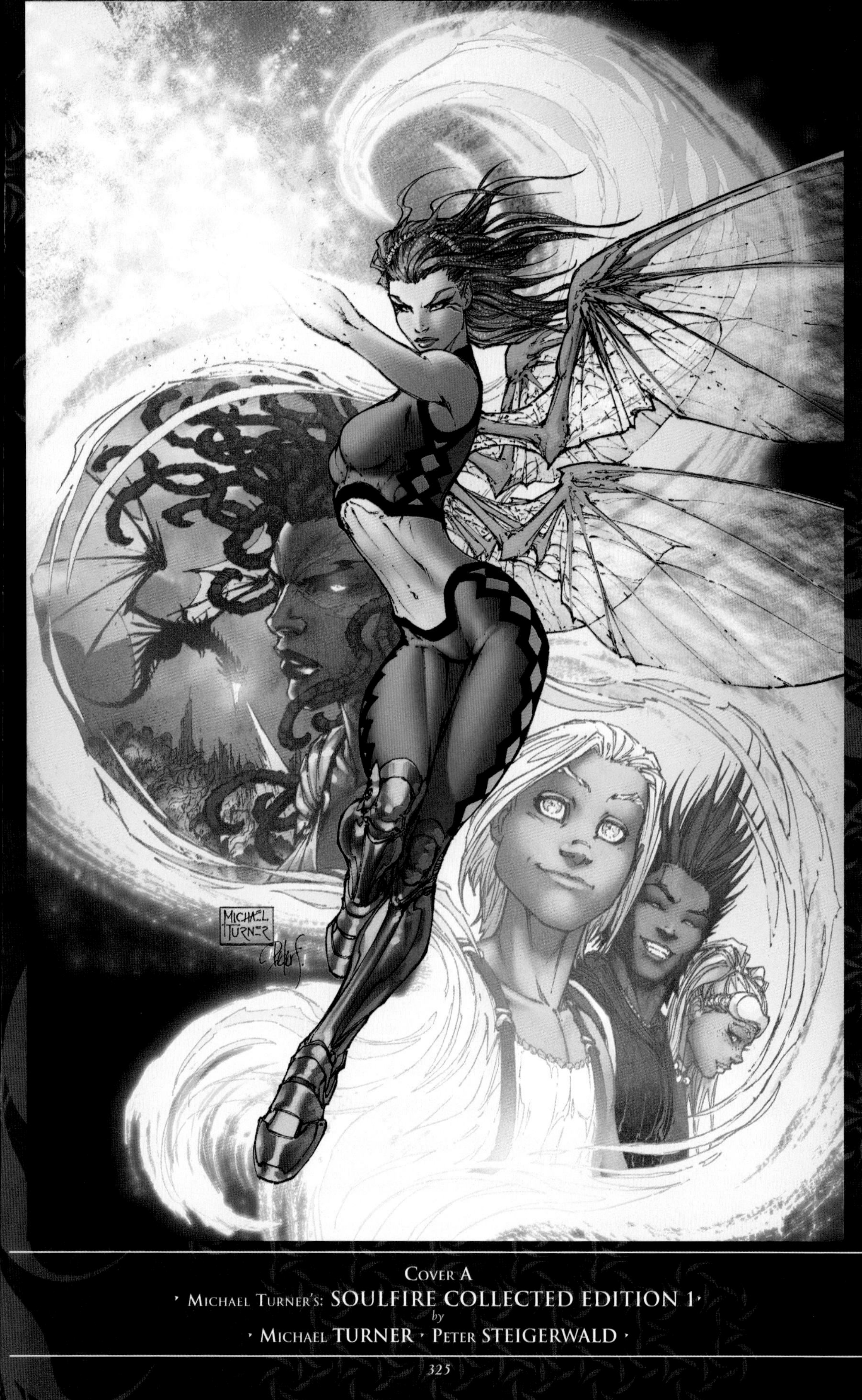
MICHAEL TURNER

COVER A
MICHAEL TURNER'S: SOULFIRE COLLECTED EDITION 1
by
MICHAEL TURNER · PETER STEIGERWALD

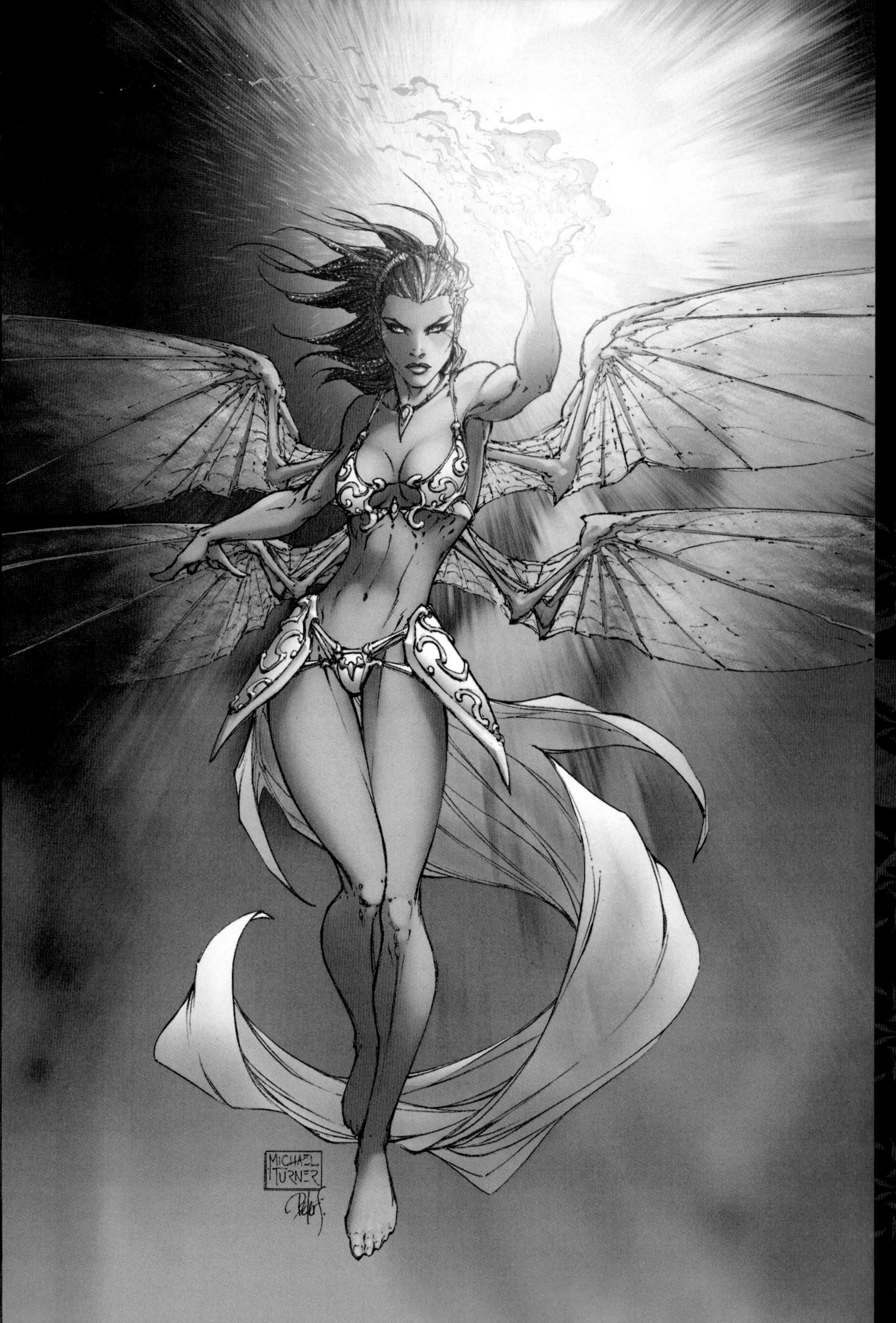
MICHAEL
TURNER

AspenStore.Com Exclusive Cover B
· Michael Turner's: SOULFIRE COLLECTED EDITION 1 ·
by
· Michael TURNER · Peter STEIGERWALD ·

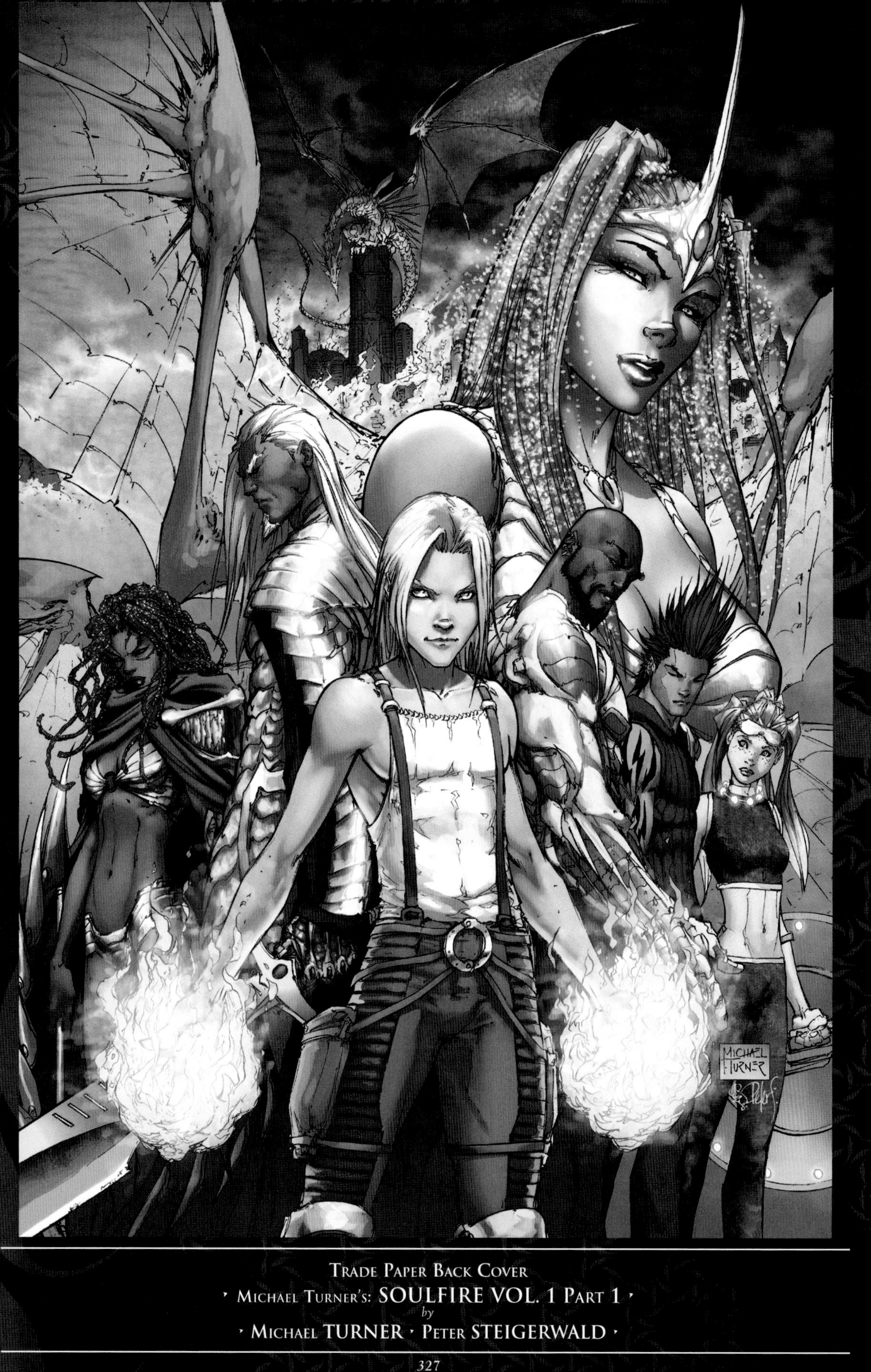
MICHAEL TURNER

TRADE PAPER BACK COVER
· MICHAEL TURNER'S: SOULFIRE VOL. 1 PART 1 ·
by
· MICHAEL TURNER · PETER STEIGERWALD ·

Michael's personal story notes are showcased here for the very first time. These handwritten notes helped him establish the tone of the story, the voice of the characters, and offer a rare inside look at the process of comic book illustrating and storytelling from the creator's point of view.

by: Michael Turner

design: Peter Steigerwald

SOULFIRE STORY NOTES

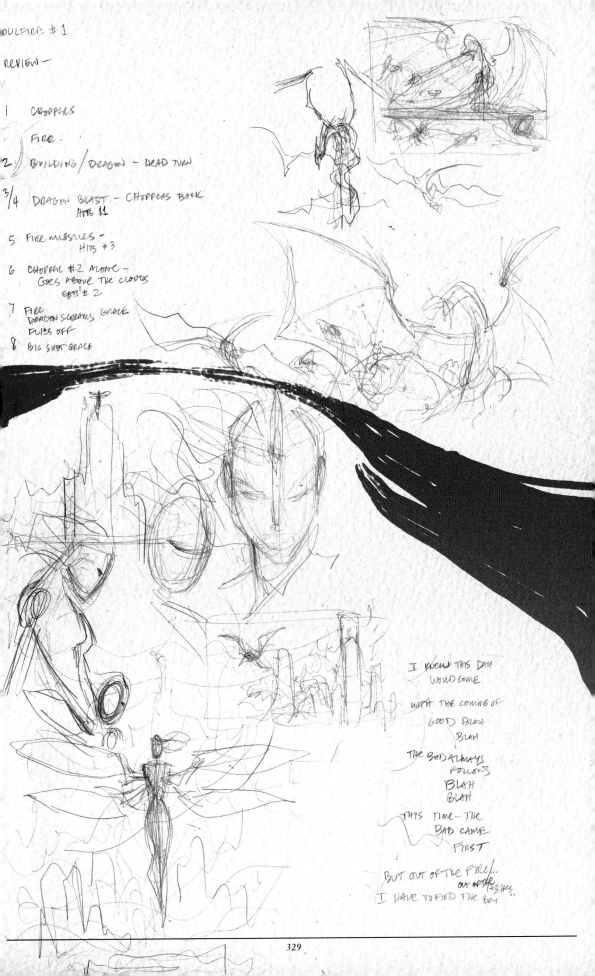

SOULFIRE #1

REVIEW—

1 CHOPPERS
   FIRE.
2) BUILDING / DRAGON — HEAD TURN
3/4 DRAGON BLAST — CHOPPERS BANK
          HITS #1
5 FIRE MISSILES —
          HITS #3
6 CHOPPER #2 ALONE —
      GOES ABOVE THE CLOUDS
          EATS! #2
7 FIRE
   DRAGON SCREAMS GRACE
   FLIES OFF
8 BIG SHOT GRACE

I KNEW THIS DAY
   WOULD COME

WITH THE COMING OF
   GOOD BLAH
          BLAH

THE BAD ALWAYS
          FOLLOWS
          BLAH
          BLAH

THIS TIME — THE
          BAD CAME
               FIRST

BUT OUT OF THE FIRE/...
               OUT OF THE ASHES...
I HAVE TO FIND THE BOY

Someone—
  5 SENSES — 5 MORE

  - TOUCH — BUT OFFENSIVE — TOUCH / HIT

  - HEAR — SOUND WAVES ...

  ...

  ~ 5 NEW —

    UNCONSCIOUS— HAVE 5 AS WELL

  - SEE — SEE YOURSELF —

  - HEAR — VOICES (SOULS TALKING...) HEAR OWN SOUL — WHAT
         LANGUAGE ?

  - TASTE —

  - TOUCH — FEEL ENERGY (LIGHT, SOUND, FEEL SMELLS

  - SMELL —
                                        --

_____

THINK — INVISIBLE MECH SUIT — AS MAGIC — THE SENSORS ARE
THE NEW SENSES — THAT IS POWER OF SOUL—
                    — DEFINE SOUL — POWER
                          - FIRE ...

+
START BOOK— WITH MAL PLAYING MINI MECH VID GAME
      — PULL BACK AND SEE HIM PLAYING — PICKED ON BY
       BULLIES—

(MAYBE SEE LITTLE MECH IN VID REACT TO MAL'S MOVEMENTS
W/O HIM USING THE CONTROLS)—METAPHOR FOR HIM
LATER CONTROLLING DRAGON—

18 —   ONYX
        KIDS W/ SONIA — BULLIES BOUT
        MULTIPLE IMAGES—GRABS MAL
        ONYX COMING AT US W/ MAL
        OUT SIDE — WINDOW BURSTS

        LANDS — 3 STORIES DOWN
19   LEAPS
        RACHET & CLANK
        UP TO TOP
        PJ/SONIA LOOK UP
        LEAPS INTO AIR

        BIG SHOT— WINGS UNFOLD
        FLY UP
        CLOSE — HAND ON CHIN
20   BLUE FLAME FROM HANDS
        BLINDED—DROPS HIM
        MAL LOOKING AT HANDS
        HANDS POINT TO SEE GOING DOWN
        FALLING INTO TARPS-
        FADE
21   FALL FALL IN TARPS
        FALL
        SWING
        LAND
        LIGHT
        LOOK UP TO ONYX DIVE BOMB
        BACK—BRIGHTER LIGHT
        LOOKS.

22   GRACE

SF #2 (US BROKEN INTO "KINGDOMS") (LIMITED TO NORTH+EAST)
GARRISON'S COMPANIES — SF? CALF? NORTH CALF.?
(CANADA/WAR w/ G. BRITIAN)
FUTURE NEWS SHOW —
SCENE— SOMETHING TALKING ABOUT NOTHING CAN FLY—
3 MULTIPLE REPORTS OF DRAGON SITINGS / HUGE FIRES
(MAYBE SITINGS OF OTHER SMALLER DRAGON THINGS ???)

(DRAGON ROASTING COWS) NO FLY   DRAG. KNIGHTS — BIG. MOTORCYCLES
                                     OR SMALL MECH. DRAGONS

— CHASE CONT.

— GET ON — HE SAYS NO — SHE SAYS SORRY — NO CHOICE — WE ARE
                                          NOT YOUR DECISION)
GOING —

CYCLE TAKES OFF — (ON GROUND)

TOWARDS EDGE — THRUSTERS— FLYS — ONYX BEHIND DIVE BOMB

FLY CHASE THRU COOL TUNNELS & FUTURE STUFF — OUT OF CITY
            SLICING w/ WEAPONS —
ONYX CLOSE — MAL ASKING WHAT ARE THE WINGS —
ONYX TAKES GRACE OFF THE BIKE
SHE SAYS GRAB THIS — PULL THIS — JUMPS OFF —
SHOWS WINGS — SHOWS WINGS   PJ/SONIA ON I-POD
                                             COMMUNICATOR — TALKING TO
HE IS LEFT TO TRY AND DRIVE (PJ — HOW DO I DRIVE A BIKE
—   (STICK IN THE MIDDLE)
GRACE/ONYX FIGHT (GO INTO SOMETHING HE CRASHES / ALMOST TOTALS
                   ALLEYS ETC.)   — HE'S UNSCATHED

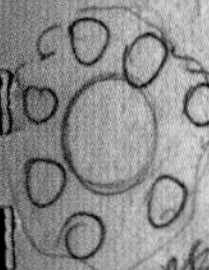

(SONIA / PJ GET INTO SOME VEHICLE OR TRY & CHASE) POWERS UP BUT
                 POWER / SEES WINGS   DOESN'T
                 THIS TOO / GRACE TO STOP HER —
BEATS ONYX — GETS AWAY (CLOCK STARTS)
                        ONYX GETS AWAY (NOW) BEFORE ONYX
— PJ — WHO THE HELL ARE YOU — TO GRACE   PJ FINDS MAL
SONIA TELLS HIM HE NEEDS TO GO ON JOURNEY .....   ON HIS BIKE
COMES IN NEED TO GET TO SEE THE FIVE MASTERS — BUT CAN'T w/
MAL   FLY — GRACE KNOWS SOMEONE WHO HAS A BOAT   I-POD
FOLLOW DRAGON OVER   THING
HEAD — SEES SEE   JET IN AIR
END w/ DRAGON ROASTING A COUPLE OF THINGS AND FLYING BY
— RIPS THROUGH JET
SHADOWY FIGURE ON TOP OF MOUNTAIN / BUILDING AND LANDING
SHE COMES UP BEHIND FIGURE — HIS BACK / HEAD DOWN   PJ KNOWS
SHE STARTS BLABBING — HE PUTS UP FINGER — SHADOW   OF BENOIST (BILLBOARD)
BIG DRAGON OVER HEAD — WIND BLOWING — SHE GOES WHAT THE HELL
RAINIER (SHADOW CLOSES) POW   SONIA HAS RICH PARENTS
NOW CONTINUE   BUT HANGS w/ STREET
POWER AT END) — DRAGON LANDS —   KIDS " YOU HAVE PARENTS?"
                — TURNS (SEE HIS FACE)   OPENS (3)
                — NOW CONTINUE
— PJ/GRACE BUMP THEN   PJ/MAL NO PARENTS —
  BOND

FUTURE ABANDONED ELEVATED "SUBWAY"

1 – SHIPPING LANES STILL REMAIN OPEN – BUT ALL PASSENGER ROUTES CANCELLED

①

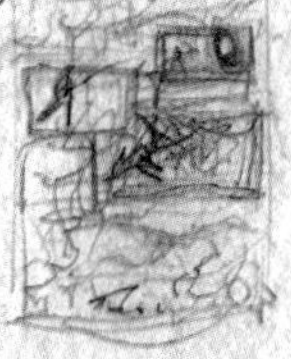

②

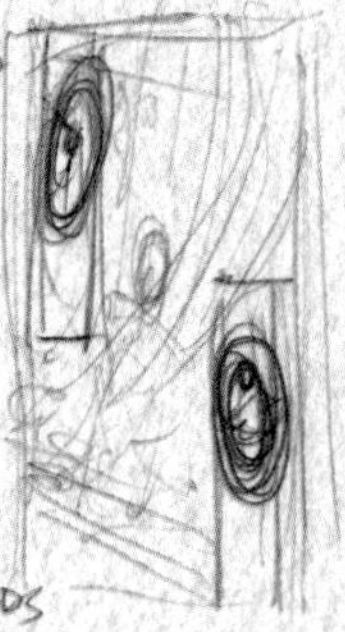

2 – SPLASH MAL W/ ONYX / GRACE

3 – ~~DPS~~ GRABS / FLIPS AROUND / ONYX ABOVE

4 PULLS OUT SWORDS
DIVE BOMB / MAL LOOKS BACK UP / GRACE HITS THRUSTERS / FLYS

5 ~~FLYING~~ (MAL/PJ I-POD) AROUND BUILDINGS – SLASHS W/SWORDS

6 – CHASE – GONE

7/8 ONYX TACKLES GRACE – THRU WALL – MAL TRY TO FLY BIKE
CRASH THRU TRANSIT SYSTEM – GRACE TURNS (CLOTHES RIPPED) TAKES OFF

13

9 SPL BIG SHOT WINGS / POWER

10 – MAL TRYING TO FLY – TALKING TO PJ (STUCK IN THE MIDDLE)

11 – FIGHTING – GRACE POWER – ONYX SCARED (REALIZES) – LEAVES

12 – DECIDES TO HELP MAL – MAL OUT OF CONTROL

13 – CRASHES

14 – PJ / SONIA SHOW UP

2

15 – GRACE SHOWS UP – PJ GUARD UP – TALK ABOUT CLOCK TICKING
– THEY KNOW ABOUT YOU / AND NOW THEY KNOW ABOUT ME NOW – HAVE TO GO TO HAWAII

16 – NEED TRANSPORT – PJ KNOWS OF BENOIST – SONIA TAKE PARENTS CAR

17 – ONYX COMES UP TO CONSTRUCTION SITE – TO FIGURE STANDING – DARK
– SHE STARTS TALKING – HE HOLDS UP FINGER

6

18 – DRAGON GOES OVER HEAD – FOLLOW DRAGON TO PORT – SEE TRANSPORTS

19/20 DPS – DRAGON ROASTING & TEARING THRU TRANSPORTS – SHIT FLYING EVERYWHERE

21 – BACK TO ONYX – RANIFER STILL SILENT – SHE'S FREAKED – WIND

22 – BIG SHOT DRAGON LANDS – CLOSE SHOT HEAD TURNED – YOU WERE SAYING?

ISSUE –
(3) – INTRO TO BENOIST – MACHINE WAR/BATTLE (ROBOT WARS)
GET THRU COUPLE OF PARTNERS – THEY GO WITH AS WELL (PIT CREW) ON BOAT
– MILITARY COMES IN TO FIGHT DRAGON
– SONIA / PJ G/M – GO TO SONIA'S HOUSE TO GET CAR
– GO TO BIG SUR

NEWS – PEOPLE LEAVING CITY...
MUSIC VIDEO
MR. DEVILLE –
SIMPSONS –
FLYING CAR COMMERCIAL
VISOR –
IN TRAFFIC – FLY ZONES (LOW)
TANKS – MILITARY FLYING
FOLLOW JET – LOCKED W/LOADED – NO DRAGON
– RAINIER HORSEMAN
– SENTINELS FLY
–

MILITARY –
– GUYS ON GROUND / TANKS
– RUMBLE
– DRAGON ON GROUND
– TANKS FIRING
– TAIL NAILS TANK
– TAKES OFF
– JETS FLYING – FIGHT
– CAN'T TAKE THIS MUCH FIREPOWER

CAN'T TAKE THIS TRAFFIC
WE'RE HERE
GET TO ARENA –
(HOW CAN PEOPLE GO TO THE ARENA W/ A DRAGON ON THE LOOSE?
– YOU KNOW PEOPLE – WAR / FOOTBALL)
– NOT YOUR AVERAGE CROWD –
– RAIDER NATION
SHOTS OF CROWD
– PULL BACK TO ARENA
– ANNOUNCER – CHANGE ARENA (FLOATING)
– CHANGE ARENA

– BENOIST
– BATTLE

BENOIST HAS A GARDEN
– HAS A GOAT
IN HIS WORKSHOP

5

– BATTLE OVER –
– GO BACK TO MEET HIM
– PEOPLE GETTING AUTOGRAPHS – ~~EATS A TOMATO~~
GRACE STARTS TALKING
– HOLD ON LITTLE LADY –
I'M HERE FOR THE KIDS
– GRABS MAL'S COMMUNICATOR
SIGNS IT W/ FINGER FLAME
MAL DOESN'T CARE / PJ TRADES
– GRACE TALKING

– ASK FOR UNDERGROUND WAY TO HAWAII –
– GETS TOMATO IN GARDEN
– NO NOT INTERESTED
– SOMEONE MENTIONS RAINIER
– SQUASHES TOMATO – GOAT LICKS
– I'M GOING MYSELF
– SHIP

8

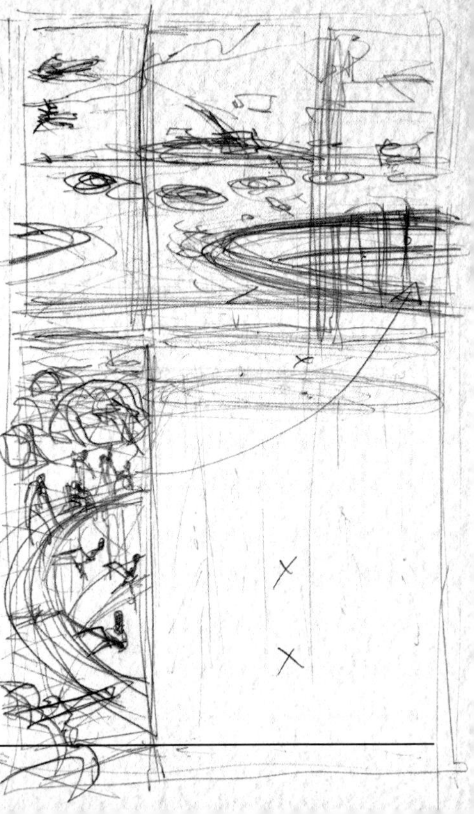

BIG SILO UNDERGROUND SHOT
2/4 SOLDIERS – LIGHTS ON –
NO READINGS (DRAGON WENT COLD)
LOOKING – LIGHTS – NOTHING
BLUE EYES

10 LIGHTS TURN –
BIG HEAD
RUNNING AS DRAGON WALKS
WALKS (ON DUDE'S RADIO)
IT'S HERE
TAIL NAILS GROUP OF GUYS

11 DRAGON PULLS BACK
BLOWS FIRE
SKREEEE
FIRE ERUPTS THRU FLOOR

SF #4

MAL

DREAM – FLYING – THEN FIRE – FALLING –

WAKE UP BY SONIA – BAD DREAM – ON BOAT

TURN OVER – HAS BUMPS ON BACK – SONIA SEES, MAYBE MENTIONS

BOAT GOING ALONG

– SENSOR FLYS CLOSE – LIGHT SCANS – SEES MAL – TAKES OFF

BENOIST COMES UP – MORNING ON SEA –

– INCIDENT W/ DECK HANDS & GRACE

– MAL STOPS IT

– SENSORS ATTACK

6
HAIR KINDA WHIPPING
PJ STILL STRAIGHT

6

- OBSERVATION DECK
- CLOSER ON BEN / GRACE
- SIMON W/ BENOIST LOOKING BACK AT GRACE
- SIMON GLARES AS WALKS AWAY – ANGLE ON BENOIST W/ GRACE
- BENOIST – A LITTLE SAD (W/ MAL – SONIA/PJ ON DECK)
- M/S/PJ LOOKING OVER SIDE
- SIMON BEHIND
- GIVES THEM SHIN STRAPS AND BELT

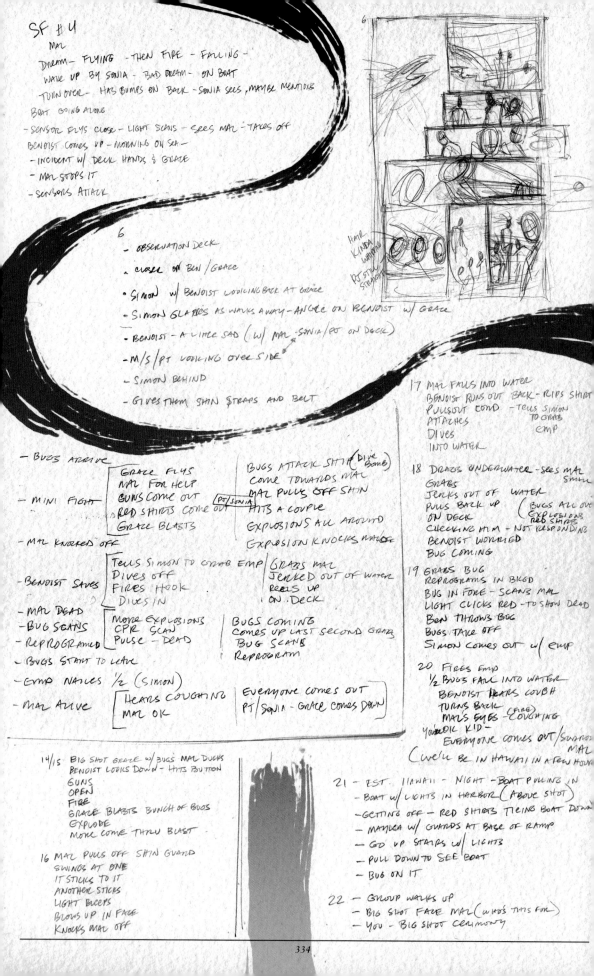

– BUGS ARRIVE

– MINI FIGHT [GRACE FLYS / MAL FOR HELP / GUNS COME OUT / RED SHIRTS COME OUT (PJ/SONIA) / GRACE BLASTS] | BUGS ATTACK SHIP (DIVE BOMB) / COME TOWARDS MAL / MAL PULLS OFF SHIN / HITS A COUPLE / EXPLOSIONS ALL AROUND / EXPLOSION KNOCKS MAL OFF

– MAL KNOCKED OFF

– BENOIST SAVES [TELLS SIMON TO GRAB EMP / DIVES OFF / FIRES HOOK / DIVES IN] | GRABS MAL / JERKED OUT OF WATER / REELS UP / ON DECK

– MAL DEAD
– BUG SCANS
– REPROGRAMED [MORE EXPLOSIONS / CPR SCAN / PULSE – DEAD] | BUGS COMING / COMES UP LAST SECOND GRABS / BUG SCANS / REPROGRAM

– BUGS START TO LEAVE

– EMP NAILS ½ (SIMON)

– MAL ALIVE [HEARS COUGHING / MAL OK] | EVERYONE COMES OUT / PJ/SONIA – GRACE COMES DOWN

17 MAL FALLS INTO WATER
BENOIST RUNS OUT BACK – RIPS SHIRT
PULLS OUT CORD – TELLS SIMON TO GRAB EMP
ATTACHES
DIVES
INTO WATER

18 DRAGS UNDERWATER – SEES MAL SMALL
GRABS
JERKS OUT OF WATER
PULLS BACK UP ON DECK (BUGS ALL OVER EXPLOSIONS RED SHIRTS)
CHECKING HIM – NOT RESPONDING
BENOIST WORRIED
BUG COMING

19 GRABS BUG
REPROGRAMS IN BKGD
BUG IN FORE – SCANS MAL
LIGHT CLICKS RED – TO SHOW DEAD
BEN THROWS BUG
BUGS TAKE OFF
SIMON COMES OUT W/ EMP

20 FIRES EMP
½ BUGS FALL INTO WATER
BENOIST HEARS COUGH
TURNS BACK
MAL'S EYES (FIRE) – COUGHING
YOU'RE OK KID –
EVERYONE COMES OUT / SURROUND MAL
(WE'LL BE IN HAWAII IN A FEW HOURS)

14/15 BIG SHOT GRACE W/ BUGS MAL DUCKS
BENOIST LOOKS DOWN – HITS BUTTON
GUNS
OPEN
FIRE
GRACE BLASTS BUNCH OF BUGS
EXPLODE
MORE COME THRU BLAST

16 MAL PULLS OFF SHIN GUARD
SWINGS AT ONE
IT STICKS TO IT
ANOTHER STICKS
LIGHT BEEPS
BLOWS UP IN FACE
KNOCKS MAL OFF

21 – EST. HAWAII – NIGHT – BOAT PULLING IN
– BOAT W/ LIGHTS IN HARBOR (ABOVE SHOT)
– GETTING OFF – RED SHIRTS TIEING BOAT DOWN
– MANUCA W/ GUARDS AT BASE OF RAMP
– GO UP STAIRS W/ LIGHTS
– PULL DOWN TO SEE BOAT
– BUG ON IT

22 – GROUP WALKS UP
– BIG SHOT FACE MAL (WHO'S THIS FOR)
– YOU – BIG SHOT CEREMONY

MAL STAIRS TO TEMPLE

ALONE
- TWO GUARDS LET HIM BY
GOES IN

MASTER BY HIMSELF
SIDE SHOT
START "TALKING"
BKGD MELTS AWAY - VISIONS
- SHOTS OF PAST / FUTURE - THINKS FATHER
VISIONS - "TBD"

SHOTS OF GROUP ENJOYING PARTY
MUSIC STOPS
MAL COMES BACK DOWN
- DRESSED DIFFERENTLY - IN ROBE - SEEMS WISER
- HEAVYIER
- - WEIGHT OF INFO
ABLE - RAINIER TALKING
TV SCREENS - SEGUE
- RAINIER SET UP OF SYSTEM - OVER PAST WEEK
- SMASH SCREEN
- INFO RAINIER / BASE
- IF HE TAKES OVER - HE CAN... OH NO I SEE WHAT HE'S TRYING TO DO
- BASE - NO SHOW - DRAGON GONE - RAINIERS BUILDING - WE FOLLOWED HIM IN - HEAT SIG DISSAPEARED - BIG BUILDING

PJ WIND SURFING - (MECH FLYING DEVICE)
- COMES IN - PASSES BY -
2 - BOAT (BENOIST / SIMON)
- SONIA / PILI - (BUSTS ASS) I WAS DONE ANYWAY
- WHERE'S MAL - ~~LOOK OVER ALL BY SELF~~
- PILI LOOK OF LONGING FOR PJ - (BUT NEEDS TO TELL HIM

"CHICKS DIG CREEPES"

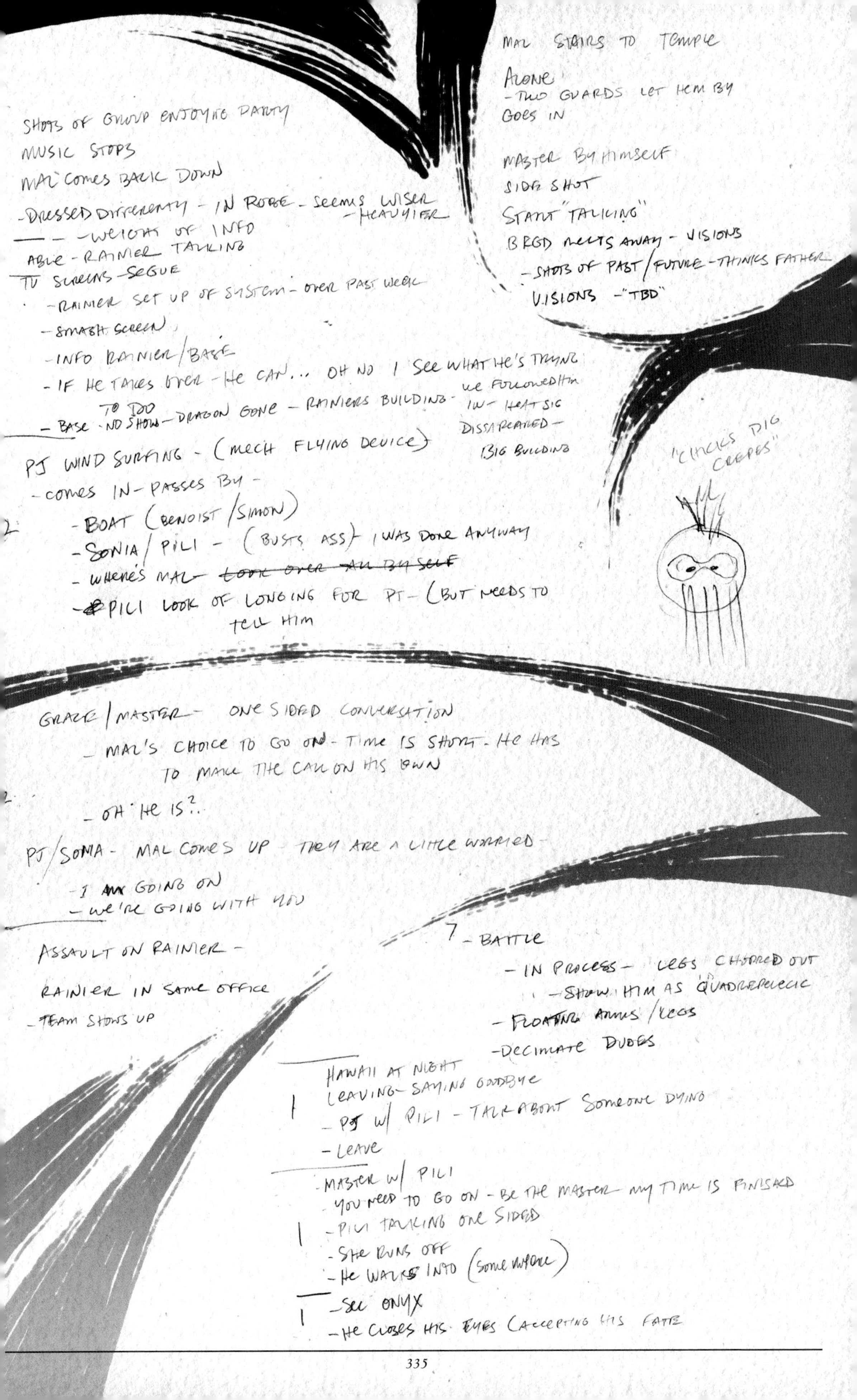

GRACE / MASTER - ONE SIDED CONVERSATION
- MAL'S CHOICE TO GO ON - TIME IS SHORT - HE HAS TO MAKE THE CALL ON HIS OWN
2 - OH HE IS?..

PJ / SONIA - MAL COMES UP THEY ARE A LITTLE WORRIED -
- I AM GOING ON
- WE'RE GOING WITH YOU

ASSAULT ON RAINIER -
RAINIER IN SAME OFFICE
- TEAM SHOWS UP

7 - BATTLE
- IN PROCESS - LEGS CHOPPED OUT
- SHOW HIM AS QUADREPELEGIC
- FLOATING ARMS / LEGS
- DECIMATE DUDES

1 HAWAII AT NIGHT
LEAVING - SAYING GOODBYE
- PJ W/ PILI - TALK ABOUT SOMEONE DYING
- LEAVE

1 - MASTER W/ PILI
- YOU NEED TO GO ON - BE THE MASTER MY TIME IS FINISHED
- PILI TALKING ONE SIDED
- SHE RUNS OFF
- HE WALKS INTO (SOMEWHERE)

1 - SEE ONYX
- HE CLOSES HIS EYES (ACCEPTING HIS FATE

14

BIG
MECH SHOT
GUNS AND MISSLES
6/7 ALL FIRING AT DRAGON AS DRAGON TURNS
COMING AT THEM
JUST MISSES AS PASS BETWEEN
OH SHIT —
SLICES ONE IN HALF

8 GRACE COMING UP TO BATTLE
GRACE IN FRONT OF COCKPIT POINTING
PILOT SAYS NO.
MAKE BIG GUN
"
"
.
GRACE FLYS OFF TO DRAGON

9 COOL SHOT SMOKING DRAGON COMING AT US
GRACE NEAR DRAGON HEAD
MAL YELLS
MECHS FIRES
GRACE ENERGY
BLOCKS HEAD
OTHER HITS WING

10 MECHS BLOCKED BY REN AS DRAGON FLYS OFF
CLOSE ON REN'S SHIP — SEE REST
DRAGON ROUNDS CORNER
LANDS
CLOSER
CLOSER
CLOSER — MAL'S EYES FIRE

11 DRAGONS HEAD FIRE COMING OUT
UP - FIRE
BLOWS
MAL COMES OUT
ON GROUND
DRAGON HEAD LOOKS AT HIM
REARS BACK
REN'S SHIP / GRACE PULL UP

12 BLAST FIRE
DRAGON TAKES OFF
THEY ALL COME RUNNING
SURROUNDING ASH
ASH STARTS TO MOVE
ARM COMES OUT

13 SPLASH —
BURNT MAL —
SMILING COMES OUT
OF GROUND

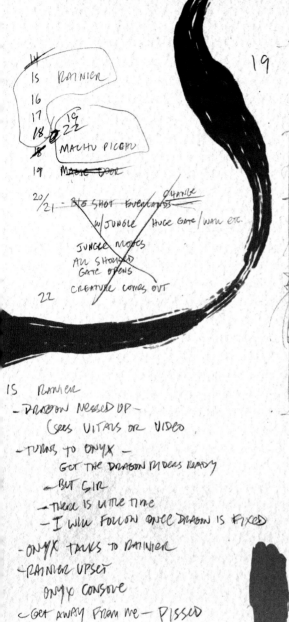

14
15 RAINIER
16
17   19
18 22
18 MACHU PICCHU
19 MAGIC DOOR

20/21 - BIG SHOT EVERYBODY ~~CHANGE~~
        w/ JUNGLE / HUGE GATE / WALL ETC.

        JUNGLE MOVES
        ALL SHOULD
        GATE OPENS

22   CREATURE COMES OUT

19

WORLD
MAP

MACHU PICCHU

15   RAINIER
- DRAGON MESSED UP -
    (SEES VITALS OR VIDEO

- TURNS TO ONYX -
        GOT THE DRAGON RIDERS READY
    - BUT SIR
        - THERE IS LITTLE TIME
        - I WILL FOLLOW ONCE DRAGON IS FIXED

- ONYX TALKS TO RAINIER
- RAINIER UPSET
    ONYX CONSOLE
- GET AWAY FROM ME — PISSED

- I KNOW HOW TO DEAL w/ RAINIER

- I REMEMBER

        — FLASH BACK BEGINS

16   FLASHBACK

17   FLASHBACK

18   FLASHBACK
        w/ RAINIER PISSED AT END

.20

SHIP LANDS
SEE TWO KIDS
ALL OUT OF SHIP
        CRATE FLIES UP
KIDS — WHOAH — WIND CHICK

3 RUNES SPARKLE
TRIANGULATES ON GROUND

21   GROUND OPENS
            WALL
        WALK THROUGH
        WALL CLOSES
        KIDS - STARING - PARENTS RETURN

        CAVERN w/ RUNES EVERYWHERE
        RUNES GROWING - GROUND SHAKING
        EVERYONE WHOAH CEILING
                        ROCK DROPPING FROM CEILING

22   SPLASH OF
        CREATURE

        MAL — I GOT THIS

SF 8 —

1. MALS FACE (CONFIDENT)
   CREATURE RISING —
   SLAMS DOWN (COVER #7)

2/3. SPLITS INTO TWO CREATURES (ONE LIGHT / ONE DARKER)
   - BOLTS FLY OFF
   - SPEAKS IN DARK TONES ABOUT DUALITY
     OF MAGIC
   - BOLD SLAM MAL TO GROUND ON STOMACH

4. MAL LOOKS AROUND / ALL ALONE
   — SPACE FIELD
   CREATURE SPLITS INTO FOUR
   FOUR SPIKES SPEAR MALS BACK
   SCREAMS

5. SHOT OF GROUP (WHATS GOING ON)
   - SEE MAL ON GROUND
   IN FRONT OF STATUE (THEY RUN DOWN TO HIM)
   MAL'S BACK IS BLEEDING
   MAL WAKES — FREAKED (WHERE'D YOU COME FROM)
   LOOKS BACK UP AT STATUE (STILL STATUE)

6. SCREAMS AGAIN
   BACK SHOOTS OUT BLOOD AND
   - WINGS
   - REACTION SHOTS

   MAL W/ WINGS

1. DONE
2. BATTLES CREATURE — SPLITS SPLITS — LOCK HIM DOWN
3/4. STAB HIM IN BACK — CREW COMES DOWN TO HIM
5. BACK TO NORMAL — WAKES UP SEES EVERYONE — SCREAMS — BLOOD OUT BACK
6. WINGS POP OUT —
7. MAL FREAKS — SONIA SCARED / CALLING
   — GRAZE YOU GO ON — CONSOLES
8. MAL / GRAZE TALK
9. REN TAKES — BENDIST TO BARRIER TO GET HIM THRU (TECH BARRIER) — GO INTO WOODS
10/11. DRAGON — BENDIST POWERS — SEPH SHOWS
12. SEPH TAKES TO CITY / MAL GRAZE JOIN
12. MAL / GRAZE JOINS
13. CITY W/ CITADEL
14. MEET MASTERS 3/4 — WE'LL TAKE MAL
15. SONIA / SEPH GO OFF W/ DRAGON — MAL LITTLE JEALOUS
16. PJ / BENDIST GET SHIP — RACE OFF — (JTA — GET SHIP NEXT BOOK ?)
17. MAL TO GET KNIFE — BIG ROOM
18/19. BATTLE W/ LIGHT DARK TO GET BLADE
20. GETS KNIFE
21. COMING BACK DOWN SEE ONYX NEAR CITADEL — GOES IN
22/23. BIG DRAGON RIDER GUARDS — STEALTH ATTACK BEGINS
24. — STEALTH ATTACK ENDS — SHUTS DOWN TECH BARRIER (BEGIN YOUR ASSAULT)

This rare gallery of Soulfire sketches and concept art features Michael Turner's various illustrations and drawings used to conceive the huge world and large assortment of characters within the Soulfire universe. Turner's design sketches would eventually form the visual foundation by which all future Soulfire stories adhere to.

pencils: **Michael Turner** - *colors:* **Peter Steigerwald**
design and production: Peter Steigerwald, Mark Roslan and Liz Brizzi

THE CONCEPT SKETCHBOOK

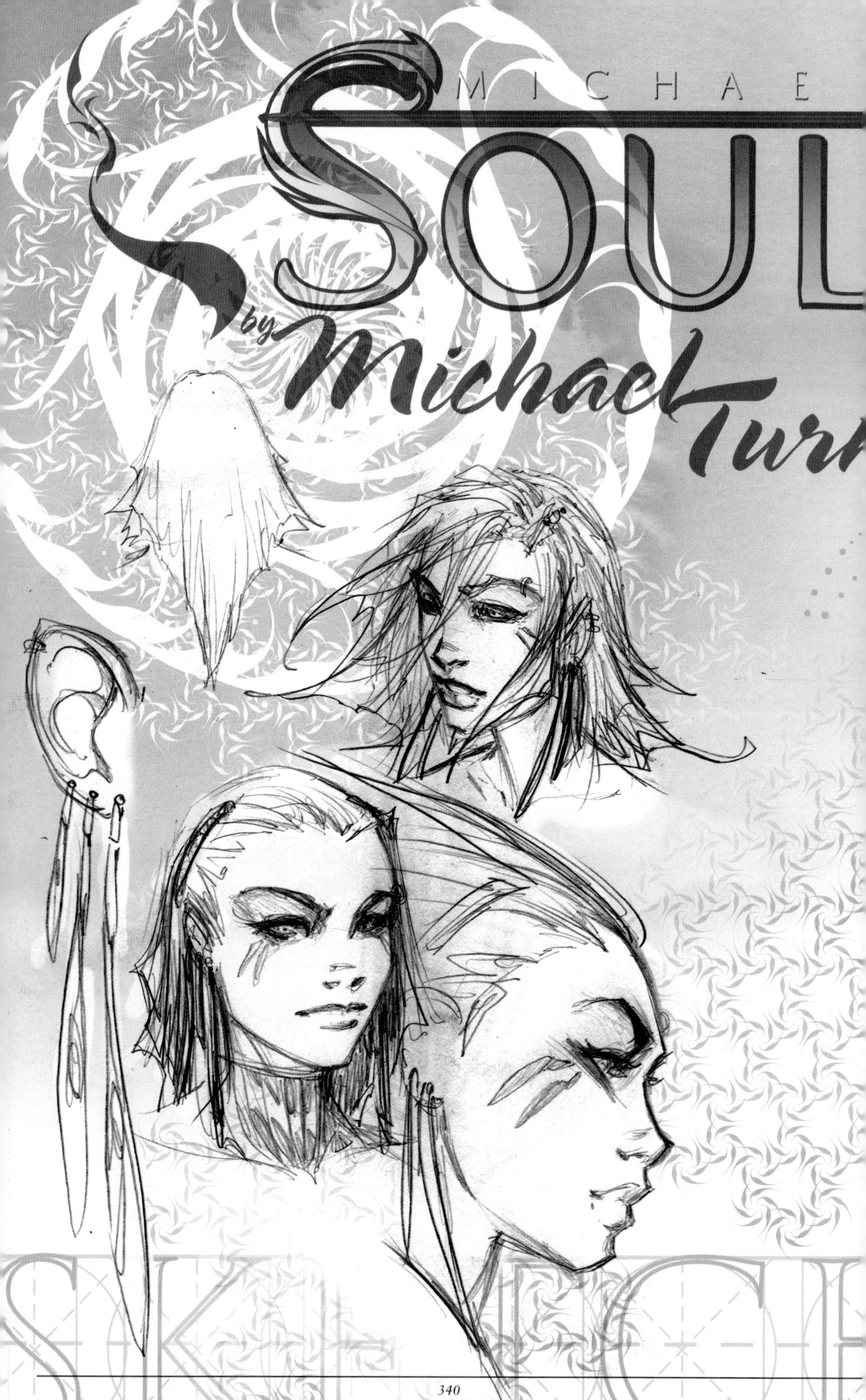
MICHAE
SOUL
by Michael
Tur

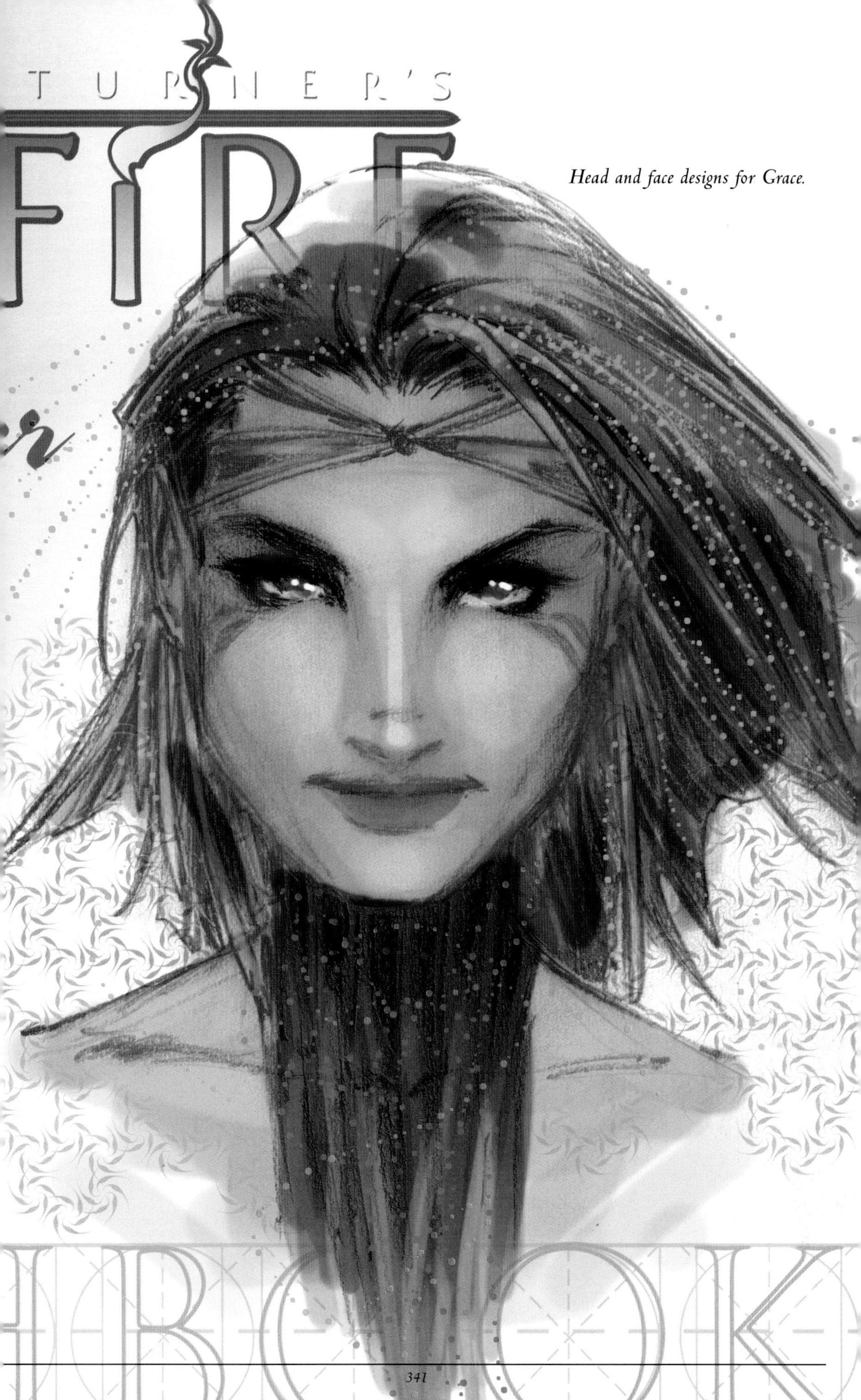
TURNER'S
FIRE

Head and face designs for Grace.

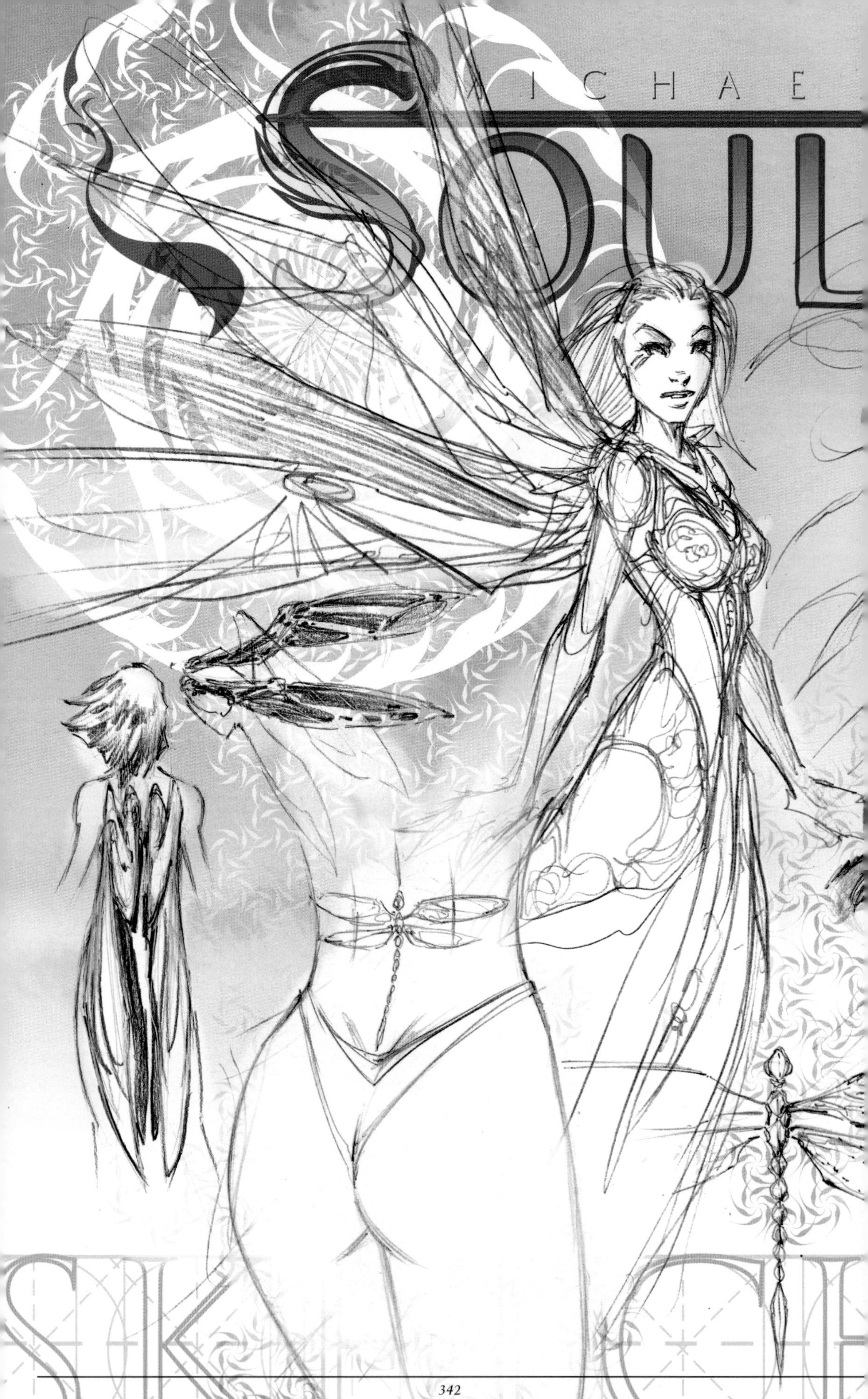
SOUL

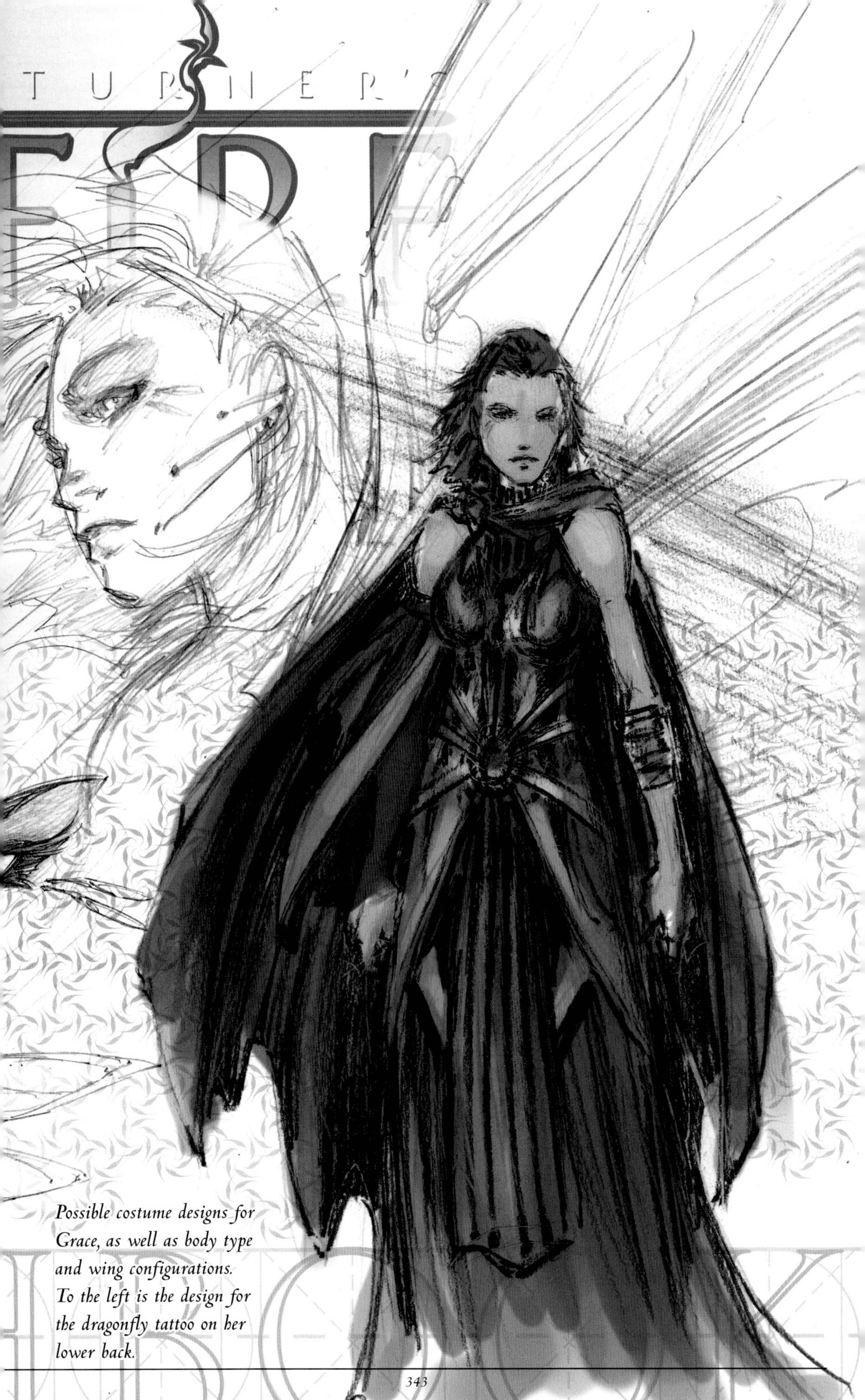
TURNER'S

Possible costume designs for Grace, as well as body type and wing configurations. To the left is the design for the dragonfly tattoo on her lower back.

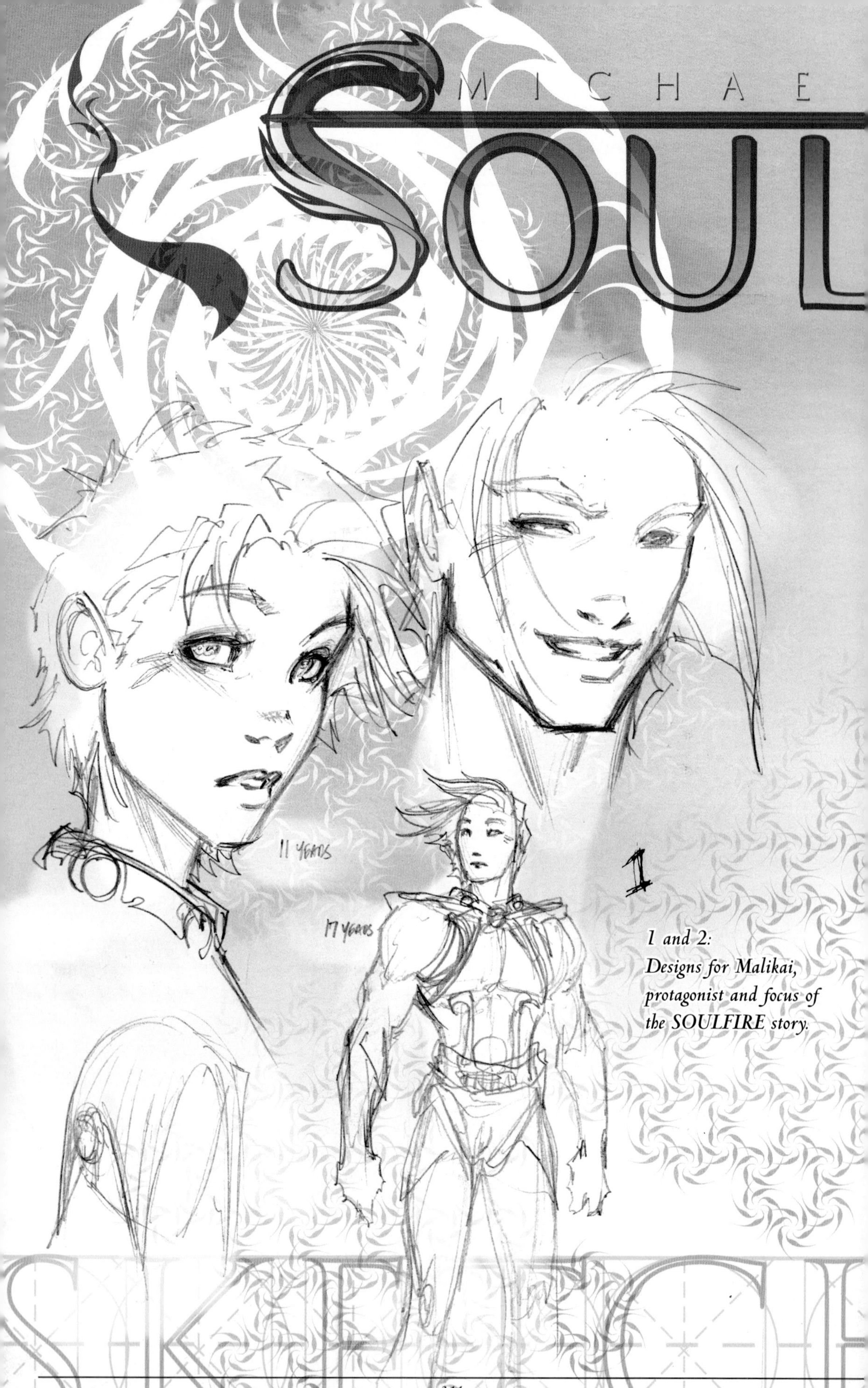
MICHAE
SOUL
11 YEARS
17 YEARS
1
SKETCH

1 and 2:
Designs for Malikai, protagonist and focus of the SOULFIRE story.

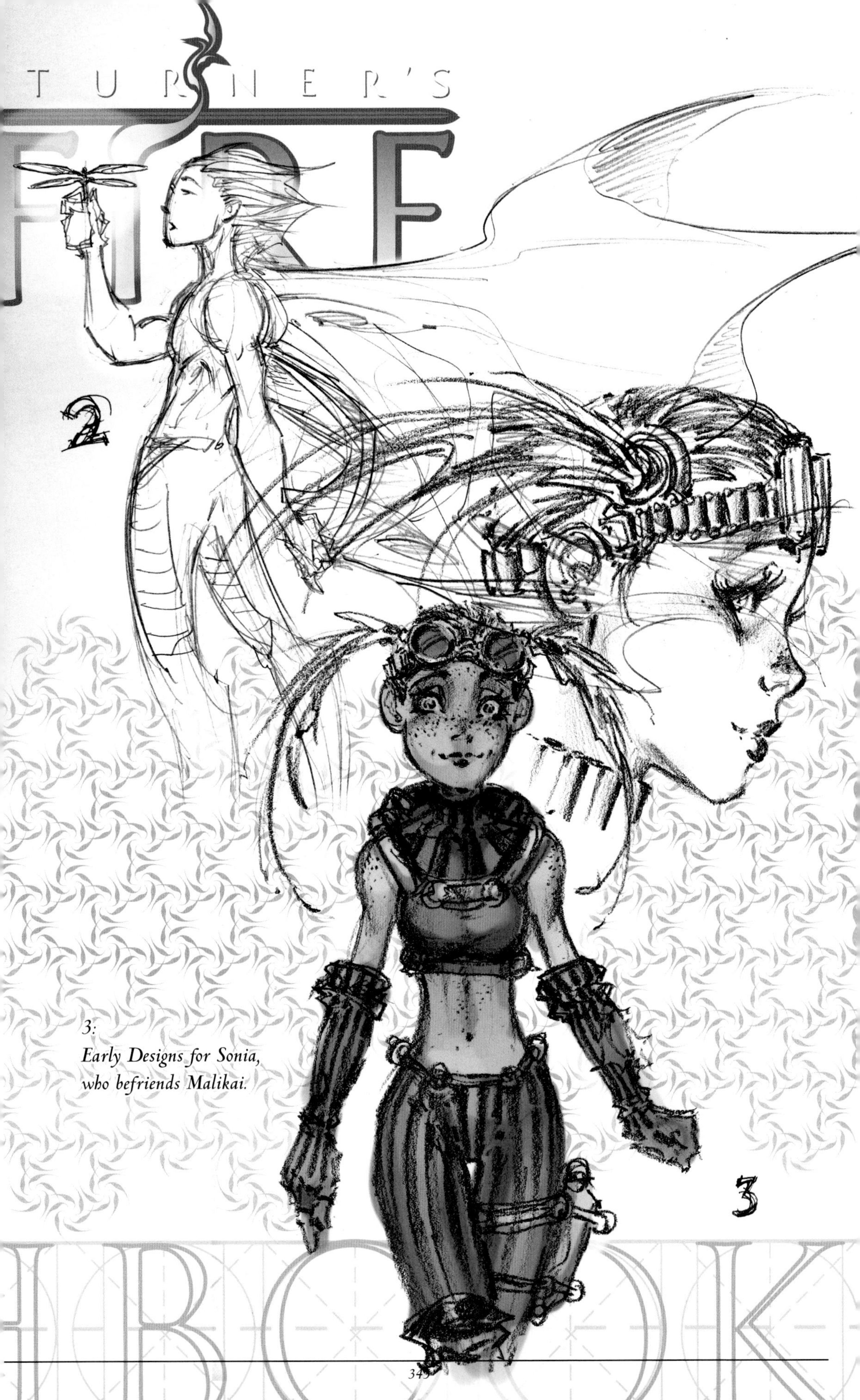
TURNER'S
FIRE
BOOK
2
3

3:
Early Designs for Sonia, who befriends Malikai.

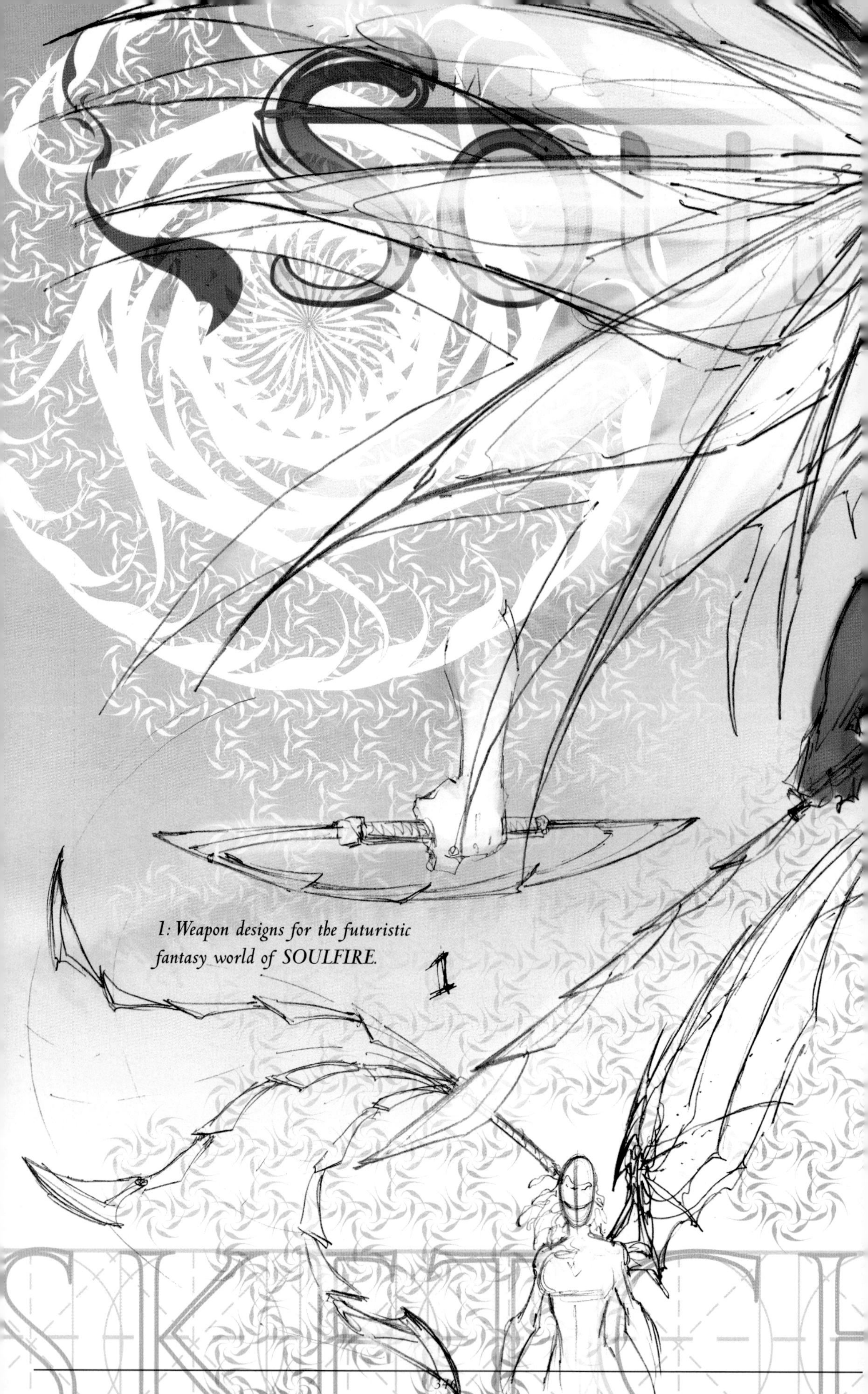
1: Weapon designs for the futuristic fantasy world of SOULFIRE.

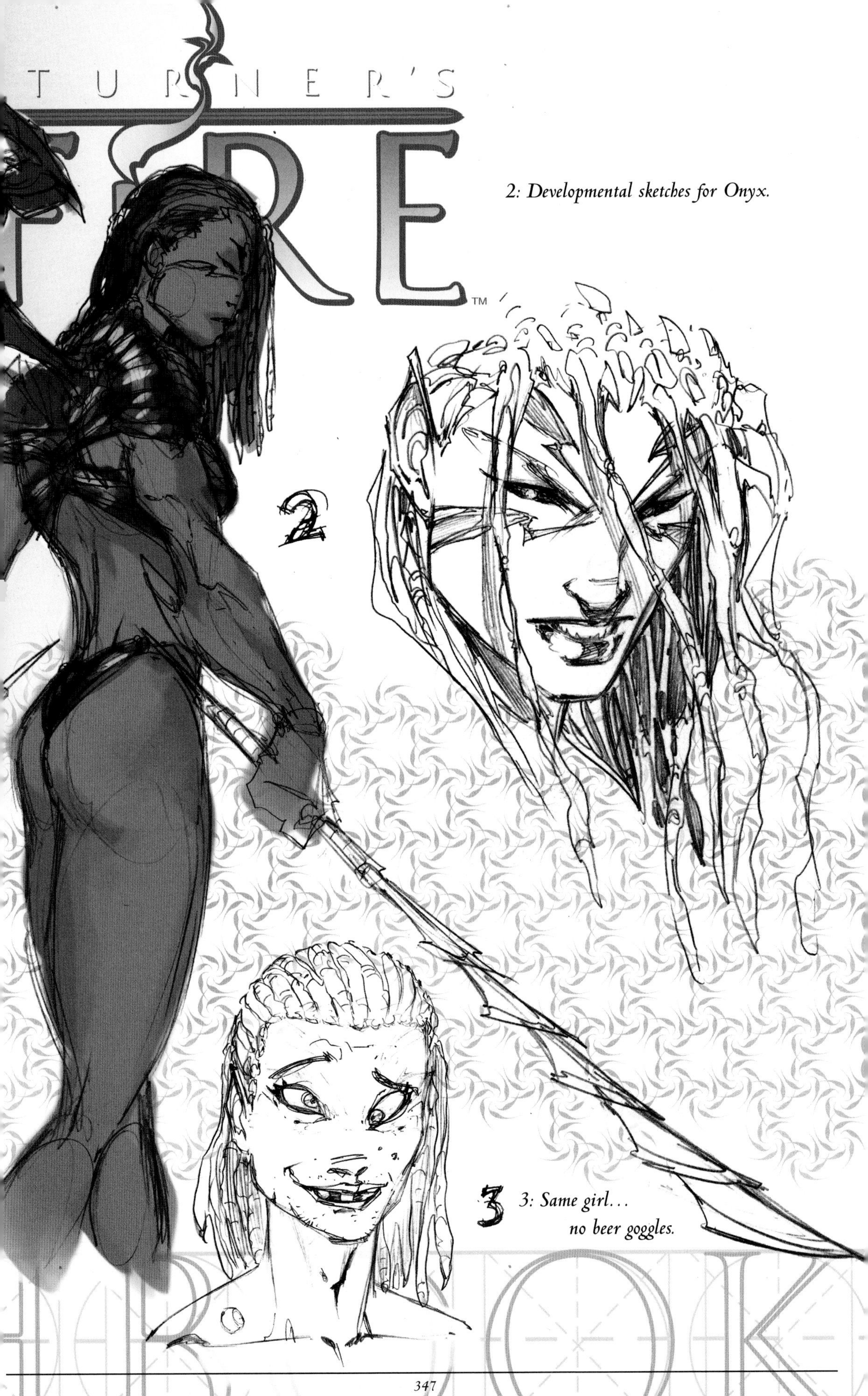
TURNER'S
2
3

2: Developmental sketches for Onyx.

3: Same girl...
no beer goggles.

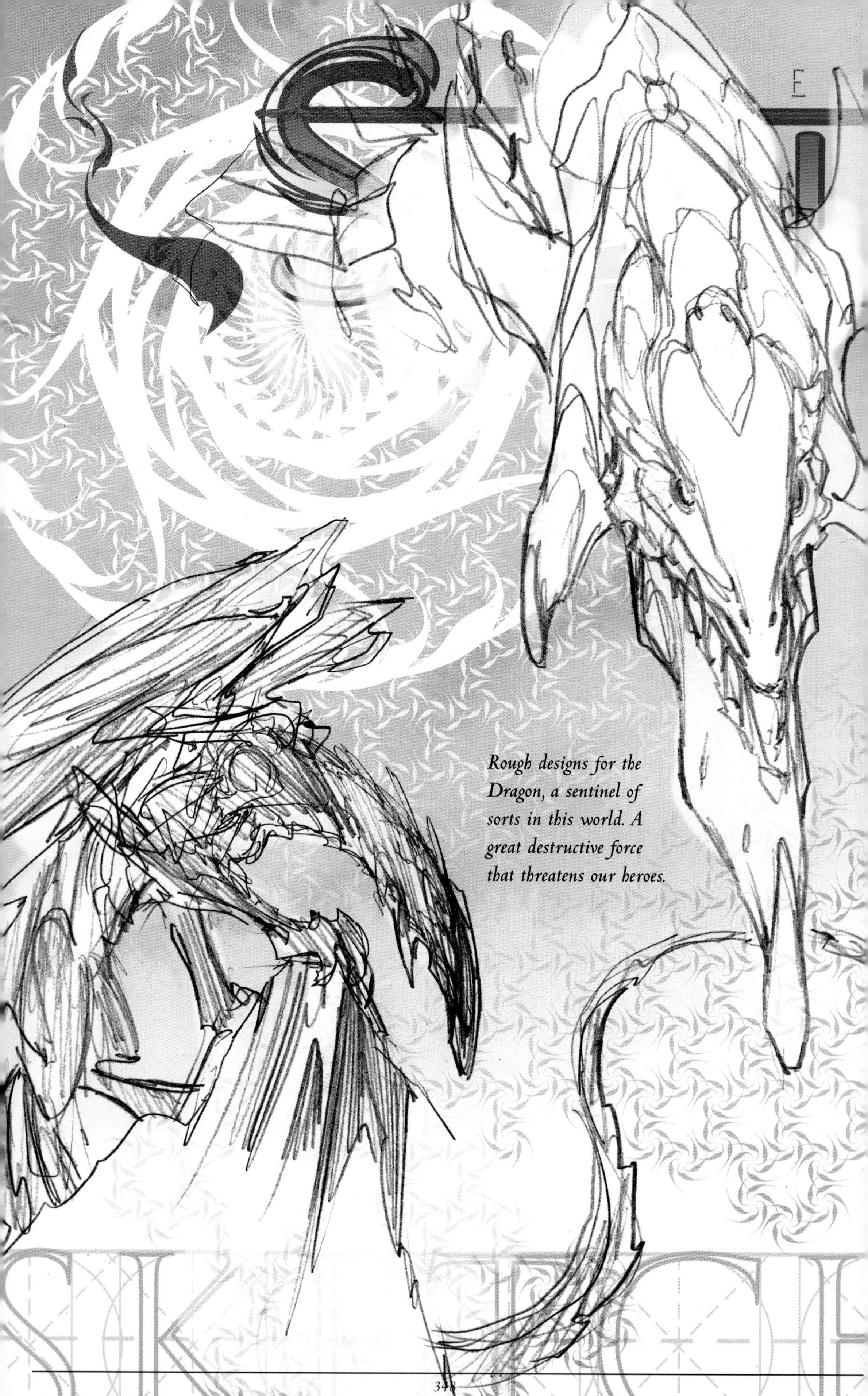

Rough designs for the Dragon, a sentinel of sorts in this world. A great destructive force that threatens our heroes.

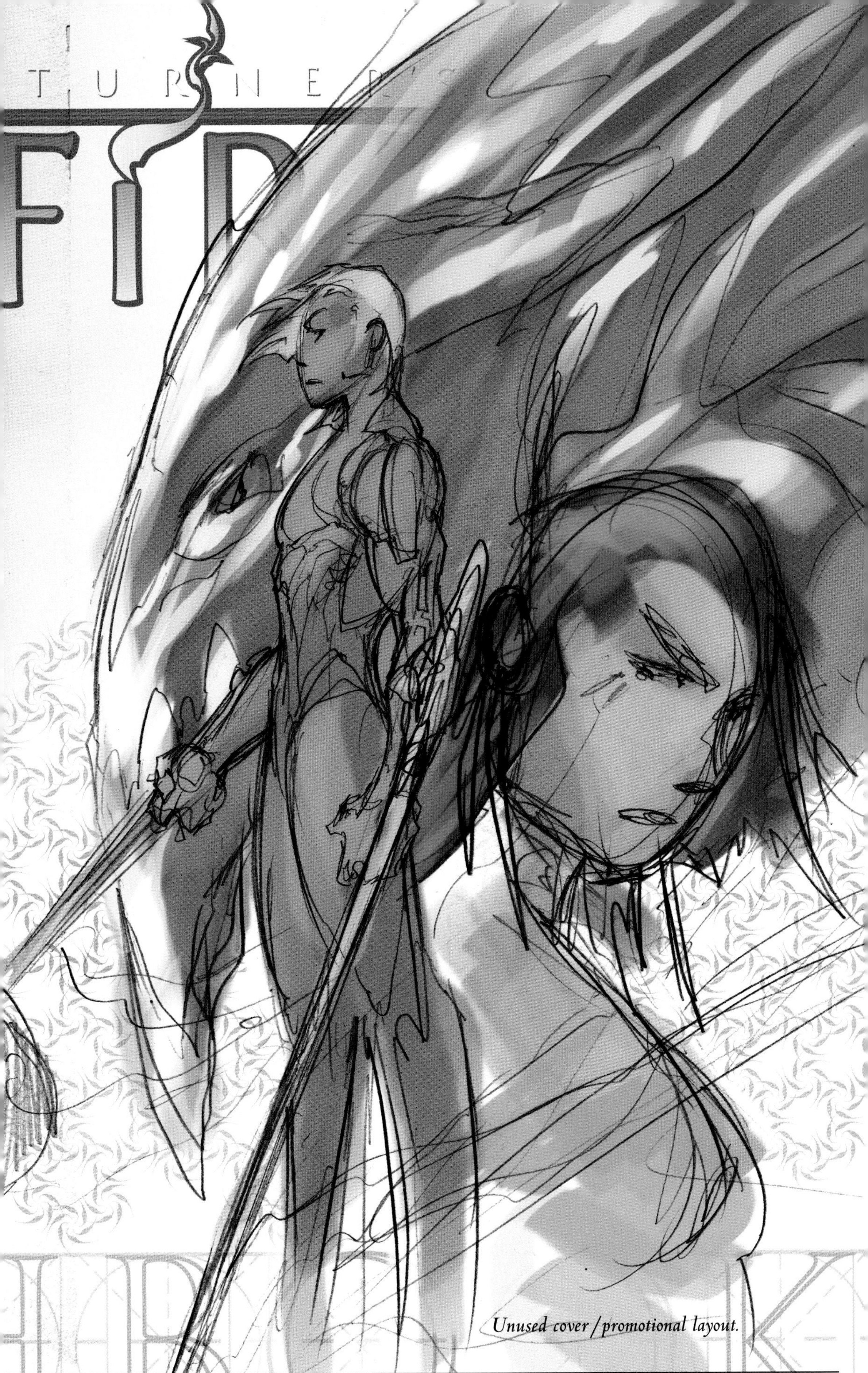
TURNER'S

Unused cover / promotional layout.

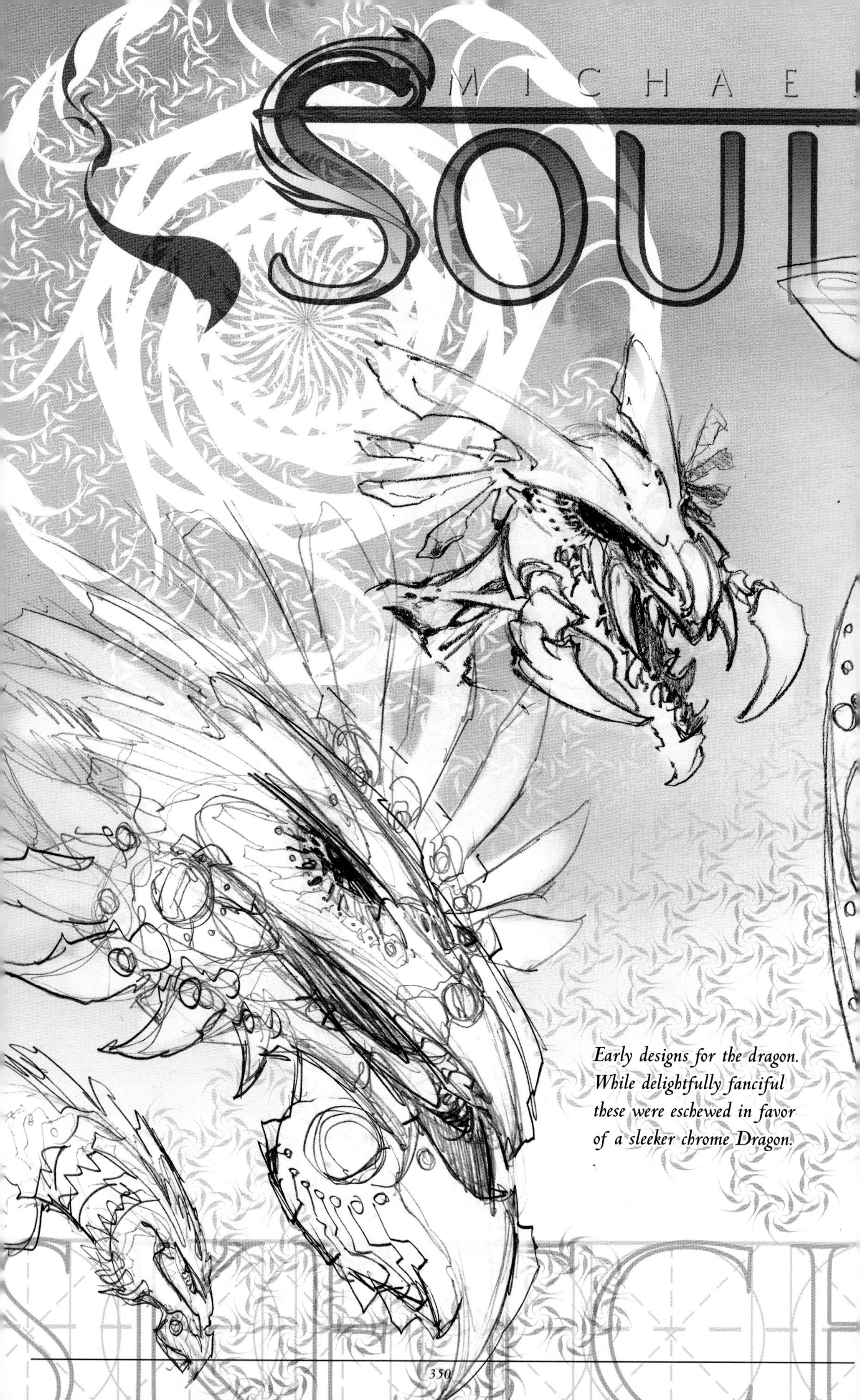
M I C H A E
SOU

Early designs for the dragon. While delightfully fanciful these were eschewed in favor of a sleeker chrome Dragon.

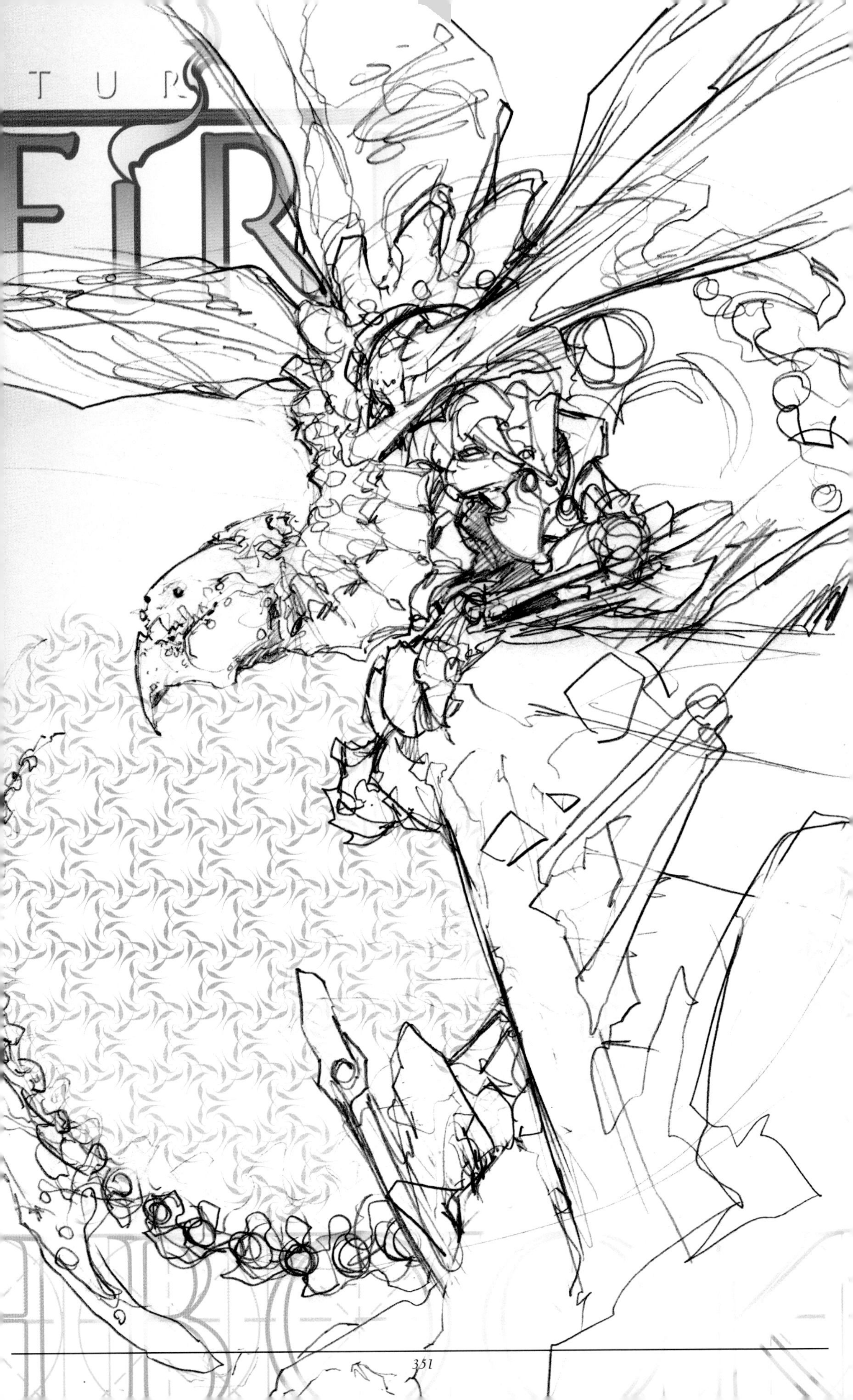

Presented for the first time is the original Soulfire Preview script by Jeph Loeb. Highlighting the working relationship between writer and artist, this nine page script presents a detailed look at the written blueprint of Soulfire that Michael Turner worked off of throughout the beginning of the first volume.

story Jeph Loeb, Michael Turner - *script:* Jeph Loeb

SOULFIRE SCRIPT

SOULFIRE
THE PREVIEW

Excerpt from Issue #1
03.30.04
Script by Jeph Loeb - 9-page story

PAGE ONE - SAN FRANCISCO - LATE NIGHT INTO MORNING

PANEL ONE

We start on ACTION. Three HEAVILY ARMED APACHE HELICOPTERS (*except there is something different about them… something futuristic -- maybe it's the blades have been replaced with jet engines…. something*) that look like three ADVANCING METALLIC BIRDS swoop under the Golden Gate Bridge. They are heavily armed with rocket launchers and missiles on their wings.

Reflected in the water, we can see the hint of FLAMES coming off the city…

CAPTION BOX #1

> *Sometime after tomorrow…*

CHOPPER #1
ELECTRONIC BALLOON #2

> *Hold pattern until point of discovery, boys and girls.*

PANEL TWO

Now, INSIDE CHOPPER #1 -- we see TWO PILOTS, helmets on, but shields up so we can see their pretty/handsome faces, but their figures are distinct -- it's a MAN and a WOMAN.

CAPTION BOX #3

> *Lt. Col. A.J. Foyt. Major Venessa Hope.*

VENESSA
DIALOGUE BALLOON #4

> *So… when <u>are</u> you going to tell your wife?*

A.J.
DIALOGUE BALLOON #5

> *That you and I have been sleeping together?*

VENESSA
DIALOGUE BALLOON #6

> *We've been doing a lot more than just sleeping…*

PANEL THREE

Now, INSIDE CHOPPER #2 -- TWO FEMALE PILOTS as they approach the city we can see FIRES reflected in their glass and helmets.
One of the women is black; the other white. In their tight fitting uniforms, they're…um… well, they look like Mike draws women. Hot.

CAPTION BOX #7

> *Captain Julienne Dominique. Captain Kristina McKenna.*

JULIENNE
DIALOGUE BALLOON #8

> *Any ideas what caused this?*

KRISTINA
DIALOGUE BALLOON #9

> *Just that we're getting heat registrations off the mark.*

JULIENNE
DIALOGUE BALLOON #10

> *I hope we get to blow something up. I haven't launched in like a month.*

KRISTINA
DIALOGUE BALLOON #11

> *You got that right!*

PANEL FOUR

And now inside CHOPPER #3, the Top Guns -- TWO Fighter Jocks, young sexy guys -- Tom Cruise and Val Kilmer back in the day. Even their angle for entry is a bit tilted as they soar INTO the city.

CAPTION BOX #12

> *Captain Carter "Cat" Wilson. Captain Mark Hennessy.*

CAT
DIALOGUE BALLOON #13

> *Dude.*

MARK
DIALOGUE BALLOON #14

> *Yeah, dude.*

CAT
DIALOGUE BALLOON #15

> *Check this out. We're gonna see some sweet action.*

MARK
DIALOGUE BALLOON #16

    Dude. That'd be sweet!

PAGES 2/3 - SAN FRANCISCO - NIGHT INTO DAWN

DOUBLE PAGE SPREAD WITH INSET PANELS
HUGE SHOT, STRETCHING ACROSS THE PAGE
The THREE HELICOPTERS, still in formation, hover over the city which looks like it's been FIREBOMBED. Entire SKYSCRAPERS are ENGULFED in flames -- lighting the city like huge Roman candles.

CHOPPER #1
ELECTRONIC BALLOON #1

    What the hell…!

INSET PANEL 2

Still in formation, the choppers now dart down along the streets, trying to find the cause of this. There are CHARRED BODIES along the piled up abandoned cars.

CHOPPER #2
ELECTRONIC BALLOON #2

    Um… guys… I'm getting a heat sig coming up that's… different.

INSET PANEL 3

Inside Chopper #3, The Guys look down at the PLASMA SCREEN DISPLAY that has one distinct color for a BUILDING on fire and on top of it.. something else …. something HUGE… burning more BLUE AND WHITE than the orange and red of the building…

CAT
DIALOGUE BALLOON #3

    Dude, we're headed right at it. Whatever it is…

MARK
DIALOGUE BALLOON #4

    Sweet.

INSET PANEL 4

The choppers arc UP a building that is FLAMING HOT -- windows shattered, the framework exposed… and nearing the top…

CHOPPER #1
ELECTRONIC BALLOON #5

    I want you all locked and loaded.

INSET PANEL 5

They find at the top… something… huge and black -- it could be part of the building… It seems sort of METALLIC -- and they seem like bugs around it…

CHOPPER #1
ELECTRONIC BALLOON #6

    I've got a baaaad feeling about this…

PAGES 4/5 - CITYSCAPE - NIGHT INTO DAWN
This is TWO HUGE PANELS -- WIDE SCREEN -- ONE ON TOP OF THE OTHER.

PANEL ONE

Okay, now REVEAL… THE DRAGON. This big dark THING they were looking at comes to life and oh, SHIT -- It SPREADS ITS WINGS and they are several blocks long -- Its TAIL unravels down several stories below them, forked at the end. And it's EYES… a cold blue… ice…

CHOPPER #1
ELECTRONIC BURST #1

    $&#! FIRE!*

PANEL TWO

HUGE SHOT of the Dragon OPENING his mouth and FLAMES ERUPTING out like the meanest, badass flame thrower you've ever seen in your life and it just INCINERATES Chopper #1 with such heat that in the flames we can ACTUALLY SEE the framework of the Helicopter and SKELETONS of A.J. and VEN fried alive!

PAGE 6 - SKYLINE - NIGHT INTO DAY

PANEL ONE

Both remaining Choppers FIRE MISSILES, ROCKETS -- HITTING The Dragon with everything they've got! As they EXPLODE off the WINGS of the creature…

PANEL TWO

INSIDE Chopper #3, The Dudes look out through the windshield, and as the smoke CLEARS… The Dragon is UNFAZED and COMING.

CAT
DIALOGUE BALLOON #1

    Duuuuude… All I think we did was piss it off!

PANEL THREE

The two remaining Choppers take PULL BACK, ARCING UPWARDS, taking EVASIVE ACTION as the Dragon pursues!

CHOPPER #2
ELECTRONIC BALLOON #2

    PULL BACK!

PANEL FOUR

Overhead shot of the city as the Dragon FLIES AFTER the two Choppers that look like Sparrows flying off from a GIANT EAGLE. Chopper #2 banks a turn *off the main boulevard*, as the Dragon bears down on Chopper #3.

PANEL FIVE

The Dragon's TAIL WHIPS AROUND and SMACKS Chopper #3 like it wasn't anything more than a hornet in its way. The Chopper SHATTERS on impact and then...

PANEL SIX

-- EXPLODES against a skyscraper, a tumbling fireball headed for the street...!

PAGE 7 - CITYSCAPE - SKYLINE - NIGHT INTO DAWN

PANEL ONE

We come back onto Chopper #3 as it BANKS a corner at a severe angle just trying to get the HELL out of this HELL!

PANEL TWO

Inside the Chopper, The Two female pilots (Julienne and Kristina) look all around... like maybe they... made it out?

> JULIENNE
> DIALOGUE BALLOON #1
>
> *Where the hell is that thing?*

> KRISTINA
> DIALOGUE BALLOON #2
>
> *You mean, WHAT the hell is that thing!*

PANEL THREE

Suddenly -- in a SHOCKING MOMENT -- The Dragon COMES UP from BELOW -- its GAPING JAWS OPEN -- GLISTENING METALLIC TEETH on either side of the Chopper --

PANEL FOUR

Inside -- the two pilots watch in horror as the TEETH start to CLOSE IN on them shredding the armored cockpit...

> JULIENNE
> DIALOGUE BALLOON #3
>
> *MOTHER FUH---*

PANEL FIVE

...and then just... blackness... =WHEW=!!!

PAGE 8 - CITYSCAPE - SKYLINE - NIGHT INTO DAWN

PANEL ONE

As the Dragon flies off into the horizon, leaving the destruction of the city behind -- either unthinking or uncaring -- we see the SILHOUETTE of a FEMALE FORM SLOWLY ENTER FRAME from above.

CAPTION BOX #1

There are few who bore witness to this day.

PANEL TWO

As the Dragon moves further away from us... The FIGURE moves closer in the foreground... an astonishingly perfect form of a woman.

CAPTION BOX #2

The dead will be buried.

PANEL THREE

The Dragon moves even further out... as the female figure has lowered enough into frame that we can see that she has WINGS!

CAPTION BOX #3

Graves will have markers.

PANEL FOUR

As the Dragon virtually disappears into the first inkling of the DAWN, we now can see, still draped in shadow, the woman's head -- her hair tumbling off her shoulders. Her head is bowed before the destruction of the city below her.

CAPTION BOX #4

In the end, all that matters isthat she has come...

PAGE 9 - SKYSCRAPER - SKYLINE - DAWN
FULL PAGE SPLASH

COME AROUND TO REVEAL - GRACE, in all her regal glory, her wings extended, as she hovers a few feet off from the edge of the building.

The City below is in even greater turmoil -- and a hint of how the world may someday become if this situation remains unchecked.

And toward that end, she says quietly:

> GRACE
> DIALOGUE BALLOON #1
>
> *I have to find the boy....*

CAPTION BOX #2

Want to See More? Be sure to Check out Soulfire #1 -- on Sale in TBD!

To be continued...

SOULFIRE EXTRAS

SOULFIRE SWIMSUIT SPLASH

pgs. 357 - 369

The following gallery of covers and pin-ups (as well as the prior items that were interspersed among the story pages) were part of Aspen's annual swimsuit issues, the Aspen Splash: Swimsuit Spectacular, released at Comic Con International in San Diego each year. Many of the industry's leading talents were given the opportunity to present their vision of Soulfire's popular heroes and villains in a more playful setting and light. The results include some of the most popular Michael Turner covers and Soulfire pin-ups ever produced.

SOULFIRE RELATED COVERS

Soulfire was featured on many covers to other publications demonstrating the power of the characters and underscoring the popularity of Grace and the Soulfire universe. We have selected a few notable ones to present to you here.

pg 370

WIZARD: THE GUIDE TO COMICS MAGAZINE #139

This cover is the first official appearance of Grace and Soulfire. In the spring of 2003, two brand new creations of Michael Turner, Soulfire and Ekos, were both previewed in Wizard. Readers were given a chance to vote on which title would be the first to be published by the then fledgling Aspen Comics. Out of many thousands of entries, Soulfire won by just a few hundred votes.

pg 371

WIZARD: THE GUIDE TO COMICS MAGAZINE #154

This issue featured the world premiere of Soulfire #1!

pg 372

PROGRAM COVER TO THE 2008 WWLA CONVENTION

Michael Turner was the featured Guest of Honor for this show, a position he held at many conventions throughout the years. This convention would mark his final public appearance.

pg 373
SOULFIRE STATUES

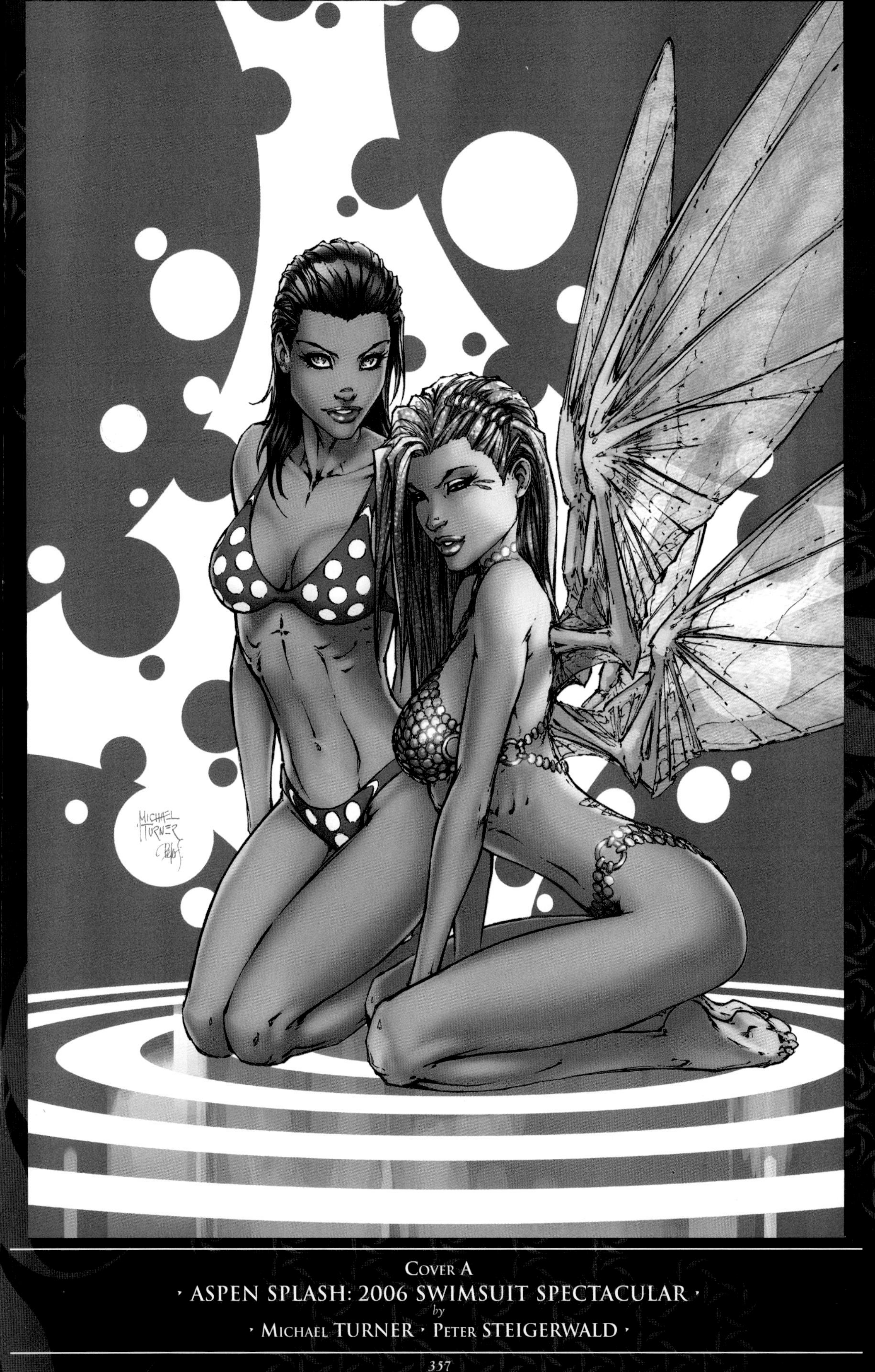
MICHAEL TURNER

COVER A
· ASPEN SPLASH: 2006 SWIMSUIT SPECTACULAR ·
by
· MICHAEL TURNER · PETER STEIGERWALD ·

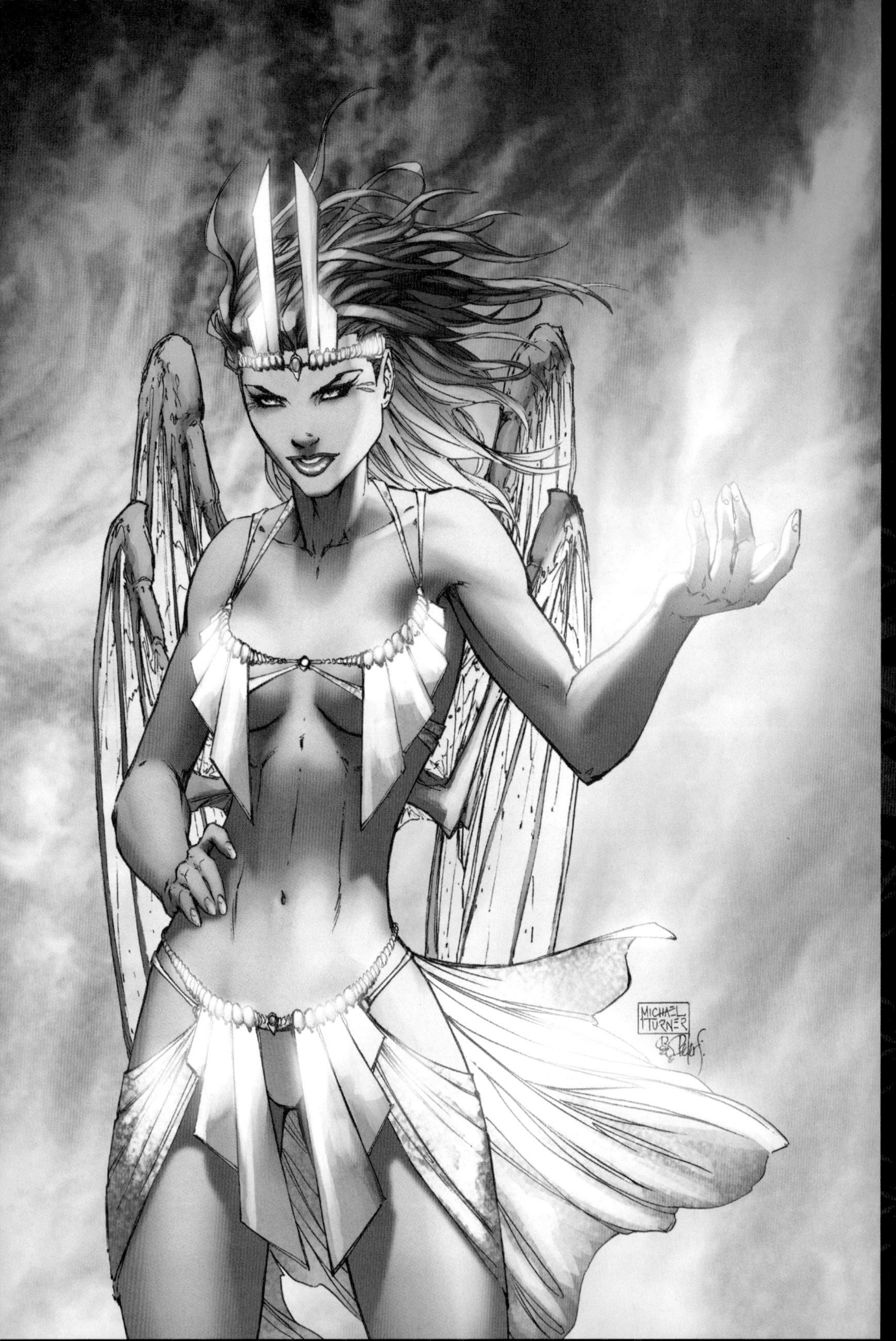
MICHAEL TURNER

Wizard World Los Angeles 2006 Convention Exclusive Cover B

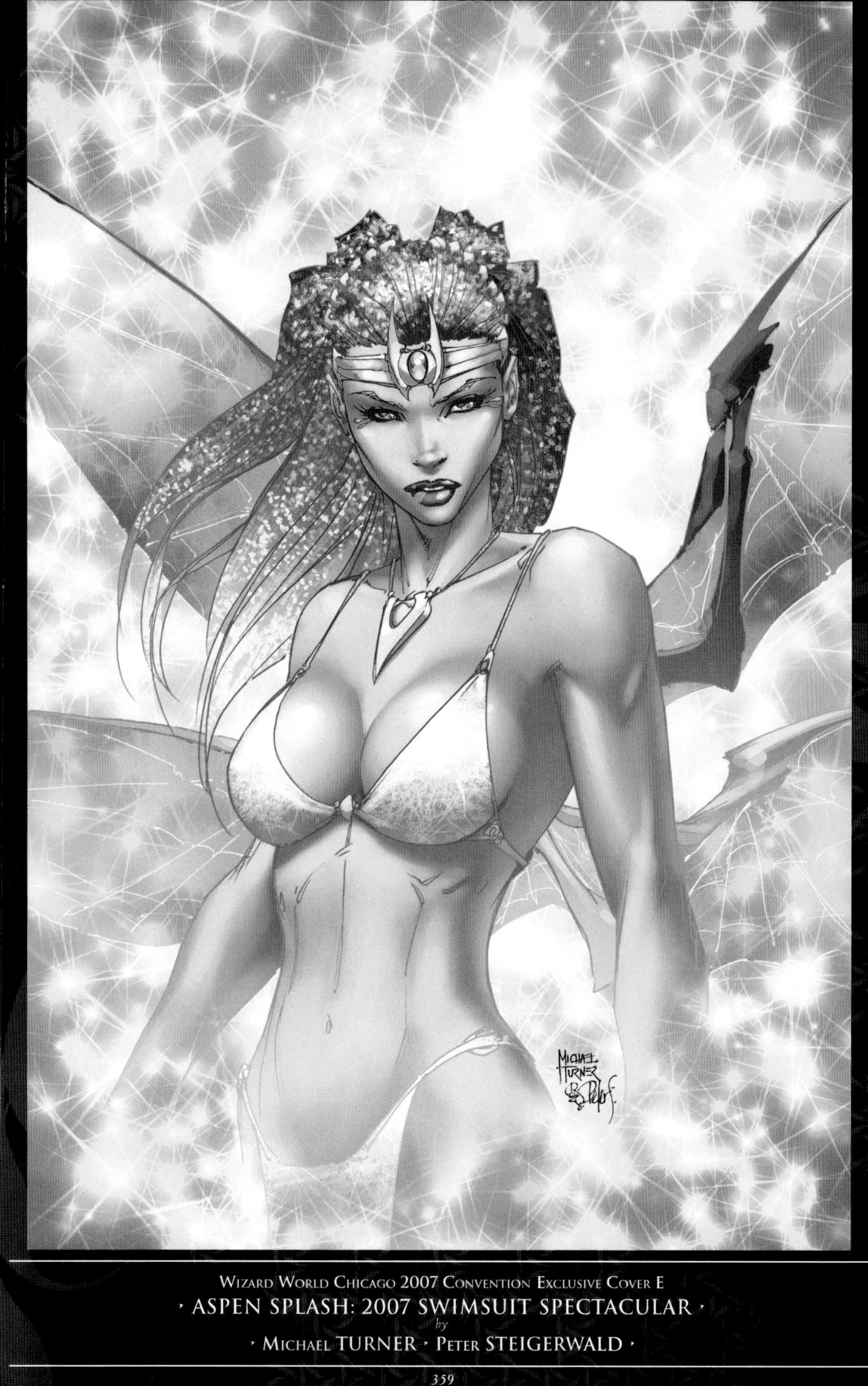
MICHAEL TURNER

WIZARD WORLD CHICAGO 2007 CONVENTION EXCLUSIVE COVER E

· ASPEN SPLASH: 2007 SWIMSUIT SPECTACULAR ·

by

· MICHAEL TURNER · PETER STEIGERWALD ·

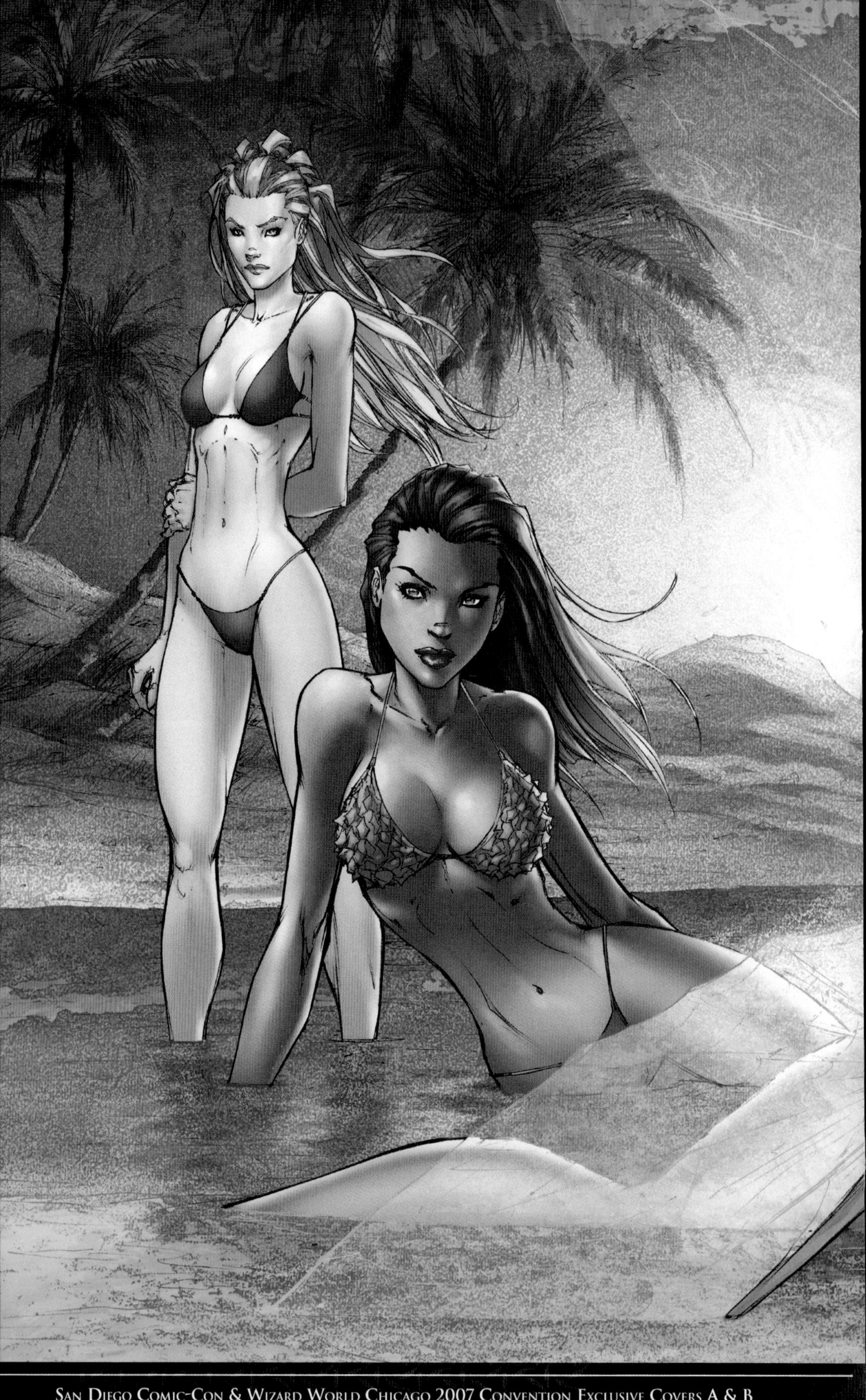

San Diego Comic-Con & Wizard World Chicago 2007 Convention Exclusive Covers A & B
· ASPEN SPLASH: 2007 SWIMSUIT SPECTACULAR ·

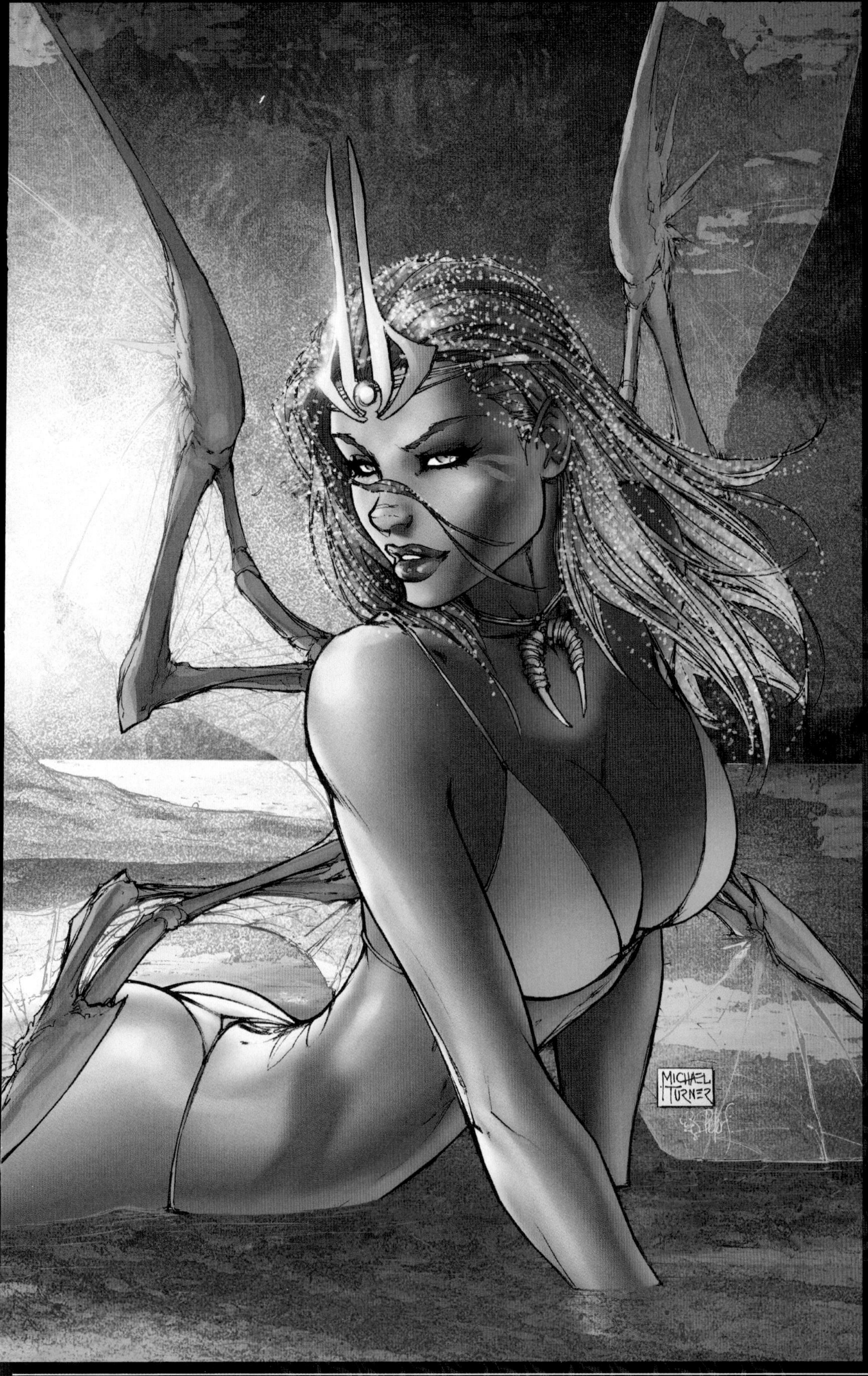
MICHAEL TURNER

by

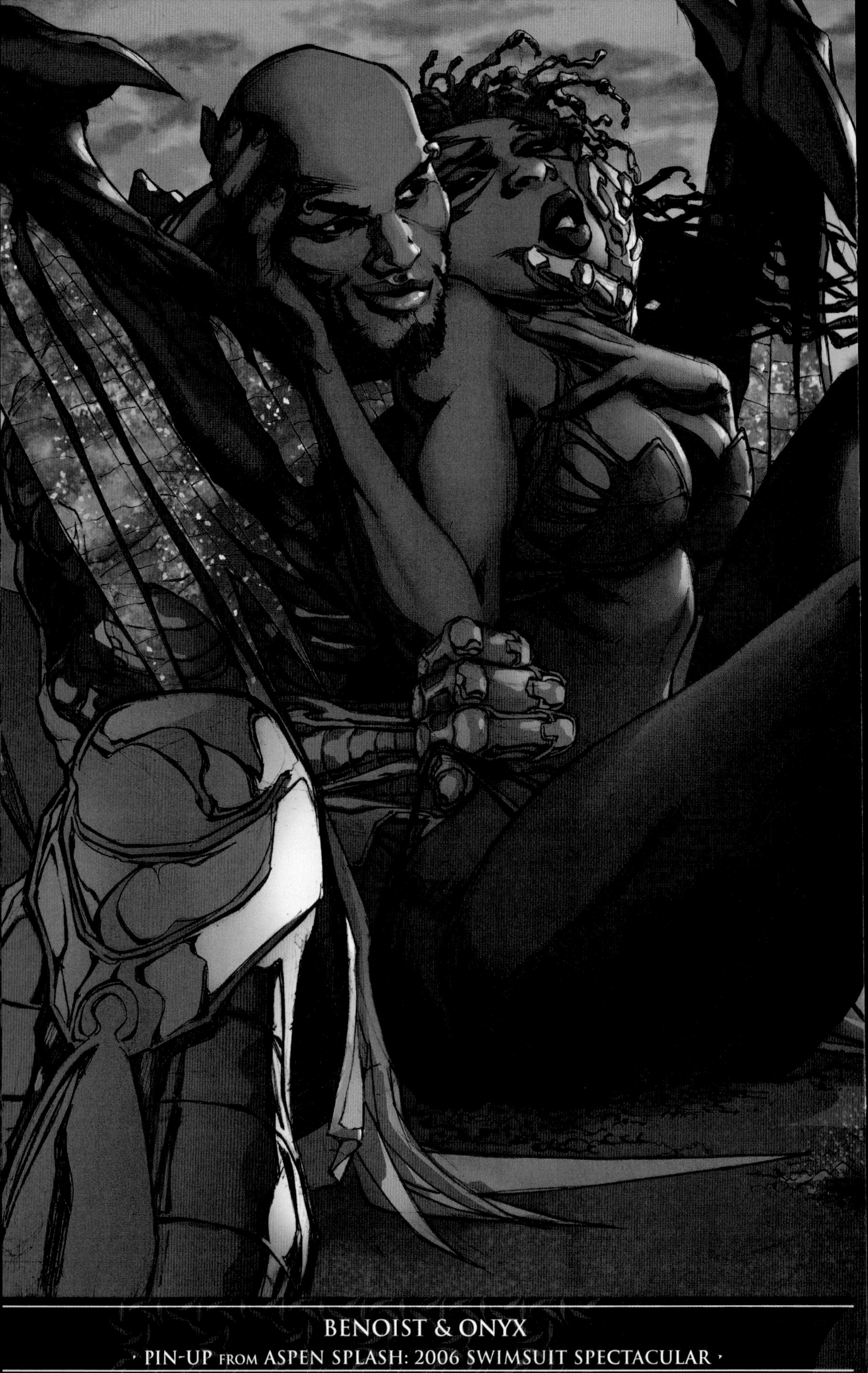

BENOIST & ONYX

· PIN-UP FROM ASPEN SPLASH: 2006 SWIMSUIT SPECTACULAR ·

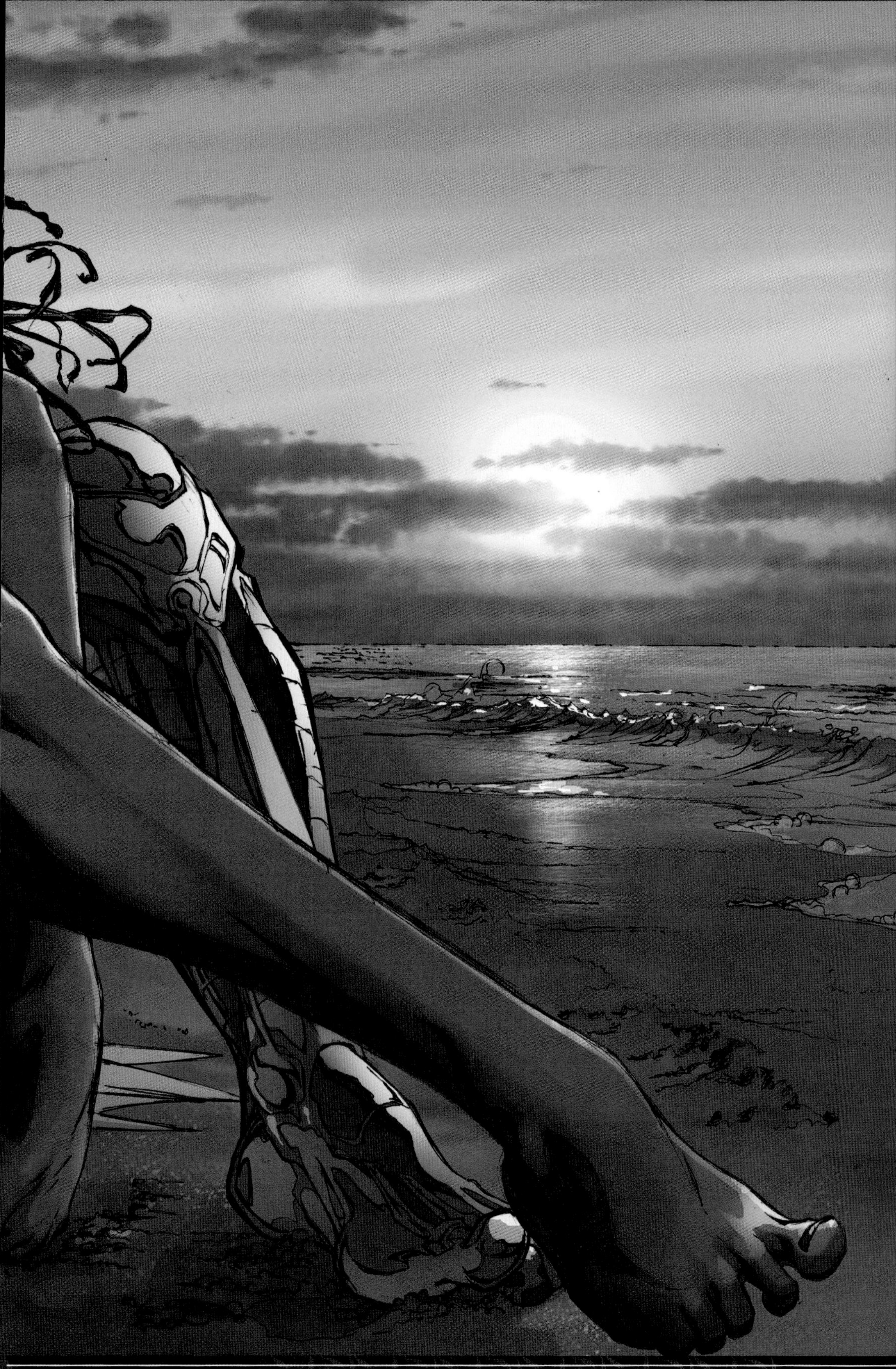

by
· Koi TURNBULL · Beth SOTELO ·

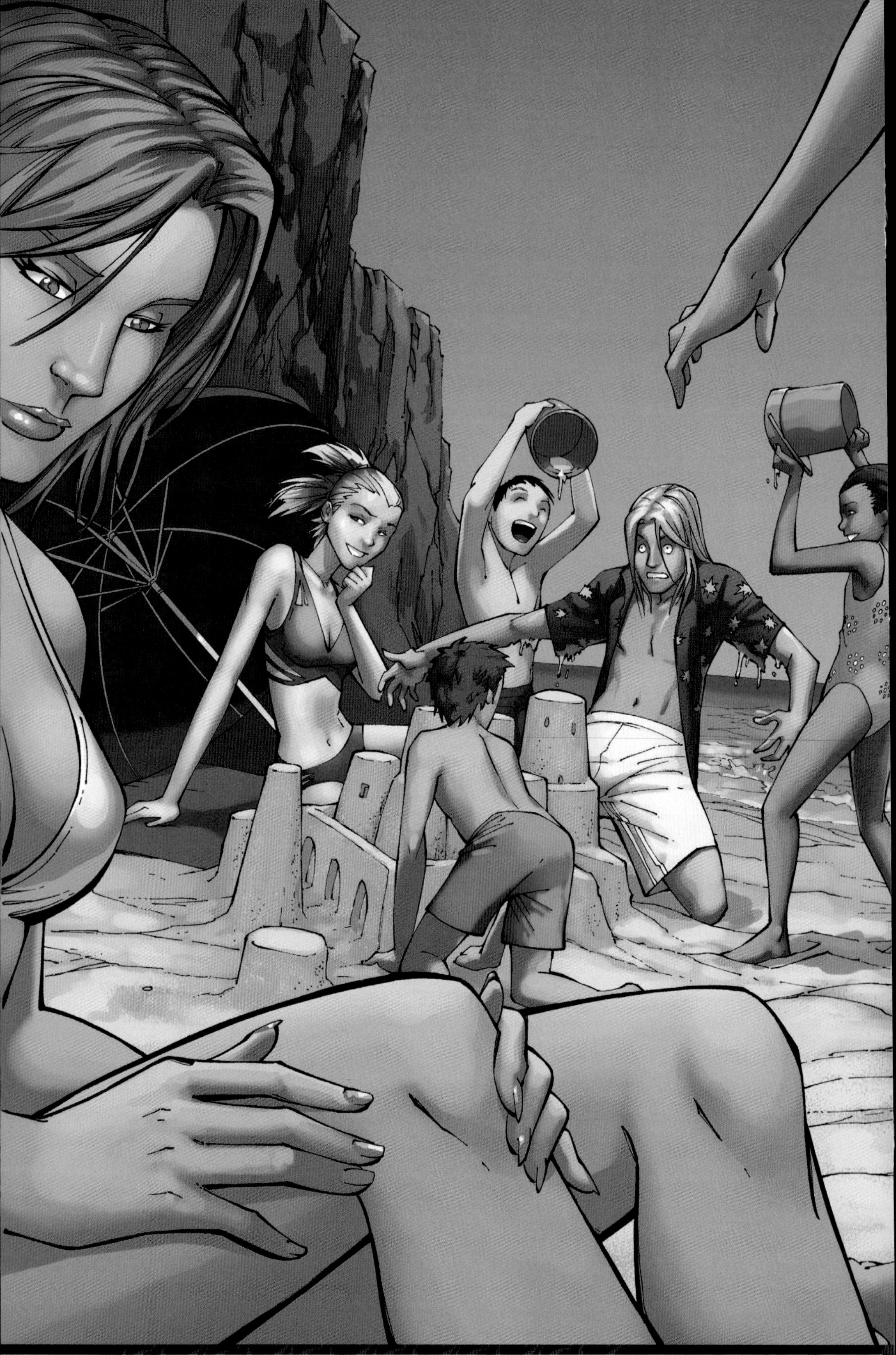

SONIA, P.J. & MALIKAI

· PIN-UP FROM ASPEN SPLASH: 2006 SWIMSUIT SPECTACULAR ·

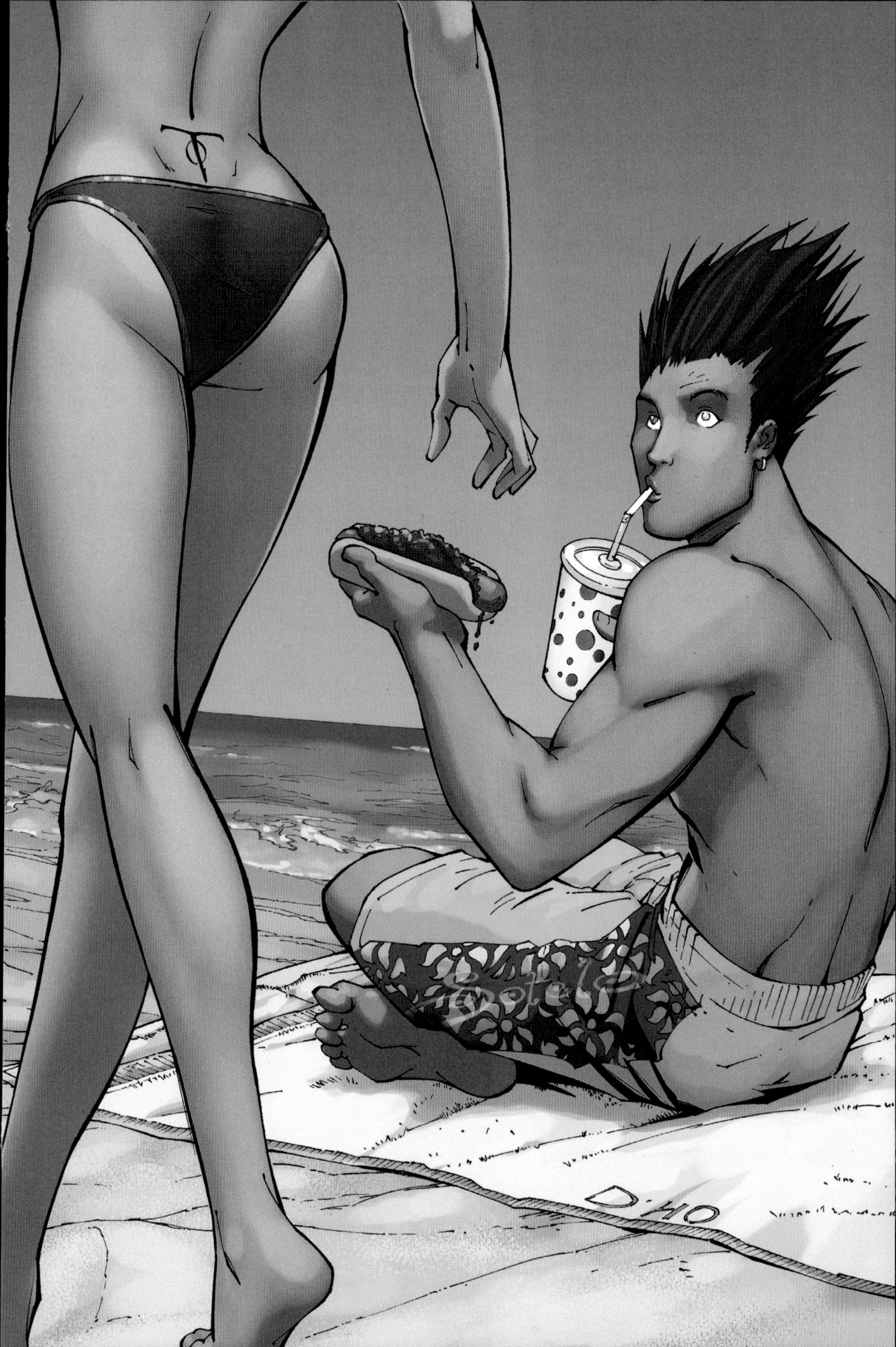
Sotelo
D·HO

by

· Marcus TO · Don HO · Beth SOTELO ·

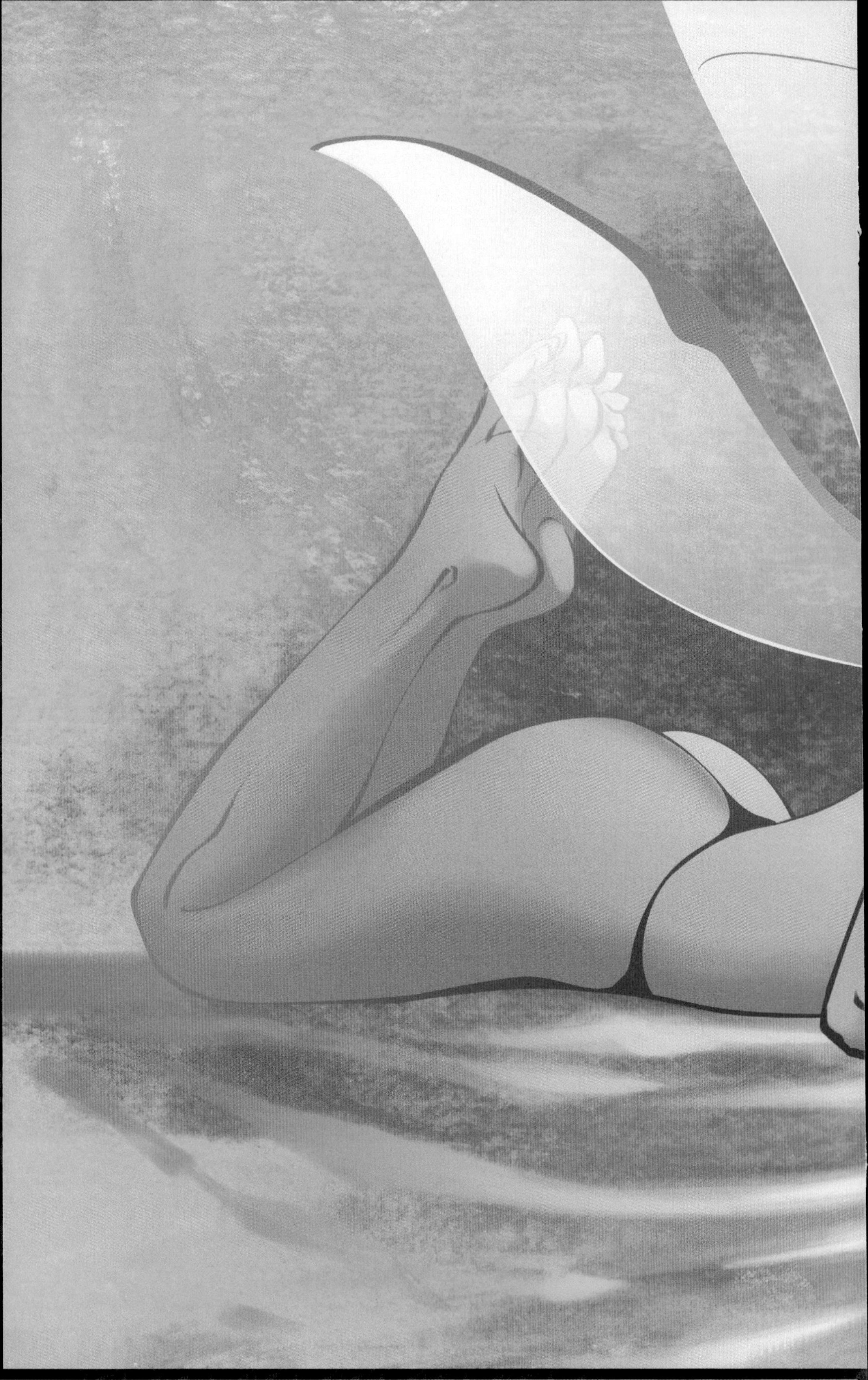

GRACE

· PIN-UP FROM ASPEN SPLASH: 2006 SWIMSUIT SPECTACULAR ·

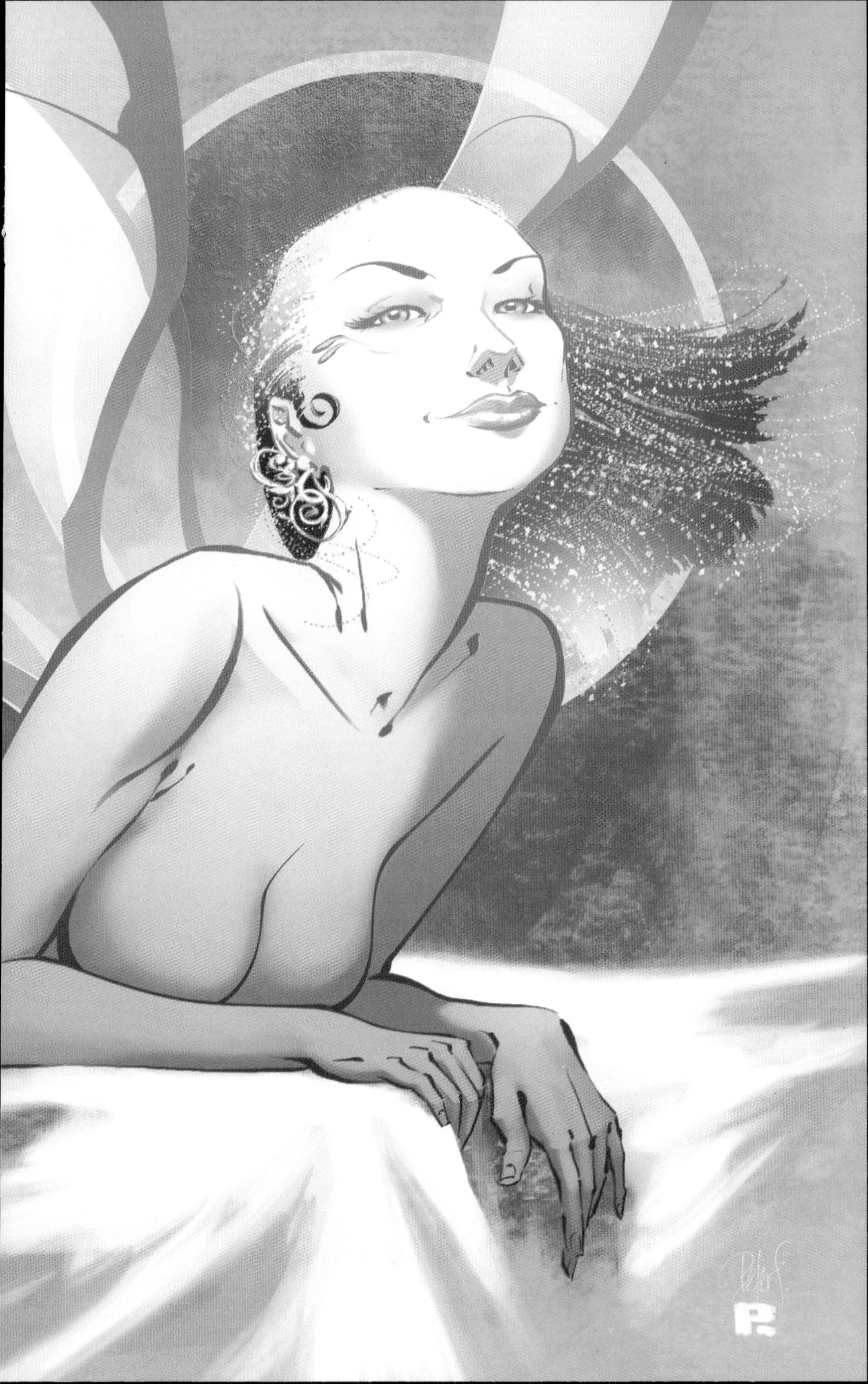

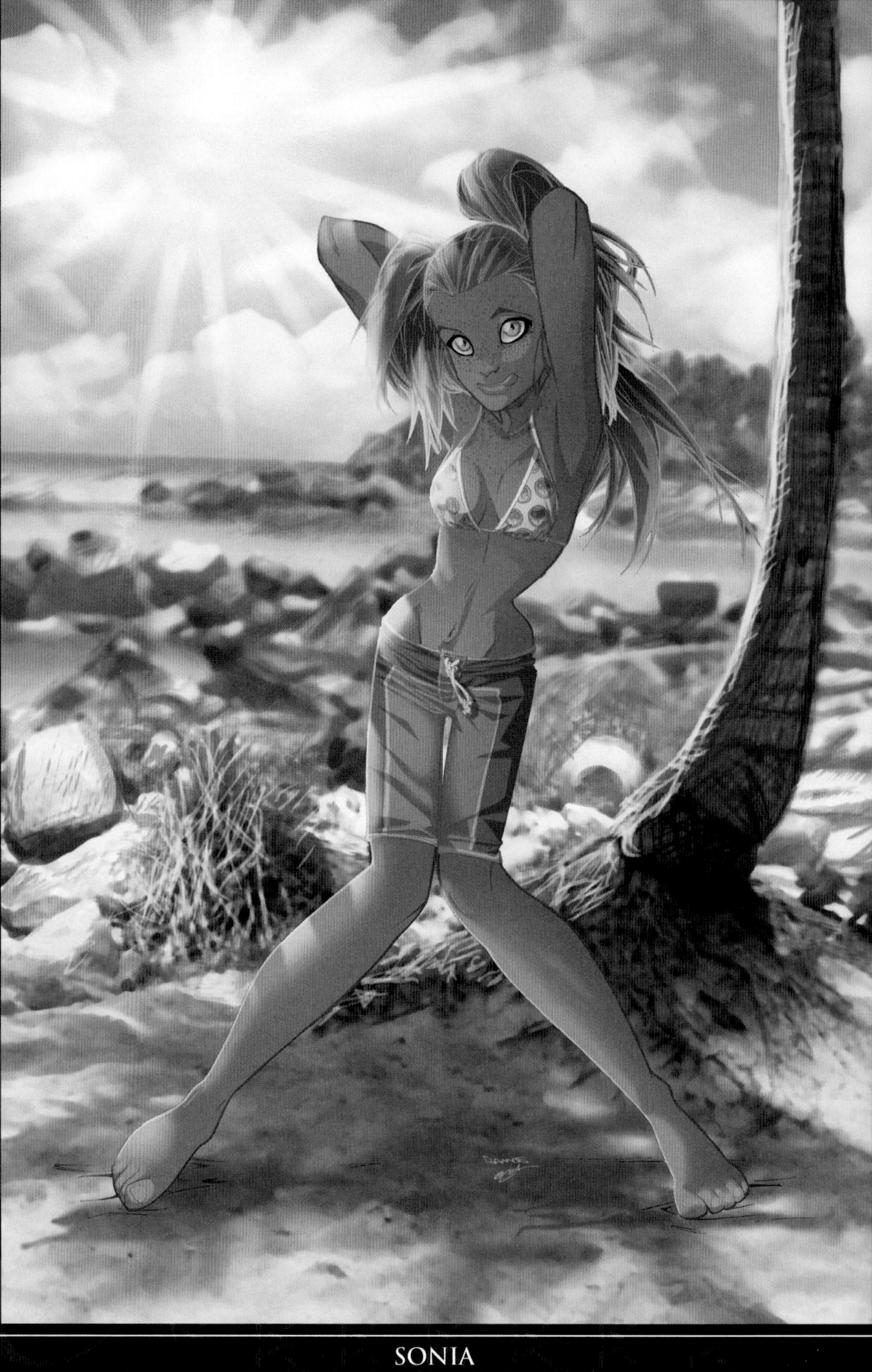

SONIA

· PIN-UP from ASPEN SPLASH: 2007 SWIMSUIT SPECTACULAR ·

by

· Humberto RAMOS · Leonardo OLEA ·

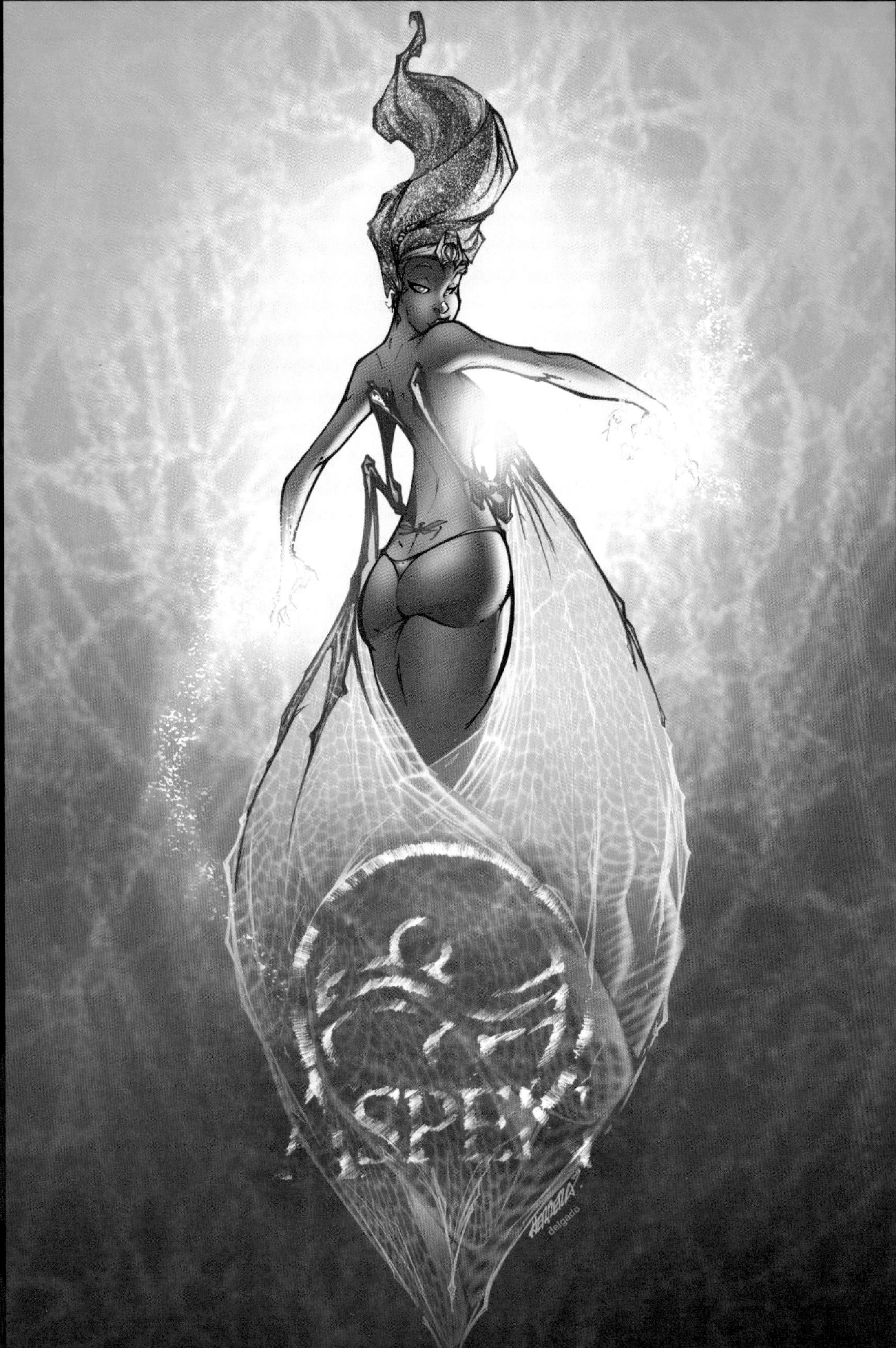

GRACE

· PIN-UP FROM ASPEN SPLASH: 2008 SWIMSUIT SPECTACULAR ·

by

· FRANCISCO HERRERA · LEONARDO OLEA ·

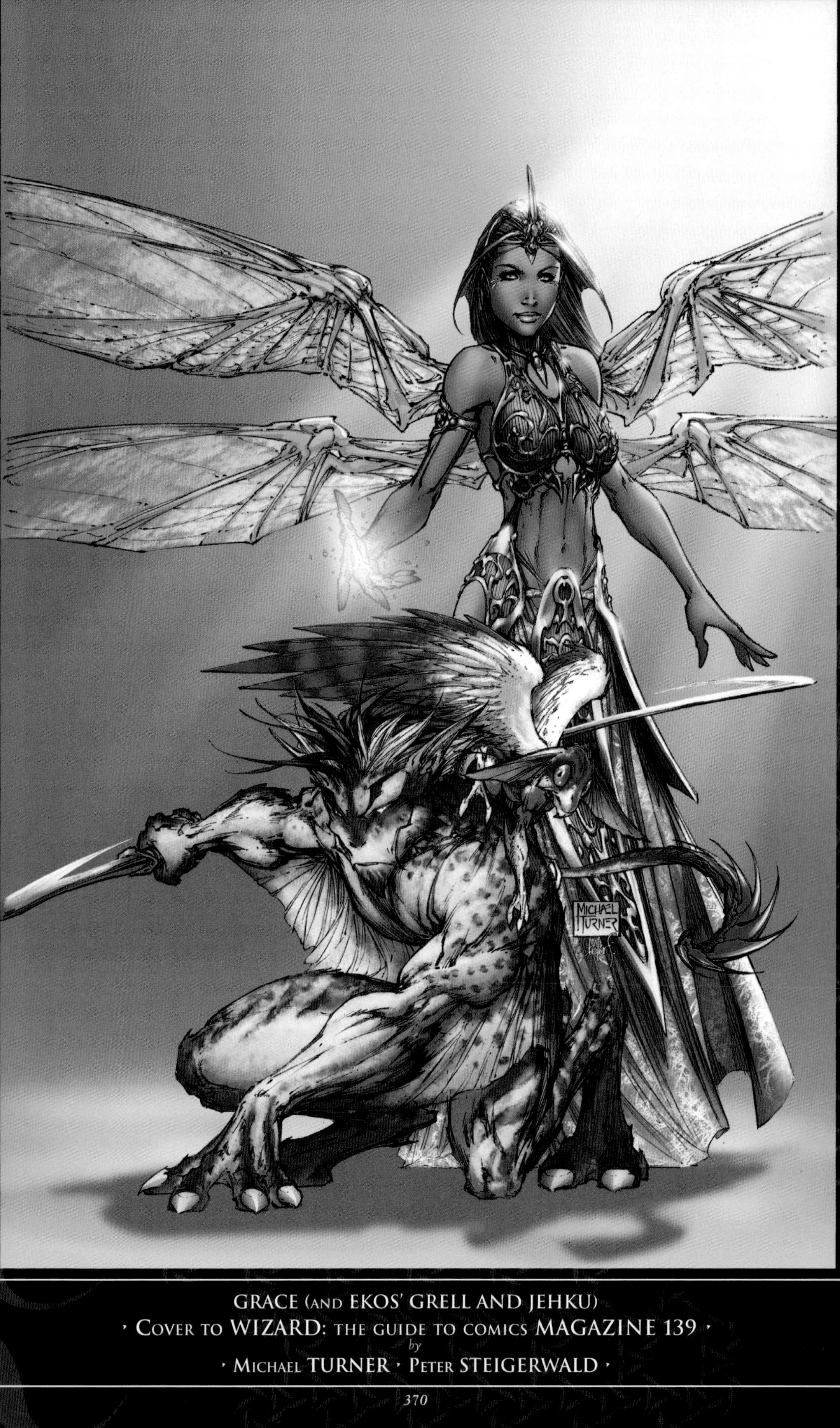
MICHAEL TURNER

GRACE (AND EKOS' GRELL AND JEHKU)

· COVER TO WIZARD: THE GUIDE TO COMICS MAGAZINE 139 ·

by

· MICHAEL TURNER · PETER STEIGERWALD ·

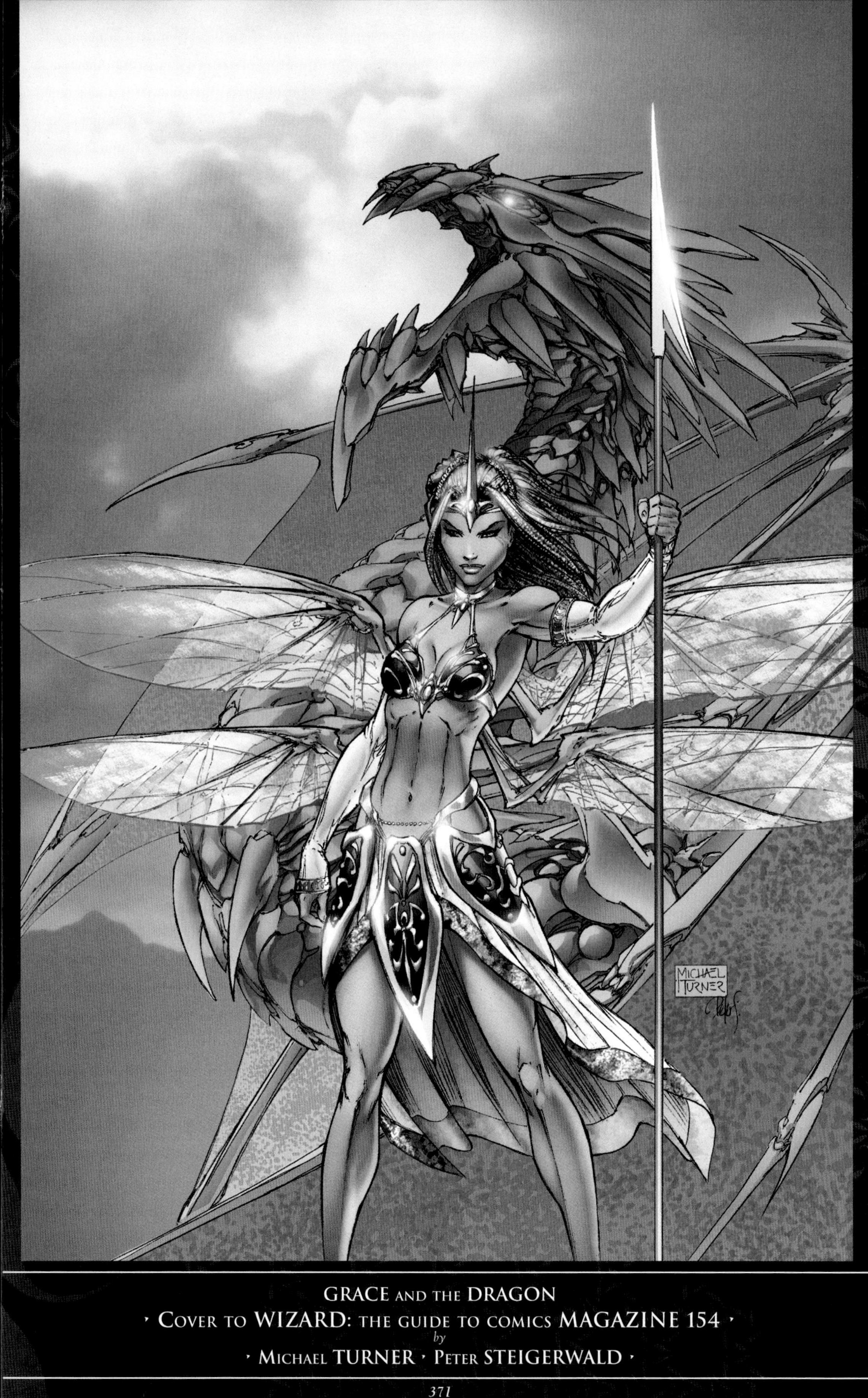
MICHAEL
TURNER

GRACE and the DRAGON
· Cover to WIZARD: the guide to comics MAGAZINE 154 ·
by
· Michael TURNER · Peter STEIGERWALD ·

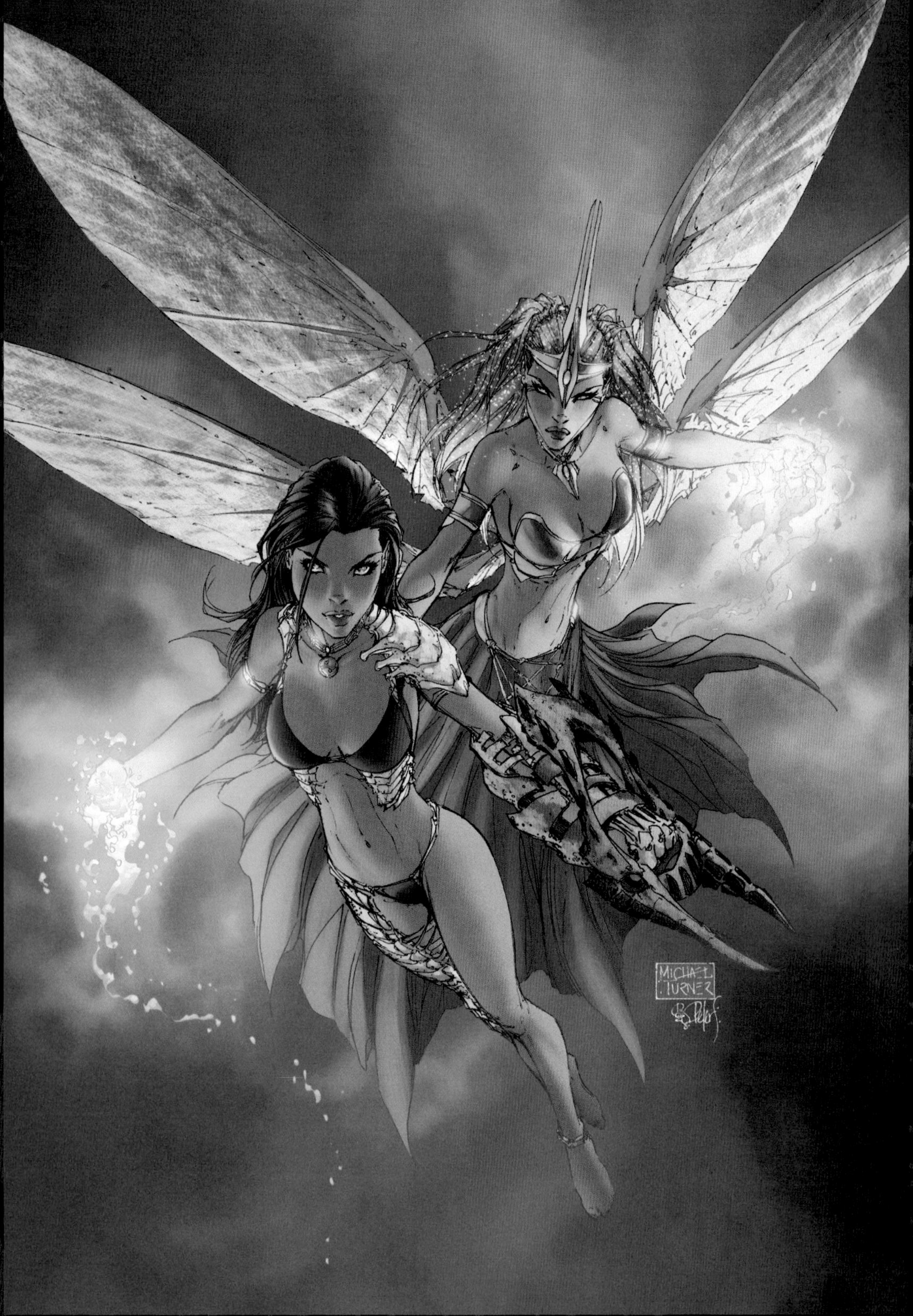
MICHAEL TURNER

GRACE (AND FATHOM'S ASPEN MATTHEWS)
· COVER TO WIZARD WORLD LOS ANGELES' 2008 PROGRAM ·
by
· MICHAEL TURNER · PETER STEIGERWALD ·

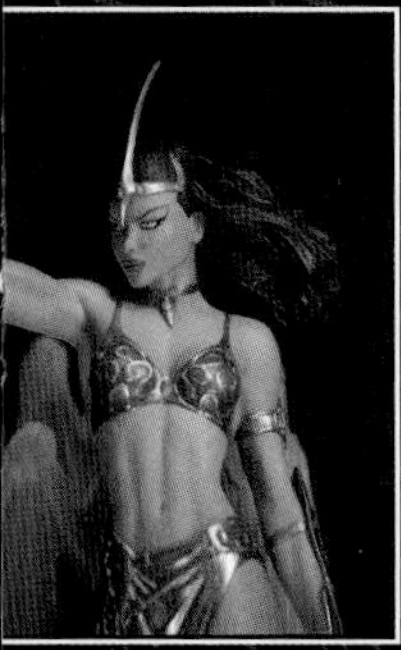

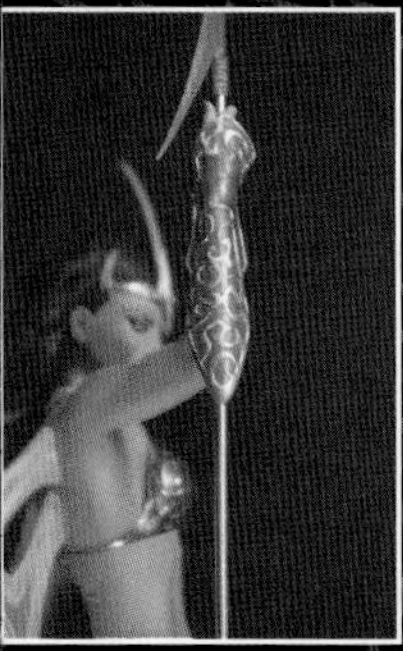

GRACE BUST CONCEPT

Designed by: Michael Turner

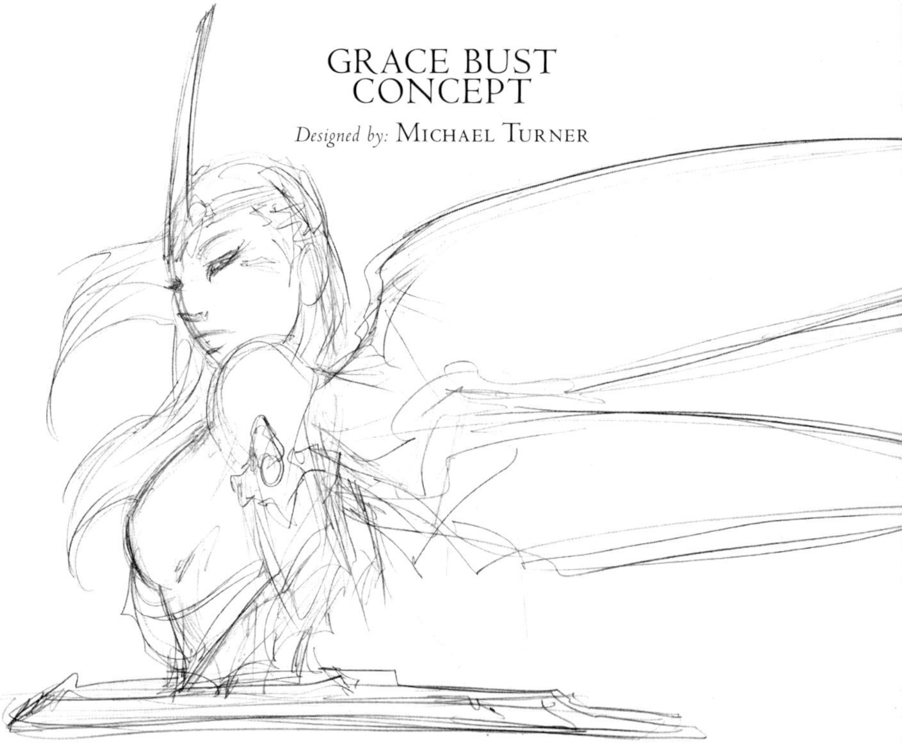

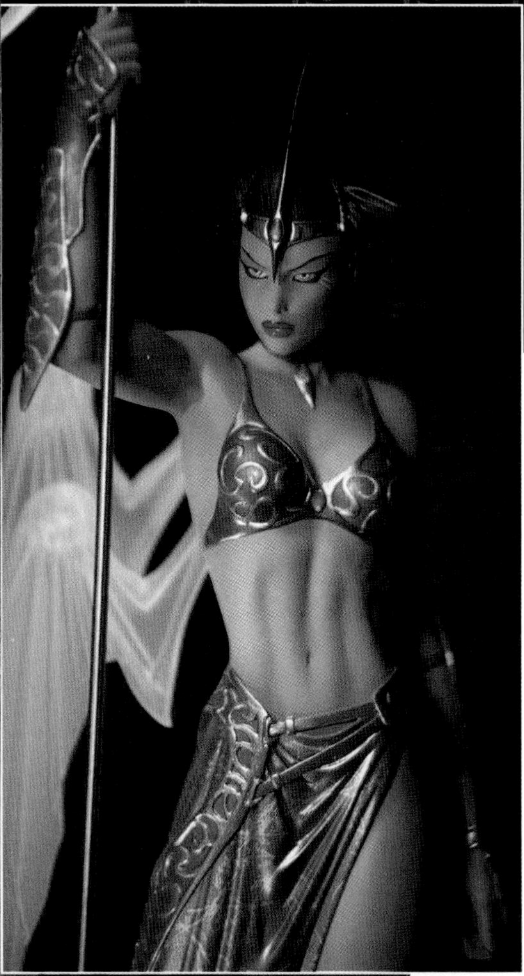

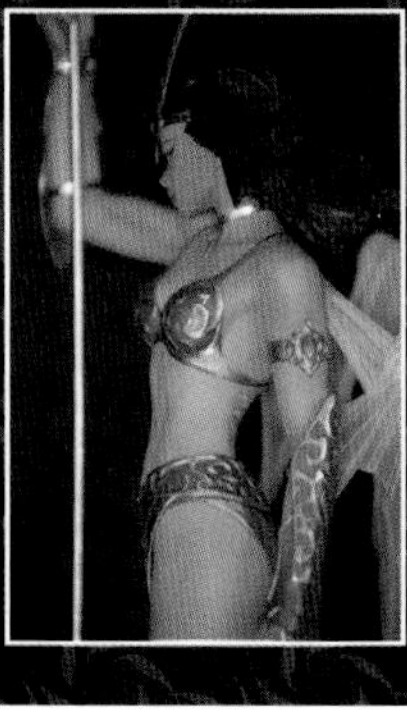

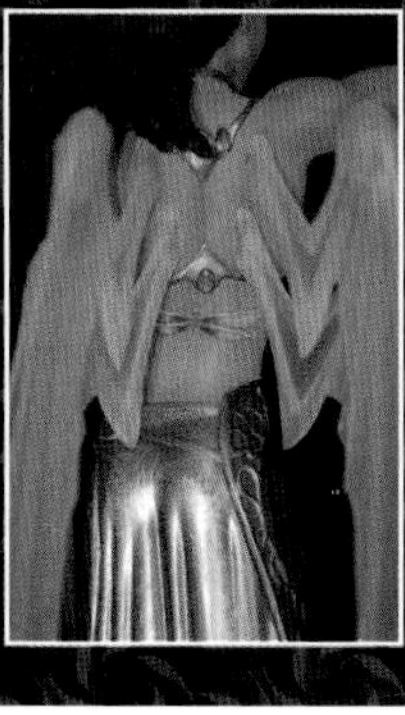

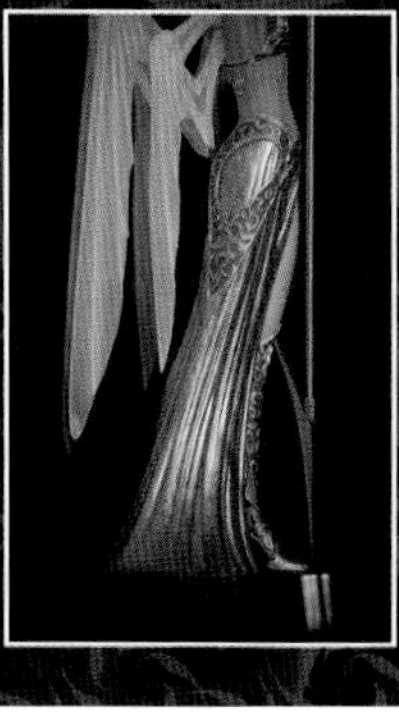

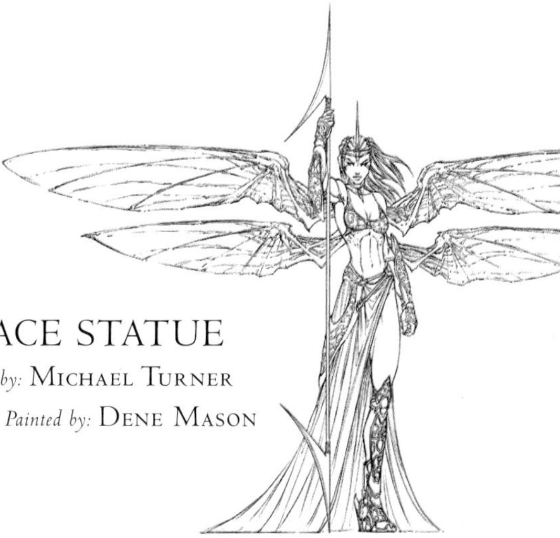

GRACE STATUE

Designed by: Michael Turner

Sculpted and Painted by: Dene Mason

Your Favorite Comic Books On The GO!
MICHAEL TURNER SKETCHBOOK
ASPEN: THE EARLY YEARS VOLUME ONE
ASPEN VOL. 1 SKETCHBOOK
ASPEN MLT inc.®
DIGITAL
Fathom series • Soulfire series
Shrugged • Executive Assistant: Iri
Now Available Online For Downloa
Comixology • Graphicly • iVerse Media
COMIXOLOGY™
www.comixology.com/Aspen-Comics
GRAPHICLY
www.graphicly.com/Aspen-Comics
COMICS+ POWERED BY IVERSE
www.comicspl.us
MICHAEL TURNER
SOULFIRE
SOULFIRE CHAOS REIGN
SOULFIRE DYING OF THE LIGHT
SHRUGGED
EXECUTIVE ASSISTANT IRIS
MICHAEL TURNER'S FATHOM
MICHAEL TURNER'S FATHOM
MICHAEL TURNER'S FATHOM
CANNON
FATHOM KIANI
FATHOM DAWN of WAR
Also Available for Download:
Broken Pieces • Charismagic • Dellec • Lady Mechanika
Mindfield • The Scourge • Michael Turner's Sketchbooks • And More
DON'T FORGET TO VISIT US ON THE INTERNET AT WWW.ASPENCOMICS.COM
All artwork, characters and their likenesses are © 2012 Aspen MLT, Inc. All Rights Reserve

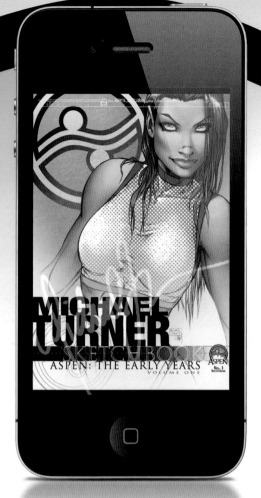

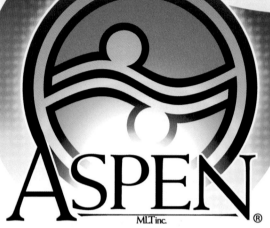

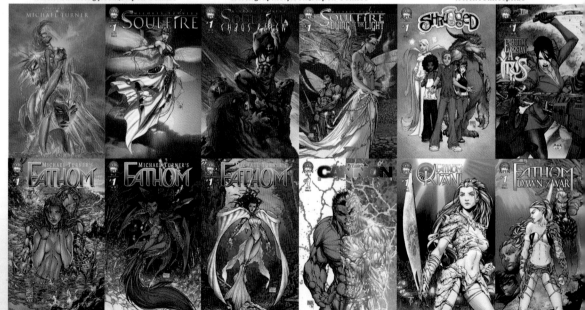

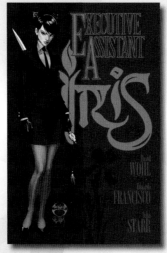

BIOGRAPHIES

MICHAEL TURNER

was born in Tennessee in 1971. In 1995 he co-created the popular smash-hit WITCHBLADE. Spawning a huge fan following of his work, Turner debuted his own creation, FATHOM, in the summer of 1998. Turner left Top Cow at the end of 2002 and founded Aspen MLT Inc., his own entertainment publishing company. Michael then teamed up with DC Comics to take the helm on some of their most popular characters. From the FLASH, to the best-selling SUPERMAN/BATMAN series, as well as providing Eisner-nominated covers for the critically acclaimed IDENTITY CRISIS series, Turner created an array of new fans with his popular take on the iconic DC characters. Returning his focus to his own properties, Michael released the fantasy-adventure SOULFIRE in 2004 and re-launched the FATHOM series in 2005 along with several spin-off titles, SOULFIRE: DYING OF THE LIGHT, FATHOM: CANNON HAWKE, and FATHOM: KIANI. Michael also created the forthcoming action adventure series EKOS and co-created EXECUTIVE ASSISTANT: IRIS before his tragic passing in June of 2008.

JEPH LOEB

is the four-time Eisner and five-time Wizard award-winning author of the critically acclaimed BATMAN: THE LONG HALLOWEEN, BATMAN: HUSH, SUPERMAN FOR ALL SEASONS, SUPERMAN/BATMAN and SUPERGIRL, all for DC Comics. His many credits at MARVEL COMICS include SPIDER-MAN: BLUE, DAREDEVIL: YELLOW , HULK: GRAY, FALLEN SON and the recently released hit titles THE ULTIMATES, HULK and ULTIMATE X. Jeph is also an Emmy and WGA nominated writer/producer whose many credits include SMALLVILLE, TEEN WOLF and LOST. Currently Jeph Loeb is Executive Vice President, Head of Television for Marvel.

J.T. KRUL

was born and raised in Michigan. He moved to Los Angeles in 1996, where he worked in television production on the legendary sitcom, SEINFELD, before breaking into the world of comics with Marvel Comics' X-MEN UNLIMITED and SPIDER-MAN UNLIMITED titles. He then joined Michael Turner and Aspen Comics, writing several projects for their flagship properties, FATHOM and SOULFIRE. In 2010 Aspen Comics published to great acclaim J.T.'s first creator-owned project, MINDFIELD. Following that success he began writing for DC Comics, where his credits include JSA CLASSIFIED, THE JOKER'S ASYLUM, TITANS, BLACKEST NIGHT: TITANS, GREEN ARROW and the new CAPTAIN ATOM. He has written for Dynamite Comics on RED SONJA and HIGHLANDER: WAY OF THE SWORD. J.T. has also worked with NBC Studios, writing several HEROES graphic novels and consulting on various online projects. J.T. has continued his long association with Aspen and SOULFIRE by writing Volumes Two and Three and being a major contributor to 2012's summer event SOULFIRE: SEARCH FOR THE LIGHT.

JOE BENITEZ

began his comic-book career in 1993 as an artist for Marc Silvestri's Top Cow Studio at Image Comics. While at Top Cow he co-created and penciled the series WEAPON ZERO and the mini-series MAGDALENA: BLOOD DIVINE. He took over the reins on Silvestri and Garth Ennis' highly successful and fan favorite title THE DARKNESS. He stepped out on his own as a creator with the 6 issue mini-series WRAITHBORN that was published by Wildstorm in 2005. As a contract artist for DC Comics he worked on titles such as JLA, SUPERMAN/BATMAN, DETECTIVE COMICS, and TITANS. In 2009 Joe stepped in to finish up Michael Turner's run on his SOULFIRE series. The winter of 2010 saw the launch of Joe's creator-owned series, LADY MECHANIKA, published by Aspen Comics. A Steampunk detective adventure, it quickly became one of the most talked-about and praised series of 2011. With a runaway success on his hand, Joe is currently hard at work on the next issue.

PETER STEIGERWALD

grew up in Honolulu, Hawai'i. He moved to Los Angeles in 1994 to work for Top Cow Productions where he filled many roles from advertising to designer, artist, colorist manager and executive. In 2001 he became the regular colorist on Michael Turner's creator-owned series, FATHOM. Wanting to return to more artistic projects Peter left Top Cow in the fall of 2002 and with Frank Mastromauro helped Michael Turner form Aspen MLT, Inc. He has provided colors for all of Michael Turner's many projects and since Turner's passing continues, with fellow co-owner Frank Mastromauro, to run Aspen MLT, Inc. and carry on Michael's legacy. Beyond SOULFIRE, Peter has also been the cover colorist on nearly all the projects from Aspen as well as too many titles to name here for Marvel and DC. One of the tops in his field he has proudly worked with many of the industry's luminaries and legends providing full interior colors for several high-profile series from Aspen, DC and Marvel including FATHOM: BLUE DESCENT, BRIGHTEST DAY, BATMAN, HULK, ULTIMATIUM, ULTIMATE X, and most recently LADY MECHANIKA. Never one to leave an empty slot in his schedule, inbetween all his other commitments he is currently working on writing, drawing and coloring his own creator-owned series, ZOONIVERSE for Aspen Comics.